Thomas Jefferson

In *Thomas Jefferson: A Modern Prometheus*, Wilson Jeremiah Moses provides a critical assessment of Thomas Jefferson and the Jeffersonian influence. Scholars of American history have long debated the legacy of Thomas Jefferson. However, Moses deviates from other interpretations by positioning himself within an older, "Federalist" historiographic tradition, offering vigorous and insightful commentary on Jefferson, the man and the myth. Moses specifically focuses on Jefferson's complexities and contradictions. Measuring Jefferson's political accomplishments, intellectual contributions, moral character, and other distinguishing traits against contemporaries like George Washington and Benjamin Franklin, but also figures like Machiavelli and Frederick the Great, Moses contends that Jefferson fell short of the greatness of others. Yet amid his criticism of Jefferson, Moses paints him as a cunning strategist, an impressive intellectual, and a consummate pragmatist who continually reformulated his ideas in a universe that he accurately recognized to be unstable, capricious, and treacherous.

Wilson Jeremiah Moses is Professor Emeritus at Pennsylvania State University and the author of six books: *The Golden Age of Black Nationalism, 1850–1925* (1978); *Black Messiahs and Uncle Toms: Social and Literary Manipulations of a Religious Myth* (1982); *Alexander Crummell: A Study in Civilization and Discontent* (1989); *The Wings of Ethiopia: Studies in African-American Life and Letters* (1990); *Afrotopia: The Roots of African American Popular History* (1998); and *Creative Conflict in African American Thought* (2004).

T0371571

CAMBRIDGE STUDIES ON THE AMERICAN SOUTH

Series Editors:

Mark M. Smith, *University of South Carolina, Columbia*
Peter Coclanis, *University of North Carolina at Chapel Hill*

Editor Emeritus:

David Moltke-Hansen

Interdisciplinary in its scope and intent, this series builds upon and extends Cambridge University Press's longstanding commitment to studies on the American South. The series offers the best new work on the South's distinctive institutional, social, economic, and cultural history and also features works in a national, comparative, and transnational perspective.

Titles in the Series

Joan E. Cashin, *War Stuff: The Struggle for Human and Environmental Resources in the American Civil War*
David Stefan Doddington, *Contesting Slave Masculinity in the American South*
Lawrence T. McDonnell, *Performing Disunion: The Coming of the Civil War in Charleston, South Carolina*
Enrico Dal Lago, *Civil War and Agrarian Unrest: The Confederate South and Southern Italy*
Daniel J. Vivian, *A New Plantation World: Sporting Estates in the South Carolina Lowcountry, 1900–1940*
Eugene D. Genovese, ed. Douglas Ambrose, *The Sweetness of Life: Southern Planters at Home*
Donald J. Mathews, *At the Altar of Lynching: Burning Sam Hose in the American South*
Keri Leigh Merritt, *Masterless Men: Poor Whites and Slavery in the Antebellum South*
Sarah Gardner, *Reviewing the South: The Literary Marketplace and the Southern Renaissance, 1920–1941*
Katherine Rye Jewell, *Dollars for Dixie: Business and the Transformation of Conservatism in the Twentieth Century*
Thomas Okie, *The Georgia Peach: Culture, Agriculture, and Environment in the American South*
Karlos K. Hill, *Beyond the Rope: The Impact of Lynching on Black Culture and Memory*
William A. Link and James J. Broomall, eds., *Rethinking American Emancipation: Legacies of Slavery and the Quest for Black Freedom*
James Van Horn *Melton, Religion, Community, and Slavery on the Colonial Southern Frontier*
Damian Alan Pargas, *Slavery and Forced Migration in the Antebellum South*
Craig Friend and Lorri Glover, eds. *Death and the American South*
Barton A. Myers, *Rebels against the Confederacy: North Carolina's Unionists*
Louis A. Ferleger and John D. Metz, *Cultivating Success in the South: Farm Households in Postbellum Georgia*
Luke E. Harlow, *Religion, Race, and the Making of Confederate Kentucky, 1830–1880*
Susanna Michele Lee, *Claiming the Union: Citizenship in the Post-Civil War South*
Ari Helo, *Thomas Jefferson's Ethics and the Politics of Human Progress: The Morality of a Slaveholder*
Kathleen Hilliard, *Masters, Slaves, and Exchange: Power's Purchase in the Old South*
Scott P. Marler, *The Merchants' Capital: New Orleans and the Political Economy of the Nineteenth-Century South*
Ras Michael Brown, *African-Atlantic Cultures and the South Carolina Lowcountry*
Johanna Nicol Shields, *Freedom in a Slave Society: Stories from the Antebellum South*
Brian Steele, *Thomas Jefferson and American Nationhood*
Christopher Michael Curtis, *Jefferson's Freeholders and the Politics of Ownership in the Old Dominion*
Jonathan Daniel Wells, *Women Writers and Journalists in the Nineteenth-Century South*
Peter McCandless, *Slavery, Disease, and Suffering in the Southern Lowcountry*
Robert E. Bonner, *Mastering America: Southern Slaveholders and the Crisis of American Nationhood*

Richard Cosway, *Prometheus*. Courtesy of the Print Collection, The New York Public Library.

"Though shalt not covet thy neighbor's wife," e.g. Maria Cosway.

Thomas Jefferson

A Modern Prometheus

WILSON JEREMIAH MOSES
Pennsylvania State University

CAMBRIDGE
UNIVERSITY PRESS

CAMBRIDGE
UNIVERSITY PRESS

Shaftesbury Road, Cambridge CB2 8EA, United Kingdom
One Liberty Plaza, 20th Floor, New York, NY 10006, USA
477 Williamstown Road, Port Melbourne, VIC 3207, Australia
314–321, 3rd Floor, Plot 3, Splendor Forum, Jasola District Centre, New Delhi – 110025, India
103 Penang Road, #05–06/07, Visioncrest Commercial, Singapore 238467

Cambridge University Press is part of Cambridge University Press & Assessment, a department of the University of Cambridge.

We share the University's mission to contribute to society through the pursuit of education, learning and research at the highest international levels of excellence.

www.cambridge.org
Information on this title: www.cambridge.org/9781108456876

DOI: 10.1017/9781108557344

First published 2019
First paperback edition 2023

A catalogue record for this publication is available from the British Library

Library of Congress Cataloging-in-Publication data
NAMES: Moses, Wilson Jeremiah, 1942– author.
TITLE: Thomas Jefferson, a modern Prometheus / Wilson Jeremiah Moses, Pennsylvania State University.
DESCRIPTION: Cambridge ; New York, NY : Cambridge University Press, [2019] | Series: Cambridge studies on the American South | Includes index.
IDENTIFIERS: LCCN 2018043272 | ISBN 9781108470964
SUBJECTS: LCSH: Jefferson, Thomas, 1743–1826 – Knowledge and learning. | Jefferson, Thomas, 1743–1826 – Influence. | United States – Intellectual life – 18th century. | United States – Intellectual life – 19th century.
CLASSIFICATION: LCC E332.2 .M67 2910 | DDC 973.4/6092 [B]–dc23
LC record available at https://lccn.loc.gov/2018043272

ISBN 978-1-108-47096-4 Hardback
ISBN 978-1-108-45687-6 Paperback

In Memoriam, Miriam, 1944–2017

Contents

Preface

Prometheus was the Titan of Greek mythology who stole fire from Olympus and gave it to mankind, along with its powers of illumination and destruction. As punishment for his offense, Zeus, the ruler of gods and men, had him chained to a desolate rock where an eagle tore diurnally at his liver. There are radically differing variations on this story, for Prometheus was a "hero with a thousand faces," a trickster god, portrayed both positively and negatively over the centuries by successive communities of ancient Greeks. To Hesiod, he was a fool, who vainly attempted to befuddle Zeus with a spoiled sacrifice, but other authors of antiquity stressed his role as mankind's instructor and benefactor. The parallels between Prometheus, the kindler of enlightenment, and Lucifer, who endowed mankind with the knowledge of good and evil, have fascinated students of comparative mythology. Even little children have been known to recognize the similarities between Bible stories, Greek myths, and Norse legends, and, with or without reference to Carl Jung's theory of archetypes, such academic luminaries as Joseph Campbell, Maud Bodkin, Northrup Frye, and Zwi Werblowsky have discussed parallels between Lucifer, Prometheus, the Norse god Loki, and the titans of William Blake's prophetic books.[1]

[1] Carl Jung wrote the preface to Zwi Werblowsky, *Lucifer and Prometheus* (London: Routledge, 1952). Joseph Campbell, *The Hero with a Thousand Faces* (Princeton University Press, 1949). J. G. Frazier mentions Prometheus in *The Golden Bough* (1890, and 1906–15). Maud Bodkin, *Archetypal Patterns of Poetry: Psychological Studies of Imagination* (London: Oxford University Press, 1934). Northrup Frye, *Fearful Symmetry: A Study of William Blake* (Princeton University Press, 1947). Other manifestations include the African tricksters, Anansi and Esu Elegbara, and the Native American trickster

Thomas Jefferson and the archetypal Prometheus were strangely overlooked by journalist Cory Pein, who almost stole my fire with his clever, amusing article, "Donald Trump: Trickster God," which presented its subject as only the most recent in a procession of slippery American presidents. Jefferson also foreshadowed Trump, setting aside the facts that Jefferson had nice manners, enjoyed Mozart, and knew classical Greek. Reflecting on the history of presidential legerdemain one may recall how George Washington once brought an audience of battle-hardened veterans to tears with "spectacular" theatrics and eighteen softly spoken words, and how Abe Lincoln supposedly wise-cracked on how often "you can fool all of the people." In graduate school I encountered a book called *The Lion and the Fox*, a study of Franklin D. Roosevelt's Machiavellian traits.[2]

John Adams, our second president, who was anything but a crowd-pleaser, learned to his chagrin during his single term in office that successful executives must be politicians. Years later he drily observed the "Stupidity with which the more numerous multitude become their Dupes, but even love to be Taken in by their Tricks." He always felt privately that his friend Jefferson had effected a "Coup de Theatre" with his "Penmanship of the Declaration of Independence," so that he "ran away with all the glory." Jefferson again stole Adams' fire when he defeated him in the venomous presidential campaign of 1800. Adams had already applied to himself the imagery of "sad Prometheus fasten'd to his Rock" in a letter to his wife, Abigail, where he accused Jefferson of encouraging "incendiaries."[3]

In Jefferson's day, allusions to the saga of Prometheus were recurrent throughout Western literature as metaphors for revolutions in thought. Prometheus appeared in the writings of Goethe, Herder, Beethoven,

"Coyote." Percy Bysshe Shelley compares Prometheus to Milton's Satan in his "Preface to Prometheus Unbound."

[2] Corey Pein, "Donald Trump, Trickster God," *The Baffler* (March 4, 2016), https://thebaffler.com/magical-thinking/donald-trump-trickster-god According to the Mount Vernon website (www.mountvernon.org/), when restless officers threatened to march on Congress with demands for backpay and provisions, George Washington, in preparing to read a letter from Congress explaining its financial difficulties, paused to put on his spectacles and apologized, "Gentlemen, you must pardon me. I have grown gray in your service and now find myself growing blind." It is said that several of the officers wept. Lincoln's purported wisecrack is untraceable. John Adams to Benjamin Rush, September 30, 1805; John Adams to Benjamin Rush, June 21, 1811.

[3] John Adams to Abigail Adams, November 26, 1794, "Jefferson it seems is to give the first Passport to these Incendiaries. Malignity seemed to have Seized upon that Mans mind as deeply as upon Paines & Callenders."

Byron, Blake, and Jefferson himself. In 1755 Kant made his ironic reference to Benjamin Franklin as the "Prometheus of the New Era, who wanted to disarm thunder ... to extinguish the fires in Vulcan's workshop, all such efforts prove the audacity of man." But Baron Turgot and the Marquis de Condorcet portrayed Franklin with less restrained enthusiasm as "le promethée moderne." The metaphor could be extended to others among America's Revolutionary founders, as it was in William Blake's visionary poem, "America, a Prophecy." Jefferson's rhetoric has inflamed many revolutionary struggles, and his words have had universal appeal, but, in his own day, the African American pamphleteer David Walker believed he was only "cramming fire down our throats."[4]

Jefferson was familiar with the titanic bearer of light and fire, and he mentioned owning a copy of *Prometheus Vinctus*, a scholarly bilingual edition in Greek and Latin of *Promētheus Desmōtēs*, the play, attributed to Aeschylus, whose English title is *Prometheus Bound*. When he founded the University of Virginia, he did not recommend that the work be placed on the list of required Greek classics. There is apparently only one specific and direct reference to Prometheus in Jefferson's writings, and that is neither sympathetic nor heroic. It is directed at Napoleon:

> and, thanks be to god, the tyger who revelled so long in the blood and spoils of Europe, is at length, like another Prometheus, chained to his rock, where the vulture of remorse for his crimes will be preying on his vitals, and in like manner without consuming them.[5]

Jefferson's contemporaries usually exploited the myth more positively. Goethe presented Prometheus as the titanic revolutionary who, in defiance of Zeus, created mankind in his own rebellious image. Percy Bysshe Shelley presented him as the heroic symbol of poetic enlightenment and creative energy. But an ironic twist came when Mary Shelley, his teenage wife – the daughter of Mary Wollstonecraft and William Godwin – achieved her own immortality in the same year that Jefferson founded the University of Virginia by publishing *Frankenstein: The Modern Prometheus*. Like the tragic protagonist of Mary Shelley's novel, Jefferson may have unwittingly unleashed a monster, by founding an

[4] Blake's "America, a Prophecy" apotheosized "Washington, Franklin, Paine, and Warren, Gates, Hancock, and Green," but ignored Jefferson, possibly, although not necessarily, because the Declaration of Independence deployed ideas of John Locke, Isaac Newton, and the construct of "Nature and Nature's God" that Blake considered nefarious.

[5] Jefferson to Antonio Dugnani, February 14, 1818.

anti-government tradition that led Theodore Roosevelt, in his capacity as progressive historian, to call him "the father of nullification, and therefore of secession," and elsewhere the twenty-sixth president said, "In my estimation Jefferson's influence upon the United States as a whole was very distinctly evil." The old Rough Rider blamed the Promethean of Monticello for kindling the Civil War.[6]

It would require Herculean labors to unbind every intricacy of the Promethean myth in Jefferson's times, and such is not my purpose. I mention only that he and his contemporaries were familiar with the legend, but my ambition is not to explore all its manifestations, either in the ancient world or in the Age of the Enlightenment. Nor have I attempted to repeat on every page that Jefferson was a Trickster God. I have been much more fascinated with the manifestations of Jefferson's erudition and genius. His brilliant rhetorical pyrotechnics and gift of hyperbole made him a Modern Prometheus when he drafted the Declaration of Independence, for nobody really thought it "self-evident" all men were created equal, regardless of how one might interpret those words, and Jefferson soon retracted them with his "suspicion only, that the blacks, whether originally a distinct race, or made distinct by time and circumstances, are inferior to the whites." He also referred to ordinary white children as "rubbish" and declared that "The tender breasts of ladies were not formed for political convulsion."[7]

It is altogether fitting and proper, but it requires little imagination, to condemn Jefferson for embodying the self-satisfied hypocrisy of the so-called "Age of Enlightenment." Accusations in the same spirit lead moralists to gnaw away at Earl Warren's unconscionable treatment of the Japanese Americans or W. E. B. Du Bois' reprehensible apology for Stalin. Those of us who are equally flawed may admit that we too have yielded to the peculiar temptations of our own time and place. Jefferson was – in Henry Cabot Lodge's words – "a child of his times." He gives somber meaning to Ralph Waldo Emerson's aphorism about "Great men" who have always "confided themselves childlike to the genius of their age." Bound to such ideas as "child of his times" and "genius of their age," we speak of the "Age of Jefferson," or the age of "Jeffersonian Democracy."

[6] Theodore Roosevelt, *The Life of Thomas Hart Benton* (St. Charles, IL: Houghton Mifflin, 1887), p. 95. Theodore Roosevelt to Frederick Jackson Turner, November 4, 1896.

[7] Authentic Jefferson quotations are easily searchable at Founders Online (see Note on Methods and Bibliography below).

We recognize that Jefferson's Democracy, like that of ancient Athens and that of the German Democratic Republic, was profoundly flawed.

Jefferson was capable of reverse snobbery and anti-intellectualism, as he showed in the following sentences to his nephew, Peter Carr:

> State a moral case to a ploughman and a professor. The former will decide it as well, & often better than the latter, because he has not been led astray by artificial rules.[8]

This seeming genuflection before folk wisdom was one of many examples of Jeffersonian hyperbole, for his communications with ploughmen were neither frequent nor familiar; his attitude towards bourgeois artisans was contemptuous, and his dealings with professors could be impatient and dismissive. Jefferson designed schools based on the classical trivium, a system for raking the best "from the rubbish," while training the rest to be content with their "condition of life."

If the "Age of Jefferson" were truly an "Age of Democratic Revolution," perhaps its "Representative Man" should be not a landed aristocrat but a small tradesman, like the Boston shoemaker George Robert Twelves Hewes, someone from that class of "artificers" that Jefferson disparaged as "panders of vice" and a threat to republican virtue. Unlike Jefferson, Hewes actually fought in the American Revolution. Slightly older, but still outlasting Jefferson by fourteen years, he lived to see the arrival of railway transportation, photography, electric communications, modern commerce, and the impending industrial capitalism. Unlike Jefferson, Hewes lived out his life among the people of the city, which allowed him to witness the coming of a newer, if still imperfect, democracy, as historian Alfred Young has famously shown. But neither man could have foreseen the economic, technological, and moral issues that confront us today, and we cannot rely on their generation for guidance. The realities of the present are such that neither the Prometheans who kindled the fires of the American Revolution, nor the proletarians who fueled them, can offer our generation much enlightenment in the darkness that threatens.[9]

[8] Jefferson to Peter Carr, August 10, 1787.

[9] Alfred F. Young, "George Robert Twelves Hewes (1742–1840): A Boston Shoemaker and the Memory of the American Revolution," *The William and Mary Quarterly*, 38, no. 4 (October, 1981), 561–623; although Jefferson hailed with enthusiasm the arrival of steamboats navigating the rivers of Tennessee, Jefferson to George W. Campbell, October 15, 1815. Jefferson's contempt for artisans is discussed in Chapter 7.

Acknowledgments

Early draft portions of this book were delivered at the W. E. B. Du Bois institute as three of the Nathan Huggins Lectures in February of 2013, on which occasion I benefitted from commentary by Professors Henry L. Gates, Annette Gordon-Reed, Tommy Shelby, Ibrahim Sundiata, Allison Blakely, Thabiti Asukile, and numerous others in the audiences. An early version was delivered at Purdue University in October of 2008, at the invitation of Professor Cornelius Bynum, where questions and comments from the audience enriched my understanding or my own unanswered questions. I was also the beneficiary of incisive and encouraging commentary by the Pennsylvania State University Society for the Study of Religion and its membership, particularly the late Paul Harvey, Annie Rose, and Gregg Roeber, when I addressed the Society on February 20, 2014. At the invitation of Professor Jonathan Brockopp, and at the kind invitation of Professor Derrick Alridge, I presented my work in progress at the University of Virginia on February 12, 2014, on which occasion Professor Peter Onuf provided a detailed commentary; this he supplemented later through correspondence. Peter also arranged a fruitful exchange with the late Peter Nicolaisen on matters related to Jefferson's German contacts. On that occasion, I also had the opportunity to dine with Mr. Henry Wiencek, who was in the audience, and later to correspond with him. Through Henry's good offices I was able to benefit from correspondence with Professor Billy Wayson, who was so kind as to share portions of his ongoing research. Professor Paul Kerry invited me to share some of my ideas in his seminar at the University of Oxford on March 10, 2016, on which occasion I benefitted from the insightful commentary of Professor Nicolas P. Cole, and the path-breaking research of Professor Jeffrey High. Professor David Waldstreicher arranged for me to offer an early draft of the chapter on Jefferson's religion at the University of Pennsylvania on January 17, 2014. He subsequently gave the manuscript two thorough readings, as a result of which I was able to eliminate or to refine several rash judgments. Professor Edward Countryman also provided a detailed and thorough reading of the manuscript's penultimate draft, and encouraged me, as others did, to eliminate the excessively redundant. My late sister, Miriam Elaine Moses (1944–2017), read more than one chapter, and saved me from several pretentious digressions, stylistic infelicities, and other self-indulgent eccentricities. My wife, Maureen, also made stylistic corrections in the process of her numerous readings and reactions to the manuscript during its five-year gestation. John Vandevanter Carter and Mark Smith helped me immensely in tightening up the Preface. Mr. Lew Bateman, who was my editor on two previous books with Cambridge University Press, offered me invaluable encouragement at the early stages of this project, and his successor, Deborah Gershenowitz, has assumed the supervision of this project with graciousness and understanding. Her assisting staff, Kristina Deusch, Rachel Blaifeder, and Julie Hrischeva, have consistently shown competency, diligence, and attention to detail. I was extremely fortunate in that the copy editing of this book was assigned to Chris Jackson, a deep scholar in his own right and magisterial in the intricacies of academic citation. If I had listened to every critical reader with the respect to which they were entitled, I am certain that this could have been a better book. For those errors that, due to my stubbornness or inattention, may have survived their scrutiny, I take full responsibility.

Note on Methods and Bibliography

I have found several bibliographies useful, although often so compendious that they served only to intimidate. For example, the overwhelming bibliography of Jon Meacham's *Thomas Jefferson and the Art of Power* (New York: Random House, 2012) is more than my poor brain could master, even if I'd begun this enterprise as an undergraduate. I have been tantalized by the much shorter, but somewhat mystifying, list of references in the guide to abbreviations of Robert M. S. McDonald's penetrating and insightful *Confounding Father: Thomas Jefferson's Image in His Own Time* (Charlottesville, VA: University of Virginia Press, 2016). This pays homage to obsolete early editions of Jefferson's writings by Paul Leicester Ford, Andrew Lipscomb, and Albert Ellery Bergh that are always interesting, but hardly essential today. A critical overview of the early editions of Jefferson's papers, and their flaws, was made by Merrill Peterson, the late dean of Jefferson scholars, in his edition of *Thomas Jefferson, Writings* (New York: Literary Classics of the United States, 1984) in the prestigious Library of America series. Peterson regularly hovered over Monticello and was ensconced in the history department of the University of Virginia. He was winner of the Bancroft Prize for his *The Jefferson Image in the American Mind* (originally printed by Oxford University Press, 1960). Other than Peterson's successor at the University of Virginia, Peter Onuf, few can approach his familiarity with Jefferson, especially now that the project for a complete edition of Jefferson's papers, begun by Julian Boyd in 1944, appears to be approaching its climax, if not its detumescence.

Before I began this project, my copy of Peterson's edition of *Thomas Jefferson, Writings* had become dirty and ragged, and I have often cited it in my footnotes as the most readily available and most authoritative compilation available. Peterson's 1,000-page *Thomas Jefferson and the New Nation* (Oxford University Press, 1970) is often disparaged for its scant attention to the Sally Hemings controversy. Fawn Brodie, Lucia Stanton, and Harvard Law School graduate Annette Gordon-Reed have argued persuasively for a paternity suit against Jefferson, the likely father of Sally Hemings' octoroon children, and they have convinced many historians, including the magisterial Peter Onuf, that in the absence of exculpatory DNA evidence Jefferson might be convicted as a predator and a pedophile in a present-day courtroom. In fact, Gordon-Reed's brilliant accomplishment reduces the DNA evidence to the status of mere "icing on the cake." But Peterson wrote *Thomas Jefferson and the New Nation* several years before discussion of Sally Hemings became mandatory. Dumas Malone did provide the chronology of Jefferson's comings and goings, to which Gordon-Reed paid homage in constructing her case. Despite the deficiencies of Peterson's superficial treatment of race relations, his work remains the best biography, with the obvious exception of Dumas Malone's six-volume *Jefferson and His Time* (Boston, MA: Little, Brown, 1948–81).

I have clambered, of course, onto the shoulders of one more giant, namely Julian P. Boyd, who oversaw the editing of *The Papers of Thomas Jefferson* (Princeton University Press) over twenty volumes published between 1950 and 1982 (a full list of the volumes, by other editors, continuing up to 2016, can be consulted at https://founders.archives.gov/content/volumes#Jefferson). My footnote citations in this study are to that edition. I used the bound volumes I–XVI, which I came to possess courtesy of the History Department of Pennsylvania State University. These were accompanied by a general index of limited usefulness, and I seldom consulted them after gaining access to Founders Online, National Archives (https://founders.archives.gov/).

It would have been cumbersome to have constantly cited all originally paper-based editions in full bibliographic form, however. It would also have been dishonest and useless to pretend that this work was conducted primarily with print editions. Perhaps those editions will stand the test of time, but of such things no one can be certain. Page numbers and volume references to earlier editions are now obsolete and completely frustrating, and who is to say what new developments will occur in the dawning age of "Artificial Intelligence"? With that thought in mind, as I advanced over the years in this study, all quotations from Jefferson and his correspondents were increasingly taken from the Founders Online edition. In the present volume, all dates are consistently entered in the format month, day, and year, e.g. "John Adams to Abigail Adams, July 3, 1776"; interested readers should bear in mind that Founders Online uniformly utilizes the format of day, month, and year, which often departs dramatically from the dating format of the original sender. In rare and hardly memorable instances I have found a Google search to prove more fruitful than a search on the Founders Online website. As explained within individual footnotes, certain other sources cited there can be found (e.g. at https://home.monticello.org/) by using the search option on the homepage. Another useful website referenced in the footnotes is the Online Library of Liberty, http://oll.libertyfund.org/ (but here one must bear in mind that the original pagination of sources may not be preserved at that site). Another useful source is Internet Archive (https://archive.org/), which offers reproductions of books, sometimes in numerous editions, with a choice between photographic facsimiles and "full-text" formats as digital reproductions.

I have in general, however, avoided giving url links at each citation, for at least one friendly scholar has kindly instructed me that I ought not to provide evidence of my having utilized electronic sources. (That said, for a small number of references a url is provided where it is felt it would be particularly helpful.) In coming decades the existing url may conceivably become as obsolete as the vaunted technologies of the "Gutenberg galaxy." The documents at Founders Online and the other websites referenced here are eminently searchable by words and phrases, but caveats are in order. What is cut and pasted into that search engine should be as short as possible, since idiosyncratic eighteenth-century punctuation will very often confuse the search engine, especially when challenged by Jefferson's inconsistent spellings, creative punctuation, and often ambiguous sentence structure.

There are many references to Jefferson's *Notes on the State of Virginia*, which I have occasionally abbreviated to *Notes on Virginia* (or even just *Notes*), as is customary. There are numerous editions, and I have no idea which will be available in future years. The standard edition of *Notes on the State of Virginia* is that edited by William Peden for the University of North Carolina Press (1955), but the most easily acquired print edition is that of Bedford Books, reliable and well-edited by David Waldstreicher (2002), and my references are to this edition unless otherwise indicated. Readers are also directed to the Avalon Project of Yale University Law School. Founders Online is the most scholarly and accessible source for reliable editions of the Madison and Adams papers, and their correspondence with Jefferson is cited copiously in this work. That site directs the researcher to the Leonard W. Labaree, Yale University Press edition of *The Papers of Benjamin Franklin*, or one may consult *The Papers of Benjamin Franklin* sponsored by the American Philosophical Society, and the Yale University digital edition by the Packard Humanities Institute, which has an exemplary search engine. While readers are reminded that they need not be fully dependent on the bound volumes, two bound scholarly editions comprising the Jefferson–Adams correspondence and the Jefferson–Madison correspondence are worthy of note, as they are well-indexed and rich in scholarly apparatus. See Lester J. Cappon, *The Adams–Jefferson Letters: The Complete Correspondence between Thomas Jefferson and Abigail and John Adams* (Chapel Hill, NC, London: University of North Carolina Press, 1959). The same holds true for James Morton Smith, *The Republic of Letters: The Correspondence between Thomas Jefferson and James Madison, 1776–1826* (New York: Norton, 1995), which has the added virtue of being aesthetically pleasing. The letters to be found in these eminently useful bound editions can also be found and searched electronically at Founders Online.

1

Introduction

TOM JEFFERSON AS TOM SAWYER: A FRONTIER GENIUS

"Mr. Jefferson tells large stories," wrote John Quincy Adams, commenting on Thomas Jefferson's boast that he learned Spanish in nineteen days. Adams, who was a splendid linguist in his own right, commented, with a touch of ambiguity, "You can never be an hour in this man's company without something of the marvelous." By all accounts, Jefferson was a gifted raconteur, and dinner at his table was, in the words of Benjamin Latrobe, "an elegant mental treat." It is said that he was a poor orator, who kept his silence in public debates, but he was pleasing and persuasive in conversation, and he knew how to tell a story to his advantage.[1]

In early childhood he displayed the qualities of a Tom Sawyer, according to his own family's tradition. His grandson, Thomas Jefferson Randolph, reports that he once tried to pull a fast one on his father, who sent him into the forest with a gun to practice self-reliance. "Inexperienced, he was unsuccessful: finding a wild turkey caught in a pen, he tied it with his garter to a tree, shot it and carried it home in triumph." But is a turkey caught in a pen free for the taking? Was this pen on someone's property? Is a bird tied to a tree a legitimate sportsman's

[1] *Memoirs of John Quincy Adams, Comprising Portions of his Diary from 1795 to 1848*, ed. Charles Francis Adams (Philadelphia: Lippincott, 1874–77), vol. I, p. 317, journal entry, November 1804, "As to Spanish, it was so easy that he had learned it, with the help of a *Don Quixote* ... in the course of a passage to Europe, on which he was but nineteen days at sea. But Mr. Jefferson tells large stories": https://archive.org/details/memoirsof johnquio8adamuoft Also see Julian P. Boyd, *The Papers of Thomas Jefferson* (Princeton University Press, 1953), vol. VII, p. 383. Benjamin Latrobe quoted in Merrill Peterson, *Thomas Jefferson and the New Nation* (Oxford University Press, 1970), p. 727. On his silence in debates on the Declaration of Independence, see Dumas Malone, *Jefferson and His Time*, 6 vols. (Boston, MA: Little, Brown, 1948), vol. I, *Jefferson the Virginian*, p. 219.

trophy? Is a boy old enough to be trusted with a gun old enough to trouble himself with such niceties? We have here the makings of a story to rival Mark Twain's "lie worthy to hold up its head and march down through history breast to breast with George Washington's lauded truth about the hatchet!"[2]

The fable of George Washington's hatchet is more famous than the story of Jefferson's turkey hunt, although the latter seems more authentic. No one knows the origins of the cherry tree legend, which was recorded for the first time by Parson Weems, years after Washington's death, although, for all we know, it may be true. The turkey story's source is known: Jefferson's remarkably candid grandson could not resist passing along an amusing anecdote of resolution and independence, despite every inclination to sanitize his grandfather's biography. The cherry tree story, whatever its source, is a parable, with the purpose of preaching "Truth, the loveliest quality of youth" to nineteenth-century schoolboys. The lad who hopes to become president, and an American hero, must realize early that "honesty is the best policy." The Jefferson turkey story carries no such burden; it is merely the portrait of a resourceful 10-year-old. "It is good to be shifty in a new country," says Captain Simon Suggs, the model for Mark Twain's conment.[3]

Jefferson never took up arms in the American Revolution, and he drafted the Declaration of Independence, more than a year after the battles of Lexington, Concord, and Bunker Hill, and almost four months after George Washington forced the British evacuation of Boston; but Jefferson deserved, and was determined to claim, his rank among the Founders. While writing his own epitaph, in which he decided not to mention his presidency, he chose words that were somehow even more imposing:

HERE WAS BURIED THOMAS JEFFERSON AUTHOR OF
THE DECLARATION OF AMERICAN INDEPENDENCE OF THE
STATUTE OF VIRGINIA FOR RELIGIOUS FREEDOM AND
FATHER OF THE UNIVERSITY OF VIRGINIA

[2] The turkey story is in *Memoirs of T. J. Randolph*, p. 3, Edgehill Randolph Papers, University of Virginia, cited by Dumas Malone in *Jefferson the Virginian*, p. 46, and Fawn Brodie in *Thomas Jefferson: An Intimate History* (New York: Norton, 1974), p. 35. In Mark Twain's *The Adventures of Tom Sawyer*, Tom lies to protect Becky Thatcher after she damages her schoolmaster's anatomy book, and takes a beating in her place. Judge Thatcher, Becky's father, chortles in joy at the beamish boy's heroism.

[3] "Johnson Jones Hooper," Steven H. Gale, ed., *Encyclopedia of American Humorists* (New York: Routledge, 1988), p. 231.

Was it modesty that led him to omit his eight years as president of the United States from his epitaph, or was it his Virginia Nationalism? His "frequent references to himself as 'a Virginian' and to Virginia as 'my own country'" have not escaped the notice of such historians as Jack Greene.[4] His purpose in the Declaration, in his epitaph, and throughout his entire life, public and private, was to place himself at the birthplace of American ideology, at the center of Virginia's life of the mind, and above the suspicious world of parties and politics. Even on his tombstone, Jefferson was a smooth, Machiavellian tactician, not contented with presenting himself merely as the third president of the United States, but aiming at something ostensibly even higher, making himself the intellectual father of his country.

OWNING THE DECLARATION OF INDEPENDENCE

He was proud of his work on and possessive of the Declaration of Independence – the document essential to his claims as an Enlightenment philosopher, and the Promethean kindler of Revolutionary fires. Over the years he became increasingly protective of his reputation as its author and insistent on the most picayune details related to its drafting.[5] He was particularly deceptive in claiming the

[4] Jack P. Greene, "The Intellectual Reconstruction of Virginia" in Peter Onuf, ed., *Jeffersonian Legacies* (Charlottesville, VA: University of Virginia Press, 1993), p. 225. Brian Steele, *Thomas Jefferson and American Nationhood* (Cambridge University Press, 2012), p. 39.

[5] Even a superficial discussion of the bibliography on the Declaration of Independence would require a book-length treatment. The basics are in Boyd, *The Papers of Thomas Jefferson*, vol. I, and Dumas Malone's *Jefferson the Virginian*. For nuanced discussions, see the notes to Pauline Maier's *American Scripture* (New York: Knopf, 1997). A quick start is provided in "Suggestions for Further Reading" in Joseph Ellis, *What Did the Declaration Declare?* (Boston, MA: Bedford, 1999). There, p. 16, Ellis says "the Declaration is more a creature of mythology than history." For Jefferson's possessiveness, see Robert E. McGlone, "Deciphering Memory: John Adams and the Authorship of the Declaration of Independence," *The Journal of American History*, 85, no. 2 (September, 1998), 411–438 note 2; Robert M. S. McDonald, "Thomas Jefferson's Changing Reputation as Author of the Declaration of Independence: The First Fifty Years," *Journal of the Early Republic*, 19, no. 2 (summer, 1999), 169–195. There are discrepancies in the most "authentic" drafts of the Declaration, i.e. that in Jefferson's manuscript *Autobiography*, in his *Notes of the Proceedings*, and in the original rough draft in Jefferson's handwriting in the Library of Congress, in which one sees the crossing-out of "sacred and undeniable," not indicated in the *Autobiography*'s version. Carl Lotus Becker, in his *The Declaration of Independence: A Study on the History of Political Ideas* (New York: Harcourt, Brace and Company, 1922), credits Franklin with this alteration, but his view is contested in Julian P. Boyd, *The Declaration of*

influences of Aristotle and Locke. He insisted that his authorship be engraved on his tombstone, having labored to ensure that he would have no competitors as the nation's original apologist. Prematurely, John Adams had imagined that Richard Henry Lee's "Declaration of Independency," July 2, would be forever commemorated as the nation's Foundation date. Adams predicted it would be "the most memorable Epochal, in the History of America ... celebrated, by succeeding Generations, as the great anniversary Festival." But this was not to be. July 4 came to be remembered as the birth date of the Republic, and the marker of Jefferson's importance in history. Adams wrote in 1805 to Benjamin Rush, asking rhetorically, "Was there ever a Coup de Theatre, that had So great an Effect as Jefferson's Penmanship of the Declaration of Independence?" And in 1811 Adams wrote to Rush again:

> The Declaration of Independence I always considered as a Theatrical Show. Jefferson ran away with all the Stage Effect of that, i.e. all the Glory of it.

But Adams admired the showmanship, and gave Jefferson all due glory. Although initially tempted, he dismissed a charge that later arose that Jefferson had copied the Declaration from the 1775 Mecklenburg Resolves, a spurious document that suddenly appeared in 1819 and was deficient in that it contained nothing approaching the philosophical significance of Jefferson's preamble. Jefferson was less concerned with the attack on his originality, something he would never claim, than with the question of the Mecklenburg declaration's authenticity, about which he expressed doubts. Adams, seemingly convinced it was a fake, wrote

Independence: The Evolution of the Text as Shown in Facsimiles of Various Drafts by Its Author: Issued in Conjunction with an Exhibit of These Drafts at the Library of Congress on the Two Hundredth Anniversary of the Birth of Thomas Jefferson (Washington, DC: Library of Congress, 1943). Pauline Maier accepts the possibility that the alteration was Franklin's in *American Scripture*, p. 136. Garry Wills, *Inventing America: Jefferson's Declaration of Independence* (New York: Doubleday, 1978), seems willing enough to attribute the revision to Jefferson and traces it to the influence of Thomas Reid's *Inquiry into the Human Mind* (1764), pp. 180, 190. Walter Isaacson's *Benjamin Franklin: An American Life* (New York: Simon and Schuster, 2003) accepts Becker's thesis concerning Franklin's alterations. Other notable works include John H. Hazelton, *The Declaration of Independence: Its History* (Boston, MA: De Capo Press, 1970); William Hogeland, *Declaration: The Nine Tumultuous Weeks When America Became Independent, May 1, – July 4, 1776* (New York: Simon and Schuster, 2010); David Armitage, *The Declaration of Independence: A Global History* (Cambridge, MA: Harvard University Press, 2007); **Lynn Hunt**, *Inventing Human Rights: A History* (New York: Norton, 2007). For some oversights, I must offer Dr. Johnson's famous excuse, "Ignorance, madam, pure ignorance."

Jefferson to declare his belief "that the Mecklenburg Resolutions are a fiction."[6]

The Declaration's opening paragraph, with its core of "self-evident" truths and its triad of "inalienable rights," is the foundation of Jefferson's claims as a political thinker, although, as he admitted, its phraseology was not original with him, and it was drafted in committee consultation with others.[7] This he admitted, while at the same time jealously insisting that he be remembered as its author. But the Declaration would be of little importance as the "exclusive property" of one man, or of one republic, a light hidden under a bushel, so he was eager to transmit its illumination to posterity. He aspired to enlighten the world, as he later revealed with the following brilliant metaphor:

> If nature has made any one thing less susceptible than all others of exclusive property, it is the action of the thinking power called an idea, which an individual may exclusively possess as long as he keeps it to himself; but the moment it is divulged, it forces itself into the possession of every one, and the receiver cannot dispossess himself of it. Its peculiar character, too, is that no one possesses the less, because every other possesses the whole of it. He who receives an idea from me, receives instruction himself without lessening mine; as he who lights his taper at mine, receives light without darkening me.[8]

He fancied himself – with a complicated mixture of hubris and humility – not only as a Prometheus to the Republic, but as a Light-Bearer to all nations. He was willing enough to acknowledge that he had lit his taper from the sacred fires of Olympus, and he was supremely generous in passing the flame. He finally explained everything in an

[6] John Adams to Abigail Adams, July 3, 1776. John Adams to Benjamin Rush, September 30, 1805; John Adams to Benjamin Rush, June 21, 1811. McDonald, "Thomas Jefferson's Changing Reputation," considers the Mecklenburg document inauthentic. John Adams to Jefferson, July 21, 1819. John Phillip Reid, "The Irrelevance of the Declaration" in Hendrik Hartog, ed., *Law in the American Revolution and the Revolution in the Law* (New York University Press, 1981), pp. 46–89. William Henry Hoyt, *The Mecklenburg Declaration .... is Spurious* (New York: Knickerbocker Press, 1907). Adams' letter to William Bentley, July 15, 1819, indicates that he probably accepted the Mecklenberg declaration's authenticity on first seeing it.

[7] Becker, *Declaration of Independence*, p. 175 note 1, speculates that Jefferson's "inalienable" was changed to "unalienable" by John Adams. Robert M. S. McDonald, *Confounding Father: Thomas Jefferson's Image in His Own Time* (Charlottesville, VA: University of Virginia Press, 2016), pp. 7, 8, addresses such matters as Jefferson's temporary and decorous anonymity as author of the Declaration and the charge of plagiarizing John Locke. "To underscore this point this book begins with a prologue describing how Jefferson's signature achievement, his 'authorship' of the Declaration of Independence, for years remained unknown."

[8] Jefferson to Isaac McPherson, August 13, 1813.

1825 letter to Henry Lee, asserting that he was neither an erudite copycat nor an entirely original writer, but the transmitter of universal verities. As Emerson would have put it, he had simply "confided himself childlike to the genius of his age."[9] Thomas Jefferson wrote:

> Neither aiming at originality of principle or sentiment, nor yet copied from any particular and previous writing, it was intended to be an expression of the American mind, and to give to that expression the proper tone and spirit called for by the occasion. All its authority rests then on the harmonising sentiments of the day whether expressed in conversations, in letters, printed essays, or in the elementary books of public right, as Aristotle, Cicero, Locke, Sidney, Etc.[10]

The attention of many scholars is drawn to the name of John Locke on this list, since it is known that Jefferson paid tribute to him as one of the three greatest men who had ever lived, but it is often observed that the Declaration's phrase, "life, liberty and pursuit of happiness," differed dramatically from the phrase "life, liberty, and estate," which Locke employed in his *Second Treatise of Government.* Merrill Peterson noted that the phrase "pursuit of happiness" did appear in Locke's *Essay Concerning Human Understanding*, where he said "the highest perfection of intellectual nature lies in a careful and constant pursuit of true and solid happiness." Jack Rakove suggests a more esoteric and more forgettable source, Jean-Jacques Burlamaqui.[11] Although the French "Declaration of the Rights of Man" is supposed to have been so profoundly influenced by Jefferson, it referred to rights of life, liberty, and "property," a word closer to Locke's "estate" than to Jefferson's "pursuit."

Whatever the source of "pursuit of happiness," Jefferson acknowledged debts to Locke and others in his letter to Lee, but he did so with

[9] Ralph Waldo Emerson, "Self Reliance" [1841], in Emerson, *Essays and Lectures* (New York: Library of America, 1983), p. 260.

[10] Anthony Gottlieb, *The Dream of Enlightenment: The Rise of Modern Philosophy* (New York: Liveright, 2016), p. 114, says that "Jefferson rather exaggerated the influence of Locke on his fellow revolutionaries," without denying that Locke's ideas were in the air and having their effects on both Revolutionaries and Royalists of the epoch. Jefferson to Henry Lee, May 8, 1825. Ellis, *What Did the Declaration Declare?*, p. 109, indicates some controversies concerning the intellectual origins of the Declaration, which I mention later. Jefferson dismissed Aristotle as a "mystic" in Jefferson to Benjamin Waterhouse, October 13, 1815.

[11] Merrill Peterson in *Thomas Jefferson and the New Nation*, p. 94. See Peter H. Nidditch, *Essay Concerning Human Understanding* (Oxford University Press, 1975), Book 2, Chapter 21, Section 51. Jack N. Rakove, in *Revolutionaries: A New History of the Invention of America* (Boston, MA: Houghton Mifflin Harcourt, 2010), says the phrase "arguably owed more to Jefferson's reading of the Swiss jurist Jean-Jacques Burlamaqui than it did to his manifest debt to John Locke," p. 300.

such intentional vagueness that a mountain of scholarship bears witness to the scholarly problem of identifying these philosophers' specific influences. Carl Becker's learned discourse of 1922, noting that scholarly treatments were already legion by that date, sometimes mildly ironic in tone, places Locke's influences within the context of Jefferson's own abstruse equivocations, but gives Locke primary credit for the ideas expressed in the Declaration.[12] Becker's treatise has often been a point of departure for subsequent discussions. Jefferson never claimed that his draft of the document was intended to duplicate the sentiments of Locke. Although he said he had "aimed at no originality," he specifically denied the charge of copying from him, while reminding more than one interlocutor that Locke's ideas were in the air of the times. There were, however, several instances over the years in which Jefferson did use the vocabulary of Locke or variations on it. We return intermittently to the matter of vocabulary and to Jefferson and Locke's notions of liberty and property, which are entwined, but not inextricably so.[13]

More than even Adams was aware, Jefferson nurtured the ideas not only that his Declaration of Independence sparked the American Revolution, but that it provided the model for the French "Declaration

[12] Becker wrote, "If the Declaration has not been forgotten, if it has been much criticized, much denounced and much applauded," in his *Declaration of Independence.*

[13] Becker says "Most Americans had absorbed Locke's works as a kind of political gospel," but also notes that Jefferson denied copying Locke in a letter to James Madison, August 30, 1823. He simultaneously confessed to and denied the charge in Jefferson to Henry Lee, May 8, 1825. Much earlier, he wrote to Madison, August 28, 1789, using the phrase, "life, liberty, property or reputation." Jefferson to J. B. Colvin, September 20, 1810 used "life, liberty, property." Jefferson in a letter to Doctor John Manners, June 12, 1817 spoke of "our right to life, liberty, the use of our faculties, the pursuit of happiness." Jefferson to Monsieur A. Coray alluded to "the protection of the life, liberty, property, and safety of the citizen." Jefferson to the General Assembly of Virginia, February 16, 1809 used "life, liberty and property." Jefferson's "Draft Declaration and Protest of the Commonwealth of Virginia," December 1825, spoke of "the enjoyment of life, liberty, property, and peace." James Tully, *A Discourse on Property: John Locke and His Adversaries* (Cambridge University Press, 1982). Scholars have asserted the primacy of Grotius, Vattel, the Scottish Enlightenment, Civic Humanism derived from Machiavelli, or other influences. Ari Helo remarks on Jefferson's erudition with respect to political authors ancient and modern, while strangely attributing to him a "stoic disregard for theory," in *Thomas Jefferson's Ethics and the Politics of Human Progress: The Morality of a Slaveholder* (Cambridge University Press, 2013), p. 5. Joseph Ellis, on the contrary, sees Jefferson as very much a theorist, in *American Sphinx: The Character of Thomas Jefferson* (New York: Knopf, 1997), p. 139, but sees him as more radical than Locke, p. 59. Staughton Lynd asserts that Jefferson and his contemporaries hijacked and radicalized Locke, in *Intellectual Origins of American Radicalism* (New York: Vintage, 1968), pp. 18–20.

of the Rights of Man." While modestly denying originality, he exploited the widely held perception of his masterpiece as radical and revolutionary. He enjoyed his burgeoning reputation as a world-historical figure and the fact that his preamble had come to be viewed as a universal statement of human rights. For, although its body was a list of grievances against one particular king, its preamble was aimed at monarchy in general. The English-speaking peoples did, after all, have an ancient tradition of bringing monarchs down a peg, and the American Revolution might be seen as one occurrence, if hardly the most overwhelming, in that tradition. The Whig interpretation of history, which Jefferson accepted, was the progressive teleology of liberty, equality, reason, and democracy. Jefferson's theory of history self-consciously placed his life and his Declaration within the world pageant of the progress of those forces.[14]

Jefferson's preamble was a brilliant display of "forensic and rhetorical skill," as David Armitage notes, and, as he says, it is "the beginning of a genre," for its words have been adapted to other declarations of national independence.[15] To that I would add that it is often cited entirely outside the context of any struggle for national independence, as a concise declaration of human equality and natural rights. The substance of the preamble is sufficiently malleable to have served divers political purposes for more than two centuries. Few persons, with the notable exception of John Adams, who participated in its creation, have dared to contest its postulate that "all men are created equal." And even Adams, although he noted the obvious fact that we all manifest unequal endowments of physique, mind, and character, believed, as I do, that every person shares in a common human dignity, despite whatever biological, mental, or socio-economic handicaps, and even despite discrepancies in moral rectitude.

As a declaration of the colonies' right to national independence, Jefferson had previously described their material grievances in his *Summary View of the Rights of British America* (1774). The Declaration, if stripped of its philosophical preamble, would be no

[14] Jefferson's Whig historiography is treated in Douglas L. Wilson, "Jefferson vs. Hume," *The William and Mary Quarterly*, 46, no. 1 (January, 1989), 49–70. Also see H. Trevor Colbourn, *The Lamp of Experience: Whig History and the Intellectual Origins of the American Revolution* (Chapel Hill: University of North Carolina Press, 1965).

[15] David Armitage, in "The Declaration of Independence and International Law," *The William and Mary Quarterly*, 59 (January, 2002); Armitage, *The Declaration of Independence*, notes the influence of the Declaration on liberation rhetoric from Haiti, to Vietnam, to Venezuela, to Rhodesia.

more than a list of protests against police actions taken by the Crown against the colonies, along with some very legitimate political complaints. But it barely alluded to the economic causes of discontent, such as restrictions on money supply, obstructions of trade, and the stifling of industrial development. As for the preamble, the nineteenth-century Southern political theorist, John C. Calhoun, made a valid observation on some of its philosophical claims. Rights do not exist in some hypothetical state of nature, which "never did nor can exist," and man's "natural state is the social and political." Brian Steele is rightly appalled by the white-supremacist assertions of Calhoun's commentary on the Declaration of Independence, as he is by those of George Fitzhugh. But black intellectuals Alexander Crummell and W. E. B. Du Bois criticized the "individualistic philosophy of the Declaration of Independence" and argued, as had Aristotle and Calhoun, for the organic state.[16]

REVOLUTIONARY WAR ERA

The Count of Monticello was fiddling in his mansion, hosting chamber music concerts and feasting with German aristocrats, while George Washington was wintering at Valley Forge. Years later, he attempted to pressure Henry Lee to suppress the record of his embarrassing performance as wartime governor of Virginia. Richard Brookhiser has starkly portrayed Jefferson's jealousy and the "pride of a snob" he directed at Alexander Hamilton, the upstart artillery captain who was charging into gunfire while "Squire Jefferson" was at his Philadelphia writing-desk. Jefferson's unpublished autobiography, with its foreword called the *Anas*, was calculated to shape the historical memory of himself as the true father of his country, while Washington was blinded by the philistine Colonel Hamilton. He was eager to deploy the most spurious second-hand rumors concerning his rival. Repeatedly, he revealed a situational ethic, and in many instances, the contrast between his public pronouncements and his private life lent credence to Hamilton's opinion of him as a "contemptible hypocrite."[17]

[16] Steele, *Thomas Jefferson and American Nationhood*, p. 300 note 50. Alexander Crummell, "The Assassination of President Garfield" in *The Greatness of Christ and Other Sermons* (New York: Thomas Whittaker, 1882), p. 325. W. E. B. Du Bois, "The Conservation of Races," *American Negro Academy Occasional Papers*, no. 2 (1898), p. 7. See G. R. G. Mure, "The Organic State," *Philosophy*, 24, no. 90 (July, 1949), 205–218.

[17] Richard Brookhiser, *Alexander Hamilton, American* (New York: Free Press, 1999). Alexander Hamilton to James Bayard, January 16, 1801.

As did most gentlemen of his class, Jefferson almost automatically held a commission in the Virginia militia at the beginning of the Revolution, but he never saw action, and, more or less informally, he abandoned the title of Colonel to succeed Patrick Henry as wartime governor of the State. Of his governorship of Virginia, John Quincy Adams wrote, "it is evident he reflected with no satisfaction upon that portion of his life." When Patrick Henry accused him of malperformance as governor of Virginia, he invited James Madison to join him in prayers for Henry's death. Even the sympathetic historian Frank Cogliano feels hesitantly compelled to entitle a paper "The Cowardice of Thomas Jefferson."[18]

A Machiavellian refinement of policy was evident in his attempt to expurgate his poor showing as military governor of Virginia from the published memoirs of Henry Lee. Cogliano and other scholars have correctly observed that no one expected Jefferson to lead a kamikaze charge against the British forces in defense of Richmond. While comparisons are odious, Jefferson's failure to offer any resistance to Benedict Arnold's invasion invites comparison to the performance of the American General Benjamin Lincoln, who withstood the siege of Charleston for six weeks before surrendering under heavy bombardment. The treatment received by General Lincoln, who was paroled after his defeat, but later returned honorably to the field and took part in the Yorktown campaign, leads us to sober reflection on what might have happened to Jefferson had he attempted to defend Richmond. Jefferson's slave Isaac, who was just a child at the time, recalled that:

> The British said they didn't want anybody but the Governor; didn't want to hurt him, only wanted to put a pair of silver handcuffs on him; had brought them along with them on purpose.[19]

Benedict Arnold commanded the army that searched for him, and one must wonder whether that embittered man would have handled a Jefferson in uniform as a fellow officer or as a captured "traitor." If the treatment of General Benjamin Lincoln provides any historical

[18] *Memoirs of John Quincy Adams*, vol. VIII; https://archive.org/details/memoirsofjohnquio8adamuoft Frank Cogliano, typescript published online, "The Cowardice of Thomas Jefferson," Inaugural Lecture, St. Cecilia's Hall, University of Edinburgh, May 12, 2009. Also see Frank Cogliano, *Emperor of Liberty: Thomas Jefferson's Foreign Policy* (New Haven, CT: Yale University Press, 2014), p. 41.

[19] Silver handcuffs: see "Isaac Jefferson's Recollections" in James Adam Bear, ed., *Jefferson at Monticello: Recollections of a Monticello Slave and a Monticello Overseer* (Charlottesville, VA: University of Virginia Press, 1967), p. 9.

parallel, we cannot think that a hypothetical "Colonel Jefferson," wearing the continental buff and blue, would have been led off in handcuffs. If Jefferson had surrendered after defending and losing a city, his fate would very possibly have been similar to that of General Lincoln. Jefferson was no pacifist: he called on others to lay down their lives in 1776, and in 1812, and his appallingly cold-blooded endorsement of the French Reign of Terror was anything but pacifistic. In 1815, he wrote a highly critical letter to Marie-Joseph-Paul-Yves-Roch-Gilbert du Motier, the Marquis de Lafayette, concerning the performance of American military commanders in the late war and joined in the scapegoating of General William Hull, accusing him of treason. Jefferson could not refrain from questioning the bravery of Hamilton on a later occasion, or generally dismissing as "a want of forethought" the courage of African Americans.[20]

His remarkably gracious treatment of captured Hessians, while perhaps within the scope of eighteenth-century norms, raises our modern eyebrows. During the winter of 1779 he entertained Hessian officers with concerts and minuets while Hamilton was enduring a rough winter in Middlebrooks, New Jersey. He saw to it that his British and German prisoners of war were ensconced in mansions, complete with African American servants. Persons of color were working at Monticello when he received a Hessian commander, Major General Baron Friedrich Adolph Riedesel, along with his baroness and three daughters, joining them in dancing, dining, and playing music for strings, but the idea of African Americans being asked to join his German guests at table would have seemed the height of absurdities. The historical memory of most Americans is closely associated with the suffering of Washington's troops at Valley Forge, not with Jefferson's entertaining Hessian officers while dancing minuets and playing chamber music, perhaps with the lovely Betsy Hemings, the mother of Sally, pouring

[20] In a letter to Lafayette, February 14, 1815, Jefferson joined in the scapegoating of William Hull, the twice-commended Revolutionary war hero who lost a son in the War of 1812, as "the traitor Hull" for abandoning Detroit, ill prepared for war, on August 16, 1812. Hull was convicted of treason and sentenced to death, but President Madison commuted his sentence. In 1825, Lafayette reportedly visited and embraced Hull, saying, "We have both suffered contumely and reproach; but our characters are vindicated; let us forgive our enemies and die in Christian love and peace with all mankind," *Publications of the Colonial Society of Massachusetts, Transactions 1904–1906* (Boston, MA: The Colonial Society of Massachusetts, 1907), vol. X, pp. 368–369. The remarks on Hamilton are in Jefferson to James Madison, September 8, 1793; on the courage of African Americans, Thomas Jefferson, *Notes on the State of Virginia*, ed. David Waldstreicher (Boston, MA: Bedford Books, 2002), p. 176. In these chapters I make much use of this edition of the *Notes* – reliable, readily available, containing an excellent introduction, and endorsed by several experts in the field.

the wine. The scene presaged things to come when, during World War II, German prisoners, being transported under the supervision of African American MPs, could eat in railroad dining cars where their guards in American uniform could not be seated.

The universal entitlement to human rights must not be chained to any claim that "all men are created equal," for that is neither factual nor fair. If all people were created equal, there would be no need for handicapped parking. There would be no need for public programs in health, education, or social security.[21] There would be no need to pay elected officials for public service in any of these realms.[22] Of course there would be no need for labor unions, or any other efforts on behalf of wage-earners, such as those that Thomas Paine promoted while he was a public employee in England and for decades thereafter.[23] John Elway, a legendary National Football League quarterback and Stanford University economics graduate, stated that he was a Republican because "I don't believe in safety nets." It may be true that the strong man has no need of a safety net. But life does not belong only to the strong. People do not enter life's competition with an equal set of talents, and it is impossible for any society to offer everyone an equal chance to pursue happiness. The African American feminist Sojourner Truth, without making the least concession of inequality, raised a crucial issue in an 1852 speech: "If my cup won't hold but a pint, and yours holds a quart, wouldn't you be mean not to let me have my little half measure full?"[24]

[21] The International Covenant on Economic, Social and Cultural Rights views access to free education, including higher education, as a basic human right. By contrast, in the presidential campaign of 2010, Mitt Romney asserted that every citizen had a right to "all the education they can afford."

[22] Benjamin Franklin wrote to William Strahan, August 19, 1784:

> You do not "approve the Annihilation of profitable Places, for you do not see why a Statesman who does his Business well, should not be paid for his Labour as well as any other Workman." Agreed. But why more than any other Workman? The less the Salary the greater the Honor. In so great a Nation there are many rich enough to afford giving their time to the Public, And there are, I make no doubt many wise and able Men who would take as much Pleasure in governing for nothing as they do in playing Chess for nothing.

[23] Eric Foner, *Tom Paine and Revolutionary America* (Oxford University Press, 1976), pp. 216–220. Pain was installed as an excise clerk and published "The Case of the Officers of Excise" in 1772. He continued to defend the workplace rights of government employees in *The Rights of Man* (1792).

[24] Sojourner Truth speech "Ain't I A Woman?" Delivered at the 1851 Women's Convention, Akron, Ohio. John Elway to Fox News: quoted in www.democraticunderground.com/1251351983

Sojourner Truth was an imposing woman, big and strong enough to do the work of a prime male field hand.[25] She had higher intelligence than most white people, greater daring than most black people, and more imagination than the majority of either. And she was wise enough to know that no one's dignity should be determined by their giftedness. While human dignity is something that must be fought for, it does not belong only to the person who is strong enough to overwhelm all opposition. Nor is it limited to the person who has the brains to escape the squalor of a New York slum or the shackles of a slave plantation. Courage and perseverance are gifts of Providence no less than good looks, mathematical aptitude, or loving parents. Thomas Jefferson's Creator gave him superior endowments of bodily strength, mental genius, and social status. When it came to the gifts of intellectual and moral consistency, he was no more fortunate than most of us.

[25] During this speech, according to legend, when a heckler in the audience questioned whether Truth was actually a woman, she is said to have bared her breasts and asked him if he cared to suck. Nell Painter, in her biography of Sojourner Truth, has questioned the accuracy of this story.

2

Lincoln and Historiography

A PRESENTISM OF THE PAST

The Gettysburg Address radically transformed the meaning of the words "all men are created equal." Lincoln was displaying the Machiavellian traits of lion and fox. As a lion, he had already spoken with the Army of the Potomac; now Lincoln the fox was masking his "great civil war" as a test of the nation's founding "proposition that all men are created equal." His Gettysburg Address was an answer to Chief Justice Roger B. Taney's *obiter dictum*, in *Dred Scott v. Sandford*, that the words of the Declaration of Independence "would seem to embrace the whole human family, and if they were used in a similar instrument at this day would be so understood. But it is too clear for dispute, that the enslaved African race were not intended to be included, and formed no part of the people who framed and adopted this declaration." But by 1863 the Civil War had evolved into a revolution towards "a new birth of freedom." The Battle of Gettysburg and Lincoln's Address that followed it were an answer to Taney's *dictum* in vigorous Jacksonian terms, to wit: "The Chief Justice has made his decision, now let him enforce it."[1]

[1] James M. McPherson follows the interpretation of Charles Beard, on the left, and Edward A. Pollard, on the right, that the Civil War transformed the Founders' America rather than preserving it, in *Abraham Lincoln and the Second American Revolution* (Oxford University Press, 1991). The Jackson quotation was conveyed to Horace Greeley by George N. Briggs, a Whig Representative from Massachusetts, and later governor of the state. Andrew Jackson, in reaction to Chief Justice John Marshall's opinion, in *Worcester v. Georgia*, that all laws of Georgia dealing with the Cherokees were unconstitutional: "John Marshall has made his decision; now let him enforce it!" See Robert V. Remini, *The Life of Andrew Jackson* (Baltimore: Johns Hopkins University Press, 1981), vol. II, pp. 276–277.

Taney, to his credit, was doing impeccable cultural history when he wrote that Jefferson's words of 1776 could not have the same meaning in 1857. He was cautioning against "presentism," which is defined by historian Douglas Wilson as "the term that historians use for applying contemporary or otherwise inappropriate standards to the past." Taney was arguing validly, however cruelly, against presentism, but Jefferson was himself a presentist. On the eve of his return from Paris to assume his duties as Secretary of State in George Washington's government, he offered his opinions on constitutional originalism to Madison, expressing his disdain for a "sanctimonious reverence for the past" and so famously saying, "The earth belongs always to the living generation." The ink was barely dry, the new government was barely launched, and already he was expressing his irreverence for the original intent, and prolonged duration of a constitution that had been in effect for a mere six months.[2]

George Bancroft, the nineteenth-century historian who has been called the "Father of American history," was committed to the idea that Jefferson was the primal abolitionist, and that Lincoln preserved Jefferson's original intent; he repeatedly made that clear in an "Address on the Life and Character of Abraham Lincoln." If Bancroft was right, then Lincoln at Gettysburg was a conservative, committed to sustaining the nation's founding principles. The best of historians are at one with Bancroft insofar as they see the historical linkage of the Declaration of Independence, the Constitution, and the Gettysburg Address. The brilliant exercises of Pauline Maier and Douglas Wilson are among the most noteworthy examples of ripe scholars doing so. Both were compelled, as every careful reader must be, to recall, as Lincoln did, the present existence of the past. But we cannot ignore Chief Justice Taney's caveat that the egalitarianism of the Declaration could not and did not mean to Jefferson's contemporaries what it meant to Lincoln's generation or to ours. As Michael Rozbicki, Maurizio Valsania, and thinkers before and after them have convincingly demonstrated, the employment of such terms as "liberty" and "equality" had variable implications in the seventeenth, eighteenth, and nineteenth centuries, and they continue to do so today. The Founders and Framers of the Constitution were sensible to the mutability of language.[3]

[2] Jefferson to James Madison, September 6, 1789; Douglas Wilson, "Thomas Jefferson and the Character Issue,"*Atlantic Monthly* (November, 1992), online edn.

[3] George Bancroft, *Memorial Address on the Life and Character of Abraham Lincoln: Delivered, at the request of both Houses of Congress of America, on the 12th*

Thomas Jefferson was always ambivalent concerning the Constitution of the United States and the mingled intentions of the "assembly of demigods" who created it. From the beginning, he expressed his uneasiness with the fact that it was drafted by conspirators, sworn to secrecy in a smoke-filled Philadelphia room, while he was several weeks and thousands of miles away in Paris. His most important objections to the Constitutional Convention and the secrecy of its proceedings were expressed at the time in private letters to James Madison and John Adams.[4] He insisted that a bill of rights be added before ratification, and he did not see it as having any perpetual validity. He later drafted his oft-quoted statement that "The earth belongs always to the living generation," an affirmation of his belief that the Constitution was *de facto* temporary, and that its laws, like all laws, ought to expire "in their natural course with those who gave them being." In this regard, he famously wrote to James Madison only a year after the Constitution's ratification that:

> Every constitution then, & every law, naturally expires at the end of 19 years. If it be enforced longer, it is an act of force, & not of right. It may be said that the succeeding generation exercising in fact the power of repeal, this leaves them as free as if the constitution or law had been expressly limited to 19 years only.[5]

And these were not merely sentiments of the present moment, for twenty-seven years later, as a senior statesman, Founding Father, and former president, he wrote to Samuel Kercheval on July 12, 1816:

> Some men look at Constitutions with sanctimonious reverence, & deem them, like the ark of the covenant, too sacred to be touched. They ascribe to the men of the

of February, 1866 (Washington, DC: Government Printing Office, 1866). Garry Wills, *Lincoln at Gettysburg* (New York: Simon and Schuster, 1992), pp. 38–40, avers that Lincoln transmogrified the Declaration by sleight of hand. Douglas Wilson puts Wills' idea more euphemistically in "Thomas Jefferson and the Character Issue." Pauline Maier, *American Scripture* (New York: Knopf, 1997), p. 208. On language, see Michael Rozbicki, *Culture and Liberty in the Age of the American Revolution* (Charlottesville, VA: University of Virginia Press, 2011). James Madison wrote of the mutability of language in a letter to Converse Sherman, March 10, 1826, cited in R. K. Matthews, *If Men Were Angels* (Lawrence, KS: University Press of Kansas, 1995), p. 220.

[4] "Assembly of demigods" is Jefferson's description of the constitutional Convention held from May 25 to September 17, 1787, and described in Jefferson to John Adams, August 7, 1787; November 13, 1787. His criticisms of the new Constitution, and the Convention's secrecy, "tying up the tongues of their members," in Jefferson to James Madison, December 20, 1787, and Jefferson to John Adams, August 30, 1787.

[5] Jefferson to James Madison, September 6, 1789.

> preceding age a wisdom more than human, and suppose what they did to be beyond amendment ... I am certainly not an advocate for frequent & untried changes in laws and constitutions ... As new discoveries are made, new truths disclosed, and manners and opinions change with the change of circumstances, institutions must advance also, and keep pace with the times. We might as well require a man to wear still the coat which fitted him when a boy, as civilised society to remain ever under the regimen of their barbarous ancestors.

Jefferson was not a constitutional conservative. He rejected the idea that "one generation has the right to bind another," repeating four times in the letter to Madison that the "earth belongs to the living" and not to the dead, and that the words set down by one generation could not perpetually constrain its successors. When Speaker of the House Paul Ryan once asserted that "Jefferson was speaking not just for his day but for all future time," he was probably not thinking about "original intent" or the semantical exercise of Chief Justice Taney, who might have added that Ryan's opinions must stand on their merits, not simply on the sanctity of Jefferson's supposed precepts.[6] By invoking the name of a Founding Father, Ryan proved Gordon Wood's observation that "We Americans seem to have a special need for these authentic historical figures in the here and now."[7] Ryan demonstrates that the charge of "presentism" can be levied not only against those latter-day moralists who would condemn Jefferson as a slaveholder and a hypocrite. Anyone is guilty of "presentism" who invokes Jefferson, as Lincoln did, to valorize contemporary goals by summoning the past.

ANDREW JACKSON'S JEFFERSON: A TOAST TO "OUR NATIONAL UNION"

Because the term "nationalism" may be defined in various ways, one must be cautious in applying it to Jefferson's conception of American destiny, although there is much to be said for the position that Jefferson was strongly committed to the National Union. Reasonable arguments have been constructed by Brian Steele and other learned hands to soften the implications of Jeffersonian regionalism, but these works never overlook the importance of Jefferson's Kentucky Resolution, which provided some

[6] See Representative Paul Ryan, "Keynote Address, "The National Association of Manufacturers Board of Directors Meeting, October 8, 2009." Italics and ellipses are in the original on Paul Ryan's official website. See more at: http://paulryan.house.gov/newsroom/documentsingle.aspx?DocumentID=193718#sthash.oy4RxCVb.dpuf

[7] Gordon Wood, *Revolutionary Characters* (New York: Penguin, 2006), p. 3.

intellectual justification for nullification in 1828 and secession in 1860.[8] Nonetheless, it is a matter of frequent ironic observation that, by 1812, Jeffersonian Republicans were among the most passionate nationalists, while the Federalist Party had become associated with disunion. If Democratic Republicans maintained their verbal hostility to "consolidating government," and if their leader seemed at times overly protective of states' rights, Jefferson was finally to assert in a letter to Lafayette that the "cement of this union is in the heart blood of every American."[9]

Jeffersonian nationalism provided the foundations on which Jacksonian nationalism was later constructed, and thereby hang the two ironies, that Jacksonian democracy is often associated with states' rights doctrine, and that Jefferson purportedly did not approve of Jackson. If Jefferson was a founder of the Jacksonian doctrine of states' rights, he also contributed to the nationalist, expansionist, and white-supremacist doctrines associated with Jackson. On the one hand, Theodore Roosevelt was correct in pointing out that Jefferson's Kentucky Resolution, along with Madison's Virginia Resolution, provided the basis for the nullification doctrine, but, on the other hand, James Madison, the last surviving Jeffersonian, repudiated the nullification doctrine at the time of the 1828–32 South Carolina crisis.

Jackson's famous words "Our Federal Union; it must be preserved" placed him in the situational irony of inadvertently supporting the "American System" of his enemy Henry Clay and opposing his erstwhile states' rights ally John C. Calhoun. Jackson spoke the words when offering a toast at the annual Democratic Jefferson Day dinner of April 13, 1830. Calhoun's famous retort was "The Union, next to Liberty, most dear." Each man sought to affirm a continuity between the party founded by Jefferson and Madison and his own political agenda. Jacksonian Democrats were determined to wrest the mantle of Jefferson from the nullification faction led by Hayne and Calhoun, but they were now obliged to perform tremendous intellectual contortions in order to defend a Hamiltonian tariff associated with the policies of Henry Clay and his detested Whig Party. The toasting duel at the Jefferson dinner of 1830 illustrates how Jefferson had become, only four years after his death, a sacred symbol for both states' rights and American nationalism, a contradiction most notable within the very party he founded.

8 Brian Steele painstakingly and thoroughly discusses the Kentucky Resolution issue in *Thomas Jefferson and American Nationhood* (Cambridge University Press, 2012), particularly on p. 240 note 15.

9 Jefferson to Lafayette, February 14, 1815.

FREDERICK DOUGLASS, ABRAHAM LINCOLN, AND JEFFERSON'S LEGACY

Abraham Lincoln was forced to confront Jefferson's theory "that a little rebellion, now and then, is a good thing," which in practice cost 700,000 American lives. At the outbreak of the rebellion, he carefully studied Jackson's Nullification Proclamation against South Carolina, to challenge the legality of that same state's secession in 1860. Jefferson's insurrectionary hyperbole has unfortunately become the perennial scripture of gun-toting anarchists. In the wake of the Oklahoma City bombing of 1995, and the Newtown, Connecticut Sandyhook massacre of 2012, extremist militias mindlessly and irrelevantly recycled what were supposed to be Jeffersonian slogans as gun sales proliferated. What makes this so tragically ironic is the fact that, while Jefferson could engage in symbolic exhortations to violence, he was pacifistic in practice, as for example when he chose to enact an embargo in order to avoid going to war in 1807.[10]

American party genealogies are spurious, as Lincoln pointed out in one of his political yarns:

> I remember once being much amused at seeing two partially intoxicated men engage in a fight with their great-coats on, which fight, after a long, and rather harmless contest, ended in each having fought himself out of his own coat, and into that of the other. If the two leading parties of this day are really identical with the two in the days of Jefferson and Adams, they have performed the same feat as the two drunken men.[11]

"All honor to Jefferson" was Lincoln's resonant conclusion to the 1859 statement, but he asserted that the party claiming Jefferson's mantle in his own epoch "hold Liberty to be nothing." His larger point was that any attempt by either party to boast of its legacy, heritage, or genealogy had become risible. Lincoln obliterated Jeffersonian democracy, thank God, by executive order, big government, and military authority. He destroyed Jeffersonian America forcibly by the same anti-democratic means that he used to emancipate the slaves – whether by proclamation, by the use of Sherman's army, or by passage of the Thirteenth Amendment. Lincoln

10 Spurious statements on the Second Amendment have also been attributed to Jefferson. The Thomas Jefferson Foundation has issued the following statement: "We currently have no evidence that Thomas Jefferson said or wrote, 'The beauty of the Second Amendment is that it will not be needed until they try to take it' or any of its listed variations": www.monticello.org/site/jefferson/beauty-second-amendment-quotation

11 Abraham Lincoln to Messrs. Henry L. Pierce and others, April 6, 1859.

was possibly influenced by Frederick Douglass' commentary on Jefferson's Declaration of Independence, as his Gettysburg Address was practically a synopsis of Douglass' widely circulated response to Taney's discourse in *Dred Scott v. Sandford.*

In the summer following the decision, the *New York Times* and other newspapers reprinted Douglass' lengthy commentary on it, which began, as Lincoln's subsequently would, with a reference to the Republic's birth date, "only eighty two years" previous, and continued with an invocation of the Declaration of Independence and its principles of liberty and equality. Douglass' article was more direct than Lincoln's Address in its deliberate and systematic attack on Taney's assertion that the Declaration's "all men are created equal" had nothing to do with the African American population. Lincoln's taciturn pronouncement in the Gettysburg Address did not mention slavery or the enslaved population. He neither implicitly nor directly reiterated Douglass' systematic counter-arguments to Taney's assertions, but simply declared his own diametrically opposed position.[12]

It has been claimed that Lincoln "hated Jefferson as a man," especially after reading Theodore Dwight's *The Character of Thomas Jefferson, as Exhibited in His Own Writings* (1839). According to William Henry Herndon, his law partner, "Mr. Lincoln never liked Jefferson's moral character after that reading." Dwight's book was a thorough, systematic, and artfully eloquent diatribe. It was written from a Federalist-Whig perspective with retrospectives on the Embargo Act of 1807, and portrayed Jefferson's administration as the embodiment of big-government tyranny. There is no evidence independent of Herndon's testimony that Lincoln read the book or that he agreed with its negative interpretation of Jefferson, but there is merit in the assertion of historian Allan Guelzo that the mature Lincoln was "an adversary of almost every practical aspect of Thomas Jefferson's political worldview." Lincoln's political legacy, like Dwight's historiography, was Federalist and Whig, but Lincoln chose to define Jefferson's moral legacy and democratic egalitarianism and to identify himself with that moral legacy.[13]

[12] See Wilson J. Moses, "'The Ever Present Now': Frederick Douglass' Pragmatic Constitutionalism," *Journal of African American History* (winter, 2013–14).

[13] Allen C. Guelzo, "What Did Lincoln Really Think of Jefferson?"*The New York Times*, Op-Ed (July 3, 2015); Allen C. Guelzo, *Abraham Lincoln: Redeemer President* (Grand Rapids: Eerdmans, 1999), pp. 3–5.

The pro-Jeffersonian Henry S. Randall countered the assertions of Dwight within a generation, also making extensive use of Jefferson's writings, and supplementing these with testimony from "a number of surviving grandchildren, who lived from ten to thirty years under the same roof with him." Randall undertook to refute the "leering, sneering, dodging way of making charges by implication, and insulting by innuendo – which has been so extensively practised by early and late calumniators of Mr. Jefferson." He constructed a sympathetic three-volume portrait that retains its influence to the present day. It is the view of Jefferson "as the conceded founder of that party which soon obtained undisputed control in our General Government and which consequently affixed its own interpretation to our federal Constitution." Despite Lincoln's caveat that party genealogies are useless, and despite the observation of numerous historians that Jeffersonian principles may be invoked by adherents of every political persuasion, Jefferson stands today, as he stood in Randall's memory, as the founder of the Democratic Party.[14]

BRAHMIN AND KNICKERBOCKER HISTORIOGRAPHY: ADAMS, LODGE, AND ROOSEVELT

At the end of the nineteenth century, three Republican historians, Henry Adams, Theodore Roosevelt, and Henry Cabot Lodge, reinvigorated Dwight's Federalist-Whig tradition. Their analysis cannot be dismissed with the simple ad hominem argument that the authors were elitists, racists, or "social Darwinists." They represented views that were associated with the Northeastern elite, but American ideological conflicts have often consisted of little more than the vendettas of elitist snobs against elitist snobs. American political leaders all claim to represent the popular causes of life, liberty, and democracy. Adams, Theodore Roosevelt, and Lodge comprised a loose tradition of a progressive-elitist historiography that was a bridge between Alexander Hamilton and the progressives of the early twentieth century, and they saw no reason to confer a demigod status on Thomas Jefferson. Henry Adams, like his father, Charles Francis Adams, continued to brood on the ancient conflicts between the Adams and the Virginia dynasty, despite the original Adams' famous reconciliation with Jefferson. Charles Francis Adams, in preserving the intellectual legacy of John Quincy Adams, referred to Jefferson as "a

[14] Henry Stevens Randall, *The Life of Thomas Jefferson* (Philadelphia: Lippincott, 1865), p. vi.

brilliant rather than a just thinker."[15] Henry Adams' historiography succeeded that of his father, Charles Francis, and was passed on to Theodore Roosevelt and Henry Cabot Lodge, who artfully portrayed Jefferson as a serpent in Eden, a cunning seducer, an elegant Mephistopheles, whose legacy was demagoguery and rebellion.[16]

Adams and Lodge were Boston Brahmins; Theodore Roosevelt was a Knickerbocker Patroon, and all three of these patrician historians were sufficiently erudite to appreciate Jefferson's mental powers without being intimidated or unduly impressed by his intellectual credentials.[17] In addition, they were unafraid of pointing out Jefferson's logical inconsistencies and pragmatic contradictions. Adams described him as among "the most aristocratic of democrats," a paradox that was not meant to invalidate him but, on the contrary, to make him a fascinating and appealing subject.[18] The dialectics of aristocracy and democracy endowed Adams' description of Jefferson's administrations with a rich mixture of admiration and irony. His own family's intellectual and political legacies gave Henry Adams critical perspectives on both the Federalists and the Republicans, and placed him in an ideal position to appreciate Jefferson's intellectual vacillation between the values of both traditions.

Flourishing in an epoch when memories of the Civil War were still alive, Adams, Lodge, and Theodore Roosevelt wrote with a bias against the party of rebellion, and particularly in the case of Roosevelt, they saw Jefferson as not only the patron saint, but the intellectual forebear of Jefferson Davis. Admitting that Jefferson's presidency had achieved at least one great thing, the Louisiana Purchase, they attributed Jefferson's primary importance to that striking monumental excursion into federalism. Theodore Roosevelt, whose theories of history were as passionate and volatile as his personality, and who defined progress partially in terms of a vigorous Union government's moral triumph over slavery, saw

[15] Charles Francis Adams, *The Life of John Adams, Begun by John Quincy Adams, and Completed by Charles Francis Adams* (Philadelphia: Lippincott, 1871), vol. II, p. 148.

[16] Direct quotations from Roosevelt's papers provided in Daniel Ruddy, *Theodore Roosevelt's History of the United States* (New York: Smithsonian Books, 2010), in particular pp. 75–91.

[17] Kathleen M. Dalton, "Theodore Roosevelt, Knickerbocker Aristocrat," *New York History*, 67, no. 1 (January, 1986), 39–65.

[18] Henry Adams, "Most Aristocratic of Democrats" in his *History of the United States during the Administrations of Thomas Jefferson* (New York: Library of America, 1986 [1890]), p. 131. Adams anticipated Richard Hofstadter's characterization of Jefferson as "The Aristocrat as Democrat" in his *The American Political Tradition* (New York: Knopf, 1948).

Jefferson as guiding "seditious agitation" with his Virginia and Kentucky Resolutions.

Both Lodge and Roosevelt also showed some sympathy for African Americans and some inclinations towards an antislavery perspective on the history of the Western hemisphere. Lodge, in editing the papers of Alexander Hamilton, sided with him not only in his role as Secretary of the Treasury, but also in his clash with Jefferson over the Jay Treaty, which happened to be partially related to the British liberation of slaves who had fought on the side of the Crown. Henry Adams treated the slave revolutionary Toussaint Louverture with admiration, and gave him greater credit than Jefferson for the Louisiana Purchase. It is necessary to note that these elitist historians, while by no means racial egalitarians, were unequivocal in their belief that slavery was an evil and that emancipation was a good. This view was hardly universal among the succeeding generation of historians, represented by Ulrich Bonnell Philips and William Archibald Dunning, who saw slavery as a benevolent institution. In this regard, we shall presently discuss Claude Bowers, who also viewed slavery as benevolent.

HENRY ADAMS' APPRAISAL OF JEFFERSON

The fine, aristocratic hand of Henry Adams placed a carefully polished stiletto beneath the sternum of Thomas Jefferson, whom he described early in his history of the Jefferson Administrations as "almost feminine," and on a later page decided that indeed "Jefferson's nature was feminine." He also called him a "deist," although he was well aware of Jefferson's preference for the terms "Unitarian" or "anti-Trinitarian." He described him as "ineffective in debate," indiscrete, inaccurate in his assertions, and a sometimes uncritical Francophile, who "seemed during his entire life to breathe with perfect satisfaction nowhere except in the liberal, literary, and scientific air of Paris in 1789." Adams' own inconsistency was that he seemed unable to decide whether to describe Jefferson as an effeminate, overly refined cosmopolite who longed for the Parisian metropole, or as a provincial frontier recluse who eventually stopped reading the newspapers, having retreated to the sanctuary of Monticello on March 15, 1809, and who "never again passed beyond the bounds of a few adjacent counties."[19]

Henry Adams said that "Ridicule of his opinions and of himself was an easy task, in which his Federalist opponents delighted, for his English was

[19] Henry Adams, *History of the United States during the Administrations of Thomas Jefferson*, pp. 100, 101, 1251.

often confused, his assertions inaccurate, and at times of excitement he was apt to talk with indiscretion."[20] But Adams was guilty of his own indiscrete contradictions. He was aware of Jefferson's condemnation of Europe, especially Paris with its effete refinements. He also knew of Jefferson's undemocratic defamation of the urban proletariat: "The mobs of great cities add just so much to the support of pure government, as sores do to the strength of the human body." He knew that Jefferson at times seemed more committed to Virginia than to American nationhood. Adams was unwilling to accept Jefferson's provincialism, his nationalism, or his cosmopolitanism at face value, and this led him to his own contradictions. His observation that Jefferson spent the entire twenty years after his retirement from the presidency in the splendid isolation of Monticello and Poplar Forest rings truer than his assertion that Jefferson was by temperament a cosmopolitan Parisian.

Although Adams' ostensible purpose was to delineate the Jefferson presidency, he felt no obligation to narrowly define that task, and his work was enriched by his interspersing it with broader commentary on Jefferson's role in the intellectual history of the Enlightenment. At one point Adams invented for Jefferson a series of questions that "in all modesty he might reasonably" have asked himself. The rhetorical questions that Adams placed in Jefferson's mind were:

> What name recorded in history would stand higher than his own for qualities of the noblest order in statesmanship? Had he not been first to conceive and to put in practice the theories of future democracy? Had he not succeeded in the experiment? Had he not doubled the national domain? Was not his government a model of republican virtues? With what offence against the highest canons of personal merit could he be charged? What ruler of ancient or modern times, what Trajan or Antonine, what Edward or Louis, was more unselfish or was truer to the interests intrusted to his care? Who had proposed to himself a loftier ideal? Among all the kings and statesmen who swayed the power of empire, where could one be found who had looked so far into the future, and had so boldly grappled with its hopes?[21]

Jefferson may indeed have asked himself these questions, as Adams hypothesized, but the examination of conscience is a task that is sometimes more easily imposed on others than on oneself. It is not known that Jefferson ever compared himself to any of the ancient or modern

[20] Ibid., p. 101.

[21] Henry Adams cunningly invents this lengthy series of rhetorical questions and places them in Jefferson's mouth in his *History of the United States during the Administrations of Thomas Jefferson*, p. 616.

figures on Adams' roster, but it is by no means ridiculous to draw such comparisons. While the enlightened ideals he articulated were noble, they were far removed from the realities of his daily existence. Jefferson's world echoed the dying feudal society. He had sat in the Paris theatre, viewing the plays of Beaumarchais and mingling with the very aristocracy that these plays criticized.[22] Returning to Virginia, he chose to live in the medieval/seigneurial domain, rather than the urbane world of his contemporaries Samuel Johnson, Benjamin Franklin, Thomas Paine, and William Blake. He retreated to Monticello and his more remote plantation, Poplar Forest, abandoning the rough and tumble of the bourgeois Enlightenment where so many of his contemporaries thrived, a world that was within his intellectual reach but beyond his emotional grasp.

Adams consistently noted, with obvious happiness and sarcasm, that Jefferson increasingly implemented the policy of vigorous government. He observed that Albert Gallatin, Jefferson's Secretary of the Treasury, advanced policies that were Hamiltonian and observed that Jefferson "eventually gave up his Virginia dogmas and adopted Gallatin's ideas." Theodore Roosevelt would later make similar observations, along with the claim that Jefferson was most successful when he behaved like a Federalist. And Adams could not resist describing Jefferson's administration of Louisiana as "despotic." He compared it to the imperial administration of the territory by the king of Spain and sided with the Federalists, who considered this colonial administration unconstitutional. One biographer of Adams notes that "The author of the Declaration of Independence now found himself in the position of George III." Adams himself wrote, "By an act of sovereignty as despotic as the corresponding acts of France and Spain, Jefferson and his party had annexed to the Union a foreign people and a vast territory, which profoundly altered the relations of the States and the character of their nationality."[23]

Adams, without invoking Hamilton, systematically set about proving Hamilton's thesis that Jefferson was not inclined to undermine either federal or executive authority. Scholars like Brian Steele and Peter Onuf are in his company when they note the themes of "federalism" and

[22] Elsewhere in this volume, I compare Jefferson to Count Almaviva in Beaumarchais' Figaro trilogy (see Chapter 10 below).

[23] Henry Adams, *History of the United States during the Administrations of Thomas Jefferson*, p. 614; also see p. 847. For the despotic administration of Louisiana, see p. 381.

"nationhood" that pervade Jefferson's writings from as early as 1774. Henry Adams, in formulating his insinuations of Jeffersonian "federalism," was aware that John Adams had opposed Hamilton, and thus Henry had no familial investment in nourishing Hamilton's reputation, and no inclination to invoke the "high federalist" tradition that had undermined his great-grandfather's administration. Even after three generations, Adams nurtured a quiet cynicism towards both Hamiltonians and Republicans, although he, like his ancestors, had some affinities to both. Thus Adams wrote with a Federalist and elitist bias, and did so without the pro-Hamiltonian sentiments that would later appear in the writings of Lodge and Theodore Roosevelt.

Adams resisted any inclination to portray Jefferson as a cynic, for he had something more subtly damaging in mind. He described Jefferson as "feminine" more than once and painted him as an ethereal idealist, going out of his way to attest to "the purity of his life." These attributions hardly prevented Adams from launching a painstakingly thorough digression on Jefferson's supposedly excessive virility, "the libels of Callender," and devoting space to Jefferson's legendary affair with a female slave, nor did it prevent his reprinting the verses of Thomas Moore, which were based on the Sally Hemings scandal that had been brought to light by James Callender. Adams delivered *en passant* a concealed blow to Jefferson's literary taste with a reference to one of Jefferson's favorite poets, Joel Barlow. He called Moore's verse "more polished, and less respectable" than that of Barlow, and then, with seeming innocence, and feigned disapproval, Adams gleefully reprinted Moore, and to good effect:[24]

> The weary statesman for repose hath fled
> From halls of council to his negro's shed,
> Where blest he woos some black Aspasia's grace,
> And dreams of freedom in his slave's embrace!

While ostensibly dismissing the assaults on Jefferson's sexual morality, Adams made certain that the charges would not remain buried in the archives, hidden from all but the most pedantic historical drudges.

[24] Henry Adams, *History of the United States during the Administrations of Thomas Jefferson*, p. 133, also see index entry, p. 1269. For Callender, see pp. 218–222. Thomas Moore is not to be confused with Charles Moore, another of Jefferson's detractors and the putative author of "The Night Before Christmas" (also see Chapter 10 note 25 below). See Paul Collins' essay "Jefferson's Lump of Coal," *The New York Times* (December 24, 2006).

Without offering any praise or endorsement of Callender, and indeed while condemning him as a drunkard and a wastrel, Adams nonetheless recorded his "libels" with barely concealed relish.

HENRY CABOT LODGE'S APPRAISAL OF JEFFERSON

Adams' doctoral student and the recipient of the first history Ph.D. granted by Harvard was Henry Cabot Lodge, a scion of the two most patrician families of Boston, where, as one satirist put it, "the Lowell's talk only to Cabots / And the Cabots talk only to God." His Brahmin credentials rivaled even those of his professor, and he was more than comfortable with Federalist elitism. But Lodge was an unabashed admirer of the social climber Hamilton, and, as the first scholarly editor of Hamilton's papers, he made no efforts to hide his sympathies. He was a Republican Party loyalist, and, as such, he had a distinguished career in both the Massachusetts and the United States legislatures. Eventually a Republican senator, and staunch supporter of the Progressive Theodore Roosevelt, he supported progressive legislation such as the Sherman Anti-Trust Act and the Pure Food and Drug Law. Lodge was hostile to Jefferson and refused to view him as the prime mover of American greatness. As did Theodore Roosevelt, Lodge subscribed, albeit for the most part tacitly, to Hamilton's view of Jefferson as a "contemptible hypocrite."

Lodge made it clear that he viewed Hamilton as Jefferson's intellectual, moral, and ideological superior. Ironically enough, he had higher regard for Hamilton, "the bastard brat of a Scotch peddler," than he did for Jefferson, a member of Virginia's cavalier elite. Henry Adams, like his brother the historian Brooks Adams, was a cultural conservative and shared Matthew Arnold's conception of the twelfth century as the peak of Western civilization. This theory of the decline of the Christian West was later taken up by T. S. Eliot, who, like Adams, was an anti-Semite.[25] While Adams viewed the Civil War as a morally justified crusade against slavery, his attitudes towards African Americans were condescending and even contemptuous, but mildly sympathetic. Like most of his contemporaries, he did not doubt that white people were culturally and intellectually superior to African Americans.

[25] There was no continuity between Adams and Eliot with respect to the broad contours of American civilization. Eliot, despite his New England roots, was contemptuous of New England and identified with Southern traditions.

Lodge's candid opinions on Jefferson appeared in his 1898 biography of Hamilton and in the editorial notes to the *Works of Alexander Hamilton* in twelve volumes. His observations and his language were vividly colored by his belief that Hamilton was "the ablest political and constitutional writer of his day." All three of the patrician historians were fond of making the same point. In Lodge's phraseology, "The democratic system of Jefferson is administered in the form and on the principles of Hamilton." Although Lodge was unfriendly to Jefferson, he did not vilify him, and indeed he credited him with a sincere "belief in Liberty and humanity which was born with him and which he did not go to Paris to learn."[26] Lodge certainly gave no credence to the paranoid claims of Jefferson's opponents in the campaign of 1800, who attempted to link him to "the wild ravings of the Jacobin clubs and the doctrines of Marat and Robespierre." He did, however accuse him repeatedly of Machiavellian machinations in his dealings with both Congress and the Washington administration.

THEODORE ROOSEVELT'S HAMILTONIAN BIAS

Theodore Roosevelt's interpretation of history was consistently, if not uncritically, Hamiltonian. He shared with Lodge an admiration for the Federalist tradition, which he revealed in his 1888 biography of Gouverneur Morris. He said, notably, "I have no use for the Hamilton who is aristocratic, or for the Jefferson who is a demagogue." In his volume on Morris, he spoke admiringly of Jefferson's "high sounding sentiments," which he considered to be sincere, but said "when it came to actions he was completely at sea." Years later he spoke admiringly of Frederick Scott Oliver's *Alexander Hamilton* (1906). His later politics were influenced by the undisguised Hamiltonian biases of Herbert Croly's *The Promise of American Life* (1909). Along with Lodge, he stands among the founders of that historiography associated with Croly and the shibboleth of "Hamiltonian means to achieve Jeffersonian ends." He enlisted the vocabulary of Croly in his 1912 presidential campaign, and today we perceive Theodore Roosevelt as a progressive politician, but seldom do we see Theodore Roosevelt being placed in the historiographical category of "progressive historians," a matter to which we shall return presently.

[26] Henry Cabot Lodge, *Alexander Hamilton* (Boston, MA: Houghton Mifflin, 1893), p. 125. Pagination differs in various editions.

Theodore Roosevelt considered Alexander Hamilton "the most brilliant American statesman who ever lived." He considered Jefferson "infinitely below Hamilton," adding "I think the worship of Jefferson a discredit to my country." That Roosevelt held these extreme opinions is well known to historians of the early republic, as well as to historians of the progressive era, and his capacity for intemperate language is known to many college graduates. He possessed a volatile personality, and his opinions could shift violently during his morning reading at the breakfast table. His opinions were also reversible, and it would surprise no one to discover if at some point he underwent a conversion experience on Thomas Jefferson, but if he ever did, the evidence is inconclusive. Daniel Ruddy has compiled a pastiche of Theodore Roosevelt's opinions sometimes irresponsibly decontextualized, but his chapter devoted to Theodore Roosevelt's opinions on Jefferson is not entirely inaccurate. He deploys such quotations as the one taken from an 1896 letter to Frederick Jackson Turner: "In my estimation Jefferson's influence upon the United States as a whole was very distinctly evil."[27]

Theodore Roosevelt characterized Jefferson in 1915 as "one of the most mischievous enemies of democracy, one of the very weakest we have ever had in public life."[28] He blamed Jefferson for sowing the seeds of disunion, and claimed his views on government nurtured the spirit of anarchy and bloodshed. He also blamed Jefferson for the embarrassment of the War of 1812, the legacy of his partisan bedfellow, James Madison. Theodore Roosevelt's views on that war were influenced by the influential book of Captain Alfred T. Mahan, *Sea Power*, and Theodore Roosevelt had served as Assistant Secretary of the Navy. One of his dramatic actions as president was to send the aptly named "Great White Fleet" on a spectacular circumnavigation of the globe. The author of his own book on the War of 1812, Theodore Roosevelt viewed Jefferson's parsimonious failure to maintain the US Navy as irresponsible.

[27] Ruddy, *Roosevelt's History of the United States*, p. 75, reprints words from Theodore Roosevelt to Frederick Jackson Turner, November 4, 1896. James MacGregor Burns and Susan Dunn see Roosevelt as doing such a "quick and thorough flipflop" as to become pro-Jefferson in 1912. It was a double flip-flop, for he called him "a slippery demagogue in 1910" and "enemy of democracy" in 1915, as cited above. Theodore Roosevelt's positions were inconsistent, as for example his abandoning the doctrine of German supremacy, his reversal of opinion on the character of Jefferson Davis, and his pandering to racism in the 1906 "Brownsville incident."

[28] Theodore Roosevelt to Albert Bushnell Hart, June 1, 1915. Theodore Roosevelt Papers. Library of Congress Manuscript Division, www.theodorerooseveltcenter.org/Research/Digital-Library/Record.aspx?libID=o212341

Theodore Roosevelt was both a progressive politician and a progressive historian, although it has not been conventional to group him with the progressive historians. For example, Richard Hofstadter's excellent book *The Progressive Historians* paid homage to Theodore Roosevelt only in passing, while focusing primarily on Beard, Turner, and Parrington.[29] It would be unfair to claim that Hofstadter ignored Roosevelt entirely, for he did mention his popular and influential *Winning of the West*, which anticipated certain insights, if not every aspect, of Frederick Jackson Turner's thesis in *The Frontier in American History*. But Hofstadter sought neither to weaken nor to reinforce the ideological bridge from Jefferson to Turner to Theodore Roosevelt. As not only a student but a celebrator of Jefferson, he was determined to make Jeffersonian democracy central to his progressive historiography, and Theodore Roosevelt had not been a Jefferson idolizer. Therefore it is not surprising that he neglected Roosevelt. It is more remarkable that Hofstadter neglected Woodrow Wilson in his work on the progressive historians, although Wilson was conventionally discussed as a progressive president, had some notoriety as an historian, and was an avowed admirer of Jefferson.

Roosevelt and Lodge conformed to Hofstadter's notions of the elitist Mugwump-Progressive genealogy, with their patrician, Northeastern biases, their unquestioning belief in the supremacy of the white race, and their preferences for upper-class Anglocentric civilization. And as Northeastern progressives, they unequivocally viewed the Civil War as a moral crusade and saw emancipation as the victory of Northern progress over Southern decadence. The Jeffersonian doctrine of weak central government, accompanied by a failure to undertake military spending, was the basis of Theodore Roosevelt's detestation of Jefferson. Theodore Roosevelt, conscious of the Democratic Republicans' unrealized imperialist aims of 1812, noted the paradox of Jefferson's cuts to military spending while pursuing an expansionist policy. He gave Jefferson little credit for the Louisiana Purchase, but believed he was sincere in his regard for the "plain people."[30]

[29] Richard Hofstadter discusses Frederick Jackson Turner's, but alludes only in passing to Theodore Roosevelt's, development of a "Frontier Thesis" in *The Progressive Historians: Turner, Beard, Parrington* (New York: Knopf, 1969).

[30] Theodore Roosevelt to William Moody, September 12, 1907, quoted in Ruddy, *Roosevelt's History of the United States*, p. 82.

In Theodore Roosevelt's eyes, the acquisition of Louisiana was inevitable; it was only one of several territories in North America, including the Floridas and California, to which Spain laid claim. France's title to Louisiana was dubious. Those who contested France's claims, Spanish-speakers and Native Americans, had proved incapable of impeding the march of the Anglo-Saxon race from the Atlantic to the Pacific. Thankfully, Jefferson, with his constitutional scruples and timidity, had not squandered the opportunity that destiny had dropped in his lap. Theodore Roosevelt gave more credit to Napoleon for making the offer than to Jefferson for accepting it, and acknowledged the negotiating role of fellow New Yorker Robert Livingston more readily than that of the Virginian, James Monroe. Theodore Roosevelt felt that the expansionist spirit of the American people could not have been contained, and his view of the winning of the West was tinged with racialism:

> The men who settled and peopled the western wilderness were the men who won Louisiana; for it was surrendered by France merely because it was impossible to hold it against the American advance. Jefferson, through his agents at Paris, asked only for New Orleans; but Napoleon thrust upon him the great West, because Napoleon saw, what the American statesmen and diplomats did not see, but what the Westerners felt; for he saw that no European power could hold the country beyond the Mississippi when the Americans had made good their foothold upon the hither bank.[31]

Theodore Roosevelt saw a danger in Jefferson as a continuing inspiration to anarchists and insurrectionists and, on the grounds of his Kentucky Resolution, called him the "father of nullification." He had no sympathy for the Democratic Societies that arose in the years of Washington's presidency, describing them as "either useless or noxious" and based "on the Jacobin clubs of France." He attributed their rise to the French ambassador, Edmond Genêt, and to "Jeffersonian doctrinaires" whose "influence in America was on the whole distinctly evil, save that, by a series of accidents, they became the especial champions of the westward extension of the nation, and in consequence were identified with a movement which was all-essential to the national well-being." Roosevelt saw Jefferson as the author of this nation's tragic, self-inflicted wound, the Civil War. As did Lodge, he believed that the secessionist threats of Jefferson's Kentucky Resolution of 1796 had fertilized the Confederate Rebellion. It was first used to justify John C. Calhoun's

[31] Theodore Roosevelt, *The Winning of the West* (New York: G. P. Putnam's Sons, 1896), vol. IV, p. 130.

nullification doctrine of 1832, and then to justify the War of the Rebellion. Jefferson's Kentucky Resolution had obliquely claimed the right of a state to armed resistance to the national government, a position refuted by Andrew Jackson's assertion that "Disunion by armed force is treason." Lincoln had consciously recycled Jackson's arguments against Jeffersonian nullification and threats of secession in his First Inaugural Address.[32]

Theodore Roosevelt criticized Jefferson's obsession with non-existent royalism, his disposition "to suppose that there was a general monarchical tendency in his time. There was not. The tendency was overwhelmingly against monarchy." In this he followed the tradition of Abraham Lincoln, whose revitalization of Jefferson's egalitarian pronouncements in the Declaration so cunningly undermined Chief Justice Taney's use of them in the Dred Scott decision. Theodore Roosevelt, like Lincoln, recognized that Jefferson's words, regardless of Taney's *caveat emptor*, had historically kindled egalitarian and democratic sentiments in America and throughout the world. Frederick Douglass had glimpsed this Hegelian teleology of "History as the progress of Freedom" even before Lincoln, who passed it on to the two Roosevelts, and thence to Arthur M. Schlesinger, Jr., Joyce Appleby, Sean Wilentz, and Douglas Wilson. Liberal historians fashioned a narrative that is humane, noble, and "usable," imposing a theory of inevitable progress on American destiny, a tradition of democratic vistas, and a view of the United States as the world's best hope. The New Deal cast this idea of Jeffersonian determinism in bronze and manufactured the Jefferson of heroic proportions who occupies his temple in Washington, but Jefferson's deifiers were not able to effect this canonization without flagrant bowdlerization of Jeffersonian texts.[33]

HAMILTONIAN INFLUENCES EVERYWHERE

Perhaps Hamilton was unfair in his famous 1801 letter to James Bayard calling Jefferson "a despicable hypocrite." It is hardly sufficient to accept either Hamilton's assessment of Jefferson as a hypocrite or the tenor of

[32] Theodore Roosevelt's opinion on the Kentucky Resolution was expressed in his *The Life of Thomas Hart Benton* (St. Charles, IL: Houghton Mifflin, 1887), p. 85. He derived his phraseology "father of nullification" from debates in Congress, February 1833; see p. 1893, "Mr. Jefferson was the father of nullification." Roosevelt on "distinctively evil" is in *The Winning of the West*, vol. II, p. 404.

[33] For "Quotations on the Jefferson Memorial," visit the website of Thomas Jefferson's Monticello, https://home.monticello.org/. The structure of Frederick Douglass' editorial on the Dred Scott decision anticipated that of Lincoln's Gettysburg Address.

Theodore Roosevelt's vituperations against him.[34] Hamilton did not specify the instances of Jefferson's hypocrisy in this letter, but certainly he recognized, as many of his contemporaries did, Jefferson's double-dealing on the slavery issue, and so too did Henry Adams and Theodore Roosevelt. They may sometimes appear harsh, but neither was taken in by Jefferson's facile egalitarian and democratic preachments. When it came to other matters, such as his record as wartime governor of Virginia, indeed not every Virginian was deceived by Jefferson. This is self-evident in the cases of Patrick Henry and the Lee family, who were unimpressed by his role in the American Revolution and felt that he had seriously mismanaged the governorship of Virginia during the war.

Hamilton was right to the extent that he saw Jefferson as neither an ideologue nor an enemy of executive power, for Jefferson contributed to the evolution of the executive order as we know it. Theodore Roosevelt was right to the extent that he saw Jefferson as being most honest and most useful when he abandoned his ideological pretentions. Henry Adams correctly perceived that Jefferson behaved as a Hamiltonian, and frequently to the dismay of his own party. Jefferson was crafty and Machiavellian, and he fulfilled his boyhood promise of a propensity for wanton and fortuitous invention. Despite his constant harping on the threats presented by monarchy, he was too intelligent to deny that democracies could be tyrannies, that proletarians could be dictators, or that republics could be empires. These were facts that literally gave him headaches. Under his administration, the United States, whether he willed it or not, became an empire disguised as a republic. He regarded this contradiction with consternation, just as he recognized with dismay and resistance Montesquieu's observation that Great Britain was a "republic disguised as a monarchy."

Jefferson's ideological positions were as "pragmatic" and contradictory as the frontier society that produced him, and his political practice contradicted his original expressions of intent. He inveighed against, but ultimately came to defend the necessity of, a vigorous government, civil religion, a powerful executive, an authoritative court system, a solid manufacturing base, a ready military, and, through the proxy of Albert Gallatin, well-regulated systems of finance and public works. Ultimately, he aided and abetted, not libertarian anarchy, but the structures of big government and the principles of law and order, consistent with the expansion of

[34] A compilation of Theodore Roosevelt's anti-Jeffersonian declamations can be found in Ruddy, *Roosevelt's History of the United States*. Also see Roosevelt, *The Winning of the West*, vol. IV.

slavery. Inadvertently to be sure, and certainly against his instincts and his will, he set the pattern for the benevolent authoritarianism of Abraham Lincoln, Franklin D. Roosevelt, and Dwight D. Eisenhower.

After 1860, the impetus for Jefferson's unrealized egalitarian preachments was advanced, not by his Democratic Party, but by the Republican Abraham Lincoln. After a long dark age, FDR, a Bull Moose Republican masquerading as a Democrat, encouraged by his wife Eleanor, reclaimed something of Jeffersonian egalitarianism. Civil Rights were subsequently championed by Dwight D. Eisenhower and Justice Earl Warren, as the Republican Party remained true to its progressive heritage. But it was the New Deal Progressive Social Democrat Lyndon Johnson who took up the fight initiated by Progressive Republicans. At this point, the Republican Party was taken over by Strom Thurmond, Barry Goldwater, and Ronald Reagan, to become the bastion of Jeffersonian reactionism. Today, on the one hand, the Republican Party conjures with the rhetoric of Jefferson's minimalist government, while, on the other, it ironically promotes what Jefferson hated and feared most, a neo-Hamiltonian program of big government working to protect the interests of bankers, businessmen, and financial elites.

PROGRESSIVE AND NEW DEAL HISTORIOGRAPHY

Charles Beard represented the second generation of progressive historians, succeeding those I have identified as the first generation, namely Henry Cabot Lodge and Teddy Roosevelt. Beard normally dominates the category that we call "progressive historians," overpowering the others, Frederick Jackson Turner and Vernon Louis Parrington. He was more skeptical of Jeffersonian democracy than were his peers. The latter two inflated the benignity of Jeffersonian democracy and ignored the fact that its author had deviously, almost treasonously, undermined the administrations of George Washington and John Adams from within. Beard's historiography was solid, despite his egregious over-reach in attributing specific venal motives to the Framers of the Constitution. He was correct in his assertion, and merely following James Madison's common sense, in observing that, for Federalists and Republicans alike, the foundation of the Republic reflected economic interests that the Constitution was designed to uphold.[35]

[35] For a defense of Beard, see Robert A. McGuire, *To Form a More Perfect Union: A New Economic Interpretation of the United States Constitution* (Oxford University Press, 2003). Also see Hofstadter, *The Progressive Historians.*

Charles Beard, who so famously appreciated *Federalist* 10, came to describe the foundation period and the origins of the United States Constitution in economic terms. He recognized correctly that Jefferson "was a planter and thus regarded as the spokesman of the agrarian interest." Jeffersonian democracy did not involve any attack on class privilege: it simply offered an alternative to the more candidly expressed elitism of Hamilton, Adams, and Madison. His famous interpretation of *Federalist* 10 was not an argument for vulgar economic determinism. It was not an example of closet Marxism, as Douglass Adair did more than to imply. Beard was following the reasoning of John Locke and Adam Smith, and had no need for Marx, Engels, or Lenin because Madison had already said, "Government is instituted to protect property of every sort." Beard seemed to understand, as Benjamin Franklin had, that "property is the creature of society," and Franklin D. Roosevelt understood, just as John C. Calhoun had, that "society would be defeated without government." FDR saved the day for capitalism – and it is well that he did so – by the Machiavellian application of the Madisonian principle that government exists for the protection of property and "the protection of different and unequal faculties of acquiring property."[36]

Beard appreciated that "Jeffersonian Democracy simply meant the possession of the federal government by the agrarian masses led by an aristocracy of slave-owning planters, and the theoretical repudiation of the right to use the Government for the benefit of any capitalistic groups, fiscal, banking, or manufacturing."[37] Beard made some methodological and factual blunders, irrelevant to his thesis, that have rightly been attacked by generations of American historians, but do not affect his main point. As historian James M. McPherson has pointed out, Beard understood that the history of the United States from the Foundation to the Civil War witnessed increasing conflict between two competing capitalist systems. In a sense, the Civil War was a triumph of Hamiltonian over Jeffersonian visions, although neither side had any prescience of the industrial capitalism looming in the not too distant future.

James McPherson's brilliant appraisal of Charles Beard indicates the semantical and ideological morass of trying to sort out the lineage of

[36] Douglass Adair, *Fame and the Founding Fathers* (New York: Norton, 1974; repr. Liberty Fund), pp. 122–123. Benjamin Franklin: Queries and Remarks on "Hints for the Members of Pennsylvania Convention" (unpublished), Tuesday, November 3, 1789. James Madison, "Property," *National Gazette* (March 29, 1792).

[37] Charles Beard, *Economic Origins of Jeffersonian Democracy* (New York: Macmillan, 1915), pp. 466–467.

American libertarianism and Jeffersonian democracy. McPherson related the conception of Jeffersonian liberty to the contrasting ideas of negative and positive liberty found in John Stuart Mill and Isaiah Berlin. The negative liberty of Jefferson's slavery-based democratic republic was superseded by the positive liberty of Lincoln's enlightened despotism, an executive order that freed the slaves, and the tyranny of a constitutional amendment ratified by only a portion of the states. Subsequently, Franklin D. Roosevelt further undermined Jeffersonian democracy when he issued executive order 8802 and banned overt racial discrimination from the military-industrial complex. McPherson notes that when President Eisenhower sent units of the 101st Airborne Division into Little Rock, Arkansas, to enforce the integration of nine black students at Central High School, he took a step towards fulfilling the promise of Lincoln's Second American Revolution.[38]

FRANKLIN D. ROOSEVELT AND CLAUDE BOWERS' BIAS

By the early twentieth century the myth of Jeffersonian democratic egalitarianism was so well established that even Theodore Roosevelt had written that Jefferson "stood for the plain people."[39] The depiction of Jefferson, at once monumental and proletarian, was, as historians Merrill Peterson, Stephen E. Knott, and Andrew Burstein observe, enhanced by the publication of Claude Bowers' 1925 book, *Jefferson and Hamilton*, which was instrumental to Franklin D. Roosevelt's Southern strategy.[40] Like the Jefferson Memorial, FDR's Jefferson was part of the New Deal legacy. The inscription on the Jefferson Memorial Rotunda amputates the

38 McPherson, *Lincoln*, p. 152.

39 Theodore Roosevelt in Ruddy, *Roosevelt's History of the United States*, p. 82.

40 Claude G. Bowers, *The Tragic Era* (Boston, MA: Houghton Mifflin, 1957 [1920]), pp. 306–326. Merrill Peterson sees the significance of Claude Bowers to the New Deal in *The Jefferson Image in the American Mind* (Charlottesville, VA: University of Virginia Press, 1998), pp. 350–357. Arthur M. Schlesinger, Jr., mentions Franklin D. Roosevelt's review of Claude Bowers' *Jefferson and Hamilton* (Cambridge, MA: Riverside Press, 1925) in his *The Crisis of the Old Order, 1919–1933* (Cambridge, MA: Riverside Press, 1957), p. 104, where the Hamilton–Jefferson conflict is interpreted in accord with Jeffersonian biases. Andrew Burstein, in *Democracy's Muse: How Thomas Jefferson Became a Liberal, a Reagan Republican, and a Tea Party Fanatic, all the While Being Dead* (Charlottesville, VA: University of Virginia Press, 2015), is among more recent historians to recognize the key role of Bowers. Others share my opinion that FDR was instrumental in reshaping the reputation of Jefferson, e.g. Robert M. S. McDonald, *Thomas Jefferson's Military Academy: Founding West Point* (Charlottesville, VA: University of Virginia Press, 2004), p. 193.

burden of Jefferson's statements on several subjects, including the matter of African American destiny.

The inscription in the Rotunda of Jefferson's Temple squares the circle of America's racial contradictions by displaying a bowdlerized quotation from Jefferson's unpublished autobiography:

> Nothing is more certainly written in the book of fate than these people are to be free . . .

But every visitor to the memorial should be made aware that the Rotunda's inscription breaks the back of Jefferson's statement. The rest of the sentence clearly places its author in the racist nightmare of the Black Muslim Movement, the Ku Klux Klan, Marcus Garvey, and the unreformed Malcolm X, rather than in the utopian dream of Martin Luther King. The Jefferson Memorial's bowdlerized quotation, when fully cited, has a painful sting in its tail:

> . . . nor is it less certain that the two races, equally free, cannot live in the same government.

In the egalitarian pronouncements of the Declaration Independence, and the sterilized and decontextualized pronouncements of his *Notes on the State of Virginia*, Jefferson is memorialized as an abolitionist, rather than as a perpetuator of slavery, racial separatism, and white supremacy.[41]

Franklin D. Roosevelt's review of Bowers' *Jefferson and Hamilton* noted rhetorically "Hamiltons we have today; is there a Jefferson on the horizon?" Andrew Burstein sees that by the 1980s American conservatives had come to view Hamilton not as the promoter of business interests, but as the founder of the Roosevelt tradition of big government and progenitor of the evils of the New Deal. Thus conservatives have transformed Hamilton into a social democrat, and seek to revive Jeffersonian libertarianism. Bowers subsequently published a history of Reconstruction after the Civil War, *The Tragic Era: The Revolution*, notable for its celebration of the Ku Klux Klan. W. E. B. Du Bois placed him among those authors who "select and use facts and opinions in order to prove that the South was right in Reconstruction, the North vengeful or

[41] The Jefferson Memorial aborts the quotation in this way, as does Peter Onuf at the conclusion of the final chapter of *Jefferson's Empire* (Charlottesville, VA: University of Virginia Press, 2000), p. 188. Onuf also quotes Jefferson's hopes for black Americans as "a free and independent people" ambiguously and out of context. The phrase is inseparable from Jefferson's elaborate program of ethnic cleansing, separating black children from their parents, and placing them in concentration camps until they can be deported.

deceived, and the Negro stupid."[42] Pro-slavery and white supremacist to the core, Bowers believed that it was in Jefferson's relations with his slaves that we "find him at his best," and he fancies their reception of him on returning from his French mission:

> At the foot of the hill all the slaves in their gaudiest attire are assembled to greet him. The carriage appears down the road. The slaves, laughing, shouting, rush forward to welcome him, unhitch the horses to draw the carriage up the steep hill, some pulling, some pushing, and others huddled in a dark mass close around the vehicle. Some kiss his hands, others his feet.

Henry Adams perpetrated no such sentimentalism. He wrote that "Jefferson's reforms crippled the gentry, but did little for the people, and for the slaves nothing." But Franklin D. Roosevelt's praise for Bowers was more cunning than it appeared to be, for it was not his only statement on the historical memory of Jefferson, which he manipulated as early as his first presidential campaign. A speech by FDR, delivered in San Francisco shortly before the election of 1932, presented Jefferson as the ancestor of progressive ideology. FDR did not yet foresee himself as the neo-Hamiltonian who exists in today's historical memory. His address attached Hamilton to "the belief that popular government was essentially dangerous and essentially unworkable." He did not question Hamilton's honesty or good intentions, but portrayed him as misguided, with his belief in "the autocratic strength of its government." FDR went so far as to attribute to Hamilton a belief "that the destiny of individuals was to serve that government."

The Jefferson he remembered in 1932 was vastly more positive than the one preserved in the writings of his cousin Theodore, and yet he included Theodore in the litany of saints, memorialized in his San Francisco speech. He recognized what he called "the new terms of the old social contract," implying that the national economy had moved beyond "the apparent Utopia which Jefferson imagined for us in 1776. He implied a linkage in the ideals that Jefferson, [Theodore] Roosevelt and Wilson sought to bring to realization." But there were no clear indications in this campaign speech that Franklin D. Roosevelt would eventually align his Democratic Party so thoroughly with the progressivism of the Old Bull Moose.

There was no hint in the San Francisco speech of the coming New Deal ideology, and apparently no idea that his own administrations would

[42] W. E. B. Du Bois, *Black Reconstruction in America, 1860–1880* (New York: Harcourt, Brace and Company, 1935), p. 732.

come to embody Croly's disparaged principles of bureaucratic government by a "strong group of central institutions, guided by a small group of able and public spirited citizens." In the long run, Franklin D. Roosevelt's practice manifested itself as more similar to the spirit of the Bull Moose Progressive Party and the Hamiltonianism of Croly than the Jeffersonianism of Bowers.

Franklin D. Roosevelt's Machiavellian fabrication of Jefferson was as cunning as Abraham Lincoln's. Where Lincoln had reshaped Jefferson into a prophet of racial equality, FDR reconstructed him as the forerunner of New Deal Progressivism. The San Francisco speech made him an advocate of "government, without whose assistance the property rights could not exist." He refashioned him as a proponent of the idea that government "must intervene" as the protector of individual rights and freedoms. He also invoked the names of both Theodore Roosevelt and Woodrow Wilson as proponents of that tradition. In fact, both had invoked the name of Jefferson in speaking of the national government as protector of the private citizen from the power of corporate interests. Franklin D. Roosevelt did not invoke the name of Lincoln in this campaign speech, but he honored Lincoln's ploy of putting his own ideas into Jefferson's mouth. In the San Francisco speech, this "trickster god" manufactured a tradition in which Jefferson was the father of a "progressive tradition" that his administration would strive to fulfill:

> Faith in America, faith in our tradition of personal responsibility, faith in our institutions, faith in ourselves demands that we recognize the new terms of the old social contract. We shall fulfill them, as we fulfilled the obligation of the apparent Utopia which Jefferson imagined for us in 1776, and which Jefferson, Roosevelt and Wilson sought to bring to realization. We must do so, lest a rising tide of misery engendered by our common failure, engulf us all. But failure is not an American habit; and in the strength of great hope we must all shoulder our common load.[43]

SCHLESINGER AND HOFSTADTER'S JEFFERSON

I would not go so far as to claim that the Thomas Jefferson we know today is the creation of Franklin D. Roosevelt, although Stephen F. Knott makes a persuasive argument along that line. There is, however, no question that

[43] Franklin D. Roosevelt, "Commonwealth Club Speech," given to the Commonwealth Club of San Francisco (September 23, 1932). Frequently anthologized. The original typescript is on file at the Roosevelt Presidential Library.

Jefferson in the mid twentieth century seemed to be the property of the Democratic Party. Since then, conservatives have staked convincingly legitimate claims on his legacy, as Burstein's researches have shown. Richard Hofstadter's 1948 work, *The American Political Tradition*, was a Brahmsian variation on the theme of FDR's San Francisco speech. Hofstadter led the several historians since Adams and Theodore Roosevelt who commented on Jefferson's necessary and proper implementation of Federalist principles. Arthur M. Schlesinger, Jr., who was fundamentally hostile to the Hamiltonian tradition, became an architect of the view that Jeffersonian democracy was somehow the forerunner of the New Deal. Schlesinger downplayed Herbert Croly's progressive slogan of "Hamiltonian means to Jeffersonian ends," and presented Jeffersonian democracy as a more simplified celebration of the sunburned and sweaty working classes. Schlesinger and Richard Hofstadter merged the overlapping view of Claude Bowers that Jefferson's heart was "with the farmer's lot" and preserved exactly the historical memory of Hamilton that Jefferson labored to institutionalize.[44]

Hofstadter recognized that, once in power, the Jeffersonians proved the truth of what had been little more than a pious platitude in Jefferson's First Inaugural Address: "We are all Republicans; we are all federalists." Jefferson's engagement in dialectics fit very neatly into Hofstadter's dialectical methodology. Hofstadter was even more astute in recognizing that he was the Republican as Federalist than he was in noting that Jefferson was "The aristocrat as Democrat." Hofstadter cited Josiah Quincy to good effect that by 1816 the Jeffersonians had out-federalized the Federalists, and pointed out that "Jefferson's party had taken over the whole complex of Federalist policies—manufactures, banks, tariffs, army, navy, and all this under the administration of Jefferson's friend, neighbor, and political heir, James Madison."[45]

Of course Hofstadter and Schlesinger knew that Jefferson could neither have foreseen nor rejoiced at the coming of the New Deal, with its military Keynesianism, government bureaucracy, and welfare state programs. They nonetheless perceived Jefferson as the New Deal's great herald, on the basis of the myth that he stood for the "common man." The facts that

[44] Stephen Knott, "The Man Who Made Modern America." Review of Chernow's *Alexander Hamilton*, in *Claremont Review of Books*, 4, no. 4 (fall, 2004). In Schlesinger's *The Age of Jackson* (Boston, MA: Little, Brown, 1945), the Jeffersonian bias was pronounced, p. 10.

[45] Hofstadter, *The American Political Tradition*, p. 42.

he belittled women, vilified African Americans, and treated Native Americans as – to recycle Kipling's metaphor – "half devil and half child" were dismissed by Schlesinger and almost entirely overlooked by Hofstadter. These flaws were barely mentioned by his biographers of that generation, who in almost all other respects did such painstaking and honest work.

Hofstadter recognized correctly the triumph of Hamiltonian ideas in the Madison administration; what he saw no need to address was the importance of ethnic nationalism as an essential element of Jeffersonian democracy. Hofstadter wrote: "Men like Hamilton could argue that manufactures ought to be promoted because they would enable the nation to use the labor of women and children, 'many of them at a tender age,' but Jefferson was outraged at such a view of humanity. Hamilton schemed to get the children into factories; Jefferson planned school systems." Hofstadter forgot that Jefferson put enslaved children to work in his factories, which he operated perhaps not so ruthlessly as Andrew Carnegie would his, in a later era, but Carnegie famously endowed the library at Tuskegee Institute, and the funding he provided to that "industrial institution" also supported the liberal training of young people destined to teach in the public schools. Whether Jefferson ever contributed to the African Free School founded in New York by Hamilton and his friends is unknown.[46]

Hofstadter overlooked the fact that Hamilton collaborated in the founding of New York's African Free School, while Jefferson's abortive proposals for public education made no provisions for colored children, and with respect to educating white children Jefferson proposed an early triage, based on a presumption of a congenital inequality of talents. More importantly, I am not aware that Hamilton – who, by the way, entered the labor market at a far more "tender age" than Jefferson – ever actually put children to work in factories. Jefferson had numerous black children laboring in the workshops of Monticello, often under unpleasant conditions that generated bullying, abuse, and violence on the job.[47]

Arthur M. Schlesinger, Jr., arguably the most influential liberal historian coming out of the New Deal era, and his contemporary rival, the liberal Richard Hofstadter, were determined to preserve the carefully

[46] Ibid.

[47] Ibid., p. 43. Peter Onuf, "Thomas Jefferson, Federalist," *Essays in History*, 35 (1993), 20–30. For an instance of adolescent mischief on the job, see Annette Gordon-Reed, *The Hemingses of Monticello* (New York: Norton, 2008), pp. 579–580.

nurtured fabrication of Thomas Jefferson as the father of democratic liberalism. They understood, very correctly, the usefulness of deploying the egalitarian rhetoric of the Declaration of Independence in order to promote a society with liberty and justice for all. They were only following in the tradition of Abraham Lincoln's Gettysburg Address, which had strategically proclaimed that the Declaration had conceived a nation "dedicated to the proposition that all ... [persons] are created equal." Lincoln had refuted the white-supremacist claims of Chief Justice Taney's Dred Scott decision. Schlesinger, Hofstadter, and other liberals, siding with the morally superior position of Lincoln, were backed by Marxist historians, both old and new, who likewise found it "necessary and proper" to nurture Lincoln's image of Thomas Jefferson as the founder of American egalitarianism.[48]

Andrew Jackson and his party were "Keepers of the Jeffersonian Conscience" in the view of Arthur M. Schlesinger, Jr. While recognizing that "the America of Jefferson had begun to disappear before Jefferson had retired from the presidential chair," Schlesinger tended to romanticize Jeffersonian ideals. He reconstructed the Jeffersonians as forerunners of the New Deal. He made them into progressives who defended the interests of the common people over the rich and powerful elites. Jacksonian democracy was "a revival of Jeffersonianism," in that it was a revolt against a monopolistic business community that threatened the freedom of "a liberal capitalistic state." This was hardly an irrational or insupportable position, but it was fundamentally different from that of another historian associated with the Franklin D. Roosevelt administration, Bray Hammond.[49]

In his history of *Banks and Politics in America from the Revolution to the Civil War*, Hammond was contemptuous of Jacksonian economics and adopted a Federalist-Whig perspective that saw Jefferson and Jackson as representing an atavistic primitive capitalism that was incapable of meeting the needs of their respective times. He was almost as critical of Nicholas Biddle, the president of the Bank of the United States, as he was of Jackson who opposed him, for Biddle, in his view, "had no sense of

[48] The notable and commendable exception is, of course, William Appleman Williams, who is discussed recurrently in these pages.

[49] Schlesinger, *The Age of Jackson*. The title of Chapter 3 is "Keepers of the Jeffersonian Conscience"; also see Chapter 24, and numerous index references. Bray Hammond was Assistant Secretary of the Board of Governors of the Federal Reserve System from 1944 to 1950, and the author of *Banks and Politics in America from the Revolution to the Civil War* (Princeton University Press, 1957).

a working organization." Nonetheless, in Hammond's view, Henry Clay's "American System" and the banking philosophy of the Whigs and Abraham Lincoln contained precedents for the banking reforms of the New Deal. It is evident that while Franklin D. Roosevelt's administration constructed a narrative that identified itself as the party of Jefferson, it resembled more closely the tradition of Hamilton, Clay, Lincoln, and Theodore Roosevelt.[50]

Some historians have pushed the case for Jeffersonian Federalism more explicitly than Hofstadter did. Peter Onuf, without any overt reliance on Hofstadter, Quincy, or Madison, maintains correctly that the roots of Jeffersonian federalism could be found as early as 1774, in Jefferson's *A Summary View of the Rights of British America*. Accordingly, Onuf observes that the "'Summary View' constituted a 'plan for Federal Union' in a reformed British empire." To this I would add that Benjamin Franklin's *Albany Plan of Union* (1754) suggested twenty years earlier an Anglo-American Federation, an idea hardly incompatible with the main contours of Jefferson's *Summary View*. Onuf's proposition that Jefferson's early thinking contained elements of federalism that later evolved into "the language of American nationhood" is not only supportable, but convincing. Jefferson's early Anglo-American imperialism was, of course, later supplanted by what Onuf calls "Jefferson's Empire."

In the process of creating the New Deal's deification of Thomas Jefferson – symbolized by that Roman temple in Washington called the Jefferson Memorial – the authoritative historians, Richard Hofstadter and Arthur M. Schlesinger, Jr., established a tendency that obscures and diminishes Henry Adams' older interpretation. The post-Depression liberal historians were curiously aligned with the reactionary Claude Bowers, whose romanticizing of Jefferson had so profoundly impressed Franklin D. Roosevelt. The previous historiography of Henry Adams, Theodore Roosevelt, and Henry Cabot Lodge was by implication so elitist and Hamiltonian as to have no continuing relevance.

The Thomas Jefferson preserved in the Jefferson Memorial is a creation of the New Deal, fabricated by that sly Machiavellian fox Franklin D. Roosevelt as part of his Southern strategy, and influenced by the popular historian Claude Bowers. Bowers was rightly denounced by W. E. B. Du Bois, as noted above, for his pro-slavery, white-supremacist, and segregationist biases, but Franklin D. Roosevelt needed the South, and furthermore he needed an interpretation of history that

[50] Hammond, *Banks and Politics in America*, p. 536.

claimed a heroic genealogy for his radically reformed Democratic Party. Thus he resurrected the patriarchal myth of Thomas Jefferson as the father of the modern Democratic Party and the prophet of democratic reform. With a bland smile, FDR fortuitously appropriated the land that had originally been set aside for a monument to his cousin, Theodore Roosevelt, to construct a Roman temple to Jefferson. The deification of Jefferson sanctified the New Deal's skillfully reconciled contradictions and its brilliantly achieved coalition of democratic socialists, Wall Street elitists, Southern populists, and racial reactionaries.

Just as Jefferson hijacked the ideas and words of John Locke and George Mason to forge the Declaration, so too did Lincoln hijack the Declaration and implicitly pretend that it was an abolitionist document. The Gettysburg Address's interpretation of "all men are created equal" had nothing to do with Jefferson's limited conception of human equality, a fact of which the still living Chief Justice Taney could have reminded Lincoln. But at Gettysburg, Lincoln was *en route* to enforcing his own transformative interpretation of the Declaration's equality clause, with the Union Armies to back him up. That Jefferson's words could be poured into the abolitionist container had been recognized by Frederick Douglass and other hijacking abolitionists. Seventy years later, the aristocratic, racialist, anti-Federalist Jefferson was magically transformed into the forerunner of Franklin D. Roosevelt's New Deal, with its military Keynesianism that pulled the nation out of its catastrophic depression. "Necessary and proper" the New Deal may have been, but, as Daniel Boorstin pointed out, it was a long way from Jeffersonian democracy.

THE MONTICELLO DYNASTY

Marie Kimball was Monticello's first curator from 1944 until her death in 1955, at which time she was working on the fourth volume of her Jefferson biography. In 1958, Monticello endowed the Thomas Jefferson Foundation Professorship of History at Jefferson's University of Virginia. From there, Dumas Malone, Merrill Peterson, and Peter S. Onuf successively emerged as the dominant figures in Jefferson scholarship. Malone's six-volume biography, *Jefferson and His Time* (1948–81), is completely sympathetic but honest. The same can be said of Peterson's two studies, *Thomas Jefferson and the New Nation* (1970) and *The Jefferson Image in the American Mind* (1988), which together total over 1,600 pages.

The complaint that Peterson in 1970 did not footnote his primary-source quotations has lost relevancy in the past decade. Many of Peterson's contemporaries cited outmoded editions of Jefferson's papers, with references to pages and volume numbers that were difficult for most readers to obtain, and are now obsolete. Since 2010, the National Archives, through its National Historical Publications and Records Commission (NHPRC), and the University of Virginia Press have created a website (https://founders.archives.gov/) that makes available primary sources and scholarly commentary on the Founders of the United States of America. The site makes available *The Papers of Thomas Jefferson*, edited by Julian P. Boyd (Princeton University Press, 1950 to the present). I have encountered no significant difficulties in locating Peterson's sources.

Peter Onuf, as author, editor, and impresario, has been more influential than "any other scholar over the past generation ... by supervising numerous Ph.D. dissertations, presiding over scholarly organizations, and collaborating with numerous scholars in the compilation of several volumes."[51]

On September 17, 2016, Monticello, along with the National Endowment for the Humanities and the University of Virginia, hosted a public summit on the legacies of race and slavery. The summit was the capstone event of Human/Ties, a four-day celebration of the NEH's 50th anniversary. We were joined by thousands on the West Lawn of Jefferson's famous home to learn from the past and grapple with issues that face us today.

This "public summit" was, no doubt, a beautiful and moving exercise in truth and reconciliation, and a noble attempt "to bind up the nation's wounds." It pointed us towards the realization of David Walker's dream that America might awaken from its racial nightmare to become "a united and happy people." Among its central concerns was a celebration of the Hemings family historiography, so brilliantly recovered by Annette Gordon-Reed, and Lucia Stanton, which has provided a path towards a more humane construction of American culture than we have heretofore witnessed. Nonetheless, we still live in a world where some men have sexual passions that many women find disgusting. A Supreme Court Justice may tell dirty jokes; a president may commit adultery in the Oval Office; a candidate for the highest office may boast of his sexual exploits in the language of a 14-year-old misfit.

[51] Frank Cogliano, review of Peter Onuf's *The Mind of Thomas Jefferson*, in *The Journal of American Studies* (August, 2008), 376.

If Jefferson's preachments of liberty and equality were "Tomfoolery," it must be admitted that they launched a rhetoric that Frederick Douglass and others were able to bend for noble purposes. Abraham Lincoln, another great American confidence man, magically reformed the words of Jefferson's Declaration of Independence so as to transform its provincial conception of liberty into a universal declaration of human rights. Pauline Maier states that it was the "American people" as a whole, not Lincoln alone, who reinvigorated the Declaration, and her point does not lack sentimental appeal, but it is undeniable that Lincoln's interpretation, backed up by the armies of Grant and Sherman, put teeth into the new interpretation.[52] Dwight David Eisenhower cited the United Nations Charter's declaration of a universal "right to life, Liberty and security of person" when he sent the 101st Airborne Battle Group to escort African American students to Little Rock High School. Whatever their original intent, the words of the Declaration have taken on a meaning for which I am personally most grateful, but it took more than the democratic egalitarianism of the American people at the grass-roots level to open up the promise of American life for me. It took the two least democratic arms of the federal government, going against much public opinion, and personified by Chief Justice Earl Warren and President Eisenhower.[53]

Abraham Lincoln's revolt against Jeffersonian democracy, while cynically invoking its shibboleths, was a necessary stage in the development of what historian James McPherson has seen as "the positive Liberty of centralized power."[54] Neither McPherson nor Beard, in their analyses of Jeffersonian democracy, specifically remarked on the irony that Andrew Jackson, when he made his famous toast to national union on Jefferson's birthday, was a prophet of nationalism, no less than his bitter enemy, Henry Clay. Jacksonian nationalism was an essential pillar of Lincoln's Whig construction of big government and presidential power. Lincoln's nationalism advanced Jackson's position that the Constitution formed "a government and not a league," that it "operates directly on the people individually, not on the states," and that it forms "a single nation." But had not Jefferson once said something similar when he referred to the

[52] Maier, *American Scripture*, p. 208.

[53] Tardy in his support of African American civil rights, Earl Warren, as governor of California, presided over the internment of Japanese American citizens during World War II. President Eisenhower's administration was responsible for the deportation of an unknown number of American citizens of Mexican origin during the 1950s.

[54] McPherson, "the positive Liberty of centralized power," in his *Lincoln*, p. 152. 101st Airborne, ibid.

Constitution not as a compact between the states, but as an "act of the whole American people"?

Lincoln employed Jeffersonian rhetoric and Jacksonian autocracy in his Gettysburg Address. The Civil War represented the triumph of Hamiltonian democracy over Jeffersonian democracy, and the triumph of Lincoln's party – the party of a nascent corporate capitalism – was a necessary stage in the eradication of slavery. History represents neither "time's arrow" nor "time's cycle." It has no more geometrical logic than a plate of spaghetti. The kaleidoscopic shifting of party ideologies and loyalties from the Revolution to the Civil War to the New Deal, to the "Republic of Social Media," offers political historians considerable opportunity to practice their craft, and it offers political rhetoricians splendid opportunities to practice theirs. Abraham Lincoln's metaphor of the two combatants confusing their coats, cited above, is in some ways as applicable to recent decades as it was to the years of Lincoln's reference, 1789–1859, each party "having fought himself out of his own coat, and into that of the other."

3

Let Our Workshops Remain at Monticello

"Let our workshops remain in Europe," Jefferson famously wrote, with deceptive rhetorical flourish. These words are the most frequently cited example of what is called Jeffersonian "agrarianism," in *Notes on Virginia*, and one of the most familiar to historians, but "agrarian" is not a term that Jefferson employed frequently or with fondness. More than once he used the term negatively, as we shall presently see, and he knew the term was ambiguous, having radical associations both in ancient Roman law and in the rhetoric of his times. For example, Thomas Paine recycled the word in *Agrarian Justice* (1797), which was a proposal for a sweeping big-government reform that Jefferson could hardly have approved. Jefferson's brand of the ideology was much more in step with the agrarianism of John Taylor, who is generally regarded its foremost American prophet, but even Taylor did not use the term frequently. In fact, neither the term "agrarian" nor "agrarianism" appears in Jefferson's *Notes on the State of Virginia.*[1]

While Jefferson is usually presented as the consummate agrarian, he has also been canonized as the patron saint of American industrialism. One textbook popular in undergraduate business courses makes him the

[1] Thomas Jefferson, *Notes on the State of Virginia*, ed. David Waldstreicher (Boston, MA: Bedford Books, 2002), p. 197. Jefferson to James Madison, June 15, 1797, Jefferson to Pierre Samuel Du Pont de Nemours, April 15, 1811. Thomas Jefferson: *Autobiography*, January 6 – July 29, 1821, Founders Online; see Merrill Peterson, ed., *Thomas Jefferson, Writings* (New York: Literary Classics of the United States, 1984). Wikipedia (as at April 17, 2013) linked agrarianism to John Taylor and listed Thomas Paine's *Agrarian Justice* in the bibliography. John Taylor, no fonder of the term than Jefferson, used it negatively at least once, saying, "the rich agrarian law-makers have most unskillfully suffered the money thus drawn to pass into the pockets of fallacious wealth," *An Inquiry into the Principles and Policy of the Government of the United States.* "Agrarianism," as an abstract noun, does not appear in Taylor's works, although the term "agrarian" appears in his manifesto, *Arator* (1814).

guiding light of America's industrial beginnings.[2] Jack McLaughlin describes the various shops at Monticello engaged in nailmaking, shoemaking, and lumber-cutting, all the work performed by Jefferson working alongside his adolescent slaves. The historian Lucia Stanton describes Monticello as a veritable beehive of industrial activity. Joseph Ellis goes so far as to suggest that Jefferson preferred the forge to the farm. It seems likely that he interacted on a regular basis with his mechanical workers, and it is not inconceivable that he may have relished his social relationship to those slaves who worked under him in his nailery, or that he enjoyed the workmanlike atmosphere of the forge.[3]

Madison Hemings asserted that Jefferson personally had little taste for farming and recalled that Jefferson spent much time in the nailery during his later years. Peter Onuf and Annette Gordon-Reed say that a visitor dropping in on Monticello might be quite likely to find him at the forge. Jefferson described himself as mornings "in my shops, my garden, or on horseback among my farms." He declared that farming necessitated familiarity with agriculture and mechanics, with "the implements of husbandry and operations with them, among them the plough and its kindred instruments for dividing the soil ... and the threshing machine." The successful small farmer did not differ from Washington or Jefferson in that he must, perforce, be a mechanic and an inventor. As a class, farmers were "those practical and observing husbandmen whose knowledge is the most valuable, and who are mostly to be found in that portion of citizens with whom the observance of economy is necessary."[4] Nonetheless, it is undeniable that he often wrote dreamily of a system of cultural and political values based on sentimental agrarianism and the self-sustaining

[2] Wallace Hopp and Mark Spearman, *Factory Physics*, 3rd edn. (Long Grove, IL: Waveland Press, 2011). Professor of Business Russell Barton brought this book to my attention at a cocktail party; however, the authors spend less than a paragraph on Jefferson.

[3] For micromanagement, see Lucia Stanton, *Slavery at Monticello* (Charlottesville, VA: Thomas Jefferson Memorial Foundation, 1996), p. 23. Also see Lucia Stanton, *Free Some Day: The African-American Families of Monticello* (Charlottesville, VA: The Thomas Jefferson Foundation, 2000); Stanton quotes Madison Hemings in *"Those Who Labor for My Happiness": Slavery at Thomas Jefferson's Monticello* (Charlottesville, VA: University of Virginia Press, 2012), p. 13. Joseph Ellis, *American Sphinx: The Character of Thomas Jefferson* (New York: Knopf, 1997), pp. 142–143. For Jefferson's delight in handworking, see Jack Mclaughlin, *Jefferson and Monticello: The Biography of a Builder* (New York: Henry Holt, 1990), pp. 111, 170–171. Annette Gordon-Reed and Peter S. Onuf, *"Most Blessed of the Patriarchs": Thomas Jefferson and the Empire of the Imagination* (New York: Liveright, 2017), pp. 15–16.

[4] See Jefferson's "Constitution for Proposed Agricultural Society of Albemarle," ca. February 1, 1811, Founders Online.

male-headed farmstead. While he obviously did not think that every farm in America could or should resemble Monticello, providing the citizen farmer with almost everything necessary to pursue happiness, he thought that most farms had the potential to be self-reliant.[5]

Self-reliance was the key idea, for "Dependency begets subservience and venality, suffocates the germ of virtue," as he wrote in *Notes on Virginia.* Jefferson wanted the mass of Americans to have farms, not jobs, for a job-holder must be dependent on the whims of his employer, while the yeoman farmer is independent. If at least once he applied the term "yeomanry" to the people of the city,[6] still, by and large, he saw an agricultural solution to the problem of perpetuating republican values. Although he did not sprinkle his writings with the word "democracy" any more than with "agrarian," Jefferson hoped to perpetuate an agrarian democracy by offering to every white male head of household the opportunity to become an independent freeholder.[7] Jefferson's political economy would offer, as historian Edmund S. Morgan put it, an opportunity "to carry the independence of the individual beyond what the world had hitherto known."

A vast amount of scholarship illustrates the conflicting definitions of the term "agrarian," and the nuances of its cultural and economic significance within the context of British, colonial, and early American law. Working definitions of "agrarianism" are also abundant, for example the useful description in a textbook by three distinguished authors, John M. Murrin, Paul E. Johnson, and James M. McPherson:

> Throughout his political life, Jefferson envisioned American yeomen trading farm surpluses for European manufactured goods—a relationship that would ensure rural prosperity, prevent the growth of cities and factories, and thus sustain the landed independence on which republican citizenship rested.

"By 1816 that dream was ended," as the foregoing authors conclude, in accord with the observations of other scholars. In fact, even Jefferson was

[5] Jefferson's reference to his time on horseback, in Jefferson to Thaddeus Kosciusko, February 26, 1810. Madison Hemings, "Life among the Lowly, No. 1," *Pike County (Ohio) Republican* (March 13, 1873), 4. Professors Peter Onuf and Annette Gordon-Reed on Madison Hemings' statement that Jefferson "had but little taste for agricultural pursuits," *"Most Blessed of the Patriarchs,"* p. 52.

[6] For example, at the time of the French ambassador Edmund Genêt's celebrated progress along the East coast, Jefferson noted his being feted by "the yeomanry of the city," Jefferson to James Monroe, May 5, 1793.

[7] James Madison, "Notes for the *National Gazette* Essays [ca. December 19, 1791–March 3, 1792]," Founders Online; Robert A. Rutland and Thomas A. Mason, eds., *The Papers of James Madison* (Charlottesville, VA: University of Virginia Press, 1983), vol. XIV, *6 April 1791 – 16 March 1793*, pp. 157–169.

never absolutely confident of his vision, for in his lifetime irresistible forces were in play, threatening any realization of a garden empire, free of slavery, free of commercialism, free of sweatshops and industrial slums. One historian has called him a "grieving optimist," and certainly by the end of his life Jefferson revealed "struggle and doubt" about the direction in which civilization was progressing. In *The Lost World of Thomas Jefferson* (1948), historian Daniel Boorstin observed with some nostalgia the vanishing of his "lost world." In that same year another historian, Richard Hofstadter, asserted that, by 1816, Jefferson's political vision was a lost cause, as his own Republican Party adopted the "whole complex of Federalist policies."[8]

The hyperbole of Query XIX of *Notes on Virginia* implied an inflexible commitment to "agrarianism," but while that term remains rightly associated with "Jeffersonian democracy," the author of that ideology vacillated and drifted on his agrarian ideal as much as he did on other aspects of his dogma, such as free markets, antislavery, the development of the US Navy, and minimal government. Jefferson was sometimes an ideologue, but he was always a pragmatist, and, as Alexander Hamilton cynically observed, he was never "zealot enough to do anything in pursuance of his principles which will contravene his popularity, or his interest."[9]

[8] The definition of agrarianism by John M. Murrin, Paul E. Johnson, James M. McPherson, et al. is in their *Liberty, Equality, Power, A History of the American People* (New York: Harcourt, 2001), p. 254. Christopher Michael Curtis probes the term in the introduction to his *Jefferson's Freeholders and the Politics of Ownership in the Old Dominion* (Cambridge University Press, 2012). For other semantic difficulties, see Thomas P. Govan, "Agrarian and Agrarianism: A Study in the Use and Abuse of Words," *Journal of Southern History*, 30, no. 1 (February, 1964), 35–47. Another highly respected study is Joyce Appleby, "Commercial Farming and the 'Agrarian Myth' in the Early Republic," *The Journal of American History*, 68, no. 4 (March, 1982), 833–849. Richard Hofstadter observes the transformation of Jeffersonian politics by 1816 in *The American Political Tradition* (New York: Knopf, 1948), p. 42. Southern intellectuals attempted to revive "agrarianism" with the publication of Rupert B. Vance's *I'll Take My Stand: The South and the Agrarian Tradition: By Twelve Southerners* (New York: Harper and Brothers, 1930). The scholarly literature "problematizing" the concept of agrarianism is immense. See, for example, Joyce Appleby, *Capitalism and a New Social Order: The Republican Vision of the 1790s* (New York University Press, 1984). Also see Appleby, "Commercial Farming and the 'Agrarian Myth' in the Early Republic." Alan Kulikoff offers a complicated and nuanced discussion of the complexities of agrarianism in *The Agrarian Origins of American Capitalism* (Charlottesville, VA: University of Virginia Press, 1992), pp. 78–79. Also see Kulikoff's notes and bibliography. Richard Hofstadter describes the "agrarian myth" in *The Age of Reform* (New York: Vintage, 1955), pp. 23–59.

[9] Charles and Mary Beard, *The Rise of American Civilization* (New York: Macmillan, 1930), contains numerous references to "agrarianism," many of them indexed. Peter Onuf

Jefferson even employed the term "agrarian" negatively in a letter to John Adams (1813), assuring his old friend that he need not fear any "agrarian and plundering enterprises of the majority of the people."[10] He knew that Adams shared with another old friend, James Madison, a suspicion of the property-less majority, and that in their vocabulary the word "agrarian" evoked something equivalent to our modern word "socialism." It was loaded with "fears of the equalization of property," and he was not insensitive to their fears, but he correctly assured Adams that the American yeomanry, presumably that represented by the likes of Daniel Shays, did not constitute a mass of "agrarians" in the sense of levelers, or plunderers, or enemies to property. In any event, Jefferson pretended that discontent among the masses was largely a New England phenomenon, since Massachusetts and Connecticut were dominated by pseudo-aristocracies. In Virginia, of course, "we have nothing of this."[11]

When he used the term "agrarian" benignly it was in his *Autobiography*, where he recalled his 1776 fight in the Virginia legislature to abolish primogeniture, a vestige of English common law, requiring that the lands and slaves of a person who died intestate pass exclusively to the eldest son. He was proud that his fight for the "equal partition of inheritances removed the feudal and unnatural distinctions which made one

indicates fundamental contradictions in Jefferson's agarianism in *Jefferson's Empire* (Charlottesville, VA: University of Virginia Press, 2000), pp. 161–163, noting how historians have problematized the term, p. 224 note 37. Sean Wilentz summarizes Hamilton's objections to agrarianism in Sean Wilentz, *The Rise of American Democracy* (New York: Norton, 2005), pp. 43–44.

Dumas Malone offers a cautionary note on the use of "agrarianism" in his *Jefferson and His Time*, 6 vols. (Boston, MA: Little, Brown, 1981), vol. VI, *Jefferson and His Time, the Sage of Monticello*, p. 146. Merrill Peterson points out some problems of definition in *The Jefferson Image in the American Mind* (Charlottesville, VA: University of Virginia Press, 1998), p. 318. Gordon Wood, *The Creation of the American Republic, 1776–1787* (New York: Norton, 1969). Also see Gordon Wood's *Empire of Liberty* (New York: Oxford, 2009), p. 8. See Thomas Paine's use of the term in *Agrarian Justice* (1797).

10 Jefferson to John Adams, October 28, 1813. The Beards, in *The Rise of American Civilization*, p. 307, refer to Shays' Rebellion as "agrarian." Gordon Wood alludes to Roman agrarian laws in *The Creation of the American Republic*, pp. 64, 69. A radical conception of agrarianism as redistribution of wealth was employed by Thomas Paine in his *Agrarian Justice*, a pamphlet Jefferson called "worth notice," Jefferson to James Madison, Philadelphia, June 15, 1797. Daniel Boorstin, *The Lost World of Thomas Jefferson* (Boston, MA: Beacon, 1948), p. 243; Hofstadter, *The American Political Tradition*, pp. 41–42.

11 Jefferson to John Adams, October 28, 1813, attributes unrest among Massachusetts farmers to "pseudo-aristocratic" traditions. Of course, no class distinctions of any sort existed with the baronial class of wealthy Virginia slaveholders.

member of every family rich, and all the rest poor, substituting equal partition, the best of all Agrarian laws," which existed in Virginia. He was confident that "these laws, drawn by myself, laid the axe to the root of Pseudo-aristocracy."[12]

He had attempted even more than that. He had tried to abolish economic obstacles to land ownership with a proposal for "every male person" of what Christopher Michael Curtis calls a "freehold entitlement." Not only would Jefferson's Draft Constitution for Virginia grant the franchise to every freeholder, and to "every resident in the colony who shall have paid his scot and lot to the government" for the last two years, but it would also increase the number of freeholders. In order to promote a broad distribution of property, he proposed that "Every person of full age [changed in the second draft to "every male person"] neither owning nor having owned [50] acres of land, shall be entitled to an appropriation of [50] acres."[13] In drafts for reform of the Virginia Constitution, and then later as president, he tried to ensure the availability of land to small farmers, expressing a vision that prefigured the homestead acts of a later epoch. He conceived of public land sales at low prices, first in the Northwest Territory and later across the Mississippi, as a way to help poor whites obtain acreage and mules.[14] Land reform necessarily implied the implementation of big government, but government must always function in a way consistent with republican ideals. The selling of public lands constituted one of the legitimate means of raising revenue that he condoned, since the best government would be the "government that governs least" and, ideally, one that does not tax at all. These were to be land reforms that would distribute wealth to the small farmer without appropriating the wealth of those who held great landed estates.

Another, more radical use of the term "agrarian laws" recalled the "Lex Sempronia Agraria" laws enacted in the late Roman Empire to guarantee the survival of the class of small farmers through the

[12] Ibid.

[13] Christopher Michael Curtis analyses Jefferson's land policies and theory of property in *Jefferson's Freeholders*. For land distribution see ibid., p. 61. Also see Stanley N. Katz, "Thomas Jefferson and the Right to Property in Revolutionary America," *The Journal of Law & Economics*, 19, no. 3, *1776: The Revolution in Social Thought* (October, 1976), 467–488.

[14] See article and document on agrarian law, 111 BC, at Project Avalon, http://avalon.law.yale.edu/ancient/agrarian_law.asp Gordon Wood notes the call for agrarian laws in 1776 in his *Empire of Liberty*, p. 8.

redistribution of lands monopolized by the upper classes.[15] Jefferson's agrarian reforms, like those of ancient Rome, called on government to assure individual liberty and preserve republican virtue, but the resemblance ended there. The Roman agrarian laws carved up the large estates of aristocratic farmers, while Jefferson's reforms never suggested anything so extreme, nor did they encompass the radical proto-socialistic agrarianism of Thomas Paine, who proposed what he called "Agrarian Justice" in his 1797 pamphlet that called for taxation of those who monopolized land and a distribution of the revenues to the landless. Paine wrote, "the earth, in its natural uncultivated state was, and ever would have continued to be, the common property of the human race. In that state every man would have been born to property ... Every proprietor, therefore, of cultivated land, owes to the community a ground-rent."[16]

Paine's was an agrarian definition of reform, certain to terrify aristocracies on both sides of the Atlantic. Jefferson's support of land taxes for the support of public schools, and his support of making public lands available to farmers who had no land, stopped short of such an extreme. The proto-socialism of Thomas Paine's pamphlet *Agrarian Justice* argued that since, in advanced civilization, all the land would be monopolized by a wealthy few, governments must make provisions to supply the masses of the people with a compensation for an inevitably exhausted supply of unclaimed land. Jefferson's theories presupposed that land would always be available, in the broad expanses of North America with a limitless frontier eternally open to a population of sturdy yeoman pioneers. Paine's agrarianism was more realistically founded in a social contract that presumed an inevitable scarcity and even a monopolization of land.

In his passionate discussion of "Jefferson and the Land Question" in the Memorial Edition of Jefferson's works, Henry George, Jr., was fascinated with a letter Jefferson wrote during his first year in Paris to the Reverend James Madison, expressing Jefferson's concern about the distribution of property rights in a democratic society. George took note of

[15] Jefferson and Paine's use of the term was probably derived from agrarian reform in ancient Rome, particularly the "Lex Sempronia Agraria" of Tiberius Gracchus, that seized public land (*ager publicus*) monopolized by the rich and distributed it to small farmers. See Howard Hayes Scullard, *From the Gracchi to Nero: A History of Rome from 133 BC to AD 68* (repr. New York: Routledge, 2003 [1959]). Roger G. Kennedy makes comparisons with Roman law in *Mr. Jefferson's Lost Cause: Land, Farmers, Slavery, and the Louisiana Purchase* (Oxford University Press, 2003), pp. 248–249.

[16] Thomas Paine, *Agrarian Justice*, in *Paine: Writings*, ed. Eric Foner (New York: Literary Classics of the United States, 1995), pp. 397–400.

Jefferson's reading of several French economists on land taxes, and recycled his father's famous proposal for a "single tax" on land, although he missed the opportunity to reference Paine's call for a universal land tax as a compensation for the natural right to land, which advanced societies must necessarily usurp.[17] George might also have mentioned Jefferson's Virginia school bill, proposing that land taxes for the expenses of public schools should be distributed such a way as to "throw on wealth the education of the poor." He skimmed over the reform in which Jefferson took the greatest pride, "the abolition of primogeniture."[18]

Jefferson envisioned an agrarianism that resembled some elements of the Roman land reforms, but not Thomas Paine's radical call for a compensatory tax based on a natural right to land. He believed, as Michael Curtis observes, that government should create opportunities for acquiring landed property, but not for breaking up and redistributing the property of wealthy landholders.[19] He thought it possible to forestall the dire trepidation of Henry Knox, that Daniel Shays' rebels were enemies of the wealthy farmers. He correctly understood Shays to be protesting an ephemeral and rectifiable debt policy, not an entire economic system. Thus, Jefferson was no hypocrite when he expressed sympathy for Shays, since he fervently shared his hostility to land speculators and moneylenders, and viewed him as a fellow capitalist freeholder, not as a leveler. Shays threatened the commercial paper of absentee landlords and parasitical speculators, not the real estate of wealthy planters.

He shared with Shays the dream of an America liberated from its bourgeoisie, the urban elite of parasitical financiers, standing above the masses of the people, dictating with pen-strokes the fortunes of honest farmers. His world would also be without a grumbling hive of urban *sans culottes*, engaged in mind-numbing factory routines. The ideal American would never be bound to a "job," and Jefferson would never have conceived of an American presidential campaign in which the sloganeers of two national parties would repeatedly mouth as their watchwords, "Jobs!

[17] Henry George, Jr. (1862–1916) was a United States Representative from New York, son of the American political economist Henry George (1839–97), famous for his proposal of a "single tax" on land outlined in his book *Progress and Poverty* (1879), which sold several million copies. Paine, *Agrarian Justice*, p. 398.

[18] Thomas Jefferson: *Autobiography*, January, 6 – July 29, 1821, January 6, 1821, Founders Online.

[19] Christopher Michael Curtis analyses Jefferson's land policies and theory of property in *Jefferson's Freeholders*. For land distribution, see ibid., p. 61. Also see Katz, "Thomas Jefferson and the Right to Property in Revolutionary America," 467–488.

Jobs! Jobs!" In the system defined in his *Notes on the State of Virginia*, having a job, being a wage-slave, would breed dependency and corrupt virtue. That was the central idea behind what we now regard as the cliché of Jeffersonian agrarianism, although, as we have seen, that ambiguous term, much over-simplified in today's textbooks, had no uniform definition in the eighteenth century.[20]

The Count of Monticello always portrayed hardscrabble subsistence farmers as if they were kindred spirits, and only later would he opportunistically express approval for the "yeomanry of the city." As did many eighteenth-century economic commentators, he viewed the rise of the urban working class, not unreasonably, as the by-product of agrarian problems. The only reason for the rise of an urban working class, in the minds of Jefferson and his peers, was the corruption of society as a result of diminishing agricultural opportunities. Many authors, even the citified Benjamin Franklin, shared the sentimental view that farmers were more virtuous than either the bourgeoisie or the working class.[21] The poet Oliver Goldsmith fretted over the threat to England's peasant vigor as aristocrats enclosed their lands and appropriated formerly common pastures in pursuit of wealth, forcing once-happy rustics to desert their villages:

> Ill fares the land, to hastening ills a prey,
> Where wealth accumulates, and men decay;
> Princes and lords may flourish, or may fade;
> A breath can make them, as a breath has made;
> But a bold peasantry, their country's pride,
> When once destroyed can never be supplied.[22]

A fictional holdover from Goldsmith's fabled "bold peasantry" flourished in the character Brom Bones of Washington Irving's short story

[20] Dumas Malone offers a cautionary note on the use of "agrarianism" in *The Sage of Monticello*, p. 146. Merrill D. Peterson indicates problems of definition in *The Jefferson Image in the American Mind* (Charlottesville, VA: University of Virginia Press, 1998 [1960]), p. 318. Wood, in his *The Creation of the American Republic*, uses the term primarily in connection with the agrarian laws of ancient Rome, pp. 64, 89, although he refers to the "standard statement of Jefferson's agrarian views" in *Notes on Virginia*. Wood also mentions Roman agrarian laws in his *Empire of Liberty*, p. 8. Govan, "Agrarian and Agrarianism," 35–47. See Thomas Paine's use of the term in *Agrarian Justice* (1797).

[21] Franklin wrote that farming was "the only honest way" for a nation to acquire wealth. "Positions to Be Examined," MS Yale University Library, April 4, 1769. *The Benjamin Franklin Papers*, MS (copy), Yale University Library.

[22] Oliver Goldsmith, lines from "The Deserted Village" (1770).

"The Legend of Sleepy Hollow." Published in 1820, the same year as the Missouri Compromise, the fiction presented the characters of Brom Bones and Ichabod Crane, contending rivals on the American rustic landscape. Ichabod desires to marry Katrina, the daughter of Squire Van Tassel, who owns an abundantly prosperous farm. Ichabod's "heart yearned after the damsel who was to inherit these domains, and his imagination expanded with the idea, how they might be readily turned into cash, and the money invested in immense tracts of wild land." Brom fortunately frightens off Ichabod, and triumphantly leads Katrina to the altar, presumably destined to ripen into a prosperous country squire. The enterprising Ichabod, however, goes on to study law, writes for the newspapers, enters politics, and becomes a judge.

In a sarcastically retrospective essay on "The Independent Farmer," Thorstein Veblen, with the economic historian's imagination, suggested that, in reality, the entrepreneurial land speculator represented American ideals much better than "the independent farmer of the poets." Ichabod Crane was probably no more on Veblen's mind than on Jefferson's, but Ichabod would have provided a rich illustration of Veblen's thesis that the yeoman farmer seeks, "by hard work and shrewd management, to acquire a 'competence'; such as will enable him some day to take his due place among the absentee owners of the land and so come in for an easy livelihood at the cost of the rest of the community."[23]

The historical process of urbanization arose from realities in addition to those represented by the movements of stricken farmers to Birmingham, Manchester, Liverpool, and London, where Blake, Hogarth, and later Dickens depicted their misery. Urbanization did not occur simply because masses of English yeomen had been dispossessed of their village greens, although that was indeed a factor, and a brutally tragic one. But cities were attractive to generations of Dick Whittingtons, Poor Richards, and Ragged Dicks who migrated to cities out of a spirit of adventure and enterprise. Even at the risk of ruination, many young people came to the cities to seek their fortunes, and early industrial workers, although often living in poverty, were not necessarily worse off than their romanticized rural forebears. And an Emma Hamilton or a Fanny Hill might discover that "the fate worse than death" was not the worst that London had to offer:

[23] Thorstein Veblen's acerbic critique of the Jeffersonian agrarian tradition and its "obstinately loyal supporters" was published in *Absentee Ownership and Business Enterprise in Modern Times* (New York: B. W. Huebsch, 1923), pp. 129–141.

> "You left us in tatters without shoes or socks,
> Tired of digging potatoes, and spudding up docks;
> And now you've got bracelets and bright feathers three!" —
> "Yes: that's how we dress when we're ruined," said she.

Cities offered opportunities to a rising class with the brains and imagination to become entrepreneurial *arrivistes*. Charles Dickens, who was the son of a petty clerk, was heading off to work as a child laborer in a blacking factory while Jefferson was opening the University of Virginia. Would Charles Dickens have endured the crash of 1819 any better if his father had been an American subsistence farmer?

Urbanization was both the cause and the effect of disruptive economic pressures. By the mid 1700s, the factory system, with its division of labor, had begun to reshape many of Europe's traditional skilled craftsmen into mechanical automatons, performing increasingly routine and unimaginative functions. "Dark satanic mills," as William Blake called them, were already presaging the emergence of Dickens' England, and a grim specter of discontent was already haunting Europe. In the year of the American Revolution, Adam Smith sadly observed that urban laborers were frequently incapable of understanding their interests or organizing to defend them.[24] Jefferson thought the prevention of a *Lumpenproletariat* seemed possible in America, due to her plenteous lands that could never be paved over. The escape hatch of a perpetual frontier would prevent the development of an urban working class, easily exploited and necessarily depraved. The German poet Johann Wolfgang von Goethe came very close to anticipating the frontier theories of both Karl Marx and Frederick Jackson Turner when he wrote: "Amerika, du hast es besser."[25]

To François Marbois, Jefferson wrote, "The mobs of great cities add just so much to the support of pure government as sores do to the strength of the human body." He described artisans or "artificers" as "lacking in husbandry," although he must be cautiously tolerant of property-owning artisans, mechanics, and merchants. He had to be tolerant, at least, of an artisan like Thomas Paine, and he was more than eager to be associated with Benjamin Franklin, who had called himself "Leather Apron."

[24] Jean Yarbrough, *American Virtues: Thomas Jefferson on the American Character of a Free People* (Lawrence, KS: University Press of Kansas, 1998), p. 60.

[25] Goethe's statement "keine verfallene Schlösser, Und keine Basalte," from the widely anthologized poem "Den Vereinigten Staaten," has puzzled interpreters. Hawthorne felt that the absence of ruined castles (verfallene Schlösser) presented challenges to the American artistic imagination. "Basalte" may have been a symbolic reference to Europe's figuratively barren, paved-over landscape in contrast to the virgin lands of the American West.

Nonetheless, farmers were the backbone of a republic, and "those who labor in the earth are the only chosen people." But Jefferson was no mystic, and his religious metaphor should not be mistaken for fanaticism. The extreme anti-industrialism he expressed in Query XX of the *Notes* was simply a matter of being swept up in his own rhetoric, and it is unlikely that he entirely believed his own purple prose.[26]

Assuming that every American had the desire, talent, and training to become an independent farmer, the American environment would preserve the moral and economic virtue of the American citizenry. Mill workers were inevitably reduced to the level of brutes, and susceptible to all manner of social vices.[27] It seemed obvious that the best mechanics were organic products of the frontier, where industrial invention sprang up in natural response to the practical needs of the yeoman. The mindless routine of urban industrial drudgery stifled imagination, but farming necessitated imagination and stimulated creativity in both the agricultural and mechanical realms. In his 1811 outline of a "Scheme for a System of Agricultural Societies," Jefferson argued reasonably enough that the independent farmer, constantly reliant on his initiative to solve a broad variety of life's tasks, had an unparalleled opportunity to develop both personal and civic responsibility. Certainly this was true in the case of the large planter, as proven by the pragmatic inventions abounding at Monticello.

CLASSICAL AGRARIANISM, GREECE, AND ROME

Following in the tradition of Douglass Adair, Gordon Wood employed the term "classical agrarianism" in one of his influential articles.[28] Republican Rome is supposed to have offered the classical model on which eighteenth-century American elites based their ideals, at least with respect to "agrarian" politics and "republican" virtue, although it was understood that the noble Romans had never instituted constitutional republicanism.[29] In the early nineteenth century Americans began to

[26] Jefferson, *Notes on Virginia*, pp. 196–197.

[27] Yarbrough, *American Virtues*, pp. 58–59. Ironic that Smith saw the worst prospects for civic responsibility within the civitas. Frederick Jackson Turner would insist that the farmer, especially on the frontier, lacked civic responsibility. Thorstein Veblen also critiqued the notion of the independent farmer (see Chapter 4 note 32 below).

[28] Gordon Wood, "The Significance of the Early Republic," *Journal of the Early Republic* 8 (1988), p. 1020.

[29] Peter Onuf and Nicholas Cole, eds., *Thomas Jefferson, the Classical World, and Early America* (Charlottesville, VA: University of Virginia Press, 2011), p. 24. Douglass Adair mentions Jeffersonian agrarianism's origins in ancient Greece in Adair, *The Intellectual*

develop the so-called "dream of a Greek democracy that generations of historians have identified as their cultural ideal."[30] The fact that classical civilizations had been dependent on slave labor was disturbing to Jefferson, and to others. George Mason and John Taylor were troubled by slavery and pontificated on its evils, but were no more prepared than Jefferson for immediate abolition or racial egalitarianism. In fact, at the end of the eighteenth century, American planters found it necessary to rationalize slavery more vigorously than the ancients ever had. Jefferson portrayed Virginia as having avoided slavery's ancient injustices.

Jefferson consoled himself with the rationalization that American slavery was less severe than slavery in the ancient world. He made his famous attempt to justify Virginia's slavery by contrasting its supposedly crueler manifestation under the Greeks and Romans: "Cato, on a principle of economy, always sold his sick and superannuated slaves." In *Notes on the State of Virginia*, he referenced the harshness of Cato the Elder and presented the example of Cato's cruelty to his slaves in contrast to the allegedly milder and more enlightened attitudes of contemporary Virginians, noting that Cato "gives it as a standing precept to a master visiting his farm, to sell his old oxen, old wagons, old tools, old and diseased servants, and everything else become useless." And Jefferson referred in righteous indignation to the writings of Romans who counseled or tolerated the exposure or outright murder of "diseased slaves whose cure was likely to become tedious."[31]

Jefferson, Madison, and their contemporaries were not impressed with Greek democracy. They distinguished between "the peaceable democracy

Origins of Jeffersonian Democracy, ed. Mark Yellin (Lanham, MD: Lexington Books, 2000 [1943, 1964]), pp. 21, 32.

30 Vernon Louis Parrington's chapter "The Dream of a Greek Democracy" is in his *Main Currents of American Thought* (New York: Harcourt Brace and World, 1927), vol. II, pp. 94–102. Wood, "The Significance of the Early Republic," 1–20, has stressed that the intellectual history of the early Republic expressed a drift away from the republican Roman ideal of the eightteenth century to the Greek democratic model "by the 1820s."

31 Jefferson, *Notes on Virginia*, pp. 178–179. Stanton, *Free Some Day*, p. 56. Marcus Porcius Cato (234–149 BC), called "the Elder," was much admired by the American Founders. So too was Marcus Porcius Cato Uticensius (95–46 BC), called "the Younger," the subject of a play by Joseph Addison and much admired by George Washington. See Carl J. Richard, *Greeks and Romans Bearing Gifts: How the Ancients Inspired the Founding Fathers* (Lanham, MD: Rowman and Littlefield, 2008), especially pp. 140–152. Cato the Elder's treatment of slaves is reported in Plutarch and is discussed in Thomas Wiedemann, *Greek and Roman Slavery* (London: Croom Helm, 1981): "even in antiquity, Cato was seen as an example of a cruel master, and his attitude towards his slaves was considered inhumane" (p. 175).

of Schwitz & the turbulent one of Athens."[32] They considered themselves republicans, and the basic difference between a democracy and a republic, said Madison in *Federalist* 10, was that democracy meant direct participation in government, while republic meant delegation of government to representatives. In *Federalist* 14 Madison went so far as to impugn the motives of anyone who would intentionally obscure the differences between the two, "applying to the former reasonings drawn from the nature of the latter," citing "the turbulent democracies of ancient Greece and modern Italy." Adams disagreed with him, saying that "A democracy is as really a republic as an oak is a tree, or a temple a building." And the democratic principle was something Adams viewed as healthy, so long as it avoided the extremes of leveling populism. Jefferson said that a democracy was "the only true republic."[33] And Jeffersonian democracy was essentially tied to the provincial capitalism of small local economies, which would guarantee the freedom of individuals in their local communities from the tyranny of a centralized imperial government.

Jefferson was an environmental determinist, and an economic determinist, for he betrayed a more than subliminal belief that primitive capitalism, rooted in the soil, would spontaneously produce republican liberty. Jeffersonian anarchism, if we may call it that, may have been a product of the frontier, as Frederick Jackson Turner maintained. Libertarian notions bordering on anarchism have always been strong in America. The governmental minimalism of Thomas Jefferson, unlike that of Marx and Engels, always preserves petty capitalism as the essential ingredient of freedom and independence. We may entertain the idea that, for Jefferson, the rights to liberty and the pursuit of happiness tacitly implied a natural right to property, that the liberties of a fee simple empire cannot belong to the natural state of man, unless there is a right, both natural and primal, to a fee simple estate. That is true, but, as Thomas Paine would later note in *Agrarian Justice*, mankind no longer lived in that primal state of nature.[34]

[32] See Thomas Jefferson's translation of Destutt de Tracy's Commentary on Book 2 of Montesquieu's *Esprit des Lois* (ca. August 12, 1810).

[33] Jefferson to Isaac H. Tiffany, Monticello, August 26, 1816.

[34] Daniel Boorstin writes of biological determinism, "The determining role of environment," in his *The Lost World of Thomas Jefferson*, p. 65, but misses the opportunity to discuss the role of economic determinism in Jefferson's frequently cited words from *Notes on Virginia*, "Dependency breeds subservience." That is to say, the Jeffersonian conception of yeoman liberty can exist only within the economic environment of the "alloidal land ownership" and "agrarian citizenship" that Christopher Michael Curtis discusses with exquisite nuance in *Jefferson's Freeholders*, p. 10.

Jefferson argued consistently that liberty is environmentally determined, and yet he maintained, in the Declaration of Independence, that it was a divinely ordained right. His theory of property is confusing, for, as we see in another chapter, he was not clear as to whether property was a natural right or a right acquired through usufruct. In practical terms, he viewed the farmer's ownership of real property as a fundamental prerequisite for liberty. There was a wonderful way for Americans to obtain land through the appropriation of Indian lands, so that white male heads of household could pursue their happiness as yeoman farmers. Indians implicitly lost their right to land by hunting on it instead of farming. He overlooked the fact that Indian women had historically been tillers of the soil. Self-evidently, it was the yeoman farmer, in his capacity as male head of household, who had a right to land, but neither Indian women nor black slaves of either gender acquired any right to own land simply by virtue of working it.

Jefferson's dream naturally depended, as did Andrew Jackson's, on the successful appropriation of America's Indian lands. This appropriation was justified, in his view, because only pre-agricultural aborigines occupied the lands. His policies of Indian removal were directly and specifically passed on to Andrew Jackson. He wrote to Jackson assuring him of his intention to press for the acquisition of Indian lands by peaceable means, but with the collaboration of the War Department.[35] Ideally, Indian people should be converted into yeoman farmers. "We wish to draw them to agriculture, to spinning and weaving," he wrote. And to William Harrison, governor of the Indian Territory, he wrote: "When they withdraw themselves to the cultivation of a small piece of land, they will perceive how useless to them are their extensive forests, and will be willing to pare them off from time to time in exchange of necessities for their farms and families."[36] This "civilizing mission" remained American Indian policy with the Dawes Act of 1887, which sought anachronistically to make yeoman farmers out of plains Indians.[37]

The enlightened despotism of "paring off" the lands of Indians could be carried out as soon as Indian people realized it was in their interest to

[35] Jefferson to Andrew Jackson, Washington, February 16, 1803.

[36] Jefferson to William H. Harrison, February 27, 1803.

[37] The Dawes Act 1887 apportioned Indian lands on the basis of male-headed farmsteads. With the depression of 1893 it was becoming clear that the idealized American family farm was succumbing to industrial pressures and international market forces. Fifteen years after the Dawes Act, Frank Norris published his short story "A Deal in Wheat," which described the unstoppable urbanization of the agrarian labor force.

become yeoman farmers rather than hunter-gatherers. It would occur painlessly as soon as they were civilized enough to cede them, gradually, and for their own good.[38] The more stubborn aborigines who could not be so convinced would be pushed across the Mississippi. This ethnic cleansing was reminiscent of Jefferson's resettlement scheme for African Americans. Jefferson hoped that the Indians could be persuaded to cultivate the wilds, to establish freeholds, to practice husbandry, and to develop agricultural habits and such mechanical arts as were necessary to sustain them, but recalcitrants could easily be reminded that "we have only to shut our hand to crush them."

Jefferson's usufruct theory, his idea that the right to property in land derived from using it for agricultural purposes, had a cognate, if not a source, in the thinking of Locke, as previous authors have noted. In Locke's theory, the right to real property derived from making legitimate use of it. As I note elsewhere, Jefferson's attitude to Indian hunting lands resembled his attitude towards the hunting preserves of the European aristocracies. Jefferson was appalled by the hereditary privilege of aristocracies to monopolize lands as game preserves. He viewed this as wasteful and barbarous as the reservation of wilderness hunting preserves by American aborigines. The fact that many Native Americans possessed "agrarian" economies when Europeans first arrived in North America, and that many had been deprived of their agrarian heritage by European settlement, did not seem to enter into Jefferson's thinking. In his letter to the Reverend James Madison of October 28, 1785, Jefferson condemned France's baronial hunting preserves, and implied they caused the poverty of the French peasants "in a country where there is a very considerable proportion of uncultivated lands." The selfish retention of a royal game preserve meant that the European peasant could not bring them under the plough. The European aristocrat was an antisocial "dog in the manger," who selfishly prevented the peasant from making use of nature's abundance. Although the American Indian was not consciously antisocial, he was just as wasteful as a European lord. Jefferson never pontificated that Indians or aristocrats should be forcibly divested of their lands, but he sympathized with the so-called "Lockean proviso" that the right to the

[38] Of course, the Indians of Virginia, like those in Massachusetts, had been farmers until the whites, or their imported diseases, devastated their ancient agricultural villages. After white settlement, some Indian peoples continued farming, and even adopted yeoman slaveholding, as did the so-called "civilized tribes." Peter Onuf acknowledges in *Jefferson's Empire*, p. 19, that Jefferson's Indian policies set the stage for Jackson, a point I address in a later chapter.

exclusive possession of property exists only "where there is enough, and as good, left in common for others."[39]

Agricultural versus industrial values were not the cause of the celebrated struggle between Hamilton and Jefferson. Hamilton is recorded as saying in 1788 that the United States, or at least New York, was destined to "remain an importing and agricultural State," a belief he shared with almost every contemporary.[40] But Hamilton found the paranoid anticommercialism of his opponents every bit as silly as their obsessive antistatism. Jefferson habitually attributed to Hamilton all the lupine ambition and vulpine cunning of a Borgia or a Medici, or, even worse, a closet royalist. It is true that Hamilton certainly placed great value on a strong central government, capable of regulating commerce, and maintaining law and order. Such ideas were central to the thinking of the royalist Hobbes, who died a hundred years before the American Revolution and to whom Hamilton apparently paid scant attention. A similar belief in the necessity of stable government was evident in the writings of Burke and Hume, both of them royalists, although both supporters of American independence. If Hamilton was inclined towards an elected monarch, he did not say so. He advocated the following: "The Supreme Executive authority of the United States to be vested in a *governor* to be elected to serve *during good behaviour*."[41]

Jefferson shared Rousseau's sentimentalization of the bucolic, but he never displayed any overt fondness for Rousseau, and I am not the first to observe that Jefferson's allusions to Rousseau are conspicuous by their rarity. There was an ocean-wide gulf between the two men's ideas on politics and society. No one has ever seriously denied that they are similar in their sentimentalization of rusticity, and in their belief that human virtue resides in the country, not the city. But Jefferson's specific thoughts

[39] John Locke's labor-theory or use-theory of property, which has been the subject of substantial discussion and numerous interpretations, derives largely from his *Second Treatise of Government*, Chapter 2, Section 33. The expression "Lockean proviso" is attributed to libertarian philosopher Robert Nozick, *Anarchy, State, and Utopia* (New York: Basic Books, 1974), p. 175.

[40] Alexander Hamilton, "New York Ratifying Convention. Third Speech of June 28, 1788," Francis Child's version, in Harold Coffin Syrett and Jacob Ernest Cooke, eds., *The Papers of Alexander Hamilton* (New York: Columbia University Press, 1962), vol. V, p. 123.

[41] In Hamilton's exceedingly skeletal notes on his speech before the Constitutional Convention he specifies an elected "executive," not an hereditary monarch. See Harold Coffin Syrett, ed.,*The Papers of Alexander Hamilton* (New York: Columbia University Press, 1962), vol. IV, pp. 207–211.

on Rousseau remain obscure. There are even fewer distinct traces of Rousseau than of Voltaire in his writings. Neither Dumas Malone, nor Merrill Peterson, nor Peter Onuf, nor any author has found significant references to Rousseau in Jefferson. J. G. A. Pocock's presentation of intellectual parallels between the two of them is dazzling, but unconvincing. The philosopher Daniel Bonevac demonstrates more effectively the contrast, arguing that, for Jefferson, human rights were natural, God-given, and inalienable, whilst for Rousseau they derived at least in a practical sense from a social contract.[42]

John Adams was a republican farmer, despite an affinity for elitist authoritarian ideas. A staunch republican, he was cautious in his support of democracy, but not hostile to it. His affinities to Jeffersonian agriculturalism were evident in his preference for his Braintree farm over the environment of the nation's capital and his hostility to commercialism. He detested at the same time, and with almost equal vigor, the presumptions of both the royalty and the bourgeoisie, as represented by the upstart Hamilton. He resisted the values of commercialism, opposed the development of a national bank, and preferred to spend his time at his farm at Quincy, Massachusetts, rather than in the center of national government. Years transpired before the two of them discovered that Adams, despite his skepticism regarding democracy, was a better Jeffersonian than a Federalist.[43]

Was it traditional rusticism, was it "country party republicanism," or was it Lockean liberalism that Jefferson was advocating? Intellectual historians have been intrigued by all three possibilities, and many have attempted to ferret out the relationship of his theory to his practice. His libertarian country values were seemingly more tied to the seventeenth than to the eighteenth century. As a country squire, his reputation for hospitality, and gracious style of living, endowed him with the respect and affection of his neighbors. He expressed little fear of peasant revolts, as the possibility of poor whites expressing any discontent with the Virginia elite

[42] Nathan Schachner, *Thomas Jefferson: A Biography* (New York: Appleton-Century-Crofts, 1957), p. 47; Daniel Bonevac, "The Forgotten Principles of American Government," originally published as a pamphlet by the Texas Public Policy Foundation, appeared in the *Texas Education Review*, 1, no. 4 (spring, 2000), 5–9.

[43] John Adams to Mercy Otis Warren, April 16, 1776, expresses admiration for republican ideals, but with the caveat that "its principles are as easily destroyed as human nature is corrupted." Adams' admiration for certain monarchs is in John Adams to Lafayette, May 21, 1782, at Founders Online.

did not worry him, and even in the wake of Gabriel's Revolt he expressed little fear of a slave uprising.[44] It was one thing for Jefferson to endorse agrarian insurrection in Massachusetts from the safety of his Paris writing-desk, especially before the guillotine was erected in the public square, but his critic Abigail Adams may well have questioned whether he would have viewed with such sanguinity the methods of Shays' rebellious farmers had they been undertaken by Virginia slaves or, for that matter, by Virginia's poor white farmers. As a big man in Virginia, and the comfortable recipient of the deference of whites and blacks alike, he was the contented country squire, a natural believer in those ideals associated with the "country party."[45]

EMANCIPATION AND ANTISLAVERY

If Jefferson's notion of agrarian liberty ever demanded the abolition of slavery, it must imply the cultivation of an economy without a need for "the peculiar institution." But the agrarian economies of the North and the South included many laborers who were not landowners. Jefferson presumed that the landless class of white agrarian workers, as well as an industrial labor force, were a prerequisite for, not an effect of, industrialism. In eighteenth-century England the potential workforce had resulted from the migration of once-happy farmers into dismal cities, and the transformation of stalwart yeomen into what Marx called a *Lumpenproletariat*, but there was a great difference between the Marxian and Jeffersonian analyses. Jefferson tended towards the physiocratic notion that workers added little or nothing of value to the articles that they produced. He accepted a radical economic theory that rejected

[44] For a concise "entry-level" summary of contending interpretations, see Sue Davis, *American Political Thought: Four Hundred Years of Ideas and Ideologies* (New York: Simon and Schuster, 1996), pp. 41–59. Also see Richard K. Matthews, *The Radical Politics of Thomas Jefferson* (Lawrence, KS: University Press of Kansas, 1984).

[45] Country, as opposed to the "court party," was an informal designation of political interests in Great Britain and the North American colonies, usually associated with the thought of Viscount Bolingbroke and James Harrington, and indicating hostility to the London-based royal court, and to monarchy in general. In the United States it meant the vigorous advocacy of republicanism. See Bernard Bailyn, *The Ideological Origins of the American Revolution* (Cambridge, MA: Harvard University Press, 1967), pp. 34–35; Wood, *The Creation of the American Republic*, pp. 14–15; and J. G. A. Pocock, *The Machiavellian Moment: Florentine Political Thought and the Atlantic Republican Tradition* (Princeton University Press, 1975), p. 519. Also see Daniel Walker Howe, *The Political Culture of the American Whigs* (University of Chicago Press, 1979), p. 87.

Aquinas' labor theory of value and did not foresee Marx's "theory of surplus value."[46]

Jefferson's *Summary View of the Rights of British America* made little reference to slavery-based agrarianism. It claimed that the colonists desired not only to free the slaves, but also spoke ambiguously of their "enfranchisement." The precise definition of this "enfranchisement" was unclear. Did he mean to enfranchise them in the sense of conferring the rights of all other British North Americans? If he did, Jefferson clearly came to oppose the idea in *Notes on Virginia*. His use of the ambiguous term "enfranchisement" in the *Summary View* is so striking that it should not have been hidden in the middle of a paragraph, but presented in its contextual entirety for emphasis. In this instance, we see one manifestation of the "temporizing" nature that Alexander Hamilton so justly attributed to Jefferson in his famous letter to James Bayard of January 16, 1801.[47] Jefferson was quick to condemn the British for having introduced North American slavery, but temporized on finding a solution to the problem that he not only inherited, but aggravated.

> The abolition of domestic slavery is the great object of desire in those colonies, where it was unhappily introduced in their infant state. But previous to the enfranchisement of the slaves we have, it is necessary to exclude all further importations from Africa.[48]

The above clauses, with "enfranchisement" embedded within them, nearly suggested a desire to convert black slaves into republican farmers. They revealed Jefferson's well-known characteristics of ambiguity and temporizing in 1774. It is obvious, however, that he had no intention of acknowledging Africans' rights to "enfranchisement" by 1785. Instead of directly promising freedom, his revolutionary writings spoke of "our repeated attempts" to abolish the slave trade by "prohibitions" and "duties," but claimed that Americans had been defeated in their humanitarian effort "by his majesty's negative." He portrayed the king as a protector of the interests of slave traders over "the lasting interests of the American states," failing to consider that the competing interests of

[46] A description of the evolution of the urban working class is not our concern in this chapter. More important is the fact that policy makers such as Benjamin Franklin and Thomas Jefferson perceived the evolution in this way. For further discussion, see E. P. Thompson, *The Making of the English Working Class* (New York: Vintage, 1966).

[47] Alexander Hamilton to James Bayard, January 16, 1801, at Founders Online.

[48] *A Summary View of the Rights of British America*, in Peterson, ed., *Thomas Jefferson, Writings*, p. 115.

the several states were famously at odds; some desired closure of the slave trade and others insisted on its continuance. John Taylor, George Mason, and Jefferson himself all accepted allusions to "the rights of human nature, deeply wounded by the infamous practice" of slavery. But humanitarian concerns were always trumped by economic necessity, and the most prominent Virginians opposed the Atlantic slave trade and continued to hold slaves for economic reasons.

Jefferson was not fond of linking American agriculture to its dependency on large slave plantations. He did, however, link the abolition of slavery to the ideas of compensation for the slaveholders and expatriation of the Africans. He toyed, from time to time, with the idea of resettling Africans in the United States. Such a program was not only embraced, but actually carried out by his distant relative, John Randolph of Roanoke, who freed many slaves and resettled them in Ohio. Jefferson's proposal for the liberation and mass deportation of African Americans in *Notes on Virginia* is well known, but, like the extreme anti-industrialism in that document, its words seem to be entirely whimsical.

ECONOMIC THEORY

Jefferson's reveries on an "agrarian" economy, at least during the years when he was writing *Notes on Virginia*, strongly resembled those of the French philosophers known in the eighteenth century as "the economists," today commonly referred to as "the physiocrats," that tribe of philosophers whose most extreme notion was that labor was the only source of value, and that wealth derived solely from agriculture. But sometimes they went to the extreme of speaking of farm produce as "the gift of the earth." Adam Smith agreed with their position that labor was the source of value, but he also believed in the economic value of free and self-interested industrial labor. Ironically, in 1768 Benjamin Franklin, despite his origins as a "leather apron" craftsman, agreed with the most extreme physiocratic notion that "the true Source of Riches is Husbandry. Agriculture is truly *productive of new wealth;* Manufactures only change Forms; and whatever value they give to the Material they work upon, they in the mean time consume an equal value in Provisions, &c. So that Riches are not *increased* by Manufacturing." This purely economic notion he supplemented with the moral statement that agriculture was the only "honest" source of wealth:

> there seem to be but three Ways for a Nation to acquire Wealth. The first is by *War* as the Romans did in plundering their conquered Neighbours. This is *Robbery.*

The second by *Commerce* which is generally *Cheating*. The third by *Agriculture* the only *honest Way;* wherein *Man receives* a *real Increase* of the *Seed thrown into* the *Ground,* in a kind of continual Miracle wrought by the Hand of God in his Favour, as a Reward for his innocent Life, and virtuous Industry.[49]

Similar agricultural biases flowed rather easily from Jefferson's pen at the time of *Notes on Virginia.* Although he modified his opinions later, there was a time, he said, when he believed "that to the labor of the husbandman a vast addition is made by the spontaneous energies of the earth on which it is employed: for one grain of wheat committed to the earth, she renders twenty, thirty, and even fifty fold, whereas to the labor of the manufacturer nothing is added." In the letter written to Benjamin Austin in 1816 he abandoned such strident expressions of agriculturalism.[50] Jefferson was as persistently inconsistent on "agrarianism" as he was on most matters of ideology. His contradictions were both theoretical and pragmatic, and they were not merely the product of changing times. His inconsistency was not teleological, not a result of the industrial revolutions that occurred during his and Madison's administrations. His belief in the necessity of American industry was a recurrent, if not a constant, theme; it was highly visible in the *Summary View* of 1774, and it was conveniently justified when he founded his nailery in 1794. His change in rhetoric was only partially a consequence of the trade embargo of 1807 and the disruption of the Atlantic trade during the Napoleonic wars.

Furthermore, traditions of patriarchal elitism were inherited from the European background. Jeffersonian republicanism shared one assumption with monarchism, in that both contained agrarian biases. Physiocratic and rustic ideology overlapped the aristocratic notion that status derived from ownership of land. An agricultural bias might as easily be interpreted to be royalist as republican, and "agrarian" biases were, in fact, nurtured by Europe's nobility. The kings and barons of Europe had always counted their wealth in terms of land, and had scorned the upstart bourgeoisie, particularly the Jewish people, whose very name in Magna Carta was synonymous with money-lending. The patricians of Jefferson's class looked down on those who worked as merchants and tradesmen and

[49] Benjamin Franklin to Cadwalader Evans, London, February 20, 1768. Carl Van Doren quoted this in his *Benjamin Franklin* (New York: Penguin, 1991 [1938]), p. 372. Actually, Franklin's physiocratic notion was "*Agriculture* the only *honest Way;* wherein Man receives a real Increase of the Seed thrown into the Ground." Franklin, "Positions to be examined," April 4, 1769.

[50] Benjamin Austin, Esq., Monticello, January 9, 1816. To John Melish, Monticello, January 13, 1813.

counted their wealth not in terms of land, but merely in terms of commercial instruments, or even precious metals.[51]

The physiocratic school was traditional in its agriculturalism, but modern and innovative in that it argued for *laissez-faire*, the idea that governments should keep their hands off the economic activities of their subjects. The physiocrats opposed state mercantilism, the policy of nations basing their economies on the hoarding of gold and silver in national treasuries. They recognized, astutely, that precious metals had no intrinsic value – only exchange value – but they also pontificated that land, not labor, was the sole basis of wealth. The modernism of the physiocrats was extremely reactionary in its attack on Thomas Aquinas' traditional labor theory of value. That is to say, Aquinas' theory, while hardly a preface to modern capitalism, was at least capable of recognizing that human initiative added value to a product and that not all wealth was simply the gift of the soil. The physiocrats' implicit attack on the "labor theory of value" was sustained by the brilliantly sophisticated mathematical conjurations of the cult's grand master, François Quesnay.

It has been demonstrated that Quesnay was influenced by Jean-Baptiste Du Halde's popular book of 1735, *Description géographique, historique, chronologique, politique, et physique de l'empire de la Chine*. The work celebrated the putative law-abiding and common-sense character of farmers and attributed to Confucianism a sentimentalism regarding rural virtue. The book is supposed to have influenced Voltaire, Rousseau, Goldsmith, and numerous other Enlightenment luminaries. There is no question that orientalism was a dominant tendency in eighteenth-century European writing, appearing in Samuel Johnson's 1759 fiction *The History of Rasselas, Prince of Abissinia*, the numerous "Turkish-inspired" works of Mozart, and perhaps most significantly Montesquieu's *Lettres persanes*, published even prior to Du Halde's *Description*, in 1721. Voltaire notably gushed that the Chinese Empire was "the wisest and best organized nation in the universe."[52]

[51] Anti-Semitic hostility to financiers and commercialists is obvious in Magna Carta: see W. D. Rubenstein, *A History of the Jews in the English-Speaking World: Great Britain* (London: Macmillan, 1996).

[52] Hyobom B. Pak, *China and the West: Myths and Reality in History* (Leiden: E. J. Brill, 1974), p. 56. An influence on Pak and others has been L. A. Maverick, *Chinese Influences upon the Physiocrats* (London: Clay and Sons, 1938). Arnold H. Rowbotham "Voltaire, Sinophile," *PMLA*, 47, no. 4 (December, 1932). Voltaire, "la nation la plus sage et la mieux policée de l'univers," *Lettres Philosophiques*, Lettre 1.

Tantalizing, if indirect, evidence of Jefferson's Confucianism appears in a remark he made around the same time as publication of *Notes on Virginia*. He wrote to one correspondent, "You ask what I think on the expediency of encouraging our States to be commercial? Were I to indulge my own theory, I should wish them to practise neither commerce nor navigation, but to stand, with respect to Europe, precisely on the footing of China."[53] It should never be forgotten that Confucianism reinforces the authority of elites for good and for ill, and that Confucian conservatism had the positive effect of promoting social stability, but the negative effect of retarding Chinese industrial development. Ironically, the Maoists of the twentieth century enforced a disguised neo-Confucian agrarianism in order to suppress "bourgeois attitudes." There is, however, no evidence that Jefferson was permanently under the influence of the Confucianism of Quesnay or other physiocrats, and it seems that he increasingly aligned his thinking with the less fashionable, but eventually more convincing, views of Smith, De Tracy, and Say. That is, with the passage of time, the anti-industrial conservatism expressed in *Notes on Virginia* in 1785 seems to be revealed as a momentary quirk, or an instance of hyperbole.

Traditional European economists, since the Middle Ages, had followed the doctrine of Thomas Aquinas and argued that labor was among the components of value. John Calvin had preserved at least this signal prominent element of Roman Catholic economic doctrine. The "labor theory of value" was revitalized by the seventeenth-century British economist William Petty, a sometime influence on the young Benjamin Franklin. Quesnay's mathematical charts provided what I would call a "Ptolemaic demonstration" that labor added nothing of economic value to any product. Quesnay used mathematics in much the same way that medieval astronomers had used Ptolemy's abstractions to support their geocentric theory of the universe. Quesnay's school of econometrists brilliantly demonstrated, at least mathematically, that the cost of industrial labor actually drained an economy of its wealth.[54]

The physiocrats, despite their bucolic romanticism, and their contempt for what Franklin called "leather apron" workers, were perfectly capable of industrial pragmatism. Jefferson's friend, Du Pont de Nemours, protégé of Quesnay and author of the term *physiocratie*, which designates the doctrine that all wealth erupts naturally from the earth, became an

[53] Jefferson to Hogendorp, Paris, October 13, 1785.

[54] Robert B. Ekelund and Robert F. Hébert, *A History of Economic Theory and Method* (New York: McGraw-Hill, 1990), p. 87.

American munitions manufacturer. On emigrating to the United States with his family, he founded the industrial dynasty that eventually encompassed Dupont Chemicals and General Motors.[55] Adam Smith, who, according to legend, idolized Quesnay and, like the physiocrats, rejected mercantilism and government monopolies, was nonetheless a champion of industrialism and a tacit sympathizer with industrial workers' rights. Jefferson responded to the views of Adam Smith as if they were an intellectual smorgasbord: he arbitrarily accepted some of Smith's ideas and rejected others. But, like Smith and the physiocrats, he believed that agricultural pursuits nurtured the morality of the worker. Ever pragmatic, if sometimes grudgingly so, Jefferson almost never denied that American industrialism could function quite nicely in accord with his agricultural principles, and he was ambivalent on the idea that the nurturing of American workshops might actually be good for national prosperity, at least for reasons of military security.[56]

The necessity of munitions manufacturing for the national defense became Jefferson's eventual rationalization for his long-simmering industrial advocacy. He came eventually to appreciate the usefulness of deploying French ideas in this connection, and became a friend and correspondent of Du Pont de Nemours, the arms manufacturing disciple of Quesnay. French machinery, French industrialism, and French munitions all played a role in Jefferson's justification of American workshops. He attempted to persuade the French manufacturer Honoré Blanc to bring to the United States the techniques of his musket factory, where machines turned out gauged parts.

Historian Robert Woodbury asserts that Jefferson introduced Eli Whitney to Blanc's methods, several months before Whitney demonstrated to President Adams and Vice President Jefferson his ability to disassemble ten muskets, separate the pieces into piles, and reassemble them from components selected at random. Woodbury's popular business

[55] Pierre Samuel Du Pont de Nemours was the author of *La Philosophie du bonheur*, (*The Philosophy of Happiness*) and putative inventor of the term *physiocratie* (rule by nature) in his book *La Physiocratie: Ou constitution essentielle du gouvernement le plus advantageux au genre humaine* (1767).

[56] According to a legend circulated by Dugald Stewart, *Life and Writings of Adam Smith* (1799), Smith admired Quesnay, and "If he had not been prevented by Quesnai's death, Mr. Smith had once an intention (as he told me himself) to have inscribed to him his *Wealth of Nations*," cited in Peter C. Dooley, *The Labour Theory of Value* (Oxford: Routledge, 2005), p. 65. P. J. O'Rourke considers this odd, given Smith's systematic dismantlement of physiocratic theories. See P. J. O'Rourke, *On the Wealth of Nations: Books that Changed the World* (New York: Grobe Press, 2007), p. 111.

history and management textbook presents Jefferson as the ideological father of American industrialism on the basis of this demonstration. Hence, we may say that the "agrarian" myth beloved of American historians is not universally taught throughout American universities. But one needs to be leery of any approach to history based on a mythos of Jefferson's genius for innovation. And, of course, it was neither the French nor the Americans who were the first to make use of such industrial techniques. The Chinese, inventors of Confucian agrarianism, were also manufacturing interchangeable parts for their crossbows from the second century AD.[57]

The physiocrats' ties to the aristocracy, both European and American, could be sometimes pragmatic and sometimes sentimental. The friendship between Jefferson and Du Pont de Nemours echoed the amity between Louis XV and François Quesnay. At the suggestion of the latter, who was also the royal physician, Louis XV hand-set the type of Quesnay's *Tableau* in order to get his daily exercise. It is interesting to note that the physician physiocrat prescribed the theoretically debasing activities of a "leather apron" workman, rather than the more ennobling activities of a peasant, such as shoveling manure or picking apples. Quesnay, despite his contempt for the class of *métiers*, prescribed a handicraft for the king instead of an agricultural pursuit, as might have seemed more appropriate. The crowned heads of Europe fancied themselves farmers. King George III enjoyed tending his apple trees and called himself "Farmer George." The court of Marie Antoinette was known for its pastoral masquerades, where the queen dressed up as a milkmaid or shepherdess at the quasi-rustic retreat of Le Petit Trianon, near the palace at Versailles.[58]

A hint of religious mysticism infected Jefferson's bucolic sentimentalism of 1785 when he celebrated farmers as "the chosen people of God, if ever he had a chosen people."[59] I have already dismissed this as rhetorical flourish; but Jefferson, like Benjamin Franklin – as we have already seen –

[57] For interchangeable parts and the Jefferson–Whitney connection, see Hopp and Spearman, *Factory Physics*, p. 19. Also see Robert Woodbury, "The Legend of Eli Whitney and Interchangeable Parts," Benjamin A. Gorman, "Discover Eli Whitney," Teachers Institute Yale–New Haven at www.yale.edu/ynhti/curriculum/units/1979/3/79.03.03.x.html and David Williams, "Mass-Produced Pre-Han Chinese Bronze Crossbow Triggers: Unparalleled Manufacturing Technology in the Ancient World," *Arms & Armour*, 5, no. 2 (October, 2008), 142–153.

[58] For "Farmer George," see Edmund S. Morgan, *The Meaning of Independence* (New York: Norton, 1978), p. 29.

[59] Jefferson, *Notes on Virginia*, p. 197.

did link farming to morality. And neither envisioned any possibility that urban industries could compensate workers for abandoning the joys and comforts of rural life. Wages could never be sufficient to sustain the happiness of urban workers. The cost of seducing an urban workforce would be prohibitively high in America unless the workers had already been debased by the process of urbanization. But America would never develop a depressed urban population, because America would never run out of land. There would never be enclosure, and there would never be a wretched *Lumpenproletariat* to man the factories. It would be impossible for any landed aristocracy to enclose acreage and drive small farmers off the lands and into the cities. There would never be any pressures for American yeomen to leave their farms and villages to supply the industrial maw. Certainly there would be no such possibility for as long as America bred patriots like Daniel Shays, whose occasional rebellions cleared the air of threats of foreclosure and enclosure. He wrote (to Abigail Adams), "I like a little rebellion now and then. It is like a storm in the atmosphere." Adams, a Massachusetts citizen, recognized the arrogance of such a position coming from a Virginian residing in Paris.[60]

The doctrines of the physiocrats, although sometimes rigorously distinguished from those of Adam Smith, cannot be entirely divorced from them. Smith admired the mathematical pyrotechniques of Quesnay, although he rejected some of the latter's conclusions. Smith shared the physiocrats' commitment to free trade and other aspects of *laissez-faire* doctrine. He shared their realism concerning the ultimate dangers of gold and silver dependency. But Smith rejected the notion that agriculture was the unique source of wealth. It is doubtful that Jefferson ever accepted such a notion, and certainly he did not maintain it in perpetuity.

Jefferson was probably put off at the outset when Smith commenced to develop his theory of wealth by describing the processes of an urban pin factory. *The Wealth of Nations*, published in the same year as the Declaration of Independence, had its opening scene on an English factory floor. This might have seemed an inauspicious beginning, even for a defender of the rights of American manufactures. Jefferson, like his physiocrat friends, would probably rather have seen a description of

[60] Jefferson to Abigail Adams, February 22, 1787. Jefferson viewed Massachusetts as culturally aristocratic and compared it unfavorably with egalitarian, democratic, Randolph-dominated, slaveholding Virginia. Jefferson to John Adams, October 28, 1813.

wealth begin where they thought it began – on the bounteous soil, which, in their view, always yielded an abundance far exceeding the efforts of the laborer. The main point on which Jefferson agreed with Adam Smith in 1776 was the latter's condemnation of British mercantilism, insofar as that system operated to the disadvantage of American planters, and the industries of their own cottages and plantations.

But he increasingly questioned the economic theories of Adam Smith and leaned towards those of Jean-Baptiste Say. In 1807, he wrote to John Norvell that "Smith's Wealth of Nations is the best book to be read, unless Say's Political Economy can be had, which treats the same subjects on the same principles, but in a shorter compass and more lucid manner. But I believe this work has not been translated into our language."[61] Later he wrote that Smith's book, "admitted to be able, and of the first degree of merit, has yet been considered as prolix and tedious." Say, on the other hand, had produced "a very superior work," in his estimation: its arrangement was "luminous, ideas clear, style perspicuous, and the whole subject brought within half the volume of Smith's work."[62] Strangely, in an earlier instance, he had remarked that he found in Jean-Baptiste Say "nothing more than a succinct, judicious digest of the tedious pages of Smith."[63] On a later occasion, he opined that "M. Tracy has written the best work on political economy which has ever appeared, he has established its principles more demonstratively than has been done before, and in the compass of one third of even M. Say's work." But in no instance did he explain precisely what he found either correct or erroneous in any of these authors. Perhaps his reasoning can be inferred from his writings, but it is not self-evident.[64]

It may be that Jefferson was unable to forgive Adam Smith for giving such centrality to factory work and departing from the ancient agricultural ideals on which his own economic theory was based. He increasingly voiced a nagging suspicion regarding Smith, whereas the theories of Say, although not entirely pure, were more agreeable to him. In his estimation, Say had corrected certain unspecified errors of Smith, and his commitment to the free market seemed purer in Jefferson's view. There was an inescapable irony in this, for while Smith was a harmless professor, Say was an

[61] Jefferson to John Norvell, Washington, June 11, 1807.
[62] Jefferson to Joseph Milligan, Monticello, April 6, 1816.
[63] Jefferson to Joseph C. Cabell, Monticello, January 31, 1814.
[64] Jefferson to Albert Gallatin, Monticello, April 11, 1816. Also see Jefferson to William Duane, Monticello, January 22, 1813.

industrialist, who operated a large spinning mill, which employed four or five hundred persons, primarily women and children.[65] Jefferson was later impressed when Say "discontinued his manufactory" and expressed a thought of removing to Virginia, where he would take up the life of a planter, presumably with slave labor.[66]

Jefferson admired both the industrialist Say and the theorist Smith not only because of their discourses on modes of production, but for other reasons. They were suspicious of paper money and opposed government-created monopolies awarded to royal or parliamentary favorites. Whether he admired Du Pont de Nemours as an industrialist or only as an economist it is impossible to say. He admired Thomas Robert Malthus, but only for his earlier work on population, not for his later work on fiscal reform. If he knew of Malthus' *Principles of Political Economy* (1820), with its reform views on government spending, he did not comment on it. Malthus' later advocacy of tax-supported public works, which were to serve as the inspiration for Keynesian economics, he may have encountered, but he expressed no admiration for them. He may have admired Jean-Baptiste Say's practical abilities at running a factory, but it was for his mystical theory that Jefferson admired him, his superstitious dogma that supply could never exceed demand. This position was a reflection of Jefferson's mechanistic, music-box theology, in which all the gears meshed in accord with the will of his rational Deity. It was a world in which legitimate interests must always be in harmony, because a God of reason would never have fashioned any other sort of world.

Jefferson's views on Smith's monetary theory may be contrasted to that of present-day economic historians, who correctly emphasize that Adam Smith was a hard-money advocate and the emblematic proponent of free markets. Jefferson, however, characterized Adam Smith as "the principal advocate for a paper circulation" and a proponent of government regulation. Smith had been willing to tolerate paper money in specific instances but "on the sole condition that it be strictly regulated." This was a second strike against him, as far as Jefferson was concerned. Paper money

[65] Say's spinning mill needs better documentation than Wikipedia, which is my only present source. Jefferson to Jean-Baptiste Say, Washington, February 1, 1804. Jefferson to Monsieur Correa De Serra, Monticello, December 27, 1814.

[66] Jean-Baptiste Say to Jefferson, June 15, 1814: "I established, fifty leagues from Paris, a cotton-spinning factory that prospered until the excessive taxes imposed by the government and the general impoverishment that befell the nation and ended almost all consumption forced me to give up my enterprise." Also see Jefferson to Jean-Baptiste Say, March 2, 1815.

supported by government regulation must be regarded with suspicion from the porch of Monticello. Smith's toleration for paper currency, limited though it was, must lead inevitably to the evil of government regulation. He pointed triumphantly to Smith's admission that "the commerce and industry of a country cannot be so secure when suspended on the Daedalian wings of paper money, as on the solid ground of gold and silver." This certainly supported his views on America's difficulties with the unstable Continental currency during the revolution. That experience had demonstrated that "the insecurity is greatly increased, and great confusion possible where the circulation is for the greater part in paper." With his intentionally cultivated obtuseness regarding Hamilton's heresy on the necessity of a public debt, Jefferson offered no theory as to how the American Revolution might have been financed in the absence of either precious metals or a fiat currency.[67]

BANKS AND "A RAGE FOR PAPER MONEY"

Jefferson agreed with Smith's opposition to government monopolies and, no doubt, with his idea that wealth could not be defined as the hoarding of precious metals. He probably did not appreciate Smith's flexibility on paper currency, although easy money was to the immediate advantage of debtors such as himself, and arguably had the democratic-egalitarian function of distributing wealth to struggling yeoman farmers. Although Smith held that hard money is the most legitimate basis of exchange, he made exceptions, notably in the case of Pennsylvania.[68] The Pennsylvanian Benjamin Franklin may have reminded Smith in one of their several conversations that, while it might be a fine thing for people to conduct business through the medium of real gold and silver coins, it was even better when exchanges could be effected through the medium of something more readily available than gold and silver, and of lesser worth. The flow of goods and services is facilitated when masses of people have faith in the exchange value of something as common and worthless as paper. Of course, a solid paper money required a stable government,

[67] Jefferson to John W. Eppes, Monticello, November 6, 1813.

[68] Adam Smith, *The Wealth of Nations*, 2 vols. (Oxford University Press, 1976), see the original index entry for paper money, subheading Pennsylvania, which reveals the complexity of Smith's opinion. Smith may have been influenced by the visit of Benjamin Franklin, whom he met in 1759, and Franklin's arguments in favor of paper money for Pennsylvania.

and a belief in that government's commitment to paying its bills on demand.

Franklin was irritated by the Empire's failure to establish consistent and efficient monetary policies throughout the colonies. Long before the Revolution, he had published *A Modest Enquiry into the Nature and Necessity of a Paper Currency*, in 1729. Some planters, like Jefferson, were contented with the provincial system of drawing credit on slaveholdings; others, like Washington, favored a diversified economy as well as a banking system similar to England's. Cosmopolitan thinkers like Franklin and Washington believed that the failure to address American monetary problems was among the causes of the Revolution. As an advocate of printing a paper currency, Franklin argued in effect that controlled inflation was a means of stimulating healthy habits of consumption. This would be surprising to anyone whose knowledge of Franklin is limited to the parsimonious maxims of "Poor Richard."[69]

The British prohibition on printing a paper currency was, of course, disadvantageous to a Boston printer like Franklin or an entrepreneur like Washington, but not equally so to a London warehouser. Tobacco or other commodities stored in England could be used as the basis of bills of trade which could be circulated throughout the Empire. The person in London who stored American goods in his warehouse assumed only the risks of any damage that might occur to them, but the American planter assumed the risks due to shipping, and the planter was more vulnerable than the warehouser to fluctuations in the price of the goods sitting in a far-away London warehouse. The theoretical price of these goods determined the value of the bills of credit that American colonials passed back and forth in the absence of both hard money and a stable paper currency.

In the absence of specie, Americans were forced to improvise paper mechanisms for commerce and to create media for the transmission of credit, such as bills of exchange. If a Virginia planter shipped tobacco to a London merchant he would draw up an order representing the price. These bills of trade had to be endorsed by the London merchant or his American agent. The signed bill, which was an agreement to pay, would endow the bill with the qualities of money. It might be accepted as money, assuming it was current (not in default). In a country where specie and paper money were scarce, it would probably be accepted as a medium of

[69] See Franklin on provincialism in Michael Rozbicki, *The Complete Colonial Gentleman: Cultural Legitimacy in Colonial Virginia* (Charlottesville, VA: University of Virginia Press, 1998), p. 5.

exchange. So long as the bill was current (hence "currency"), its value rested on the faith and credit of the persons doing business.[70]

Jefferson's position regarding Smith became even more bizarre when he seemingly approved the old mercantilist program of hoarding precious metals in the national treasury, with the specious argument that a portion of the gold flowing out would be exchanged for "foreign wines; silks, etc., to be consumed by idle people who produce nothing; and so far the substitution promotes prodigality, increases expense and corruption, without increasing production." With this justification, he seemed to argue for a monetary mercantilism that the colonies had once so militantly opposed. He reproved Adam Smith for his admitted inability "to determine what is the proportion which the circulating money of any country bears to the whole value of the annual produce." But he went even farther in his condemnation with the argument that the policies of Adam Smith, whom he characterized as paper currency's "principal advocate," would corrupt the morals of the people, lessen the capital of the nation, and undermine native industries.[71]

Jefferson's turn to manufacturing, on his resignation from Washington's cabinet in 1794, has never escaped the interest of his biographers. When he returned to Monticello in 1794, he came to grips with his difficulties as a self-sustaining farmer, and, seeking a solution to his financial difficulties, began the manufacture of nails in hopes of keeping his plantation solvent. The nailery made Monticello a factory whose products were sold on the open market, and a participant in the modern industrial process. It was a textbook illustration of the principles of division of labor, noted by Adam Smith, principles that allowed industry to be broken down into simple, routine tasks. It did not require that anyone master every step of the industrial process. Nor did it require the consummate skill that one associates with the medieval guild craftsmen at their best. Presumably the industrial processes at Monticello did not bring out the best in its workers, did not encourage the habits of creativity and independent entrepreneurship that are associated with a village blacksmith, functioning as an independent entrepreneur. In the removal of the yeoman craftsman from the industrial process Jefferson foresaw moral hazards that likewise discomfited Adam Smith.[72]

70 Jonathan Hughes and Louis P. Cain, *American Economic History* (New York: HarperCollins, 1994), p. 76.

71 Ibid.

72 James Adam Bear, ed., *Jefferson at Monticello: Recollections of a Monticello Slave and a Monticello Overseer* (Charlottesville, VA: University of Virginia Press, 1967).

Jefferson, great planter and slaveholding aristocrat though he was, could always in good conscience consider himself a working man, and now he had become in the truest sense "industrious." He asserted, indeed, in a letter to his French acquaintance Jean-Nicolas Démeunier, that "every honest employment is deemed honorable," and referred to his "new trade of nail-making," thus representing himself with some degree of accuracy and irony as a working man.[73] This self-characterization was reasonably true, for he was at that moment as much an industrial foreman as a plantation proprietor. Despite his well-known contempt for the artisan class, he plunged pragmatically into the routines of nail-making. His innate curiosity, his personal ethic, and his impulses to invention drove him to constant activity, and reports by his slaves acknowledged him to be a man of perpetual energy. The historical descriptions of his work habits demonstrate a virtuosity born of necessity. He wrote to Adams that it was his custom to spend half his day on horseback, micromanaging his plantations, and the other half at his industrial pursuits.[74]

He was now more intimate than Adam Smith with the factory floor. The hands-on practice of a nail-making factory bore an uncanny resemblance to the abstract description in Smith's pin factory. Monticello's nailery dealt with a simple process, or, as Smith called it, "a very trifling manufacture." Smith described the division of labor and other industrial routines that were the hallmarks of eighteenth-century industrialism, whether in London or at Monticello. Smith's commentary on the routine and standardization in pin-making stressed that the mechanic need not be particularly skilled, and that the industrial process is broken down into "eighteen distinct operations." A nail, like a pin, is a fairly simple instrument, simply a piece of iron, relatively inflexible, with a point at one end and a head at the other. The relative simplicity of the product may have led Jefferson to choose nails, as opposed to horseshoes or ploughshares, to manufacture.[75] Anything more complicated than a nail would have required a more skilled and specialized worker. He wrote to Démeunier that his workers were "a dozen little boys from 10 to 16 years of age." It turned out, however, that the job did indeed require

[73] Jefferson to Jean-Nicolas Démeunier, April 27, 1795, cited in Dumas Malone, *Jefferson and His Time*, 6 vols. (Boston, MA: Little, Brown, 1962), vol. III, *Jefferson and the Ordeal of Liberty*, p. 217.

[74] Jefferson to John Adams, May 27, 1795.

[75] See McLaughlin, *Jefferson and Monticello*, p. 110.

expert supervision, especially in Jefferson's absence. In 1801, the year he left to become president, Jefferson employed William Stewart, a white nailsmith who, despite a proclivity for drinking, remained at Monticello until 1812, that is to say, four years after Jefferson's return from Washington. Whether Jefferson's tolerance in this instance indicates a laxness in his management practices that affected his business success is not known. But it is clear that a drunk should not be supervising or working around adolescent boys.[76]

The work at the nailery consisted of cutting and finishing nail rod, supplied from an outside source. Not all of the boys were under 16, but the age of their employment indicates that Alexander Hamilton was not exceptional when he reflected on the economic advantages of putting children to work at young ages. Lucia Stanton's considerable investigation into nail-making and other manufactures at Monticello has revealed much on Jefferson's techniques of labor management and discipline. Stanton and Annette Gordon-Reed have provided a glimpse into the world of interpersonal relations between the boys and young men at the forge. They shed considerable light on the murky incident of the attack on Brown Colbert by another nail boy, an 18-year-old named Cary. The incident and its aftermath have drawn the attention of other scholars. We do not know for how long or how persistently Cary was provoked until he approached Colbert from behind with a hammer and struck him on the head "with his whole strength."[77]

We know that Colbert had been harassing Cary in some way, but the chroniclers of the incident did not provide much information on the exact nature of the harassment, or whether it involved a sexual element. A sexual element is almost always involved in the traditions of "signifyin'" and "playing the dozens." Anthropologists and folklorists often describe such behavior as amusing, but it masks an underlying self-hatred and mutual contempt among young black males. A signifying monkey is not a beloved member in any community, and he can often make the life of

[76] Lucia Stanton, *Free Some Day*, pp. 132–133, describes Stewart as a skilled ironworker who trained young workers at the forge and sometimes, when drunken, turned over its management to one of them named Joe Fossett: "From 1807, when Stewart was finally fired, until 1827, Fossett ran the shop."

[77] For a brief overview of industrial slavery at Monticello, see Stanton, *Slavery at Monticello*, p. 22; Stanton, *Free Some Day*, pp. 47–48, 74–76; Annette Gordon-Reed, *Thomas Jefferson and Sally Hemings: An American Controversy* (Charlottesville, VA: University of Virginia Press, 1997), pp, 150–151. Also see Annette Gordon-Reed, *The Hemingses of Monticello* (New York: Norton, 2008), pp. 579–580.

his victim almost unbearable. We do not know what the final straw was that led Cary to take his "most barbarous revenge." Violence among workers in factory environments is not uncommon. Unskilled workers in strenuous conditions often take out their anger and frustration on one another. The interaction between Cary and Colbert is a striking example of industrial violence, but apparently the only notable case that made it into the historical record of Monticello. It provides us with only one fleeting illustration of the conditions that prevailed among the nail boys, and the common tendency of industrial workers to turn their hostilities towards one another. It seems that Jefferson knew whereof he spoke when he maintained that factory work was debasing.

Adam Smith said that 10 persons could make up to 48,000 pins in a day. Jefferson's output in nails was one ton per month in 1796, which was, at least in that year, sufficient to cover his grocery bills. What this productivity meant in terms of cash flow or monetary gain is difficult to estimate. Jefferson's nails often functioned merely as the basis for barter because of "the great difficulty of getting cash for anything in Virginia," as Dumas Malone put it, recounting an incident in which he proposed to one creditor a swap of nails for goose feathers.[78] The nailery assisted him in meeting plantation expenses, but did not make him a member of the entrepreneurial class of manufacturers. He enacted at once the roles of the independent farmer, the proud plantation owner, and the struggling American industrialist. This was through necessity as much as choice, for the plantations of Virginia were unsustainable without slave labor, both agricultural and industrial – industrial, because in order for the southern plantation economy to be as independent as its mythology claimed, it had to furnish and keep in repair its own industrial machinery. Jefferson could legitimately claim that his farms were to some degree self-sustaining, and capable of producing agricultural and industrial surpluses. And while he entertained traditional fantasies about a perpetually bucolic South, with the independent farmer at its political and economic center, his own industrial enterprises were necessary and undeniable.

With inconsistent degrees of success, Monticello represented a widespread pattern of nineteenth-century industrialism. Manufacturing was not limited to the cities, but was performed in both urban and rural households. Jefferson's industrialism was not confined to the nailery, but encompassed a variety of manufactures necessary to the maintenance

[78] Malone, *Jefferson and the Ordeal of Liberty*, pp. 217–219.

of a frontier farm. There is less information on the earlier than on the later years of Jefferson's industrial productivity. It is known that he embarked on numerous ventures both before and after his sojourns in the cities of Philadelphia, Paris, and Washington. These included tin-making, flour milling, ironworking, and tobacco processing. Textile manufacture, although neither so voluminous nor so efficient as in the factories of Lowell, Massachusetts, during the early 1820s, was also performed at the plantation. Carpentry, ironworking, and furniture making were largely performed at Monticello by trained slave laborers and slave foremen.[79]

INDUSTRIAL WORKERS AS CORRUPT

Jefferson's attitude towards Americans who worked with their hands was at best condescending, and those who worked for wages were pitiable wretches. He could not see how anyone other than a frustrated farmer would look for a job. Factory workers in eighteenth-century Europe and America were still few in number, and the working class, as it would evolve in the industrial cities known to Charles Dickens and Karl Marx, was only beginning to evolve. Jefferson viewed such persons as wage-slaves, whose dependency bred submission and stifled their virtue. The handworker or craftsman lived, as Gordon Wood has posited, with a "sense of obligation and dependency." The artisan class is unavoidably "dependent on the spending habits of the rich."[80]

Holding a "job" implied an obsequious relationship to an employer, but even the self-employed handworker was suspect. Tacitly, Jefferson endorsed Edmund Burke's opinion that while "no honest employment was disgraceful," not every occupation was "honorable." As Burke put it, "The occupation of a hair dresser, or a working tallow-chandler, cannot be a matter of honor to any person—to say nothing of a number of other more servile occupations."[81] We need not guess at whether Burke applied

[79] Lucia Stanton's three aforementioned titles present the wide variety of trades in which Monticello slaves were engaged, as well as the above-mentioned managerial responsibilities of Joe Fossett. Note particularly her index entries in "*Those Who Labor for My Happiness*" under the headings "Monticello plantation," "nailery," and "slave laborers." Also note the managerial responsibilities of George Granger.

[80] Gordon Wood, *The Radicalism of the American Revolution* (New York: Vintage, 1991), pp. 63–64.

[81] Edmund Burke, *Reflections on the Revolution in France* (1790), cited in Bernard Wishy, et al., *Introduction to Contemporary Civilization in the West*, 3rd edn. (New York: Columbia University Press, 1963), p. 91.

such opinions to Thomas Paine, a maker of women's corsets.[82] Artisans, plying their trades in cities and earning their bread by meeting the needs of patrons, were presumably dependent on the latter's tastes and, since they were ever dependent on the whims of bourgeois fashion, ever corruptible. Jefferson sentimentalized the yeoman farmer as a sunburned and sweaty, but independent and enterprising, capitalist, the industrial worker as a sullen, malcontented threat.

In a 1785 letter to John Jay, he wrote, "I consider the class of artificers as the panders of vice & the instruments by which the liberties of a country are generally overturned."[83] And yet this is a statement that reveals his ideological bias, rather than his practical policy. "Dependency begets subservience and venality, suffocates the germ of virtue." He had elsewhere written, and often recapitulated, a nightmare scenario of a corrupt mechanical class undermining the virtue of his garden republic. At this epoch, at least, he viewed menial workers, wage-enslaved craftsmen, and all elements of the emergent working class as rendered by economic necessity servile and dependent. He recorded at the time, and never forgot, John Adams' argument in the Continental Congress of 1776 "that the condition of the labouring poor in most countries, that of the fishermen particularly of the Northern states is as <painful> abject as that of slaves." By the mid nineteenth century Southern sentimentalists such as John C. Calhoun, George Fitzhugh, and William Grayson would actively assert that the industrial worker of the North was worse off than the African slave. Jeffersonian America would presumably be a world with neither hirelings nor slaves. And thereby hangs a tale, for, in reality, Jefferson was not committed to the elimination of the merchant, the fisherman, the handworker, or the hired man from his republic, any more than he was to the elimination of the African industrial slave.[84]

82 The authors of the Thomas Paine article at Wikipedia offer no support for their contention that Paine's work actually was to manufacture the stay ropes used on sailing ships. Most biographers maintain that his work was the making of corsets; for example, see Eric Foner, *Tom Paine and Revolutionary America* (Oxford University Press, 1976), p. 2.

83 Jefferson to John Jay, Paris, August 23, 1785.

84 Jefferson recorded John Adams' argument in "Notes to the Proceedings of the Continental Congress" (June 7 to August 1, 1776), Julian P. Boyd, *The Papers of Thomas Jefferson* (Princeton University Press, 1950), vol. I, p. 321. Calhoun's positions are discussed at length in Hofstadter, *The American Political Tradition*, Chapter 4. Fitzhugh is discussed in Eugene Genovese, *The World the Slaveholders Made* (New York: Vintage, 1969). See Grayson's *The Hireling and the Slave*, treated in Parrington, *Main Currents of American Thought*, vol. II, pp. 98–103.

"I think our governments will remain virtuous for many centuries; as long as they are chiefly agricultural; and this will be as long as there shall be vacant lands in any part of America."[85] Bucolic sentiments were shared by many of Jefferson's contemporaries, notably Adam Smith, and they were sustained well into the twentieth century.[86] Common sense and anecdotal evidence indicated that a lack of farming opportunities was the only cause for any mass migration to cities, and the conventional wisdom was that urban living damaged the moral and intellectual sensibilities of those forced to inhabit them. His hopes of preserving America's small-farming economy received a fortuitous boost with the surprise opportunity to purchase Louisiana. He could hardly have employed the anachronistic metaphor of the frontier as "safety valve," suggested by Frederick Jackson Turner in 1893. He did anticipate the thesis that the frontier provided Americans with an escape from the cesspool of European industrial life.

As the forest primeval was transformed gradually into an empire of independent freeholds, slavery would wither away. As he saw it in 1785, the American frontier would eventually be populated with independent small farmers, who would have no need of slaves. The abolition of slavery was an important, if not an essential, ingredient of the Jeffersonian teleology, in which a benevolent anarchy would accompany the secular millennium. Ethnically cleansed of both the African and the Indian populations, America would become a homogeneously white society, characterized by neoclassical but homely simplicity. In the fee simple empire, all politics would be local; the tax collector would disappear; the only visible trace of polity would be in the direct democracy of the local shire, limited to a mere hundred families.

His opportunity to purchase Louisiana allowed a proper extension of his plan for a fee simple empire. Territorial expansion would enable development of a nation of free farmers. Originally, he had argued that the contamination of slavery should be kept out of the territories, but Louisiana from the day of its purchase was a slave territory. And alas, Jefferson eventually came to believe in the inevitability of slavery in Louisiana, and its possible expansion into all the lands across the wide Missouri. The destiny of the frontier was inseparable from the discussion, and inevitably the subject of Jefferson's famous letter to John Holmes in which he compared the momentous Missouri question to a "fire-bell in the night" and lamented that "we have the wolf by the ears." Emancipation

85 Jefferson to James Madison, December 20, 1787. This opinion is expressed at greater length in *Notes on Virginia*, Chapter 19, pp. 196–197.

86 Jean Yarbrough compares Jefferson's ideas to Smith's in *American Virtues*, pp. 57–60.

would be advanced by a "diffusion" of the slavery impulse. He was forced to accept the serpentine reasoning of James Madison's *Federalist* 10, which had argued that large land expanses were automatically more conducive to Democratic Republicanism than smaller communities, and he revealed his almost mystical faith in the power of frontier geography to generate republican values and libertarian ideals. He was led to the specious argument that the extermination of slavery would become more likely if it were allowed to expand freely to the West.[87]

Rustic virtue is associated with a broad range of ideas that have developed in Western civilization over the millennia, but which achieved particular articulation among British social theorists in the seventeenth and eighteenth centuries. These ideas included the myth of the happy rustic, an ancient notion harkening back to the bucolic traditions of ancient Greece and Rome. Literary pastoralism was enough of a cliché to be satirized memorably in Shakespeare's *As You Like It*. But by the time Shakespeare wrote, England had already long sustained, side by side, and perhaps illogically in the context, its rigid, royalist class structure, a myth of yeomanry, and a nascent egalitarianism. This egalitarianism was deeply rooted before the rise of the Tudors and Stuarts, and was destined to flourish by the eighteenth century. It was inseparable from the rise of an urban class of tinkers, tailors, weavers, merchants, journalists, and staymakers. And this remarkably vital class had already produced the genius of a Shakespeare, a Franklin, and a Paine. This was an actuality that every American inescapably realized at the time of independence.

Nonetheless, Jefferson's ideology was founded on the idea that independent farmers, not craftsmen or shopkeepers, must perpetually constitute the majority of the "middling classes." The American democratic republic was to be solidly anchored in a literate, rural populace, primarily agricultural but managing cottage industries on the side. Of course they must be literate and possessed of common sense. Eventually, perhaps, as he intimated in a letter to Du Pont de Nemours, it might someday be practicable to limit the rights of citizenship to those who could read and write, "Enlighten the people generally, and tyranny and oppressions of body and mind will vanish like evil spirits at the dawn of day."[88]

[87] I follow the standard practice of accepting Douglass Adair's attribution of *Federalist* 10 to James Madison. See Adair, "The Authorship of the Disputed Federalist Papers," *The William and Mary Quarterly*, 1 (1944), 97–122, 235–264. Jefferson to John Holmes, Monticello, April 22, 1820. See Ellis, *American Sphinx*, pp. 265ff.

[88] Jefferson to Pierre Samuel Du Pont de Nemours, April 24, 1816.

A stalwart population of literate and informed white males would select good leaders from the best among themselves. Voting citizens would resemble Addison and Steele's Roger de Coverley, or the financially independent Squire Van Tassel, memorialized by Washington Irving. These responsible individuals would choose from among themselves the best representatives for Congress and, indirectly, those for the Electoral College. Jeffersonian democracy provided, as has often been said, not a mirror of society, but a filter. Democratic Republicanism had no confidence in the political judgments of the hireling or the wage-slave, and it did not seek to represent their views and values. It was based on an implicit trust in the wisdom, justice, and common sense of the virtual representative of the farming class.[89]

The countryside, if we are sensitive to all its historical connotations, can conjure up contradictory images, either of peasants storming the castle with pitchforks, or of slack-jawed yokels easily duped by the trickery of priests and the pageantry of kings. It can also evoke the image of the Jeffersonian squire, who describes his mornings on horseback surveying his domains and his afternoons reading the classics. The historian J. G. A. Pocock, in *The Machiavellian Moment*, associates Jefferson with the philosophers of a country party, a movement of rural, landowning elites seeking to provide a balance against the party of the court. An indirect influence of Machiavellian republicanism reached Jefferson through Algernon Sidney, whose name Jefferson invoked as one of the influences on the Declaration of Independence. Monarchs were easily seduced by the flattery of sycophants and courtiers; right-thinking country Whigs owed little to the favoritism of kings. An agrarian party was seen as a necessary and healthy counter-balance not only to the ancient corruptions of king and court, but to the rising power of what Gordon Wood has called "the fiscal-military state."[90]

JEFFERSONIAN INDUSTRIALISM

In every respect, citizenship in a fee simple empire was a self-contradictory notion, in that it was both future-oriented and nostalgic. In the

89 The problem of "representation" in the early republic, as mirror and/or as filter of the will of the people, is fruitfully discussed in Wood, *The Creation of the American Republic*, pp. 506–518, and Jack N. Rakove, *Original Meanings* (New York: Vintage, 1997), pp. 202–242.

90 Jefferson to Henry Lee, May 8, 1825. Gordon Wood, *Revolutionary Characters* (New York: Penguin, 2006), Chapter 4.

"Machiavellian Moment" of the early Enlightenment, rustic sentimentalism was tied as much to reactionary royalism as it was to Democratic Republicanism – no more and no less.[91] Civic humanism was counterrevolutionary in that it sentimentalized and sought to encourage a contented grass-roots populace, but it was modern and "progressive" to the extent that it nurtured the egalitarian notion of plebeian citizenship. By the mid eighteenth century, the enclosure movement and the displacement of a traditional peasantry had generated the *Lumpenproletariat* of London and Paris, and produced the fodder for European sweatshops. Jefferson was not the only one to see this, or the only voice insisting on the virtues of maintaining a class of independent farmers, but he presumed that these farmers would also be engaged in cottage industrialism.

While it is not entirely erroneous to see a shift in Jefferson's views from ideological agriculturalism to opportunistic industrialism, we should recall that throughout his public life he entertained conflicting visions of American economic destiny. These shifted kaleidoscopically during the Revolution, during his years in the White House, and during his lengthy retirement. He continued to hope that America offered the opportunity to develop a new concept of individual freedom, and to believe that the repository of republican virtue existed in the countryside. But one should entertain with caution the idea that he ever desired for all, or even most, American industrial needs to be met in Europe. The younger Jefferson made several enthusiastic statements, which, after more profound reflection, he modified; among these were his antislavery pronouncements and his rhetorical "agrarianism."[92]

The British public must have been amazed when they first read *Notes on Virginia*, in which he was willing to consign the bulk of American manufacturing to European, presumably English, workshops. In his *Summary View of the Rights of British America* he had been indignant at parliamentary restrictions on colonial manufacturing, but, surprisingly, the Declaration of Independence barely mentioned trade, although

[91] Ekelund and Hébert, *History of Economic Theory*, p. 87. J. G. A. Pockock's *The Machiavellian Moment: Florentine Political Thought and the Atlantic Republican Tradition* (Princeton University Press, 2003) is an extremely influential work which is concerned less with the author of *The Prince* than with conceptions of Machiavelli's republican thought that achieved prominence in English and American thought during the seventeenth and eighteenth centuries.

[92] *Notes on Virginia* was completed in 1781, and revised in 1782 and 1783. The first edition, published anonymously in Paris in 1785, was in French. Jefferson published the first English edition in 1787. He later considered revisions, especially of Chapter 19. See Jefferson to Mr. J. Lithgow, January 4, 1805.

published in the same year as Adam Smith's famous attack on trade restrictions, *The Wealth of Nations*. Jefferson understood that Americans gained from participation in the global economy. Farmers in the British colonies who sought to produce a surplus in sugar, tobacco, or rum were all tied in to an international commerce, which handled in silks, firearms, textiles, and, of course, slave agricultural labor. But even for purely local needs, industrial production had also become a matter of concern to plantation economies. Farms and plantations were the sites of cottage industries, which fell under the restrictions of the rather silly Hat Act, whereby "an American subject is forbidden to make a hat for himself of the fur which he has taken perhaps on his own soil," and the more serious Iron Act, which forbade producing finished articles, even for domestic needs.[93]

At the onset of the Revolution, Jefferson revealed no inclination to abandon manufacturing to Europe, since that would have meant, of course, abandoning manufactures to England, Europe's most important industrial power. And even in *Notes on Virginia* he tolerated, even endorsed, the fact that in America "The erecting of iron-works and mills is encouraged by many privileges." One detects a note of vicarious pride as he describes the "remarkable toughness" of the iron cast at two furnaces: "Pots and other utensils, cast thinner than usual, of this iron, may be safely thrown into, or out of the waggons in which they are transported. Salt-pans made of the same, and no longer wanted for that purpose, cannot be broken up, in order to be melted again, unless previously drilled in many parts." He neglected to mention that developing these American workshops implied a class of American industrial workers, and at his own initiative many of these were destined to be black children. The African ironworker was a hidden presence in his earlier writings, although increasingly important in the American economy.[94]

In any event, he was never opposed to American development of "Mechanical arts, so far as they respect things necessary in America, and inconvenient to be transported thither ready-made, such as forges, stone quarries, boats, bridges, (very especially,) etc., etc." In 1788 he saw a need for heavy manufacturing, but lesser need for "Lighter mechanical

[93] *A Summary View of the Rights of British America* is published in Peterson, ed., *Thomas Jefferson, Writings*, p. 109. The text is also available at the online edition of the Avalon Project, Yale University Library. Also see Jefferson, "Note on the instructions given to the first delegation of Virginia to Congress, in August, 1774."

[94] S. Sydney Bradford, "The Negro Ironworker in Ante Bellum Virginia," *Journal of Southern History*, 25 (May, 1959), 194–206.

arts, and manufactures ... circumstances rendering it impossible that America should become a manufacturing country during the time of any man now living."[95]

Jefferson fancied himself an independent farmer, but what farmer was ever independent of market forces? He was forced to be a businessman, and an industrialist as well. And so, like George Washington, John Taylor, and all his frontier contemporaries, he must entertain contradictory visions of his personal enterprises and of American destiny. For the farmer, in order to be independent, had no choice but to become a tradesman and an industrialist, and if the nation was to be politically independent, it must also be industrially independent. Monticello was hardly unique as a center of mechanical invention. Washington's Mount Vernon was no less a center of experimentation and invention; George Washington was constantly on the watch for agricultural and industrial novelties, and supremely efficient at turning knowledge to profit.[96]

After 1795 Jefferson was willing to acknowledge that he existed in a state of mutual dependency not only with slavery, but with industrial slavery. He was reinforcing his position in the *Summary View of the Rights of British America* of 1774, which was entirely different from his rhetorical flourish in *Notes on Virginia*:

> My idea is that we should encourage home manufactures to the extent of our own consumption of everything of which we raise the raw material. I do not think it fair in the ship-owners to say we ought not to make our own axes, nails, etc., here, that they may have the benefit of carrying the iron to Europe, and bringing back the axes, nails, etc. Our agriculture will still afford surplus produce enough to employ a due proportion of navigation. Wishing every possible success to your undertaking, as well for your personal as the public benefit, I salute you with assurances of great esteem and respect.[97]

Later Jefferson boasted that "Our manufacturers are now very nearly on a footing with those of England." He had accepted the fact that our workshops were not to remain in Europe. The industrial culture was fully engaged at Monticello, although he admitted that "many others in this

[95] Jefferson, "Travelling notes for Mr. Rutledge and Mr. Shippen," June 3, 1788.

[96] Washington's interest in manufacturing is revealed in a diary entry. For November 4, 1789 (Founders Online): "In Haverhill is a Duck manufactory, upon a small but ingenious scale, under the conduct of Colo. At this manufactory one small person turns a wheel which employs eight spinners, each acting independently of each other, so as to occasion no interruption to the rest if any one of them is stopped whereas at the Boston manufactory of this article, each spinner has a small girl to turn the wheel."

[97] Jefferson to Colonel David Humphreys, Washington, January 20, 1809.

business" had advanced farther than himself. The women and girls working in Monticello's spinning and looming industries were African American:

> My household manufactures are just getting into operation on the scale of a carding machine costing $60 only, which may be worked by a girl of twelve years old, a spinning machine, which may be made for $10, carrying 6 spindles for wool, to be worked by a girl also, another which can be made for $25, carrying 12 spindles for cotton, and a loom, with a flying shuttle, weaving its twenty yards a day. I need 2,000 yards of linen, cotton and woolen yearly, to clothe my family, which this machinery, costing $150 only, and worked by two women and two girls, will more than furnish.[98]

Jefferson's appointment of Albert Gallatin as Secretary of the Treasury might have appeared to signal a reversion to extreme "agarianism." A Pennsylvania farmer, Gallatin had served as clerk for a Philadelphia protest meeting against the whiskey excise, but took no part in the tarring and feathering of federal agents. Although a Swiss immigrant, and somewhat cosmopolitan, Gallatin had quickly adopted an American localist ideology and been elected to Congress. There he had represented the interests of farmers who sought liberation from commercial and banking interests. But, as Secretary of the Treasury, Gallatin made pragmatic adjustments to such ideas as central banking, a protective tariff, an embargo, a plan for internal improvements, and a national program to stimulate commerce. He seemed to be promoting a national policy far removed from Jefferson's bucolic localism. Indeed Gallatin's policies, initiated under the administration of Jefferson and advanced even further under Madison, were never supported by the "Old Republicans" in Congress.

During the Whiskey Rebellion, Gallatin's was a moderating voice, as he called for a non-violent solution to the crisis, but he later regretted even this mild involvement, referring to it as "my only political sin." He made his first impression on national politics with his attack on Alexander Hamilton's policies in "A Sketch of the Finances of the United States" (1796) and "Views of the Public Debt, Receipts and Expenditures of the United States" (1800). Rhetoric and ideology were later cast aside when the Louisiana Purchase and the War of 1812 made elimination of the debt impractical and abolition of Hamilton's bank inconvenient. Surrendering to the spirit of his age, Gallatin gave

[98] Jefferson to General Thaddeus Kosciusko, Monticello, June 28, 1812.

substance to the conciliatory rhetoric of Jefferson's inauguration statement, "We are all federalists."[99]

And if this was true, then Gallatin's career proved it by overturning all the clichés of "agrarianism" imbedded in Jefferson's *Notes on Virginia.* His 1808 "Report on Roads and Canals" called for increasing the national debt with the development of internal improvements.[100] Jefferson had in fact written to George Washington in support of internal improvements in 1784, while he was putting the finishing touches to his *Notes*. Gallatin's 1810 "Report on Manufactures" was another matter: it proposed a debt of $20 million in order to develop the industrial sector. His ideas anticipated the economic nationalism of the emergent Whig Party and the "American Plan" of its leader, Henry Clay; it was anathema to the emergent Democratic Party under Andrew Jackson. Ironically, it was to be the Whigs and the Republican Party – Lincoln's rising party of business and industrial interests – that inherited Gallatin's schemes. "Old Republicans" opposed Gallatin's radicalism, which to their relief was never implemented.

The storm clouds of international relations hovered over Jefferson's bucolic America like the forces of darkness over peaceable Hobbits in the fragile fastness of their Shire. At the beginning of his second term, the British Navy amplified its policy of impressing American seamen and disrupted American trade with France. Jefferson, a pacifist at heart, had neglected to build on the policies of his predecessor, John Adams, often called "father of the US Navy," who had extended George Washington's policies of naval development and secured the funds for completing the five original frigates, sister-vessels of the famous USS *Constitution.* Jefferson, whose policy of parsimonious taxation and generous government expenditures had no means of building a navy, must resort to economic pressures in response to French and British attacks on American shipping. Thus, he secured from Congress passage of an Embargo Act prohibiting all foreign trade. The consequences to American commerce during the two years of the Act's operation were devastating, but its effects on industrialism were positive.

Now, it is true that Jefferson's own Embargo Act forced him to step back from extreme "agrarian" sermonizing. And subsequently American industrial development was accelerated by the War of 1812, which disrupted trade with British manufacturers. Consequently, he was forced to

[99] Raymond Walters, *Albert Gallatin: Jeffersonian Financier and Diplomat* (University of Pittsburgh Press, 1957), pp. 66, 69.

[100] Jefferson to George Washington, March 15, 1784.

face in 1812, as he had in 1807, the pragmatic necessity of American industrial independence, offering the justification that it was in the interest of national security. It is true, as is often said, that war had the unintended consequence of stimulating American industry, and that Jefferson's embargos made it necessary for America to develop its own workshops. These facts, which are undeniable, should not lead to minimizing the importance of Jefferson's pre-Revolutionary, earlier support for domestic industry.[101]

The claim, reinforced by Jefferson himself, that he underwent a change from "agrarianism" to "industrialism" is based on the false presupposition that his cry of "Let American workshops remain in Europe" was ever to be taken literally. If he did undergo a transformation, it would have been long before he imposed the embargo. In a letter addressed to a Mr. J. Lithgow in 1805 he was already negating his earlier position in Chapter 19 of the *Notes*, saying, "Had I time to revise that chapter, this question should be discussed, and other views of the subject taken, which are presented by the wonderful changes which have taken place here since 1781, when the *Notes on Virginia* were written." He was somewhat disingenuous in pushing back the composition date to 1781, because the first English edition had appeared in 1787. By the time of his arrival in Europe in the mid 1780s, he was certainly becoming aware that the world was entering the age of iron, coal, and steam.[102]

He wrote David Humphrys, formerly a colonel in the Continental Army but by 1809 the proprietor of a woolen mill in Connecticut, to acknowledge receipt of a sample of cloth "which does honor to your manufactory, being as good as any one would wish to wear in any country." Humphreys' enterprise demonstrated that "Amidst the pressure of evils with which the belligerent edicts have afflicted us, some permanent good will arise; the spring given to manufactures will have durable effects." While he still believed that most spinning and weaving would be performed in the country homestead, "in our families," he recognized that, ultimately, "For finer goods we must resort to the larger manufactories established in the towns." While "commercial men" engaged in

[101] Jefferson to William Duane, August 4, 1812; Dumas Malone, *Jefferson and His Time*, 6 vols. (Boston, MA: Little, Brown, 1981), vol. VI, *Jefferson and His Time, the Sage of Monticello*, p. 109. With respect to Canada, Malone calls Jefferson an "inveterate expansionist," in ibid., p. 339.

[102] Jefferson to Mr. J. Lithgow, January 4, 1805. Editor's Note, in A. E. Bergh, ed., *The Writings of Thomas Jefferson* (Washington, DC: The Thomas Jefferson Memorial Association, 1907), vol. XVI, p. vii, "Jefferson and the Land Question." See reference to this letter in Bergh, ibid., and www.constitution.org/tj/jeff16.htm

Atlantic commerce might not like this and be angry at their loss of profits, Jefferson had come to feel that "we should encourage home manufactures to the extent of our own consumption of everything of which we raise the raw material." Already Americans had begun to make their own farm machinery. He trusted that in time "the good sense of our country will see that its greatest prosperity depends on a due balance between agriculture, manufactures." But, for the time being, he still envisioned these manufactures in terms of cottage industries.[103]

The farmer as mechanic was undeniably an American asset, while those who depended on the Atlantic trade were holding us back. He wrote to Thomas Leiper excoriating the New England merchants, whose "doctrine goes to the sacrificing of agriculture and manufactures to commerce." He now viewed manufacturing as honorable, to be compared with agriculture, and to be encouraged, as a countermeasure against commerce. Depending on foreign manufactures was likely to draw people from the interior country to the sea-shore and turn yeoman farmers into merchants, "and to convert this great agricultural country into a city of Amsterdam." He hoped that the danger would be averted, and that the "good sense of our country will see that its greatest prosperity depends on a due balance between agriculture, manufactures and commerce," rather than on the Atlantic merchants and their policy of dependency, "which has kept us in hot water from the commencement of our government, and is now engaging us in war."[104]

In 1816, with the experience of the embargo far behind, and the economic disruptions of the Napoleonic wars at an end, he revealed his perpetual ambivalence on domestic manufactures and free trade. He ended with another of his characteristic rhetorical questions:

> experience has taught me that manufactures are now as necessary to our independence as to our comfort; and if those who quote me as of a different opinion, will keep pace with me in purchasing nothing foreign where an equivalent of domestic fabric can be obtained, without regard to difference of price, it will not be our fault if we do not soon have a supply at home equal to our demand, and wrest that weapon of distress from the hand which has wielded it. If it shall be proposed to go beyond our own supply, the question of '85 will then recur, will our surplus labor be then most beneficially employed in the culture of the earth, or in the fabrications of art?

In his *Notes on Virginia*, Jefferson preached agrarian democracy with an almost mystical enthusiasm, but by the end of James Madison's first

[103] Jefferson to Humphrys, Washington, January 20, 1809.
[104] Jefferson to Thomas Leiper, Washington, January 21, 1809.

presidential administration, experiments with steamships and locomotives had proven commercially successful in Europe, signaling the dawn of a new age. Jefferson was already learning to be cautiously tolerant of artisans, mechanics, and even merchants as constituents of his republic. The essential feature of the fee simple empire was an American government drawing on the values of a property-owning, literate, and self-interested, if not necessarily urbane, population. A republican electorate would select good leaders from the best among their own, an educated and financially independent agriculturally productive gentry. Jeffersonians had little confidence in the political judgments of the hireling or the wage-slave, but came to appreciate the thrifty handworker, even in an urban setting. Clearly such republican businessmen as Jean-Baptiste Say, William Duane, and Benjamin Franklin Bache could not be dismissed as corruptible hirelings, and they did not languish under dependency, subservience, or a suffocation of virtue.

Jefferson's later compromise on the expansion of slavery into the territories, despite his pastoral, physiocratic, or agrarian preachments, makes questionable whether, after 1817, he sincerely believed in what Henry Nash Smith called the "fee simple empire."[105] Big government might subsidize Indian and Negro resettlement, but would yeoman farmers or large plantation owners automatically be the ultimate beneficiaries? Slavery, like military expenditure, taxation, banking, commerce, vigorous government, and even the inclusion of religion in functions of state were all elements of civilization that Jefferson saw theoretically as evil, but he accepted them as pragmatically necessary. Industrialism, a national debt, a naval establishment, loose construction, and miscegenation were evils that Jefferson could tolerate. He stuck to his principles when possible, and accommodated when necessary.

At the age of 58, in his First Inaugural Address, no political naïf at that point, President Jefferson famously paid lip-service to national unity, saying "we are all Federalists; we are all Republicans." He was old enough and experienced enough to have understood his own rhetoric when he spoke of the rising power of a people engaged in commerce "traversing the seas with the rich productions of their industry." Josiah Quincy believed that the Jeffersonians ultimately out-federalized the Federalists.

[105] Henry Nash Smith pointed out the conflict between the idea of a plantation society and a "fee simple empire" made up of independent small property owners in *Virgin Land: The American West as Symbol and Myth* (Cambridge, MA: Harvard University Press, 1950).

The presidential historian Theodore Roosevelt was convinced that Jefferson accomplished most when he behaved pragmatically as an opportunistic Federalist.[106] Jefferson, indeed, spoke more accurately than he knew when he said "we are all federalists," if he meant by that statement that the self-interest of Americans was inseparable from promoting a powerful, centralized economic empire in which industrialism, including industrial slavery, was to play a part.

But Jefferson seemingly took back these conciliatory words more than once, both during his presidency and thereafter. His *nunc dimittis* on the Federalist–Republican (or industrial–agrarian) controversy was to insist that throughout history there had always been two eternal parties – the aristocratic and the democratic. The idea that both parties were aristocratic and that the party system consisted of conflicts between elites seemed to make little impression on him. Thus, towards the end of his life, he confided to Lafayette his opinion that:

> in truth, the parties of Whig and Tory, are those of nature. They exist in all countries, whether called by these names, or by those of Aristocrats and Democrats, *Cote Droite* and *Cote Gauche*, Ultras and Radicals, Serviles and Liberals. The sickly, weakly, timid man, fears the people, and is a Tory by nature. The healthy, strong and bold, cherishes them, and is formed a Whig by nature.[107]

It was a strange interpretation of history that made northern Roundheads into aristocrats and southern Cavaliers into Whiggish egalitarians, but Jefferson saw himself as a country Whig. How could he have any presentiment that the meaning of that term was changing? Paradoxically, by the mid 1820s the term "Whig" would come to designate the party of the industrial Northeast. It was, in his view, the Southern agrarian slaveholders who were the true Whigs. If he had lived to the age of 91, as John Adams did, he would have witnessed a transmogrification of the Federalist Party and the appropriation by industrialists of the name of Whigs. In Jefferson's view, Daniel Shays did not represent the irrepressible Revolutionary tradition of Puritan Massachusetts. Shays' Rebellion was seen as the reaction of agrarians to the aristocratic predilections of the Northeast. He saw nothing incongruous about lumping Shays' Yankee farmers together in the same category with Southern Cavaliers, attended by liveried slaves. He blended these two

106 Jefferson to Lafayette, November 4, 1823.
107 Jefferson to Lafayette, Monticello, November 4, 1823.

incompatible classes together as republican liberals and egalitarian democrats.

Even more remarkably, he decided that antislavery could never be anything more than a conspiratorial cover-up for elitism. The Missouri Compromise, which banned slavery from a portion of the territories, must be interpreted not as a move by Whiggish business and industrial interests, but as the conspiracy of an eternal aristocratic party, the perpetual opponents of libertarian and egalitarian values, who had "got up the Missouri question, under the false front of lessening the measure of slavery." Their only true concern was to divide the nation into parties along geographical lines, in order to capture the presidency. The ordinary people of the North were mere dupes, laudable though their moral zeal might have been. Hopefully they were becoming sensible "that they were injuring instead of aiding the real interests of the slaves." Antislavery sentiment was merely a tool employed "for electioneering purposes," a trick of hypocrisy, doomed to failure.[108]

Although he never actually denied that the Missouri Compromise involved a moral issue, he dismissed practical efforts by Northern politicians to halt slavery's spread as mere political cynicism. He had come to view American regional frictions as arising not from the problem of slavery, an opinion he had shared with James Madison thirty years earlier, but as a manifestation of reactionary, elitist notions that predominated in the North. He viewed the slavery debate at the root of the Missouri Compromise as epiphenomenal. The real issue was a crude aristocratic grab for power, rooted in a fear of democracy, for democracy in his mind had become inseparable from protecting the freedom of the South to expand its slavery empire.

From its very beginnings, Jeffersonian democracy always contained an industrial element, and industrial slavery was always accommodated within it. Like its author's beloved Monticello, Jeffersonian democracy was always a work in progress, and from beginning to end it lacked the elements of a systematic or cohesive ideology. It reflected what Hamilton identified as Jefferson's "temporizing" disposition. Jefferson's commitment to the practical necessities of independent farming made him a small-time manufacturer. The African slave therefore was always a factor in his exercises in expedient pragmatism. The Monticello economy of necessity bore less resemblance to the bucolic idealism celebrated by Rousseau than to the industrial realities that Adam Smith described. Smith began his

[108] Ibid.

treatise on *The Wealth of Nations* with a description of a pin factory that was uncannily similar in its production routines to Jefferson's nailery, and it is worthy of repetition.

To reiterate, Jefferson's anti-industrial rhetoric in 1787 could be taken no more seriously than his pronouncements on ending slavery. There is no doubt that he demonstrated an ideological preference for farms over factories, and for free soil over factories in the fields. But antislavery rhetoric diminished after the Revolution, and not only because the invention of the cotton gin increased the demand for slaves. Yankee merchants and Southern planters both profited from slavery and the slave trade. With the arrival of independence, the slave economy was no longer a source of embarrassment, and patriotic Americans had come to care less about "the opinion of nations" as slavery was becoming increasingly attractive to land developers and agricultural entrepreneurs. This is not the same thing as saying that slavery was dying before the cotton gin, but it was a fact that, at least in the South, economic forces overwhelmed moral rhetoric as Americans no longer apologized for slaveholding, and even began to argue that slavery was beneficial for blacks and whites alike.

Slavery was a "machine in the garden." By 1837 the Tredegar Works in Richmond was destined to become a major iron producer, and industrial slavery was becoming a factor in the developing South. Not only in factories, but on plantations, the industrial model provided what historian James Oakes has called "factories in the fields." Slave production undermined the bucolic ideal and converted the entire region into one gigantic industrial plant, or, as Alexander Crummell described things towards the end of the century with some awareness of the irony of the fact that slavery brought factory organization to the fields:

> The Race was one great machine, every member in his place; working with severest regularity, and producing vast and valuable results. Within a range of both narrow and material interests, but alas, with a constant muzzling of our personal wills, the whole world saw the physical value of the Negro Race. Every man was made to stand in his own place; every man to do his own work; every man to yield a distinct and telling product! Out of this came labour; industrial order; servile systematized energy and activity; great increases of Negro population; vast crops of Corn, Rice, Tobacco, and Cotton; enormous revenues to individuals, and to the national treasury.[109]

[109] Alexander Crummell, "The Discipine of Freedom" in Wilson J. Moses, ed., *Destiny and Race: Selected Writings of Alexander Crummell* (Amherst, MA: University of Massachusetts Press, 1992), p. 246. Also see James Oakes' chapter entitled "Factories in the Fields" in Oakes, *The Ruling Race* (New York: Norton, 1988), pp. 153–191,

"Let our workshops remain in Europe" was never more than a wisecrack, a hyperbolic quip – facetious, flippant, and frivolous, and it should not be viewed as representing a serious statement of policy. Although Jefferson never became a big cotton planter, and Whitney's cotton gin had no direct effect on his enterprises, Monticello had an incipient factory culture, constantly struggling to keep pace with the industrial revolution. Jefferson knew that the rhetoric of *Notes on Virginia*, whether on slavery or agriculture, was practically unsustainable. True enough, he was enraptured with the concept of bucolic virtue, but he certainly never intended to discourage the varieties of manufacturing that all farmers and planters necessarily practiced to sustain their domains. But Jefferson was not by any means encouraging factories in big cities, after the patterns that were emerging in Europe. He still viewed manufacturing in terms of small towns and local shires.

Jefferson's thinking in the area of political economy exemplified the pragmatism and temporizing disposition that Hamilton so cynically and accurately observed. The economic theory of *Notes on Virginia*, like its biology, thus underwent some evolution, if we are to believe Jefferson's later correspondence.[110] The temporary and exceptionally dismissive attitude towards manufacturing expressed in the *Notes* was neither a thorough nor an honest expression of Jefferson's industrial philosophy at any time. I have noted earlier that he heaped opprobrium on the class of artisans and mechanical workers in a 1785 letter to Jay, but by 1809 he had returned to his position of 1774, which vigorously insisted that American workshops neither could nor should remain in Europe.

Celebrating the rise of American industry in 1813, he wrote from a memory that was both true and false when he said "I have not formerly been an advocate for great manufactories. I doubted whether our labor, employed in agriculture, and aided by the spontaneous energies of the earth, would not procure us more than we could make ourselves of other necessaries. But other considerations entering into the question, have settled my doubts."[111] His theory that only farmers were capable of republican virtue oscillated, so that by 1808 he had returned to a position of 1774, a "policy which plants the manufacturer and the

which also plays on the irony that slavery introduced industrial organization into the garden of Jeffersonian agrarianism.

110 Jefferson's biological revisionism involved his eventual acceptance that animals could become extinct, as discussed elsewhere in the present work.

111 Jefferson to John Melish, Monticello, January 13, 1813.

husbandman side by side, and establishes at the door of every one that exchange of mutual labors and comforts, which we have hitherto sought in distant regions, and under perpetual risk of broils with them." By 1816 he was saying, "We must now place the manufacturer by the side of the agriculturist."[112]

The village blacksmith, the weaver, the tailor, and the joiner were all capable of republican virtue, insofar as they were all independent small capitalists, and often they were not exclusively members of an artisan class. They were cottage industrialists, and the same yeoman farmers he considered essential to his shires. Industry was something to be carried out in the country, not the city. Henry Wadsworth Longfellow, born while Jefferson was in office, wrote the following well-known tribute to the independent village artisan, composed around the time Henry Ford was born:

UNDER a spreading chestnut tree
 The village smithy stands;
The smith, a mighty man is he,
 With large and sinewy hands;
And the muscles of his brawny arms
 Are strong as iron bands.

His hair is crisp, and black, and long,
 His face is like the tan;
His brow is wet with honest sweat,
 He earns whate'er he can,
And looks the whole world in the face,
For he owes not any man.[113]

But the village blacksmith, no less than Brom Bones, was an independent small capitalist, not a routine wage-earner in Adam Smith's pin factory who, for Smith's purposes of illustration, might be lacking in craftsmanly skills. And the celebrated "yeomenry of the city" were not like the grumpy African American teenagers employed in Jefferson's own workshops. It was understood that the spirit of white youth must be preserved from the pestilence of factory life. Much as he praised the independence and good husbandry of the mechanic farmer, Jefferson's

[112] Jefferson to the Society of Tammany, or Columbian Order, No. 1, of the City of New York, Washington, February 29, 1808. Jefferson to Benjamin Austin, January 9, 1816.

[113] Longfellow wrote "The Village Blacksmith" (1840) as a tribute to his ancestors, one of whom, Stephen Longfellow, worked a forge in Portland, Maine, where Longfellow was born.

practical interest in manufacturing was tied to slavery. His interest in manufactures, which in his case meant plantation enterprises, was expressed in public at least as early as 1774, and sporadically thereafter. He did not, as is sometimes implied, come to support manufactures tardily, as a result of the Napoleonic wars, or the embargo of 1807, or the War of 1812, and solely as a national security measure.

Since he did not see slaves as present or future participants in "Jeffersonian democracy," he did not have to worry about the corrupting effects of industrial slavery on them. Mind-numbing industrial routines, which were to be tolerated only on large plantations such as his own, would have no detrimental effects on his ideal American citizen. The yeoman farmer could be left alone to follow his freedom-loving instincts. Slaves required strict supervision and were even capable of perpetrating acts of violence on one another, as in the case of worker-on-worker harassment resulting in serious injury described by historian Annette Gordon-Reed; thus the need for a class of white overseers. But the white yeoman farmer was the principal component of an ideal republican democracy. Manufacturing was as essential to Jeffersonian democracy as slavery was to Monticello, and despite its sporadic rhetoric of agrarian idealism, Jeffersonian republicanism always rested squarely on the factory floor, where black boys and girls were among its indispensable workers.

4

Life, Liberty, Property, and Peace

"THE BOISTEROUS SEA OF LIBERTY"

The Declaration of Independence, with its appeal to "the opinions of mankind," was clearly intended to gain recognition from other nations, particularly the French monarch, but paradoxically it contained an almost gratuitous anti-monarchist dig that was at best undiplomatic and might even have proven counter-productive. Its egalitarian language implicitly assailed not only the divine rights of George III, but those of all kings, and could not have warmed the heart of Louis XVI. Yet one of its drafters, Benjamin Franklin, departed on his mission to secure that monarch's assistance only three months after helping to frame the Declaration's anti-royalist rhetoric. The Declaration expressed the shared perspectives of a particular disgruntled elite, whose emotions were neither harmonious nor egalitarian. The doctrine that all men are created equal was obviously untrue, and had less to do with "harmonizing sentiments of the day," as Jefferson later called them, than with igniting the emotions of domestic mobs.[1]

The Declaration's anti-monarchism inflamed both vulgar and elite passions, and fed the smoldering resentments against a king who was charged with believing he was better than Americans of Jefferson's class, who considered themselves the equal of any European noble, but superior to a shoemaker, shopkeeper, shipwright, or shoveler of manure. The Declaration was an emotional appeal, not to mankind in general, but it did aim at the machismo of more ordinary American white males, who might be enlisted in its call for manly retaliation. It circumvented the

[1] Jefferson to Henry Lee, May 8, 1825.

fact that most English abuses resulted from acts of Parliament and laid all the crimes on the head of a hereditary monarch, an evil man, who had "plundered our seas, ravaged our coasts, burnt our towns, and destroyed the lives of our people."[2]

Its immediate consequence was that it provoked a riot four days after its drafting, when George Washington delivered it to one of its intended audiences, the Continental Army. Washington read it aloud to the troops on July 8, at John Hancock's behest, and was dismayed as a mob proceeded to race through the town, toppling the equestrian statue of King George, dismembering it, and carrying the severed head through the streets. Washington's General Orders marking the occasion read:

> 'Tho the General doubts not the persons, who pulled down and mutilated the Statue, in the Broadway, last night, were actuated by Zeal in the public cause; yet it has so much the appearance of riot and want of order, in the Army, that he disapproves the manner, and directs that in future these things shall be avoided by the Soldiery, and left to be executed by proper authority.[3]

Nonetheless, Hancock and the Congress had rightly anticipated that mass sentiments would be more easily aroused by the dehumanizing of King George than by any systematic discussion of the economic and industrial issues more precisely delivered in Jefferson's *Summary View of the Rights of British America* two years earlier.

Jefferson's draft of the Declaration contained only one sentence directed at the economic causes of the revolution in progress – a cursory reference to "cutting off our trade," which was misleading, since American traders drew both advantages and disadvantages from their colonial status within the Empire. American merchants, including

[2] Carl Lotus Becker opines that "one is likely to think the poor king less malevolently guilty than he is made out to be," *The Declaration of Independence: A Study on the History of Political Ideas* (New York: Harcourt, Brace and Company, 1922), p. 23. He also notes the absence of references to grievances against Parliament, p. 21 ibid., which Jefferson had addressed in *A Summary View of the Rights of British North America* (1774).

[3] David Waldstreicher, *In the Midst of Perpetual Fetes: The Making of American Nationalism, 1776–1820* (Chapel Hill: University of North Carolina Press, 1997), pp. 19–52, describes the "Funeral of the Monarchy." Ron Chernow, *Washington: A Life* (New York: Penguin, 2010), p. 237; "General Orders, 10 July 1776," Founders Online: http://founders.archives.gov/documents/Washington/03–05-02–0185 (ver. 2014-02-12). Source: Philander D. Chase, ed., *The Papers of George Washington*, Revolutionary War Series (Charlottesville, VA: University Press of Virginia, 1993), vol. V, *16 June 1776 – 12 August 1776*, pp. 256–257. Jay Fliegelman, *Declaring Independence: Jefferson, Natural Language, and the Culture of Performance* (Stanford University Press, 1993), argues that Jefferson wrote the Declaration to be read aloud.

Yankee slavers, enjoyed a favored trading status. In a few years' time, a provision of the Jay Treaty of 1794, which Jefferson's party bitterly opposed, was aimed at restoring the West India Trade. The Declaration made no mention of the problems of banking and money supply. It did not mention parliamentary obstacles to industrialization such as the Iron Act. It ignored such historic grievances as the Stamp Act, which Benjamin Franklin had opposed so tardily as to enrage the people of Philadelphia against him. It did not mention the Tea Act, which that same luminary had viewed as an almost trivial nuisance, but which Boston hotheads saw as a matter of honor.[4]

The Declaration's complaints against the Empire's unwieldy bureaucracy were undoubtedly legitimate, but, as Henry Steele Commager notes, "Increasingly the Enlightenment encouraged, developed, and relied on bureaucracy, which increasingly frustrated it."[5] The Declaration itemized several complaints regarding the administration of justice. The complaints were as legitimate as the frustrations were unavoidable. Individuals at the far reaches of any empire inevitably experience frustrations when dealing with bureaucracies located in the metropole, whether that be London, Paris, or Washington. The Founders did not imagine that the United States would someday become an imperial bureaucracy west of the Atlantic. Benjamin Franklin was possibly the only one who envisioned a United States destined to supplant England in the way that Constantinople had supplanted Rome.[6] No one, with the possible exception of Benjamin Franklin, envisioned the United States as the new center of a future Anglo-American hegemony, destined to bestride the world as an economic and political colossus. For Jefferson and the tradition he nourished, American independence held out the utopian illusion of an American exception, an empire without bureaucracies.

[4] Edmund S. Morgan appreciates Franklin's vacillations and ambivalences in his *Benjamin Franklin* (Yale University Press, 2002), pp. 152–165, 171–173; Gordon Wood, *The Americanization of Benjamin Franklin* (New York: Penguin, 2005), pp. 107–113, 144.

[5] Henry Steele Commager, *The Empire of Reason: How Europe Imagined and America Realized the Enlightenment* (Garden City, NY: Anchor Press / Doubleday, 1977), p. 121.

[6] Benjamin Franklin, "Observations Concerning the Increase of Mankind," printed in [William Clarke], *Observations On the late and present Conduct of the French, with Regard to their Encroachments upon the British Colonies in North America ... To which is added, wrote by another Hand; Observations concerning the Increase of Mankind, Peopling of Countries, &c.* (Boston, MA: Printed and Sold by S. Kneeland in Queen-Street, 1755) at: https://founders.archives.gov/documents/Franklin/01-04-02-0080

Except for acts against Indian people, the Revolutionary war was not characterized by mindless and indiscriminate terrorism either on the Loyalist or on the Patriot side. The Empire took police actions to suppress the ongoing rebellion, but King George's measures were hardly as brutal as William the Conqueror's "Harrowing of the North," or the looting of the monasteries by Henry VIII. A future generation would witness the deeds of William T. Sherman in a later police action against rebellious individuals, and scorched earth was not a rampant policy. The American General John Sullivan conducted a brutal campaign to destroy the villages and food supplies of the Iroquois allies of the British.[7] These actions against Indian "terrorists" were not, and still are not, conceived as the moral equivalent of King George's comparatively restrained efforts to put down the rebellion.

It was easy enough to whip up the manly emotions of ordinary Americans, and some were inspired to undergo the hardships of Valley Forge. Listing instances of police brutality aroused their combative instincts, but the Declaration offered no systematic or rational presentation of what a ragged volunteer might ultimately gain from the fighting. Those who successfully incite wars or revolutions seldom if ever express a desire to overturn the structures of private wealth. The task of revolutionary leaders is to convince the masses that their interests are identical with those of the wealthy. Foot soldiers in every war are largely people who lack property, but the ultimate cause of the American Revolution was the desire of propertied classes to increase or retain their holdings in land and other forms of wealth, including slaves.

The British Empire was not hostile to slavery, a system that included three related, but discrete, elements: its first element was the Atlantic trade in human cargoes, which Jefferson's original draft of the Declaration blamed on King George. Its second element was the ownership of human beings as property and the exploitation of their labor, which served the interests of many British subjects, whether in England or in America. Its third element was the racial degradation of African peoples, and the doctrine that they were a separate and inferior branch of the human family, a position defended by David Hume and other intellectuals of the British Enlightenment. Jefferson's draft Declaration condemned only the first element of slavery, skimmed over the second, and ignored

[7] See the biography of Sullivan, Library of Congress website. Since destruction of civilian food supplies was not banned until 1977, under Article 54 of Protocol I of the Geneva Conventions, I plead guilty to presentism.

the third. In fact, Jefferson was entangled by marriage in the first, and he was no less culpable than King George of the second and third atrocities that constituted slavery in the eighteenth-century Enlightenment.

In 1772 Lord Mansfield, speaking for Parliament, in the case of *Somerset v. Stewart*, declared that slavery was "so odious" as to be inconsistent with English tradition, but two years later Jefferson was still blaming slavery on the British. Mansfield's decision did not render the colonial ownership of slaves illegal, but it frightened some American slaveholders, and slavery continued to be legally ambiguous even on English soil.[8] The decision nurtured paranoia and uncertainty among slaveholders throughout the Empire, but Mansfield's celebrated animadversions were hardly inconsistent with the thinking of those Virginians who pretended to detest slavery. Furthermore, some Yankee merchants had nothing against the perpetuation of the slave trade. In short, Americans could not agree on whether membership in the Empire provided a bulwark to slavery or an undermining of its foundations. The Constitutional Convention was still incapable, seven years later, of abolishing the slave trade "prior to the Year one thousand eight hundred and eight." Britain did not outlaw the slave trade until 1807, one year before the American constitutional provision took effect, and did not abolish slavery in its New World colonies until 1833.[9]

The historian Gerald Horne has argued that the American War of Independence was a counter-revolution sparked by an American dread of British abolitionism. Horne's position is rational, but not unassailable, for Jefferson and many others hardly viewed either Parliament or the king as abolitionists. And even if they did, it was more tactically advantageous for them to pretend that the Empire was pro-slavery, and that Americans were its innocent victims, the position Jefferson had taken in his *Summary View*. Of course, he had no power to abolish either slavery or the slave trade, but he certainly had the power to free his own slaves and need not

[8] Scholars continue to debate the precise implications of Mansfield's decision. Some argue that it theoretically, if not effectively, rendered slavery illegal in England. Others maintain that it simply rendered invalid the sale of Somerset to an owner in the Indies. Peter P. Inks, John R. Michigan, and R. Owen Williams, *Encyclopedia of Antislavery and Abolition* (Westport, CT: Greenwood Publishing Group, 2007), p. 643.

[9] Lord Mansfield, the chief justice, declared from the Court of King's Bench in 1772 that slavery was unsupported by existing law in England and Wales. See Jerome Nadelhaft, "The Somersett Case and Slavery: Myth, Reality, and Repercussions," *Journal of Negro History*, 51, no. 3 (July, 1966), 193–208. It is interesting to note that Hamilton used Lord Mansfield's word "odious" to describe slavery in *Camilus*, vol. III (1795), his defense of the Jay Treaty, over Jefferson's opposition.

have waited either for King George or for the Virginia legislature. He always had the option of becoming an independent yeoman farmer, relying solely on his own labors for his livelihood, or he could have supported himself as a Philadelphia lawyer, had he so desired. But his attempt to drag a red herring across the trail of his own involvement, both as a profiteer from the slave trade and as a slaveholder, by a personal attack on King George was an act of hypocrisy so transparent that even the Continental Congress blushed at endorsing it.[10]

Jefferson's references to the slave trade ignored the substantive point that if there were no buyers, there would be no sellers. The international slave trade undermined the interests of Virginians, much of whose capital was invested in slaves. By continuing to import slaves, the British were devaluing the property and reducing the debt collateral of Thomas Jefferson. This section of the Declaration was removed out of deference to Georgians and South Carolinians, who recognized that the deflation of slave prices was in their interest. None of Jefferson's drafts of the Declaration mentioned such matters. In fact, they never provided the real reasons for bushwhacking Redcoats or surprising somnolent Hessians. Neither those poor wretches nor most of the Americans who would engage them in battle had much grasp of the issues that had led to the Revolution in the first place.

The Declaration said nothing about commodities, precious metals, banking, manufacturing, or the balance of trade, all of which affected ordinary American farmers like Daniel Shays. It took Shays ten years to suspect that he might have been duped, but Shays' Rebellion did not perturb Jefferson, for two reasons: it was not, as General Knox feared, an attack on private wealth, and second, it took place in Massachusetts, not Virginia. Abigail Adams lost patience with him, knowing he would not have viewed with such sanguinity the methods of Shays' rebels if they had been the acts of Virginia slaves. It was one thing for Jefferson to endorse a Massachusetts insurrection from the safety of his Paris writing-desk, another to encourage French suppression of an insurrection in Haiti. Later he would endorse Parisian bloodshed, while his erstwhile Parisian French dinner companions were facing the guillotine in the public square. It was, of course, unthinkable that Virginia's white yeoman farmers might

[10] Gerald Horne, *The Counter-Revolution of 1776: Slave Resistance and the Origins of the United States of America* (New York University Press, 2014). Alfred W. and Ruth G. Blumrosen, *Slave Nation: How Slavery United the Colonies and Sparked the American Revolution* (Chicago: Sourcebooks, 2005).

harbor resentments against the plantation aristocracy. The yeomen eagerly volunteered as "paddy rollers," slave patrollers, members of a "well-armed militia." As Hinton Rowan Helper would later observe, this class worked against their own interests by helping to secure a system that undermined the value of their own labor.[11]

TABULA RASA, PURITAN DEPRAVITY, AND INNATE MORAL SENSE

Whether the Declaration is fundamentally a religious document is debatable, albeit Jefferson's invocation of God within it is so frequently cited by evangelical Christians and "right-to-lifers" in support of religious agendas. Historians have long noted that the Declaration has to be read against numerous intellectual and social currents, including not only the heterodox Christianity of Locke, but also Jefferson's conception of Republican virtue, and also in the context of the various competing "deisms" of the era. Allen Jayne offered a timely reminder of the importance of religion to Jefferson's Declaration, and more recently Jeffry Morrison, Gideon Mailer, and others have shown the subtleties within the contested ideas of moral sense in dialogue with residual Calvinism in the Presbyterianism of the Scottish Enlightenment. It should be remembered that not only did Roger Sherman, a respectable Presbyterian theologian, sit on the Declaration's drafting committee, but that another one of its signers, the theologian John Witherspoon, had presided over the faculty while Madison was a student at Princeton.[12]

We don't know how thoroughly he chewed and digested the "elementary books of public right" to which he so vaguely alluded in the famous letter to Henry Lee, but it is obvious that he chose not to produce critical

[11] Carl T. Bogus, "The Hidden History of the Second Amendment," *University of California at Davis Law Review*, 31 (1998), 309. "The Georgia statutes required patrols, under the direction of commissioned militia officers, to examine every plantation each month and authorized them to search 'all Negro Houses for offensive Weapons and Ammunition' and to apprehend and give twenty lashes to any slave found outside plantation grounds," Sally E. Hadden, *Slave Patrols: Law and Violence in Virginia and the Carolinas* (Cambridge, MA: Harvard University Press, 2003). See Hinton Rowan Helper, *The Impending Crisis of the South* (New York: Burdick Brothers, 1857).

[12] Allen Jayne, *Jefferson's Declaration of Independence: Origins, Philosophy, and Theology* (Lexington, KY: University Press of Kentucky, 1998). Political scientist Jeffry H. Morrison argues that John Witherspoon came "to conclusions in moral anthropology identical to those drawn by his American colleagues like Jefferson." See Jeffry H. Morrison, *John Witherspoon and the Founding of the American Republic* (University of Notre Dame Press, 2005).

analyses of them.[13] It is certain that he viewed certain republican theories "of public right" with dismay, such as Montesquieu's proposition that a republican form of government would be unworkable in a large and populous nation. His taste in philosophy was oriented towards the past, rather than the contemporary, as we can see from the authors he listed when he claimed that the principal influences on the Declaration were Aristotle, Cicero, Sidney, and Locke. He consistently privileged English Renaissance thinkers, such as Bacon and Sidney, over philosophers of the French Enlightenment, such as Voltaire, Montesquieu, and Rousseau. Cicero and Sidney, although ages apart, held high place as martyrs for republicanism, and Locke he revered as the champion of government by the consent of the governed. Therefore it is easy to see how these three names mentioned in the letter to Lee would fit into the American Revolutionary world picture.

Aristotle's influence is more problematic, although, of course, cultural literacy, then as now, required that some occasional lip-service be paid to Aristotle. But Aristotelianism was under attack on two fronts, on the one side from Bacon, on the other side from Locke. Jefferson was not alone in his revolt against the organic theory of the state, implicit in the works of Plato and Aristotle, who saw politics and the state as the natural condition of man. At the same time, Jefferson rejected "the principle of Hobbes, so humiliating to human nature, that the sense of justice & injustice is not derived from our natural organisation, but founded on convention only." Somehow, he must reconcile his rejection of Plato and Aristotle's organic state with his belief that the Creator had "formed man for the social state" and provided him "with virtue and wisdom enough to manage the concerns of the society." Several Enlightenment authors had already covered this territory.[14]

Although his admiration for Locke, prophet of the doctrine of *tabula rasa*, is incontestable, Jefferson was nonetheless attached to the Scottish common-sense concept of innate ideas lodged in a moral sense, the idea that principles of right and justice were engraved on the human heart.[15] In a letter to Doctor John Manners of June 12, 1817, he wrote, "The evidence of this natural right, like that of our right to life, liberty,

[13] Jefferson to Henry Lee, May 8, 1825.

[14] On Hobbes, Jefferson to Francis W. Gilmer, June 7, 1816; on social state, Jefferson to John Adams, October 28, 1813. On the Enlightenment's putative rejection of Plato and Aristotle's organic state, see G. R. G. Mure, " The Organic State," *Philosophy*, 24, no. 90 (July, 1949), 205–218.

[15] He used the phrase *tabula rasa* in Thomas Jefferson, *Notes on the State of Virginia*, ed. David Waldstreicher (Boston, MA: Bedford Books, 2002), p. 189.

the use of our faculties, the pursuit of happiness, is not left to the feeble and sophistical investigations of reason, but is impressed on the sense of every man." Jefferson attempted, as did the celebrated moral philosopher Francis Hutcheson, to reconcile his empiricism with a belief that moral ideas were innate. Such a belief placed him in the same camp as Adam Smith, whose *Theory of Moral Sentiments* asserted the existence of an "invisible hand" of morality, working in accord with the better-known "invisible hand" of self-interest, which appeared in his later-developed *Wealth of Nations.*[16]

Jefferson's eclectic moral ideology yoked together the Lockean epistemology with a concept of innate sentiments. It accepted the doctrine of innate moral ideas and encompassed the thought of such seventeenth-century authors as Francis Hutcheson, Thomas Reid, and Anthony Ashley Cooper, the 3rd Earl of Shaftesbury who, without repudiating Locke, argued that morality was innate.[17] Smith had written that society was regulated not only by the invisible hand of the market, but, prior to that, as he had argued with equal conviction, by the existence of the invisible hand of moral sentiments. Although Smith had so famously written that "It is not from the benevolence of the butcher, the brewer, or the baker that we expect our dinner," he had also argued with reason and compassion that the wealth of nations depended on civilized behavior. Mankind's innate moral instincts regulated selfishness with wholesome restraint. Smith recognized, furthermore, that whatever the ultimate source of property rights, the actual enjoyment of property was dependent on law and order. This was tacitly acknowledged by Thomas Jefferson, and more explicitly by Franklin and Paine.

Jefferson's approach to *laissez-faire* liberalism was not anarchic; it was tempered not only by the invisible hand of moral sentiment, but regulated by reason, and imbedded in a concept of civic humanism. The anarchic selfishness of the Social Darwinists who were to invoke Adam Smith's economic laws in the nineteenth century broke free from his theory of

[16] There has been considerable discussion of the supposed contradictions between Adam Smith's metaphor of the "invisible hand" as deployed in the *Theory of Moral Sentiments* and in *The Wealth of Nations*. See D. D. Raphael and A. L. Macfie, eds., *Theory of Moral Sentiments* (Oxford University Press, 1976), pp. 20–25. Garry Wills has no difficulty reconciling the two in his *Inventing America: Jefferson's Declaration of Independence* (New York: Doubleday, 1978), p. 232.

[17] A concise introduction to the problems of "moral sense" is to be found in the online article "Moral Epistemology," in *The Stanford Encyclopedia of Philosophy* (https://plato.stanford.edu/), first published February 4, 2003, with substantive revision November 18, 2015.

moral sentiments. Herbert Spencer made an effort at social responsibility, with his argument that "survival of the fittest," despite its apparent cruelty, could be reconciled with morality. Allowing the strong to crush the weak would be ultimately beneficial to society, by the process of eliminating inferior stocks. In the ensuing twentieth century, "Austrian school libertarians," such as Friedrich Hayek, Ludwig von Mises, and Murray Rothbart, and the "objectivist" Ayn Rand repudiated even the reverse-altruism of Herbert Spencer. For the extreme libertarians of the twentieth century, any function of government other than the protection of private property was the equivalent of slavery. Within such a strict definition of liberty, even such a modest proposal for civic welfare as Thomas Jefferson's tax-supported public education would be seen as abusive. [18]

But one finds nothing in Jefferson, in Smith, or in Locke approaching Ayn Rand's so-called "virtue of selfishness," because she was a coolly rational atheist, and her system lacked the erudite irony of Mandeville's *Fable of the Bees*, which made the satirical and paradoxical observation that acts of selfishness work to the good of society. Rand and the Social Darwinists offered a humorless and superficial reformulation of Bernard Mandeville's position, and were remote from the idea of selfless public service, putatively idealized in the Jeffersonian conception of civic virtue. Jefferson's republicanism rests on the idea of a good God, who endows natural aristocrats and virtuous yeomen alike with social instincts. The components of a free republic must always comprise the homely virtue of the yeoman class, the leadership of the "wise and good," the benevolence of "natural aristocrats," with "virtue and wisdom enough to

[18] A seminal expression of the Lockean liberal thesis is Louis Hartz, *The Liberal Tradition in America* (New York: Harcourt, Brace and Company, 1955). The pivotal study in the civic humanist tradition, sometimes referred to as the republican tradition, is J. G. A. Pocock, *The Machiavellian Moment: Florentine Political Thought and the Atlantic Republican Tradition* (Princeton University Press, 2003). For additional nuances on American republican ideology, the writings of Bernard Bailyn and Gordon S. Wood are essential, e.g. Bailyn, *The Ideological Origins of the American Revolution* (Cambridge, MA: Harvard University Press, 1967), and Wood, *The Creation of the American Republic, 1776–1787* (New York: Norton, 1969). An early summary of the supposed dichotomy between the paradigms of Lockean liberalism and civic humanism is in Isaac Kramnick, "Republican Revisionism Revisited," *The American Historical Review*, 87, no. 3 (June, 1982), 629–664. It should be noted that antebellum racists such as Calhoun and Fitzhugh rejected *laissez-faire* economics, which they interpreted as a key component of heartless, Northern industrial capitalism. By contrast, post-bellum racists like Spencer accepted *laissez-faire* economics as a fundamental correlative of their Social Darwinist biological theories.

manage the concerns of the society," deriving their authority from an electorate endowed with moral instincts and common sense.[19]

GOVERNMENT AND STATE OF NATURE

Jefferson accepted Locke's premise that freedom is mankind's natural state; that life is a natural right; that governments exist in order to "ensure these rights."[20] But although government did not create rights, natural rights were implicitly in jeopardy without the existence of government. Aristotle, who was on one occasion denounced by Jefferson as a mystic, but cited as an authority in the letter to Lee, had argued "that man is by nature a political animal," whose natural state was to be under government. Aristotle never said that the function of government was to protect liberty, as Jefferson implied in the letter to Lee. It is debatable whether there ever has been a government that made the protection of liberty its primary function, as Jefferson implied in the Declaration. *Par contra*, Hobbes and Locke had argued or implied that governments are instituted to protect life and property, sometimes at the price of liberty. Life and property are otherwise uncertain, due to what Locke calls the "inconveniences" of the natural state. This amounts to admitting that whatever rights and freedoms humans might have in a natural state are theoretically present, but practically useless, outside the social contract. Jefferson says governments "ensure" liberty, but others say that the very nature of a social contract is to sacrifice liberty for security.[21]

John C. Calhoun later carried this notion much farther, implicitly and directly attacking Jefferson, Smith, Paine, Hobbes, and anyone else who claimed that government is an artificial state of mankind.[22] Calhoun saw government as "of Divine ordination" and asserted moreover that society "would be defeated without government," an essential to human culture,

[19] Jefferson to John Adams, October 28, 1813.

[20] Locke, *Second Treatise of Government*, Chapter 9, Section 123, lists freedom as a right, but also acknowledges that its existence in the state of nature, like the right of property, is tenuous, hence the necessity of law and government. See also *Second Treatise of Government*, Chapter 2, Section 4.

[21] Jefferson to Benjamin Waterhouse, October 13, 1815, referred to "the jargon of Plato, of Aristotle & other mystics."

[22] Needless to say, both Locke and Jefferson rejected Hobbes' idea that the natural state of mankind was a state of "Warre," since they believed that human beings were naturally inclined and divinely fashioned for harmonious living in a social state.

and to everything that made human existence meaningful.[23] Calhoun was joined in this assertion not only by other white supremacists and defenders of slavery, like George Fitzhugh, but subsequently by black abolitionists like Alexander Crummell, who wrote in the tradition of Cambridge Platonism. Law and order were among the most basic needs of mankind, and *laissez-faire* libertarianism, as Crummell and his younger associate W. E. B. Du Bois well knew, did not necessarily sustain the rights and liberties of weak and powerless minorities.

Jefferson wisely recognized that governments do not automatically guarantee rights and liberties either, and he was at least as uncomfortable as Locke with any suggestion that rights derived from government, or that the price of security in society must be the sacrifice of personal liberty. Anyone might appreciate the famous paradox identified by Benjamin Franklin that "Those who would give up essential Liberty, to purchase a little temporary Safety, deserve neither Liberty nor Safety."[24] On the other hand, it could not be denied that Hobbes and Burke were correct in stating what Locke only tacitly admitted, that there is a wide gap between the nebulous theoretical rights that the individual may possess in a mythical state of natural liberty and the practical and enforceable rights they derive from a social contract.[25]

Jefferson was economically chained to a social contract that he claimed to despise, and within that system the contradiction between the *state* of liberty and the *right* to property was everywhere self-evident. Jefferson was not fond of quoting Aristotle, and yet Monticello's very existence confirmed the Aristotelian principle that slavery was based on a perceived economic necessity. Whether or not they are born free, both the slaveholders and their slaves are everywhere in the psychological chains that bind every individual in every social relationship. It is the nature of the social contract to curtail liberty, and the fundamental nature of the social contract is that liberty must be moderate in order to ensure life and

[23] John C. Calhoun's attack on Jeffersonian egalitarianism appeared in the posthumously published *Disquisition on Government* (1851) as a systematic attack on the principles of the Declaration of Independence. He served in Congress during the War of 1812 and was a leader of the "War Hawks." His career illustrated the shifting ideology of the Democratic Party, and splits within it, during the Age of Jackson. Similar attacks on the egalitarian notions of the Declaration of Independence were launched by George Fitzhugh and by the black intellectuals Alexander Crummell and W. E. B. Du Bois.

[24] It is necessary to digress at this point on Benjamin Franklin's well-known comment, "Pennsylvania Assembly: Reply to the Governor," November 11, 1755; as cited in Leonard W. Labaree, ed., *The Papers of Benjamin Franklin* (New Haven, CT: Yale University Press, 1963), vol. VI, p. 242.

[25] Locke, *Second Treatise of Government*, Chapter 8, Sections 95, 96, 97.

property. Aristotle had defended slavery as necessary to the functioning of society, but Jefferson's religious beliefs and Enlightenment liberalism did not allow him to endorse Aristotle's position, although he listed Aristotle as a fundamental influence on the Declaration of Independence.

Jefferson's genius at reconciling this and other intellectual contradictions – not to mention his pragmatic ones – remains impenetrable, due to his own cavalier vagueness. Joseph Ellis' depiction of him as an "American Sphinx" is not without merit, at least with respect to his ideological impenetrability.[26] He remains enigmatic despite the rich commentaries on his words, his reading habits, and his personal life provided by generations of such scholars as Kevin Hayes and John Boles, who have so impressively reconstructed the relationship between his daily experiences and the thoughts he set down in writing.[27]

Jefferson's intellectual biographers have been cautious about identifying which of Aristotle's ideas are supposed to have influenced his writing of the Declaration. Jefferson received repeated queries from Isaac H. Tiffany asking him to explain his reverence for Aristotle. They mostly went unanswered, except for one response regarding republicanism: "the introduction of this new principle of representative democracy has rendered useless almost every thing written before on the structure of government: and in a great measure relieves our regret if the political writings of Aristotle, or of any other antient, have been lost." This serves to make his later references to Cicero and Aristotle in the letter to Henry Lee even more puzzling.[28]

Jefferson's altruistic, egalitarian rhetoric led him inevitably into conflict with Edmund Burke, for while the Dublin-born statesman accepted the idea that the Revolution was justifiable, his opinions were linked to his

[26] Joseph Ellis, *American Sphinx: The Character of Thomas Jefferson* (New York: Knopf, 1997).

[27] Glimpses of Jefferson's private life are provided by Fawn Brodie's *Thomas Jefferson: An Intimate History* (New York: Norton, 1974). Jon Meacham's *Jefferson and the Art of Power* (New York: Random House, 2013) is laudatory, but "humanizing." Kevin J. Hayes' excellent *The Road to Monticello: The Life and Mind of Thomas Jefferson* (New York: Oxford University Press, 2008) at times resembles a log in its detail. Annette Gordon-Reed and Peter S. Onuf's *"Most Blessed of the Patriarchs": Thomas Jefferson and the Empire of the Imagination* (New York: Liveright, 2017) is sometimes speculative. Also see John B. Boles, *Jefferson: Architect of American Liberty* (New York: Basic Books, 2017).

[28] Becker, *Declaration of Independence*, cites Jefferson's reference to Aristotle once in passing. Merrill Peterson's mention is likewise cursory. As of this writing, the *Jefferson Encyclopedia* and the Monticello website mention the several queries from Isaac H. Tiffany, but do not quote Jefferson's response, which I cite here, Jefferson to Isaac H. Tiffany, August 26, 1816.

sympathies for the rights of the rising British middle-class elite. Burke voiced the standard refrain that liberty is the opposite of slavery, although "slavery" was an inappropriate metaphor for the American colonial condition. Burke's good friend, Samuel Johnson, asked, "How is it that we hear the loudest yelps for liberty among the drivers of negroes?" – a question that cannot be repeated often enough. Johnson was quick to observe that taxation was no tyranny, and unlike Burke accepted the spurious notion that Americans needed no representation other than the virtual representation they already had in Parliament.[29]

Recondite discussions of eighteenth-century British constitutionalism are stimulating to the mind and satisfying to its aesthetic demands, but what is pertinent right here is that persons of various political persuasions, regardless of whether or not they supported the American cause, expressed objections to the reasoning of Paine's *Common Sense* and Jefferson's Declaration. Jefferson might have responded to Johnson by anticipating John Stuart Mill's rationalization that the temporary subordination of "barbarians" was justifiable until they are fit for self-government. Burke did not voice any sentiment approximating that, but he did share Johnson's bourgeois conservative fear of anarchy. His support of the Revolution had little or nothing to do with the Declaration's implicit radicalism, as became evident years later, when he saw the French Reign of Terror as a manifestation of egalitarian extremism.

Jeremy Bentham shared Johnson's view that the Declaration was a hypocritical protest written by the drivers of slaves. He collaborated with John Lind in publishing a critique of the Declaration with a passing reference to its charge that the king had "excited domestic insurrections amongst us." The following paragraph may be read as a defense of Lord Dunmore's promises of freedom to African Americans who would take up arms on the side of the Loyalists.

> Is it for *them* to say, that it is tyranny to bid a slave to be free? to bid him to take courage, to rise and assist in reducing his tyrants to a due obedience to law? to hold out as a motive to him, that the load which crushed his limbs shall be lightened; that the whip which harrowed up his back shall be broken, that he shall be raised to the rank of a freeman and a citizen? It is their boast that they shall have taken up arms in support of these their own *self evident truths*—that "all men are *equal*" – "that all men are endowed with the unalienable rights of life, liberty and the *pursuit of happiness*." Is it for them to complain *of the offer of freedom* held out

[29] *Speech of Edmund Burke, Esq., on Moving His Resolutions for Conciliation with the Colonies*, March 22, 1775. Samuel Johnson, *Taxation No Tyranny* (1779).

to these wretched beings? of the offer of reinstating them in that *equality* which, in this very paper, is declared to be the *gift of God to all;* in those *unalienable rights,* with which, in this very paper, God is declared to have *endowed all* mankind?[30]

Bentham and Lind's objections were not only political, but philosophical as well. Their essays took umbrage at something more than the Declaration's attack on a monarch whom they considered a "patriot king." They challenged the document's basic philosophical assumptions concerning human nature and natural rights. Bentham apparently agreed with the philosophical objections to the Declaration contained in Lind's essay, and presented his contribution to the volume "A Short Review of the Declaration" by saying, "Of the preamble, I have taken little or no notice. The truth is little or none does it deserve." He nonetheless affixed his remarks to a document that analyzed the preamble, and his collaborator made the following statements:

What difference these acute legislators suppose between the laws of Nature, and of Nature's God, is more than I can take upon me to determine, or even to guess. If to what they now demand they were entitled by any law of God, they had only to produce that law, and all controversy was at an end. Instead of this, what do they produce? What they call self-evident truths. "All men," they tell us, "are created equal." This surely is a new discovery; now for the first time, we learn, that a child at the moment of his birth has the same quantity of natural power as the parent, the same quantity of natural power as the magistrate.[31]

The foregoing allusion to the "natural power" that a parent holds over their child placed Bentham and Lind in the same camp as Locke, who also saw the powers of government as analogous to those of parents within a family. But they deviated from Locke's position with their unequivocal assertion of the "natural" legitimacy of magisterial power. Basing a theory of government on an analogy to the parent–child relationship must

[30] Jeremy Bentham, "A Short Review of the Declaration" in John Lind and Jeremy Bentham, *An Answer to the Declaration of the American Congress* (London: T. Cadell, J. Walter and T. Sewell, 1776), pp. 119–132. Robert G. Parkinson, *The Common Cause: Creating Race and Nation in the American Revolution* (Chapel Hill: University of North Carolina Press, 2016), p. 51. David Armitage in "The Declaration of Independence and International Law," *The William and Mary Quarterly*, 59 (January, 2002), 39–64. Armitage argues convincingly that the book's philosophical objections to the Declaration were in accord with Bentham's opinions, as he "remained consistently critical of the principles that underlay the American Declaration to the end of his life," 54. Jeremy Bentham's attack on the Declaration is reprinted in Robert Ginsberg, ed., *A Casebook on The Declaration of Independence* (New York: Thomas Y. Crowell Company, 1967), pp. 9–17, although it is there attributed to John Lind.

[31] Bentham, "Short Review," 120.

logically undermine any assertion that "all men are created equal," since all men are born into the status of children. But there are more effective arguments against the congenital equality of mankind, such as those later made by Adams and Madison. We have felt obliged to return to Madison and Adams' agreements for the unequal distribution of talents and faculties several times throughout these pages. All human beings are born with obvious inequalities, first in terms of their mental, physical, and character traits, and secondly with respect to legal faculties and property rights.

JEFFERSONIAN LIBERTY INSEPARABLE FROM LANDED PROPERTY

How was it that Jefferson managed to leave property rights out of the Declaration of Independence, since the concept of liberty is so intertwined with property in Jeffersonian thought, and especially since he had made efforts in redrafting the Virginia Constitution to make free land available to those who did not yet possess it? Anticipating this question, Stanley Katz cites Jefferson's often-quoted letter to Madison, October 28, 1785:

> Wherever there is in any country, uncultivated lands and unemployed poor, it is clear that the laws of property have been so far extended as to violate natural right. The earth is given as a common stock for man to labour and live on. If, for the encouragement of industry we allow it to be appropriated, we must take care that other employment be furnished to those excluded from the appropriation.

The answer is that Jefferson never said that property was a natural right, as Paine's agrarianism had implied. He saw the right to land as deriving from usufruct, as was appropriate for a disciple of Locke. Locke's labor theory of property averred that when someone brings land under cultivation, "It being by him removed from the common state nature hath placed it in, it hath by this labour something annexed to it, that excludes the common right of other men." From this Jefferson deduced that tillers of the soil had a justifiable right to land "at least," as Locke had said, "where there is enough, and as good, left in common for others."

Those who brought virgin land under cultivation might justify their right to it. Those who hogged up uncultivated lands were in violation of nature, and thus Jefferson's lamentation that, in France, the right to property had come into conflict with the law of nature, but this could happen only in a nation where kings monopolized lands purely so they could enjoy the luxury of their hunting preserves. In America there were no kings, and his reform of the Virginia Code had done away with primogeniture and other medieval abuses that limited the common people's access to land. Jefferson was obviously not so radical as to maintain that "those who labor for my happiness" were by right of usufruct entitled to the lands they worked. It was sufficient in his mind that he had somewhat increased possibilities for white males to own land.

William Jennings Bryan, in his essay for the *Jefferson Papers* Memorial Edition, declared that "The rights of life, liberty and the pursuit of happiness carry with them the inherent, unalienable, equal right of all to land."[32] Bryan extended Jeffersonian reasoning farther than Jefferson did, although Jefferson clearly believed that without a fee simple estate there could be no independent yeoman farmer and no "Jeffersonian democracy." It is therefore interesting that Jefferson did not declare, at least in this instance, the existence of a natural right to property. By avoiding the word "property," the Declaration of Independence avoided the abstract philosophical debate over whether property was a natural right, and left it to government to legislate any homestead act. Jefferson wrote later, and in a different context, that it was "a moot question whether the origin of any kind of property is derived from nature at all."[33]

The philosopher Ayn Rand makes a rational, if disputable, claim that the right to liberty and all other rights derive from property rights.[34] "Dependency breeds subservience," and the individual is always beholden unless he possesses property. The farmer realizes republican liberty through ownership of a farm "in full and absolute dominion." Liberty, in the "lost world of Thomas Jefferson," is inseparable from farm ownership. One has a right to place one's feet on an acre and breathe the air above it if one owns that acre. His efforts as a lawyer were "agrarian," in the sense that he called for the distribution of forfeited and unappropriated lands as a precursor to the later homestead acts.

[32] William Jennings Bryan, "Jefferson and the Land Question" in A. E. Bergh, ed., *The Writings of Thomas Jefferson* (Washington, DC: The Thomas Jefferson Memorial Association, 1907), vol. XVI. Cf. Thorstein Veblen's skeptical critique, "The Independent Farmer" in *Absentee Ownership* (New York: Huebsch, 1923), pp. 129–141.

[33] Jefferson to Isaac McPherson, August 13, 1813.

[34] Robert Nozick, one-time head of the philosophy department at Harvard University, indicated a weakness in Ayn Rand's argument, which he found to be circular. Since property rights and right to life seemed to be interdependent, the right to one could not provide the foundation for the other. See Nozick, *Anarchy, State, and Utopia* (New York: Basic Books, 1974), p. 179. Ayn Rand, "Man's Rights" in *The Virtue of Selfishness* (New York: Signet, 1964), p. 94.

Liberty would be most secure in a fee simple empire of small farmers. "They are the most vigorous, the most independent, the most virtuous, and they are tied to their country, and wedded to its liberty and interests, by the most lasting bonds." Jefferson employed his presidential powers to oppose the concentration of public lands in the hands of big investors and speculators, but in his libertarian society public lands should be available for development by private entrepreneurs.[35] Jefferson wanted sales of public lands in the West to go to small farmers. Republicans in control of Congress passed the Land Law of 1800, reducing the minimum individual purchase of land in the West to 320 acres. In 1804 they reduced it further, to 160 acres. At least theoretically this would remove big land speculators from the market and keep the family farm within the purchasing power of small farmers.[36]

NUNC DIMITTIS ON LIFE, LIBERTY, PROPERTY, AND PEACE

Dumas Malone may have been correct in classifying Jefferson as "a philosophical statesman rather than a political philosopher."[37] He made no attempt to formally eliminate all contradictions from his philosophy, and the Declaration's ideas, as he admitted, were not novel. In fact, Jefferson's political ideology was unclear, but the magical cloudiness of the words "pursuit of happiness" perhaps contained more of a revolutionary spark than the word "property." Still, property appeared forcefully in one of his later statements. "Life, liberty, property and peace" were the goals of Jeffersonian democracy, as their author expressed them in December of 1825, after almost fifty years of reflection, and only a few months before his death.[38] This mature and considered iteration differed from the words "life, liberty and pursuit of happiness" a half century earlier in the Declaration of Independence, as much as it did

[35] The libertarian Cato Institute offers "a blueprint for auctioning off all public lands over 20 to 40 years." See Terry L. Anderson, Vernon L. Smith, and Emily Simmons, "How and Why to Privatize Federal Lands," The Cato Institute, *Policy Analysis*, 363 (December 9, 1999): www.cato.org/publications/policy-analysis/how-why-privatize-federal-lands

[36] Johnson, S. Lyle, "Fight for the Pre-Emption Law of 1841," *Arkansas Academy of Science Journal*, 4 (1951), 165–172. Retrieved January 27, 2013.

[37] Malone, "Jefferson," in *The Concise Dictionary of American Biography* (New York: Charles Scribner's Sons, 1964).

[38] Jefferson, *Draft Declaration and Protest of the Commonwealth of Virginia* (December, 1825), in Merrill Peterson, ed., *Thomas Jefferson, Writings* (New York: Literary Classics of the United States, 1984), p. 484.

from Locke's actual words, "life, liberty and estate."[39] Substitute the word "property" for "estate," and Jefferson's 1825 utterance resembles more closely the better-known of the two Lockean phrases. The French "Declaration of the Rights of Man" elevates the security and enjoyment of property to the status of an inalienable right.[40] If, as Edmund S. Morgan and others have ably demonstrated, the citizen freeholder is the core constituent of Jeffersonian liberty, it is not absurd to infer that ownership of real estate is absolutely essential to Jeffersonian liberty.[41]

Despite Jefferson's possessiveness about the Declaration's wording, it is known that he presented a draft to Benjamin Franklin, and presumably discussed it with him. Other members of the Committee of Five presumably reviewed and discussed Jefferson's drafts with him. Benjamin Franklin is supposed to have made immediate minor corrections, and Congress made substantive changes after that. Franklin might have had something to do with the omission of property from the Declaration's list of natural rights and the substitution of "pursuit of happiness." Benjamin Franklin, like Jefferson, rejected the idea of an inalienable right to property. In fact, Franklin once wrote: "Private Property is a Creature of Society ... and is subject to the Calls of that Society, whenever its Necessities shall require it, even to its last Farthing."[42] Jefferson never

[39] The Virginia Declaration of Rights, June 12, 1776, written by George Mason, mentions happiness among "the fundamental natural rights of mankind." Jack N. Rakove, *The Annotated US Constitution and Declaration of Independence* (Cambridge, MA: Belknap Press, 2009), p. 78. Scholars debate whether the "Founding Documents" of the United States are based on "Lockean liberalism," "civic humanism," "the Scottish Enlightenment," or other sixteenth-, seventeenth-, and eighteenth-century schools of thought.

[40] Jefferson's influence on the French Declaration of 1789 is difficult to ascertain; his influences on the never-adopted version of 1793, even more obscure. Jefferson's influence on Lafayette and the French "Declaration of the Rights of Man" is undeniable, but also problematic. A commentary on the Library of Congress website notes that "In a July 9, 1789 letter to Jefferson, General Lafayette (1757–1834) asked for Jefferson's 'observations' on 'my bill of rights' before presenting it to the National Assembly." See www.loc.gov/exhibits/jefferson/jeffworld.html

[41] The theme runs throughout Christopher Michael Curtis, *Jefferson's Freeholders and the Politics of Ownership in the Old Dominion* (Cambridge University Press, 2012), although he offers sage words of caution and nuance. In particular, see his splendid Introduction. Edmund S. Morgan, *The Meaning of Independence* (New York: Norton, 1978), pp. 69–70.

[42] Franklin, like Rousseau, sees private property as a product not of natural right, but of the social contract. See Benjamin Franklin's letter to Robert Morris, December 25, 1783, which is reproduced in J. A. Leo Lemay, ed., *Benjamin Franklin: Writings* (New York: Library of America, 1987), pp. 1081–1082. Also see Benjamin Franklin, "Queries and Remarks Respecting Alterations in the Constitution of Pennsylvania" in Albert H. Smyth,

went quite that far, but he too believed that "stable ownership is the gift of social law," and he was not prepared to say unequivocally that private property had its origins in nature. He had built much of his intellectual career on undermining antiquated conventions of property, such as the inalienability of estate, as it had been defined under the tradition of primogeniture.

Franklin apparently raised no more objection to the facile manipulation of the word "liberty," and he questioned whether property was a natural right. Fifty years earlier, he had problematized "liberty" in his precocious "Dissertation on Liberty," published at the age of 19. He almost immediately sought to withdraw it from circulation, but fortunately he failed. He had questioned whether the concept of liberty had any validity at all. How could we speak of political liberty if human beings did not have free will? The clever lad had demonstrated that the notion of liberty could be challenged on Calvinistic or on Newtonian grounds. Furthermore, even at age 19, Benjamin Franklin was aware that the concepts of political liberty and justice could not be divorced from the Calvinistic concept of predestination or the Newtonian concept of causality. Before discussing political freedom, he must first of all confront the question of whether the human condition allows for any freedom at all. Voltaire addressed the same question, and his more mature reflections on the nature of liberty showed that the concept might be as easily ridiculed by a ripe scholar as dissected by the teenaged Franklin. Every literate person in 1776, having encountered St. Paul, Martin Luther, John Milton, and Thomas Hobbes, realized that the definition of liberty was neither common-sensical nor self-evident.[43]

Of course, Thomas Jefferson believed in private property; that is beyond question, but he could not come to a permanent position on whether private property was a natural right. He believed that everyone had a right to pursue the happiness of owning property, but he did not believe that the right to inherit land was "inalienable," because people owned land only in usufruct. The right to own land derived from occupying it and farming it. For this reason it was very easy for him to justify his

ed., *The Writings of Benjamin Franklin* (New York: Macmillan, 1905–07), vol. X, pp. 58–60.

43 Voltaire is the author of sometimes inspirational and sometimes sarcastic opinions on liberty and free will. On the more abstract question of free will, he denied it and took a position similar to that of the young Franklin. Voltaire, "Franc Arbitre," *Dictionnaire philosophique* [1764] in *Œuvres complètes de Voltaire* (Oxford: Voltaire Foundation, 1968), vol. XXXVI.

policy of "persuading" the Indians to give up their lands. The matter is discussed elsewhere in this volume in connection with his correspondence with William Henry Harrison and Andrew Jackson. Since only those who made legitimate use of the land were entitled to it, the "barbarian" Indians had no more right to their game lands than the decadent French nobility to their hunting preserves. By the logic of usufruct, Indians were no better than Louis XVI and other monarchs, who retained lands only for hunting.[44]

Jefferson's position on property in patents "changed over the years," states Russell L. Martin, but Jefferson's positions were mutable on many things. His most eloquent argument against patents was in his 1813 letter to Isaac McPherson, discussed in the introduction to the present volume.[45] He was an inveterate tinkerer, and Monticello was replete with his clever inventions, also discussed elsewhere. If Jefferson's importance as an inventor had ever paralleled that of Eli Whitney, who lost considerably from patent infringement, he might have shown greater toleration for patents. He understood the logic of the Constitution's Article 1, Section 8, which gives Congress power "to promote the progress of science and useful arts, by securing for limited times to authors and inventors the exclusive right to their respective writings and discoveries." Given his devotion to strict construction, and the flexibility with which he was able to modify his principles in accord with his interests, it is interesting to speculate that if any of his inventions had ever met a mass-market demand, and if he had held a valid patent on it, he might have taken a strong position on the right to patents, as he languished increasingly under the burden of debt.

More than once over the course of fifty years Jefferson made reference to the rights of "life, liberty, and property," but if he believed, as he stated, that the question of a natural right to property was moot, he was in fundamental disaccord with the French "Declaration of the Rights of Man," which enumerated a right to property. Jefferson is frequently mentioned as Lafayette's collaborator in the drafting of the French

[44] Jefferson to William H. Harrison, Washington, February 27, 1803: "When they withdraw themselves to the culture of a small piece of land, they will perceive how useless to them are their extensive forests, and will be willing to pare them off from time to time in exchange for necessaries for their farms and families."

[45] Jefferson's position on property in patents "changed over the years," observes Russell L. Martin in a signed article in *The Thomas Jefferson Encyclopedia*, at www.monticello.org/site/research-and-collections/tje Martin cites Jefferson to James Madison, August 28, 1789. His opposition to patents on ideas is cited in the introduction to the present work, Jefferson to Isaac McPherson, August 13, 1813.

Declaration, although his autobiography says little about that collaboration and does not mention his participating in any discussion as to the insertion of property as a natural right. He mentions that Lafayette asked him to host a meeting in his home, at which he describes himself as "a silent witness." On the following day, he assured Count Montmorin, the foreign minister, that although the meeting had taken place in his house, he participated in the "character of a neutral and passive spectator."[46]

Jefferson never mentioned the French Declaration's insistence on a right to property. There exists in his own hand a Draft of a Charter of Rights, which Boyd believes he "evidently" sent to Lafayette. Malone speculates that "Jefferson's influence on the Marquis in this connection was probably greater than appears in any formal record, but neither Conor Cruise O'Brien, nor William Howard Adams makes any great claims for Jefferson's participation."[47] The draft, which is in English, includes the wording that "No person shall be restrained in his liberty" without due process of law, but mentions neither property nor the pursuit of happiness. There were certainly other discussions with Lafayette and other French patriots concerning their "Declaration of the Rights of Man," but the final wording, with its provisions on property, were closer to those of Locke than to those of Jefferson's American Declaration. Article 2 declares that "The aim of all political association is the preservation of the natural and imprescriptible rights of man. These rights are liberty, property, security, and resistance to oppression." Article 17 declares that "property is an inviolable and sacred right." Words such as "natural," "imprescriptible," "inviolable," and "sacred" assert that property rights are natural and self-evident, not "moot."

Usufruct was a convenient idea for Jefferson's denial of the claims of Marie Antoinette or Chief Tecumseh to ancestral hunting preserves, but it does not preclude giving land to one's children, or for claiming territories for the United States in perpetuity. On the land question, he hedged both theoretically and pragmatically, as he did on numerous other matters, including the church–state question, the elasticity of the Constitution, the expansion of slavery into the territories, and the very existence of slavery itself. Jefferson was no more willing to divest himself and his heirs of

[46] Jefferson's description of this meeting is in his *Autobiography*, in Peterson, ed., *Thomas Jefferson, Writings*, p. 96.

[47] See William Howard Adams, *The Paris Years of Thomas Jefferson* (New Haven, CT: Yale University Press, 1997), pp. 284–286, 291–293. Dumas Malone, *Jefferson and His Time*, 6 vols. (Boston, MA: Little, Brown, 1951), vol. II, *Jefferson and the Rights of Man*, p. 223.

uncultivated real estate than he was to divest himself and his heirs of slaves. In sum, Jefferson's concept of "usufruct" was as flexible and "pragmatic" as his concept of liberty.

Jefferson and Adams were more sympathetic to democracy than was Madison, and both rejected Madison's republic–democracy dichotomy, and maintained that a republic was only another form of democracy. "*The Federalist* is a valuable work," he wrote, "and Mr. Madison's part in it as respectable as any other. But his distinction between a republic and a democracy cannot be justified. A democracy is as really a republic as an oak is a tree, or a temple a building." Jefferson, on this abstract issue, sided with Adams against Madison, calling "a democracy the only pure republic, but impracticable beyond the limits of a town."[48] One thing that must be borne in mind is that all three authors could vary their opinions over a lifetime, if not from day to day, and would certainly have objected to their ideas being taken out of context and deployed by demagogues. All three believed in a republican form of government in which interested landholders would elect the best from among themselves, and in which political culture would provide not a mirror of the society, but a filter.[49]

It was not difficult for Franklin D. Roosevelt to find in the historian Claude Bowers the anticipation of progressivism in Jefferson's preachments and actions. Bowers could not have predicted one obvious parallel that must eventually have occurred to the author of the New Deal. Jefferson effected a gigantic land purchase as a means to ensure the future of agrarian capitalism; Roosevelt effected tremendous military purchases towards the end of saving the day for industrial capitalism.[50]

Jefferson's libertarian reasoning was never so thorough as the rational "objectivism" of Ayn Rand, when she asserted that the right to life could not be implemented without presuming the existence of a right to

48 John Adams expressed his disagreement with Madison's dichotomy in a letter to J. H. Tiffany, March 31, 1819. Also see Jefferson to Isaac H. Tiffany, August 26, 1816.

49 Jack Rakove addresses the issue in the chapter "The Mirror of Representation" in his *Original Meanings* (New York: Vintage, 1997), and Gordon Wood, "The Nature of Representation," confronts it in *The Creation of the American Republic*. Wood revisits the problem of representation in *The Radicalism of the American Revolution* (New York: Vintage, 1991), pp. 245, 257, 259, 294.

50 Arthur M. Schlesinger, Jr., commented on Roosevelt's review of Claude Bowers, *Jefferson and Hamilton* (Cambridge, MA: Riverside Press, 1925) in Schlesinger, *The Crisis of the Old Order, 1919–1933* (Cambridge, MA: Riverside Press, 1957), p. 104. Roosevelt's review was in the *New York World* (November, 1925). An incisive commentary on Bowers is contained in Andrew Burstein, *Democracy's Muse: How Thomas Jefferson Became a Liberal, a Reagan Republican, and a Tea Party Fanatic, All the While Being Dead* (Charlottesville, VA: University of Virginia Press, 2015), pp. 4–6.

property. "Without property rights no other rights are possible," says Rand.[51] According to her logic, "The right to life is the most basic of all rights." But since the right to property is necessary to life, did she mean to say that only those who are capable of owning property could assert a right to life? No one has a right to till the land or to breathe the air above it unless they own that land, otherwise they must establish their farm or factory at the sufferance of some other individual, the person who does own it. Jefferson believed that every person had an inalienable right to life, but as for the bread, the staff of life, the individual had only a right to "pursue" his daily bread. If his right to work implied that he possess land and farming implements, no one should stand in the way of a white yeoman farmer's pursuing 40 acres and a mule, but no government should provide them, or guarantee them.

If, as Ayn Rand asserts, "The right to life is the source of all rights—and the right to property is their only implementation," then the right to property is inseparable from the right to life.[52] And there's the rub, for someone owned most of the arable real estate in Jefferson's Virginia, and thus only those clever enough to become land-owning yeoman farmers could enjoy Jefferson's "inalienable" right to life. Those who had no property could live only at the sufferance of those who did own property. The libertarian economists and Randian objectivists assert an inalienable and absolute right to property such that no one has a right to work except on the terms dictated by whatever proprietor will allow them to work on his property. And anyone who must ask an employer to provide their bread must be willing to submit to whatever terms are dictated by that employer if they wish to eat and live. Thus, Jefferson's summation is as correct as it is tidy: "Dependency begets subservience and venality, suffocates the germ of virtue." Ayn Rand's objectivism carries Jeffersonian logic to an inescapable conclusion – that a servant can have no interests independent of the interests of the master. If Leporelo is appalled by Don Giovanni's "barbaro appetito," he is perfectly free to seek a better boss, "padron miglior," but his dependency on the Don will suffocate any possibility of virtue.

Historian Christopher Michael Curtis is convincing when he writes of "the conflation of liberty with ownership" in Jefferson's thinking, for rights and liberties were inseparable from his theory of yeoman independence. Jefferson undertook a remedy in the form of legislative efforts at land reform

[51] Robert Nozick's rebuttal in *Anarchy, State, and Utopia*, noted above, is logically formidable, but Rand's position and Jefferson's are, in a practical sense, convincing.

[52] Ayn Rand, "Man's Rights" in *The Virtue of Selfishness* (New York: Signet, 1961), p. 94.

in Virginia through the eradication of primogeniture and entail. His ideology of freedom was not only based on sentimental notions of the traditional freedoms of the English freeholder. His practical efforts at the eradication of primogeniture and entail were designed to extend the rights and liberties that derived from land ownership in an agricultural political economy. By implication, there is a contradiction between the natural rights theory of liberty and the social contract theory of liberty. If rights derive ultimately from the traditions of Anglo-Saxon law, they cannot be attributed to the Christian God or any other God. Jefferson's legal land reforms were an attempt to restore a concept of rights that had sprung up naturally in the forests of Germany and been transported by the Saxons to English soil.

While Franklin and Paine believed that property was "the gift of society," or the "effect of Society," John Locke asserted that property, or "estate," was a natural right, and that theft should be a capital crime. That is, Locke went so far as to imply that, on the mere suspicion that someone might potentially steal from him, he had a right to deprive that person of his life. Garry Wills and others have rightly addressed, without resolving it, the problem of Jefferson's leaving the right to property out of the Declaration's pontification on rights. Other discussions of life and liberty have recognized the linkage of property to any discussion of rights. Every modern philosopher, from John Locke to Ayn Rand, has found it necessary to address the problem of this linkage.

ETERNALLY IN PURSUIT OF HAPPINESS

In February of 1787, midway through the years of his residency in Paris, still plagued by his difficulties with the language and ill at ease with the sophisticated salon environment in which Benjamin Franklin had thrived, Jefferson wrote the following remarks to Anne Willing Bingham:[53]

> You are then engaged to tell me, truly and honestly, whether you do not find the tranquil pleasures of America preferable to the empty bustle of Paris. For, to what does that bustle tend? At eleven o 'clock, it is day, *chez madame* ... Thus the days of life are consumed, one by one, without an object beyond the present moment; ever flying from the ennui of that, yet carrying it with us; eternally in pursuit of happiness, which keeps eternally before us.

[53] Jefferson to Mrs. Bingham, February 7, 1787. Jefferson to St. John de Crèvecoeur, July 11, 1786: "Being unable to write in French so as to be sure of conveying my true meaning, or perhaps any meaning at all, I will beg of you to interpret what I have now the honour to write."

In this letter Jefferson's phrase "pursuit of happiness" is deployed more ironically, and with greater nuance, than is readily evident in the Declaration of Independence. The word "happiness," in the vocabulary of sophisticated English speakers, has always been more complicated than is recognized in the vernacular. Certainly, it meant something quite different to John Dryden, Samuel Johnson, and John Locke than it does to most of us, for to them "happiness" was not a synonym for "joy." The word "hap" is quite ancient, and shares etymological roots with Old Norse, Old English, and even some Old Slavonic words related to luck, fate, and circumstance. Jefferson would have used the word "happiness" as it was commonly employed in his era, to mean good fortune or good luck, as well as economic contentment. To this we might add that he delighted in ancient languages, including Anglo-Saxon, that he seldom selected any word without reflection, and that, as his letter to Anne Bingham reveals, he was hardly unaware of the ironies embedded in the Declaration's phrase "pursuit of happiness."

In Ralph Ellison's novel, *Invisible Man*, the malicious Dr. Bledsoe writes a damaging letter of reference for the novel's unsuspecting protagonist: "I beg of you, sir, to help him continue in the direction of that promise which, like the horizon, recedes ever brightly and distantly beyond the hopeful traveler."[54] Jefferson, himself a master of the poisoned pen, might have appreciated the character of Dr. Bledsoe and the image of a naïve black youth perpetually in pursuit of an illusion. It is pretty clear in Jefferson's letter to Mrs. Bingham that he was exquisitely aware of the irony imbedded in any allusions to an "eternal pursuit," and it is just as clear that the irony was, and remains, lost on persons of lesser genius than James Madison, John Adams, George Washington, and others on the list of Jefferson's ideal readers.

The phrase "pursuit of happiness" bore a similarity to that of the Virginia Declaration of Rights, attributed to George Mason and adopted June 12, 1776, which stated that "all men ... have certain inherent rights," including "the means of acquiring and possessing property, and pursuing and obtaining happiness and safety."[55]

54 A. Herbert Bledsoe's letter of recommendation in Ralph Ellison, *Invisible Man* (New York: Random House, 1952). Jefferson's poisoned pen and capacity for damning with faint praise are discussed elsewhere in the present work, e.g. in his obituary of George Washington.

55 Virginia Declaration of Rights, Articles 1 and 2, cited by Pauline Maier in *American Scripture* (New York: Knopf, 1997), p. 134.

The implication of the Virginia Declaration's wording is that people have natural rights that are congenital and innate, and that take precedence over any social contract, and that these include a right to property. This is presumably the meaning of that word "inalienable" or "unalienable." It means that no one has the power to give them up; nor can they be removed "by any compact."[56] Based on this, we must infer that Jefferson employed the term "inalienable" in accord with the Lockean prescription that fathers have certain rights over their children that they can neither give away nor have taken from them. Locke had gone so far as to insist that no persons had the power to enter into any social contract that deprived them of their inherent rights to life, to liberty, or to property, but then he had also said that anyone with a reputation as a thief could be summarily deprived of his life. Jefferson's Declaration of Independence paraphrased not Locke, but Mason in such a way as to offer a tacit confirmation of the latter's adaptation of John Locke. But Locke contained much that was unclear and equivocal, and Jefferson's word "inalienable" clearly had much more power in rhetoric than viability in law.[57]

Locke had discussed the human rights to life, liberty, and estate after a fashion, but neither the first nor the second Treatise on Government had directly asserted that these rights were "inalienable." Garry Wills argues that Jefferson probably derived his use of "inalienable" from Hutcheson, rather than from Locke. Be that as it may, I am in complete accord with Wills that Jefferson, as a practicing lawyer, had devoted considerable effort to undermining the conception of inalienability. Jefferson never offered any systematic definition of "inalienable" or any justification for his use of it. He does not tell us why he attempted to persuade Lafayette to omit property from the list of "inalienable" rights listed in the French "Declaration of the Rights of Man."[58] My point is that "inalienable" is

[56] Every draft of the Declaration in Jefferson's handwriting prefers the spelling "inalienable," although the printed draft on parchment and John Adams' rough draft prefer the spelling "unalienable." Eighteenth-century English spelling was irregular, and the writings of the Founders reflect the lack of standardization prevalent in their times. See www.ushistory.org/index.html

[57] One must ask whether Locke's proposition makes any rational sense. Jefferson approved of the guillotining of French aristocrats, thus providing a pragmatic contradiction of his abstract "right to life" principle. The duke of Windsor gave up his inalienable right to be king of England. American courts deny that criminals convicted of capital crimes have an inalienable right to life.

[58] Gilbert Chinard, *Thomas Jefferson, the Apostle of Americanism* (Boston, MA: Little, Brown, 1929), pp. 84, 85, 88, 233. Wills, *Inventing America*, p. 230.

a concept that has no practical manifestation in the course of human events, and whatever place it ever had in American law was obliterated thanks in part to Thomas Jefferson's revision of Virginia's property law.

POSITIVE AND NEGATIVE LIBERTY

The fact that the Declaration lists "liberty" and "pursuit of happiness" as separate entities reminds one of the distinction between "negative liberty" and "positive liberty" drawn by John Stuart Mill and later developed by Isaiah Berlin.[59] Negative liberty recognizes that in a state of nature there exists an absolute freedom from constraint. Positive liberty implies that in a state of nature there is an opportunity to pursue happiness. Positive liberty is in accord with the idea of Thomas Paine, argued in *Agrarian Justice*, that liberty from restraint guarantees no equality of opportunity. Paine raised the question of how one can exercise the liberty to pursue happiness if one is born into a world where all the land and all the water are already the property of other persons. The rights to life, liberty, and property and pursuit of happiness exist in the state of nature, but only in the negative sense that nobody has a right to kill, enslave, rob, or restrain someone else in their pursuit of happiness. But no one is obliged, in the state of nature, to found a land grant university, to provide lands for the yeomen, to free the slave, to enact Albert Gallatin's program of internal improvements, or to feed the hungry, clothe the naked, or provide health insurance. Was Paine saying that positive liberty implies the necessity of big government?

Jefferson's rights doctrine was inseparable from his theory of human nature, in that he believed in a moral instinct and an invisible hand that regulates human moral behavior. The invisible hand of God is detectable in a moral instinct, akin to and interactive with the aesthetic instinct, according to Adam Smith. The invisible hand is not confined solely or even primarily to the world of market forces: it is in the world of human senses. Jefferson's notion of a moral sense deviated from the epistemology of Locke's *Essay on Human Understanding*, which was based on the primacy of the traditional five senses in Lockean empiricism. Jefferson

[59] In a presentation by the present author at the University of Virginia in February of 2014, Peter Onuf very generously commented on an earlier version of these remarks and questioned whether my insertion of Mill's distinction between positive and negative liberty was appropriate. My response is that, in Jefferson's writings, there is ample evidence that he understood the distinction between "freedom from" and "freedom to," which is the principal distinction that Mill made in his discourses on liberty.

came much closer to the Earl of Shaftesbury's, Francis Hutcheson's, and Adam Smith's idea that there was also a "moral sense."[60] He objected to the "principle of Hobbes, that justice is founded in contract solely, and does not result from the construction of man. I believe, on the contrary, that it is instinct."[61]

Locke seems forced to imply, at least, some element of the moral instinct, as he hedges on the matter of what exactly liberty or freedom meant in the state of nature, and for this reason generations of scholars, including many in his own time, were unconvinced by Locke's assertions.[62] Locke was annoyed by certain critics, whom he did not always identify, who wanted to know how the champion of empiricism could assert the existence of a state of nature that neither he nor anyone else had ever seen. Thomas Hobbes and many of his contemporaries believed they had seen the state of nature during the Thirty Years War and the English Civil War. Hobbes had argued that only in the unnatural state of civilization did it make any sense to speak of rights. Hobbes' state of nature was a world of absolute and disgusting freedom, from which any sane person might wish to escape. Liberty made every man literally an outlaw, or outside the law, with the freedom to murder, rape, and steal. The source of all rights was thus, obviously, in a social contract, not in some indefinable and indemonstrable prior state of nature, whose existence was every bit as spurious as the Garden of Eden. The nineteenth-century Cambridge polymath William Whewell felt that Locke was, tacitly and effectively, if not openly or articulately, in the same camp with Hobbes. Locke obviously would have disagreed with this notion.[63]

Jefferson, like Locke and Rousseau, rejected the Hobbesian fear that perfect liberty is a state of war, but for differing reasons: Locke disagreed with Hobbes because of his arbitrary pontification that "true" liberty can

[60] Ernest Tuveson, "The Origins of the 'Moral Sense'," *Huntington Library Quarterly*, 11, no. 3 (May, 1948), 241–259.

[61] Jefferson to John Adams, October 14, 1816.

[62] Locke was squeamish about using the term "liberty" without qualifying it in some way, e.g. as "natural liberty," because unless he defined or limited it in accord with his own moral or religious biases, it would have to mean exactly what Hobbes said it meant, a state of "Warre," in which neither life nor property could be secure. Locke insisted that governments are established to protect rights, but he was more successful in arguing for the right to change a government, i.e. revolution. See Locke's *Second Treatise of Government*, Chapter 8, Sections 113–119, Chapter 16, Section 222, where his influences on the Declaration are most evident.

[63] See discussion of Whewell in Wilson J. Moses, *Alexander Crummell: A Study of Civilization and Discontent* (Oxford University Press, 1989).

exist only when the individual has a respect for the freedom of others. Bentham scoffed at Locke's semantic ploy of "true liberty," saying that liberty meant by definition the ability to do whatever one pleased, without any restraint whatever. Rousseau also disagreed with Locke for semantic reasons: he quibbled over Hobbes' equation of the state of nature with the state of "Warre," because Rousseau insisted that the word "war," properly speaking, refers to a relation between states, not between autonomous individuals (*Social Contract*, Book 1, Chapter 4).

At a glance, Bentham appears to be opposed equally to Jefferson's position on "natural rights" and to the theory of "social contract." He specifically rejects both as they are presented in "the masters of the science—Grotius, Puffendorf, Burlamqui, Vattel, even Montesquieu himself, Locke, Rousseau, and the crowd of commentators." He presents all these authors as equally misleading when "They speak of a natural right, of a law anterior to man, of the divine law, of conscience, of a social contract, of a tacit contract, &c. &c." Bentham nominally dismisses both natural law theory, an idea that he denounces in one instance as "nonsense on stilts" and elsewhere as "pernicious to morals." He deems "social contract" equally pernicious. But this equivalency is only apparent, for he squarely places himself on the side of social contract theory and reveals himself to be a social contract man no less than Thomas Hobbes. Although Bentham nominally rejects the idea of a "social contract" in the sense of a "tacit contract," existing prior to or independent of government, he indisputably asserts that rights exist only as the creation of governments. Rights are not the gift of God, and not the gift of Nature, but the creation of the state, for right is "the child of the law." Rights are "the fruits of the law, and of the law alone. There are no rights without law—no rights contrary to the law—no rights anterior to the law."[64]

Jefferson was deliberately obtuse when it came to understanding Bentham's notion that governments create rights, or Hobbes' notion that the state of nature was a state of "Warre." Hobbes' observation

[64] Jeremy Bentham, *The Works of Jeremy Bentham*, ed. John Bowring (Edinburgh: William Tait, 1839), vol. III, part 9; the works were originally printed in 1816. Also see Jeremy Bentham, "Anarchical Fallacies" in Jeremy Waldron, ed., *Nonsense upon Stilts: Bentham, Burke, and Marx on the Rights of Man* (London: Routledge, 2014), p. 69. Waldron offers a useful discussion of Bentham. Also see Bentham's *Panomial Fragments*, www.laits.utexas.edu/poltheory/bentham/pannomial/index.html at the Classical Authoritarianism website, which is maintained by Dan Bonevac, Department of Philosophy, University of Texas. Bonevac uses the Bowring edition cited in this footnote: *The Works of Jeremy Bentham*, vol. II, *Judicial Procedure, Anarchical Fallacies, Works on Taxation*, Online Library of Liberty (http://oll.libertyfund.org/).

was empirical, based on the religious history of Europe. "Warre" was the state of anarchy, famine, and disease that had devastated the German states in the seventeenth century. Given Locke's almost "Machiavellian" definition of the "state of nature" as the relation between absolute monarchs, one wonders how Locke, any less than Hobbes, could have derived his ideas of natural liberty from any other empirical evidence than that of the Thirty Years War, which still survived in living memory. Hume's royalism, which Jefferson abhorred, was based on a fear of anti-governmental excesses. Hume perceived the beheading of Charles I as a bit excessive, and Burke was appalled by the humiliation of Marie Antoinette. Jefferson's fear of government, focused on a detestation of monarchy and couched in egalitarian rhetoric, allowed him to completely disregard the stench of rotting corpses.

The defense of monarchy in Hume and Plato was an obvious source of Jefferson's displeasure with both, although Plato gave him at least one additional reason. Without specifically naming his objections, he described to Adams in his later years his general impressions on re-reading Plato's *Republic*:

> it was the heaviest task-work I ever went through. While wading thro' the whimsies, the puerilities, & unintelligible jargon of this work, I laid it down often to ask myself how it could have been that the world should have so long consented to give reputation to such nonsense as this?[65]

If Jefferson found Plato's *Republic* offensive, he must have found his dialogue, the *Crito*, downright blasphemous, for in the *Crito* Plato seemed to be abandoning divine justice in favor of social contract theory and placing in the mouth of Socrates words that elevated the social contract above the self-evident rights to life, liberty, and pursuit of happiness that Jefferson had called the endowment of God. Not only Jefferson's fear of monarchs and the powerful centralizing state, but also his horror of any social contract theory that might justify the one or the other were the sources of his hostility.

Locke repudiated and Jefferson loathed the doctrines of Plato's *Crito*, which had Socrates mouthing the most authoritarian version of social contract theory, as it appeared in Hobbes and Hume. Not only had they justified royalism, they had made the social contract, through the instrument of the state, which created law and order, into the source of all rights and security. Jefferson could not forgive Plato for fabricating – as he saw

[65] Jefferson to John Adams, July 5, 1814.

it – the heresies of the *Crito*, which denied the right to defy the government, or to replace or to overthrow it. Plato had made Socrates say that, in a conflict between the rights of the state and those of the individual, the government was right.

Jefferson could not drink the cup of Socrates, for he believed, as had Locke, that rights existed prior to the social contract, which existed only to protect natural rights. The *Crito* repudiated that theory and therefore undermined those very Lockean principles on which the Declaration of Independence was based and the American Revolution was mythically justified. Plato had replaced the natural rights given by the Creator with an artificial social contract practically synonymous with the power of the state. Plato had made Socrates willingly subordinate himself to that contract and its unjust legal processes. Plato's Socrates must submit to the laws, irrespective of their fairness, because he had benefitted from those laws and lived under their protection for his entire life. Plato's *Crito* had Socrates arguing against the fundamental principles of Lockean reasoning, and also against the doctrine of natural rights. If Plato was telling the truth, then Socrates believed that contract law supersedes natural liberty, and that governments derive their authority not from the consent of the governed, but from a debt that the individual owes to society.

But Jefferson's hero, Locke, had recognized, if Jefferson had not, a problem with demonstrating a truth that Jefferson called "self-evident." A fundamental challenge to Locke's reasoning was that no one had ever witnessed the hypothetical "state of nature" on which he based his *Treatises of Government*. Locke had anticipated the question of where the empirical evidence was that rights and liberties existed, or ever had existed – and where was this state of nature? His stunning response was that "all rulers of independent governments all through the world are in a state of nature." The only empirical evidence for any state of nature, the only place where a state of nature could be observed, was in the relationship between competing princes (the only truly autonomous individuals), who are constrained from attacking one another only by the fear of retaliatory violence.

Locke's views on the natural relationship between monarchs did not lead him to the conclusion that monarchs struggled naturally to eat each other up. Locke pontificated that the natural state was one in which princes agreed tacitly, informally, and automatically to enter into implied contracts. Hobbes came closer to the truth when he viewed the anarchic state of nature in which princes lived as a "Warre," a "brutish" state that he also attributed to "the savage people in many places of America." He believed that Native Americans, "except the government of small Families, the concord whereof dependeth on naturall lust, have no government at all." And Hobbes in 1651 viewed government as a necessary positive good, while Thomas Paine in 1776 saw it as a necessary evil. It was the artificial, not the natural, that Hobbes viewed as beneficial to mankind, and even Paine was forced to make a partial concession on this point, as we shall later observe. Hobbes anticipated the nineteenth-century thinking of Lester Ward, who said that the genius of humanity is not in the *laissez-faire* doctrine of submission to any "law of nature," but rather in the subjugation of nature to the artifice of mankind.[66]

Locke did not offer Hobbes' "savages" of North America but the European prince as his prime example of man in the natural state; however, Locke required an additional empirical example, so he presented a second piece of evidence, taken from a once popular work published in 1633 which he cited as Garcilasso (sic) de la Vega's *Historia des Yncas de Peru*. De la Vega, a soldier of fortune born in Peru of mixed Spanish and Indian parentage, was an authority on whom Locke relied in his *Treatises* for more than one rhetorical purpose. One of de la Vega's stories, to which Locke apparently gave credence, was the anecdote of a Spaniard who found himself marooned on an island off the coast of Peru with an indigenous Indian.[67] However familiar this story may have been to Locke's contemporaries, it is not well known today outside of the numerous scholarly discussions of it in treatments of Locke's political theory. Garcilaso recounted the story of a hypothetically spontaneous social contract in which two men supposedly dealt honorably with one another in a fancied state of nature, and Locke repeated the tale.[68]

Jefferson's library contained a copy of de la Vega's *Comentarios reales de los Incas del Peru*, which even in his day was remembered mostly by scholars and pedants.[69] Vastly more popular was a kindred narrative in the fiction of Daniel Defoe's *Robinson Crusoe*. Jefferson's reading of Defoe confirmed his white-supremacist beliefs, and those of many others, as Defoe had Crusoe enter spontaneously and immediately into

66 Lester Ward, "Mind as a Social Factor," *Mind*, 9, no. 36 (October, 1884), 563–573.

67 John Locke, *Second Treatise of Government*, Chapter I, Section 14.

68 In one scholarly edition of Locke's *Treatises of Government*, Peter Laslett says that Locke was referring to a French translation of the *Comentarios Reales* of Garcilaso de la Vega, published in 1633. See Peter Laslett, ed., *Locke: Two Treatises of Government*, student edn. (Cambridge University Press, 2003 [1960]), p. 182.

69 Jefferson's library contained a copy of both the *Historia* and the *Comentarios* of Garcilaso de la Vega.

a master–slave relationship with his man Friday. In so doing, he was viewing new world contacts between the races with more historical pessimism than Locke's narrative of Garcilaso de la Vega. Every schoolchild knows the story of Friday's debasing himself before Robinson Crusoe and placing Crusoe's foot upon his head, but few remember Garcilaso's non-confirmable claim on which Locke depended for his theory. One must ask, at least rhetorically: which of these two narratives, Garcilaso's memoir or Defoe's fiction, is the truer depiction of racial contacts in the New World? Jefferson once reported his delight in seeing that the Cherokees had begun to read *Robinson Crusoe*, and one may imagine without difficulty the lessons of white supremacy they were supposed to have gleaned from Crusoe's relationship to Friday.[70] Jefferson's bowdlerized version of the Bible for Native Americans and his secret communications with Andrew Jackson concerning the destiny of Native Americans are both discussed elsewhere in this volume. Reflecting on Jefferson's advocacy of *Robinson Crusoe* and his cut-and-paste New Testament, abridged for the Indians, confirms the observation of Sean Wilentz that Jefferson handled them with "Machiavellian benevolence."[71]

INALIENABLE RIGHTS

The existence of a "self-evident" right to life was hardly axiomatic, and "right to life" was not clearly defined in contemporary discourses. People who draft a Declaration justifying war and rationalizing violence must concede that they are asking people to take the lives of others, and possibly sacrifice their own. Since the Declaration of Independence is a justification of violence, nothing can be more obvious than its drafters' pragmatic admission that the right to life is "alienable"; therefore some reflection is in order on the circumstances that allowed them to alienate people from their right to life. When a general gives an order for a frontal assault, the footsoldier is expected to accept the reasoning of Plato's *Crito* and give up his life for the state. Molly Pitcher is lauded when she fires grapeshot into the bodies of enemy soldiers. Thomas Jefferson may preach in the abstract that the right to life is "inalienable," but George Washington has to make concrete decisions about whether or not to shoot deserters.

70 Jefferson to Governor James Jay, Monticello, April 7, 1809.

71 Sean Wilentz, *Major Problems in the Early Republic 1787–1848* (Lexington, KY: D. C. Heath, 1992), p. 130.

It is ironic that Jefferson's name should be so associated with the term "inalienable rights," synchronic with his drafting the Declaration, since he bore some responsibility for undermining that concept in American law. Locke had obliquely addressed inalienable rights in connection with the rights of fathers over their children and the rights of kings over their ancestral lands. His *Treatises of Government* were sprinkled with the terms "alienate," "alienable," "alienation," and he addressed the special conditions under which certain rights, such as the rights of a parent or a monarch, could be alienated. Locke specifically stated that while parents or monarchs might dispossess themselves of certain legal and moral rights, private individuals had no right to divest themselves of their lives or to place themselves in a condition of slavery:

> a man, not having the power of his own life, cannot, by compact, or his own consent, enslave himself to any one, nor put himself under the absolute, arbitrary power of another, to take away his life, when he pleases. No body can give more power than he has himself; and he that cannot take away his own life, cannot give another power over it.

Locke did assert that while persons cannot alienate themselves from their own lives, they can forfeit their lives by committing acts that deserve death, and by this logic they may alienate themselves from their right to life. Locke arrives, after much circumlocution, at the admission that the right to life is not absolutely inalienable.

Alienability, as Jefferson well knew, was essentially a legal concept.[72] It had to do with whether or not an owner could legally cede a claim to some property, and whether a property owner could legally be divested of his claim. Jefferson's prominent engagement with the question occurred in 1776 before his drafting of the Declaration, as he drafted reforms to the Virginian Constitution. The laws of entail had traditionally required that estates be passed down within particular family lines from generation to generation, usually through primogeniture, i.e. inheritance by the eldest son. Jefferson's attack on entail was the clearest manifestation of his contempt for the concept, and a pragmatic demonstration of its legal vulnerability. Jefferson had proven that inalienable rights were not permanent, absolute, or immutable. Thus, on employing the term "inalienable" in the Declaration, he was certainly aware that inalienability of rights was a legal convention, not a logical impossibility. A triangle cannot

[72] Stanley N. Katz, "Thomas Jefferson and the Right to Property in Revolutionary America," *The Journal of Law & Economics*, 19, no. 3, *1776: The Revolution in Social Thought* (October, 1976), 467–488.

be alienated from its three-sidedness, but a person can certainly be alienated from his or her life, and, as far as Grotius and Locke were concerned, by means that are perfectly justifiable in both the moral and the legal senses.[73]

And yet Jefferson and the Declaration's drafting committee, unlike Locke, asserted that the right to life was "inalienable." This is strange, for he and the drafting committee accepted both capital punishment and homicide on the battlefield. Was it an innate reverence for the right to life that kept Jefferson out of combat throughout the Revolution? This is difficult to believe, for he had no compunctions about urging other men to shed human blood. He provided much evidence that he was no pacifist – in the American Revolution, in the French Revolution, in the war on the Barbary pirates, and in the failed campaign to annex Canada. Much of the problem with fathoming Jefferson's concept of a right to life has to do with his careless employment of the term "inalienable." Among Jefferson's contemporaries, some of the most brilliant authors considered the idea of "inalienable rights" problematic, if not downright nonsensical, whether or not they accepted social contract theory. Literally hundreds of historians have addressed the problem of that definition, without approaching a consensus.[74]

Even Jefferson's intellectual heroes, Bacon and Locke, had not attempted to show that a right to life was self-evident, inalienable, or unequivocal.[75] Neither the Old nor the New Testaments of the Bible made any such claims regarding a right to life or any other rights. Indeed, Alexander Cruden's *Complete Concordance of the Holy Scriptures*,

[73] Locke and Jefferson's intellectual engagement with Grotius, although certain, has seldom dominated discussions of the Declaration. Few scholarly works have completely exhausted the entire catalogue of ancient and modern authors or descanted on such modern authors as Grotius, Vattel, Machiavelli, or the entire canon of figures who most certainly influenced Jefferson both directly and indirectly. Jefferson felt less of a compulsion than Adams to be specific about references.

[74] The matter is problematized by Garry Wills in his *Inventing America*, pp. 213–214, 216, 229–237, 246.

[75] Thieves and murderers have surrendered their right to life, according to Locke's *Second Treatise of Government*, Chapter 3, Section 18:

> This makes it lawful for a man to kill a thief, who has not in the least hurt him, nor declared any design upon his life, any farther than, by the use of force, so to get him in his power, as to take away his money, or what he pleases, from him; because using force, where he has no right, to get me into his power, let his pretence be what it will, I have no reason to suppose, that he, who would take away my liberty, would not, when he had me in his power, take away every thing else.

a reputable reference work of Jefferson's era, does not even contain an index entry under "rights." But Jefferson obviously needed neither biblical authority nor philosophical proofs on the matter of rights: he simply held his truths to be as "self-evident" as the axioms of Euclid. He did not use anything resembling a Baconian method of induction to arrive at his theory of rights: he deduced them on the basis of his private enthusiasm and his personal revelation of the mind of God.

The Declaration of Independence, like its predecessor, the 1775 Declaration Setting Forth the Causes and Necessity of Their Taking Up Arms, was a justification of homicide. Historian Carl Van Doren once argued that the Founders justified violence in political terms because they found the language of political rights more dignified than the language of economic rights. "Their rich and lofty political eloquence clouded their economic realism."[76] Warfare is definable as any group's more-or-less justifiable homicide in defense of its political and economic interests. The Declaration was a rationalization for violence, and it offered a list of reasons for engaging in acts of violence. It was a justification for depriving British Redcoats and Hessian mercenaries of their "inalienable" right to life. The imperial armies on American soil were the representatives of a Parliament that sought to deprive Americans of the entitlements, primarily economic, that Jefferson had enumerated in his *Summary View of the Rights of British America*.[77]

Locke had insisted that homicide was justifiable in defense of property, or in a state of war, while at the same time maintaining that the right to life was a natural, if not inalienable, right. In other words, the fact that one could, under certain circumstances, legitimately deprive someone of their right to life apparently would not affect that right's inalienability, in Locke's reasoning. This must lead one to question whether the concept of "inalienability" makes any sense at all, either in theory or in practice. Locke makes clear in Section 17 of his *Second Treatise of Government* his position that "he who attempts to get another man into his absolute power, does thereby put himself into a state of war with him," and, as

76 Carl Van Doren, *Benjamin Franklin* (New York: Penguin, 1991 [1938)], p. 361.

77 Eric Nelson, *The Royalist Revolution, Monarchy and the American Founding* (Cambridge, MA: Belknap Press, 2014), pp. 58, 156. Jefferson felt the king should be authoritarian at home and negate the actions of Parliament; Nelson puts it mildly in calling Jefferson "conflicted" or "ambivalent" and describing the *Summary View* as "heterodox." Jefferson was in fact contradictory, but he was correct in asserting that Parliament had no legitimate authority over the colonies. On p. 156 Nelson is also useful on Jefferson's anti-royalism.

a result, may be deprived of his own life. From this "state of war" argument Locke derives his belief that he has the right to kill a thief "when he sets on me to rob me but of my horse or coat."

The right to life, according to Locke, may be alienated for a horse or a coat, but there is more. A person has a right to kill not only in self-defense, but in defense of his property, and "it is lawful for a man to kill a thief, who has not in the least hurt him, nor declared any design upon his life." In other words, a person loses his right to life if he poses a threat to my property. By putting on the Hessian or Redcoat uniform, an individual forfeits his right to life and he may be killed because, by donning that uniform, he has become a threat to the American rights of life, liberty, and property. More abstractly, an American is entitled to kill a Hessian mercenary or a Lobsterback because he represents that British power that would steal from him his right to convert pig iron into ploughshares. In practical terms, a common footsoldier may be alienated from his own right to life and stand before a firing squad if he refuses to kill someone George Washington considers a threat to the ownership of his horse or of his coat.

Since the Declaration of Independence must unavoidably be regarded as a justification for the taking of human life, it is difficult to overlook the irony that the right to life should be the first of those rights that it listed as "inalienable." Fundamental human rights might be theoretically "inalienable," whatever the meaning of that ancient legal term, but in practice the divine rights of "all men" were no more inalienable than the divine rights of kings.

EQUALITY, REPRESENTATION, AND THE CONSTITUTION

Jefferson believed his Declaration to be based on immutable, universal, and eternal truths, as self-evident as the laws of geometry, but not so the Constitution. He famously advocated rewriting the Constitution every nineteen years, insisting that the world belongs to the living, and yet he believed that its underlying principles of government were sustainable. The index of his mind did not reveal a man "voyaging on strange seas of thought alone." Ideologically, he was sometimes a presentist, but more often a traditionalist. The Greeks, the Romans, and the canonical writers of the late Renaissance were the sources where he sought vindication. He was not always launched on "the boisterous sea of liberty," but often anchored in the secure harbor of deductive logic, traditional thinking, and religious dogma.

Samuel Adams' cry of "taxation without representation is tyranny" was a silly and irrelevant statement, since under any "democratic republic" or "representative" government there will always be some "taxation without representation." All representation is "virtual," by definition. There has never been, nor can there ever be, any "democratic" system of taxation without an ineluctable "tyranny of the majority," except, of course, where there is a "tyranny of the minority." For the American farmhand or day laborer, representation under the British Parliament was not radically different in 1776 from representation as codified, eleven years later, under the Constitution of the United States. In both instances, representation was purely geographical, and thus merely "virtual," whether in the House or the Senate. Ironically enough, the Framers of the Constitution of the United States codified the principle of virtual representation in 1787 not only by the compromise that allowed for inflating the population to be "represented" by counting three-fifths of the slaves in the census, but also by the creation of the Senate, the Electoral College, and other elements of government in which the ordinary American ploughman or milkmaid had no voice. Edmund Burke supported American independence, but not by any reasoning acceptable to Samuel Adams, with his unqualified assertion that "taxation without representation is tyranny." Burke's concept of representation viewed representation in terms of persons, not their opinions, and in like respect the Framers of the Constitution saw representation not as a mirror, but as a filter of opinion. Elected officials represented not interests or opinions, but warm bodies, or in some cases, three-fifths of a warm body.[78]

EQUALITY AND VIRTUAL REPRESENTATION – MADISON'S HONESTY

That Thomas Jefferson and Edmund Burke were in fundamental agreement on the idea of "virtual representation" is so obvious as to require little argument. Although that ought to be self-evident, some explanation may be necessary for the deliberately obtuse. The Constitution of the United States, while democratic, does not establish pure democracy, but representative government. Nonetheless, many of the persons "represented" under the Constitution at the time of its ratification were not allowed to vote, were not considered "equal," and were not entitled to the rights of "life, liberty, and pursuit of happiness." Indeed, Jefferson's own bill extended the

[78] See Rakove's chapter on "The Mirror of Representation" in his *Original Meanings*, and Gordon Wood, "The Nature of Representation," in Wood, *The Creation of the American Republic*.

franchise only to freeholders and taxpayers.[79] They were nonetheless "represented" in the Congress of the United States, although not represented to the extent that Madison and Jefferson would have preferred. They had to be contented that a mere three-fifths of their slaves would be "represented" in the census for the purpose of apportioning seats in Congress.

The meaning of the three-fifths compromise is unfortunately distorted by Floyd McKissick's valid indignation at the fact that the Constitution considered an African slave as a mere "three fifths of a man."[80] McKissick's anger and attention should not distract from another important issue. The crucial point is that African Americans, although effectively deprived of citizenship in the slave states in 1787, were counted in calculating the number of congressional seats to which slave states were entitled. Every slave state got to add three-fifths of its slaves to the census when calculating the number of "representatives" for that state. That same principle remains alive in 2017, since the Republican Party counts the black population in apportioning seats in Congress, while actively engaged in suppression of the black vote. The Constitution leavened the idea of democracy with the republican concept of "representation," but the meaning of representation was problematic in eighteenth-century political culture. Jefferson would have denied it, but his idea of "representation" was annoyingly similar to the notion defended in Edmund Burke's November 3, 1774 "Speech to the Electors of Bristol," which anticipated the principle of the three-fifths compromise in the United States Constitution. An elected official, according to Burke, represented the bodies, but not the minds, of those within his district, and a representative had no obligation to advance his constituents' opinions.

Burke's "virtual representation" involved two fundamental principles: first, and of lesser importance, was the idea that every member of the House of Commons spoke for every subject of the Empire, represented collectively and organically. More important was the idea that no member of Parliament was responsible for soliciting the opinions of his constituents before casting his vote. The American Revolution demonstrated that although virtualism was not an acceptable doctrine for the representation of upper-class white males, it was considered perfectly appropriate for Africans, for women, and for landless white males. This idea of virtual representation is retained in the United States today, where the Supreme Court supposedly interprets the

[79] Katz, "Thomas Jefferson and the Right to Property in Revolutionary America," 470.
[80] Floyd McKissick, *Three-Fifths of a Man* (New York: Macmillan, 1969).

collective will of "the people" as expressed in the Constitution. Virtual representation exists when a senator, congressional representative, or the Speaker of the House makes the ridiculous claim of representing the will of "the American people."

Madison once honestly admitted that the governments of the several United States privileged aristocracies, and that the Southern states, in particular, privileged a minority of 25 percent over a majority of 75 percent:

> In Virginia the aristocratic character is increased by the rule of suffrage, which requiring a freehold in land excludes nearly half the free inhabitants, and must exclude a greater proportion, as the population increases. At present the slaves and non-freeholders amount to nearly ¾ of the State. The power is therefore in about ¼. Were the slaves freed and the right of suffrage extended to all, the operation of the Government might be very different. The slavery of the Southern States, throws the power much more into the hands of property, than in the Northern States. Hence the people of property in the former are much more contented with their established governments, than the people of property in the latter.

Madison added in French a short passage from a currently popular French translation of the *Voyage du jeune Anacharsis en Grèce*, which translates to the effect that after the Athenians had dispensed with the Persian threat and extended the franchise to a broader band of the populace, history witnessed the decline of constitutional government and the rise of the demagogue. Jefferson was not inclined to accept Madison's pessimism regarding the people and did not see them as susceptible to demagogues.[81] Madison feared the tyranny of an "unjust and interested majority," a possibility that seemed remote to Jefferson. In theory, of course, it was possible to experience tyrannies of more than one sort, identified by John Adams as the tryannny of "the many, the few, or the one," but the danger presented by the first of that triad was minimal, at least in America, Jefferson felt, because "the yeomanry of the US are not the Canaille of Paris," as he wrote to Lafayette, February 14, 1815. The fact that the United States was an empire of frontier settlements boded well for the possibility that it might remain perpetually republican.[82]

[81] James Madison, *Notes for the National Gazette Essays* [ca. December 19, 1791 – March 3, 1792], in Founders Online. The French quotation is from the biography of Aristides in Plutarch's *Lives*: "Mais c'est principalement aux victoires que les Athéniens remportèrent contre les Perses, qu'on doit attribuer la ruine de l'ancienne Constitution (Arist: de rep: 1. 2. cap. 12.). Après la bataille de Platée, on ordonna que le citoyens de derniers classes exclus par Solon de principales magistratures, auroient désormais le droit d'y parvenir. Le sage Aristides, qui presenta ce decret."

[82] This was, in fact, one of the presuppositions of Madison's *Federalist* 10.

VACILLATION ON THE EQUALITY DOCTRINE

After 1776, Jefferson made clear on several occasions that he did not think universal human equality was "self-evident" after all. He said specifically that not all schoolchildren demonstrated an equal genius, and people seemed to demonstrate innate deficiencies in character. His attitudes on women lacked "a seriousness," putting it mildly, as historian Joyce Appleby does. His views on women are explored more fully in a separate chapter, and elsewhere in this text.[83] He expressed the gravest doubts concerning the physical and mental abilities of black people, not necessarily assigning them an inferior link in nature's Great Chain, but in *Notes on Virginia* he expressed "a suspicion only" that blacks might be "inferior to the whites." Still he postponed judgment on their potential equality, and allowed that their propensity for stealing was due to their condition, and not to any depravity of the moral sense.[84] But some individuals might have a congenital deficiency of character. The biography of Napoleon Bonaparte proved "that nature had denied him the moral sense, the first excellence of well organised man."[85]

John Adams' committee that drafted the Massachusetts Constitution, several years after Adams endorsed the proposition that all men are "created," borrowed some of Locke's ideas about liberty and equality, but they did not replicate his words. The Massachusetts Constitution, putatively drafted by Adams, read "All men are born free and equal, and have certain natural, essential, and unalienable rights," substituting the secular word "born" for the more religious word "created."[86] The Declaration of the Rights of the Inhabitants of the Commonwealth of Massachusetts stated that "all men are born free and equal."[87] But Locke's words, by Adams' own later admission, were contestable. Adams and Jefferson were presumably aware, and Locke as well, of Aristotle's pontification in Book IV of his *Politics*, which would not have seemed obscure to any student of "political science" as that discipline was understood in Jefferson's time.

[83] Joyce Appleby writes, "One can only hope that future assessments of Jefferson will confront his views of women with a seriousness that eluded him," *Thomas Jefferson* (New York: Times Books, 2003), p. 143.

[84] Jefferson did not use the medieval notion of the "Great Chain of Being" in connection with black Americans, although he employed the metaphor in Query VI of *Notes on Virginia*, denying that the mammoth was a "link in her [nature's] great work so weak as to be broken."

[85] On Napoleon's natural moral inferiority, Jefferson to John Adams, February 25, 1823.

[86] Constitution of Massachusetts (1779).

[87] *The Massachusetts Gazette*, 7, no. 403, Boston (January 25, 1788).

But is there any one thus intended by nature to be a slave, and for whom such a condition is expedient and right, or rather is not all slavery a violation of nature? There is no difficulty in answering this question, on grounds both of reason and of fact. For that some should rule and others be ruled is a thing not only necessary, but expedient; from the hour of their birth, some are marked out for subjection, others for rule.

In a brilliant exchange of letters from August through October of 1813, Jefferson and John Adams debated the meaning of the words "all men are created equal." Adams had decided in the years since he had approved this "self-evident" axiom of the Declaration of Independence that all men were not born equal, and Jefferson finally conceded that Adams had a point. He admitted the existence of a natural aristocracy of "virtue and talents," but he still rejected the legitimacy of "an artificial aristocracy founded on wealth and birth."[88] Adams was not satisfied with this partial concession, however. He argued that the distinction between natural and artificial aristocracies was specious, in that "both artificial aristocracy and monarchy, and civil, military, political, and hierarchical despotism, have all grown out of the natural aristocracy of virtues and talents."

Expanding on the traditional allegorical significance of the word "talent" as it was employed in the New Testament, Adams defined a talent as any of the gifts with which God might endow a person at the moment of their conception.[89] Adams proclaimed that in the traditional, if not in the contemporary, vocabulary, the word "talent" might imply

[88] John Adams to Jefferson, August 14, 1813, and Jefferson to John Adams, October 28, 1813, skirt the notion of eugenics, more directly approached in Jefferson, *Notes on Virginia*, p. 176, discussed later in the present work. The exchange of letters between August and October on the subject of equality, to which reference is made above, may be conveniently traced in Lester J. Cappon, *The Adams–Jefferson Letters: The Complete Correspondence between Thomas Jefferson and Abigail and John Adams* (Chapel Hill, NC, London: University of North Carolina Press, 1959), pp. 364–414. The debate is by no means limited to the letters referenced here. It underlies or is recurrent in much of the correspondence between Adams and Jefferson. It should be noted that neither Jefferson nor Adams at the time of this discussion viewed the US Senate primarily as what it was to become later in the century – the bulwark of states' rights and the bastion of the pro-slavery faction. The 1813 debate focused on the Senate as the embodiment of class privilege, analogous to the British House of Lords.

[89] See the parable of the talents, Matthew 25:14–30, where a master not only distributes the talents (a Greek coin) to his servants unequally, but teaches a very harsh doctrine. When two of the servants invest their talents, they are rewarded, but the third does not invest his money, and to him the master says, "You knew that I was a harsh master, and that I reap where I do not sow." Then he binds the unproductive servant and casts him out into darkness saying, "To him who hath shall be given, and from him that hath not shall be taken away even that which he hath."

any number of attributes: "wealth, strength, beauty, stature, birth, marriage, graceful attitudes and motions, gait, air, complexion, physiognomy, are talents, as well as genius, science, and learning." In other words, people were created unequal, not only in terms of their mental and physical endowments, but also in terms of the rights and privileges that societies confer, including those accompanying property, family connections, and the status of caste and class. Jefferson had already conceded that traits of character such as wisdom, goodness, and justice were unevenly distributed by the entity he called "Nature's God."

Adams pushed his advantage, proceeding to argue that talents were not necessarily associated with wisdom and justice. In a council made up of a hundred men, twenty-five would be aristocrats with Machiavellian influence over their peers. An "aristocrat" could sway votes by virtue of "birth, fortune, figure, eloquence, science, learning, craft, cunning, or even his character for good fellowship, and a bon vivant." He insisted that "talent," as he used the term, had very little to do with "virtue," and that it might easily go hand-in-hand with vice. Avarice, the result of appetite, was universal, and Adams rejected Jefferson's distinction "between natural and artificial Aristocracy," saying, "I would trust one as soon as the other with unlimited Power." He recognized not only "the Stupidity with which the more numerous multitude become their Dupes, but even love to be Taken in by their Tricks." Certainly, he recalled Hamilton's observation that demagogues have a talent for courting "the people" and Madison's that a "favorite leader" might "varnish his sophistical arguments with the glowing colors of popular eloquence."[90]

Jefferson felt compelled to admit the existence and the legitimacy of a "natural" aristocracy, founded on laudable talents. Adams more cynically insisted that natural aristocracy could be founded on wealth, social position, or a predisposition to guile. These were equally "talents," and these talents were dangerous. Furthermore, Adams saw, as Madison had thirty years earlier, that differences in talents led to diverse economic interests in society. The premises of the Declaration's equality clause were debatable, if not entirely false; they contradicted both reason and the empirical evidence. It was obvious that talents were conferred on some and denied to others, "imperiously" as Adams said, and "by Nature."

Adams employed the word "talents" in his letter to Jefferson decades later in much the same way Madison had used the word "faculties" in

[90] John Adams to Jefferson, November 15, 1813. Alexander Hamilton, *Federalist* 1 (1787); James Madison, "Vices of the Political System of the United States," April, 1787.

Federalist 10, but they were talking about the same thing: the unequal distribution of brains and beauty, of wealth and power, fortitude and adroitness, and moral character in any assembly of people. Wealth and power, as well as mental and physical endowments, could be listed among the "talents" and "faculties" of an individual. God had chosen to distribute talents and faculties, genius and knowledge, vices and virtues, as he saw fit. He was no respecter of persons and had unequally and arbitrarily distributed talents and faculties by an act of divine will, without a need for reason or explanation. No truth could be more "self-evident" than that whatever rights and talents "Nature's God" may have bestowed, he clearly had not bestowed them equally.

FIREARMS AND THE FORTUITOUS CONCOURSE OF BREEDERS

Jefferson admitted to differences in military prowess, masculine strength, and male sexuality in his letter to Adams of October 28, 1813. His approach in this letter was entirely masculinist, and, as Appleby notes, Jefferson was morally and intellectually vulnerable on matters of gender. He asserted that superior males of the master race were congenitally fit to rule because of their heritage, but he expressed a reservation. In ages past, "mere bodily powers gave place among the aristoi," but "the invention of gunpowder" had changed all that, opening the way for the ascendancy of a natural aristocracy of "virtue and talents." Natural aristocrats might emerge as "accidental aristoi, produced by the fortuitous concourse of breeders." But natural aristocrats were best selected by the citizens through the process of "the free election." His tone was sometimes facetious, and his argument discontinuous, but he was clear about his belief that sex and breeding played a role in determining the traits of any aristocracy, whether natural or artificial, "For experience proves that the moral and physical qualities of man, whether good or evil, are transmissible in a certain degree from father to son."

Jefferson's use of the term "equal" in the Declaration was time-bound and space-bound. It did not imply any renunciation of social hierarchy. It did not imply that he or the drafting committee doubted their own mental and moral superiority to small farmers, indentured servants, milkmaids, and tallow chandlers. The nation's foundation documents contained no implicit challenge to their authors' belief in the superior rights of their own ruling class. These documents certainly did not imply an equal birthright with respect to property or family status. The Declaration's phrase "created equal" reflected no more than Jefferson's implacable hostility to kings in general and to King George in particular. But Jefferson, as his exchange with Adams proved, was an elitist, and he believed that elite capacities were hereditary.

Periodically after drafting the Declaration Jefferson expressed a belief that a cadre of morally and physically superior men cropped up, sometimes fortuitously, in society. They were agreed that superior character traits were hereditary, and, as Adams asserted to Jefferson in a letter of August 14, 1813, intelligent men selected their wives with an eye to her antecedents and forebears. There were natural aristocrats, and the best government was that which "provides the most effectively for a pure selection of these natural aristoi into the offices of government." Despite his hatred of hereditary nobility and hereditary landed titles, it is certain that neither he nor Adams intended to deny the existence of hereditary inequality, whether physical, moral, or intellectual. In the 1813 correspondence with Adams, he flirted with human eugenics, as he had in Query XIV of *Notes on Virginia,* and his ideas on congenital equality were selective and inconstant.[91]

THE HEREDITARY POWER OF A FRONTIER ARISTOCRAT

Jefferson did exactly as he pleased for the greater part of his life. His obsessive fear of authority is difficult to explain, for he was blessedly spared contact with persons of superior status. During his youth on the Virginia frontier, no arbitrary power was exercised over him. Any arbitrary power exercised in his vicinity was his own power over his slaves. Sometimes, but not often, Jefferson's writings betrayed a subliminal nuance of awareness concerning his privileged status. Jefferson was undeniably the scion of a rural master class. "He used to mention as his first recollection, being handed up and carried on a pillow by a mounted slave," says his friendly biographer, Henry Stevens Randall.[92] Monticello was a frontier outpost, but nonetheless a stately mansion, and Jefferson, ensconced in this setting, could combine the better of two worlds, viewing them simultaneously as both frontiersman and patrician. But although he lived on the frontier, he was not a trail-blazer in any sense;

[91] Jefferson to John Adams, October 28, 1813.

[92] The source of the pillow legend is a family tradition reported by Henry Stevens Randall, *The Life of Thomas Jefferson* (New York: Derby and Jackson, 1858), vol. I, p. 11. Dumas Malone cites Randall in Dumas Malone, *Jefferson and His Time*, 6 vols. (Boston, MA: Little, Brown, 1948), vol. I, *Jefferson the Virginian*, pp. 19–21, 428.

the overriding reality was that he belonged to the class of slaveholding great planters, and he could not have escaped a poignant awareness that, surrounded by vassals and serfs, he resembled a European aristocrat. Perhaps the source of his almost paranoid dread of being controlled derived from the putatively anarchic tradition of the frontier. But his resentment of monarchs was also imbedded in an intellectual tradition, a discomfort with religious and political tyranny, inherited from the seventeenth century, and its obscure martyr, Algernon Sidney, whom he mentioned in the letter to Lee.[93]

Hostility to vigorous government was by no means a local Virginia phenomenon: this hostility had revealed itself periodically elsewhere in the colonies, as when Cotton Mather and the Boston bourgeoisie imprisoned and then deported Governor Andros, and when Nathaniel Bacon's rebels assailed Governor Berkeley. In the colonial history of Massachusetts and Virginia, big government had been the power of a hereditary aristocracy that was remote, alien, and irrelevant. The Declaration was rooted in an ancient tradition of rebellion as much as it was on the "harmonizing sentiments of the day," or the contemporary ideas in the air.[94] It was based on a feudal heritage of elite rebellion, at least as ancient as Magna Carta. Like the hoary warlords who had confronted John Lackland, the Founding Fathers had a notion of equality that was confined to a selfish and exclusive system of caste and class.

THE "DEMIGODS" AND THE CONSTITUTION

Between 1776 and 1790, Jefferson drafted the Declaration, witnessed the drafting of the French "Declaration of the Rights of Man," and, via correspondence with Madison, indirectly influenced the United States Constitution, a document about which he had mixed feelings. His opinions were sometimes steadfast, sometimes flexible as he developed them in a volatile political environment that he was helping to generate. His relationship to the Constitution was necessarily characterized by fortuitous compromises with his avowed principles, but his Machiavellian genius was always present. Writing to John Adams from Paris, he

[93] John Milton was the author of *Tenure of Kings and Magistrates* (1649), a presumed defense of regicide. He had visited Galileo under house arrest and was a contemporary of Algernon Sidney (1623–83), who opposed regicide but was executed for treason as the author of *Discourses Concerning Government*, a justification for armed resistance to oppression, written between 1681 and 1683.

[94] Jefferson to Henry Lee, May 8, 1825.

expressed objections to the Framers' oath of secrecy. He was "sorry they began their deliberations by so abominable a precedent as that of tying up the tongues of their members. Nothing can justify this example but the innocence of their intentions, and ignorance of the value of public discussions."

This was the same letter in which he made his famous reference to the Constitutional Convention as "an assembly of demigods."[95] Absent from the Convention, did Jefferson fear that history would forget him, and that his role as a founder of the republic would some day fade from collective memory? John Adams' peevish remarks in a letter of 1790 made clear that he already resented the apotheosis of Franklin and Washington:

> The History of our Revolution will be one continued lye [sic] from one end to the other. The essence of the whole will be that Dr. Franklin's electric rod smote the earth and out sprang General Washington. Then Franklin electrified him ... and thence forward those two conducted all the Policy, Negotiations, Legislations, and War.[96]

Adams did not appreciate until years later that Jefferson had guaranteed his own apotheosis, despite his absence from the Constitutional Convention. While historians will always marvel at Adams' keen acerbic brilliance and Madison's controlling political mind, the more ordinary American is unaware of the role of either in the Foundation. Americans revere Washington for his bedrock character and admire Franklin for his wit, but Jefferson, despite his admitted faults, is remembered as the author of American Liberty, and the prophet of democratic egalitarianism.

JUSTICE TANEY'S DECLARATION AND CONSTITUTION

The decision to mandate what Annette Gordon-Reed has called "blacks' perpetual alien status" was made at the inauguration of the republic, along with the decision to use race, as Robert Parkinson maintains, as a means of shaping national character and national unity.[97] The truth of

[95] Jefferson to John Adams, Paris, August 30, 1787. Other than Washington, the most likely other "demigod" to whom he might have been referring was Benjamin Franklin. John Adams' envious remarks concerning Washington and Franklin are in John Adams to Benjamin Rush, April 4, 1790.

[96] John Adams to Benjamin Rush, April 4, 1790.

[97] See Annette Gordon-Reed, "The Captive Aliens Who Remain Our Shame," *The New York Review of Books* (January 19, 2017), 54, which is a review of Robert Parkinson's *The Common Cause: Creating Race and Nation in the American Revolution* (Chapel Hill: University of North Carolina Press, 2016).

at least one of Chief Justice Roger B. Taney's premises is inescapable: words cannot be extracted from the time and place at which they are spoken or written. Taney had a valid point when he said that the libertarian and egalitarian preachments of the Declaration did not mean what they implied to later generations. Numerous scholars and politicians have sought to reconcile the Declaration of Independence's preachments of liberty and equality to the pro-slavery content of the United States Constitution.[98] Of particular interest has been its application to Abraham Lincoln's appropriation of its words, "all men are created equal." Taney famously opined that those words should not be taken out of their historical context or their original intent. "If they were used in a similar instrument at this day," he allowed, in 1857, they "would seem to embrace the whole human family." Jefferson's words could have had no such intent in "the language as understood in that day." It was "too clear for dispute that the enslaved African race were not intended to be included and formed no part of the people who framed and adopted this declaration." Thus, not only did Taney give quasi-constitutional authority to the Declaration, he took a position consistent with that of William Lloyd Garrison, the most prominent abolitionist of his day. Garrison publicly burned a copy of the Constitution, calling it "a Covenant with Death, an Agreement with Hell," and for more than a decade Frederick Douglass agreed with him.

Responding to the *Dred Scott v. Sandford* decision, Frederick Douglass cynically and deliberately ignored the Chief Justice's historically accurate interpretation of Jefferson's words, "all men are created equal," disingenuously transforming Jefferson into an abolitionist icon. I discuss elsewhere Jefferson's famous belief that blacks were inferior and must be deported in order to prevent genetic contamination of the white race. Douglass and Lincoln performed Machiavellian acts of sorcery, as they shrewdly advanced an interpretation of the Declaration that was as "presentist" as it was utilitarian. It is clear that Lincoln followed Frederick Douglass' as opposed to Taney's interpretation of Jefferson in his Gettysburg Address. Historian Douglas Wilson was disturbed by the idea that Lincoln's words might be seen as a "presentist" distortion, but they were.[99] The Gettysburg Address followed Frederick Douglass, who

[98] E.g. Garry Wills, Douglas Wilson, and Pauline Maier.

[99] See Wilson J. Moses, "'The Ever Present Now': Frederick Douglass' Pragmatic Constitutionalism," *Journal of African American History* (winter, 2013–14), 71–88. Douglas Wilson and Lynn Hunt, "Against Presentism," *Perspectives on History,*

strategically heroized Jefferson and invoked him as a prophet of human rights and racial egalitarianism. Alexander Crummell was having none of this. Born a "Free-African," proud of his "Simon Pure" black complexion, and a University of Cambridge graduate, he attacked both Jefferson and the purportedly Lockean principles of the Declaration of Independence.[100] Cambridge Platonists like Crummell were not fond of Locke. Crummell, like his young protégé, W. E. B. Du Bois, rejected Jeffersonian individualism and accepted an organic conception of the state similar to George Fitzhugh's or John C. Calhoun's.[101]

Garrison's opinion remained accurate: "That the author of the Declaration of Independence should have been a slaveholder and a slave-breeder, and have died without emancipating a single slave, is a most glaring inconsistency of human nature."[102] Garrison was obviously right, but Douglass decided that nothing was to be gained by drumming on the hypocrisy of Jefferson. It was much more useful to seize on the egalitarian language of the Declaration and follow Taney's precedent of affixing it to the Constitution, but to make the Constitution egalitarian. So Douglass thumbed his nose at Taney's originalist principle, and interpreted

The Newsmagazine of the American Historical Association (May, 2002), www.historians.org/publications-and-directories/perspectives-on-history/may-2002/against-presentism; Michael Rozbicki, *Culture and Liberty in the Age of the American Revolution* (Charlottesville, VA: University of Virginia Press, 2011); Greg Roeber, "The Limited Horizons of Whig Religious Rights" in Barry Shain, ed., *The Nature of Rights at the American Founding and Beyond* (Charlottesville, VA: University of Virginia Press, 2007), pp. 198–229; Peter S. Onuf, "The Scholars' Jefferson," *The William and Mary Quarterly*, 50, no. 4 (October, 1993), 671–699. Paul Finkelman has problematized the concept of "presentism" in *Slavery and the Founders: Race and Liberty in the Age of Jefferson*, 2nd edn. (Armonk, NY: M. E. Sharpe, 2001), pp. 170–173, and on p. 173 is particularly critical of Julian Boyd, Joseph Ellis, and Alf J. Mapp.

100 Alexander Crummell, the son of an African father and a black mother, took a degree from Cambridge University in 1853. He attended the lectures of William Whewell, who attacked the materialism of Locke and led a revival of "Cambridge Platonism" during Crummell's years at the University. See Moses, *Alexander Crummell*, pp. 77–78.

101 Philip S. Foner, ed., *The Life and Writings of Frederick Douglass* (New York: International Publishers, 1952), vol. III, pp. 284, 325, 328, 439–441. W. E. B. Du Bois, "Democracy does not and cannot mean freedom. On the contrary it means coercion. It means submission of the individual will to the general will," in W. E. B. Du Bois, "The Revelation of St. Orgne the Damned," Commencement Address, Fisk University, 1938, repr. in Nathan Huggins, ed., *W. E. B. Du Bois, Writings* (New York: Library of America, 1986), pp. 1048–1070.

102 William Lloyd Garrison to R. W. Ingraham, February 16, 1873, condemned Jefferson for having children by a slave woman "to be bought and sold in the market like merchandise," Walter M. Merrill and Louis Ruchames, eds., *The Letters of William Lloyd Garrison*, vol. VI (Cambridge, MA: Belknap Press, 1981), p. 267.

Jefferson's words as applying to the present. He outlined in 1857 the basic contours of an assertion that would appear six years later in Lincoln's Gettysburg Address.[103] The words "all men are created equal" were ostensibly meant to include African American persons, whether slave or free, or at least that is the interpretation usually attributed to them. The Constitution's references to persons bound to service and Madison's statement in *Federalist* 54 could be forgotten or ignored. Although some persons were born into a state of inequality, as the property of others, all men were created equal. What could be clearer than that?

All men were created equal, if you had the guns to make them equal. On citing Jefferson at Gettysburg, Lincoln not only accepted Douglass' serviceable, but ahistorical, re-interpretation of the Declaration and the Constitution, but tacitly accepted Andrew Jackson's position on executive authority, to boot: "The Chief Justice has given his interpretation of the Constitution, now let him enforce it." Lincoln, not Taney, was the man with the army, and hence his was the *ultima ratio.* Colonel George Armstrong Custer and General William T. Sherman provided the final reasoning that he would use to enforce his interpretation. Abraham Lincoln's expansion of the Declaration's egalitarian principles was an expression of the most radical and violent presentism, and simultaneously of benevolent humanitarianism, but it was the logic of Thrasymachus in Plato's *Republic*, the logic that might makes right. *Ultima ratio*, the final argument, was the slogan that Cardinal Richelieu and Frederick the Great engraved on their cannons, and it might have been stamped on Lincoln's just as well.

CONCLUSION: EQUALITY AND INALIENABLE PURSUITS

Jefferson was not an egalitarian, but a snob; he saw himself as the equal of King George, but definitely felt superior to a merchant, a clockmaker, or Alexander Hamilton. His remarks on Hamilton were among "the iciest and ugliest" of his career, as Richard Brookhiser has accurately perceived.[104] Jefferson was his own very model of a natural aristocrat. The only person he ever acknowledged as an equal was Benjamin Franklin, who was his superior in every way. His role in the history of American law, his administration

[103] Frederick Douglass, "Speech before the American Antislavery Society" on May 11, 1857.

[104] Richard Brookhiser, *Alexander Hamilton, American* (New York: Free Press, 1999), pp. 109–110.

of Monticello, and most importantly his philosophical musings in his own hand demonstrated that no rights were ever inalienable or unalienable, regardless of how it was spelled. "Inalienable" for Jefferson, shaper of a society where moral values were as flexible as spelling rules, seems to be a rhetorical term, since both Jefferson and his idol, Locke, were perfectly willing to deprive people of life when necessary, and Jefferson systematically deprived them of liberty when convenient.

The Declaration of Independence was founded not in reason, but in rhetoric, much of which was thankfully excised by the Continental Congress, when it blushed at Jefferson's blaming the king for the slave trade. Jefferson had assumed the debts of his father-in-law acquired through that trade, hoping to profit from the maneuver, but his plans went awry. As for the Declaration's attacks on monarchy in general, they were counterproductive in that they probably retarded France's decision to support the Revolution. John Adams was correct in calling it theatrics. It was drafted after the battles of Lexington, Concord, and Bunker Hill, and the capture of Fort Ticonderoga. Washington had already forced the British evacuation of Boston. Until the performance of Donald Trump in the presidential debates of 2016, never in modern history has any politician pulled off an equally impressive coup of self-aggrandizement. Jefferson used words on parchment rather than actions on the battlefield to establish himself as the creator of the Republic, urging others to lay down their lives while making only the most half-hearted attempt as wartime governor of Virginia. He was absent from the country while the Constitution was being framed, and he returned just in time to continually bushwhack George Washington's administration, as in his attack on the Jay Treaty, his authorship of poison-pen letters, and his shady collusion with Edmund Genêt.

As for a right to property, as we have seen, Jefferson considered the question "moot," and the "pursuit of happiness" could not be narrowly defined as equivalent to "pursuit of property." But although in conversations with Lafayette he opposed the idea that property is an inalienable right, Jeffersonian economic theory made security of a yeoman's life and liberty impossible without land ownership. The Declaration of Independence failed to consider the question, commonly addressed by philosophers before and after Jefferson, of whether liberty is to be subsumed under the category of rights, or whether liberties and rights are distinct ontological categories. Thomas Jefferson for at least a moment in his career viewed rights as inalienable possessions, and viewed liberty as a right. Nonetheless, the rights to life, liberty, and property were not consistently absolute, either in the activities or in the writings of lawyer

Jefferson. Without the yeoman's having a natural right to property, a question that Jefferson considered "moot," happiness must remain, in Dr. Bledsoe's words, an eternal pursuit, a "promise which, like the horizon, recedes ever brightly and distantly beyond the hopeful traveler."[105]

[105] Ellison, *Invisible Man*, p. 191.

5

What is Genius? "Openness, Brilliance, and Leadership"

A stunning array of mechanical and scientific devices invented or owned by Thomas Jefferson is presented in the catalogue entitled *Monticello, a Gift Collection*, distributed by the Thomas Jefferson Memorial Foundation. In this catalogue, and in several handsomely illustrated scholarly and popular studies, we gain an impression of Jefferson as scientist and inventor. Those who have visited Monticello never, or only once, can gain or supplement the experience by viewing the handsome pictures available online of such inventions as his writing-desk, his cipher lock, his "polygraph," and his revolving bookstand, as well as other handsome objects he possessed, such as the orrery, the portable writing-desk, and a framed replica of the Declaration of Independence. The internet even provides us with the apocryphal information that Jefferson invented macaroni and cheese.

Two more serious studies are those by Martin Clagett and Keith Thomson, published by university presses and directed at the more sophisticated reader. Both of these acknowledge their debt, as we all must, to the prior exhaustive publications of Sylvio Bedini, and all of these are careful to distinguish between those objects Jefferson invented, those he adapted or improved, and those he simply admired or possessed. Clagett notes that "in the area of science, he is remembered almost exclusively for the ingenuity of his gizmos." Thomson points out that the polygraph or copying machine, which he used to make a copy of each of his letters as he wrote them, was invented by an Englishman, John Isaac Hawkins, and improved by the American Charles Willson Peale. His most impressive invention was a by-product of his mathematical instincts, the "wheel cipher machine," a device for sending messages in code.

A prototype, according to all authorities, had been previously introduced as early as the 1500s, and there was a description of a similar coding machine in Diderot's *Encyclopédie Ancienne* in 1750. Jefferson collected and read in their French editions several books on the subject and perfected a version that remained in use by the United States Army during the World War II.[1]

Jefferson also applied his penchant for mathematics to designing his moldboard plough – as well as to calculating the admixture of "the unit of blood" in a mulatto. The plough, according to all reports, was a good one, but George Washington also invented a plough, making no mention of resorting to mathematics, and John Deere, relying primarily on his mechanical expertise, eventually had more impact than either of them.[2] The French Society of Agriculture was impressed with this invention by the author of the Declaration of Independence, and awarded him a gold medal. Jethro Wood, who invented a moldboard plough in 1814, died in poverty, ineffectively protesting violations of his patent. Jefferson, with characteristic disdain for the craftsmen who brought his ideas to fruition, wrote "I have imagined and executed a mould-board which may be mathematically demonstrated to be perfect, as far as perfection depends on mathematical principles, and one great circumstance in its favor is that it may be made by the most bungling carpenter, and cannot possibly vary by a hair's breadth, but by gross negligence." [3]

As yet, no historian has explained whether the mathematical calculations that Jefferson made on the backs of bills and scraps of paper were anything other than rigorous intellectual gymnastics, and there is no record of his personally executing the work on this plough that he declared could be constructed by "the most bungling carpenter."[4] As a frontier farmer and inventor, Washington is said to have excelled him, according to at least one scholar, who makes the following invidious comparison:

[1] Sylvio A. Bedini, *Thomas Jefferson: Statesman of Science* (New York: Macmillan, 1990); Martin Clagett, *Scientific Jefferson: Revealed* (Charlottesville, VA: University of Virginia Press, 2009), p. 95; and Keith Thomson, *Jefferson's Shadow: The Story of His Science* (New Haven, CT: Yale University Press, 2012), p. 169.

[2] Bedini, *Thomas Jefferson*, pp. 260–262. Clagett, *Scientific Jefferson*, pp. 12–14; Thomson, *Jefferson's Shadow*, pp. 172–173.

[3] See the article on "Moldboard Plow" at https://home.monticello.org/, based on Russell L. Martin and Lucia Stanton, Monticello Research Report, October, 1988. Also see Frank Gilbert, *Jethro Wood, Inventor of the Modern Plow. A Brief Account of his Life, Services, and Trials; Together with Facts Subsequent to His Death, and Incident to His Great Invention* (Chicago: Rhodes & Mcclure, 1882).

[4] Clagett, *Scientific Jefferson*, p. 12.

Jefferson designed a plow that nobody ended up using, but mathematically it is supposed to be the perfect plow. Washington designed a plow that drops seeds while plowing, and farmers came from all around the region to copy and use it.[5]

As a clockmaker, Jefferson's standards were so exacting that he once criticized Isaac Newton's method for calculating the length of a pendulum, but he had difficulty in calculating the length of the counterweights for the great clock at Monticello. He solved the problem by cutting holes in the floor so they could pass into the cellar. To this day Monticello's great clock, situated over the main doorway in the Entrance Hall, raises the admiration of visitors. It is powered by two sets of weights, attached to cables that extend across the ceiling to opposite corners of the room, and descend into the basement through holes cut in the floor. There are markings on the wall in one of the corners, corresponding to the days of the week. According to Martin Clagett, it was "a miscalculation in the construction" that necessitated cutting the holes in the floor, and the marking for Saturday was located in the basement.[6]

Garry Wills has referred to Jefferson's clock-making efforts as a "clumsy mimicking of the clockmaker's real achievements in the eighteenth century."[7] Along these lines, one thinks today of Dava Sobel's fine work on John Harrison, the self-educated English carpenter who invented the marine chronometer. Also noteworthy was the Englishman John Whitehurst, a member the Royal Society; I mention him elsewhere, and Jefferson once mentioned him in disparaging tones. The Monticello polymath turned over the actual construction of his clock to a craftsman named Spurck, according to Bedini, although numerous spellings of that name have cropped up in discussions of the ensuing result. Jefferson wrote numerous letters complaining about the clock, supposedly made to his own specifications, although he attributed its malfunctions to the "bungling manner" in which Spruck (sic) made it. Regardless of who was at fault, the designer was not able to identify where the craftsman had gone wrong, and it was not until many years later that historians discovered that the mechanism was one tooth short in the gear for winding up the weights.[8]

[5] See podcast and transcript, "Doug Bradburn on George Washington: The Tantalizing Man behind the Myth," The Grateful America Foundation.

[6] Clagett, *Scientific Jefferson*, p. 96.

[7] Garry Wills, *Inventing America: Jefferson's Declaration of Independence* (New York: Doubleday, 1978), pp. 109–110. Dava Sobel, *Longitude: The True Story of a Lone Genius Who Solved the Greatest Scientific Problem of His Time* (London: Penguin, 1995).

[8] Bedini, *Thomas Jefferson*, p. 246.

In the conflict with Spurck, Jefferson revealed his characteristic contempt for ordinary handworkers, as displayed in his aforementioned statement that his plough could be "made by the most bungling carpenter." The practical implementation of craftsmanship was something to be relegated to that "class of artificers," and he regarded them as pedestrian and deficient in republican virtue. On a more equestrian level, like most planters of his generation and region, he was familiar with the practical and theoretical literature on farming methods. Still, if his financial success as a farmer was any indication, he does not seem to have been George Washington's practical equal.[9] The British ambassador, Sir August John Foster, described him as a "bad farmer," although acknowledging that farming the hillside of his estate presented serious challenges. Jefferson was comparable to Washington as a clever fellow who brought a spirit of invention to what was still a frontier society. As a farmer and a problem-solver, however, Washington was the more gifted in fiscal management, as well as scientific and technical accomplishments.

THE POSTHUMOUS IQ SCORE

In 2006, Dean Keith Simonton, who held the title of Distinguished Professor of Psychology at the University of California Davis, published a study of presidential genius in the journal *Political Psychology*, which was subsequently popularized in *US News and World Report*, *Scientific American*, *The Chronicle of Higher Education*, and the *History News Network*. Simonton had "discovered" that Jefferson was the second-smartest president of all time, outranked only by John Quincy Adams, and in the process he created for Jefferson a hypothetical IQ of 160. Jefferson never had an IQ, of course, since he never took the test; like most of the presidents included in the study, he lived and died before IQ-testing was invented. Simonton's study contained other interesting features, such as inventing a score of 159.8 for John F. Kennedy, although his biographers have, rightly or wrongly, maintained that his score was 119.[10]

[9] No great believer in fertilizers: Dumas Malone, *Jefferson and His Time*, 6 vols. (Boston, MA: Little, Brown, 1962), vol. III, *Jefferson and the Ordeal of Liberty*, p. 202.

[10] Dean Keith Simonton, "Presidential IQ, Openness, Intellectual Brilliance, and Leadership: Estimates and Correlations for 42 US Chief Executives," *Political Psychology*, 27, no. 4 (August, 2006), 511–526. Summary of Simonton, "Presidential IQ ... " in *Chronicle of Higher Education* (July 12, 2006). Lindsey Cook, "Poindexter in Chief: Presidential IQs and Success in the Oval Office," *US News and World Report* (May 27, 2015). David Z. Hambrick, "How Smart Should the President Be? A Historical

There have been numerous attempts, notably that of Catherine Morris Cox in 1926, to estimate the intelligence quotients of world-historical figures, such as da Vinci, Newton, and Napoleon, but Simonton confined himself in this study to United States presidents.[11] Those who are fascinated by the matter often illustrate genius by referring to legends of precocity, such as Mozart's juvenile symphonies, or his legendary transcription of Lassus' *Miserere*, after one hearing at the age of 14. There are no such anecdotes related to Thomas Jefferson, and youthful precocity was not the controlling factor in Simonton's study. The most important indicators of intelligence were "Openness, Intellectual Brilliance, and Leadership." These qualities are difficult to define, and even more difficult to quantify. Simonton placed exceptional stress on the quality of "openness," in which he awarded Jefferson a score of 99 percent, which was higher than any other US president. He fails to explain convincingly how he quantifies "openness," or why he awards it higher importance than other criteria, such as auto-didacticism, multi-lingualism, aesthetic sensibility, or mathematical talent.[12]

Simonton rightly credits Jefferson with "intellectual brilliance," but whether he merits the 99 percent rating given him for the trait of "openness" is a question that many of his contemporaries found debatable. As for "leadership," 370 lines of rhymed satire in flawless iambic

Analysis Suggests a Link between IQ and Performance," *Scientific American* (May 26, 2015). Unsigned article, "Rating American presidents' IQ's," *History News Network* (copyright 2015). Kennedy's IQ score was reported as 119 by Thomas Reeves in *A Question of Character: A Life of John F. Kennedy* (New York: Three Rivers Press, 1997), and the same score is attributed by Robert Dallek in *An Unfinished Life: John F. Kennedy, 1917–1963* (New York: Little, Brown, 2003).

11 Catherine Morris Cox, *The Early Mental Traits of Three Hundred Geniuses* (Stanford University Press, 1926), vol. II, *Genetic Studies of Genius*. Nicolas Macintosh says that Cox often had "no evidence worthy of the name," in *IQ and Human Intelligence*, 2nd edn. (Oxford University Press, 2011), p. 207. The pop-cultural pastime of guessing the IQs of historical figures, on internet sites and blogs, often follows after Cox in ranking J. S. Mill higher than Copernicus. Skeptics often note that Nobel Prize-winning physicist Richard Feynman is said to have scored 125, which relegates him to the status of "superior," lower than the "genius" scores Simonton fabricated for Jefferson, Kennedy, and most other American presidents.

12 Darin McMahon, in his *Divine Fury: A History of Genius* (New York: Basic Books, 2013), pp. xix–xx, observes the contrast between Thomas Jefferson's declaration that all men are created equal and his subsequent description of a natural aristocracy. He remarks on p. 249 that surprisingly little work has been done on the history of the idea of quality, and notes that "Jefferson is cited and discussed in John Carson, *The Measure of Merit, Talents, Intelligence, and Inequality in the French and American Republics, 1750–1940* (Princeton University Press, 2007)."

pentameter describing Jefferson as "weak and erring" were penned by William Cullen Bryant, a boy of 14:[13]

> Ye who rely on Jeffersonian skill,
> And say that fancy paints ideal ill,
> Go, on the wing of observation fly,
> Cast o'er the land a scrutinizing eye;
> States, counties, towns, remark with keen review,
> Let facts convince, and own the picture true . . .
> When shall this land, some courteous angel say,
> Throw off a weak and erring ruler's sway?
> Rise, injured people, vindicate your cause,
> And prove your love of liberty and laws.

THE GIFTS OF PROVIDENCE

Although Jefferson did not display the precociousness of a Bryant, Providence endowed him with an impressive physical appearance, musical talent, mathematical aptitude, and linguistic ability, as well as the character traits of perseverance and assiduity and circumspection. He was not lazy and by his teens had developed the work ethic that served him well in adulthood. From early youth, he rose early and committed every available hour to reading, writing, and cataloguing. What survives of his adolescent correspondence reveals an intelligence that was notable, if not remarkably daring. His mature correspondence skimmed over every aspect of contemporary intellectual life. Jefferson managed to enjoy a fulfilling life of the mind, while managing an impressive schedule of appointments, receptions, and soirees with scientists, politicians, and inventors.

Like King George III, who fancifully called himself "Farmer George," Jefferson had inherited horses and pastures, vassals and serfs, as well as an enviable family background.[14] Fortune had also bestowed on him the virtue of industry, along with intellectual talent, and the blessings of wealth and leisure that made it possible for him to thrive as a man of letters. Had not Jesus himself observed, "many are called but few are chosen"? As a Virginia

[13] William Cullen Bryant's "The Embargo; or, Sketches of the Times" (1808). For a delightful discussion of the circumstances surrounding Bryant's youthful prolusion, see Julius Kahn, *Muck-Rakers of Other Days: Speech of Hon. Julius Kahn of California in the House of Representatives Saturday, March 26, 1910* (Washington, DC: Government Printing Office, 1910).

[14] For "Farmer George," see Edmund S. Morgan, *The Meaning of Independence* (New York: Norton, 1978), p. 29, and Chapter 3 of the present work.

planter, he was among the chosen, for planters were tillers of the soil, and therefore, as he famously pontificated, among God's elect, "if he ever had a chosen people." Jefferson's mother was a Randolph and his father a striving entrepreneur of the gentry class, who by powers of body and mind improved on his upward mobility. Like his father, Peter, Thomas Jefferson easily fit the definition of a "natural aristocrat," taller, handsomer, more robust, and more intelligent than the average man.

Jefferson graduated from the College of William and Mary at 19, but this was neither rare nor remarkable in the eighteenth century. It was then common for a boy to start college in his mid teens and to complete in two years. James Madison, although he entered Princeton at 18, was graduated in two years. Alexander Hamilton's age when he started college is not certain, due to his contested birth date. He was 17 or 19 when he entered King's College (later Columbia University) in 1774, but he discontinued his studies after two years, when the Revolution brought classes to a halt, and joined the Continental Army. Gouverneur Morris had already graduated from King's College at 16. John Adams entered Harvard at 16 and graduated at 20, but most delegates to the Constitutional Convention who graduated from university did so by their late teens. In 1826, Jefferson expected that an entering freshman at the university would be 16.[15]

Before the Revolution, college preparation in Great Britain and the United States consisted primarily of classical languages, for which reason the elementary schools were called grammar schools.[16] Whether in England or America, boys of the privileged classes were introduced, as Jefferson was, to Latin, Greek, and (usually) French, by private tutors before the age of 10. In the eighteenth century, the prerequisite for matriculation at Harvard included the ability to translate extended biblical passages into grammatical Latin. Full matriculation at Yale, Princeton, and King's College (renamed Columbia) presumed a thorough preparation in Latin, if not in Greek. College preparation in grammar school was based on the mastery of the "trivium," which comprised Latin grammar, rhetoric, and logic, and, prior to the Revolution, usually some introduction to Greek, plus solid geometry, trigonometry, astronomy, and ethics. Mathematical expectations were not high by

[15] Graduation dates are provided in *The Concise Dictionary of American Biography* (New York: Charles Scribner's Sons, 1964). For Jefferson's expectations at the University of Virginia, see Jefferson to John Patten Emmett, May 2, 1826.

[16] In England, private academies such as Eton, Harrow, and Rugby were (and still are) traditionally called "public schools." The term "grammar school" was less rigidly defined.

today's standards; it is not uncommon for freshmen at William and Mary today to have met already the mathematical requirements for graduation in 1770. By contrast, it is rare for anyone currently studying at an elite American university to meet the 1770 Latin requirement for freshman matriculation. Peter Jefferson placed Thomas, his older son, in Latin school from the age of 9. He lived in the home of the schoolmaster, the Reverend William Douglas, who taught him Greek, Latin, and French. Soon after the untimely death of his father, Jefferson found a surrogate parent in the Reverend James Maury, an excellent linguist, with whom he boarded until the age of 17.

During his ensuing two-year sojourn at the College of William and Mary he was blessed with the mentorship of George Wythe, an enduring friend, and he was taken under the wing of a young and gifted mathematician, William Small. Jefferson was undoubtedly a brilliant, industrious, and early maturing scholar. His accomplishments in classical languages met the highest expectations. He was naturally inclined towards intellectual pursuits, and by the age of 20 he was developing a reading knowledge in Anglo-Saxon and discovering Italian. He was naturally gifted, and not only in the ability to read, memorize, and understand. He had that third attribute that God gives purely at will, and without which a scholar is lost: this was the talent for working deliberately, consistently, and for long hours at a time.

Little is known of his mathematical training prior to the age of 17, when he arrived at the College of William and Mary, but it is obvious that during the two years he studied and boarded with Maury he had sufficient diligence and curiosity to master the fundamentals of Euclid. This was hardly uncommon for bright lads in colonial Virginia's master class, for a knowledge of surveying had a practical use in a frontier society. By consequence he was well prepared to benefit from the two years of what amounted to an almost constant private tutorial with William Small, in the intimate environment of the college, where he refined his knowledge of geometry and was introduced to Newton's *Principia*. He learned to read music, and his gravitation to the violin seemed to be founded in formal traditions, not confined to country fiddling. He somehow resisted the social pressures that drew many young men to gaming, cockfights, horse-racing, ribaldry, and drunkenness. Such temptations were abundant in Virginia's frontier villages, but they apparently did not seduce Thomas Jefferson, as they did others. [17]

[17] Memorandum of Nicholas Trist, Jefferson's private secretary and executor of his estate, cited by Henry Stevens Randall, *Life of Thomas Jefferson*; cf. Monticello.org article on Jefferson, "Violins."

PRECOCIOUS GENIUS, SOME OTHER CONTENDERS

Benjamin Franklin was markedly precocious. He had only one year of grammar school, but as a small child he taught himself to read, starting with Cotton Mather's *Essays to Do Good*, with its argument that "there is no popish nation but would, by embracing the protestant religion, not only introduce itself into a glorious liberty, but also would double its wealth immediately." Mather contended that the value of Protestantism could be precisely calculated in sterling; this was the ideological root of the "Protestant Ethic" that Max Weber sought to identify in Franklin's "spirit of capitalism."[18] At the age of 15 he published his famous *Dogood Letters*, slipping them under the door of the printer's shop where he was apprenticed to his elder brother. At 16 he took temporary charge of publishing the *New-England Courant*, while his brother, James, its editor, was imprisoned for violating the censorship laws. At the age of 19, he published his essay on *Liberty and Necessity, Pleasure and Pain*, where he irreverently brought Calvinist predestination into harmony with Newton's proof of "intelligent design." With veiled sarcasm, he argued against the existence of free will and wielded that talent for ambiguous satire he would display for the rest of his life. At 23, Franklin published *A Modest Enquiry into the Nature and Necessity of a Paper-Currency*, showing an awareness of American needs in banking and finance that Jefferson lacked throughout his life.

George Washington also showed promise as a very young man, for despite a lack of formal schooling he mastered geometry, geography, law, and accounting to become a professional surveyor at the age of 17.[19] Everything Washington touched turned to gold, and even in times of economic volatility he magically acquired wealth. Washington, like Franklin, had the ability to multiply money, unlike Jefferson, who started life with sizeable resources and died on the edge of bankruptcy. Jefferson's childhood circumstances were superficially comparable to Washington's, except that Jefferson's deceased father had provided well for him. George Washington, whose habits were more literary and intellectual than is sometimes recognized, possessed a good library, and repeatedly

[18] For Mather's argument that Protestantism can be specifically valued in pounds sterling, see "A catalogue of desirable things" in his *Essays to do Good* (London, 1816), p. 159. Weber called Franklin "a colorless deist" but traced his capitalist ethos to his Puritan father, seemingly unaware of the direct influence of Mather's essays.

[19] John Rodelhamel, note to George Washington, *Writings* (New York: Library of America, 1997), p. 1056.

demonstrated his infatuation with Joseph Addison's play *Cato.* Washington's writing style can display a cool acerbic wit that indicates habits of literacy. He would unavoidably have possessed second-hand knowledge of such a phrase as *Et tu, Brute*, although he had not studied Latin grammar.[20]

Patrick Henry spent his youth at fiddling and dancing, but demonstrated his intellectual nimbleness when he passed the bar examination after a scant six weeks of preparation, and embarked on a flashy political career.[21] Jefferson, whose intellectual regimen included fifteen hours of study a day, was appalled by his superficiality as a scholar, referring to him as "the laziest man in reading I ever knew." Henry may have been lazy in reading, but he was vigorous in debate, and William Wirt, an early biographer, credited him with the slogans, "If this be treason, let us make the most of it," and "Give me liberty or give me death." Henry, at 39, did almost as much to ignite revolution with his oratory as Jefferson at 33 did with his pen. Jefferson later recalled hearing "the splendid display" of Henry's talents "such as I have never heard from any other man. He appeared to me to speak as Homer wrote."[22]

Another boy genius was Jefferson's rival, Alexander Hamilton. "The bastard brat of a Scottish peddler," as John Adams called him, he was the son of Rachel Lavien, a resolutely independent, highly intelligent, and heroically courageous single mother, who taught him basic arithmetic and rudimentary French. There is some uncertainty as to whether he was born in 1755 or 1757, so we cannot say whether he was 11 or 13 years old when history did "first stoop to notice him," as Jefferson put it.[23] He was

[20] Peter Onuf and Nicolas Cole, *Thomas Jefferson and the Classical World in Early America* (Charlottesville, VA: University of Virginia Press, 2011). Carl J. Richard, *Greeks and Romans Bearing Gifts: How the Ancients Inspired the Founding Fathers* (Lanham, MD: Rowman and Littlefield, 2008), p. 151. Speculations on Washington's classical knowledge in Kevin J. Hayes, *The Road to Monticello: The Life and Mind of Thomas Jefferson* (New York: Oxford University Press, 2008), p. 23. Also see Adrienne M. Harrison, *A Powerful Mind: The Self Education of George Washington* (Lincoln, NE: Potomac Books, 2015).

[21] Malone, *Jefferson the Virginian*, p. 90. Thomas Jefferson: *Autobiography*, January 6 – July 29, 1821, January 6, 1821, Founders Online.

[22] Thomas Jefferson: *Autobiography*, January 6 – July 29, 1821, January 6, 1821, Founders Online.

[23] Jefferson disparages Hamilton with the comment that the Secretary of the Treasury is "a man whose history, from the moment at which history can stoop to notice him, is a tissue of machinations," Jefferson to George Washington, September 9, 1792. Conservative historian Richard Brookhiser, *Alexander Hamilton, American* (New York: Free Press, 1999), pp. 109–110, calls the phrase "one of Jefferson's iciest and ugliest."

in any case exceedingly young in 1768 when, at the death of his mother, he went to work at the import and export firm of Beckman and Cruger on the Caribbean island of St. Croix, the courts having stripped him entirely of the few possessions she left him. He showed early signs of administrative genius, however, and his employers gave him increasing responsibility. In 1772 – he may have been 15, or he may have been 17 – he successfully managed the firm for six months during the absence of its principal head, who travelled to North America for medical reasons. As an adolescent, he could function as an adult in the business world, gaining a knowledge of Atlantic trade routes and the circulation of paper drafts on wares in London storehouses. He was around 19 in the winter of 1774–75 when he published two pamphlets, *A Full Vindication of the Members of Congress* and its lengthier supplement, *The Farmer Refuted* – both published within six months of Jefferson's completing, at age 31, his *Summary View of the Rights of British America*, and, like it, these were no mere polemics against tyranny and taxation, but treatises addressing the material causes of colonial discontent.

Jeremy Bentham, by the time he was 5, had learned to read music, read Latin, and play the violin. At the age of 12 he distinguished himself as a composer of Greek and Latin verse, and was admitted to Oxford University, where he took the B.A. degree before the age of 16. He was an influence on John Stuart Mill, another precocious genius, who learned Greek at 3. Johann Wolfgang von Goethe, like Bentham, was a precocious classicist, who, by the age of 20, had already produced two extended scholarly works in Latin. He launched his public career with mighty impact at 25, publishing his notorious *The Sorrows of Young Werther.* He later contributed significant reflections on various aspects of science, including evolutionary biology. Jefferson's friend Pierre Samuel Du Pont de Nemours, by the age of 29, had published several works on economics, including, with François Quesnay, *Physiocratie, ou constitution naturelle du gouvernement le plus avantageux au genre humain* (1768). Wolfgang Amadeus Mozart, by the age of 33, had completed most of his major works, knew German, Italian, and English, and maintained a playful but tender correspondence in French with his wife, Constanze.

Even a Prussian prince did not necessarily share Jefferson's educational advantages: Frederick II was beaten by his father for reading poetry and discouraged from any interest in the classics. The young prince acquired Greek, Latin, and Hebrew in secret. He learned French with his governess, in infancy, but his father forced him to perform his studies exclusively in German. When, at the age of 18, Frederick and his friend Hans Hermann von Katte plotted to escape to England, the old king had them tried and convicted for treason and desertion; then he forced Frederick to witness von Katte's beheading. Despite these traumas, Frederick became one of Europe's comparatively tolerant and enlightened intellectuals, and a patron of the arts and letters. His book, the *Anti-Machiavelli*, was written in French, a language that Jefferson read very well, but could sometimes find intimidating to speak or write. Frederick wrote whole volumes in French, their content ranging from military science to poetry, some composed according to the strict conventions of the Italian sonnet form.

EXTRAORDINARY LITERARY ERUDITION

The depth and breadth of Jefferson's studies, even by the exacting standards of his times, were imposing. There were few subjects in which he lacked an interest, and, requiring no stimulation other than curiosity, he accumulated knowledge for the purest love of learning. He was a bibliophile, and from every indication he loved books for their contents, for their reputations, for the texture of their paper, for the style of their bindings, and the smell of their ink. Like most intellectuals, he had in his library those books that were, according to Bacon's precept, to be "tasted" and those to be "swallowed whole." There are several hints, but few proofs, in his letters as to which of the books in his reading lists fell into which of these categories. Not every book in his library fell into the Baconian category of those to be "thoroughly chewed and digested." Jefferson could be a name-dropper, and, when he failed to acknowledge the essential role of militarism in Spartan history, he revealed that he did not always give evidence of deep reflection on what he read.

What Samuel Johnson said of the erudite John Dryden may justly be applied to Jefferson, for it can be surmised "that his studies were rather desultory and fortuitous than constant and systematical."[24] He was as opinionated as Johnson, and his views, the majority of which are preserved in private correspondence, on the arts and letters reveal a profound capacity for absorption and an uninhibited capacity for pontification. He characterized the work of David Hume as "elegant lies," and, while generally

[24] For example, he possessed a copy of *Sparrman's Voyage* (1786 – see Chapter 8, note 25, below), which opened the mind of Herder with respect to the merits of African cultures, but which Jefferson apparently ignored when he dismissed the possibility of appraising the same.

appreciative of Adam Smith, accused him of prolixity.[25] Thomas Paine had far less formal education than Jefferson, but was at least as articulate, and more systematic. Under vastly more trying circumstances, he published more. In matters of religious thought, Jefferson never equaled the imagination or the wit of William Blake. Jefferson's reaction to the pageant of Toussaint Louverture was inferior to Wordsworth's, and his comments on the humanity of Africans in general fell short of Herder's.[26]

Jefferson's influence on the literary tradition of the frontier is indirect, if undeniable. Literary historian Henry Nash Smith called him "the intellectual father of the American advance to the Pacific," acknowledging Jefferson's role in the creation of "the American West as symbol and myth." Jefferson's 1824 letter to William Ludlow foresaw the disappearance of native cultures before the march of civilization:

> I am 81 years of age, born where I now live, in the first range of mountains in interior of our country. and I have observed this march of civilisation advancing from the sea coast, passing over us like a cloud of light, increasing our knolege and improving our condition insomuch as that we are at this time more advanced in civilization here than the seaports were when I was a boy. and where this progress will stop no one can say. barbarism has in the mean time been receding before the steady step of amelioration; and will in time I trust disappear from the earth.[27]

JEFFERSON AND CLASSICAL CULTURE

In Jefferson's lifetime, as today, even a genius might employ a tricky simile, "like a cloud of light," and even an "ignoramus" knew something about the classics. While presumably the young Jefferson read Plutarch's *Lives* in the original Latin, it would not have been necessary for him to do

[25] Henry E. May, *The Enlightenment in America* (Oxford University Press, 1978), p. 294. Jefferson's neglect of Rousseau has inspired little scholarly reflection. Hume sometimes elicited his grudging admiration, while Voltaire (see *Notes on Virginia*) caught his attention for his scientific, but not his literary or philosophical, opinions.

[26] Winthrop Jordan was the first to compare Jefferson with Herder on racial issues. See Winthrop Jordan, *White over Black: American Attitudes toward the Negro, 1550–1812* (Chapel Hill: University of North Carolina Press, 1968), p. 230. Emanuel Chukwudi Eze, while recognizing the humanitarian ideals of Herder, noted that on the whole the Enlightenment had the effect of strengthening rather than ameliorating the pain of white supremacy. See Eze, ed., *Race and the Enlightenment* (Oxford: Blackwell, 1997), p. 5. To Eze's astute observation, I would add that Enlightenment rationality necessitated the scientific justification of slavery, colonialism, and white supremacy.

[27] Henry Nash Smith, *Virgin Land: The American West as Symbol and Myth* (Cambridge, MA: Harvard University Press, 1950), p. 15. Jefferson to William Ludlow, September 6, 1824.

so. Centuries before, Shakespeare knew Plutarch and other classical authors only in translation, or by oral tradition, but it is to Shakespeare that Jefferson's generation, and succeeding generations, have turned for their impressions of Julius Caesar and when quoting his spurious last words.

Jefferson's mastery of Latin would have been excellent, since he began to study it at an age when the brain is receptive to foreign-language acquisition. He quoted Greek texts, although not extensively, in correspondence with John Adams, who responded by teasing him gently:

> Lord! Lord! What can I do, with So much Greek? When I was of your Age, young Man, i.e. 7 or 8 or 9 years ago I felt, a kind of pang of Affection, for one of the flames of my youth, and again paid my Addresses to Isocrates and Dionissius Hallicarnassensis &c &c &c I collected all my Lexicons and Grammers and Sat down to περι ενθεςεως ονοματων &c. In this Way I amused myself for sometime: but I found, that if I looked a word to day, in less than a Week I had to look it again. It was to little better purpose, than writing Letters on a pail of Water.[28]

As a source of moral as well as intellectual discipline, he valued the classics and scorned the Old Testament. He selected eternal verities arbitrarily from the ancients according to the virtues he admired and tended to overlook more cynical appraisals of classical culture.[29] This practice he inherited from medieval, Renaissance, and other Enlightenment authors, and he sometimes extracted lessons that could not withstand the most casual scrutiny. So, for example, he insisted that "The Greeks and Romans had no standing armies, yet they defended themselves."[30] This, despite the evidence of the Peloponnesian Wars, in which the perpetually mobilized Sparta defeated Athens, and the testimony of Polybius that Rome had a standing army by the third century BC. All the Greek city-states, with the notable exception of militaristic Laconia, eventually submitted to Philip and Alexander. It is certain that Jefferson read and admired Plutarch and Xenophon, both of whom were quite specific about the Spartans' universal military socialization and warlike culture. This leads to the conclusion that Jefferson could be deliberately obtuse when the books he read did not confirm his ideological presuppositions.[31]

[28] John Adams to Jefferson, July 9, 1813.

[29] Christopher Marlowe mocked the Greek myths as tales of "heady riots, incest, rape" in his *Hero and Leander*. Cotton Mather's opinion may be intuited.

[30] Jefferson to Thomas Cooper, September 10, 1814.

[31] Clifford Hindley, "Xenophon on Male Love," *The Classical Quarterly*, new series, 49, no. 1 (1999), 74–99.

It seems reasonable to presume that Jefferson was silently perturbed by the relationship between homosexuality and Greek military culture, but it is more likely that he ignored it. The Spartan demand for universal military service, and the lack of any surviving tradition in Spartan arts and letters, left Jefferson with few ideas of Greek civilization other than those of the Athenians. The slavery-based Athenian democracy, while close to what he practiced, was far removed from the egalitarianism he professed. The Spartans' organic conception of the state reveals that they thought of liberty in purely collectivist terms, which was anathema to the ideal of personal freedom professed by Jefferson.

Obsessed with discovering the patterns that led to the decline of Greek, Roman, and other civilizations, he sought to discover the eternal principles of time's arrow and time's cycle – what led to progress and what led to repetition. He was, of course, aware of the historiography of decline, as expressed in Tacitus, Bolingbroke, and Gibbon, and was anxious to discover the laws of nature that determined the trajectories of civilizations. It is difficult to say whether he agreed with Volney that the ancient Ethiopians and Egyptians had discovered the principles of government by studying the laws of nature, and then fallen into decline by allowing their foundational values to decay. Certainly he accepted the view that the ancients had discovered the first and most enduring of nature's principles in literature, the arts, and sciences.

While devising slogans of Democratic Republicanism, Jefferson delighted in the demonstration of his elite classicist erudition. As for modern languages, his supportive biographer Dumas Malone says that Jefferson learned to speak French "eventually." This seems to be faint praise, for apparently he could communicate adequately soon after his arrival in France. He tells of conversing with an economically distressed peasant woman, whom he met by chance walking along a country road in 1785. Assuming that this uneducated woman spoke little or no English, Jefferson functioned impressively for a 40-year-old with little previous exposure to speakers of colloquial French.[32] Of course he had never experienced the practical need to speak French as a youth, unlike his daughters, or John Quincy Adams. He therefore never mastered it as fully as did continental intellectuals of his generation. Jefferson read Montesquieu and De Tracy, but he recorded his reactions to them minimally. This is not remarkable, for he was also sparse in his commentary on

[32] Jefferson described this conversation to the Reverend James Madison, president of William and Mary, October 28, 1785.

all authors. The Scottish authors, such as David Hume and Adam Smith, received no more specific commentary than their French contemporaries.

LITERARY IMAGINATION, ART, AND AESTHETICS

Jefferson's literary theory was didactic; his reading tastes reflected the classical belief that we read in order to learn moral lessons. His aesthetics were not limited by his grounding in the classics, for he was affected by the "cult of sensibility," but we do not discover in his writing much discussion of classical or neoclassical, or proto-romantic literary theory. To the extent that he believed literature should encourage morality, he was in agreement with the traditional Aristotelian–Horatian precepts. But by the mid eighteenth century a cult of sensibility had begun to resuscitate the neoclassical idea that morality was encouraged more by emotional sympathy than by rationality and didacticism. There is little in his writings that reveals the theoretical basis of his taste in eighteenth-century authors. Certainly nothing that reveals his attitudes towards the theatrical productions he witnessed in France, or the novels and poetry produced by French authors during this extremely fruitful period of French literature.

Jefferson's ideas of literature were utilitarian, in the Aristotelian or Horatian sense: that is, he justified literature for its function of instructing through pleasure. Literature must teach by pleasing, and its lessons might be strictly didactic with a clearly stated moral lesson, or literature might teach by arousing sympathy with a protagonist, or it might arouse our pity and fear as we witness the downfall of a great man. Percy Bysshe Shelley, who was a generation younger, and incidentally an admirer of Jefferson, recognized neo-Aristotelian defenses of poetry when he said that poesy takes us out of ourselves and makes us sympathize with another, thereby teaching us morality not by preaching, but by awakening sympathy. What Jefferson's contemporaries said of literature they often said of history as well: the value of Plutarch was to teach virtues, drawn from the lives of noble Greeks and Romans, not in a relativistic conceptualization of the past, and not in the search for any peculiar Zeitgeist in a representative man. The purpose was not to illustrate historical particularities, but to celebrate what were assumed to be eternal verities.

At the age of 28, Jefferson wrote to Robert Skipwith, the husband of his wife's half-sister, evincing a theory that was a typical, if somewhat unoriginal, expression of traditional literary utilitarianism, stating "that the entertainments of fiction are useful as well as pleasant." We read history and literature to the same effect, for "the fictitious murther of Duncan by

Macbeth in Shakespeare" must excite in the sensitive reader "as great horror of villainy, as the real one of Henry IV by Ravaillac."[33] It seems likely that Jefferson clung to such notions for the next fifty years, and there is some indication that he did. Jefferson's relish for the seemingly contradictory elements in his literary world, such as the blend of sentimentality and Horatian satire found in Laurence Sterne's *Tristram Shandy* and the romanticism in James Macpherson, has inspired delightful commentary from E. M. Halliday. The Marquis de Chastellux describes an evening at Monticello in 1782 that he spent in drinking punch and discussing James Macpherson's contrived Celtic epic, *Ossian*, well into the night.[34] Jefferson's discussions of literature reveal greater interest in Macpherson's romanticism than in the biting sociological realism of Voltaire's *Candide* or the pastoral reflections of Rousseau's *Reveries*.

He viewed the aesthetic sense and the moral sense as innate and closely related, an idea disseminated by Francis Hutcheson. The human moral and aesthetic senses were analogous and mutually reinforcing in the systems of Hutcheson and Adam Smith. Beauty and virtue were implicitly linked in Hume, that is to say what is moral must be beautiful, and that which is beautiful must be moral. For a person with a bias towards the classics, this would seem natural and normal, for the ideas of wickedness and disharmony were etymologically related in the Greek language, where the terms for evil and cacophony have the common stem, "*kakós*." But there were some classical ideas that Jefferson shied away from, for example, Longinus suggesting that the sublime can also be terrifying, nuancing a similar idea in Aristotle. The idea that even the shocking, the cruel, and the destructive may have a sort of beauty was an underlying paradox of Lessing's *Laocoön*. While Jefferson had a sufficient sense of irony to appreciate the wit of Laurence Sterne, he was not fond of paradox and ambiguity, and his excursions into literary theory did not exploit the full range of classical or contemporary discussions – at least not when he put his ideas into writing.

[33] The editors of Jefferson's papers at Princeton University Press describe the defense of fiction in this letter as "less noteworthy" than its inconsistencies of spelling, "since it represents the views of English critics from Sir Philip Sidney to Addison and Johnson than the up-to-the-minute character of the list." See editorial note, "From Jefferson to Robert Skipwith, with a List of Books for a Private Library, 3 August 1771," Founders Online: http://founders.archives.gov/documents/Jefferson/01–01-02–0056 (ver. 2015-09-29).

[34] E. M. Halliday, *Understanding Thomas Jefferson* (New York: HarperCollins, 2001), p. 188.

In literature, as in the natural sciences, Jefferson is noted for his appreciation of excellence, rather than for his contributions to the field. He wrote to John Adams in 1818 of his "canine appetite for reading," adding with an ironic twist that it was reading "which occupies the mind without the labor of producing ideas from my own stock."

As a literary critic, Jefferson was whimsical and unsystematic. While the breadth and sophistication of his reading were impressive, he left few clues as to his criteria of literary excellence. Jefferson's reading tastes reflected his grounding in the classics, although we do not discover in his writing much discussion of classical or neoclassical literary theory. He seems to have accepted without question the moral criteria of Milton, Pope, and Samuel Johnson. The *Poetics* of Aristotle, and their influence on Horace, would have been inescapable. One suspects that he would have encountered, at least indirectly, the neoclassical principles of Philip Sidney, Joseph Addison, and Richard Steele, and found them satisfactory. But like Samuel Johnson's, and unlike Voltaire's, Jefferson's critical theory was only moderately neoclassical; he was open to Shakespearean and other post-Aristotelian literary values. That is to say, his tastes were, in many respects, modern.

The Enlightenment was sometimes an age of irrationality, and its authors often displayed hostile reactions to reason and common sense. One of the landmarks of what Paine called "The Age of Reason," but probably unknown to Paine, was an attack on empiricism in Immanuel Kant's *Critique of Pure Reason*. The Age of Reason was also the age of enthusiastic religion, ceremonial spirit possession, heart over head, tearful virtue, the cult of sensibility, and the "sentimental novel," usually associated with Oliver Goldsmith and Samuel Richardson. One of the most influential of all romantic novels was Johann Wolfgang von Goethe's *Die Leiden des jungen Werther*, the story of a young man who commits suicide when the woman he loves marries another man. Goethe's Werther did not conform to Aristotelian criteria of excellence, but the book was a landmark of pre-romanticism, and it was an international bestseller. Young men all over Europe began dressing in imitation of him, and there was even a rash of "Werther suicides," as some even went so far as to take their own lives in imitation of Goethe's hapless hero.

The literature of the British Enlightenment contained contradictory elements of romanticism and reason, of sense and sensibility, of social conscience and individualism. A poet like Samuel Johnson might spend an afternoon idling in the meadows, meditating on the pleasures of solitude, then of an evening repair to Will's coffee-house. Not surprisingly we see in

Benjamin Franklin a man whose literary habits resembled those of Johnson, as much as his politics eventually differed. A frontiersman who could negotiate firearms and rum with Indians, Franklin easily found himself at home in his London gentleman's club. The Anglophone Enlightenment was a world rich in scope, intellectually as well as geographically. John Adams was a biting satirist, a social conservative, and a heretical individualistic deist, who willingly paid taxes to support the established church. There was no uniformity in the British literary Enlightenment. The various individuals contradicted one another, and they contradicted themselves.

William Godwin, a major contemporary figure in literature and philosophy, was a name that naturally arose in the correspondence between Jefferson and John Adams. Adams brought it up, but Jefferson did not respond. Jefferson paid no attention to Mary Wollstonecraft, who just happened to be William Godwin's wife, as well as the best-remembered feminist of her day. He may have been unaware of Jane Austen, who did not achieve her standing as a major British stylist and social commentator until decades after her demise. Mary Shelley, daughter of Godwin and Mary Wollstonecraft, published her widely reviewed work, *Frankenstein, or the Modern Prometheus*, in 1818, when Jefferson was only 75. There is no reason he would have noticed it, and indeed it made little impression on his American contemporaries. The work is important as an early critique of the age's sometimes uncritical fascination with science, and today it is better remembered than anything Percy Shelley ever wrote.

A product of the imagination of a 21-year-old, *Frankenstein* has become the emblematic expression of scientific skepticism for all subsequent ages. There was hardly any way for an aging physiocrat in rural Virginia to have anticipated the moral problematic of science and society that Mary Shelley addressed. Skepticism regarding science was a matter to be developed by the next generation of American romantics, and would find expression in the writings of Hawthorne and Emerson. Unlike certain of his literary contemporaries, the somewhat younger Blake, and the much younger Wordsworth, Jefferson viewed scientific progress with seldom-alleviated optimism.

His tastes were conventional, and he was captivated by the contemporary enthusiasm for Fingal, the legendary Celtic hero, whose story was represented in James Macpherson's Ossian cycle. Macpherson was a Scottish writer who collected and translated verses that he claimed to have discovered in the Highlands, and which he attributed to a third-century poet named Ossian. The popularity of this work, be it a restoration or a fabrication, is more understandable to cultural historians than to most readers of the present day. Jefferson and Goethe admired it, Voltaire satirized it, and Samuel Johnson dismissed it as a hoax. Jefferson seems to have shared a common opinion that Macpherson's translation was on a level comparable to Homer. When Charles Mcpherson, the poet's kinsman, toured the United States, Jefferson met him, and later wrote to him saying, "The tender and the sublime emotions of the mind were never before so wrought up by the human hand. I am not ashamed to own that I think this rude bard of the North the greatest poet that has ever existed."[35]

Perhaps it was his quest for a northern European equivalent of the classical poets, or perhaps it was the quest for an authentic noble savage that ignited Jefferson's admiration for Ossian. He was fascinated with the oratorical powers of the Native American, and wrote in *Notes on Virginia* of the stirring speech of Logan, Chief of the Mingos, delivered to Lord Dunmore: "I may challenge the whole orations of Demosthenes and Cicero, and of any more eminent orator ... to produce a single passage superior to the speech of Logan." The authenticity of the speech, like that of Ossian's verses, was dubious. Even more curious was Jefferson's recollection at the age of 69 of a speech he had heard when he was 14. He recalled being present in the camp of "the great Outassetè [Outacity], the warrior and orator of the Cherokees," when that man delivered a "farewell oration to his people." He recalled how the speaker's voice "filled me with awe & veneration, altho' I did not understand a word he uttered." Many years later, he expressed a bias that Native Americans were gifted in oratory, while African Americans were not. His empirical evidence for this bold assertion was a publication of dubious provenance and a dimly recalled speech he heard in his youth, delivered in a language that he could not understand.[36]

He professed an understanding of several languages, and wrote to Joseph Delaplaine, "I read Greek, Latin, French, Italian, Spanish." In some of the books he owned that were written in these languages, indeed he made marginal notes.[37] He seems to have read French with ease, although he avoided corresponding in it. The several volumes edited by Chinard, one of them comprising his correspondence with Lafayette, and two more his

[35] James Macpherson and Charles Mcpherson spelled their names differently; James addressed Charles as "My Dear Sir" in a letter of August 7, 1773, saying, "I seldom hear from you." Boyd refers to him as "a shadowy figure" in Julian P. Boyd, *The Papers of Thomas Jefferson* (Princeton University Press, 1953), vol. I, p. 96.

[36] Thomas Jefferson, *Notes on the State of Virginia*, ed. David Waldstreicher (Boston, MA: Bedford Books, 2002), pp. 123–124. Jefferson to John Adams, June 11, 1812.

[37] Jefferson to Joseph Delaplaine, April 12, 1817.

correspondence with Volney, Say, Tracy, Comte, and others, almost invariably reveal him answering French letters in English. So too when German correspondents, such as Friederich von Geismar and Alexander von Humboldt, wrote to him in French, he responded in English. Jefferson's independent mastery of Anglo-Saxon dialects, which he sometimes reproduced in his writings on legal history, was singularly impressive. His papers include a few examples of his diplomatic correspondence in French and some letters to wine merchants. If may be that he secured assistance in writing this French business correspondence, but we can say of a certainty that his butler, Adrien Petit, was neither his amanuensis nor his editor, as Petit wrote French far more poorly than Jefferson.[38]

It is more likely that Jefferson was regularly aided by William Short, his private secretary, who resided with him in the Hôtels de Landron and Langeac. Short was 25 when he arrived in Paris in 1784, and, sixteen years younger than the middle-aged Jefferson, he advanced with greater rapidity towards a mastery of the language. For several months, Short isolated himself from English speakers by boarding with an educated middle-class French family in the town of Saint-Germain-en-Laye, where he apparently developed a romantic interest. His French abilities were apparently well advanced, even at the point of his arrival, for the Duchess Rosalie de La Rochefoucauld d'Enville wrote to Short as follows: "I cannot tell you, Monsieur, how I am amazed at the skill with which you write French. I truly marvel that a foreigner can so idiomatically and precisely use expressions which must be strange to him in his own tongue, and in a manner that many Frenchmen would envy who pride themselves on writing well." An intense love affair with the young matron, commencing shortly after his arrival, may have provided means, motive, and opportunity for a more rapid mastery of the language. It seems clear that Short pursued his studies in French with greater assiduity than most Americans, and if the duchess' testimony was more than flattery, he was well equipped to serve Jefferson as a splendidly useful translator, as well as secretary.[39]

38 Gilbert Chinard, *Volney et l'Amérique d'après des documents inédits et sa correspondance avec Jefferson* (Baltimore: Johns Hopkins University Press, 1923). Gilbert Chinard, *Jefferson et les idéologues d'après sa correspondance inédite avec Destutt de Tracy, Cabinis, J.-B. Say et Auguste Comte* (Baltimore: Johns Hopkins University Press, 1925). Gilbert Chinard, *The Letters of Lafayette and Jefferson* (Baltimore: Johns Hopkins University Press, 1929).

39 Marie Kimball, "William Short, Jefferson's Only 'Son'," *North American Review*, 223 (1926), 471–486; Yvon Bizardel and Howard C. Rice, "Poor in Love Mr. Short," *The William and Mary Quarterly*, 21, no. 4 (October, 1964), 516–533.

But although he was never strong in spoken or written French, Jefferson could communicate functionally with the natives upon his arrival. He was also able to get around, after a fashion, in Italy, although he did not measure up to the extraordinary genius of Goethe as a modern linguist any more than he matched him as a classicist. Jefferson knew very little of German authors in translation and nothing of them in the original, despite the increasing interest in German that Anglophone intellectuals began to show by the end of the 1790s. Nonetheless, Jefferson's linguistic accomplishments were excellent by eighteenth-century standards, and few twenty-first-century American intellectuals can approach him.

ANGLO-SAXONISM, LANGUAGE, LAW, AND LITERATURE

Jefferson began young to master late "Old English," or Anglo-Saxon, as it is more properly called, and this was among his many impressive intellectual achievements. It is a challenging language, which bears closer resemblances to Old Norse than to modern English. It antedates by several centuries the Middle English of Geoffrey Chaucer, and is even more distant from the Early Modern English of Shakespeare and the King James Bible. Jefferson began the study of Anglo-Saxon as part of his law studies. In his bill for the revision of Virginia's code of crimes and punishments, he wrote to George Wythe, "The extracts from the Anglo-Saxon laws, the sources of the Common law, I wrote in their original for my own satisfaction." In numerous later instances one notes an insistence that Anglo-Saxon ought to be an important part of the training of lawyers, and thus his efforts to guarantee that it would be competently taught at the University of Virginia.[40]

As in the case of his French, it is difficult to assess how thorough Jefferson's mastery of Anglo-Saxon was. Stanley Hauer, writing in the flagship journal of the Modern Language Association, *PMLA*, is of the opinion that his studies were impressive, but that his mastery was limited, and that he showed little sensitivity for the 500-year difference between the Anglo-Saxon language of Alfred the Great and the eminently more readable Middle English of Chaucer.[41] This is difficult to explain, because

[40] Jefferson to George Wythe, November 1, 1778. Jefferson to John Waldo, August 16, 1813, Jefferson to John Adams, August 15, 1820.

[41] Stanley R. Hauer, "Thomas Jefferson and the Anglo-Saxon Language," *PMLA*, 98, no. 5 (October, 1983), 879–898.

Jefferson quoted so often from ancient English texts that he had to be aware of the relative difficulty of reading the two languages. Although he showed little interest in Anglo-Saxon literature, he was able to translate legal documents from Anglo-Saxon, which indicates something more than the ability to make use of a bilingual dictionary. There seems little doubt that he was able to read and translate the language, and that his capacity was not limited to the East Midlands dialect of Chaucer's fourteenth century. Hauer comments that "had his library contained the early works of Grimm and Rask that were in print during his lifetime, his studies would have been the more profitable."

POETRY, PROSODY, AND CRITICISM

Phillis Wheatley was a pretty, chocolate-skinned, 7-year-old girl, who showed up on the docks of Boston, Massachusetts, in 1761. Were her eyes wide with fright, or was she apathetic with hunger and fatigue when the benevolent John Wheatley purchased her, brought her home, and treated her almost as a member of his family? She was converted to Christianity, and taught to read and write English, and John Wheatley even thought she showed "great inclination to learn the Latin Tongue," in which she "made some progress."[42] In 1773, she published *Poems on Various Subjects, Religious and Moral*, most of them composed while she was in her teens. The following are among her more often quoted lines:

> Should you, my lord, while you peruse my song,
> Wonder from whence my love of *Freedom* sprung,
> Whence flow these wishes for the common good,
> By feeling hearts alone best understood,
> I, young in life, by seeming cruel fate
> Was snatch'd from *Afric's* fancy'd happy seat:
> What pangs excruciating must molest,
> What sorrows labour in my parent's breast?
> Steel'd was that soul and by no misery mov'd
> That from a father seiz'd his babe belov'd:
> Such, such my case. And can I then but pray
> Others may never feel tyrannic sway?

[42] Vincent Carretta, *Phillis Wheatley: Biography of a Genius in Bondage* (Athens, GA: University of Georgia Press, 2011), briefly mentions Phillis Wheatley's beginnings in Latin, p. 40, and cites, p. 209 note 35, John Wheatley's letter that prefaced her *Poems on Various Subjects, Religious and Moral* (London: Archibald Bell, 1773).

If we are to evaluate Wheatley's verse, the first question to be posed is that of methodology. The expression of one's likes or dislikes may be of less interest than an explanation of how one arrives at an opinion. The question of whether Wheatley's poetry has merit should be preceded by a presentation of the method whereby we arrive at our judgment. How do we decide that it is inferior to or superior to the verse of Joseph Addison, a poet whose merit Jefferson found self-evident?

> OH Liberty, thou goddess heav'nly bright,
> Profuse of bliss and pregnant with delight!
> Eternal pleasures in thy presence reign,
> And smiling Plenty leads thy wanton train;
> Eas'd of her load, Subjection grows more light,
> And Poverty looks cheerful in thy sight;
> Thou mak'st the gloomy face of nature gay,
> Giv'st beauty to the sun and pleasure to the day.[43]

Jefferson, although he never produced any comparable verse at any age, quoted Addison without raising an eyebrow, and was cruelly contemptuous of Wheatley's accomplishments. He never revealed the touchstone he applied to Phillis Wheatley's poetry, nor did he ever reveal the methodology that allowed him to place Joel Barlow and Philip Freneau at a high position in the chain of Anglophone poets. Phillis Wheatley had "small Latin, and less Greek," like William Shakespeare, Benjamin Franklin, and Thomas Paine, but her poetry was informed by a secondary knowledge of the classics, and it demonstrated discipline and taste. Anyone is entitled to entertain whatever opinions of Phillis Wheatley's poems they wish, but it is weak practice to declare Wheatley's poetry "beneath criticism," as Jefferson so famously did, without revealing what his critical methodology might be.

His "Thoughts on English Prosody" is the only extended essay in which he approached literary theory. On the level of prosody, according to Jefferson's own standard, Phillis' outpourings were in no way inferior to Addison's. Indeed, Jefferson detected inelegance in the final line of Addison above, having accepted the dogma of Alexander Pope that the "Alexandrine," or six-feet, line is "Like a wounded snake [that] drags its slow length along." Even Addison was not above criticism for inserting

[43] Kevin J. Hayes, in *The Road to Monticello*, p. 308, comments on Jefferson's literary taste, including his preference for the poet William Shenstone, and opines that "Jefferson obviously found the apostrophe to Liberty from Joseph Addison's 'Letter from Italy' inspiring."

one into his verse, Jefferson pontificated. The six-feet line "only is tolerated now and then, and is never a beauty."[44] For over a century, French neoclassical poets had considered the Alexandrine to be the most noble and heroic of lines, but that was, of course, in another language and represented a different national taste, a matter Jefferson might have addressed, since he wrote the essay while living in Paris.[45] In any case, he offered no other commentary on Addison's lines: on neither the strained syntax nor the vulgar juxtaposition of the image of pregnancy against smiling Plenty, wantonly aborting her load in the sight of cheerful Poverty.

Later in the essay, he juxtaposes Milton's account of creation against that of the King James translation of Genesis 1:6, presumably to the disadvantage of Milton. This was hardly a bad judgment. The problem is not, however, in Milton's decision to render the account of creation in blank verse, but in his gilding of a lily. The King James version is not only more familiar to the ear, but more natural. A critic more picayune than Jefferson might have noted that the words being compared were not in the Hebrew of the Jewish Bible but the English of Sir Launcelot Andrews' committee, which rendered the Bible into English at King James' behest. By the time Jefferson was making his observations, presumably around 1785, biblical scholars had already begun to question whether the author of Genesis actually was Moses. In any case, Jefferson's facetious reference to Moses as the author revealed a certain intellectual flippancy – a refusal to present the grounds on which he considered either the King James or the Miltonic version to be superior.

Would Jefferson have argued for a systematic aesthetic theory, a standard equally applicable to Milton, Pope, Joel Barlow, and Philip Freneau? Could he have formally explained the grounds for his admiration of Joseph Addison? Was he sensitive to the clumsy imagery, the vulgar neoclassicism, or the sometimes strained rhythms of Addison's verse? He proclaimed by fiat the inferiority of Wheatley's verse, as if the assertion required neither evidence nor argument, resorting to the facile expedient that prevails in so much of his thinking and taking refuge in the self-evident.

44 Jefferson might have mentioned the fact that there are two Alexandrine lines in Addison's "The Blessings of Liberty," which is an extract from his "Letter from Italy."

45 Racine's exemplary Alexandrine couplet from *Phèdre*: "Je le vis, je rougis, je pâlis à sa vue/ Un trouble s'éleva dans mon âme éperdue" (I, 3, vv. 273–274).

MUSIC AS PURE AESTHETICISM AND OPERA WITHOUT SOCIAL COMMENTARY

Jefferson possessed impressive musical gifts, including the indispensable talent for practice. Apparently without being pressured by parents or teachers, he is said to have practiced three hours daily. At least twice in his life, injuries to his wrist would have impaired his violin playing: once in 1781, during the period of his governorship of Virginia; and once in 1786, during a Parisian promenade, while leaping a fence in the Cours-la-Reine in an apparent attempt to impress Maria Cosway.[46] The latter injury affected his ability to write for several weeks and sadly impaired his bowmanship on the violin. The site at Monticello.org reports that he continued to purchase violin bows and strings, which leads to the supposition that he was probably able to continue playing after these accidents.

There are few works by Mozart in the catalogue of Jefferson's music, and none by Beethoven. Although Haydn, Handel, and J. C. Bach are present, works by minor Italian and French composers far outnumber those by the greatest Germans. A portion of his music collection was the donation of the Prussian prisoner of war Baron von Geismar, with whom Jefferson occasionally performed during 1779.[47]

Unfortunately, we know little of his performance style at a time when styles of performance on string instruments made demands very different from those of today.[48] His love of music and his listening tastes are only partially documented. There is nothing of music criticism in his writings, and he made no attempts to relate his musical experience to broader elements of Enlightenment culture. He certainly knew that music, especially the opera, was associated with political ideas, but this reality does not seem to have interested him. There is no evidence that he attributed any importance to Beethoven, the musician we think of today as inseparable from the Age of Revolution. There is no reason news should have reached the White House of when Napoleon's occupation of Vienna

[46] Jon Kukla, *Mister Jefferson's Women* (New York: Vintage, 2008), p. 96.

[47] Michael Kranish, *Flight from Monticello* (Oxford University Press, 2010), p. 297. Peter Nicolaisen, "Thomas Jefferson and Friederich Wilhelm von Geismar: A Transatlantic Friendship," *The Magazine of Albemarle County History*, 64 (2006), 5.

[48] We do not know, for example, whether Jefferson utilized a "constant vibrato" or a more traditional baroque "vibrato-free" technique, where bowing putatively had a more important role in expression. Greta Moens-Haenen, *Vibrato as Expressive Ornament: Translation of Summary Chapter from* Das Vibrato in der Musik des Barock (1988), translated by Frederick K. Gable (1992, revised 2009), available at: www.york.ac.uk/music/conferences/nema/haenen/

temporarily interrupted the debut of Beethoven's *Fidelio*, that testament to political freedom. The supposedly apolitical Vivaldi is well represented in the catalogue of Jefferson's works listed by the University of Virginia Music Library. This catalogue, to be sure, contains only music acquired before 1783, so it is possible that Jefferson may eventually have become familiar with later composers.[49]

Mozart and his librettist, Lorenzo Da Ponte, offer disturbing contemporary commentaries on gender and sexual issues that were central to Jefferson's world. I discuss elsewhere how the Italian libretto of Mozart's *Don Giovanni* and the text of *Le Nozze di Figaro*, which was adapted from a trilogy by Beaumarchais, addressed poignant issues of sexual and class exploitation that any slaveholder would have witnessed or experienced in eighteenth-century Virginia. Mozart's *Die Zauberflöte* presents the high priest Sarastro, said to embody the enlightened ideals of freemasonry, and his *Entführung aus dem Serail* presents the character Pasha Selim, an enlightened despot. Both operas circulate impressions of oriental enlightenment also found in Samuel Johnson's *Rasselas* and Montesquieu's *Persian Letters*.

Beethoven's outraged reaction to Napoleon's coronation as emperor is legendary, but one finds no similar immediate reaction to that event in Jefferson's papers. Unlike Beethoven or Mozart, Jefferson gives no evidence of seeing music as a commentary on political happenings. Eighteenth-century opera was often highly political, albeit the baroque tradition of *opera seria* continued to avoid direct commentary on contemporary political events and made its points indirectly by reference to Greek mythology or Roman history. *Opera buffa* often focused on more contemporary, and thus more sensitive, themes. Commentaries on politically sensitive issues, even obliquely stated, could lead to a work's being censored, as was Beaumarchais' *Le Marriage de Figaro*, by the official censor under Louis XVI. It seems unlikely that Jefferson could have witnessed a performance of the operatic version, which premiered in Vienna in 1786. The catalogues of his musical library do include arias from Mozart's *Don Giovanni*, namely that parody of feminine submissiveness, "Beat me, beat me, oh pretty Masetto; beat your poor Zerlina." Its lines certainly touched the sensibilities of eighteenth-century feminists.

[49] This catalogue is a transcription of "The Music Section of Jefferson's Catalogue of 1783" and "An Inventory of the Collections of Jefferson Family Music," Appendices I and II of Helen Cripe, *Thomas Jefferson and Music* (Charlottesville, VA: University of Virginia Press, 1974), pp. 97–128.

One assumes that Jefferson understood what he listened to, but he never reacted to the inescapable social implications of the Mozart operas he apparently encountered.[50]

The operatic world of the eighteenth-century Enlightenment contained three seemingly antagonistic movements: classicism, revolutionism, and romanticism. The first element appears in Mozart's *opere serie*, such as *Idomeneo*; the second in Don Giovanni, with its cry of "Viva la libertà!"; and the third in the proto-romanticism of *Die Zauberflöte*, which Jefferson might have appreciated as part of an eighteenth-century romanticization of Nilotic culture that historian Scott Trafton has called "Egyptomania."[51] Produced in Vienna in 1791, it was a mélange of masonic musical references and pseudo-Turkish musical themes placed in an Egyptian setting. It might have interested American Masons like George Washington, who probably never saw it, or Benjamin Franklin, who died the year before its debut. The scene in which Monostatos, a Moorish slave, hovers menacingly over an unconscious white virgin is Jeffersonian in its attribution of lascivious instincts to black men.

THE DISTRACTION OF PUBLIC AFFAIRS

It might be suggested that the overwhelming burden of public affairs kept him from publishing a treatise on political theory, but Jefferson certainly enjoyed as much solitude and leisure as any of his continental or American contemporaries. In fact, nothing ever kept him from his writing-desk; he simply chose not to systematically develop his ideas, although he had the mental capacity, the writing talent, and the time to do so. Even during his years in the White House, he was less burdened with governmental affairs than other heads of state, then or now. In comparison with European contemporaries, like Frederick the Great, Edmund Burke, David Hume, or Johann Wolfgang von Goethe, Thomas Jefferson, whether at Monticello or Poplar Forest, or in the relatively slow-paced environment of rural Washington, DC, always had great blocks of time available for reading,

[50] Sandor Salgo, *Thomas Jefferson, Musician and Violinist* (Charlottesville, VA: The Thomas Jefferson Foundation, 2000), p. 66. In this aria, *Batti, batti, o bel Masetto*, the inconstant peasant girl, Zerlina, caught in a flirtation with Don Giovanni, invites her lover to "Beat me, beat me, oh pretty Masetto." While certain that there is no danger of his following through, she renders frivolous a brutal aspect of traditional male dominance.

[51] Scott Trafton, *Egypt Land: Race and Nineteenth-Century American Egyptomania* (Durham, NC: Duke University Press, 2004).

writing, and reflection, more than those of his contemporary intellectuals, who were distracted by the affairs of London, Paris, or Berlin.[52]

Jefferson worked under less frenetic circumstances than Theodore Roosevelt, who was immensely busier in his day. Roosevelt wrote two books while still a Harvard undergraduate.[53] Thereafter he produced voluminous speeches, essays, and historical works, although distracted by telephones, telegraphs, railroads, coal strikes, war, and assassins. Jefferson lived at a more leisurely pace, and neither the three years and nine months he served as Secretary of State, nor even the eight years he spent in the White House kept him from his studies. In Washington he followed a schedule not much different from that he had enjoyed during his previous seven years in Virginia, where he was able to confine himself to "the enjoyments of my family, my farm, my friends and books."[54] If interrupted in his studies, he casually answered the door of the White House clad in robe and slippers.[55] According to his slave, Isaac Jefferson, he spent much of his day enjoying the lifestyle of the solitary scholar:

> Old Master had an abundance of books; sometimes would have twenty of 'em down on the floor at once—read fust one, then tother. Isaac has often wondered how Old Master came to have such a mighty head; read so many of them books; and when they go to ax him anything, he go right straight to the book and tell you all about it.[56]

Leisure is not to be confused with idleness, and Jefferson's leisure hours, whether in private or at his dinner parties, always displayed intellectual vigor and catholicity.[57] His erudite loquaciousness at the table, as opposed to his public reticence, has never escaped the notice of biographers and historians. While remarkably lacking as a public speaker, and

52 His brilliantly attractive personality is well elucidated in the works of Peter Onuf, Annette Gordon-Reed, John Meacham, and Lucia Stanton.

53 Roosevelt wrote his senior thesis at Harvard on the "Practicability of Equalizing Men and Women before the Law." At the same time, he largely completed work on his *The Naval War of 1812* (New York: G. P. Putnam's Sons, 1900).

54 Jefferson to W. D. G. Worthington, Esq., Monticello, February 24, 1810.

55 He once received the British ambassador informally clad. For a discussion of this controversy, see Thomas Edward Watson, *The Life and Times of Thomas Jefferson* (New York: D. Appleton & Company, 1908), pp. 399–400.

56 James Adam Bear, ed., *Jefferson at Monticello: Recollections of a Monticello Slave and a Monticello Overseer* (Charlottesville, VA: University of Virginia Press, 1967), p. 12.

57 Joseph Pieper, in *Leisure: The Basis of Culture*, trans. Alexander Dru, with an introduction by T. S. Eliot (New York: Pantheon, 1963), p. 20, makes the point that the Latin word for leisure is *scolia*, from which we derive the word "school." The cover illustration of an early English edition showed Isaac Newton relaxing under a tree with an apple about to fall on his head.

refusing to participate in debate, he was a magnificent host and raconteur at Monticello and in the White House, and every bit as charming as he was voluble. His well-recorded personal attractiveness, the broad range of his interests, and his superior intellect placed him at ease in the company of other quick minds. But many of his thoughts were buried in unpublished writings, secret lucubrations, or unpublished drafts of public, but anonymous, documents.

ORIGINALITY AS THINKER AND PHILOSOPHER

Despite his boast of sailing "the boisterous seas of liberty," he was fundamentally conservative, and it gave him migraines to put up with human instability and caprice.[58] Like the medieval scholiasts, he preferred to see the world as governed by immutable verities, and he deduced principles from what he believed to be eternal truths. He was masterful in reconciling his reputation as a political and scientific innovator with his reliance on premises reflecting the laws and nature and of nature's God. Although he obviously had a theory of progress and social change, he simultaneously conceived the world as in a state of being, rather than becoming. The human condition forces most of us to entertain contradictory models of the cosmos, and Jefferson was no exception to this Orwellian paradox. So while he championed the progress of science, commerce, and industry, he could not free himself from sentimental notions of a conservative agricultural republic, an Eden without workshops.

His quest for stability led him to rely on a God of reason who provided order and meaning to his universe. As a scientific thinker, he lingered in the world of 1687, the early Enlightenment of Isaac Newton's mechanistic certainties, and he does not seem to have grasped the radical implications of Laplace's challenge to Newton's deistic cosmos.[59] While he impatiently rejected the social thought of such traditionalists as Edmund Burke, David

[58] John D. Battle, Jr., "The 'periodical head-aches' of Thomas Jefferson," *Cleveland Clinic Quarterly*, 51 (1984), 531–539. Monticello.org devotes a page to Jefferson's headaches: www.monticello.org/site/research-and-collections/headaches

[59] Laplace was not able to create a mathematical model of a stable and rational universe, but he famously challenged the theologically determined Newtonian hypothesis of divine intervention in the regulation of the cosmos. When Napoleon Bonaparte asked Laplace for the place of God in his system, he is said to have denied any need for such an hypothesis. Morris Kline, *Mathematics in Western Culture* (Oxford University Press, 1953), pp. 266–267.

Hume, and Samuel Johnson, his thinking was sometimes more conservative than theirs. He conspicuously ignored the liberalism of Jean-Jacques Rousseau, and he was apparently unaware of William Blake's critique of Lockean and Newtonian thought. The dialogues between Mary Shelley's Frankenstein and the monster he created eluded him entirely. Jefferson's scientific methods were more speculative and deductive than practical and inductive, and his approach to natural philosophy was closer to Voltaire's flights of fancy than to Benjamin Franklin's experiments. Indeed the present-day scholar may appreciate the hands-on bustle of Franklin's urban workshop as much as the isolated contemplativeness of Monticello. Franklin, although much older than Jefferson, impresses us as the more "modern" of the two, reveling in his position as bourgeois journalist, apologist for commercial capitalism, and creator of the modern success manual.

Dumas Malone cautiously described Jefferson as "a philosophical statesman rather than a political philosopher," but in fact he did a great deal of writing, some of it abstract and philosophical, although most of his writing was, like Benjamin Franklin's, aphoristic, occasional, and unsystematic. Kevin Hayes has challenged "the single biggest cliché in Jefferson's literary life," that Jefferson produced only one book, and offers two more examples, *A Manual of Parliamentary Practice*, and the ninety-page *Proceedings of the Government of the United States, in Maintaining the Public Right to the Beach of the Mississippi*, and he also lists Jefferson's incomplete and unpublished autobiography.

The overwhelming bulk of this writing consisted of letters, almost 20,000 in his lifetime. On January 11, 1817, he complained to John Adams as follows:

> from sun-rise to one or two oclock, and often from dinner to dark, I am drudging at the writing table. and all this to answer letters into which neither interest nor inclination on my part enters; and often for persons whose names I have never before heard. yet, writing civilly, it is hard to refuse them civil answers. this is the burthen of my life, a very grievous one indeed, and one which I must get rid of.

He wrote to Adams again, on June 27, 1822, describing the demands of his correspondence, much of it "requiring answers of elaborate research, and all to be answered with due attention and consideration." He was certainly reflecting that, over a period of forty years, his reactions, requiring "elaborate research," included *Notes on Virginia*, which was not intended as a complete or thorough expression of his philosophy, or as an exhaustive description of his country.

WHAT IS GENIUS?

By the standards of any time, Jefferson's intellectual achievements were high, even for a person of his class. He knew Greek and Latin classics, but his references to them were allusive rather than interpretive. Jefferson, as we have noted, came to know French rather well, but was obviously hesitant to write in it. One encounters many young people today in American and European universities who speak perfect English and a second European language in addition to their native Japanese, Chinese, or Yoruba. We can assume that his mathematical attainments were equal to those of today's strong freshmen in engineering at the University of Virginia. There is no foundation for comparing him to an Isaac Newton, an Edmund Halley, or a Pierre-Simon Laplace. He would probably perform quite well as an undergraduate in any science or engineering program today, but perhaps he would choose to study anthropology or music, or even art history.

There are African Americans today achieving at Jeffersonian levels, some of unadulterated Africoid stock, and others of Afro-European ancestry, whose intellectual accomplishments disprove his doubts and suspicions. Condoleezza Rice, who ascended to his office as Secretary of State in 2005, began to learn French, ballet, and figure skating at the age of 3, and at 15 she performed Mozart with the Denver Symphony. She graduated from university at 19 and took a Ph.D. in Soviet studies at the age of 26. Mathematician John Urschel earned a master's degree from Pennsylvania State University at 22 with grades of straight A while starring on the football team, teaching undergraduate calculus, and co-authoring a professional-journal article in the field of astronomy. He became a starting player in the National Football League at the position of center, one of the most mentally demanding positions, while simultaneously pursuing a Ph.D. at MIT.

Jefferson's genius, unlike that of Donald Trump, was not limited to marketing. His linguistic and mathematical powers were so obvious as to render meaningless any hypothetical IQ score. He had extraordinary social intelligence, refined manners, and an air of gravitas, in addition to which he possessed Machiavellian pragmatism and the ability to adjust his positions rationally and in accord with circumstances. He was able to present himself as an egalitarian while maintaining the bearing of an aristocrat, and living as such. He financed an elegant mode of existence by the ingenious manipulation of personal debt while earning a reputation as the prophet of balanced budgets.

In short, he was brilliant, both in the resolution of contradiction and in the sleight of hand that allowed him to get away with it. He was not materially or politically ambitious, and why should he have been? The material and spiritual pleasures of Jefferson's Poplar Forest were as satisfying as those of Marie Antoinette's Petit Trianon. Puttering in his shops and gardens, he enjoyed more freedom and peace than King George could in his retreat at Kew Palace. The Count of Monticello had his scientific amusements, his French wines, his excellent library, and a comely handmaid to serve him ice cream on imported china. He enjoyed freedom from want, and his happiness was in the knowledge of his position as a world-historical figure, having made his epoch "The Age of Jefferson" and himself the center of "Mr. Jefferson's Empire."[60] He was stupefyingly successful at the exploit attributed to great men by Hegel, Carlyle, and Emerson – that of making his personal genius identical with the genius of his age.

[60] Peter S. Onuf, *Jefferson's Empire: The Language of American Nationhood* (Charlottesville, VA: University of Virginia Press, 2000).

6

A Renaissance Man in the Age of the Enlightenment

Thomas Jefferson has been celebrated both as a "Renaissance Man" and as the embodiment of the "American Enlightenment." One might reasonably ask how one understands these contradictory accolades and how one perceives the overlapping epochs to which they refer. A bibliography of either would require a multi-volume treatment, taxing to the persistence of most authors and to the endurance of most readers.[1] I wade gingerly into these waters, paying some attention to the less cumbersome, but often overlooked, topic of Jefferson‘s limited contact with the German Enlightenment. In prior scholarship, French influences have been exaggerated, and the few German influences almost entirely neglected. The matter seems to have attracted the attention of very few scholars, but the notable exceptions include Jeffrey High and the late Peter Nicolaisen. Professors Susan Buck-Morss and Sandra Rebok also deserve kudos in this regard, and I have touched lightly on their discussions of the later phases of the German Enlightenment. The Scottish Enlightenment had a profound effect on Jefferson directly and indirectly. With respect to the Italian Renaissance, I naturally acknowledge J. G. A. Pocock's well-known linkage of Jefferson's thinking to the eighteenth-century's "Machiavellian moment," but I do this with some

[1] The problematics of defining the Renaissance have long captured the attention of scholars. See Ernst Cassirer, Francis R. Johnson, Paul Oskar Kristeller, Dean P. Lockwood, and Lynn Thorndike, "Some Remarks on the Question of the Originality of the Renaissance," *Journal of the History of Ideas*, 4, no. 1 (January, 1943), 49–74; Theodore E. Mommsen, "Petrarch's Conception of the "Dark Ages'," *Speculum*, 17, no. 2 (April 1942), 226–242. As for the Enlightenment, one usually begins with, or encounters in due course, the works of, *inter alios*, Ernst Cassirer, Peter Gay, Henry Steele Commager, and Henry May.

reservations, and with a more somber inflection than Professor Pocock intended.[2]

AN AMERICAN LEONARDO IN A "MACHIAVELLIAN MOMENT"

Historian Norman Risjord calls Jefferson "truly the American Leonardo, the last Renaissance Man," in imitation of James Parton, who gushed in 1874 that Jefferson could "calculate an eclipse, survey an estate, tie an artery, plan an edifice, try a cause, break a horse, dance a minuet and play the violin."[3] Franklin D. Roosevelt famously stated in a 1936 speech at Monticello that Jefferson's mind "encompassed the full scope of the knowledge of his time." John Kennedy, while entertaining a group of Nobel laureates at the White House in 1962, enthused that this was "the most extraordinary collection of talent, of human knowledge, that has ever been gathered together in the White House, with the possible exception of when Jefferson dined alone," and reiterated the Parton catalogue of Jefferson's accomplishments. But "Renaissance man," like the word "renaissance" itself, is a nebulous concept. Michelangelo, as painter, draftsman, anatomist, sculptor, poet, and architect, exceeded Leonardo. The painter of Mona Lisa and designer of whimsical flying machines was a very clever fellow, but Leonardo did not contribute to modern science as significantly as Copernicus or Galileo, and he was no Columbus.[4] Neither was Thomas Jefferson, although ironically, and in accord with the strict humanist definition, he might meet the standard of "Renaissance man"

[2] Douglass G. Adair, *The Intellectual Origins of Jeffersonian Democracy*, ed. Mark Yellin (Lanham, MD: Lexington Books, 2000 [1943, 1964]), p. 32, agrees with Gilbert Chinard, *Thomas Jefferson, the Apostle of Americanism* (Boston, MA: Little, Brown, 1929), that French influences on Jefferson were negligible. J. G. A. Pocock, *The Machiavellian Moment: Florentine Political Thought and the Atlantic Republican Tradition* (Princeton University Press, 2003). Daniel N. Robinson, "The Scottish Enlightenment and the American Founding," *The Monist*, 90, no. 2, Scottish Philosophy (April, 2007), 170–181.

[3] Norman K. Risjord, *Representative Americans: The Revolutionary Generation* (Boston, MA: Madison House, 2001) pp. 231, 307. James Parton, *Life of Thomas Jefferson, Third President of the United States* (Boston, MA: J. R. Osgood and Company, 1874), p. 165. Horsebreaking in Jon Meacham, *Thomas Jefferson and the Art of Power* (New York: Random House, 2012), pp. 286, 289–290.

[4] Franklin D. Roosevelt, "Address at the Home of Thomas Jefferson, Monticello, Virginia," July 4, 1936, at http://www.presidency.ucsb.edu/ws/?pid=15317. John F. Kennedy, "Remarks at a Dinner Honoring Nobel Prize Winners of the Western Hemisphere," April 29, 1962. Published by Gerhard Peters and John T. Woolley, eds., *American Presidency Project* (accessed 2014), at http://tjrs.monticello.org/letter/1856

better than either Leonardo or Michelangelo because, in contrast to them, he studied Greek and Latin.

The first use of the term *rinascita* is attributed to the humanist Giorgio Vasari, although the idea of a "renaissance," or rebirth, of classical learning appeared in the Late Middle Ages, with the Italian humanist Francesco Petrarca (Petrarch, 1304–74). Petrarch distinguished between the times that he called the "dark ages" and his own era, with its rediscovery of classical Latin texts. But some scholars rightly suggest that the origins of the Renaissance predated Petrarca. The historian Charles Homer Haskins famously spoke of a "renaissance of the twelfth century, with its revival of the Latin classics and of Latin poetry and Roman law, the recovery of Greek arts and science, with its Arabic additions, and of much of Greek philosophy." Some scholars discover Renaissance characteristics in Dante Alighieri, or even in the somewhat older Thomas Aquinas, for whom Jefferson showed some respect as a theologian. Some scholars have even spoken of a Carolingian Renaissance. It has become common to use the term broadly, and without reference to any specific historical period, to designate a person whose achievement in mathematics, science, or technology is complemented by some accomplishments in arts and letters.[5]

When we consider the impressive breadth of his interests and knowledge, Jefferson merits the accolade "Renaissance man," but no more than many of his contemporaries, who lived before our own age of specialization. We may list many, but among the more prominent one thinks of Frederick II of Prussia, Benjamin Franklin, Johann Wolfgang von Goethe, and Jefferson's severe critic, Samuel Johnson, who was a solid classicist, a brilliant poet, and a knowledgeable student of chemistry.[6] It would not be unreasonable to place George Washington in the category, for although he knew "small Latin and less Greek," he had a practical knowledge of Euclid. His reading dealt mostly with practical affairs, and his small English library contained little in the way of *belles lettres,* with Addison's *Cato* being a striking exception, but he was reflective, and he understood what he read.

[5] Charles Homer Haskins, *The Renaissance of the Twelfth Century* (Cambridge, MA: Harvard University Press, 1957 [1927]), p. vi. Haskins' introduction refers to several "renaissances," including a "Carolingian," an "Ottonian," a "Medieval," etc. Also see G. W. Trompf, "The Concept of the Carolingian Renaissance," *Journal of the History of Ideas*, 34, no. 1 (January–March, 1973), 3–26.

[6] Frederick Kurzer, "Chemistry in the Life of Dr. Samuel Johnson," *Bulletin for the History of Chemistry*, 29, no. 2 (2004), 65–88.

Washington lacked Jefferson's erudition in arts and letters, but Jefferson lacked Washington's military accomplishment. Acclaimed by Frederick II for military genius, and by George III for political wisdom, Washington, due to his lack of formal education, was excessively modest about his intellectual attainments. He sometimes called on Madison or Hamilton to polish his writing, although he demonstrated that he possessed a literary style that was terse, subtle, and acerbic. As agricultural innovators Washington and Jefferson were on a par, but Washington was superior as a frontiersman, businessmen, and humanitarian. He began life with fewer advantages than Jefferson, but he died a wealthy man, while Jefferson died attempting to wrest special economic favors from the Virginia legislature.[7]

Much of Jefferson's scientific thought was rooted in a convention known as the Great Chain of Being, a doctrine that was taught to the present author by the Dominican nuns, long before he had heard of A. O. Lovejoy's scholarly 1936 study by that title. The idea was that God had ordered the universe as a hierarchical chain, which linked together, in immutable rank, all of nature's creatures, including rocks, stones, and trees, as well as animals, humans, and nine ascending choirs of angels. Lovejoy, from his twentieth-century vantage point, made the observation that the chain represented being, rather than becoming, and that the dogma was eventually weakened by eighteenth-century notions of progress, and ultimately broken by nineteenth-century notions of evolution. But Jefferson's ideas, in this instance, were neither progressive nor evolutionary. In Jefferson's understanding, nature's God, whose laws were as inviolable as Euclidean geometry, had formed this chain, and Nature had never "formed any link in her great work so weak as to be broken."[8]

[7] Jefferson pressured the Virginia legislature to establish a lottery to help him avoid bankruptcy. See Merrill Peterson, *Thomas Jefferson and the New Nation* (Oxford University Press, 1970), pp. 992, 1007. Jefferson, "Thoughts on Lotteries," February, 1826, Founders Online. Also see "Jefferson Lottery" at www.monticello.org/

[8] Jefferson makes use of the chain metaphor in Query VI. See Thomas Jefferson, *Notes on the State of Virginia*, ed. David Waldstreicher (Boston, MA: Bedford Books, 2002), p. 116. Also see Arthur O. Lovejoy, *The Great Chain of Being: A Study of the History of an Idea* (Cambridge, MA: Harvard University Press, 1936). Keith Thomson agrees, in his *Jefferson's Shadow: The Story of His Science* (New Haven, CT: Yale University Press, 2012), p. 90, that the chain metaphor is present in *Notes on Virginia*, but does not recognize Jefferson's hesitancy to depart from the inflexible chain metaphor at a time when other thinkers were beginning to conceive of a dynamic and evolutionary universe. Ari Helo cites Lovejoy's *The Great Chain of Being*, pp. 206–207, and notes Daniel J. Boorstin's discussion of Jefferson's link and chain cosmology in his *The Lost World of*

Jefferson's deployment of the "link" metaphor was more reminiscent of the Middle Ages than of the Renaissance or the Enlightenment, and classical and medieval thinking usually dominated his approaches both to natural philosophy and political science. Despite the homage he so famously paid to the nascent empiricism of Bacon, Newton, and Locke, as previously noted, his methods were usually deductive rather than inductive, and his pronouncements sometimes owed more to religious axioms than to empirical observations. His scientific and political thinking were based on truths that he held to be "self-evident," and yet, his practice often deviated from his avowed principles. His overriding intellectual imperatives were based on conceptions of "Nature and Nature's God," and he deduced truth from postulates that he perceived as axiomatic. While he was not a mainstream Christian, professing a belief in the doctrine of Jesus' atonement on the cross, he regarded mainstream American religion as "benign." He once asserted that government must rest on the belief of the people in divine retribution, and he was opportunistic in appealing to a non-denominational civil religion. Like the Emperor Constantine, he claimed to know God's will, and like Constantine he opportunistically wielded the religious imagination to establish an empire.

Jefferson was a remarkable *amateur* of the arts and sciences, but it was as a Renaissance politician that he excelled. Maurizio Valsania is not wrong in comparing him to Niccolò Machiavelli, that emblematic figure of Renaissance subtlety, observing that he "internalized Machiavelli's *ragion di stato*." Paul Rahe has written on "Jefferson's Machiavellian Political Science," and Sean Wilentz has referred to Jefferson's "Machiavellian benevolence towards the Indians." The foregoing scholars appear to use the term "Machiavellian" in the *Oxford English Dictionary*'s sense of "the employment of cunning and duplicity in statecraft or in general conduct" in referring to Jefferson's theory and practice.[9] The Monticello website, as of the time of writing, records the

Thomas Jefferson (Boston, MA: Beacon, 1948), pp. 35–36. Also see interesting reference in J. A. Leo Lemay, *The Life of Benjamin Franklin* (Philadelphia, PA: University of Pennsylvania Press, 2006), vol. I, p. 272.

[9] Wilentz refers to his Machiavellian Indian policies in *Major Problems in the Early Republic, 1787–1848* (Lexington, KY: D. C. Heath, 1992), p. 130. Paul A. Rahe, *Machiavelli's Liberal Republican Legacy* (Cambridge University Press, 2005), "Thomas Jefferson's Machiavellian Political Science," Chapter 2, pp. 208–228, says that Jefferson's references to Machiavelli were confined to attacks on the philosophy expressed in *The Prince*. Of related interest is Alissa M. Ardito, *Machiavelli and the Modern State: The Prince, the Discourses on Livy, and the Extended Territorial Republic* (Cambridge University Press, 2015).

information that in 1764 he purchased an Italian–English dictionary, two works in Italian, and the works of Machiavelli. This acquisition seems to have accompanied an effort to master Italian, in which his prior knowledge of French and Latin were no doubt of some usefulness. Most likely, Jefferson sampled the Italian editions of *The Prince* with grammar books and English translations in hand, a method he admitted to employing with *Don Quixote* in Spanish.[10]

Jefferson's idol, Francis Bacon, famously wrote, "Some books are to be read only in parts."[11] It is a rare bibliophile who has "thoroughly chewed and digested" every book in their library, and there is no evidence that Jefferson was preoccupied or obsessed with deep reflection on Machiavelli. Whatever he found in the original or in translations of Machiavelli does not seem to have risen above the most common clichés. His references to the author of *The Prince* are few, fleeting, and negative. He did not like Machiavelli, used his name purely as a term of opprobrium, and would have been unhappy with any comparisons between himself and the man he made the symbol of "a melancholy age," an epoch characterized by "the mean, wicked and cowardly cunning."[12]

J. G. A. Pocock argues that Thomas Jefferson participated, at least passively, in what he calls a "Machiavellian moment," defined as the moment at which Western civilization moved towards its current republican discourse.[13] He sees certain of the lesser-known writings of Machiavelli as having stimulated this movement both directly and indirectly, and argues that Machiavelli's significance cannot be reduced to the content of *The Prince*, which at least one scholar believes may reasonably be viewed as satire.[14] Pocock alludes, as do other historians, to Jefferson's Machiavellian "justification of frontier expansion," without mentioning the Machiavellian displacement of Native Americans that Sean Wilentz observes.[15] Pocock argues that Machiavelli provided models and context

10 Maurizio Valsania, *Nature's Man: Thomas Jefferson's Philosophical Anthropology* (Charlottesville, VA: University of Virginia Press, 2013), p. 140.

11 Monticello.org contains references to Jefferson's purchase of Machiavelli. John Quincy Adams' skepticism concerning Jefferson's mastering Cervantes in nineteen days has been cited earlier in this volume.

12 Jefferson to William Duane, April 4, 1813. "Jefferson sincerely despised Machiavelli," Valsania, *Nature's Man*, p. 140.

13 Pocock, *The Machiavellian Moment*.

14 G. Mattingly, "Machiavelli's Prince: Political Science or Political Satire?" *The American Scholar*, 28 (1958), 482–491.

15 Pocock, *The Machiavellian Moment*, p. 539; Willentz, *Major Problems in the Early Republic*, p. 130.

for seventeenth-century republicanism and for Jeffersonian "discourses," directly and indirectly through Lord Bolingbroke and James Harrington. It was Harrington, in his *Oceana*, who employed the phrase "the empire of laws and not of men," transformed by John Adams into the more elegant iambic pentameter of "A government of laws and not of men." In recent scholarship the term "civic humanism" is coterminous with the agrarianism of the "country party," although in Jeffersonian thought the *civitas* is the antithesis of the *agra.* Adams and Jefferson retired to their farms at every opportunity, despite their "civic humanism."[16]

Pocock presents an analysis in which "Jefferson and Hamilton "may emerge in a broadly discernable relationship to Rousseau and Marx."[17] The comparison, however imaginative and alluring, is confusing. While Jefferson and Rousseau shared overlapping notions about natural man in a state of nature, Jefferson and his party would have seen in Rousseau some of the evils that ultimately came to pass in the Marxist–Leninist state. But while he would have recoiled in horror from the Marxist "dictatorship of the proletariat," which hints unavoidably at Rousseau's concept of the "general will," Jefferson might have romanticized the "withering away of the State." He never recorded his ideas on Rousseau's general will, an idea he might have considered an unacceptable restraint on individual liberty of conscience. The governmental minimalism of Jefferson shares no genealogy with the anarchist teleology of Marx, but it seems to point in that same utopian direction. Pocock's discussion of the Hamilton–Jefferson rivalry is more imaginative than convincing, for he slips into the convention of using "Machiavellianism" as a synonym for cunning. He might have extrapolated more fully on the idea that both men manifested that trait.[18]

Frederick II's treatise, the *Anti-Machiavel*, surprisingly receives no analysis in J. G. A. Pocock's discussion of the Machiavellian moment. The document was reputedly drafted with the encouragement and

16 Gordon Wood, "The Significance of the Early Republic," *Journal of the Early Republic*, 8, no. 1 (spring, 1988), 12. Daniel T. Rodgers, "Republicanism: The Career of a Concept," *The Journal of American History* 79, no. 1 (June, 1992), 11–38. Jacob Soll, "J. G. A. Pocock's Atlantic Republicanism Thesis Revisited: The Case of John Adams's Tacitism," *Republics of Letters: A Journal for the Study of Knowledge, Politics, and the Arts*, 2, no. 1 (December 15, 2010), at https://arcade.stanford.edu/rofl/j-g-pocock%E2%80%99s-atlantic-republicanism-thesis-revisited-case-john-adams%E2%80%99s-tacitism

17 Pocock, *The Machiavellian Moment*, p. 462.

18 Alexander Hamilton to James Bayard, January 16, 1801. John Randolph, Note to Joseph H. Nicholson, January 1, 1801.

collaboration of Voltaire in 1739, four years before Jefferson's birth.[19] But, while Pocock offered no discussion of either Frederick or Voltaire, he oddly enough wrapped Jefferson in the mantle of Machiavellian republicanism and placed Jefferson in what he called the "Machiavellian moment." And from thence things proceeded to become, as Alice in Wonderland said, "curiouser and curiouser," because next Professor Pocock found in Jean-Jacques Rousseau a bridge between Machiavelli and Jefferson.

Jefferson made occasional passing references to Rousseau, and his biographers have reasonably assumed that Jefferson and his contemporaries were familiar with Rousseau's work.[20] Pocock's Rousseau thesis is nonetheless purely inferential, as is historian Donald Livingston's thesis that Jefferson was influenced by David Hume. Jefferson showed no demonstrable infatuation with Rousseau, and considered Hume's work to be fundamentally misguided, writing: "Hume seems intended to disguise and discredit the good principles of the government, and is so plausible and pleasing in its style and manner, as to instill its errors and heresies insensibly into the minds of unwary readers." Jefferson's references to Rousseau are so vague, but Pocock is correct in seeing that both men's writings have fueled libertarian ideals.[21]

Philosophy professor Daniel Bonevac shows a fundamental opposition between Jefferson and Rousseau, arguing that Jefferson saw the most basic human rights as natural, while Rousseau implied that they were contractual.[22] Pocock not only places Jefferson in a Machiavellian moment, but also says, "Jefferson is placing himself and America at a Rousseauan moment." This might seem valid enough, for one recalls, as Merrill Peterson does, that Jefferson's critics sometimes linked him disparagingly, and unfairly, with Rousseau, but any decisive influence is difficult to identify. Peterson must certainly have investigated the matter, but his noteworthy studies barely mention Rousseau, who is absent from

19 Thomas Paine, in *The Rights of Man*, called Voltaire "the flatterer and the satirist of despotism," and the same may be said of Machiavelli in *The Prince*.

20 Nathan Schachner, *Thomas Jefferson: A Biography* (New York: Appleton-Century-Crofts, 1957), refers to a "well-thumbed copy of Rousseau's work in his library," p. 47. Albert Taylor Bledsoe and Mrs. Sophia M'Ilvaine Bledsoe Herrick referred to a "well-thumbed" copy of *The Social Contract*, in an article in *The Southern Review*, 9 (1871), 671.

21 Jefferson to John Norvell, June 11, 1807. Donald W. Livingston, "David Hume and the Republican Tradition of Human Scale," *Anamnesis*, Online Essays, October 26, 2011, at http://anamnesisjournal.com/2011/10/donald-w-livingston/

22 Daniel Bonevac, "The Forgotten Principles of American Government," originally published as a pamphlet by the Texas Public Policy Foundation, appeared in the *Texas Education Review*, 1, no. 1 (spring, 2000), 5–9.

the index of his compilation of Jefferson's writings. If Rousseau was important to Jefferson, then there must be a conspiracy to minimize this importance in the works of his major recent biographers. True enough, the foxlike cunning of Machiavelli's prince occupied a place in the behavior of both men. Both have been charged with hypocrisy, and if either of them was fundamentally committed to Machiavelli's republican principles, they were, like Machiavelli himself, famously capable of temporizing. Jefferson's real Machiavellian moment arrived with the Louisiana Purchase, achieved through an executive order, a fiat that more than fulfilled Hamilton's prediction that he would be an able guardian of presidential powers. Indeed, he amplified the prestige and powers of the government in Washington DC. By imperial edict he shattered the moribund treaties that had granted an immense wilderness to Spain, and replaced the spurious archaic legalisms of long dead popes and kings by contracting with the dictator Napoleon.[23]

FROM RENAISSANCE TO ENLIGHTENMENT

The "Age of Enlightenment" has nebulous boundaries, as noted by J. B. Shank and many others. Three symbolic, although arbitrary, events might be used for dating its onset: these are the first publication of Isaac Newton's *Philosophiæ Naturalis Principia Mathematica* in 1687, the Glorious Revolution of 1688, and Locke's *Two Treatises of Government* in 1689. Its terminal date in many reference works is the French Revolution in 1789. Settling on this date conveniently lops off the horrors of the 1790s and allows historians to avoid certain troublesome irrationalities of the so-called "Age of Reason." *The Stanford Dictionary of Philosophy* proposes an opening somewhere in the late seventeenth century and a termination corresponding to the 1789 storming of the Bastille. *Wikipedia*, in its English, French, German, and other language editions, offers a similar periodization, and excludes such embarrassing content as the beheading of Marie Antoinette, Napoleon's coup d'état, the continuation of African slavery, and the codification of white supremacy in the works of Kant, Hume, and Jefferson. [24]

[23] Pocock, *The Machiavellian Moment*, pp. 533, 541, 545. Merrill Peterson, *The Jefferson Image in the American Mind* (Charlottesville, VA: University of Virginia Press, 1998), pp. 44, 117, 133, 214, 269.

[24] J. B. Shank, *The Newton Wars and the Beginning of the French Enlightenment* (University of Chicago Press, 2008).

It would be fiendishly iconoclastic to argue that the Salem witch trials (1692) and the French Reign of Terror (1793–94) were the Enlightenment's "bookends." Henry F. May more reasonably presents the terminal dates for the American Enlightenment as 1688 to 1815; these correspond to dates offered by Oxford University Press in its four-volume *Encyclopedia of the Enlightenment* (2003), "Covering the 'long' Enlightenment, from the rise of Descartes' disciples in 1670 to the restoration of the Bourbon monarchy in 1815." These dates also correspond roughly to what some historians have called the "long eighteenth century," a phrase that usually designates the years from the Glorious Revolution in 1688 to the battle of Waterloo in 1815. Henry F. May sees a decline of the Enlightenment in the United States after the presidential election of 1800, when Americans became "conscious that they were living in a new period."[25] My own arbitrary date for the terminus is 1804, when Napoleon, in the presence of Pope Pius VII, crowned himself "Emperor of the French" in Notre Dame Cathedral. That was the point at which Ludwig von Beethoven, in a fit of rage at the news, supposedly scratched Napoleon's name from the dedication of his third symphony, *The Eroica*, tore the first page of the manuscript in half, and threw it on the floor. His act symbolized many of the frustrations, unintended consequences, and disappointments of the Age of Enlightenment, or alternatively the Age of Reason.[26]

DEFINING THE ENLIGHTENMENT QUALITATIVELY

If the term "Age of Reason" may function as a rough equivalent for "Era of the Enlightenment," then the publication dates of the first two volumes of Thomas Paine's *The Age of Reason* (1794–95) would seem to be crucial, although they come at the end, rather than at the climax, of the epoch. Paine wrote *The Age of Reason* while he was awaiting his scheduled, but narrowly evaded, beheading during the Terror, and he published

[25] Henry E. May, *The Enlightenment in America* (Oxford University Press, 1978), commences his learned study by dividing the Enlightenment into four phases. See pp. 275, 307.

[26] Beethoven's secretary, Ferdinand Reis, wrote that he tore the dedication in two and threw it on the floor, so that the first page had to be rewritten. "Beethoven ging an den Tisch, faßte das Titelblatt oben an, riß es ganz durch und warf es auf die Erde. Die erste Seite wurde neu geschrieben und nun erst erhielt die Symphonie den Titel: Sinfonia eroica." As of the date of writing (2018), an image of the original first page of the Third Symphony is available at Wikipedia: https://en.wikipedia.org/wiki/Symphony_No._3_(Beethoven)

it in two parts (1794 and 1795). He mentioned a third installment in his letter to Jefferson of October 1, 1800, but postponed publication until 1807, conceivably due to the controversies surrounding the presidential campaign of 1800. During that campaign Jefferson's name was widely linked with that of Payne; Jefferson's Federalist opponents made every effort to associate him with the putatively atheistic writings of Paine. Philip Foner and other scholars have asserted that Jefferson "advised and requested him" not to publish the third volume, even as late as 1802, well after Jefferson had taken the oath of office. Paine made very clear his belief not only in a God, but in a personal deity, and the immortality of the soul, although the neo-Federalist historian Theodore Roosevelt referred to him as a "filthy little atheist."[27]

Bernard Bailyn refers to Paine as "an ignoramus both in ideas and in the practice of politics, next to Adams, Jefferson, Madison, or Wilson." Bailyn was nominally correct, since, as he pointed out, Paine was ignorant of Latin, and he notes, as does Gordon Wood, the importance of the classics in impressing Roman republican ideals, if not lasting cultural influences, on the American Revolutionary period. But, as Wood notes, classical ideals, "by the last half of the eighteenth century," had been "attenuated and transformed," and were fated to give way to the "scrambling, acquisitive individualistic society that emerged after the Revolution." Eric Foner, overlooking the lacunae in Paine's formal education, describes him as "a member of a transatlantic group of cosmopolitan intellectuals." Indeed, he was a scrambling urban entrepreneur who bore a closer resemblance to William Blake and Benjamin Franklin than to a country party classicist like Jefferson. Paine, for his part, made the irreverent observation that "The best Greek linguist, that now exists, does not understand Greek as well as a Grecian ploughman did, or a Grecian milkmaid." Precisely because its author was an "ignoramus," Paine's *Common Sense* encompassed as strong a current of Enlightenment egalitarianism as its title signified. Paine and Franklin symbolize the

[27] A final volume was completed in 1802. Edward H. Davidson and William J. Scheick say that the volume was suppressed until 1807 at Jefferson's suggestion, but do not provide a source for this contention, in *Paine, Scripture, and Authority: The Age of Reason as Religious and Political Idea* (Bethlehem, PA: Lehigh University Press, 1994), pp. 103–106. Philip Foner, in *The Complete Writings of Thomas Paine* (New York: Citadel, 1945), p. 848, asserts that Jefferson counseled Paine not to publish Part III, placing the words "advised and requested him" in quotation marks, but offers no source for the quotation. Roosevelt's description of Paine as a "filthy little atheist," a clear case of academic dishonesty, was in Theodore Roosevelt, *Gouverneur Morris* (Cambridge, MA: The Riverside Press, 1892), p. 289.

American Enlightenment because their lack of formal education revealed the democratic-egalitarian notion of universal common sense. Jefferson's classical education did, however, symbolize the Americanization of the Enlightenment because it presented the paradox of frontier erudition in the context of American provincialism.[28]

Common Sense was an egalitarian testament that offered a more systematic attack on the so-called "divine right of kings" than is present in Jefferson's Declaration of Independence. It was no more original than the Declaration, but it was a more systematic and scholarly exposition of the Revolution's egalitarian foundations, providing a theological foundation for attacking the divine right of kings. As a result of his fame in America and his notoriety in England, Paine was enthusiastically received by the French Revolutionary government and elected a deputy to *Parlement*. Imprisoned and sentenced to death by the Montagnard faction for protesting the execution of Louis XVI, he was released through the influence of Jefferson and the offices of James Monroe, at that time the American Minister to France.[29] Paine remained in France, where he continued to wield appreciable influence, and on his return to the United States in 1802 he continued to communicate vigorously with Jefferson, although his correspondence diplomatically avoided references to slavery.

Writing for publication, as Paine did, was one of the emergent features of Enlightenment intellectualism, but it was a practice that Jefferson often considered beneath his dignity as a gentleman. Henry Steele Commager, in his book *The Empire of Reason*, asserts that "The Old World imagined, invented and formulated the Enlightenment, the New World—certainly the Anglo-American part of it—realized it and fulfilled it."[30] This work is a sequel to his other masterful work on the epoch, *Jefferson, Nationalism, and the Enlightenment*. Both are stunning displays of erudition, as well as

[28] Bernard Bailyn, *Faces of Revolution: Personalities & Themes in the Struggle for American Independence* (New York: Knopf, 1992), p. 82; Bernard Bailyn *The Ideological Origins of the American Revolution* (Harvard University Press, 1992 [1967]), pp. 23–29; Gordon Wood, *The Idea of America* (New York: Penguin Press, 2011), "Afterword to Chapter Two." See also Wood, *The Creation of the American Republic, 1776–1787* (New York: Norton, 1969), pp. 48–53. For Paine's ploughman and milkmaid observation, see Foner, *Complete Writings*, p. 696.

[29] Monroe saved Paine by stating that Paine was a US citizen, but Gouverneur Morris was later instrumental in denying Paine the New York franchise, with the specious argument that Paine's indictment by the French proved he was not a citizen of the United States.

[30] Henry Steele Commager, *The Empire of Reason: How Europe Imagined and America Realized the Enlightenment* (Garden City, NY: Anchor Press / Doubleday, 1977). The subtitle of this book is expanded on p. ix in the Preface. Henry Steele Commager, *Jefferson, Nationalism, and the Enlightenment* (New York: G. Braziller, 1975).

academic patriotism, that make Jefferson the principal political philosopher of the epoch. While it was appropriate to acknowledge Jefferson's genius and the tribute paid to him by contemporaries, it was something of a stretch to make him the greatest intellectual of the time, surpassing even Voltaire, Rousseau, and Goethe.[31]

Commager praised Jefferson's religious tolerance, comparing him to Voltaire, but awarded him greater acclaim because he "toppled the Established Church in his own Commonwealth." Jefferson did not "topple" the Episcopal Church in Virginia: he disestablished it, a worthy accomplishment, but, unlike Voltaire, Jefferson was never imprisoned for his beliefs or exiled because of them. His attack on the tradition of a tax-supported clergy had wide support in Virginia, and Jefferson was never so acerbic in his criticism of his Episcopalian background as was Voltaire in his attacks on the Jesuits who educated him. Both men were "deists," but it is said that Jefferson continued to attend the Episcopal Church throughout his life. Jefferson endorsed "civil religion" throughout his presidency. His disestablishment of the Church was not equivalent to the French Revolution's promotion of *laïcité*, the ideal of removing religion from the public sphere. Few governments have ever undertaken a program of secularization so radical as Atatürk's reforms in Turkey. Jefferson's religious views were never so extreme as the Federalists claimed, and he produced nothing so iconoclastic as Voltaire's *Poem on the Lisbon Disaster*.

Commager presents a heroic, indeed martyr-like, "Mr. Jefferson who gave up a brilliant career at the bar for public service."[32] But following a career at the bar could hardly have kept Jefferson from assuming the presidency, as he did, at close to 60. Others have managed to serve the public and to have brilliant careers at the bar before going to Washington, for example Abraham Lincoln. It falls on many people to make difficult and courageous value judgments by the age of 30 that affect the remainder of their lives. Mr. Jefferson was free, early in his brilliant career, to liberate his slaves, give up his plantation, and become a Philadelphia lawyer, decisions he would have found uncomfortable, for he chose to be surrounded by rustic menials rather than bourgeois intellectuals. Commager vastly exaggerates Jefferson's sacrifice, for with the exception of five years in Paris he spent his life in rural Virginia, doing pretty much as he pleased.

[31] Alexandre Beljame, *Men of Letters and the English Public in the Eighteenth Century, 1660–1744*, 2nd edn., edited and with an introduction by Bonamy Dobrée, translated by E. O. Lorimer (London: Kegan Paul, 1897). Commager, *Empire of Reason*, p. 89.

[32] Commager, *Empire of Reason*, p. 131.

It will not be contested that Jefferson possessed intellect, imagination, and knowledge approaching the best of contemporary minds on both sides of the Atlantic. But other than the preamble to the Declaration of Independence, his contributions to Western thought and writing are few. His attainments, while strong, were not overwhelming for a person of his class. Commager compares Jefferson to continental intellectuals in general and to Johann Wolfgang von Goethe, specifically as follows:

> Jefferson knew everything the naturalists and philosophes knew and responded not only to their ideas and their interests, but to their sentiments as well. He shared Goethe's passion for Italy and, what is more, translated Palladio to Virginia—something that Goethe could not do for Weimar.[33]

The elegance of Commager's rhetoric might easily seduce us, if we did not recall that Goethe's mastery of Italian was superior to Jefferson's smattering. Commager's serpentine "translation" metaphor is strikingly inappropriate, because Jefferson never actually "translated" anything out of the Italian of Andrea Palladio or anyone else. In a style inspired by Palladio, he sketched Monticello's original facade, but neither Monticello, the elegantly tasteful mansion that we rightly admire today, nor its minor version, Poplar Forest, bears much resemblance to that sketch. Goethe wrote, "Amerika, du hast es besser," and Jefferson did have it better, with hundreds of vassals and hod-carriers, but Goethe's contributions to architectural theory are more memorable than Jefferson's sparse, conventional, and past-oriented remarks. Goethe, like Jefferson, had a sophisticated appreciation of Renaissance, neoclassical, and medieval style. He had an excellent understanding of the rules of design, but he was also a pioneer and pace-setter in the architectural tastes of the nineteenth century. He outdistanced Jefferson and other contemporaries in rediscovering the sublimity of gothic style, and his maxim, "ancient temples concentrate God in humans," could today be engraved as a sarcastic commentary on the Jefferson Memorial that stands as an antique temple deifying a graven image.[34]

[33] Ibid., p. 89.

[34] Like most poetry and philosophy, Goethe's aphorism translates poorly: "Antike Tempel konzentrieren den Gott im Menschen; des Mittelalters Kirchen streben nach Gott in Höhe." Johann Wolfgang Goethe, *Maximen und Reflexionen. Aphorismen und Aufzeichnungen.* Nach den Handschriften des Goethe- und Schiller-Archivs, ed. Max Hecker (Weimar: Verlag der Goethe-Gesellschaft, 1907), www.aphorismen.de/zitat/10436. One possible rendering might be that antique temples make humans godly, but another might be that antique temples bring the sublime down to the human level. Taken in context, Goethe may be interpreted as saying that while antique temples are profound,

Jefferson and Goethe were close contemporaries, born only six years apart. Both enjoyed privileged childhoods, benefitted from private tutors, studied the law, and dabbled in the natural sciences. Jefferson was a performer, but not a composer, on the violin. The influence of Goethe's poetry and drama on German lieder and French opera was tremendous. Both men struggled internally to reconcile the conflicting impulses of classical, Enlightenment, and romantic intellectualism. Both knew the contradictory pulls of cultural patriotism and civilized cosmopolitanism, and both intellectually straddled the Enlightenment and the romantic movements. We know for certain that Goethe had several children outside of marriage, as Jefferson almost certainly did, although Goethe eventually married the mother of his extramarital children. Goethe and Jefferson were both accomplished amateurs in the natural sciences, and shared an enlightened, if unrealized, conception of human progress. But while Jefferson's name is familiar to every educated German of today, it may safely be said Goethe's name is not only unpronounceable to most Americans but, for the most part, unknown.

Since Goethe spent his youth in Frankfurt and Leipzig, not on the colonial frontier, he obviously had vast intellectual opportunities that the young Jefferson never enjoyed. One reads Goethe's description of his journey to Leipzig, where his father sent him at the age of 16, and shares his fascination with the commerce, the bustle, the architecture, the moments of activity and silence, as he wandered the streets observing the polyglot population, and the peculiar costumes of Russians and Poles, and Greeks. He described his frustrations with theology and his beginning studies in the law, while still only 16, which culminated in his completing a scandalous and heretical doctoral thesis at the age of 20. This youthful exercise shocked the faculty, who rejected it, although many years later the university awarded him an honorary doctorate.[35]

Jefferson's Greek and Latin were not meager, a result of his innate brilliance, unassailable work ethic, and the fact that he commenced his studies with paternal encouragement at the age of 9. Goethe wrote his dissertation entirely in Latin, and as a classicist he was indisputably superior to Jefferson, and he could apply Hebrew as well as Greek to his biblical studies. Neither Jefferson nor Goethe encountered the difficulties of the young Prince Frederick, which are mentioned elsewhere in these chapters.

medieval churches are sublime. Goethe's art, like that of William Blake, and unlike that of Phillis Wheatley and Joel Barlow, displayed intentional ambiguity.

[35] Siegfried Unseld, *Goethe and His Publishers* (University of Chicago Press, 1996), p. 11.

As scientists, both Jefferson and Goethe had the temerity to challenge Isaac Newton, Jefferson in the calculation of the length of a pendulum, and Goethe in the fields of optics and particle physics. Jefferson's challenge was of no consequence. We admire Goethe's optics for its audacity and his particle theory of light for its fortuitous correctness, but in neither case did Goethe make a lasting contribution to scientific method.[36]

Goethe's autobiography, *Dichtung und Wahrheit*, is not lacking in arrogance, but its title hints at its lower frequencies of irony and introspection, and its author often approaches his life experiences with an almost sociological detachment. Jefferson's autobiographical writings offer little introspection; they are self-righteous, rumor-mongering, and backbiting. He neither seeks nor arrives at the transparently supercilious self-deprecation that one discovers in Goethe. Jefferson is too often self-justifying and self-satisfied, and always contented with self-evident truth. Goethe is famous for acknowledging his inner conflict and self-contradiction, "Zwei Seelen wohnen, ach! in meiner Brust." Jefferson was not known for his self-directed irony, but remarkable for his apparent self-satisfaction, and for taking himself very seriously. Other American authors, notably Franklin, Lincoln, and Twain, and Jefferson's friend Adams, show a greater capacity for mocking their occasional intellectual ungainliness.[37]

It is uncertain at what point Jefferson became aware of Goethe's *Faust*, but Kevin J. Hayes notes the presence of the work illustrated by Moritz Retzsch in Jefferson's retirement library. The edition was well-known and much admired, and although Jefferson could not read German, he would definitely have had some idea of its content, both religious and philosophical, although it is true that Jefferson was not always profoundly engaged with every author whose works he possessed. I mention elsewhere that John Adams advised Jefferson to acquaint himself with Goethe's exercises in biblical interpretation, as he was in the process of drafting his *Life of Jesus of Nazareth*, but Jefferson did not take up the challenge. When he told Adams he was unacquainted with Goethe's theology, it probably slipped his mind that *Faust*'s prologue in heaven is a commentary on the Book of Job. His failure to pursue an interest in

[36] Jefferson mentioned "The works of the king of Prussia. The Berlin edition is in 16. vols. 8vo." in a letter to Joseph Willard, president of Harvard. See Jefferson to Willard, Paris, March 24, 1789.

[37] "Zwei Seelen wohnen, ach! in meiner Brust," translated as "Two souls dwell, alas, in my breast," has been interpreted variously as signifying the human conflict between worldly and ethereal love, or Goethe's two souls of classicism and the German romantic sensibility, or his straddling the Enlightenment and romanticism, etc.

Goethe is, however, no more significant than his failure to offer commentaries on Cervantes and Rousseau.[38]

Jefferson demonstrated genius in one area unknown to Goethe, the avoidance of battlefield experience. This matter would not deserve comment if Jefferson had not been so righteous when urging others into battle, so insensitive to the loss of life, and so critical of the performances of combatants. Goethe, although he was obviously no George Washington or Frederick the Great, could claim to have encountered minor military experience, having been present at the battle of Valmy, an attempt by the Prussian Army to suppress the French Revolution. History was not on his side, but, with characteristic irony, and cold comfort, he offered a commentary on the moment that is memorable: "From this place and from this day forth commences a new era in the world's history and you can all say that you were present at its birth."[39]

It is unclear whether it was a matter of honor or merely of curiosity that led Goethe to place himself at least once within range of enemy fire. Although he never fired a shot or engaged in hand-to-hand combat, he shared a flask of pilfered wine with fellow soldiers thereafter. Jefferson never placed himself under the rockets' red glare. It is difficult to imagine him sharing comradeship or drinks with ordinary soldiers; much easier to picture Squire Jefferson as he danced minuets with Hessian officers. Goethe did not derive his notoriety from a document advocating bloodshed and violence, but from his poignant depiction of a pregnant girl without a husband, the inspiration for Schubert's song.[40]

REASON AND SENSIBILITY

Jefferson's rationalism led to a fixation with classical and seventeenth-century models, Aristotle, Cicero, Locke, and Sidney, and he called Bacon,

[38] Kevin J. Hayes, *The Road to Monticello: The Life and Mind of Thomas Jefferson* (New York: Oxford University Press, 2008), p. 575. Jefferson to Robert Skipwith, with a List of Books for a Private Library, August 3, 1771, lists Rousseau's *Eloisa*: "Eng. 4 v. 12-mo. 12 and *Emilius and Sophia*. Eng. 4 v. 12mo. 12/."

[39] For Goethe on his experiences at the battle of Valmy, see Johann Wolfgang von Goethe, *Kampagne in Frankreich* (Berlin: Karl-Maria Guth, 2016 [1792]).

[40] Franz Schubert's famous song, "Gretchen am Spinnrad" (Gretchen at the spinning wheel), has a young woman singing of her seduction and abandonment "My peace is gone, my heart is heavy," based on words taken from Goethe's *Faust* I. Jefferson has been accused of impregnating the three-quarters-white teenager Sally Hemings when she was 16. See Annette Gordon-Reed, "Thomas Jefferson and Sally Hemings: A Brief Account," at https://home.monticello.org

Newton, and Locke "my trinity of the three greatest men the world had ever produced."[41] But the Age of Reason offered a critique of reason, following after Kant and Rousseau. Emotional religion, encouraged by John Wesley, and the cult of sensibility and sentimental fiction produced by Samuel Richardson and Oliver Goldsmith were at some remove from rationalism and empiricism. Immanuel Swedenborg, who was a scientist and a mystic, was among the more important challengers of mechanistic deism, while William Blake lambasted Newton and Locke, rejecting the heresy of "Nature and Nature's God," and depicting the "natural man" as the mad and degraded Nebuchadnezzar described by the prophets as reverting to bestiality. Voltaire attacked this tendency towards romantic naturalism and expressed his contempt for Rousseau's primitivism when he wrote, "you are trying to turn us into brutes: to read your book makes one long to go about on all fours."

Despite the sentimentalization of rural virtue in Rousseau and Jefferson, the Enlightenment was a creature of the cities, even, by Jefferson's own admission in his 1788 travel notes, an urban movement. He praised, in particular, Frankfurt, for which he gave the gallicized spelling Francfort; he even generalized that its urban environment went hand in hand with prosperity, commerce, and republicanism, as we shall see later in this chapter. The prophet of the yeoman farmer – although he later made casual reference to "the yeomanry of the city" – was notable for theoretically restricting republican virtue to bucolic life. In honest moments, however, Jefferson was willing to allow that urban environments and bourgeois economies were perfectly suited to nurture republican values, even in Europe. Our historical conception of the Enlightenment is indebted to the bucolic meanderings of Rousseau, but inconceivable without the cities. Its natural meeting places were in Frederick II's Berlin, in Samuel Johnson's London coffee-house, and in the salons of Paris that Franklin and Jefferson attended.

PARIS AND THE FRENCH ENLIGHTENMENT

Jefferson's experience with urban life was paltry before his1785 arrival in Paris, and so too was his face-to-face contact with persons on his own intellectual level. Henry Adams expressed the opinion that Jefferson's happiest days were in Paris, and Carl Becker, seemingly without any direct reference to Adams, came to the same conclusion. Becker wrote, "Not

41 Jefferson to Doctor Benjamin Rush, Monticello, January 16, 1811.

without reason was Jefferson most at home in Paris." But Jefferson was as disapproving of French cosmopolitanism and decadence as Henry Adams' ancestors, John and Abigail, had been, and Jefferson issued a warning on the moral temptations to be encountered by innocents abroad.[42]

> While learning the language in France a young man's morals, health and fortune are more irresistibly endangered than in any country of the universe: in Canada he would be acquiring a knolege of the country and it's inhabitants which cannot fail to be useful in life to every American. On this point I have long ago made up my mind, that Canada is the country to which we should send our children to acquire a knolege of the French tongue.[43]

Henry Adams' opinion is difficult to explain, although he was by no means aiming at an accurate portrayal of Jefferson's personality, and he certainly did not seek to exaggerate Jefferson's cosmopolitan sophistication. Adams invented this description of the Francophile Jefferson in pursuit of an old family feud, long after his great-grandfather had ostensibly buried the hatchet. On the one hand, as Adams noted, Jefferson's Paris had a "liberal, literary and scientific air" that a man of his intellectual tastes might have enjoyed.[44] On the other hand, it was, after all, a city, and thus it was a breeding-ground for corruption. Jefferson was inescapably provincial, and thus ambivalent about the French metropolis. While he had ample opportunities for contact with the more cosmopolitan French intellectuals, he does not seem to have become truly intimate with any of them. His heart did not bleed when French friends and acquaintances were imprisoned, executed, or driven into exile. After the revolution in France he continued his friendship with Du Pont de Nemours, who shared his romanticization of the rustic, and he nurtured Du Pont de Nemours' French physiocratic notions, while encouraging him to undertake slave-based manufacturing.[45]

Jefferson could read French before he arrived in Paris in 1784. Neither his strengths nor his deficiencies should be exaggerated, but a judicious and appreciative chronicle of his strivings with the language is long

42 Henry Adams, *History of the United States during the Administrations of Thomas Jefferson* (New York: Library of America, 1986 [1890]), pp. 101–102. For John and Abigail's disapproval, see Edmund S. Morgan, *The Meaning of Independence* (New York: Norton, 1978), pp. 18–19. Carl Lotus Becker, *The Declaration of Independence: A Study on the History of Political Ideas* (New York: Harcourt, Brace and Company, 1922), p. 217.

43 Jefferson to Dugald Stewart, June 21, 1789.

44 Henry Adams, *History of the United States during the Administrations of Thomas Jefferson*, p. 102.

45 Jefferson to Pierre Samuel Du Pont de Nemours, November 8, 1812.

overdue. On August 30, 1785, after he had been in France for over a year, he wrote to his brother-in-law, Francis Eppes: "Patsy is well. She speaks French as easily as English; Humphries, Short and myself are scarcely better at it than when we landed." After three years in Paris, he was still not at ease with the language, and he wrote to Stephen Cathalan, Jr., saying, "I am honored with your father's letter of June the 30th [1787]; and, as he does not read English, and I cannot write French, I must beg leave to answer him through you."[46] This was an exaggeration, for there are French letters from this period written in Jefferson's hand – albeit they are brief, formal, unexciting, and reveal almost nothing of his engagement with French literary or intellectual culture. It has been noted already that Jefferson wrote a more correct French than did his French butler, Adrien Petit.[47]

Jefferson's spoken French, like his chess game, was uncultivated when he arrived in Paris, and he was self-conscious respecting his deficiencies in both. It is rare even for adolescents to master the idiom and grammar of a foreign language, and Jefferson had passed 42. For adults, even after a limited fluency has been achieved, it may take considerably longer before they are at home in every situation. As late as July 11, 1786, after two years in Paris, he wrote to St. John de Crèvecoeur, "Being unable to write in French so as to be sure of conveying my true meaning, or perhaps any meaning at all, I will beg of you to interpret what I have now the honour to write." It is difficult to say how much time Jefferson spent in French conversations, but Jefferson was not a lazy man, and it seems almost certain that his studious habits would have compelled him to read French every day. The practice would have strengthened his vocabulary, his reading comprehension, and his aesthetic appreciation for the language, but would have had limited effect on his writing or oral skills. His private secretary, William Short, who arrived in Paris with limited competency at 25, made greater progress, and so did Benjamin Franklin, although he was much older. An imperfect but vigorous and sometimes flirtatious French flowed from the old rascal's pen, and he apparently enjoyed a richer socio-cultural experience, by seizing every opportunity to improve his French and his chess. In one notable instance he practiced both skills simultaneously in the presence of a French observer while she relaxed in her bathtub.[48]

[46] Jefferson to Stephen Cathalan, Jr., July 21, 1787.

[47] See letter of his butler, Adrien Petit, to Jefferson, July 28, 1792.

[48] Jefferson's chess defeat is mentioned by John Meacham in *Jefferson and the Art of Power*, p. 189. Benjamin Franklin's chess game with a mutual friend while Madame Brillon

Jefferson certainly had conversational ability in French from the day he arrived, and he probably reached in due course the same level as a modern American university student with a strong French minor. He presumably could interact "with a degree of fluency and spontaneity that makes regular interaction with native speakers quite possible without strain for either party."[49] Jefferson had regular contact with Du Pont de Nemours, Condorcet, La Rochefoucauld, and Lafayette frequently in person, and he did not find it necessary to correspond with them by letter, so he left behind only limited evidence of his skills. We know that once Jefferson developed strength at any mental activity, he loved to exercise it, even to flaunt it. With respect to mathematics, music, and architecture, he was *homo ludens*, a man at play, demonstrating a sense of intellectual satisfaction even when his experiments were not perfect. With French, we do not discover a parallel expression of aesthetic enjoyment to that he found in mathematical exercises. It is remarkable that while he claimed to speak several of the Romance languages, he avoided writing in any of them. One searches in vain for any evidence that Jefferson took the same variety of delight in the intellectual exercise of modern languages that he found in toying with algebra.

If one were to believe his account of the Paris years, dictated later to Daniel Webster, one might assume he was at ease with French society and manners from the beginning of his residency, but this is contradicted by his own writings. Although he naturally found the new environment and the duties of his office stimulating, he at first disparaged "the brilliant pleasures of this gay capital." At 42 he felt himself to be "of an age which does not easily accommodate itself to new manners and new modes of living." He was "sick and confined to his house for six weeks towards the end of 1784," and then in January he was staggered by news that Lucy, his youngest daughter, left behind in Virginia, had died of whooping cough. As the months passed, he suffered from depression and longed "for the woods, the wilds, and the independence of Monticello." He looked forward to his return to Virginia, "for tho' there is less wealth there, there is more freedom, more ease and less misery." It was not until July of 1787

reclined in her bath is described in Walter Isaacson, *Benjamin Franklin: An American Life* (New York: Simon and Schuster, 2003), p. 362.

[49] Jefferson's French competency by today's standard of the Cadre européen commun de référence pour les langues would have been at level B2: "the student can understand the main ideas of complex text on both concrete and abstract topics ... Can interact with a degree of fluency and spontaneity that makes regular interaction with native speakers quite possible without strain for either party."

that he was cheered by the arrival in Paris of his surviving daughter, Polly, accompanied by Sally Hemings.[50]

At first he was reluctant to join a salon, perhaps due to his initial difficulties with the language, but eventually he did pay his visits "chez Madame." He described one such occasion disparagingly in a letter to Anne Willing Bingham, comparing the effete emptiness of the Parisian scene to "the tranquil pleasures of America." Jefferson chose as the symbol of ennui his unnamed hostess, "propped on bolsters and pillows." The ungenerous description presented in this letter of 1787 differs greatly from the recollections of 1822, in the often-referenced interview with Webster. The "Madame" of his letter to Anne Bingham probably referred to Madame d'Houdetot, or, with lesser likelihood, to Madame Helvétius, as these were among the prominent female contacts that he inherited from Franklin, although he dropped the names of numerous women of the aristocracy in his correspondence.[51]

FRENCH INFLUENCES AND THE ENLIGHTENMENT

Jefferson often dropped the names of French authors in his letters, although he did not always explain his references with precision. The following to Madison is representative of his usual vagueness:

> I send you a book of Dupont's on the subject of the commercial treaty with England. Tho' it's general matter may not be interesting, yet you will pick up in various parts of it such excellent principles and observations as will richly repay the trouble of reading it. I send you also two little pamphlets of the Marquis de Condorcet, wherein is the most judicious statement I have seen of the great questions which agitate this nation at present.[52]

The letter is tantalizing, in that it offers not a word of what Jefferson considered meaningful in the content of these authors. We may say with absolute confidence that Jefferson never attempted a systematic critique of

[50] The account by Daniel Webster is in Fletcher Webster, ed., *The Private Correspondence of Daniel Webster* (Boston, MA: Little, Brown, 1857), p. 371. Reprinted in Kevin J. Hayes, *Jefferson in His Own Time* (University of Iowa Press, 2012), p. 99. Abigail Adams mentions Jefferson's illness in a letter to Mrs. Cranch, December 9, 1784. Jefferson's discontent and longing for Virginia are in his letter to von Geismar, September 6, 1785.

[51] Hayes, *The Road to Monticello*, pp. 294–295, describes Jefferson's first visit to the Comtesse d'Houdetot on June 30, 1785.

[52] Jefferson to James Madison, July 31, 1788.

any French author comparable to John Adams' *Defense of the Constitutions of the United States* – an elegant, erudite, brilliant, but unnecessary refutation of Anne-Robert-Jacques Turgot's essay, disparaging some of America's states' constitutions.[53] Jefferson offered little or no commentary on any of the principal writings of the French Enlightenment. He expressed his approval of Jean-Baptiste Say and his reservations on Montesquieu, but offered little explanation of his agreements or disagreements.[54] It is not surprising that we find fewer references to Rousseau than to Voltaire in Jefferson's writing, since most Anglophones find Voltaire easier to read than Rousseau. He made references in his *Notes on Virginia* and in his "Notes of a Tour into the Southern Parts of France" to Voltaire's speculations on geology, an area in which Voltaire has had no lasting influence, and he challenged some of his wildly imaginative speculations with equally ungrounded ruminations of his own. More than once his papers contain references to Voltaire's *Questions Encyclopédiques*, but how could he have guessed that posterity would remember Voltaire primarily for his *Candide*, while forgetting his neoclassical dramatic works that are no longer performed?[55]

In his lifetime Jefferson was "criticized for his supposed foible for the French Revolution," as his sympathetic biographer, Gilbert Chinard, noted many decades ago. But Chinard shows that the criticisms were inspired more by partisan bias than by anything substantive, and there is little merit in the idea that Jefferson's ideology was largely French-influenced. While he had an appreciation for French achievements in the arts and sciences, and relished his chance to experience Parisian society, during his five years as minister to France, "curiously enough," as Chinard notes, during his formative years, "the direct influence of the French

[53] Gordon Wood approaches the problem of Adams' *Defense of the Constitutions of the United States against the Attack of Turgot in his Letter to Dr. Price*, 3 vols. (London: C. Dilly, 1787–88) and the Constitution in "The Relevance and Irrelevance of John Adams," *Revolutionary Characters* (New York: Penguin, 2006), pp. 173–202, although Wood makes little reference to Turgot.

[54] Tracy, who offered a critique on Montesquieu, wrote to Jefferson on several occasions in French, e.g. February, 1816 and March 10, 1819, concerning Jefferson's project of translating and distributing Tracy's critique. Jefferson's letters to Tracy are in English. As in his preference for Jean-Baptiste Say over Adam Smith, Jefferson leaves to the reader's imagination the reasons for his preference for Say over Montesquieu.

[55] Jefferson, "Notes of a Tour into the Southern Parts of France, &c., 3 March–10 June 1787"; see http://founders.archives.gov/documents/Jefferson/01-11-02-0389 (Original source: Julian P. Boyd, *The Papers of Thomas Jefferson* (Princeton University Press, 1955), vol. XI, pp. 415–464.) There are further allusions to Jefferson and Voltaire in the present volume.

philosophers was negligible. As a young man, he encountered Voltaire's *Essai sur les moeurs*, and heavily annotated Montesquieu's *Espirit des Lois*, but he used both books as repertories of facts rather than founts of ideas."[56]

And even as "repertories of facts," he seldom found the works of French authors overwhelmingly convincing. His *Notes on Virginia* was largely an attack on errors he discovered in the naturalist, Georges-Louis Leclerc, Comte de Buffon. He mentioned Voltaire in the *Notes* only by way of dismissing that *philosophe*'s observations on historical geology. During his five years in France, Jefferson encountered such French intellectuals as Madame d'Houdetot, Madame Helvétius, Lafayette, Condorcet, Cabanis, Du Pont de Nemours, and l'Abbé Morellet. But although he was sometimes accused of returning to the States with a head full of French ideas, and although he surveyed French authors respectfully, he does not seem to have been blown off his feet by any of them. The economic theorist Jean-Baptiste Say's *Traité d'économie politique*, published in 1803, received Jefferson's enthusiastic endorsement, but as a welcome confirmation of ideas he already held.[57]

VOLNEY AND THE HISTORIOGRAPHY OF DECLINE

Two French authors who received Jefferson's most remarkable and painstaking attention were Constantine Volney and Destutt de Tracy. He devoted considerable effort towards the translation and dissemination of works by both authors. Recent scholars accept Gilbert Chinard's judgment that Jefferson contributed significantly to the Tracy translation, but their investigations do not proceed far beyond his surmise as to how far he actually got with Volney's *Les Ruines, ou méditations sur les révolutions des empires*. In neither case did Jefferson seek credit for the translation,

[56] Chinard, *Thomas Jefferson*, pp. vii, 366. This volume, as its full title (*Thomas Jefferson, the Apostle of Americanism*) indicates, hints at the idea that Jefferson's influence was at least a symbolic inspiration, if not an ideological influence, on France. The same may certainly be said of George Washington and to a greater extent of Benjamin Franklin. Chinard places heavy emphasis on Jefferson's interactions with Volney and Tracy, both overlooked in Conor Cruise O'Brien's *The Long Affair: Thomas Jefferson and the French Revolution, 1785–1800* (University of Chicago Press, 1996). Merrill Peterson commented on Jefferson's twenty-seven entries from Montesquieu's *Espirit des lois* "in his commonplace book—more than any other book or author," in *Thomas Jefferson and the New Nation*, p. 61.

[57] He preferred Say's work to Adam Smith's *Wealth of Nations*. Jefferson to Joseph Milligan, Monticello, April 6, 1816.

and the exact amount of his contribution to each is less than certain. Dumas Malone and Merrill Peterson demonstrated little interest in his translation of Volney. Julian Boyd and his successors at the Jefferson Papers project present their cumulative knowledge of Jefferson's engagement with the translations, and have made more substantive contributions towards our understanding of his efforts.

The translation was published in 1802, and there have been numerous printings of that edition. Eventually Jefferson, or Volney with Jefferson's understanding, consigned the translation to Joel Barlow, who completed the final four chapters, and we cannot say what finishing touches were added to the rest by Volney or Barlow. The translator's preface to the English edition, published in Paris in 1802, introduces some ambiguities as to authorship. It credits the influences of an earlier translator and adds, "we have been aided by his labors; and what is of still more importance, our work has been done under the inspection of the author, whose critical knowledge of both languages has given us a great facility in avoiding such errors as might arise from hurry or mistake."[58]

Few scholars have commented on Volney's relationship to Jefferson; Fawn Brodie is a notable exception. In describing the Frenchman's visit to Monticello, Brodie notes Volney's comments on seeing Jefferson about brandishing a whip while walking among his slaves. She also notes Volney's astonishment on witnessing that some of the slave children were indistinguishable from whites: "Mais je fus étonné de voir appeler noirs et traiter comme tels des enfants aussi blancs que moi." Brodie notes that Jefferson blamed this admixture on the sexual adventures of white hired men with mulatto slave women, but she speculated on whether these children may actually have been Jefferson's own. Since Brodie's concern was primarily with Jefferson's "intimate history," she devoted no conspicuous attention to Jefferson's efforts as translator of *Les Ruines* or their romanticization of the African past.

[58] See the translator's note to the 1802 edition. For the present work I have used *The Ruins of Empires* (Baltimore: Black Classic Press, 1991), which is a photographic reproduction of the American edition by Peter Eckler (New York, 1890). The Eckler edition is in turn a republication of the Paris 1802 edition, and includes the preface to the London edition of 1851, and the preface to the Eckler edition was reproduced from that of the 1833 edition printed in Boston by Charles Galord. Volney's additional chapters are on "The Law of Nature" and "Volney's Answer to Dr. Priestley," and an "Appendix: The Zodiacal Signs and Constellations." In the compilation of this book I have also consulted various editions, both French and English.

In the Introduction, which was the most eye-catching portion of the translation attributed to Jefferson, one discovers the following sentimental reverie on the lost heritage of the black African race, and the decline of Nilotic civilization from its ancient glories:

> Behold the wrecks of her metropolis of Thebes with her hundred palaces, the parent of cities, monument of the caprice of destiny. There a people, now forgotten, discovered, while others were yet barbarians, the elements of the arts and sciences. A race of men now rejected for their sable skin and frizzled hair, founded on the study of the laws of nature, those civil and religious systems which still govern the universe.[59]

Volney's footnote, which is preserved in the Jefferson–Barlow translation, declared that it was "incontrovertible that by the term Ethiopians, the ancients meant to represent a people of black complexion, thick lips and wooly hair." Why did Jefferson, the prophet of white supremacy, decide to translate, and contribute to the distribution of, a volume that seemed to argue for the past glories of African peoples? The answer is that he was interested in speculation on the reason for their presumed decline. Gordon Wood says that eighteenth-century Anglophones' study of the classics "was highly selective, focusing on decline and decadence."[60] Such an obsession may have been the motivation for Jefferson's undertaking. Believing that blacks were inferior, he asked himself what original sin against nature had led to the unfortunate fall that Volney's work bemoaned. Jefferson sought to discover, if I may borrow the terminology that Wood transmits in Edward Montagu's words from *Reflections on the*

[59] Volney's original French reads as follows:

> Voilà les débris de sa métropole, Thèbes aux cent palais, l'aïeule des cités, monument d'un destin bizarre. C'est là qu'un peuple maintenant oublié, alors que tous les autres étaient barbares, découvrait les élémens des sciences et des arts; et qu'une race d'hommes aujourd'hui rebut de la société, parce qu'ils ont les cheveux crépus et la peau noire, fondait sur l'étude des lois de la nature des systèmes civils et religieux qui régissent encore l'univers.

There is a French-language 1802 edition of *Les Ruines* online at Internet Archive, https://archive.org/details/newtranslationofoovoln/page/n11 There is also an English-language edition at http://knarf.english.upenn.edu/Volney/volneytp.html The "sable skin and frizzled hair" of the Thebans were omitted from some early editions but were included in the introductions to both the 1785 edition and the Jefferson–Barlow translation. See Gilbert Chinard, *Volney et l'Amérique d'après des documents inédits et sa correspondance avec Jefferson* (Baltimore: Johns Hopkins University Press, 1923), pp. 111–114, and cf. Jefferson to Volney, March 17, 1801, and Volney to Jefferson, June 24, 1801.

[60] Gordon Wood, *Creation of the American Republic*, pp. 48–53.

Rise and Fall of the Ancient Republics (London, 1759), "the principal causes of that degeneracy of manners, which reduc'd those once brave and free people into the most abject slavery."

The Jefferson–Barlow translation preserved intact Volney's two-page footnote, declaring that it was "incontrovertible that by the term Ethiopians, the ancients meant to represent a people of black complexion, thick lips and wooly hair." Jefferson's allusions to the cycles of civilizations and the vicissitudes of fortune reiterated themes that were familiar to him before he began his translation. A notable instance of this theory of the rise and fall of civilizations, cyclical and organically predestined, was already familiar to readers of Lord Bolingbroke, who famously wrote in 1738:

> The best instituted governments, like the best constituted animal bodies carry in them the seeds of their destruction; and though they grow and improve for a time, they will soon tend visibly to their dissolution.[61]

This historiography of decline and fall, and the cycles of civilization, themes well known to readers of Bolingbroke and in the process of being refined by Edward Gibbon, were familiar to Jefferson. He alluded to them in his *Notes on Virginia*, completed in the same year that *Les Ruines* was published.[62] His allusions naturally excited the imagination of the African American (eponymous) author of *David Walker's Appeal*, a work published five years after Jefferson's death by a literate Free African, who operated a used clothing store in Boston's Brattle Street. Walker's *Appeal* commenced with, and was dominated by, Jefferson's allusion in the *Notes* to the wheel of fortune. The present cycle, said Walker, had given Europeans their ephemeral power over Africans. Jefferson's mention of the possibility of another cycle of history in Query XIV of the *Notes* was well known to David Walker and his circle, including the editors of the first African American newspaper, *Freedom's Journal,* published in New York, and the *Notes on Virginia* elicited his sustained commentary. When Jefferson wrote the following lines, he was thinking not

61 Bolingbroke, *The Patriot King* (1749). See Stow Persons, "The Cyclical Theory of History in Eighteenth-Century America," *American Quarterly*, 6, no. 2 (summer, 1954), 147–163. Also see Gordon Wood, *The Creation of the American Republic*, pp. 48–53.

62 For the publication history and other relevant dates, see Jefferson, *Notes on the State of Virginia*, pp. iv, 18–20, 39, 78, 218. Also see Douglas L. Wilson, "The Evolution of Jefferson's *Notes on the State of Virginia*," *The Virginia Magazine of History and Biography*, 112 (2004), 98–133.

progressively of "time's arrow" but in terms of "time's cycle," after the fashion of Bolingbroke:

> Indeed I tremble for my country when I reflect that God is just: that his justice cannot sleep for ever: that considering numbers, nature and natural means only, a revolution of the wheel of fortune, an exchange of situation, is among possible events.[63]

The laws of nature, even without special divine intervention, predicted that America might have rough times ahead due to the inevitable patterns of history. There was a question as to whether American society would follow the upward evolutionary teleology of "time's arrow" or whether America's future would proceed in accord with the cheerless laws of "time's cycle." Was America's historical arrow so exceptional that its arc was not subject to the laws of gravity? Did God make adjustments in the trajectory of history similar to those that, according to Newton's hypothesis, He made in the orbits of the planets? Would the Creator intervene in American history to keep it ever in the ascendancy, or would he exact his divine tribute on a slaveholding nation? One wonders what comfort American slaves might have taken from meditating on the slow movement of God's pendulum of justice as they endured the daily burdens of their status.

It was neither the matter of race nor the matter of slavery that made Volney's work so intriguing as to deserve an English translation, but his theory of "the law of nature." Although almost forgotten today, Volney was widely read during the Enlightenment, and was taken so seriously that Joseph Priestley mounted a significant attack on him for his atheism. Jefferson, who called himself a Christian (although an anti-Trinitarian, who denied the divinity of Jesus), was in the same "deistic" camp as Priestley and must have sided with him in this clash; nonetheless, he devoted great energy to the secret sponsorship of Volney's work. *Les Ruines* does not seem to have influenced Jefferson's fundamental religious beliefs or moral philosophy in any demonstrable way. The larger issue that Volney had approached, and which is encountered

[63] In Jefferson to James Monroe, July 14, 1793, Jefferson expressed a fear that the revolt in Santo Domingo would eventually spread to encompass the entire West Indies. Forrest MacDonald, in his biography, *Alexander Hamilton* (New York: Norton, 1979), p. 279, says Jefferson feared the Gulf States of North America would also fall. Philip Foner notes that in the election of 1800 some Federalists made fantastic claims that Jefferson desired to import the Haitian Revolution, due to his negrophilism, as evidenced by the reported liaison with Sally Hemings.

in the *Notes on Virginia*, was the historiography of decline, an idea already of interest to Jefferson, and previously encountered in Bolingbroke.

Jefferson's position with respect to an imbroglio between Volney and Joseph Priestley, evident in Volney's letter to Priestley appended to later editions of *Les Ruines*, is discernable, and we shall never know all the nuances, because Jefferson provided no editorial notes to his anonymous translation, even ordering that Volney destroy his copy. The work was criticized by Priestley, an avowed deist, whom Jefferson much admired, for the atheism that Priestley attributed to Volney's writings. It is well known that Jefferson was often labeled, rightly or wrongly, as an atheist by association with the views of authors he had befriended, read, or admired. His secret sponsorship of Volney and his labors on a translation of an author who was so roundly denounced as an atheist by his much-admired friend, Priestley, are unexplained by anything in Jefferson's writings.

Jefferson's positions on religion, as expressed in letters, are vague and variable, in contrast to his profession of religion in political rhetoric, as in the Declaration of Independence or on state occasions and his First Inaugural Address. His profound interaction with and promotion of *Les Ruines* bespeaks an accord with those of its author. The role he played in the translation of *The Ruins* is ambiguous, since, as previously noted, we have neither a complete manuscript in Jefferson's handwriting, nor a statement from him in which he unequivocally lends his support to any of the encyclopedic content of the work. Jefferson, Priestley, and Volney all professed a belief in a "law of nature," which Volney defined in an appendix to later editions as "the constant and regular order of events by which God governs the universe; an order which his wisdom presents to the senses of men, as an equal and common rule for their actions."[64]

MONTESQUIEU, TRACY, AND THE AXIOMS OF POLITICS

Jefferson regarded Charles-Louis Montesquieu's *Spirit of Laws* as admirably learned, but fraught with error. As early as 1790 he had decided that the work contained "a great number of political truths; but also an equal number of heresies: so that the reader must be constantly on his guard."

[64] Quoted from the first page of Volney, "The Law of Nature," appendix to *Les Ruines* (New York: Eckler, 1890 [1802]), p. 177.

He was vague as to his reasons, other than the standard objection that Montesquieu raised uncomfortable questions about the viability of the American experiment. In 1810 Jefferson was translating Destutt de Tracy's *Commentary and Review of Montesquieu's Spirit of Laws*, which provided warnings as to where exactly the pitfalls might be encountered.[65] Malone cautiously describes Jefferson as overseeing the Tracy project. There is some doubt as to how much of a role he played in the translation, but there is no doubt that he sponsored the completion and distribution of Tracy's work.

Jefferson rendered the publication history of Tracy's text intentionally murky at the time of its initial circulation. Tracy wanted it that way, for he feared Napoleon's censors, and therefore published the work anonymously.[66] The confusion has been described by other scholars, who point up the problematic of Jefferson's relationship to it. Du Pont de Nemours, believing at the time that Jefferson was the author, even began to undertake a translation into French. Jefferson hastened to correct the misapprehension. Today one finds even more frustrating than Jefferson's secretiveness his failure to be open about the authorship of the preface.[67]

As in the case of Volney, Jefferson was being scientific. He defined "scientific" as efforts to discovering a law of nature, then constructing syllogistic deductions based on that aphoristic law. He was sympathetic to the common presupposition of Volney and Tracy that political science

[65] Jefferson to Destutt de Tracy, January 26, 1811, in Merrill Peterson, ed., *Thomas Jefferson, Writings* (New York: Literary Classics of the United States, 1984), p. 948. Dumas Malone, *Jefferson and His Time*, 6 vols. (Boston, MA: Little, Brown, 1981), vol. VI, *Jefferson and His Time, the Sage of Monticello*, pp. 207–212. Jefferson also undertook, but did not complete, a translation of Volney's *The Ruins*, which he consigned to Joel Barlow, and completed four pages of a translation of Condorcet's *De l'influence de la révolution*. Jefferson read French well and spoke conversational French. He was not comfortable writing it, even for relaxed social purposes; see Jefferson to Stephen Cathalan, Jr., July 21, 1787.

[66] Decades of research into the publication history of Jefferson's translation of Tracy have led to a maze of speculations as to authorship. Gilbert Chinard, Dumas Malone, Merrill Peterson, and the editors of the Julian Boyd edition of Jefferson's papers are difficult to decipher on the matter of this edition. Jefferson apparently began the translation of this work, but the Boyd edition makes use of the passive voice and such expressions as "probably composed" and "probably created." The editors of Jefferson's papers cite a notation in Jefferson's hand, reading "it was translated by W. Duane." See note from Jefferson to William Duane, 16 September 1810, Founders Online.

[67] See Gilbert Chinard, *Jefferson et les idéologues d'après sa correspondance inédite avec Destutt de Tracy, Cabinis, J.-B. Say et Auguste Comte* (Baltimore: Johns Hopkins University Press, 1925), p. 63. Malone, *The Sage of Monticello*, p. 209.

was a natural science. What Alexander Pope had written (in *An Essay on Criticism* [1711]) concerning the rules of art was applicable to Jefferson's perception of all the arts and sciences, including political science.

> Those rules of old, discover'd, not devised,
> Are Nature still, but Nature methodized.

Jefferson's Natural Law approach to political science was founded in the idea that the laws of government were as axiomatic as those of geometry – and, like Pope's rules of poetry, "discover'd, not devised." A common thread in Volney, in Montesquieu, and in Jefferson's writing was the belief that political science could and should be a natural science. Montesquieu's contributions to "political science" were welcomed, if only cautiously, by the early republic's political theorists, most notably John Adams and James Madison, who accepted Montesquieu's division of governmental powers into executive, legislative, and judicial branches. They were, however, disturbed by Montesquieu's assertion that republican government was not applicable to large territories so extensive as the thirteen United States.

A nagging fear existed in American minds that the reason for the failure of ancient Rome's republican experiment had to do with its territorial expansion. Since the United States had begun as an extensive land empire, one of the several tasks of the Federalist Papers was their attempt at a refutation of Montesquieu's contention concerning the incompatibility of republican government with a great land empire. Jefferson wrote, "I suspect that the doctrine, that small States alone are fitted to be republics, will be exploded by experience, with some other brilliant fallacies accredited by Montesquieu and other political writers."[68] Rather than attempting an original and systematic exposition of Montesquieu's "brilliant fallacies," Jefferson chose to champion a critique in the form of Tracy's *Commentary and Review*, and recommended his authorized translation of it to the College of William and Mary as a basic text.[69]

Another of Tracy's points of agreement with Montesquieu was bothersome to Jefferson – the idea that the English government was "a republic disguised as a monarchy." Jefferson was adamant in his belief that the two forms of monarchy and republic were dichotomous. A democratic republic was founded in "the good sense of the people," he wrote, and if it was capable of any evils, they would be self-correcting, "whereas the evils of

[68] Jefferson to Monsieur D'Ivernois, Monticello, February 6, 1795.
[69] Malone, *The Sage of Monticello*, p. 211.

monarchical government are beyond remedy."[70] Montesquieu and Tracy were less adamant, and they saw the two systems as neither contradictory nor mutually exclusive; furthermore, Tracy found the terminology nebulous. On p. 9 of Jefferson's authorized translation Tracy stated that "The word republican is itself a very vague term," and "Moreover the term republic cannot be contrasted with that of monarchy, for the United Provinces of Holland, and the United States of America, have each a single chief magistrate, and are yet considered republics."[71]

Such opinions were unsettling to Jefferson and Madison, devout acolytes at the altar of republicanism, and constantly inciting crowds by conjuring up royalist bogeymen. It seems strange that he would transmit Tracy and Montesquieu's words into a university textbook without footnote or commentary, when we consider the vigor with which Jefferson so frequently accused his political opponents of "squinting" at monarchy or being "Anglomen." How could Jefferson conscientiously have accepted a definition asserting that "The word monarchy properly designates a government in which the executive power is vested in a single person"? This may have been etymologically true, but to Jefferson it would seem to muddy the waters with an extremely broad and incautious definition. As Tracy maintained, it did encompass the American presidency. Montesquieu offered the qualification that concentration of executive power is "only a circumstance which may be connected with others of a very different nature, and which is not essentially characteristic of the social organization. What we have said of Poland, Holland, and the American government, confirms this."

Jefferson's disagreements with Tracy and the legacy of Montesquieu are barely revealed in private correspondence, and nowhere completely explicated. He must have been annoyed that Tracy compared the office in which he had served to that of the king of Poland, although this was exactly the critical comparison he had made in a letter to Adams decades previously.[72] He must have recognized the irony that, as president of the United States, he exercised his office with considerably more independence of action than some kings could command. In 1803, George III could not have independently decided to purchase a vast land empire

70 Jefferson to David Ramsay, August 4, 1787.

71 [Destutt de Tracy], Montesquieu, *Commentary and Review of Montesquieu's Spirit of Laws* (Philadelphia: William Duane, 1811), p. 9.

72 Jefferson to John Adams Thomas, November 13, 1787, "How do you like our new constitution? ... [the] President seems a bad edition of a Polish king."

extending from the Mississippi river to the Rocky Mountains. Tracy and Montesquieu described "republic" with an obvious sense of irony that Jefferson must certainly have found irksome. In fact, they obscured the boundaries between monarchy and democracy to such an extent as to make their definitions functionally useless.

NATURAL LAWS AND POSITIVE LAWS

Thomas Jefferson reminds us of Thomas Aquinas, whom he admired, because natural law is the cornerstone of their thinking. Tracy too was obsessed with natural law, which must have been the magnet that drew Jefferson to his work. Tracy begins with a distinction between natural laws and positive laws. The first were universal, eternal, and immutable; the latter were laws created by society, "laws which are artificial and conventional," and which were quite different than the "laws of Nature," which are universal and eternal. Positive law is the creation of society, and we apply the term to nature only in a metaphorical sense. The conventions of the positive law may be either just or unjust. "The just law is that which produces good, the unjust that which produces *evil.*" Tracy was in agreement with Montesquieu, who said that "Positive laws ought to be consequent of the laws of nature: this is the spirit of laws." Tracy said:

> that fundamental justice is that only which is conformable to the laws of nature; and that radical injustice is that which is contrary to the laws of nature; and consequently that our posterior and consequent laws should be in unison with those more ancient and inevitable laws. This is the true spirit, or genuine sense, in which all positive laws ought to be established.[73]

The term "political science," which Jefferson and his contemporaries frequently used, meant the discovery of axioms on which governments should be founded. It did not necessarily imply the ceaseless accumulation of data that we find intrinsic to political science methods today, but an attempt to shape government in accord with discoverable laws. The invocation of "the Laws of Nature and Nature's God" in the Declaration of Independence bears an affinity to Montesquieu's *Spirit of Laws*, and it is not surprising that Jefferson recommended Tracy's systematic endorsement of Montesquieu's natural law principle for the essential reading list at the University of Virginia.

[73] De Tracy, *Commentary and Review*, pp. 5–7.

With the exception of the introduction to Tracy's *Commentary and Review*, his analyses of political writers are seldom more than jottings, but he certainly knew which authors to address. It is sometimes difficult to discern what he found valuable in a given theorist; it can be equally difficult to see what he found objectionable. His wide range of references to political theorists is stunning, but his references to these authors are often vague, and, as to content, he is seldom clear as to what he finds worthwhile and what condemnable in them, and he was so reluctant to stoop to the level of published polemics that we have very little in the way of a systematic expression of his ideas. Jefferson's theoretical writings were never as prominent or public as those of Hamilton or Madison, or as pungent as those of John Adams or Thomas Paine, although their political effects were great.[74]

Jefferson's responses to the writings of Adam Smith, of which he apparently approved, are also tantalizing in this respect. In 1790 he referred to *The Wealth of Nations* as "the best book extant" in political economy, but later amended this statement to declare it was "the best book to be read, unless Say's *Political Economy* can be had, which treats the same subjects on the same principles, but in a shorter compass and more lucid manner. But I believe this work has not been translated into our language." As for "Locke's little book on Government," he called it "perfect as far as it goes." Astonishing indeed was his 1790 declaration that, in the field of political science, "there is no better book than the Federalist." Was he aware when he wrote this that most of the *Federalist*'s contents were the work of Alexander Hamilton, a fact that Madison must surely have revealed to him? One must wonder how critically he had studied the *Federalist* and some of the other works of "political science" that he praised.[75]

If the American presidency did resemble, as Tracy and Montesquieu averred, that of a king, Jefferson resembled Bolingbroke's ideal of the

[74] Jefferson's use of the term "political science" is in Jefferson to John Adams, January 19, 1819; Jefferson to Eleuthère I. Pierre Samuel Du Pont de Nemours, December 25, 1812. Jefferson to John Adams, January 19, 1819. Hamilton uses the term in *Federalist* 66, writing as Catullus III, in an article for the *Gazette of the United States* (September 9, 1792), and again, pejoratively, in his *Views on the French Revolution* (1794), and the phrase "science of politics" in *Federalist* 9.

[75] Jefferson to Thomas Mann Randolph, New York, May 30, 1790. In calling the *Federalist* a "book" Jefferson was no doubt referring to the two-volume compilation of these essays and eight others, reprinted as *The Federalist: A Collection of Essays, Written in Favour of the New Constitution, as Agreed upon by the Federal Convention, September 17, 1787* (New York: J. & A. McLean, 1788).

"patriot king." George III's pathetic attempts to fulfill the role of "patriot king" deserve more pity than scorn, for George had sought anachronistically to play the citizen monarch at a time when regal functions, at least in England, were drifting inevitably into irrelevance. His wistful admiration for George Washington as potentially "the greatest character of the age" reveals King George's recognition that Washington had attained the role of patriot king to which he had so unsuccessfully aspired. Washington and Jefferson, with their rejection of Napoleonic ambitions, advanced the course of the American empire, assuming the powers of patriot kings while wisely avoiding all the uneasiness laid upon crowned heads. Washington and Jefferson silently grasped a truth that had been recognized in political theory since the early 1700s, and stated by Montesquieu. If the British government had evolved since the English Civil War into a republic masquerading as a monarchy, Washington, Adams, and Jefferson created an empire masquerading as a republic.[76]

JEFFERSON AND THE GERMAN ENLIGHTENMENT

Jefferson's connections to the French Enlightenment, as Chinard posited, may have been exaggerated, but were never in danger of being ignored. Less frequently observed are his impressions of German intellectual life of the late eighteenth and early nineteenth centuries, although he obviously gave much greater notice to French authors. German has never been the first foreign language mastered by American intellectuals, but then it was only in the eighteenth century that Germans began to prefer German. Leibniz, who wrote in Latin, which Jefferson read, is mentioned only once in the correspondence, where his name is spelled "Leibnitz," and where Jefferson makes an oblique reference to his mathematics. Kant, whose definition of "Enlightenment" is often cited today, is difficult for most people to read, including most Germans, and his "categorical imperative" was still unknown to most English speakers before the nineteenth century. Fichte and Herder, whose attitudes on race have been compared and contrasted to Jefferson's, were probably never studied by him. Whether he had read any Hegel cannot definitely be determined from a global search of his papers, and his knowledge of Goethe was superficial.

[76] Bolingbroke, *The Patriot King* (1749). King George III's statement is quoted in Benjamin West to Rufus King, May 3, 1797, cited by Richard Brookhiser, courtesy of William Allen, from Robert Spiller, et al., *A Literary History of the United States* (New York: Macmillan, 1963), p. 200.

German philosophy had little influence in England or America until after his death, and therefore Jefferson's friendship with Alexander von Humboldt at the tail-end of the Enlightenment was a point of contact with German intellectual life unusual for an American of his generation.

WASHINGTON, JEFFERSON, AND FREDERICK THE GREAT

Jefferson's destiny was intertwined with that of the emblematic "Enlightened Despot," Frederick II, King of Prussia, when he launched the Seven Years War in 1754, accidentally intertwining his ambitions with American destiny. Prussia was an ally of the British Empire and set in motion a series of events that led to the loss of France's Canadian territories and, in due course, to the French intervention on the American side in the War for Independence. Immanuel Kant saw him embodying the ideals of the Enlightenment, primarily on the basis of his religious toleration. If it is true, as a respected colleague has noted, that Frederick was "one of the most rapacious scoundrels in Europe at the time, land-greedy, cunning, duplicitous," it is also true that American continental ambitions proved to be equally "Machiavellian."[77] Jefferson collaborated with Andrew Jackson in plans for the resettlement of Indians and blacks, and he planned or promoted an ethnic cleansing of African Americans equally dishonorable.[78] Frederick, as did Jefferson, made anti-Semitic remarks, and, like Jefferson, he thought of the Jews as a separate people.[79] Jefferson made one of his most disturbing allusions to their ethnic otherness in a letter to Lafayette of 1817 in the midst of an attack on Quakers: "Dispersed, as the Jews, they still form, as those do, one nation, foreign to the land they live in ... forgetting all duties to their country in the execution of the policy of their order."[80]

[77] Peter Onuf, e-mail to Wilson Moses, February 4, 2013.

[78] For a brief summary of Frederick's measures against the Jewish people, see JewishEncylopedia.com, which reproduces "the unedited full text of the 1906 *Jewish Encyclopedia*": www.jewishencyclopedia.com/articles/6334-frederick-ii

[79] The Jewish Virtual Library is an online source that vigorously defends Jefferson as a promoter of all religious freedom, although admitting that "While Jefferson advocated for Jewish liberty, he held certain aspects of Judaism in low regard." (See www.jewishvirtuallibrary.org/thomas-jefferson-and-the-jews) He referred in passing to the Jewish people as a perpetual minority with either a "peculiarity" or "perversity" of character, depending on which transcription of his remarks one is reading. See Jefferson to John Taylor, June 4, 1798, and the editorial note at Founders Online.

[80] Jefferson to Lafayette, Monticello, May 14, 1817. Jefferson's attitudes on Jews, Unitarians, and Quakers are discussed in another chapter.

Jefferson refers almost affectionately to the emperor as "Old Frederic" in his *Anas*, but not surprisingly, given his support to the American struggle for independence. On hearing of Washington's rout of the Hessians at the battle of Trenton, Frederick sent his congratulations, and he notably refused to allow armies hostile to the American cause to pass through his territories.[81] Washington is said to have admired Frederick, and to have studied his ideas on military tactics and strategy. Frederick enthusiastically celebrated, even exaggerated, the genius of George Washington, whose triumphs he called "the most brilliant of any recorded in the annals of military achievements."[82] Jürgen Overhoff compares Frederick to Washington and intimates that Washington was the more perfect embodiment of Enlightenment ideals.[83] Both Frederick and Washington knew battlefield triumphs and humiliations. Frederick had more than one horse shot out from under him, but Jefferson showed little eagerness to take up arms, although, in more than one war, he urged others to hazard their lives.

Jefferson interacted indirectly with Frederick in 1785, conducting a commerce treaty through proxies, and he wrote, "Of all the powers not holding American territory, a connexion with him will give us the most credit." Jefferson's autobiography contains the confusing statement that, at the court of Versailles, "Old Frederic, of Prussia, met us cordially, and without hesitation, and appointing the Baron von Thulemeyer, his minister at the Hague, to negotiate with us, we communicated to him our Project, which, with little alteration by the King, was soon concluded."[84] Jefferson's confusing sentence, with its dangling participle and imprecise word choice, implies a cordial meeting with the emperor that did not occur, but it reflected his appreciation for "Old Frederic's" gracious reception of the new republic. Jefferson noted that most of the European nations "listened to our propositions

81 Ron Chernow, *Washington: A Life* (New York: Penguin, 2010), p. 283. Robert Asprey, *Frederick the Great: The Magnificent Enigma* (New York: The History Book Club, 1986), pp. 603–604, 616–617.

82 Chernow, *Washington*; Jürgen Overhoff, *Friedrich der Große und George Washington* (Stuttgart: Klett-Cotta Verlag, 2011), p. 283.

83 Overhoff, *Friedrich der Große und George Washington.*

84 Jefferson negotiated "The Treaty of Amity and Commerce" of September 10, 1785 between the Kingdom of Prussia and the United States that was later signed by Frederick the Great and George Washington. This made Prussia one of the first nations to recognize the United States. For comments on "Old Frederic," see Peterson, ed., *Thomas Jefferson, Writings*, p. 57, and Jefferson to Elbridge Gerry, May 11, 1785.

with coyness and reserve; old Frederick alone closing with us without hesitation."[85]

As a Renaissance man, Frederick mastered music, literature, and philosophy; his legendary reputation as a patron and practitioner of the arts, and his position in the history of Western music and architecture, while pursuing a long military and political career, is astonishing. Frederick is noted for numerous compositions for the flute and several orchestral pieces, and for transcribing the works of other composers. The anecdote of his donation of the theme for "The Musical Offering" to Johann Sebastian Bach is well known. As an architect, he also had accomplishments, and although he was no more responsible than Jefferson for the actual engineering, carpentry, or masonry of his residences, Frederick was involved in the oversight and design of his palaces in Berlin. He is rightly given credit for developing the style called "Frederican Rococo" that is represented in the palaces at San Souci and Potsdam. In comparing the "typical houses of the American aristocracy" with the "vast domestic palaces" of European nobles, Bernard Bailyn has called them of "a different world, remote and irrelevant."[86]

Jefferson's first significant contact with cultivated Germans occurred during the Revolution. Some of the music that made its way into Jefferson's library was the parting gift of a minor German noble, Baron Friedrich Wilhelm von Geismar. The young Hessian officer had arrived in Albemarle County, Virginia in 1779 as a prisoner of war, having been with General Burgoyne's army at its surrender at Saratoga. During the winter of 1778–79 Jefferson hosted several chamber music concerts at Monticello, he and his wife performing along with his talented German prisoners. Jefferson had extensive contact during this period with a higher-ranking officer, Baron Riedesel, often misidentified as von Riedesel, while the baron was paroled after Saratoga and quartered close by Thomas Jefferson's plantation as a prisoner of war. He and the baroness joined with other members of the Albemarle community for the chamber music concerts during the epoch of Washington's legendary hard-winter encampments.

Eventually Riedesel was exchanged for the American General Benjamin Lincoln, who had been captured and paroled by the British after his heroic but unsuccessful stand at the siege of Charleston. Jefferson technically

[85] Jefferson to John Quincy Adams, Monticello, March 30, 1826.

[86] Bernard Bailyn, *To Begin the World Anew: The Genius and Ambiguities of the American Founders* (New York: Knopf, 2003), pp. 11–12.

held the rank of militia colonel prior to the Revolution and until he assumed the governorship of Virginia. One of his German prisoner–guests referred to him in a letter as "Colonel Jefferson, Governor of Virginia."[87] Riedesel resided in Jefferson's custody under comfortable conditions, vividly illustrating that officers and enlisted men are not created equal.[88] Riedesel's wife and family had accompanied him to the battle of Saratoga, after the custom of the time, which brought many non-military personnel onto battlefields as "camp followers" – the term and the concept had not taken on the pejorative implications affixed in later times – and therefore his family was with him during his sojourn in the vicinity of Monticello.

Jefferson's biographer, Marie Kimball, treats with admirable candor, as indeed does Dumas Malone, Jefferson's interactions with the two German barons. Kimball groups these interludes among "the most stimulating and agreeable experiences of his life," which is certainly believable, for these were the days before the untimely loss of his beloved Martha, who was not only his hostess, but a talented musician, demonstrating a fine touch at the keyboard. The Baroness Riedesel joined them in their chamber entertainments with her admired singing voice, and Jefferson and Geismar played violin. Along with the Germans, the British Major-General William Phillips was also in Jefferson's custody, and the cordial, even friendly, relations between Jefferson and his captives was typical of the era. Although Jefferson supposedly "despised royalty and its trappings, he was," as Merrill Peterson notes, "charmed by Phillips, Riedesel, and their like."[89] Amicable relationships with his war prisoners are not the only example of his friendly attitudes towards French and German aristocrats. Jefferson did not deny the Riedesels freedom to travel, and wrote them a letter of safe conduct when the baron decided to visit the medicinal springs in Louisa, Berkeley, and Augusta.[90]

87 Marie Kimball, *Jefferson, War and Peace, 1776 to 1784* (New York: Coward-McCann, 1947), p. 20: "'My only recuperation at present,' writes this unnamed officer, who may very well have been [Baron Wilhelm] Geismar or [John Louis] De Unger, 'is to learn the English language. I have free access to a copious and well-chosen library of Colonel Jefferson, Governor of Virginia. The father of this learned man was also a favorite of the muses.'"

88 Silver handcuffs: see Isaac Jefferson's recollections, in James Adam Bear, ed., *Jefferson at Monticello: Recollections of a Monticello Slave and a Monticello Overseer* (Charlottesville, VA: University of Virginia Press, 1967), p. 9.

89 Peterson, *Thomas Jefferson and the New Nation*, pp. 164–165.

90 Jefferson to Riedesel [n.d. 1779].

The baroness describes this excursion in her memoir, but she makes no mention of Jefferson's good offices. The Count of Monticello and the Baroness Riedesel apparently did not pay much attention to one another. He never mentioned her, other than to extend his polite regards in his correspondence with the baron, and he may have found her intimidating. She was his first encounter with any woman even marginally related to the continental Enlightenment, and she seems to have had a formidable intellect and a critical disposition. She comments more than once in her memoir on the condition of "the Negroes" who were treated "very badly," although they prospered sufficiently to provide her family with fresh poultry and vegetables at a time when the troops at Valley Forge were ragged and starving. She avers that the slaves "consider it a misfortune to have children, as they in turn will become slaves and wretched men." She describes their children as "allowed by their masters to run naked until they are fifteen and sixteen years old, and the dress which is then given them, is scarcely worth wearing."[91]

Unimpressed by Jefferson's solicitousness, the baroness took pains to portray the Revolutionaries in negative terms, and she was critical of popular culture, describing a public spectacle of "two naked men boxing with the greatest fury ... their blood flowing, and the rage that was painted in their eyes (48)." In another passage she described a reprisal taken against the loyalist John Fenton, whose wife and 15-year-old daughter were putatively seized by a mob that "without regard to their goodness and modesty, stripped them naked, besmeared them with tar, rolled them in feathers, and in this condition, led them through the city as a show" (141). Her descriptions of the poor whites included the shocking example of one farmer who impregnated his two young daughters, and another who traded his wife to his son in exchange for his daughter-in-law, throwing in two cows and two horses to sweeten the pot. These pejorative views of frontier morality reiterate opinions, famously expressed by the loyalist Charles Woodmason, the itinerant South Carolina preacher, who also was appalled by the morality of the backwoods yeoman farmer.[92]

91 Baroness Friederika Luise (von Massow) Riedesel, *Letters and Journals Relating to the War of American Independence and the Capture of the German Troops at Saratoga* (Albany: Joel Munsell, 1867 [1827]), p. 159. Also see this online version, which includes both the paternal incest passage and an incident describing paternal incest: https://archive.org/details/lettersjournalsrooried

92 Ibid. The reader is to be cautioned that the electronic resources at Internet Archive pp. 159–160 were physically excised, along with portions of pp. 161–162, before the

Jefferson renewed his contact with von Geismar shortly after arriving in France as Minister Plenipotentiary in Paris on March 3, 1785. He had allowed the friendship to lapse, but the baron was delighted to renew it, and in 1788 he visited the baron at his home in Hanau; the two spent four days together, touring the Moselle valley. They corresponded thereafter, well into Jefferson's presidency and until von Geismar's fortunes took him to the court of Frederick II Eugene, duke of Württemberg, where he held the rank of general adjutant and major-general.[93] Jefferson initiated the correspondence in English, and von Geismar, claiming that he had forgotten his English, responded in French, in a very gracious letter of March 28, 1785. Jefferson replied in English, and so it went in every exchange over four years' correspondence, until Jefferson's final letter from von Geismar on April 13, 1789. This pattern of corresponding with Germans through the medium of French prevails years later in his exchanges with Alexander von Humboldt, who wrote to Jefferson, Madison, and Hamilton in French. Von Geismar seemed comfortable writing in fluent but imperfect French, while Jefferson squeamishly avoided French, for the same reason that von Geismar refrained from English.

It would be a great mistake to assume that the friendships with von Geismar and Riedesel were Jefferson's only exposure to eighteenth-century Germany, "das Land der Denker und Dichter." He gained more direct impressions in 1788, when he left Paris and travelled through Holland to the Rheinland, which at the time included the westernmost province of the Kingdom of Prussia. Crossing into German territories, he commented on the abject condition of the peasantry, saying:

> The transition from ease and opulence to extreme poverty is remarkable on crossing the line between the Dutch and Prussian territory. The soil and climate are the same. The governments alone differ. With the poverty, the fear also of

book was reproduced as an online document. Pages describing the regular beating of slaves and testimony concerning slave teenagers "running around naked" until the age of 16 were removed. The Google Books version that I have utilized is undamaged (see p. 128); also undamaged was the Arno Press 1968 edition I procured from the Penn State University libraries and the edition cited by Michael Kranish, *Flight from Monticello* (Oxford University Press, 2010), p. 112, and note on p. 347. "Captain Fenton" was John Fenton, a loyalist whose case is recounted with quotations from Riedesel's *Letters* and *Journals* in *Proceedings of the Massachusetts Historical Society*, 2nd series (Cambridge, MA: Massachusetts Historical Society, 1892–94), vol. III, pp. 412–413.

[93] Peter Nicolaisen, "Thomas Jefferson and Friederich Wilhelm von Geismar: A Transatlantic Friendship," *The Magazine of Albemarle County History*, 64 (2006), 1–27.

slaves is visible in the faces of the Prussian subjects. There is an improvement however in the physiognomy, especially could it be a little brightened up.

He recorded his shock at the poor state of agriculture, the primitiveness of the local plough, the poverty of the German peasants. In Hanau, "the silence and quiet of the mansions of the dead."[94]

On entering the "Land-graviate of Hesse," he recorded positive impressions, but remarked that "In the Republic [of Frankfurt], every body being allowed to be armed, and to hunt on their own lands, there is very little game left in it's territory." He recorded certain positive impressions of a larger city, which he attributed not only to a republican government, but to "the tendency which the neighborhood of such a commercial town as Francfort [sic] has to counteract the effects of tyranny in it's vicinities, and to animate them in spite of oppression." In nearby Hanau, by contrast, there was "no sound of the saw, the hammer, or other utensil of industry. The drum and fife is all that is heard." Frankfurt, the birthplace of Goethe, had once been the site of Germany's major book fair, but by the time of Jefferson's arrival it had been eclipsed by Leipzig. Still, although Frankfurt was not the center of the German Enlightenment, he wrote, with seeming approval, that "In Francfort all is life, bustle and motion." His observations were confined mostly to the local economies, particularly agriculture, with considerable attention paid to the quality of the wines.[95]

He made a notation about the lack of bookstores, which is puzzling, since he did not read or speak German, although this was hardly remarkable at the end of the eighteenth century. Frederick the Great of Prussia was legendary for his disdain for his native German, and literate Germans were only beginning to overcome their preference for speaking French and publishing in Latin. Jefferson's descriptions of his travels reveal little likelihood of contact with persons immersed in Germany's emergent high literary culture. His contact with the various German peoples was limited, for he could communicate neither with poets nor with peasants, and the Germany that Jefferson saw during his brief tour was not the land of Goethe and Schiller. Any German authors Jefferson knew before or after were those he read in translation. Eventually, he read, and highly recommended, William Enfield's "judicious abridgment of Johann Jakob

[94] "Das Land der Denker und Dichter" (the land of thinkers and poets) is a frequent saying of unknown origin in Germany's self-portrait. The "transition" described is in Peterson, ed., *Thomas Jefferson, Writings*, p. 634.

[95] Jefferson's remarks on "Francfort" are in Jefferson's "Travel Journals" in ibid., p. 639, where Peterson restores the German spelling of Frankfurt.

Brucker's *History of Philosophy*," on which he based his exceedingly negative opinions of the Talmud, although it would be unfair on this basis to link either Brucker or Jefferson to the horrific anti-Semitism of Nazi Germany.[96] Eighteenth-century Germans were only beginning to develop the concepts of Volksgeist that would eventually evolve into nationalism. It would require generations of musicians, folklorists, linguists, and commercialists, an invasion of France, conflicts with Austria, and a fusion of interests between Protestant Prussia and Catholic Bavaria before German nationalism could be achieved late in the nineteenth century by Otto von Bismarck. Before returning to France, Jefferson managed to have at least one conversation, with "a peasant of Hocheim," that focused on crop prices.

Jefferson's life overlapped the generations of Immanuel Kant and Georg Wilhelm Friedrich Hegel, the former dying while Jefferson was in the White House and the latter outliving him by five years. Although he was contemporary with both, he was only superficially conscious, if at all, of either philosopher. It is noteworthy that their negative comments on the potential of Africans, like those of David Hume, were on a par with his own. By contrast, the German proto-nationalist Johann Gottlieb Fichte denounced slavery and argued against Germans becoming involved in Atlantic slavery and African colonialism, "wishing to draw a profit from the sweat and blood of a poor slave across the seas."[97] Kant and Hegel, although every bit as white-supremacist as Jefferson, were never slave traders and did not conspicuously interact with black women; nor is there any record of their having any intimacy with such assimilated, English-speaking, Christianized persons of mixed blood as the Hemingses of Monticello.

The German historian and philosopher Johann Gottfried Herder, who was a year older than Jefferson, was presumably more humanitarian, and refused to classify Africans or any other humans as kin to the apes. In one of his short fables, *Der Afrikanische Rechtspruch* (*The African Verdict*),

[96] William Enfield (1741– 1797) was a British Unitarian who published an abridgement. See *Enclosure: Thomas Jefferson's Supplemental List of Recommended Books* [ca. October 4, 1809], Founders Online: http://founders.archives.gov/ documents/Jefferson/ 03–01-0 2–0450-0002 (ver. 2015–02-20). Source: *The Papers of Thomas Jefferson*, Retirement Series (Princeton University Press, 2004), vol. I, *4 March, 1809 – 15 November, 1809*, ed. J. Jefferson Looney, pp. 576–577.

[97] Johann Gottlieb Fichte, *Address to the German Nation*, lectures delivered 1807–1808, repr. in Justus Buchler, et al., *Introduction to Contemporary Civilization in the West* (New York: Columbia University Press, 1963), p. 157.

which depicts a purely fictitious encounter between Alexander the Great and an African king, Herder portrays Africans as virtuous barbarians with traits of honesty and generosity. Herder had no means of anticipating the twentieth-century discovery that all human beings share 95 percent of their DNA with chimpanzees. His position, although uninformed, represented a complete rejection of the racism expressed by his contemporary, Johann Friedrich Blumenbach. Despite limited contact with Africans, Herder's opinions of them were sometimes based on his reading, at other times on his proto-romantic sentiments.

Hegel is more difficult to defend, but Professor Susan Buck-Morss makes an attempt in a discussion focused on his reaction to Toussaint Louverture's Haitian Revolution.[98] Hegel's notion of liberty, like Jefferson's, is caught up in the contradiction that the Enlightenment carried European racism to new heights in order to rationalize the Atlantic slave trade.[99] Although Hegel developed a theory of the progress of liberty, we speak of "Jeffersonian democracy," not "Hegelian." It was Jefferson, not Hegel, who succeeded in affixing his name to the notion of liberty, thereby seizing a reputation not only as a philosopher of the Enlightenment, but as a prophet of freedom. Jefferson was probably unaware of Hegel's "great man" theory or his principle that "The history of the world is progress in the consciousness of freedom." The German philosophers, Kant and Hegel conceived of liberty, in terms that were marred by white supremacy, but Hegel's teleology of liberty has nonetheless made him appealing to such black thinkers as W. E. B. Du Bois and Martin Luther King.[100]

Jefferson, as an eponymous symbol for his age, might have met G. F. W. Hegel's definition of a "World Historical Figure." Historians employ the phrase "Age of Jefferson," but rarely does anyone speak of the Age of Washington or the Age of Franklin. Such designations as "Age of

98 Susan Buck-Morss, "Hegel and Haiti," *Critical Inquiry*, 26, no. 4 (summer, 2001), 832.

99 Winthrop Jordan, *White over Black: American Attitudes toward the Negro, 1550–1812* (Chapel Hill: University of North Carolina Press, 1968), mentions Herder's opinions on p. 230.

100 Martin Luther King, Jr., called Hegel his favorite philosopher in an interview with Tom Johnson, *Montgomery Advertiser* (January 19, 1956). King paid tribute to his *Philosophy of History*, i.e. his teleology of liberty, in his *Stride Toward Freedom* (New York: Harper & Row, 1958). Du Bois made reference to the Hegelian element in the philosophy of Martin Luther King in "Will the Great Gandhi Live Again?" *The National Guardian* (February 11, 1957). Du Bois called Kant's *Critique of Pure Reason* one of the four "certain books in the world which every searcher for truth must know," *The Crisis* (May, 1933).

Jefferson" and "Age of Jackson" are familiar, and so are their names with corresponding varieties of "democracy."[101] Jefferson embodies the "spirit of an age," and he is preserved for us as the monumental symbol of a concept of liberty. Hegel pontificated, as Jefferson did, on notions of progress and freedom, but no one speaks of an "Age of Hegel." And while Hegel never owned 600 slaves, it is Jefferson's name, not Hegel's, that became the trope for an age associated with liberty and democracy.[102]

However that may be, Jefferson felt more socially at home with German aristocrats than with yeoman farmers or the despised "class of artificers." Several times in June of 1804 he received the celebrated Prussian naturalist and explorer Baron Friedrich Wilhelm Heinrich Alexander von Humboldt at the White House. The much younger man, who was only 7 years old at the time of the Declaration of Independence, was naturally impressed by Jefferson's reputation as the author of the American Revolution. He stopped in Washington on his way home from a four-year expedition to Central and South America, and praised the president, who was easily old enough to be his father, as "the most virtuous of men." We do not know if Humboldt was one of those guests whom the president met at the door in robe-and-slippers, but Humboldt remarked on being received "with the simplicity of a philosopher," and the two engaged in a series of wide-ranging discussions.[103] Humboldt's friendship with Jefferson resembled his friendship with Johann Wolfgang von Goethe, who was also his senior. Of the two, he came to know Goethe much better, and the relationship was strengthened by the fact that the two Germans could communicate in their own language. Humboldt's letters to Jefferson, Hamilton, and other American correspondents were often written in French, but Jefferson always responded in English.

[101] The University of Virginia launched an online course, "Age of Jefferson," February 17, 2014. Paul Finkelman uses it as the subtitle of his *Slavery and the Founders: Race and Liberty in the Age of Jefferson*, 2nd edn. (Armonk, NY: M. E. Sharpe, 2001).

[102] Georg Wilhelm Friedrich Hegel, *Vorlesungen über die Philosophie der Geschichte* (1837), "Die Weltgeschichte ist der Fortschritt im Bewußtsein der Freiheit" (World-history is progress in the consciousness of freedom).

[103] Quoted in Gerhard Casper, "A Young Man from 'ultima Thule' Visits Jefferson: Alexander von Humboldt in Philadelphia and Washington," *Proceedings of The American Philosophical Society*, 155, no. 3 (September, 2011), and in Peterson, *Thomas Jefferson and the New Nation*, pp. 738–739. Sandra Rebok, "Enlightened Correspondents: The Transatlantic Dialogue of Thomas Jefferson and Alexander von Humboldt," *Virginia Magazine of History and Biography*, 116, no. 4 (2008), 229–369. Sandra Rebok, *Humboldt and Jefferson: A Transatlantic Friendship of the Enlightenment* (Charlottesville, VA: University of Virginia Press, 2014).

Humboldt was a critic of slavery, but so charmed – as were most people – by Jefferson as host and raconteur that he kept diplomatic silences on the subject of abolitionism, presumably taking Jefferson at his word that he was working towards the eventual emancipation of African Americans. Humboldt's attitude towards Africa and its peoples, like that of the majority of his contemporaries in Europe or the Americas, was in any case not radically egalitarian. Robespierre had abolished slavery, and Napoleon re-established it, but the Germans had never had African colonies, nor a need for African slaves. Humboldt shared Jefferson's abstract, ideological opposition to slavery, as historian Sandra Rebok has demonstrated, but neither played a role in its eventual extermination.[104]

If, by "Renaissance man," we mean a person whose intellectual achievements revealed a broad interest in the knowledge of his time, and an attempt to survey it, Jefferson met the definition, as did many of his contemporaries, for his was not an age of specialization. If, by "Citizen of the Enlightenment," we mean a person who questioned ancient dogmas, Jefferson sometimes succeeded; at other times he did not. His greatest impact on the age and on all of history was his Preamble to the Declaration of Independence. It was a masterpiece of rhetoric. It captures our imaginations in the same way as the first four notes of Beethoven's Fifth. It is on that one work of genius that his reputation rests, and it is that one work that guarantees his place in history. Whatever is meant by "Renaissance man," he probably deserves the title as much as any of his contemporaries. It is probably better to keep him in his own epoch, and describe him as he was seen by one of the fiercest of his contemporary critics, an African American merchant and pamphleteer of Boston. David Walker was certainly unaware that Jefferson's hand was in the secret translation of Volney's *Ruins*, with its melancholic references to the faded glory of ancient Ethiopia. He would certainly have found this astonishing in comparison with the statements Jefferson made publicly. I quote from David Walker's appraisal of Jefferson in a spirit even more bitterly ironic than the author intended:

> Comparing our miserable fathers with the learned philosophers of Greece, he says: "Yet notwithstanding these and other discouraging circumstances among the

[104] See Rebok, "Enlightened Correspondents" and Rebok, *Humboldt and Jefferson*. Also see Sandra Rebok, "La Révolution de Haïti vue par deux personnages contemporains: Le Scientifique Prussien Alexander von Humboldt et l'homme d'état américain Thomas Jefferson," *French Colonial History*, 10 (2009), 75–95.

Romans, their slaves were often their rarest artists. They excelled too, in science, insomuch as to be usually employed as tutors to their master's children; Epictetus, Terence and Phædrus, were slaves – but they were of the race of whites. It is not their *condition* then, but *nature*, which has produced the distinction." See this, my brethren!! Do you believe that this assertion is swallowed by millions of the whites? Do you know that Mr. Jefferson was one of as great characters as ever lived among the whites? See his writings for the world, and public labours for the United States of America. Do you believe that the assertions of such a man, will pass away into oblivion unobserved by this people and the world? If you do you are much mistaken.[105]

Walker would have been perplexed if he had known of Jefferson's sponsorship of Volney's *Ruins* and the transmission of those lines where he had allowed the "sable skin and frizzled hair" of the Thebans to stand. Walker might have wondered whether Jefferson had been dozing while he effected the translation, for if Jefferson had been aware of Ethiopia's monumental past, how could he question the African's exalted place in the family of nations? But Jefferson had not been oblivious to what he was translating, or to the meaning he saw imbedded in Volney's words. It was certainly possible within Jefferson's worldview to perceive the Ethiopians as having lapsed from a state of civilization and political liberty to one of barbarism and enslavement. White supremacy did not require that African people be devoid of a past, only that they currently occupy such a position of mental and cultural inferiority as to justify at least their temporary enslavement. Enlightenment rationalism did not require the immediate emancipation of the slaves: it only required an immediate justification for their degradation.

Jefferson's vision surveyed that broad expanse where the Renaissance meets the Enlightenment, and his mind compulsively imposed on that landscape his ideal of a mathematically harmonious and stable continuum, governed by immutable rules of symmetry and balance. He was a "Renaissance man" both in the sense of Pocock's "Machiavellian Moment" and in the popular Machiavellian sense of craftiness, for, as Alexander Hamilton observed, he was too wily a fox "to do anything in pursuance of his principles which will contravene his popularity, or his interest." And, like Machiavelli, he paid homage to republican principles

[105] *Walker's Appeal, in Four Articles; Together with a Preamble, to the Coloured Citizens of the World, but in Particular, and Very Expressly, to Those of the United States of America, Written in Boston, State of Massachusetts, September 28, 1829. Third and Last Edition, With Additional Notes, Corrections, etc. Revised and Published By David Walker* (Boston: David Walker, 1830), p. 18. Walker quotes from Jefferson, *Notes on Virginia*, cf. Waldstreicher's edition, Jefferson, *Notes on the State of Virginia*, p. 179.

that he himself obscured by expedient adaptations of his theories to the exigencies of political reality and his personal economic needs. Although Jefferson admired Algernon Sidney, who is perceived as one of the important transmitters of Machiavelli's lesser-known republican ideals, there is no evidence in Jefferson's writings that he associated Sidney with this variety of Machiavellianism. Jefferson despised Machiavelli as much as he admired Sidney, but in Jefferson's life and letters we sometimes witness the refined authoritarianism of a renaissance prince, and the restrained munificence of an Enlightened Despot.

7

Baconism and Natural Science

It was 1790, and Jefferson was still enraptured with Francis Bacon and his *Novum Organum Scientiarum* published in 1620. If that work, which had deeply influenced the generation of Voltaire, had one dominant theme, it was the need to rid the mind of prejudices and prior conceptions. Jefferson, although still capable of growth, was nonetheless inclined to smirk at ideas that contradicted truths he held to be "self-evident."[1] At the time of his 1785 arrival in Paris his worldview was still grounded in the medieval cosmology of the Great Chain of Being, and his understanding of science was still rooted in deductions from "the laws of nature." He could show respect for experimentalism, as late as his 80s, when he had a burst of excitement for vivisection as practiced by Jean-Pierre Flourens in the field of brain physiology. He remained skeptical, however, of advances in geology, where his own speculations were as unfounded as Voltaire's and no more empirically based than others he dismissed. Although he did not lead the ridicule when John Quincy Adams proposed funding for astronomical observatories, neither did he come to Adams' defense. He was flippant and dismissive on the subject of meteorites. These instances reveal an obstinate temperament although his stubbornness was mitigated by his perpetual curiosity.

[1] Carl Lotus Becker, *The Declaration of Independence: A Study on the History of Political Ideas* (New York: Harcourt, Brace and Company, 1922), p. 142 note, speculates that the words "self-evident" were contributed to the Declaration by Benjamin Franklin, but Julian P. Boyd, in *The Papers of Thomas Jefferson* (Princeton University Press, 1950), vol. I, pp. 427–428, argues that the phrase was Jefferson's own. I define enthusiasm here according to Dr. Johnson's *Dictionary*, "A vain belief of private revelation; a vain confidence of divine favour or communication" (see note 3 below). Jefferson's belief that Bacon was one the three greatest men in history is recurrent in this volume.

Jefferson ranked Bacon higher even than Galileo, who, Jefferson asserted, "was sent to the inquisition for affirming that the earth was a sphere."[2] This compulsive swipe at big government, especially one headed by Catholics, led him to run roughshod over facts. He certainly knew that the expedition of Ferdinand Magellan and Juan Sebastián Elcano circumnavigated the globe before Galileo and Bacon were born, and that two of the most ruthless enforcers of the Inquisition, Ferdinand and Isabella, sponsored Columbus' attempt to reach India by sailing westward. Jefferson can be forgiven that, in his eagerness to make a political point, he ignored the existence of Ptolemaic geography, which had conceived the earth as a sphere but situated it at the center of the universe. It was the stationary placement of the globe, not its shape, that Galileo had challenged, but the fact that he could so muddle the sequence of historical events in his magnum opus gives an indication of the hyperbole that permeates *Notes on Virginia.* It was only one instance in which the author's gift for sarcasm overreached his requirements for scientific exactitude. There may be instances of the same propensity in my own work.

Jefferson admired Bacon as much for his celebrated English essays as for his guidelines to science. Bacon, in conformity with academic tradition, had published his scientific theories in Latin, but his appeal was in his iconoclasm, his call for overthrowing revered "idols" of the past, and his mitigation of the Aristotelian methodology of syllogistic logic, inherited from darker ages. But Bacon, and Jefferson's other idols, John Locke and Isaac Newton, who published their masterworks in the seventeenth century, retained many traditional ideas and approaches. Like them, Jefferson betrayed a fondness for axioms, "laws of nature," and "self-evident" truths. That is to say, he was always more comfortable deducing his ideas from known facts than inducing them from observable phenomena. The doctrine of self-evident truths was present not only in the Declaration of Independence, but also in his scientific methods. Incontrovertible axioms existed for him not only in Euclidean geometry, but also in the natural and the social sciences. His scientific as well as his political inspiration illustrated Dr. Johnson's definition of "enthusiasm," for he sometimes wrote as if he were the recipient of revelations directly from the mind of "Nature's God."[3]

2 Thomas Jefferson, *Notes on the State of Virginia*, ed. David Waldstreicher (Boston, MA: Bedford Books, 2002), Query XVII, p. 193.

3 For "enthusiasm," see Johnson's *Dictionary of the English Language* (London, 1755). "ENTHUSIASM. n.s. A vain belief of private revelation; a vain confidence of divine favour

As a scientific work, *Notes on Virginia* illustrates well that Jefferson was "a Renaissance man" in terms of breadth, but in terms of methods he lagged behind the Renaissance of Galileo. The methodology of *Notes* was not even "Baconian," if by that we mean predominantly inductive, as opposed to predominantly deductive. In that respect, it fell short of the best practices of Jefferson's much older contemporary, Benjamin Franklin, and it was never completely updated in the light of early nineteenth-century scientific advances in biology, geology, and ethnology. Jefferson was not inflexible in all matters, and over the forty years following the original publication of his *Notes* he modified some of its rash assertions in the realm of "natural history." In the field of political economy, he admirably demonstrated a capacity to tone down his agrarian rhetoric in accord with the exigencies of the times. Still, new ideas gave him headaches, and he showed little capacity to entertain ideas that deviated from his preconceptions of "the known operations of nature."[4]

In 1952 the independent scholar Edward T. Martin saw the historian's need "to distinguish between the meaning of the word *science* which signifies 'all knowledge' and that meaning which signifies systematized and formulated knowledge related to the facts of the physical world and the laws which regulate their operation."[5] Jefferson used the term "science" in both senses, and he also used the terms "natural philosophy"

or communication. *Enthusiasm* is founded neither on reason nor divine revelation, but rises from the conceits of a warmed or overweening brain. —Locke."

4 For example, Jefferson to Benjamin Austin, January 9, 1816, says that times and his opinions regarding "let our workshops remain in Europe" had changed "within the 30 years which have since elapsed" since the publication of the *Notes*. For a discussion of variant editions and the updating of *Notes on Virginia*, see Coolie Verner, *A Further Checklist of the Separate Editions of Jefferson's* Notes on the State of Virginia (Charlottesville, VA: Bibliographical Society of the University of Virginia, 1950). Also see the introduction and scholarly notes in William Peden, ed., *Notes on the State of Virginia. By Thomas Jefferson* (Chapel Hill: University of North Carolina Press, 1955) for contemporary reactions and Jefferson's planned revisions. David Waldstreicher's 2002 edition (Jefferson, *Notes on the State of Virginia*) contains an informative introduction and several well-chosen contemporary documents.

5 Edward T. Martin, *Thomas Jefferson: Scientist* (New York: Henry Schuman,1952), p. 261. The standard work is Silvio Bedini, *Thomas Jefferson: Statesman of Science* (New York: Macmillan, 1990). See especially pp. 260–262. Also insightful are Martin Clagett, *Scientific Jefferson: Revealed* (Charlottesville, VA: University of Virginia Press, 2009), and Keith Thomson, *Jefferson's Shadow: The Story of His Science* (New Haven, CT: Yale University Press, 2012). Morris Kline, a professor of mathematics at New York University, offered a clever discussion of the uses of the term "law" in the mathematical and legal professions. See Morris Kline, *Mathematics in Western Culture* (Oxford University Press, 1953), pp. 463–464.

and "natural history" in the same sense that we use the word "science" today. In his own times, people did not anticipate our modern quirk of placing the arts and the sciences in discrete, mutually exclusive categories, and commonly spoke of the "mechanical arts" and the "moral sciences."[6]

In an 1814 letter to his nephew, Peter Carr, Jefferson sketched out a proposal for a system of scientific education that was to encompass the educational needs of both the rich and the poor according to their condition in life, from the most elementary through the university level. The term "science" encompassed every field, including "I. Language. II. Mathematics. III. Philosophy." Science included the practical and the theoretical disciplines, comprising classical languages, mathematics, theology, and ethics, and a discipline that he called "ideology," which he assigned to the "Philosophical department," along with "the law of Nature & Nations."[7]

Jefferson thought in terms of "nature" and of the discovery of, and obedience to, "natural law," as had Lucretius, Aquinas, Thomas Hobbes, John Locke, Alexander Pope, and Isaac Newton. Jefferson of course employed the phrase "laws of nature" in the Declaration of Independence. Raymond Williams says, "Nature is perhaps the most complex word in the language," and offers several pages of definitions in their historical contexts, mostly from the thirteenth to the eighteenth centuries. Destutt de Tracy, whose work Jefferson vigorously championed, pointed out that there is no such thing as a "law of nature," since the word "law" refers properly to a breakable human convention. Those phenomena that we call "laws of nature" are unbreakable and therefore are not, properly speaking, "laws." Tracy remarked that law is the creation of society, "a rule of action, prescribed by an authority," and that only after society had progressed beyond a primitive state did human beings begin to systematically describe the forces of nature.[8]

6 Jefferson used the term "mechanical arts" in numerous letters, for example Jefferson to John Page, May 4, 1786, Jefferson to James Madison, March, 1809, and "moral sciences" occasionally, as in a letter to Abigail Smith Adams, May 15, 1817.

7 Jefferson to Peter Carr, September 7, 1814. The plan was somewhat more elaborate than what he had proposed thirty years earlier in *Notes on Virginia*.

8 A search of the Jefferson papers at Founders Online reveals ninety-one instances of the phrase "law of nature" or "laws of nature." Destutt de Tracy, *A Commentary and Review of Montesquieu* (Philadelphia: William Duane, 1811), p. 6. As Montesquieu and Volney had been, so Jefferson was in accord with Tracy's belief that "Positive laws ought to be consequent of the laws of nature," Tracy, ibid., p. 7. Some definitions of "nature" are presented in Raymond Williams, *Keywords* (Oxford University Press, 1976), pp. 184–189. Jefferson's uses of the term "nature" are discussed in Charles A. Miller, *Jefferson and*

These were metaphorically denominated the *laws of nature*, being only an expression significant of the manner in which the phenomena constantly act. Thus with reference to the descent of heavy bodies, we say that it is the effect of gravitation, one of the laws of nature, *that a heavy body abandoned to itself, falls by an accelerated motion proportionate to the series of odd numbers, so that the spaces passed through are as the squares of the times of its movement.*

Despite Tracy's erudite quibbling, Jefferson continued to throw around the expression, and his approach to science was reasonably enough based on the search for unbreachable laws of nature. Science must be based on propositions as unassailable as Euclid's rules and Newton's laws, and had to accord with the laws of nature. After all, crude sensory perceptions could be deceiving. Empiricism was not triumphant in Jefferson's work. The sensual impressions of an ignoramus were unreliable, and naïve perceptions must be fallacious if they did not agree with what were understood to be the laws of nature. He was a living proof that empiricism did not suddenly triumph with the dawn of the Enlightenment, nor did inductive reasoning suddenly replace syllogistic deduction or the medieval cosmology of the Great Chain of Being.

The word "empirical" could have a pejorative connotation well into the eighteenth century. Jefferson was not eager to accept ideas "disfigured by a fantastical mixture of superstician and empiricism."[9] Negative implications of the term can be located in the correspondence of Hamilton and Adams, and in the *Oxford English Dictionary*. In *Notes on Virginia*, Jefferson frequently deduced conclusions from the "law of nature" rather than inducing them from systematic observations. "Self-evident" axioms corrupted their ethnology and their political science as much as they did their zoology. Jefferson's and the Enlightenment's concepts of nature were significantly static, and implied the existence of a set of absolute laws that had been progressively discovered as the scales of superstition fell from the eyes of the unenlightened.

Jefferson found little occasion in the *Notes* to apply the experimental methods associated with Robert Boyle in the seventeenth century or Benjamin Franklin in the eighteenth. By the time of Jefferson's death in 1826, *Notes on Virginia* was a work behind its times, with questionable

Nature: An Interpretation (Baltimore: Johns Hopkins University Press, 1988), which offers a discussion of Jefferson and Lucretius. Matthew Stewart, *Nature's God: The Heretical Origins of the American Republic* (New York: Norton, 2014), is erudite and provocative. Also see Mario Valsania, *Nature's Man: Thomas Jefferson's Philosophical Anthropology* (Charlottesville, VA: University of Virginia Press, 2013).

[9] Jefferson to Richard Peters, February 20, 1822.

axioms and proceeding from non-demonstrable postulates about "Nature and Nature's God."[10] Sometimes Jefferson's approach to establishing truth could be inferential and inductive, but usually he proceeded from axioms. He could be incautious in deciding what constituted the "laws of nature," and he was impatient or derisive when presented with anything that did not conform to his understanding of those laws. His faith in scientific progress was such that he believed the laws of nature had been largely codified, and he shared in the Enlightenment's premature satisfaction so famously expressed by Alexander Pope in his epitaph intended for Newton:

> Nature and Nature's laws lay hid in night:
> God said, Let Newton be! and all was light.

Jefferson considered Newton, Bacon, and Locke "the three greatest men that have ever lived, without any exception, and as having laid the foundations of those superstructures which have been raised in the Physical & Moral sciences." This trinity resembled one that had been constructed by Voltaire in his essay *Sur le chancelier Bacon*. Jefferson asked John Trumbull to design a drawing of all three within a circular compound portrait, "three busts in three ovals ... Bacon at the top: Locke next then to Newton." Jefferson would not wish any of them "confounded at all with the herd of other great men." It is questionable whether the scientists Jefferson criticized in *Notes on Virginia*, or those he admired, like Benjamin Rush, consistently paid more than lip-service to Bacon's methodological caveats. It seems strange to our modern thinking that Jefferson elevated Bacon above Galileo. Bacon, born in 1561, did not make the permanent contributions to the body of scientific knowledge made by his contemporary, Galileo, born in 1564, nor did he equal Galileo in the application of experimental methods.[11]

Bacon's method in practice bore a superficial resemblance to that of Thomas Aquinas, who in his *Summa Theologica* employed a ritual of making lists, then posing and answering a series of objections to the

[10] The terms "empirical" and "empiricism" had negative meanings until well after 1700. See entries in the *Oxford English Dictionary*. Neither Bacon nor Newton, Jefferson's putative heroes, practiced anything resembling twentieth-century "empiricism." For negative employment of the term, see John Adams to *Boston Patriot*, July 27, 1810: "last resource of little wits and mercenary Empirics, the vainest men alive"; Alexander Hamilton to Timothy Pickering [May 14, 1800]: "men of real integrity & energy must unite against all Empirics." Both letters are at Founders Online.

[11] Jefferson to John Trumbull, February 15, 1789. Voltaire, *Lettres philosophiques*, 1734, *Douzième lettre, Sur le chancelier Bacon*.

propositions he set out to prove.[12] These lists were not exhaustive, and Aquinas was more interested in validating Christian dogma than challenging it. Bacon would have repudiated the comparison, but he also made and tested lists, although in the process he attempted to be exhaustive, and he rigorously questioned conventional wisdom, rather than seeking to confirm doctrines that he had already accepted on faith. Much as he idolized Bacon, Jefferson's practice sometimes seemed closer to that of Aquinas, some aspects of whose thinking Jefferson admired. Often he failed to anticipate counter-arguments, or to consider objections that were being raised by his contemporaries. He could rashly deduce from axioms before considering the possibility of negations. It was not only in his political rhetoric, but in his scientific judgment that he proceeded from his ideological convictions to the "self-evident" truth.[13]

Bacon's *Novum Organum Scientiarum* advised caution in the formulation of hypotheses. A similar, if not identical, idea was associated with Isaac Newton, who issued his famous pejorative definition of "hypothesis" as a proposition not deduced from phenomena. Deductive logic could be valid only when its syllogisms were based on axioms inferred or induced from "phenomena," or experimental evidence. A translation of the clauses in which Newton originally declared the Latin watchword with which he is associated, "Hypotheses non fingo," reads as follows:

> I do not feign hypotheses. For whatever is not deduced from the phenomena must be called a hypothesis; and hypotheses, whether metaphysical or physical, or based on occult qualities, or mechanical, have no place in experimental philosophy. In this philosophy particular propositions are inferred from the phenomena, and afterwards rendered general by induction.[14]

Despite his famous boast that he would "feign no hypotheses," and would base no conjectures on questionable or unsupported notions, Newton deduced a portion of his theory from the *a priori* notion of

[12] Joseph Piper describes the method of *disputatio* in his *Guide to Thomas Aquinas* (New York: Pantheon, 1962). Aquinas, in his *Summa Theologica*, lists a series of objections to be refuted, often by appeals to the authority of the Bible or Aristotle. Juergen Klein, in *The Stanford Encyclopedia of Philosophy*, writes that Bacon repudiates the medieval "emphasis on syllogism and dialectics." Hegel redefined dialectics around the time Jefferson resumed correspondence with John Adams.

[13] Becker, *Declaration of Independence*, p. 142 note, speculates that the words "self-evident" were contributed to the Declaration by Benjamin Franklin, but Julian P. Boyd, in *The Papers of Thomas Jefferson*, vol. I, pp. 427–428, argues that the phrase was Jefferson's own.

[14] Isaac Newton, *General Scholium*, appended to the second (1713) edition of the *Principia Mathematica*.

a rational watchmaker God, his axiomatic belief in a God of Reason. When Newton's science could not account for the trajectories of all heavenly bodies, he found it necessary to fall back on a belief in a God whose guiding hand kept the planets from falling into the sun. The French scientist Pierre-Simon Laplace rejected such an explanation. According to legend, when Napoleon asked Laplace for the place of a Newtonian God in his system, Laplace responded that he had "no need of such an hypothesis."[15]

Well into the nineteenth century, science was almost exclusively the preserve of gentleman dilettantes and amateurs.[16] The chivalric courtesies that predominated in the world of scientific exchange are illustrated in Jefferson's sense of gentlemanly propriety regarding the protocols of sharing research. He sent a revealing letter to the Marquis de Chastellux, accompanying a copy of *Notes on Virginia*, and requesting that the marquis forward two enclosed copies to the French naturalists Georges-Louis Leclerc, Comte de Buffon, and Louis Jean Marie Daubenton. When it came to initiating contact with these fellow members of the scientific gentry, who were outside his proper circle of acquaintances, he was squeamishly punctilious:

> The other copy [of the *Notes*] delivered at your hotel was for Monsr. de Buffon. I meant to ask the favour of you to have it sent to him, as I was ignorant how to do it. I have one also for Monsr. Daubenton: but being utterly unknown to him I cannot take the liberty of presenting it till I can do it through some common acquaintance.[17]

Notes on Virginia was a series of responses, of varying length, to twenty-three Queries put to Jefferson by the Marquis de Marbois in 1783, and originally published in Paris in 1785. Its subsequent publication history is not without scholarly interest, but by consensus the edition that best represents Jefferson's intentions is the authorized English edition published by John Stockdale in London in 1787. It was Jefferson's most ambitious scientific work and was intended as a descriptive treatise encompassing several realms of the physical, biological, and social sciences. It is debatable as to whether the work was "state of the art" by the standards of its time.[18] In fact, it was a polemic against the positions

[15] Bedini, *Thomas Jefferson*, pp. 322, 474.

[16] These attitudes are evidenced by the relationship between Sir Humphrey Davy and his brilliant protégé, Michael Faraday, who was once compelled to serve Davy as a valet, due to Faraday's working-class background and the fact that he had not attended university.

[17] Jefferson to the Marquis de Chastellux, June 7, 1785.

[18] Jefferson, *Notes on Virginia*, pp. 1–2. The present work also makes use of Peden, ed., *Notes on Virginia*.

circulated by French naturalists of that era, in particular the Comte de Buffon, whose opinions seemed important at the time but would be almost forgotten today if Jefferson had not attacked them. In effect, they were also an attempt to quieten Jefferson's own fears in the face of the spurious claim that the North American climate might predestine the republic and its inhabitants to degeneracy.

Nonetheless, a powerful and voracious intellect was everywhere evident in the *Notes*, although Jefferson inadvertently proved himself the victim of one of the idolatries that Bacon had particularly condemned, *idola specus.*[19] He was imprisoned in the cave of his own prejudices, as when he speculated on African inferiority that he would "advance as a suspicion only." This speculation violated the Newtonian principle of "Hypotheses non fingo." Jefferson used the term "hypothesis" throughout, applying it to numerous vague suspicions and uninvestigated propositions. He tossed around ideas with cavalier abandonment and offered unsupported axioms.

The work was a mixture of science and rhetoric, undertaken when he was 40 years old and about to embark on his four-year tour of duty as Minister to France.[20] By contemporary or by twenty-first-century standards, the book was worthy of regard, and yet, like many scientific works of its day, it often revealed patterns of thinking that were more traditional than revolutionary. It was an ambitious text, for it compressed into some 200 pages a wide range of data and opinions, ranging over topics as diverse as geography, biology, ethnology, commerce, and politics. It was compiled and revised between 1782 and 1787, during which time

[19] Translated as "idols of the cave." The associated logical fallacy is denoted by Bacon as follows:

> The Idols of the Cave are the idols of the individual man. For everyone (besides the errors common to human nature in general) has a cave or den of his own, which refracts and discolors the light of nature, owing either to his own proper and peculiar nature; or to his education and conversation with others; or to the reading of books, and the authority of those whom he esteems and admires; or to the differences of impressions, accordingly as they take place in a mind preoccupied and predisposed or in a mind indifferent and settled; or the like. So that the spirit of man (according as it is meted out to different individuals) is in fact a thing variable and full of perturbation, and governed as it were by chance. Whence it was well observed by Heraclitus that men look for sciences in their own lesser worlds, and not in the greater or common world. (*Novum Organum Scientiarum*, Aphorism XLII)

[20] Jefferson arrived in Paris on August 6, 1784, William Howard Adams, *The Paris Years of Thomas Jefferson* (New Haven, CT: Yale University Press, 1997), p. 37. His departure, three weeks after the storming of the Bastille, was well timed to avoid the rising violence and the forced removal of the royal family from Versailles to Paris in early October.

Jefferson saw more than one edition go into print, but the opinions reflected in it did not always undergo revision. It did not always exhaust every aspect of the contemporary scientific knowledge or method. Sometimes he refused to investigate the works of more direct observers.

From the outset, Jefferson was not completely satisfied with his *Notes on Virginia*, but he never fully updated it. In 1811, he sent a copy to Alexander von Humboldt, apologizing that it was *chétif* (undeveloped), but offering no specifics as to where he felt it needed improvement.[21] It was never completely revised even in areas where changing times made some ideas appear obsolete. For example, Merrill Peterson offers an observation on his "change of opinion on manufactures," which Jefferson justified in terms of the thirty years that had elapsed. Jefferson had in fact painted himself into a corner on manufacturing in 1787, after insisting in 1774 on the colonies' manufacturing independence, and his statement in the *Notes* about letting "our workshops remain in Europe" had been excessively feverish. When he was approached by a publisher with a plan for updating *Notes on Virginia*, he demurred, with the explanation that his words of 1787 had been inspired by what he knew of manufacturing in European cities, but that manufacturing America had not produced such dark satanic mills.[22]

His working assumptions were not always derived from the masses of data that he assiduously collected, but were often based on his orderly theology into which he forced his facts. He was often determined to prove his sacred presuppositions, rather than to test them. His interests demonstrate a superior mind and boundless curiosity, but his observations were not systematic, and, despite his interest in mathematics, not quantitative. Neither he nor most of his contemporaries fully appreciated the method of formulating testable generalizations based on systematically assembled quantities of data. They paid lip-service to the Baconian ideal, but the scientific method had yet to be institutionalized.[23]

[21] Jefferson to Alexander von Humboldt, April 14, 1811, says, "In sending you a copy of my Notes on Virginia, I do but obey the desire you have expressed. they must appear chetif enough to the author of the great work on South America." It is possible that Jefferson may have admitted to errors or reconsiderations in his conversations with Humboldt.

[22] Jefferson to Benjamin Austin, January 9, 1816, mentions that the times and his opinions had changed with regard to letting our workshops remain in Europe "within the 30 years which have since elapsed" since the publication of the *Notes*. Merrill Peterson, ed., *Thomas Jefferson, Writings* (New York: Literary Classics of the United States, 1984), p. 1530.

[23] That Jefferson assembled admirable collections of biological and geological specimens with avidity is well known. See, for example, Henry Schuman, *Thomas Jefferson: Scientist* (New York: H. Wolff, 1952); Bedini, *Thomas Jefferson*.

In the so-called Age of Enlightenment, mechanics and clock-smiths often had a more refined understanding of the natural world than did university professors, although they were seldom taken seriously, simply because they had not mastered Greek and Latin. Eighteenth-century medicine remained largely guesswork and superstition, and a delivering mother was often safer in the hands of a midwife than those of a trained physician. It is to be remembered that Presidents Washington and Garfield, at opposite ends of the long nineteenth century, were both killed by doctors who never sanitized their instruments and rarely washed their hands. Despite the universal homage to Bacon, empirical and inductive methods had little impact on the biological sciences until very late in the history of medicine. Jefferson, like his learned friend Benjamin Rush, was more imaginative than scientific. He strove towards a scientific methodology in his avid collecting of specimens in the areas of geology, biology, and mineralogy, but he tended to force his observations into pre-existing hypothetical boxes.

PROBLEMS IN MATHEMATICS

Most discussions of Jefferson's mathematical interests have been sketchy, focusing chiefly on his prescriptions for mathematical instruction at the University of Virginia. By today's standards, he might have sufficient mathematical knowledge to teach a freshman course at that institution, but assessments of his abilities and achievements are uncommon and indeterminate. Students of the matter have found numerous references to his obsession with mathematical problems in his papers.[24] He obviously loved mathematics, which he called the "most sublime of all sciences." His youthful accomplishments were outstanding, by virtue of his sharp mind, his internal motivation, and the "enlightened & affectionate guidance" to his studies offered by William Small, the professor of mathematics at the College of William and Mary.

Jefferson later recalled that the young teacher was "to me as a father," although Small was only nine years older than himself. It would have been perfectly normal, almost expected, for the shy, studious 16-year-old to develop a Platonic affection for the young mathematician. "He, most happily for me, became soon attached to me & made me his daily

[24] Jefferson's tribute to Small is in his letter to Louis H. Girardin, March 18, 1814. Jefferson's "most sublime of all the sciences" appears in Jefferson to Nathaniel Bowditch, September 25, 1815.

companion when not engaged in the school." With Small, he discussed many branches of the arts and sciences, studied a text by William Emerson called *Doctrine of Fluxions*, and was introduced to Newton's *Principia Mathematica*. Jefferson advanced magnificently during this intensive two-year private tutorial, and his knowledge may have exceeded that of some artillery officers of his day, such as Alexander Hamilton and Napoleon Bonaparte, but he had no need of that application, and he loved mathematics mainly for their aesthetic value.[25]

As heir to a plantation, he needed, and he achieved, a surveyor's practical knowledge of Euclid, as did George Washington and other frontier farmers, but he basically saw mathematics as one of the liberal arts, and he approached mathematics from the purest intellectual motives. Numbers were a pleasant diversion, aside from their application to such matters as the moldboard plough. Annette Gordon-Reed has examined, and Barbara Chase-Riboud has gently satirized, his use of a mathematical formula to establish the effects of miscegenation, which he calculated in an 1815 letter to Francis Gray:

> it becomes a Mathematical problem of the same class with those on the mixtures of different liquors or different metals. as in these therefore, the Algebraical notation is the most convenient & intelligible. let us express the pure blood of the white in the capital letters of the printed alphabet, the pure blood of the negro in the small letters of the printed alphabet, and any given mixture of either, by way of abridgment in MS. letters. let the 1st crossing be of **a**, pure negro, with **A**. pure white. the Unit of blood of the issue being composed of the half of that of each parent, will be **a**/2 + **A**/2 call it, for abbreviation, h (half-blood).[26]

Thomas Jefferson might have wondered about the capacity of mulattoes for inheriting and passing to their descendants "the circumstance of superior beauty," his actual words in *Notes on Virginia*, which are quoted in the chapter dealing more specifically with Jefferson's thoughts on African American colonization. Here we are concerned with his application of mathematics to his breeding experiments. Jefferson's letter to Gray of March 4, 1815 shifted to the subject of merino sheep, in order to make a comparison. The matter could not easily have been examined by direct

[25] Jefferson to Robert Patterson, March 30, 1798: "I possess Emerson's fluxions at home, & it was the book I used at College." Jefferson to Nathaniel Bowditch, May 2, 1815; Jefferson to L. H. Girardin, January 15, 1815; Jefferson mentions Small's friendship and support in Peterson, ed., *Thomas Jefferson, Writings*, p. 4.

[26] Jefferson to Francis Gray, March 4, 1815. See Barbara Chase-Riboud, *Sally Hemings: A Novel* (New York: Viking Press, 1979).

experimentation even on African Americans, due to some misgivings related to the matter of father–daughter incest:

> a Merino ram being crossed 1st with a country ewe, 2dly with this daughter, 3dly with this grandaughter, and 4thly with the great grandaughter, the last issue is deemed pure Merino, having in fact but 1/16 of the country blood. our Canon considers 2. crosses with the pure white, and a 3d with any degree of mixture, however small, as clearing the issue of the negro blood. but observe that this does not reestablish freedom, which depends on the condition of the mother, the principle of the civil law, partus sequitur ventrem, being adopted here. but if e. be emancipated, he becomes a free white man, and a citizen of the US.

With respect to the effects of inbreeding on the likelihood of emancipation, Jefferson could not have forgotten his 1770 plea in the case of *Howell v. Netherland*, nor could he have forgotten what he had written about the maintenance of racial purity in *Notes on Virginia*. The presence of Jefferson mulattoes on his plantations, regardless of their fatherhood, made the matter "worthy of attention." We know not whether the Ptolemaic mathematics of his letter to Francis Gray were in agreement with empirical evidence, or what might have been induced from the more Galilean experiments of contemporary farmers. Scientific animal breeding was still in its infancy. In 1810, Robert Bakewell, the geologist, sent him a copy of his *Book upon Wool*. Jefferson was most likely aware of another Robert Bakewell, the agriculturalist whose contributions to selective breeding of livestock are now considered an important development in the history of agriculture. In any case, Jefferson should have had adequate opportunity to observe that his predictions of the phenotypic characteristics of persons of black/white admixture are not reliably the same as those he deduced from his mathematical calculations based on sheep.[27]

He calculated the effects of inbreeding at the age of 72, which shows that his interest in mathematical games continued as he advanced in years. He was aware of advancements in mathematics, both in England and in France, and insisted on the importance of offering differential calculus on proposing a curriculum for the University of Virginia.[28] He tried to keep up with British and French developments in the field, and he reported rumors that the mathematicians at Cambridge lagged behind those of Paris, but, given his voluntary isolation at age 81, it is difficult to know

[27] Robert Bakewell to Jefferson, December 23, 1810. James Mease to Jefferson, February 27, 1809, describes some of the refinements of sheep-breeding and mentions both the "Merino breed" and ewes of "the Bakewell breed."

[28] Jefferson to Joseph Priestley, January 18, 1800; Jefferson to Patrick Kerr Rogers, January 29, 1824.

how well he was keeping up, due to "the rust of age and long continued avocations of a very different character."[29]

This did not stop him from making disparaging remarks about the Italo-English mathematician and inventor Tiberius Cavallo, who was born in 1749 and became a Fellow of the Royal Society at the age of 30. It is not impossible that Jefferson was jealous of Cavallo, who was, like himself, an amateur violinist, and whose publications on mathematics, music, and electricity were neither so trifling nor fatuous as Jefferson claimed.[30] He expressed a much higher regard for his French contemporary Pierre-Simon Laplace, although, in mentioning him, he did not make the observation that Laplace had improved on some of Newton's ideas in mathematics and cleansed astronomy of the seventeenth-century theological mysticism from which Jefferson never escaped.

ASTRONOMY AND HOROLOGY

He proudly possessed an orrery, a beautiful mechanical invention, named for its modern inventor, Charles Boyle, 4th Earl of Orrery (1674–1731). One such device was described by George Washington as "a curious piece of Mechanism for shewing the revolutions of the Sun, Earth, and many other of the Planets." These instruments were sophisticated mechanical abstractions, offering a fascinating analogy, but not a recreation, of astronomical reality. They presented the orbits of earth and moon as perfect circles, and necessarily misrepresented the distances between the heavenly bodies, as well as their spatial relationship to a miniaturized sun. The orrery was a curiosity, like the eighteenth-century music boxes and other mechanical toys that connoisseurs like Washington and Jefferson could appreciate mathematically and aesthetically, but which neither could fashion with his own hands. Jefferson found the machine worthy of possession, but he was dependent on a member of the despised artisan class to make one.[31]

Jefferson's conception of science, like Newton's, was theistic and rational. A disorderly event, such as a meteorite falling to earth, was as

[29] Jefferson to Patrick Kerr Rogers, January 29, 1824.

[30] Tiberius Cavallo (1749–1804) published numerous studies on electricity, including a *Treatise on Electricity* (1795). He was a violinist and also published *Of the Temperament of Those Musical Instruments, in Which the Tones, Keys, or Frets, are Fixed, as in the Harpsichord, Organ, Guitar, &c.* (Philosophical Transactions of the Royal Society of London, 1788).

[31] Diary of George Washington, Thursday, October 29, 1789.

annoying as the idea of a species going extinct. It did not accord with the reasonable, geometrical universe of Jefferson's quasi-Newtonian God. Although he was aware of theories that the earth had undergone drastic changes over the aeons, he was almost flippant regarding them, and he had difficulty accepting and reconciling evolutionism with the idea of an orderly creation and an intelligent design.[32] He expressed skepticism and unease when confronted by theories that the Earth and its creatures were mutable – had not always existed in exactly the same form. If he had any notion of geological evolution in 1786, it was fragmentary and unsystematic. When confronted with the phenomenon of a meteorite, he was not simply cautious, but almost lacking in curiosity. When Daniel Salmon wrote to him of a stone that had seemingly fallen from the sky, Jefferson's response, while not entirely derisive, was effectively disparaging:

> It may be very difficult to explain how the stone you possess came into the position in which it was found. But is it easier to explain how it got into the clouds from whence it is supposed to have fallen?[33]

Jefferson's flippancy reflected a widespread contemporary skepticism that discounted reports of stones falling from the sky as superstitions or old wives' tales. By 1795, however, the climate of scientific opinion was changing with the famous case of the Wold meteorite. Serious scientists were beginning to entertain the possibility that rocks could indeed fall from the sky. Nonetheless, in 1807, two Yale scientists who declared their belief in meteorites were roundly jeered. According to an undocumented rumor, Jefferson is supposed to have said it "was easier to believe that two Yankee professors could lie than to admit that stones could fall from heaven." While some historians doubt that Jefferson actually made this remark, it cannot be denied that his letter to Salmon was in a similar vein, not only skeptical, but summarily dismissive.[34] The skepticism that he expressed demonstrated the limitations of his, and much eighteenth-century, empiricism when observable phenomena clashed with presuppositions about the laws of nature, self-evident truths about the cosmos.[35]

[32] Jefferson to Charles Thompson, Paris, December 17, 1786.

[33] Jefferson to Daniel Salmon, Washington, February 15, 1808.

[34] Bedini, *Thomas Jefferson*, p. 387.

[35] According to historian Anna Berkes of the Monticello staff, the words attributed to Jefferson first appeared in *American Contributions to Chemistry: An Address Delivered on the Occasion of the Celebration of the Centennial of Chemistry, at Northumberland, PA, August 1, 1874, by Benjamin Silliman, of Yale College* (reprinted from the *American*

There is, however, no question of Jefferson's sophistication with respect to astronomy or his ability to apply his mathematical knowledge to it. Although Jefferson was no Copernicus, James Parton's endlessly quoted exclamation that he could "plot an eclipse" is no doubt accurate. He gave ample evidence of being able to discuss both solar and lunar eclipses with knowledgeable correspondents, such as David Rittenhouse, who clearly took him seriously. There was, of course, no need for him to plot an eclipse, as the knowledge of how to do so was ancient and the methods were readily available in published form. The most prominent of recent books describing his scientific studies, curiously, do not contain chapters on his adventures along the lines of predicting either solar or lunar phenomena, and the word "eclipse" occurs in only one of the indexes, that of Sylvio Bedini.[36] An impressive article related to Jefferson's astronomy appears in the Monticello website with an entry courtesy of the *Thomas Jefferson Encyclopedia* under the entry "Longitude," describing his interests and beginning with the years at William and Mary, as well as containing a description of his calculating the longitude of Monticello, based on the 1811 solar eclipse.[37]

There were other amateur astronomers in the United States, such as the self-taught African American surveyor, Benjamin Banneker, who sent Jefferson a letter in August of 1791 expressing his indignation over slavery, and including a copy of an almanac that he had compiled, containing some of his own astronomical calculations. It would be pretty if we were able to compare Jefferson and Banneker as clockmakers, but since Banneker's clock does not survive, we have no way of knowing whose timepiece was the better. Both of them made attempts to master the scientific knowledge of their day, but neither of them made a singular contribution to scientific method or to any field of science. Silvio Bedini has written excellent biographies of both men, but supports no such claim for either of them.[38]

Chemist for August–September and December, 1874). The sarcasm of the remark is consistent with Jefferson's flippancy in the letter to Daniel Salmon, which undermines Berkes' assumption that Silliman's statement was "a lie. By a Yankee professor."

[36] Bedini, *Thomas Jefferson*. Cf. Clagett, *Scientific Jefferson* and Thomson, *Jefferson's Shadow*.

[37] The article is based on Lucia Stanton, "Interrogating the Moon," *Monticello Keepsakes*, 59 (April 13, 1996).

[38] Bedini, *Thomas Jefferson*. Also see Bedini's *The Life of Benjamin Banneker* (New York: Charles Scribner's Sons, 1972).

Jefferson forwarded a copy of Banneker's almanac to the Marquis de Condorcet in France, along with a letter in which he described Banneker as "a very respectable mathematician," and presenting himself as one of his strongest promoters. "I procured him to be employed under one of our chief directors in laying out the new federal city on the Patowmac, and in the intervals of his leisure, while on that work, he made an Almanac for the next year, which he sent me in his own handwriting." Banneker had, in that same letter, rebuked Jefferson for "detaining by fraud and violence so numerous a part of my brethren, under groaning captivity and cruel oppression." Jefferson responded to him by saying "no body wishes more than I do to see such proofs as you exhibit, that nature has given to our black brethren, talents equal to those of the other colours of men, & that the appearance of a want of them is owing merely to the degraded condition of their existence both in Africa & America."[39]

There was, however, beneath Jefferson's apparent equanimity, an irritation that seethed for many years, and he later described both Banneker's opinions and his almanac in quite different tones in an 1809 letter to Joel Barlow. There he wrote disparagingly that:

> The whole do not amount, in point of evidence, to what we know ourselves of Banneker. We know he had spherical trigonometry enough to make almanacs, but not without the suspicion of aid from Ellicot, who was his neighbor and friend, and never missed an opportunity of puffing him. I have a long letter from Banneker, which shows him to have had a mind of very common stature indeed.

Sylvio Bedini opines that Jefferson's puzzlingly contradictory estimations of Banneker may have reflected the passage of time, and the fact that his "widely publicized letter" to Banneker was used against him in the presidential election of 1800. What seems more likely is that Jefferson was bent on cultivating his reputation as a philosopher of freedom on one side of the Atlantic, while maintaining his position as a respectable Virginia planter on the other.[40]

Comparable to Jefferson's accomplishments in the natural sciences were his contributions to the social studies; both showed marks of flashing brilliance, mingled with stunningly inept methodologies and medieval

[39] Jefferson to Benjamin Banneker, August 19, 1791. The standard biography of Benjamin Banneker is Bedini, *The Life of Benjamin Banneker*, cited in the previous note. Also see Charles A. Cerami, *Benjamin Banneker: Surveyor, Astronomer, Publisher, Patriot* (New York: John Wiley & Sons, 2002). Bedini supports the idea that Jefferson knew of and approved Banneker's appointment, p. 109.

[40] Bedini, *Thomas Jefferson*, p. 225.

superstitions. His frequent references to books and authors offer many tantalizing but incomplete glimpses into his philosophical values, his scientific imagination, and his literary tastes. Contrary to our expectations, he gives us very few clues as to how his reading influenced his political and economic thought. His commentaries on political authors are impressionistic; his private thoughts on literature, the arts, and the sciences are rare and fleeting. A person of similar congenital endowments, born 200 years after him could probably have achieved professorial status in any discipline at most American universities today, but – as in his own time – he might be more impressive for his mastery of current knowledge than for any singular contributions to its advancement.

In the natural sciences, as in other areas, Jefferson embodied the contradictory principles of provincialism versus cosmopolitanism, of agriculturalism versus industrialism. He was, as Hamilton so astutely observed, no rigid ideologue, and he had only a few unyielding biases, but he was limited by unconscious metaphysical preconceptions. He was a committed cottage industrialist even when writing against industrialism, and thus, of necessity, an amateur inventor. In pressing his farming-based localized economy, he early made disparaging remarks about "the class of artificers as the panders of vice, and the instruments by which the liberties of a country are generally overturned." Nonetheless, two of his highly admired associates, Benjamin Franklin and Thomas Paine, were members of the artisan class. Thus, while his contempt for the class of handworkers is well known, it was mutable and inconstant. Besides, he said elsewhere that merchants were even less trustworthy.[41] He depended necessarily on the hands of craftsmen, black and white, in order to realize the inventions that often existed as mere half-formed images in his mind, and he possessed neither the functional knowledge nor the practical expertise, nor the patience, to actually construct a plough, a clock, or an orrery with his own hands.

MAMMOTHS, MEGALONYX, AND A MOOSE

Whether pontificating on mammoths, meteors, the moose, or the megalonyx, Jefferson's methods and his conclusions were deficient by the vaunted standards of Bacon, for they were always designed to prove

[41] Jefferson to John Jay, August 23, 1785. Neither did merchants have the makings of loyal republican patriots: as he wrote to Horatio G. Spafford, March 17, 1814, "merchants have no country."

a political point. One of the aims of Jefferson's *Notes on Virginia* was to make the argument that the North American climate and geography were conducive to the success of transplanted Europeans and their enlightened ideals. The logical steps in this argument were that: first, the continent had always supported vigorous mammalian life, both indigenous and transplanted; second, that it could therefore sustain a vigorous human population of whites transplanted from Europe; third, that it could sustain not only the people, but the republican form of government that these transplanted Europeans sought to establish. It is for this reason that the *Notes* demonstrated such an obsession with the large animal species of North America. American scientists were immersed in an ongoing controversy concerning the healthiness of the American biosphere.

An impromptu and inconclusive, but nonetheless amusing, experiment related to this controversy was conducted at a Parisian dinner party hosted by Benjamin Franklin, where half the guests were Americans and the other French. One of the assembled was the French naturalist Guillaume-Thomas-François Raynal, Abbé de Raynal. "During the dinner he got on his favorite theory of the degeneracy of animals, and even of man, in America." Franklin at length said, "M. l'Abbé, let us try this question by the fact before us. We are here one half Americans, and one half French ... Let both parties rise, and we will see on which side nature has degenerated." It happened that while the Americans were mostly above average height, the French present were "remarkably diminutive, and the Abbé himself was a mere shrimp." Franklin's amusing demonstration proved nothing, of course, although Raynal's negative assessment of the American environment was without scientific merit. David Waldstreicher points out in his introduction to *Notes on Virginia* that this "seemingly childishness" argument concealed graver issues, for he is correct in viewing publication of the *Notes* as an "extended attempt to explain and justify the American republican experiment."[42]

Franklin's dispute with Raynal was echoed in Jefferson's quarrel with the Comte de Buffon, although Jefferson admitted that the count had never made any claims "as to the degeneracy of the man of Europe transplanted to America." He did feel, however, that the comte had come "within one step" of doing so. He saw it as his patriotic and scientific duty to demonstrate that North America could produce animal species as

[42] Waldstreicher, introduction to his edition of Jefferson, *Notes on Virginia*, p. 1. Jefferson to Richard Walsh, December 4, 1818.

robust as any in Europe.[43] The task related to an ongoing discourse concerning the possibility of inevitable moral degeneration of Europeans in North America. An important theme in the science of the early republic was a defense of the geography and climate of North America from charges that it was deleterious, or incapable of sustaining the manners, customs, and morals that make life meaningful and refined. In popular history Jefferson is presented as a tough-minded defender of America from the harebrained speculations of a silly *philosophe*, and his efforts are presented as proof of the superiority of America's pragmatism over French dogma. Jefferson was zealous in the refutation, writing to his American friends with requests for specimens of American animals, including the "skin, the skeleton, and the horns of the Moose, the Caribou, and the Orignal or Elk ... but most especially those of the Moose."

At this moment, the Monticello website concludes its remarks on Jefferson's efforts with the observation that "Jefferson as diplomat, scientist, and citizen went to unusual lengths and personal expense to dispel unfavorable myths about his country by attempting to prove once and for all that the American moose was as large as or even larger than its European counterparts." The moose story is an interesting diversion for the entertainment of schoolchildren. We do better to inform them of the distortion of his opinions that encircle the dome of the Jefferson monument.[44]

In constructing the tables listing the quadrupeds for the *Notes*, he relied on Buffon to some extent, but was not clear as to where exactly he departed. In fact his table includes animals that were unknown in any territory ever belonging to the State of Virginia, such as the mammoth and the "white bear." In one confusing paragraph he launched a series of attacks on Buffon's descriptions, pausing in mid-stream to say, "These, I think, are the only instances in which I have departed from the authority of Mons. de Buffon in the construction of this table. I take him for my ground work, because I think him the best informed of any Naturalist who has ever written." It is difficult to ascertain whether this apparent instance of irony was intentional or inadvertent.[45]

[43] Lee Alan Dugatkin, *Mr. Jefferson and the Giant Moose: Natural History in Early America* (University of Chicago Press, 2009).

[44] William Peden's introduction to the *Notes*, like the inscription on the dome of the Jefferson Memorial in Washington, DC, renders harmless Jefferson's views on slavery and masks his efforts to preserve it. For example, see p. xvii, where Peden speaks of Jefferson's "cherished goal ... the emancipation of slavery in Virginia," Peden, ed., *Notes on Virginia*.

[45] Ibid., p. 118.

In listing the fauna of North America in *Notes on Virginia* he included the Pleistocene mammoth, hoping against hope that it might still roam the plains of the American Northwest. Jefferson's wishful thinking was a combination of national chauvinism imposed on a medieval superstructure when he made this telling allusion to the Great Chain of Being, and his hope of discovering a missing link:

> It may be asked, why I insert the Mammoth, as if it still existed? I ask in return, why I should omit it, as if it did not exist? Such is the oeconomy of nature, that no instance can be produced of her having permitted any one race of her animals to become extinct; of her having formed any link in her great work so weak as to be broken. To add to this, the traditionary testimony of the Indians, that this animal still exists in the northern and western parts of America, would be adding the light of a taper to that of the meridian sun.[46]

The above paragraph reveals a characteristic tendency to derive ideas from the Great Chain metaphor and a willingness to accept the light of any taper, even American Indian testimony, if it would reinforce his intelligent design dogmas. He grasped even at the most preposterous assertion of Buffon that the mammoth was "six times the cubic volume of the elephant." He quoted at length an American Indian legend of great behemoths that once roamed, and still might roam, the plains. "Of these the Mammoth, or big buffalo, as called by the Indians, must certainly have been the largest." In this instance he was not certain whether the animal under discussion was an elephant or a buffalo, whether it was vegetarian or carnivorous, whether it was extinct or extant. All that mattered is that it be mammoth! "Their tradition is, that he was carnivorous, and still exists in the northern parts of America." And even the most spurious of myths and legends contain some shred of truth to support the hope that some variety of "great bull" might survive above the Great Lakes even to the present day.[47]

Jefferson used the Chain of Being metaphor in expressing his hopes for the survival of the North American megalonyx, as he called it, as well as the legendary mammoth or big buffalo. Both the giant animals and the chain on which they were suspended recur in Jefferson's correspondence, but his position on their survival within the *Notes* is inconsistent. In 1782 and 1783 he persisted in hoping for the survival of the "big buffalo,"

[46] Ibid., p. 116.

[47] Jefferson on Buffon's descriptions: "Our quadrupeds have been mostly described by Linnaeus and Mons. de Buffon." Ibid, p. 107; Jefferson cites Buffon on the size of the mammoth, p. 109; Jefferson on American Indian testimony, pp. 107–108.

caring little whether this animal was identical with the mammoth. He wrote to George Rogers Clarke in the same year as the first draft of the *Notes* thanking him for his efforts "in procuring for me some teeth and bones of the big buffalo." The single consistency was that over the next fifty years his letters concerning extinct species tended to stress size, robustness, and possible ferociousness, as if his principal concern was not purely scientific, but rhetorical. It was as if the capacity of the American continent to support such fearsome animals as the mammoth, the mastodon, and the megalonyx would somehow guarantee the prospects for supporting the republican ideal.[48]

Jefferson's "Memoir on the Megalonyx," presented to the American Philosophical Society on February 10, 1797, required that he invoke nature, personified as a woman who ran a planned economy, as he had in his commentary on the mammoth. Jefferson's paper provided an opportunity to demonstrate the falsity of Buffon's outdated conjectures on the classification of the species, although he did not belabor the point that he had once accepted Buffon's conjecture that the megalonyx was a member of the cat family. Julian Boyd notes that, just as he was completing his paper, a fortuitous reading of an article by Georges Cuvier led him to suspect that the megalonyx was neither a lion nor a carnivore.[49] He quickly grasped that his megalonyx was probably

[48] For discussions of Jefferson's references to large animals of the western hemisphere, see the online edition of the Jefferson papers at the Founders Online website that refer to "Jefferson to George Rogers Clark Philadelphia Jan. 6. 1783 Th: Jefferson RC (WHi). TJ's Letter . . . of the last month was that of 26 Nov. 1782. Clark's letter about the Bones of the big buffalo (though he did not employ the term) was that of 20 Feb. 1782"; [Jefferson to Louis of Parma, February 25, 1799] "of two such animals as the Megalonyx and Mammoth, with a thousand other facts, will surely . . ."; [Jefferson to Lacépède, February 24, 1803] "it is not improbable that this voyage of discovery will procure us further information of the Mammoth, & of the Megatherium also, mentioned by you page 6. for you have possibly seen in our Philosophical transactions"; [Jefferson to Benjamin S. Barton, October 10, 1796] "This with the bones I have would enable me to give the actual stature of the animal, instead of calculating it on the principle of ex pede Herculem." The allusion, ex pede Herculem, derives from a legend that Pythagorus once said "from his foot [we can measure] Hercules." [Jefferson to William Clark, September 10, 1809]:

> these have enabled them to decide that the animal was neither a Mammoth nor an elephant, but of a distinct kind, to which they have given the name of Mastodont, from the protuberances of it's teeth. these from their form & the immense mass of their jaws, satisfy me this animal must have been arboriverous. nature seems not to have provided other food sufficient for him; & the limb of a tree would be no more to him than a bough of Cotton tree to a horse.

[49] Julian Boyd made two strong contributions to understanding Jefferson's studies of Megalonyx or Megatherium. See Boyd's note, "Drawing of the Megatherium Sent to

identical to Cuvier's megatherium, an extinct New World giant sloth. Although he used the past tense, he still clung to the idea that nature was not so improvident as to allow the extinction of North America's large animal species. Although Cuvier's work led to the conclusion that megatherium "probably was not carnivorous," Jefferson clung to the hope that megalonyx might prove to be a separate species and a ferocious predator, greater than a lion, as he had imagined the previous year in a letter to Archibald Stuart that:

> the animal must have been as preeminent over the lion, as the big buffalo was over the elephant. The bones are too extraordinary in themselves, and too victorious an evidence against the pretended degeneracy of animal nature in our continent, not to excite the strongest desire to push the enquiry after all other remains of the same animal which any industry can recover for us.[50]

The fact that the "big buffalo" and now the megalonyx might be extinct did not detract from Jefferson's conviction that even their past existence was a refutation of Buffon's thesis. It raises questions of whether science should be enlisted in support of republican ideology, and whether science should take us wherever it leads us, regardless of however embarrassing or inconvenient. Revising his paper and scrupulously acknowledging Cuvier, he made no inappropriate claims to originality. His paper became simply an admission that his and Buffon's observations had been less accurate than Cuvier's. Nonetheless, in 1822, the French naturalist Anselme Gaëtan Desmarest called the animal *megalonyx jeffersonii*. This was flattering to the author of the Declaration of Independence, but it was a political honor rather than a scientific distinction. It demonstrated the homage often paid by the French Revolutionary generation to the principles of liberty and egalitarianism with which Jefferson had associated himself so successfully. Desmarest ignored the fact that Jefferson had neither discovered the species nor correctly identified it.[51]

Cuvier had been almost as impressed as Desmarest, and in his 1796 article he had not only paid tribute to Jefferson's "talents and virtues"

Jefferson from Madrid," in Boyd, *The Papers of Thomas Jefferson*, vol. XIV, pp. xxv–xxxiv; also see Julian P. Boyd, "The Megalonyx, the Megatherium, and Thomas Jefferson's Lapse of Memory," *Proceedings of the American Philosophical Society*, 102, no. 5 (October 20, 1958), 420–435; Silvio A. Bedini, *Thomas Jefferson and American Vertebrate Paleontology* (Charlottesville, VA: Virginia Division of Mineral Resources Publication, 1985).

50 Jefferson to Archibald Stuart, May 26, 1796.

51 Boyd, "The Megalonyx, the Megatherium," p. 433. Thomas Jefferson, "Memoir on the Megalonyx [10 February 1797]," Founders Online.

and contributions to humanity, but also credited him with being "le premier qui ait fait connoitre cette interessante expèce d'animale fossile." But Cuvier did not say that Jefferson had correctly identified it, and apparently Cuvier had not done so either. That honor went to José Carriga in his 1796 publication, *Description del esquelleto de un quadrupedo muy corpulento y raro que se conserva en el Real Gabinete de Historia Natural de Madrid.* Julian Boyd notes that Jefferson had come into possession of a copy of the Carriga paper by the time he left Paris in 1789, but forgot that he had seen it. Stephen Rowland, an expert in geoscience, also notes the Carriga paper. It seems surprising that, if Jefferson had read the paper in 1789, he would have forgotten it seven years later, since his letters in the intervening time reveal an absolute obsession with the megalonyx such that he could hardly have suffered from what Boyd called "a lapse of memory." It seems more likely that Jefferson had read the paper superficially, or – since his Spanish was not perfect – that he had set it aside unread.[52]

Jefferson's biological theories were subordinate to, and inseparable from, his patriotic fervor. The metaphysical ramblings of this prophet of the American Enlightenment were often just as specious as the legends of Native Americans. Jefferson's deistic suppositions regarding the "oeconomy of nature" illustrate that he was often more seventeenth than eighteenth century in his thinking. Indeed, he sometimes retained biases that were even more outmoded, such as his medieval Great Chain of Being, which impaired the struggle of his mind towards a scientific method. With respect to extinctions, the *Notes* revealed a striking ambivalence, for on a subsequent page of the *Notes* he was able to imagine that under unfavorable conditions a species might be extirpated: "Animals transplanted into unfriendly climates, either change their nature and acquire new senses against the new difficulties in which they are placed, or they multiply poorly and become extinct." By 1823 he had finally come to believe that "certain races of animals are become extinct," as he admitted in a letter to John Adams.[53]

52 Boyd, "The Megalonyx, the Megatherium." Stephen M. Rowland, "Thomas Jefferson, Extinction, and the Evolving View of Earth History in the Late Eighteenth and Early Nineteenth Centuries" in Gary D. Rosenberg, ed., *The Revolution in Geology from the Renaissance to the Enlightenment* (Boulder, CO: The Geological Society of America, 2009), p. 245.

53 Jefferson, *Notes on Virginia*, pp. 116, 200; Jefferson to John Adams, April 11, 1823. Arthur O. Lovejoy, *The Great Chain of Being: A Study of the History of an Idea* (Cambridge, MA: Harvard University Press, 1964 [1936]). Lovejoy discusses the tension between being and becoming and the idea of a God "that never is, but is only coming to be" and the idea that God and his creation metamorphose, ibid., pp. 244ff, 300ff, 318–325.

Where Jefferson stood in the budding controversy between evolutionists and those who believed in the permanently fixed Great Chain of Being cannot be ascertained definitively.[54] This is due to the fact that evolution and the natural mutability of species were theories only gradually gaining ground, and Jefferson's reactions to them were in flux. There were advancements, reversals, and dead-ends in biological theories, for example the evolutionary dead-end in the theory of Lamarck, who was right about evolution, but mistaken about how it occurred. Jefferson was certainly familiar with Lamarck's ideas, for he received a letter from Thomas Cooper asserting that "in natural history, the French authors undoubtedly take the lead. What Englishman competes with ... La Marck."[55] Jefferson was presumably aware of Lamarckian evolution by 1814, when he received this letter, but none of his biographers have identified a specific Lamarckian influence on him. The idea that the North American environment might improve newly introduced species never entered his discussion. Years after Jefferson's death, Frederick Douglass, influenced both by Lamarck and Darwin, toyed with the idea that the American populations, both white and black, were undergoing evolutionary progress, due to the salubrious influences of North America. This optimistic application of Lamarckian theory did not become predominant in the eighteenth century, and if he ever encountered it, Jefferson did not include it in his philosophical meanderings.[56]

In his *Notes on Virginia* and elsewhere, he took pains to answer French calumnies, especially the charges of Buffon, who had made some uninformed remarks about the North American environment.[57] While it is true

[54] For another view, consult Stephen M. Rowland, a professor of geoscience at the University of Nevada, who takes the view that "Jefferson never abandoned the basic elements of his completeness-of-nature worldview." See Rowland, "Thomas Jefferson, Extinction, and the Evolving View of Earth History," *Memoir of the Geological Society of America*, 203, nos. 225–246 (January, 2009), 245.

[55] Thomas Cooper to Jefferson, September 15, 1814.

[56] Rowland, "Thomas Jefferson, Extinction, and the Evolving View of Earth History." Frederick Douglass, "Pictures and Progress: An Address Delivered in Boston, Massachusetts, on December 1861," in John W. Blassingame, ed., *The Frederick Douglass Papers* (New Haven, CT: Yale University Press, 1986), series 1, vol. III, pp. 452–473. Douglass briefly commented on evolutionism in "'It Moves' or The Philosophy of Reform: An Address Delivered in Washington, D.C. on November 20, 1883" in John W. Blassingame and John R. McKivigan, eds., *The Frederick Douglass Papers* (New Haven, CT: Yale University Press, 1992), series 1, vol. V, pp. 124–144.

[57] Gaye Wilson, "Jefferson, Buffon, and the Mighty American Moose," *Monticello Newsletter*, 13 (spring, 2002). Lee Alan Dugatkin, "Jefferson's Moose and the Case against American Degeneracy," *Scientific American*, 304, no. 2 (2011), 84–87.

that Buffon's methods were often indistinct from pure speculation, and while many of his theories are dismissed today as totally without foundation, it would be wrong to assume that Jefferson's attempts to refute him were any more solid in terms of scientific method. Jefferson and Franklin alike had trivialized and facetiously dismissed a scientific problem that merited serious discussion. Admittedly, Raynal had not made a scientific argument but an invidious comparison, and the question he raised differed somewhat from Buffon's.

Buffon had introduced legitimately, if inadvertently, an important question concerning the effects of natural environment on political culture. How did one explain the fact that no civilizations comparable to the Greek and Roman Empires had arisen in the Americas? Buffon did not raise his question in modern scientific terms. He was not aware, as future generations of paleontologists would be, that the absence of the horse and other large domesticable animals had deeply influenced the history of indigenous American peoples. The absence of the horse, the ass, the camel, the elephant, and other beasts of burden meant that neither sub-Saharan Africa, nor the Western hemisphere had produced a Greece, a Rome, or a China.[58]

Long after the deaths of Franklin and Buffon, Jefferson was still contesting the antiquated conjectures that Buffon had published in 1778. Ironically, Jefferson persisted in some of Buffon's errors for the rest of his life. By 1797, the unripe opinions of both men were superseded by the researches of Cuvier, and Buffon had been dead for over a decade. Peter Gay and David Brion Davis have shown that the discourses of Raynal and his cohort were primarily concerned not with pessimism about the physical environment, but with optimism about the future prospects of America. While critical of slavery, and aware that slavery was "intimately connected with the very meaning of America," Raynal entertained a prophetic vision of America's future as the land of promise.[59]

Buffon may be defended on one point, albeit as a matter that neither he nor Jefferson could have appreciated at the time. Buffon was well aware that the North American continent, unlike the Eurasian continent, lacked the same breadth and diversity of large animal species, for example the

Dugatkin, *Mr. Jefferson and the Giant Moose*. Keith Stewart Thomson, "Jefferson, Buffon and the Moose," *American Scientist*, 96, no. 3 (2008), 200–202.

[58] Jared Diamond, *Guns, Germs, and Steel: The Fates of Human Societies* (New York: Norton, 1999).

[59] David Brion Davis, *The Problem of Slavery in Western Culture* (Ithaca, NY: Cornell University Press, 1966), p. 16.

horse, which disappeared from North America until it was reintroduced by the conquistadors. Today every schoolchild knows that the horse evolved in the New World, and then went extinct for reasons that no one can currently explain. Elephants survived on the Eurasian continent, and performed important economic functions, even north of the thirtieth parallel, where they had served as domesticated beasts of burden. The Americas had panther-like cats such as the jaguar, which resembled Eurasian leopards, and other fairly large cats assigned various names, such as cougar, puma, and mountain lion. Very large cats, such as lions and tigers, did not exist either in North or South America, and taxonomists were not yet aware of extinct species such as the smilodon. Jefferson clung to the hope that his megalonyx might be a great cat, even larger than the Eurasian lion, but his hopes faded on that score, as we have seen.

Buffon had inadvertently placed his finger on a very important point in world history, which today is widely acknowledged, although denied by Jefferson and even by Franklin. Jared Diamond observes in his book *Guns, Germs, and Steel* that much New World history was determined by the lack of large draft animals in the pre-Columbian Americas. Lacking beasts of burden, Native North American civilizations, like those of sub-Saharan Africans, had been severely disadvantaged in the struggle to achieve technological cultures similar to those of China, Egypt, India, and Mesopotamia. The lack of native wheat was also a deficiency in the North American environment of which Buffon was unaware. Native Americans had corn, but corn is deficient in protein and B-vitamins. Neither Jefferson nor Buffon can be blamed for not knowing of Indian corn's vitamin deficiency. They cannot be faulted for not understanding vertebrate paleontology or the study of phylogeny as it would develop in the nineteenth century. But the answer to Buffon's exceedingly important challenge was not going to be found in a stuffed moose, and geographical patriotism should not have been a substitute for seriously considering Buffon's discomfiting assertions.

VOLTAIRE, GEOLOGY, SHELLS, AND MOUNTAINS

At one point, Jefferson was willing to consider Voltaire's imaginative theories in the field of historical geology. In the first edition of *Notes on Virginia*, he took seriously Voltaire's speculations on the origins of fossilized seashells in mountainous rock formations.[60] After that, he revealed

[60] See Peterson, ed., *Thomas Jefferson, Writings*, pp. 251, 252, and Jefferson, *Notes on Virginia*, p. 102. Jefferson to Mr. Rittenhouse, Paris, January 25, 1786: "It will not be

surprisingly little interest in Voltaire, other than in these few remarks on geology. Jefferson adhered to an early variety of uniformitarianism, the idea that the earth and the seas were stable and not given to radical transformations. He was uncomfortable with the theory that fossilized seashells might give evidence of past geological disruptions, resulting in the uplift and draining of ancient seabeds. During 1786–87, he exchanged correspondence on the matter with David Rittenhouse, who agreed with Voltaire's assumption on the matter. Jefferson simply could not accept the idea of a cataclysm that could have deposited sea creatures atop a mountain. He made a list of the explanations he was aware of:

> 1. That they have been deposited by a universal deluge .... 2. They are animal remains. 3. That they grow or shoot as chrystals do .... I find that I could swallow the last opinion sooner than either of the others; but I have not yet swallowed it. Another opinion might have been added, that some throw of nature has forced up parts which had been the bed of the ocean ... But ... No such convulsion has taken place in our time, nor within the annals of history ... and the forcing the bed of the sea fifteen thousand feet above the ordinary surface of the earth ... It is not possible to believe any of these hypotheses; and if we lean towards any of them it should be only till some other is produced more analogous to the known operations of nature.[61]

"The known operations of nature" – that was the key phrase. Sometimes he personified nature as a feminine force, but he always relied on preconceptions about what constituted "the ordinary economy of nature," and scientific judgments must not depart too rapidly from what was already known of "her" economy.[62] Forty years later he still could address questions within the known operations of nature. A letter addressed to John Patten Emmett, a newly appointed chemistry professor at the University of Virginia, made that clear. In clarifying Emmett's duties Jefferson delivered his precise recommendations as to how a professor should organize his time in the lecture hall:

> I should think that mineralogy, geology, and chemistry might be advantageously blended in the same course. then your year would be formed into two grand

difficult to induce me to give up the theory of the growth of shells, without their being the nidus of animals. It is only an idea, and not an opinion with me."

61 See commentary in Peden, ed., *Notes on Virginia*, pp. 266–267. Jefferson to David Rittenhouse, Paris, January 25, 1786. Jefferson to David Rittenhouse, September 18, 1787. Brooke Hindle, *David Rittenhouse* (Princeton University Press, 1964), p. 285. Also see commentary of Garry Wills, *Inventing America: Jefferson's Declaration of Independence* (New York: Doubleday, 1978), p. 110.

62 Jefferson, "Memoir on the Megalonyx" [February 10, 1797], Founders Online.

divisions, ⅓ to botany and zoölogy and ⅔ to chemistry and it's associates mineralogy and geology. to the last indeed I would give the least possible time. to learn, as far as observation has informed us, the ordinary arrangement of the different strata of minerals in the earth, to know from their habitual collocations, and proximities, where we find one mineral, whether another, for which we are seeking, may be expected to be in it's neighborhood is useful. but the dreams about the modes of creation, enquiries whether our globe has been formed by the agency of fire or water, how many millions of years it has cost Vulcan or Neptune to produce what the fiat of the Creator would effect by a single act of will, is too idle to be worth a single hour of any man's life.[63]

He was far too intelligent and inquisitive to consider any scientific speculation a complete waste of time. Thus, in the final months of his life he resorted to sarcasm, as he did in at least one other instance, when confronted with the unexplainable problem of meteorites. In this instance, he dismissed historical geology as a waste of time, with flippant allusions to Roman mythology and an invocation of the Creator. He showed that he remained, in his eighty-third year, a sharp ironist, but, in the end, he rejected both Voltaire's speculation and Rittenhouse's arguments because what they suggested was self-evidently wasteful, disorderly, and inconsistent with the economy of nature's God. His position on the shell fossils is a good illustration of how Jefferson's scientific mind functioned. Postponement of judgment in the absence of definitive proof was an idea that he understood.

Jefferson's science retained both the strengths and the weaknesses of Newton's God hypothesis. He could not shake free of seventeenth-century theological mysticism. Thus he wrote dismissively of the careful and painstaking work of John Whitehurst, *An Inquiry into the Original State and Formation of the Earth* (1778).[64] Whitehurst, a self-educated man of humble origins, was a superior scientist to Jefferson, and his conclusions have held up, not because of guesswork, but due to his methodological rigor. Eventually elected to the Royal Society, Whitehurst came from the class of "artificers" that Jefferson despised, a mere maker of watches and compasses. His artisanship in these realms was as superior to Jefferson's as was his painstaking methodology in the realm of science. Whitehurst's theory of geological evolution was based on a scrupulous collection of data, far beyond Jefferson's patience. His nascent thesis that the Earth had undergone vast evolutionary change

63 Jefferson to John P. Emmett, May 2, 1826.
64 Jefferson to Charles Thompson, Paris, December 17, 1786.

has stood the test of time. Jefferson's response to Whitehurst was not to challenge his method or his evidence, but to revert to theological babble:

> I give one answer to all these theorists. That is as follows. They all suppose the earth a created existence. They must suppose a creator then; and that he possessed power and wisdom to a great degree. As he intended the earth for the habitation of animals and vegetables, is it reasonable to suppose, he made two jobs of his creation, that he first made a chaotic lump and set it into rotatory motion, and then waited the millions of ages necessary to form itself? That when it had done this, he stepped in a second time, to create the animals and plants which were to inhabit it? As the hand of a creator is to be called in, it may as well be called in at one stage of the process as another. We may as well suppose he created the earth at once, nearly in the state in which we see it, fit for the preservation of the beings he placed on it.

In the forty years between 1786 and 1826 Jefferson's scientific concepts evolved, but not uniformly. As the aforementioned letter to Emmett demonstrates (see note 63 above), his ideas were petrified in theological sediment throughout his life. By the 1780s, John Whitehurst and James Hutton were advancing theories of a changing geological universe. These theories, along with Voltaire's speculations on fossilized seashells, were ultimately to be accepted, with the rising influence of Charles Lyell in the decade following Jefferson's death.[65] But he rejected on theological grounds both the emerging and ultimately dominant concepts of geological evolution and biological evolution. He died a few years too early either to accept or reject the contemporary theories that eventually stood the test of time.

CLASSICS AND THE SCIENCES

In 1743, the year of Jefferson's birth, Benjamin Franklin founded the American Philosophical Society and, in that same decade, the University of Pennsylvania.[66] Franklin opposed the overemphasis on Latin and

[65] Uniformitarianism has more than one definition, due to the fact that the theory evolved over a period of fifty years. It is most commonly associated with James Hutton and Charles Lyell, whose approaches implied gradual but nonetheless dramatic changes in the structure of the earth. The more traditional form of uniformitarianism advanced by Jefferson and Voltaire presumed that the universe was governed by constant processes, observable in the present. It did not acknowledge the gradual but uniform theory of change found in the theory of their contemporary, James Hutton, or in the later development of Lyell.

[66] The University of Pennsylvania claims as its founding date 1740 because a building erected in that year, although originally intended for different purposes, was eventually

Greek but lost that battle. Jefferson, on the other hand, remained committed to the classics, and reserved admission to the university for those who had been winnowed in the Latin grammar schools. Jefferson understood that the historic functions of the university have seldom been the preservation of the humanities for their own sake. It might be argued that utilitarian, technological training has usually been the underlying reason for the existence of universities. Since the Middle Ages, university students had traditionally studied Greek in order to read Galen, because it was assumed that Galen understood something about anatomy and the curing of disease.

Jefferson was still caught up in the tradition in which people studied Latin in order to understand Roman law and politics. Furthermore, not only were the crucial documents of British government such as Magna Carta written in Latin, it was also the original language of Bacon's *Novum Organum Scientiarum* and Newton's *Philosophiæ Naturalis Principia Mathematica.* To be sure, translations were readily available by the late eighteenth century, but Jefferson expected that students entering his University of Virginia would be "previously so far qualified" in ancient languages "that one year in our schools shall suffice for their last polish." His prospectus stressed a gentleman's grounding in the classical humanities, as well as a central role for science, technology, mathematics, and engineering. His specifications, while not lacking any appreciation of the arts and humanities for their own sake, contained echoes of the idea that Latin was good for the mind. With respect to its breadth, his syllabus anticipated the civilizing mission of the modern university, but not the degree of specialization of the modern engineering or business school.

Jefferson, while an impressive amateur scientist, made no significant contribution to scientific knowledge or to scientific method. In a previous century, Galileo had devised methodological experiments that were less dramatic, but more important, than his celebrated experiment at the Leaning Tower of Pisa. Leonardo da Vinci's attempts to design a flying machine were more fanciful than scientific, and he made no lasting contribution to the theory of aerodynamics, but his *Codex on the Flight of Birds* showed a commitment to patient and systematic scientific observation. Closer to Jefferson in time and space was Benjamin Franklin, whose experiments with the Leyden jar led to explanations of its functions rivaling those of the man for whom it was named. His Franklin stove

taken over by it. Benjamin Franklin first convened the Trustees of the University in 1749, and instruction began in 1751.

was never perfected, and was not a great success, which is probably why it was never adopted to solve the heating problems at Monticello. But Franklin did perfect the lightning rod, and his contributions to the theory of electricity comprised much more than his celebrated kite-flying experiment.

Jefferson was elected to membership in the American Philosophical Society (APS) in January 1780, almost forty years after Benjamin Franklin founded it. His commitment to the Society, like his commitment to the University of Virginia, focused on science, both theoretical and practical. He served on numerous committees, including the "Bone Committee," whose charge was "to procure one or more entire skeletons of the Mammoth."[67] In 1793, Jefferson got the Society to finance an expedition by French botanist André Michaux, and to support the celebrated expedition of Meriwether Lewis and William Clark in 1804–06; it thereby became the repository for many of their expedition's original journals. Jefferson also donated fossils to the APS from Big Bone Lick, Kentucky, when he financed an 1807 excavation by William Clark. On March 3, 1797, Jefferson was installed as president of the APS. He served as the Society's president for the next eighteen years, although the last entry listing Jefferson present at a meeting was May 2, 1800. The Society refused his offers to resign the presidency on three different occasions, but finally acceded to his wishes at the meeting of January 20, 1815, "with great reluctance."

It is not difficult to understand why Jefferson so highly idolized Bacon and Newton: they both viewed nature as a stable economy. But while he paid lip-service to Bacon's iconoclastic principles, he found it difficult to adhere to them. He enshrined Bacon, the man who called for the abandonment of idols, and those of his works that he most revered were products of the seventeenth, not the eighteenth, century, and even more removed from the nineteenth. Jefferson was still alert and vigorous when steamboats appeared on the Hudson and the first working telegraph was invented.[68] Nonetheless, his flippancy regarding meteorites and developments in geology, and his reluctantly abandoned hope of finding

[67] Minutes of June 16, 1797, referenced in Gaye Wilson, *Monticello Research Report*, November 1997, available at www.monticello.org/site/research-and-collections/american-philosophical-society (ver. 2018-10-01).

[68] Katharine Park and Lorraine Daston, eds., *The Cambridge History of Science* (Cambridge University Press, 2006), vol. II, *Early Modern Science*, p. 13: "Even the canonical texts, for example Galileo, Bacon, or Isaac Newton (1642–1727), appear modern, only if read (as they often are) with the greatest selectivity."

a mammoth, showed a resistance to the new models of the universe that were evolving in his time and a reliance on the "law of nature" paradigm. He reluctantly modified his views on the Pleistocene megaspecies by keeping abreast of the work of Cuvier. His methods of collecting specimens through the use of untrained menials left something to be desired, but demonstrated that his curiosity led him to focus on the accumulation of data from which others might be able to draw conclusions. But his conclusions derived from thought experiments about how an orderly nature would order her economy. Although thought experiments were never going to be abandoned by future scientists, they were no longer to be the predominant mode. Reproducible experiments conducted under controlled conditions were becoming the more respectable practice.[69]

Towards the end of his life, Jefferson wrote to John Adams and François Adriaan Van der Kemp, appraising the experiments of Jean-Pierre Flourens. To Van der Kemp, he wrote:

> I have been lately reading a most extraordinary book, that of M. Flourens on the functions of the nervous system, in vertebrated animals. he proves by too many, and too accurate experiments, to admit contradiction, that from such animals the whole contents of the cerebrum may be taken out, leaving the cerebellum, and the rest of the system uninjured, and the animal continue to live, in perfect health, an indefinite period. he mentions particularly a case of 10½ months survivance of a pullet. in that state the animal is deprived of every sense, of perception intelligence, memory and thought of every degree, it will perish on a heap of grain, unless you cram it down it's throat. it retains the power of motion, but, feeling no motive, it never moves unless from external excitement. he demonstrates in fact that the cerebrum is the organ of thought, & possesses alone the faculty of thinking.[70]

Jefferson's fascination with vivisection might remind the reader of the visionary stare and the self-hypnotized expression on the face of the bath-robed scientist in Joseph Wright of Derby's 1768 painting, *An Experiment on a Bird in the Air Pump*. The progress of science was not without the moral hazards that Mary Shelley, a young woman of 20 years, imagined while completing her novel *Frankenstein* in 1818. Meanwhile, Jefferson was dictating the scientific curriculum for the University of Virginia and still recommending Bacon's Latin works from the 1600s for a list of readings in the "sciences," but failing to grasp Professor Emmett's need

[69] Jefferson to François Adriaan Van der Kemp, January 17, 1813, mentions Cuvier's discovery of the mastodon, and Jefferson's donation of specimens to the American Philosophical Society at Philadelphia.

[70] Jefferson to François Adriaan Van der Kemp, January 11, 1825.

to focus on his specialty. While his letters concerning the work of Flourens reveal an amateur's seeking to stay abreast of new research, his letter to Emmett reveals that he had not yet overturned all the idols that Francis Bacon had sought to banish. As Alexander Pope saw it, Isaac Newton had "girded up his loins" to manfully take up the challenge of John Milton "to assert eternal providence, and justify the ways of God to man":

> Nature and Nature's laws lay hid in night:
> God said, Let Newton be! and all was light.

Jefferson's communications on science still spoke of the "known operations of nature," as Newton had seen them, and the "power of reason to maintain itself against error." His political science still invoked nature's God, decades after Laplace had declared that he "had no need" of Newton's hand-of-God "hypothesis." Whether in the natural or in the social sciences, Jefferson's method was to first discover Nature's laws, then utilize them as axioms, from which all other useful knowledge could be deduced through flawless syllogisms. Jefferson the Baconian had ended up an Aristotelian after all, but his was a new Aristotelianism, based on flawless Newtonian truths. Unfortunately for those certainties in which the Enlightenment rejoiced, scientists were already born who were destined to witness the dismay of Albert A. Michelson and Edward W. Morley when their "failed experiment" at a university on the Western Reserve presented classical physics with the first of many unanticipated questions for which Newton had no answers. New problems were beginning to arise more rapidly than science could even formulate them. Jefferson's faith in Enlightenment progress and Alexander Pope's exuberant certitude would now seem premature, for once again it appeared as if "Nature and Nature's Laws lay hid in night." The Enlightenment was an age of self-assurance; the nineteenth century was to end at a precipice of doubt.[71]

[71] I refer, of course, to the experiment performed in 1887 by Albert A. Michelson and Edward W. Morley at Western Reserve University, which failed to detect the phenomenology of an "aether" and led to the inference that the speed of light is a constant and unaffected by the movement of the object from which a beam of light is projected. The experiment was the first warning to future generations that the number of scientific questions was increasing, and that mankind might never be able to formulate, much less to "shed light" on, the continual multiplication of new questions in the field of physics. At present, new questions seem to be appearing more rapidly than they can be solved.

8

Anthropology and Ethnic Cleansing: White "Rubbish," Blacks, and Indians

BACONIAN METHOD AND JEFFERSON'S SOCIAL SCIENCE

As certainly and unequivocally as Thomas Aquinas' *Summa Theologica* was intended to defend his Church's dogmas, so was Jefferson's *Notes on Virginia* intended to defend the reputation of his country. As soon as it was published, Jefferson began to distribute it to selected Parisian men of high social standing. One of these, the Marquis de Chastellux, received also a cover letter that was clearly a polemic in defense of a polemic. The *Notes* were compiled as a refutation of the views of the French mathematician Georges-Louis Leclerc, Comte de Buffon, "on the general question of the degeneracy of animals in America." They were also a response to claims of the Abbé Raynal, "as to the degeneracy of the man of Europe transplanted to America."[1] It was fundamentally and deliberately patriotic in its goals. He conceived his country first and foremost as Virginia itself, although throughout the text he made it clear that he was beginning to imagine his country as a continental empire extending beyond the Mississippi, and to the Great Plains where the buffalo and perhaps even the mighty mammoth still roamed. Why did he think there might be elephants wandering the Great Plains? Aside from reasons grounded in his metaphysical presumptions, it was because he had heard there were American Indian legends to that effect.

Thomas Jefferson's ethnic and racial concepts were prime examples of what Francis Bacon had called "*idolus speculi*," prejudices one derives from "his education and association with others, or the books he reads and the several authorities of those whom he cultivates and admires." But

[1] Jefferson to the Marquis de Chastellux, June 7, 1785.

while Jefferson's attitudes on the future of African and Native Americans were common among his contemporaries, they were not universally shared. David Ramsay, Gilbert Imlay, and William Short were among those who took exception to at least some of them.[2] In social studies, as in natural science, he struggled to maintain an open mind, but often failed to keep abreast of the broad variety of contemporary opinion. His lack of methodological rigor, his lapses of intellectual discipline, and his failure to practice the best of scholarly traditions are difficult to ignore. Thomas Aquinas, whom Jefferson once cited with respect, set a standard for the anticipation of counter-arguments, systematically applying the scholastic method of dialectics, or *disputatio*.[3] By contrast, Jefferson tended to overlook alternative opinions to which he had access, sometimes bypassing items in his own library, such as the previously mentioned article on the megalonyx by José Carriga. With respect to Indian people, his philosophy was coldly rational. His most consistent resettlement policy towards the Indians was to convince them to cede their lands in the East and to push them towards the West. His attitudes, as we shall see, were seamlessly continuous with those of Andrew Jackson. Both men's policies – and they understood one another very well – were what we would today call "ethnic cleansing." He wrote to George Rogers Clark concerning Indian removal in language that was disturbing: "we must leave it to yourself to decide on the object of the campaign. If against these Indians, the end proposed should be their extermination, or their removal beyond the lakes or Illinois river. The same world will scarcely do for them and us."[4]

[2] Nicholas Guyat, in *Bind Us Apart: How Enlightened Americans Invented Racial Segregation* (New York: Basic Books, 2016), p. 26, notes that David Ramsay and Gilbert Imlay took issue with Jefferson's comments on African Americans in *Notes on Virginia*, citing Ramsay to Jefferson, May 3, 1786, and Gilbert Imlay, *A Topographical Description of the Western Territory of North America* (Dublin: William Jones, 1793), pp. 184–185. Ta-Nehisi Coates, in "The Myth of Jefferson as 'a Man of His Times'," *Atlantic Monthly* (December 2, 2012), offers an excellent discussion of Jefferson's close friend, William Short, and his efforts to persuade Jefferson towards a more immediate emancipationism, citing Short's lengthy letter to Jefferson, February 27, 1798.

[3] As noted in another chapter, Jefferson quoted approvingly a theological opinion attributed to St. Thomas Aquinas.

[4] Jefferson to George Rogers Clark, January 1, 1779 [i.e. 1780]; José Carriga in his 1796 publication, *Description del esquelleto de un quadrupedo muy corpulento y raro que se conserva en el Real Gabinete de Historia Natural de Madrid.* Julian P. Boyd notes that Jefferson had come into possession of a copy of the Carriga paper by the time he left Paris in 1789, but forgot that he had seen it. Stephen Rowland, a historian of geology, also notes the Carriga paper. See Steve Rowland, "The Fossil Record," published lecture notes for "The Fossil Record" course at the University of Nevada, Las Vegas, August 2010. Also see Julian P. Boyd, "The Megalonyx, the Megatherium, and Thomas Jefferson's Lapse of

The first choice was "extermination," the second was "removal," and both words should be disturbing. Jefferson's Indian policies, like Frederick the Great's resettlement policies towards the Jews, called for a brutal displacement. Both Jefferson and Frederick viewed the Jewish people as non-assimilable; in Jefferson's case, this was a result of their own character. Political enemies might be compared to the Jewish people. The Federalists were a tribe "marked, like the Jews, with such a peculiarity of character, as to constitute from that circumstance the natural division of our parties."[5] Neither Jefferson nor Frederick was anti-Semitic in identical thuggish manner to the Nazis. Frederick was not guilty of genocide, although he resettled Jewish and other populations to suit his interests, but, quite aside from the Jewish people, his national policy consisted of sacrificing human lives to gain land. Jefferson saw America's Manifest Destiny as a trade of lives for land. The difference was that Jefferson was less willing to risk his own neck and dirty his own hands on the battlefield than Frederick was.

In a letter of June 23, 1812, John Adams opined to Jefferson that the ancient history of the Native American populations "was of no moment to the present or future happiness of man." Jefferson did not respond specifically to Adams' pontification, for he found Native American studies intellectually intriguing not for utilitarian purposes, but in their own right. The history of vanished civilizations had no bearing whatever on whether transplanted Europeans in America might be on a trajectory of decline – or did it? Suppose Buffon's degeneration theory had been correct, what would have been the consequences of his theory for American republicanism? If, indeed, the continent of North America was inhospitable to human progress, and if the American experiment was inevitably doomed, it mattered little what Buffon or Jefferson had to say about the matter. If Buffon was wrong, then time and the vigor of the American yeoman would demonstrate the falsity of his theories.

Jefferson's letter to Chastellux made some of the most sweeping and unsupported claims, offering no justification or explanation for its assertion that the Indians of South America do not manifest the "original character" of their race, or that those of North America do. The South Americans had fallen from their earlier state of civilization and had degenerated "through ten generations of slavery." The letter to

Memory," *Proceedings of the American Philosophical Society*, 102, no. 5 (October 20, 1958), 420–435.

[5] Jefferson to John Taylor, June 1, 1798.

Chastellux was commendable in that it held out hope for the evolution of native North Americans, but it also demonstrated Jefferson's intellectual inconstancy. Within a few pages of *Notes*, Jefferson could shift from the mechanical metaphor of the fixed link to the organic metaphor of the mutating organism. On the whole, his statements in the *Notes*, as elsewhere, reveal a fundamental bias against the evolutionary metaphysic of his contemporary, Jean-Baptiste Lamarck (1744–1829), which allowed species to evolve in response to environmental factors. It is therefore startling that he suggested to Chastellux not only that the Indian might be elevated and improved, but perhaps even the African American:

> I believe the Indian then to be in body and mind equal to the whiteman. I have supposed the blackman, in his present state, might not be so. But it would be hazardous to affirm that, equally cultivated for a few generations, he would not become so.[6]

For the *Notes*, Jefferson constructed an impressive statistical chart of selected Indian nations in the East, and eventually he was destined to read Lewis and Clark's reports on Indian peoples of the far West. He lamented the disappearance of ancient Indian languages, although there is no evidence that he ever learned to speak any of those that remained extant.

> Of the Indian of South America I know nothing; for I would not honor with the appellation of knowledge, what I derive from the fables published of them. These I believe to be just as true as the fables of Aesop. This belief is founded on what I have seen of man, white, red, and black, and what has been written of him by authors, enlightened themselves, and writing amidst an enlightened people. The Indian of North America being more within our reach, I can speak of him somewhat from my own knowledge.[7]

Jefferson does not make clear whether he is speaking of the Inca of Peru, the Maya of Guatemala, or the Aztecs of Mexico. He says he knows nothing of South America, having heard nothing but "fables published of them," but he does not name the works that he considers fabulous. As far as Native Americans were concerned, he knew only those east of the Mississippi, and even there, Jefferson was not one of those who could speak most knowledgeably about their manners and customs. He had never fought against them, as had Andrew Jackson, never been adopted by an Indian family, as was Daniel Boone, never negotiated with them on

[6] Jefferson to the Marquis de Chastellux, June 7, 1785.

[7] Thomas Jefferson, *Notes on the State of Virginia*, ed. David Waldstreicher (Boston, MA: Bedford Books, 2002), p. 121.

their own turf, as had Benjamin Franklin, and he did not know their languages.

He supervised the excavation of an Indian mound on his own property, and he has long been credited with being among the first persons ever to excavate a site stratigraphically.[8] His efforts have been described as advanced for their date, and superior to those of Heinrich Schliemann, the German businessman, later famous for the excavation and partial destruction of the site that he believed to be ancient Troy. Both men, in their amateurish enthusiasm, "murdered to dissect," for in the process each damaged or destroyed much of the site.[9] Like Napoleon's invasion of Egypt, which discovered the Rosetta Stone and mutilated the Sphinx, Jefferson's activities had mixed consequences and obliterated much of the very history that he believed himself to be unearthing. Jefferson devoted several pages of *Notes on Virginia* to describing his approach, which, although systematic, reflected, as did Schliemann's, a failure to anticipate methodological questions that might be posed by later researchers. It should also be noted that he conducted his excavations with almost no regard for the fact that he was violating sacred ground.

Jefferson is to be commended for his spirit of investigation, and perhaps he may even deserve the accolade "father of American archeology," although we know very little of his methods or his findings, other than what he preserved in a few paragraphs in *Notes on Virginia*, and a few subsequent references in his correspondence. These indicate that he maintained an interest in Native American languages and cultures that persisted

[8] Karl Lehmann-Hartlebe, "Thomas Jefferson, Archaeologist," *American Journal of Archaeology*, 47 (1943), 161. William H. Stiebing, Jr., "Who First Excavated Stratigraphically?" *Biblical Archaeology Review* (January–February, 1981), 52–53.

[9] William R. H. Cunnington (1754–1810) was responsible for early modern excavations in the vicinity of Stonehenge and elsewhere in England. His methods were no less destructive than Jefferson's, and it was not until the twentieth century that archeologists began to understand that the excavation of a site, even at best, always necessitates its destruction, and hence the irretrievable loss of the artifacts' historic context. See William R. H. Cunnington, *From Antiquary to Archaeologist: Study of William Cunnington of Heytesbury*, ed. James Dyer (London: Shire Publications, 1975). Also see David Boyd Haycock, "William Cunnington," in the *Oxford Dictionary of National Biography*. Wikipedia says that the eighteenth-century archeologist John Aubrey was "ahead of his time" (whatever that means) and references a work by Michael Hunter, *John Aubrey and the Realm of Learning* (London: Duckworth, 1975), pp. 156–157, 162–166, 181. Wikipedia also mentions William Cunnington's excavations in Wiltshire ca. 1798; Paul Everill, "The Parkers of Heytesbury: Archaeological Pioneers," *Proceedings of the Society of Antiquaries of London*, 90 (2010), 441–453; Paul Everill, "Invisible Pioneers," *British Archaeology*, 108 (2009), 40–43.

throughout his life. As president, he notably charged the expedition of Lewis and Clark with the exploration of and amassing of data on Native American life and customs. In comparison with many Americans in the early nineteenth century, he showed amazing intellectual curiosity, but in the main Jefferson's approach to indigenous cultures was destructive.[10]

Unlike John Adams, Jefferson did not consider studies of Native Americans to be "of no moment." Nonetheless, he commented disparagingly on the content of the Indian mounds, saying, "I know of no such thing existing as an Indian monument: for I would not honour with that name arrow points, stone hatchets, stone pipes, and half-shapen images." This was puzzling to the anthropologist A. F. C. Wallace, who thought that Jefferson must have known of Indian earthworks in Virginia more impressive than those he famously excavated.[11] Jefferson's blanket disparagement of all Indian earthworks is puzzling in view of the fact that he was certainly aware of other "Indian mounds" in Virginia than those he excavated. Some of these massive earthworks and pyramids had been thoroughly discussed in literature antedating the *Notes*, and it is difficult to imagine that Jefferson could have spent his entire life in Virginia without having overheard or participated in conversations concerning them. It is clear that he continued to receive reports on the lost civilization of the mound builders throughout his life. In 1820 he acknowledged receipt of a copy of Caleb Atwater's *Description of the Antiquities Discovered in the State of Ohio and Other Western States.* He thanked the sender, Isaiah Thomas, and the American Antiquarian Society, of which he was president, saying, "It is truly pleasing to hope that, by their attentions, the monuments of the character and condition of the people who preceded us in the occupation of this great country will be rescued from oblivion before they will have entirely disappeared."[12]

In the course of his excavation, he was aware that these burial mounds had "considerable notoriety among the Indians." He recalled that the site had once been visited by an Indian party:

[10] John Adams to Jefferson, "of no moment," in a letter of June 28, 1812. Lehmann-Hartlebe, "Thomas Jefferson, Archaeologist," 161. See also Stiebing, "Who First Excavated Stratigraphically?" 52–53. Also see Waldstreicher, introduction to Jefferson, *Notes on Virginia*, previously cited. For "father of American archeology," see Brian Steele, "Jefferson's Legacy" in Francis D. Cogliano, ed., *A Companion to Thomas Jefferson* (Malden, MA: Wiley-Blackwell, 2012).

[11] Anthony F. C. Wallace, *Jefferson and the Indians: The Tragic Fate of the First Americans* (Cambridge, MA: Belknap Press, 2001), Chapter 5, pp. 130–160; also see p. 338. For stone pipes, see p. 133.

[12] Jefferson to Isaiah Thomas, October 14, 1820.

passing, about thirty years ago, through the part of the country where this barrow is, [and] went through the woods directly to it, without any instructions or enquiry, and having staid about it some time, with expressions which were construed to be those of sorrow, they returned to the high road, which they had left about half a dozen miles to pay this visit, and pursued their journey. [13]

As previously noted, he referred disparagingly to the contents of the mounds, "arrow points, stone hatchets, stone pipes, and half-shapen images," but in this context, he does not systematically chart or describe any such artifacts. He also records having found and examined human teeth and bones. The Native Americans who were accustomed to visit this site might have expressed sadness at his disturbing these human remains, but Jefferson did not mention it.

In Query XI of his *Notes on Virginia*, Jefferson asserted that Native Americans lived without "any shadow of government" and that they had no laws. This is remarkable in comparison to Benjamin Franklin's observations of three decades earlier with reference to the Iroquois confederation – "It would be a strange thing if Six Nations of ignorant savages should be capable of forming a scheme for such an union, and be able to execute it in such a manner as that it has subsisted ages and appears indissoluble."[14] Some historians have made exaggerated and romantic claims concerning the influence of the Iroquois Federation on the political traditions of the United States. It has even been gushingly suggested that the Constitution of the United States owes its fundamentals to the Iroquois model. While one need not accept any such extravagant notion, it is certainly appropriate to recognize that Indian peoples were capable of complicated and sophisticated political institutions.[15]

Jefferson's later admission in the same chapter that the Native Americans established confederacies is difficult to reconcile with his belief that they had neither laws nor governments. This contradiction between fact and opinion is poor evidence of a Baconian dedication to discovery through observation; it shows a compulsion to "feign hypotheses" in

[13] Jefferson mentions a visit by Indians to their ancestral mounds in *Notes on Virginia*, p. 150.

[14] Elizabeth Tooker, "The United States Constitution and the Iroquois League," *Ethnohistory*, 35, no. 4 (autumn, 1988), 305–336.

[15] The online journal, *History Network* (July 21, 2005), http://historynewsnetwork.org/article/12974, contains Jack Rakove's "Did the Founding Fathers Really Get Many of Their Ideas of Liberty from the Iroquois? Fact & Fiction," and a quotation from Gordon Wood's attack on the "implausible assertion" that the Iroquois' "Great Law of Peace" had a direct influence on the United States Constitution. Rakove also references Tooker, "The United States Constitution and the Iroquois League," cited above.

service to an ideological purpose. Perhaps his agenda was to support his *a priori* notions regarding the *hypothetical* state of nature, in which government was unnecessary, a state in which noble savages enjoyed a state of happy anarchy. Even Thomas Paine, as he revealed in *Common Sense*, was open to the "common sense" argument that people, though in a primitive state, must have a rudimentary notion of statecraft.[16] Jefferson, on the basis of no apparent investigations, simply asserted that Native Americans had no concept of law and no "shadow of government." Modern scholars may disagree as to the nature of government among the original peoples of the Eastern United States, and they are correctly skeptical as to whether these peoples' institutions provided a model for the United States Constitution, but Franklin knew that Native Americans were able to institutionalize codes of political conduct and develop authoritative notions of social organization.

A letter of February 16, 1803, written to General Andrew Jackson illustrates what Sean Wilentz, in another instance, has called Jefferson's "Machiavellian benevolence towards the Indians." It also reveals continuity between Jeffersonian and Jacksonian Indian policy.[17] In the letter to Jackson, he expressed his discomfort with the handling of land policy by Indian agent Benjamin Hawkins. The policy must be officially directed "towards the attainment of our two objects of peace and lands." He was happy that Hawkins had gained the confidence of the Indians, but – and here he slipped into the passive voice – "doubts are entertained by some whether he is not more attached to the interests of the Indians than of the United States." Jefferson liked to make the claim that he was "not willing to substitute suspicion for proof" when he had already made a negative judgment, and, as we have seen, he had definitely asserted a proof. This we can readily see in his judgments on African abilities in Query XIV of *Notes on Virginia*. So he turned to the judicious and fair-minded Andrew Jackson, asking that he keep a sharp eye on Hawkins:

I shall always be open to any proofs that he obstructs cessions of land which the Indians are willing to make; and of this, Sir, you may be assured, that he shall be

[16] Thomas Paine, "Of the Origin of Government in General . . ., " in *Common Sense* (1776).

[17] Sean Wilentz characterizes Jefferson's policies as "Machiavellian" in *Major Problems in the Early Republic 1787–1848* (Lexington, KY: D. C. Heath, 1992), p. 130, using an excerpt from the letter from Jefferson to Benjamin Harrison, February, 1803. Also see Robert M. Owens, *Mr. Jefferson's Hammer: William Henry Harrison* (University of Oklahoma Press, 2011). Peter Onuf, *Jefferson's Empire* (Charlottesville, VA: University of Virginia Press, 2000), p. 49, also contains critical observations on Jefferson's Indian policy expressed in this letter.

placed under as strong a pressure from the executive to obtain cessions as he can feel from any opposite quarter to obstruct. He shall be made sensible that his value will be estimated by us in proportion to the benefits he can obtain for us.[18]

In writing directly to Hawkins, on February 18, two days later, he was subtle in the application of the "pressure" that he had promised in the letter to Andrew Jackson. He did not accuse Hawkins of obstruction, as he had in the letter to Jackson, but wrote to him as a sympathetic friend. Rather than speaking of the inevitable disappearance of Indian peoples and cultures, he spoke of converting them to civilization, and even possibly assimilating them. As Americans, the Native Americans would come to see the superior value of cultivated over uncultivated lands. In the same letter, he wrote as if "the natural progress of things" would be to blend them in with white Americans. But he also wrote in contradictory fashion, "surely it will be better for them to be identified with us, and preserved in the occupation of their lands," which shifted in mid clause from a separate to an assimilated destiny. Then he swiveled suddenly back to assimilationism, for surely it was better for them to be absorbed "than be exposed to the many casualties which may endanger them while a separate people." The structure of this vacillation between preservation of Indian lands and their acquisition, between mixing and preservation, reveals a deep ambivalence regarding the ultimate destiny of Native Americans. But whatever their fate, be it assimilation or separatism, they ought to be paring off their lands:

the wisdom of the animal which amputates & abandons to the hunter the parts for which he is pursued, should be theirs, with this difference that the former sacrifices what is useful. the latter what is not. in truth the ultimate point of rest & happiness for them is to let our settlements and theirs meet and blend together, to intermix and become one people, incorporating themselves with us as citizens of the US. [19]

In a letter to William Henry Harrison, February 27, 1803, he was tough again. Eventually the Indians might possibly be expected to "incorporate with us as citizens of the United States," but a better "termination of their history" would be for them to "remove beyond the Mississippi." He expressed his desire to see Indian people converted to the culture of the American small farmer; assuming incorrectly that all Native Americans were hunter-gatherers, and, observing correctly that the decrease of game in the West was inevitable, he wished "to draw them to agriculture, spinning, and weaving." Once they had become small farmers, they

[18] Jefferson to General Andrew Jackson, Washington, February 16, 1803.
[19] Jefferson to Benjamin Hawkins, February 18, 1803.

would presumably "perceive how useless to them are their extensive forests," and they would be "willing to pare them off from time to time in exchange for necessaries for their farms and families." It was, of course, "essential to cultivate their love," but more important to reinforce their fear, for they must see that "we have only to shut our hand to crush them."[20]

Jefferson's letter of August 28, 1807, to his Secretary of War, Henry Dearborn, was even more ominous:

> learning that some of them meditate war on us, we too are preparing for war against those, & those only who shall seek it: and that if ever we are constrained to lift the hatchet against any tribe, we will never lay it down till that tribe is exterminated, or driven beyond the Missisipi: adjuring them therefore, if they wish to remain on the land which covers the bones of their fathers, to keep the peace with a people who ask their friendship without needing it, who wish to avoid war without fearing it. in war they will kill some of us; we shall destroy all of them.

In giving advice to the Indian nations in 1806 his language was tough, ominous, and sternly paternalistic, consistent with the threats of his letter to Harrison. He said, "I have now an important advice to give you ... my children, we are strong, we are numerous as the stars in the heavens, & we are all gun-men." What gave him the right to speak to the Indian representatives as "My friends & children?" He was speaking to adults. Indians were as aware as whites that the world was a complex place, and that Europeans had guns. Indians had long been conscious of their precarious position with respect to the Euro-American empire and the global economy. This consciousness was already evident in 1620, when Tisquantum greeted the Pilgrims. He had already crossed the Atlantic and mastered European languages. Indians had not forgotten Joseph Brand's frustrated attempts during the Revolution to conduct a foreign diplomacy, or their increasingly vain attempts to win "a descent respect" in "the opinion of nations." Jefferson must certainly have imagined that Native Americans harbored resentments towards settlers, for he had alluded elsewhere to the resentments of black Americans towards whites. One wishes that in addressing Native Americans he had respected their intelligence sufficiently to make his threats more direct, and not have resorted to such disgustingly affected poetic diction. His condescending address to the chiefs was not only a deliberate insult, but a thinly veiled display of power.[21]

[20] Jefferson to William H. Harrison, February 27, 1803.

[21] Jefferson to Chiefs of Nations, January 4, 1806. Jefferson's Speech to a Delegation of Indian Chiefs, printed in Donald Jackson, ed., *Letters of the Lewis and Clark Expedition*

Jefferson's position on Indian Territory was founded in his more fundamental doctrine of "usufruct," an assertion that the right to landed property was limited to those who accepted his definition of its proper use. The right to land was tied to both Jeffersonian morality and Jeffersonian utility. Cultivation of land was the source of any right to it, and neither French aristocrats nor Native Americans had an unalienable right to lands that they were not putting to use as farms or plantations. The culture of the large planter was legitimate for Jefferson and his class, and so too "the culture of a small piece of land," in the case of Indian people, just as it was in the case of the ideal American citizen. Jeffersonian political economy, whether in the *Notes* or in his later presidential policy, always stressed the small farmer, not the big planter. But he never denied that the legitimate use of land also allowed for the preservation of pleasing prospects, such as the vistas he could survey at Monticello and Poplar Forest. Neither the Native Americans nor the crowned heads of Europe had a right to preserve such broad landscapes.

Jefferson's complicated attitudes towards the Native American population represent the continuing ambivalence of the people of the United States towards its indigenous peoples. While North America was no Garden of Eden when the first Europeans arrived, it was not a howling wilderness either. The settlement of North America by its European elites and their slaves and indentured servants involved the suppression and displacement of Indian people as a result of imported diseases, warfare, and appropriation of territory. It is impossible to reconcile the egalitarian morality of the Declaration of Independence with the westward march of civilization across the American continent. Although the descendants of African slaves and ragged European emigrants cannot be blamed for America's history of Indian massacre and displacement, honesty requires us to admit that even those of us whose ancestors arrived through Ellis Island or the slaver's auction blocks currently sit on land gained by the ruthless policies of William Henry Harrison, Andrew Jackson, and Thomas Jefferson.

ANTHROPOLOGY OF AFRICAN AMERICANS

Although by his own admission he "could not understand a word," as noted earlier, Jefferson compared Indian orators to Demosthenes and Cicero. He was quick to make invidious comparisons between the abilities

with Related Documents 1783–1854 (Urbana, Chicago, London: University of Illinois Press, 1978), vol. I.

of African Americans and Native Americans. He regretted "that though for a century and a half we have had under our eyes the races of black and of red men, they have never yet been viewed by us as subjects of natural history." Nonetheless, he continued to venture comparisons with respect to verbal abilities. As noted previously, he considered Phillis Wheatley's linguistic achievements "below the dignity of criticism." He damned Ignatius Sancho with faint praise, and was duplicitous in describing the book written by Benjamin Banneker. It was "self-evident" that Africans transplanted in the Americas showed little capacity for intellectual or artistic development; their cultural inferiority was possibly congenital and irremediable. But since he had "suspicion only," he would postpone judgment.

He observed in the *Notes* that Native Americans "often carve figures on their pipes not destitute of design or merit." But elsewhere in the *Notes* he disparaged the pipes and carvings he unearthed in Indian mounds. He had apparently never encountered any Africans in Virginia who showed an interest in wood-carving, or sewing, or other simple handicrafts. Had none of his slaves ever stitched a quilt, whittled on a stick, made a doll for her child, or drawn a pattern in the dust? In contrast to the disparaging comments above, there is the report of La Rochefoucauld of his visit to Monticello in 1796. The visiting nobleman was impressed by Monticello's African American skilled workers engaged in a wide range of arts and crafts:

> As he cannot expect any assistance from the two small neighbouring towns, every article is made on his farm; his negroes are cabinet-makers, carpenters, masons, bricklayers, smiths, &c. The children he employs in a nail-manufactory, which yields already a considerable profit. The young and old negresses spin for the clothing of the rest. He animates them by rewards and distinctions.[22]

It has long been maintained that New World slavery was not conducive to the preservation of West African arts, and this is partially true. West African arts, such as sculpture or mask-making, were intrinsically religious, and thus frightening to superstitious Europeans, who regarded African traditional masks and graven images as sinister and threatening. Throughout the Americas, the craft of drum-making was commonly

[22] François Alexandre, Duc de La Rochefoucauld-Liancourt, *Travels through the United States of North America, the Country of the Iroquois, and Upper Canada, in the years 1795, 1796, and 1797*, 2nd edn. (London, 1800), vol. III, pp. 157–158.

suppressed, because of a fear that drumming might be used for insurrectionary purposes.[23]

Jefferson considered contemporary travellers' accounts of African manners and customs unworthy of comment. With the striking exception of the footnotes in his translation of Volney's *The Ruins*, he seemed untouched by anything that might vindicate the history or the potential of African people for any achievements, and so he wrote of African Americans, "it would be unfair to follow them to Africa" to investigate their manners and customs. There is no indication that he ever contemplated a trip to Africa, and in any event the implication was that Africans self-evidently had no Old World traditions that merited observation. It would not have been in his nature to undertake an expedition of exploration in order to employ the Baconian process of collecting evidence, as had the Comte de Bougainville in his explorations in North America and the South Seas.[24] Perhaps he meant to imply that travellers' accounts of Africans were unreliable. He was dismissive of such accounts respecting South America, as we have seen, although he offered no specific grounds for his skepticism. As far as accounts of African peoples were concerned, as we shall see, some were available to him, but apparently he did not consider these worthy of examination or appraisal.

[23] African traditions in sculpture, while only rarely preserved in North America, were more frequently retained in the Caribbean. See Robert Farris Thompson, *Flash of the Spirit* (New York: Random House, 1983). Banning of drums, *National Geographic* online, Thursday, October 28, 2010. John Michael Vlach, "Rooted in Africa, Raised in America: The Traditional Arts and Crafts of African-Americans across Five Centuries" in *Freedom's Story: Teaching African American Literature and History* (George Washington University, National Humanities Center, 2008, online at http://nationalhumanitiescenter.org/tserve/freedom/1609-1865/essays/africa.htm), describes a drum in the British Museum collected in Virginia ca. 1730–45 and decorated after the mode of the Akan peoples of what is now Ghana. Sharon Patton, *African-American Art* (Oxford University Press, 1998), mentions the carpentry skills of John Hemings and other African American artisans in the early republic. Also see Richard Powell's article, "Art, African American" in Henry Louis Gates and Anthony Appiah, eds., *Africana: The Encyclopedia of the African and African-American Experience*, 2nd edn. (Oxford University Press, 2005). James E. Newton, "Slave Artisans and Craftsmen: The Roots of Afro-American Art," *The Black Scholar*, 9, no. 3 (November, 1977), 35–42. James E. Newton and Ronald L. Lewis, *The Other Slaves: Mechanics, Artisans, and Craftsmen* (Boston, MA: G. K. Hall and Co., 1978). James Sidbury, "Slave Artisans in Richmond Virginia, 1780–1810" in Howard B. Rock, Paul A. Gilje, and Robert Asher, eds., *American Artisans: Crafting Social Identity, 1750–1850* (Baltimore: Johns Hopkins University Press, 1995), pp. 48–62. S. Sydney Bradford, "The Negro Ironworker in Ante Bellum Virginia," *Journal of Southern History*, 25 (May, 1959), 194–206.

[24] Bougainville's travels influenced the myth of "the noble savage" in *Le Voyage autour du monde* (1766).

It would not be "unfair" to expect Jefferson to consult such contemporary travellers' accounts of African peoples as were available, but he displayed his usual penchant for either ignoring the research of his contemporaries or dismissing it without explanation. We know that as early as 1797, and certainly by the time of the later editions of the *Notes on Virginia*, Jefferson was acquainted with Anders Sparrman's *Voyage to the Cape of Good Hope*, translated from Swedish into English in 1785. He cited it at least once, but there is no evidence that he read it before or after issuing his revised American edition of the *Notes*.[25] By contrast, the German philosopher Herder based his opinions of Africa on Sparrman's *Voyage*, with its lofty appraisal of African virtues. Mungo Park published his *Travels in the Interior Districts of Africa* in 1799; Jefferson eventually possessed a copy, but there is no record of his reaction to it.[26] He had no need to entertain such sources, beginning with the premise that "it would be unfair to follow them to Africa" and that African Americans, once freed, must be removed, either to Africa or elsewhere. Self-evidently they must be isolated from the possibility of any additional admixture, a process that was obviously advancing at Monticello, but which he irrationally presumed would be prevented by their continued enslavement.

ETHNIC CLEANSING OF AFRICAN AMERICANS

Jefferson's ethnic cleansing policy with respect to the black population may not have been sincere, in that it involved an elaborate big-government program and considerable expense. His attitude towards African Americans was dichotomous, since it was based on two mutually exclusive and mutually contradictory premises – that African slavery was necessary, but that the African population must be expunged. Neither Jefferson and

[25] Anders Sparrman, *A Voyage to the Cape of Good Hope, towards the Antarctic Polar Circle, and round the World: But Chiefly into the Country of the Hottentots and Caffres, from the Year 1772, to 1776 ... Translated from the Swedish Original*, 2 vols. (London: G. G. J. and J. Robinson, 1786). Jefferson cited this volume in his "Memoir on the Megalonyx" [February 10, 1797], Founders Online. By 1800 Jefferson felt obliged to defend some of the statements he had made in the *Notes on Virginia*, but apparently not those on the abilities of Africans, and certainly none that might have been influenced by Sparrman.

[26] Mungo Park, *Travels in the Interior Districts of Africa: Performed ... in the Years 1795, 1796, and 1797 (2 Volumes)* (London: John Murray, 1799, 1815). For Sparrman's *Voyage*, see James Gilreath and Douglas L. Wilson, eds., *Thomas Jefferson's Library: A Catalog with the Entries in His Own Order* (Washington, DC: Library of Congress, 1989), entry number 156.

his class nor the "Free Africans" flocked to the Society for the Colonization of Free People of Color of America when it was founded in 1816. The black ship-captain Paul Cuffe, who resettled a small company of African Americans in Sierra Leone, chose not to migrate himself. His wife was Native American. While never contented with their subordinate position in America, few African Americans were inclined to make an exodus. Jefferson's resettlement plans for African Americans were, in any case, ambivalent, and the plans never took any concrete, practical form.[27]

Paul Finkelman assumes, reasonably enough, that Jefferson did not like black folks, citing the negative description of Africans in *Notes on Virginia*, and observing that Jefferson complained of their odor and denied the physical attractions of unmixed Africans. Finkelman's inferences are rational, but Jefferson certainly spent a great deal of time breathing the same air as "his people," in the fields, in the sweaty environment of the forge, and in the dining-room, where his food was prepared by Sally Hemings' brother. Respecting interracial sex, it is a well-known fact that Senator Strom Thurmond fathered a child with an underage black house servant, then proceeded to serve consecutively as governor of North Carolina and United States senator from that same state until 2001, while celebrated for his advocacy of racial segregation. Jefferson's attitude resembles that of white boys I knew in my youth, who, although they told insensitive racist jokes, enjoyed cavorting nude in the locker room with black boys, hugged and kissed their black teammates after a spectacular play, and visited black prostitutes with exuberance.

> Thick pouting lips! How sweet their grace!
> When passion fires to kiss them! [28]

[27] Peterson, *Thomas Jefferson, Writings*, pp. 998–1000. See Osmane K. Power-Greene, *Against Wind and Tide: The African Struggle against the Colonization Movement* (New York University Press, 2014); Floyd Miller, *The Search for a Black Nationality* (Chicago: University of Illinois Press, 1975); Wilson J. Moses, *Liberian Dreams: Back-to-Africa Narratives from the 1850s* (Philadelphia, PA : University of Pennsylvania Press, 1998). As of this writing, the article at Wikipedia presents a nuanced and complicated treatment of the American Colonization Society and its contradictory and competing objectives, and intelligent footnotes offering a guide to sources, not all of which are duplicated in the bibliography; see https://en.wikipedia.org/wiki/American_Colonization_Society

[28] Paul Finkelman, *Slavery and the Founders: Race and Liberty in the Age of Jefferson*, 2nd edn. (Armonk, NY: M. E. Sharpe, 2001), pp. 180–181. Satirical ballad from the anti-Jefferson press in 1802, quoted in Winthrop Jordan, *White over Black: American Attitudes toward the Negro, 1550–1812* (Chapel Hill: University of North Carolina Press, 1968), p. 468. Michael Janofsky, "Thurmond Kin Acknowledge Black Daughter," *The New York Times* (December 16, 2004).

Historians such as Roger Abrahams and Michael Sobel have noted the cultural contacts between white and black Southerners under slavery. Even some of the most bigoted Americans enjoy consuming food prepared by Negroes, and watching them dance, sing, and play sports. James Hugo Johnston and others have shown that race relations in Virginia and miscegenation in the Old South involved frequent violations of supposed cultural norms.[29] Isaac Jefferson, a Monticello slave, reported that Jefferson's brother, Randolph, "used to come out among black people, play the fiddle and dance half the night." Members of the Jefferson family attributed Negro-loving pursuits to Jefferson's nephew, Peter Carr.[30] By the same token, African Americans have been attracted to various white American cultural norms. Blacks of all social classes and all regions adopted American Christianity in both its enthusiastic and more sedate forms. Africans learned to read, and were exposed to the better aspects of European and American culture, coming, as one eighteenth-century African author put it, to relish their society and manners.[31]

Despite the "ten thousand recollections, by the blacks, of the injuries they have sustained," at Monticello as elsewhere in America, blacks and whites, whether they liked it or not, were bound together biologically, socially, and emotionally.[32] While the majority bitterly resented racial subordination, they were not constantly plotting violence against whites. In the course of a lifetime, the behavior of a slave might reveal variable expressions of acceptance, accommodation, and resistance. Why Jefferson chose to emphasize the supposedly ineffaceable resentments that blacks felt towards whites is puzzling, since some of his enslaved people were friendly and loyal to him. One even helped to conceal the family silver when Jefferson fled Monticello before the advance of British troops. But in peacetime and in war, Jefferson was constantly exposed to specific examples of slave loyalty everywhere he looked, and the

[29] James Hugo Johnston, *Race Relations in Virginia and Miscegenation in the South* (University of Chicago Press, 1939). Roger D. Abrahams, *Singing the Master: The Emergence of African-American Culture in the Plantation South* (New York: Penguin Books, 1992). Michael Sobel, *The World They Made Together: Black and White Values in Eighteenth-Century Virginia* (Princeton University Press, 1987).

[30] Isaac Jefferson, *Memoirs of a Monticello Slave as Dictated to Charles Campbell in the 1840s by Isaac, one of Thomas Jefferson's Slaves* (Charlottesville, VA: University of Virginia Press, 1951), p. 49. For Peter Carr, see Fawn Brodie's *Thomas Jefferson: An Intimate History* (New York: Norton, 1974), pp. 494–497.

[31] *The Interesting Narrative of Olaudah Equiano or Gustavus Vassa, the African, Written by Himself* (New York: Penguin, 1995 [1794]), p. 77.

[32] Jefferson, *Notes on Virginia*, pp. 175–176.

motivations of African Americans ranged from the self-interested to the sentimental.[33]

Both the British Empire and the United States sought to manipulate African American loyalties during the wars from 1776 to 1815, and both undertook plans for their resettlement in West Africa. Jefferson received a letter from William Short in 1798 mentioning C. B. Waldstrom's 1794 *Essay on Colonization, Particularly Applied to the Western Coast of Africa*, published in London, which contained a description of the colony of Sierra Leone, where the British had settled some of the black loyalists evacuated after the American Revolution. Waldstrom collaborated with Sparrman in an enterprise to "promote the civilization" of Africa. Representing himself to be "a zealous friend to the Africans," the author sought "to diffuse among them a spirit of liberal commerce." Cultivation and commerce, by "rendering the mind active, would early dispose it for the reception of pure moral instruction, [and] could not fail to become the vehicles of ideas and inventions ... Morality or religion would of consequence soon prevail; and the human species thereby would be ultimately improved and exalted."[34] Waldstrom praised the virtue of the pristine Africans, remarking on their probity, hospitality, and sense of justice. Short mentioned the explorations of several recent travellers, reporting that "one of them has discovered a city larger than London." Admitting the possibility of exaggeration, "still it leaves enough to suppose a state of civilization far advanced." Short believed "that our posterity at least will see improved, populous & extensive nations of the black color, formed into powerful societies who will par in every respect with whites under the same circumstances."[35]

SLAVERY AND MISCEGENATION

Jefferson's thoughts on slavery and miscegenation are well known and are mentioned in proximity to his comparison of American with Roman slavery. He noted that Roman slaves were, to begin with, "their rarest artists. They excelled too in science," although unlike Benjamin Franklin and Alexander Hamilton, he had never sponsored a school for black

[33] Annette Gordon-Reed discusses the legend of Martin Hemings' hiding the Jefferson's silver in *The Hemingses of Monticello* (New York: Norton, 2008), pp. 139–140.

[34] C. B. Waldstrom, *An Essay on Colonization Particularly Applied to the Western Coast of Africa* (London: Darton and Harvey, 1794), p. iii.

[35] William Short to Jefferson, February 27, 1798.

children. *Notes on Virginia* summarized the ways in which slavery in the Roman republic had been harsher than in the United States. Claiming, as seen earlier in this chapter, that he was "not willing to substitute suspicion for proof," he observed that Roman slaves had advanced to high levels in the arts and sciences, whereas Africans had not, and this "proves that their inferiority is not merely of their condition of life."[36]

True, the Romans had sometimes freed their slaves, but:

> Among the Romans emancipation required but one effort. The slave, when made free, might mix with, without staining, the blood of his master. But with us a second is necessary, unknown to history. When freed, he is to be removed beyond the reach of mixture.

The mixing of races came from slavery, not freedom. On southern plantations the truth of racial mixing was self-evident. White males were the progenitors of a mulatto population, and yet Jefferson argued, against reason and experience, that slavery prevented sexual interaction rather than encouraged it. The product was mulatto women, often with "the fine mixtures of red and white," graced with "flowing hair" and other "circumstance of superior beauty," temptingly beautiful hybrid women who could produce that son white enough looking to mix with "the blood of his master."

Short did not think the absorption of a black population presented an insuperable problem, in the biogenetic sense, and their social assimilation could be solved if "the owners of slaves begin to prepare them as well as themselves for the gradual transmutation."[37] The matter of color, he thought, would be mitigated by the North American climate. The physical traits of black people that Jefferson felt undesirable would eventually disappear. At the time no one understood how many millennia it had actually required for blue-eyed blonds to evolve out of the prehistoric populations that had once migrated out of Africa. But Short was also willing to consider racial admixture and mulaticization as a solution. The white population was large enough to absorb the blacks eventually, perhaps not without a trace, but probably the end result would be a population resembling that of southern Italy:

> Even in our own country there are some people darker, than the gradual mixture of the blacks can ever make us, & yet I do not know that they suffer from thence—I don't know if you ever saw, a Mrs. Randolph afterwards Mrs. Tucker,—There is

[36] Jefferson, *Notes on Virginia*, pp. 175–180.
[37] William Short to Jefferson, February 27, 1798.

no country that might not be content to have its women like her—There is no sentiment arising from the contemplation of beauty that they would not be capable of inspiring equally with those who can boast the perfect mixture of the rose & the lilly.[38]

Irrationally, Jefferson viewed slavery as a safeguard against miscegenation, an opinion that contradicted empirical observation as well as common sense. Jefferson was, as we have observed, an imperfect empiricist, but common sense alone should have revealed the fallacy of his theory of miscegenation. Mulaticization does not merely represent the whitening of the black race but, by Jefferson's own admission, the "staining" of the white race as well. American law attempted to nullify this fact by classifying every mulatto as "black," when it would have been equally rational to classify every mulatto as white. Jefferson had tacitly admitted that classifying mulattoes as black had the function of preserving the prideful myth of white racial purity and the shameful myth of black racial pollution. Furthermore, Jefferson knew who fathered the mixed children on Virginia plantations, and, as a scientific observer, he was in a position to know that the mixing of races had nothing to do with the lasciviousness of black men and everything to do with the inability of white men to keep their hands off black women.

Jefferson might have dismissed the speculations of William Short with all the patient toleration that an indulgent parent might have for an adopted son, but Benjamin Rush had to be taken more seriously. Short wrote to Jefferson, "If I do not mistake, the blacks in our country several generations removed from their imported ancestors are sensibly less dark than the Africans themselves—some part of this may be imputed perhaps to a mixture of the whites in their production, but a part also to the climate."[39] Rush came close to anticipating the later views of Gobineau and Spengler that the biological mixing of races might actually be beneficial to humanity. Rush made the more challenging, and amusing, observation that "the mulatto has been remarked, in all countries to exceed, in sagacity, his white and black parent."[40]

38 Short to Jefferson, ibid.

39 Short to Jefferson, ibid.

40 Benjamin Rush, *Introductory Lectures*, p. 117, quoted in Daniel Boorstin, *The Lost World of Thomas Jefferson* (Boston, MA: Beacon, 1948), p. 268. I shall leave it to the readers to investigate for themselves the often misrepresented views of Gobineau and Spengler. For such investigations, primary sources in the original languages are more useful than digests of translations.

Jefferson's pessimistic observations on African capacities are sometimes compared to those of the provincial and naïve Immanuel Kant, who was known for his uninformed appraisal of the talents of African people. Pedantic and isolated, poor Kant encountered very few black people in the quiet regularity of his life in a German college town. He never visited Virginia, where blacks and mulattoes were omnipresent as storytellers, musicians, and skilled artisans. Unlike Jefferson, he never resided in Paris, where Africans became musicians, soldiers, entrepreneurs, and skilled workers. Jefferson, on the other hand, had lived in Paris and Philadelphia, and he was surrounded by assimilated Negroes his entire life. They constituted a meaningful portion of the artisan class in colonial Virginia, and, as La Rochefoucauld had noted, played a role in the industrial, as well as the agricultural, life of the South.[41]

Jefferson spoke of nature as having formed each species as a "link in her great work" in Query VI of his *Notes on Virginia*. It is unclear whether Jefferson's anthropology in 1785 was in accord with that of James Burnett, Monboddo, and Jean-Jacques Rousseau, who placed man in the category of anthropoid apes, or with that of Buffon and Herder, who rejected that idea.[42] Jefferson's pontification that black males preferred white women "as uniformly as is the preference of the Oranootan for the black women over those of his own species" is a statement on inter-species attraction. It reveals that he perceived the African as a link between anthropoid apes and Europeans. Historian John B. Boles supports the conclusion of the present author that Jefferson's preferred view of creation was the medieval notion of a Great Chain of Being, and I would extend this point to include Jefferson's use of such phrases as "rank in the scale of beings" and "gradations in all the races of animals," and I would accord with the view of medievalist A. O. Lovejoy, according to whom the links of the chain represented unalterable rankings, states of superiority that simply existed and did not evolve. Unlike Larmarckism, the theory was non-evolutionary.[43]

[41] La Rochefoucauld-Liancourt, *Travels*, vol. III, pp. 157–158, notes for June 22–29, 1796.

[42] James Burnett, Lord Monboddo (1714–99), was a Scottish scholar whose theory of evolution classified human beings among the other primates. A. O. Lovejoy writes of Monboddo: "With some wavering, he extended Rousseau's doctrine of the identity of species of man and the chimp into the hypothesis of common descent of all the anthropoids, and suggested by implication a general law of evolution." See Lovejoy, "Monboddo and Rousseau," *Essays in the History of Ideas* (Baltimore: Johns Hopkins University Press, 1948), p. 61, first appearing in *Modern Philology*, 30, no. 3 (February, 1933), 275–296.

[43] Jefferson did not directly employ the term "Great Chain of Being" in connection with black Americans, although he employed the metaphor in Query VI, denying that the

There is no evidence that Lord Monboddo had any direct influence on him, but Jefferson was tacitly aligned with Monboddo's notion that humans were closely linked to anthropoid apes, and in this he demonstrated a point of disagreement with Buffon.[44] Jefferson was ambivalent, perhaps, as to whether the African was a link in the chain between orangutans and Caucasians, so it is unclear whether he saw black people as a sub-species within the human link, or as a separate link between humans and apes. If they were a sub-species of ape, then miscegenation amounted to bestiality or zoophilia. Jefferson's recommendation for revising the Virginia Code discussed penalties for bestiality. He had commented on the penalties for bestiality, and knew of the occasional cases in colonial justice in which white males were convicted of sexual acts with animals and suffered severe punishments. At one point in *Notes on Virginia* he indicated a belief that whites and blacks were both human, if not equally human. At another point he betrayed a belief that blacks were a link between apes and whites.

The chain-link metaphor was a telling remnant of medieval theology, persisting into the "Enlightenment" anthropology of Jefferson, the "Renaissance man." This "natural history" of mankind straddled the Linnaean world of being and the Lamarckian world of becoming. The chain-link metaphor was implicit in his ranking of apes, blacks, and whites. He had already applied it to the mammoth; now he would apply it to humans. Perhaps Jefferson employed the metaphor as a mere literary device, but that does not seem to be the case. He intended to apply it as a scientific principle. "Will not a lover of natural history, then, one who views the gradations in all the races of *animals* with the eye of philosophy, excuse an effort to keep those in the department of MAN as *distinct* as nature has formed them?" Use of the term "gradations" implies discrete sections, in ascending rank. And it is clear that he perceived each race in "the department of MAN," as a separate link in "her [nature's] great work."[45]

mammoth was a "link in her [nature's] great work so weak as to be broken." One noted historian has forcefully denied this in a televised public forum, but the weighty scholarship of historian John B. Boles supports the conclusion of the present author. See John B. Boles, *Jefferson: Architect of American Liberty* (New York: Basic Books, 2017), p. 174, but Boles does not mention that Jefferson uses such phrases as "rank in the scale of beings" and "gradations in all the races of animals." Jefferson, *Notes on Virginia*, p. 180.

44 On the Monboddo–Buffon debate, see Jordan, *White over Black*, pp. 234–239. M. Andrew Holowchak and Brian W. Dott, eds., *The Elusive Thomas Jefferson: Essays on the Man behind the Myths* (Jefferson, NC: McFarland, 2017).

45 Jefferson, *Notes on Virginia*, p. 180.

ETHNIC CLEANSING AND THE REMOVAL OF FREE AFRICANS

Jefferson presented a complicated plan for general abolition in *Notes on Virginia*, where he cited a proposed revision of the Virginia Code. He proposed to declare that all slaves born after a certain date should be gradually emancipated. First, they would be separated from their parents at a certain (unspecified) age:

> then be brought up, at the public expence, to tillage, arts or sciences, according to their geniusses, till the females should be eighteen, and the males twenty-one years of age, when they should be colonized to such place as the circumstances of the time should render most proper, sending them out with arms, implements of houshold and of the handicraft arts, feeds, pairs of the useful domestic animals, &c. to declare them a free and independant people, and extend to them our alliance and protection, till they shall have acquired strength.[46]

He suggested sending out ships to Europe to recruit masses of potential white immigrants who would take the place of the departing Negroes. Such massive deportations and importations were an astonishing proposal for a man who loathed government spending and who viewed bureaucracies with horror. A few years later, he suggested, in ambiguous language, another idea. He wrote to Edward Bancroft with a proposal to import German sharecroppers:

> I shall endeavor to import as many Germans as I have grown slaves. I will settle them and my slaves on farms of fifty acres each, intermingled, and place all on the footing of the Metayers (Medictani) of Europe.[47]

The 1788 project would not involve expelling the blacks at all, nor would it involve government expenditures. At his own expense, he planned to import European peasants, presumably as indentured servants, and "intermingle" them with blacks. This whimsical or half-serious reverie, announced in the year following publication of the American edition of *Notes on Virginia*, has rightly puzzled those scholars who are aware of it. It is not clear whether he intended to intersperse these farms, or to encourage some sort of experiment in eugenics aimed at creating a mulatto population. As we shall presently see, he was not above considering experiments in human genetics.

There is an intriguing letter, written to Robert Pleasants in 1796, that hints at the possibility of educating the slaves in connection with "the

[46] Ibid., p. 175.

[47] Jefferson to Edward Bancroft, January 26, 1788. "Metayers" were sharecroppers.

establishment of the plan of emancipation if it should precede I am not prepared to decide." He then mentions that in "the Revised code printed in 1784 was a bill entitled 'for the more general diffusion of knowledge'," and adds:

> Permit me therefore to suggest to you the substitution of that as a more general and certain means of providing for the instruction of the slaves, and more desirable as they would in the course of it be mixed with those of free condition. Whether, for their happiness, it should extend beyond those destined to be free, is questionable. Ignorance and despotism seem made for each other.[48]

He reflected on a resolution of the Virginia legislature for colonizing freed African Americans on the Western territories, in the wake of Gabriel's Conspiracy of 1800. James Monroe wrote to him in the early days of Jefferson's presidency concerning this proposal for purchasing lands "without the limits of this state, to which persons obnoxious to the laws or dangerous to the peace of society may be removed." Jefferson presumed that Monroe referred to "that description of persons who brought, on us the alarm, and on themselves the tragedy, of 1800," clearly referring to Gabriel's Conspiracy. He wrote back to Monroe on November 24, 1801, concerning the resolution, but dismissed it. He doubted "whether that race of men could long exist in so rigorous a climate" as the American Northwest. He suggested rather that the West Indies would offer "a more probable & practicable retreat for them. inhabited already by a people of their own race & colour; climates congenial with their natural constitution; insulated from the other descriptions of men." For some reason he considered Africa only as "a last & undoubted resort, if all others more desirable should fail us."[49]

With respect to expatriation, several scholars have cited this letter to Monroe, in which Jefferson supported resettling rather than hanging the conspirators and wrote, "there is a strong sentiment that there has been hanging enough. The other states & the world at large will for ever condemn us if we indulge a principle of revenge, or go one step beyond absolute necessity."[50] Dumas Malone interprets these words as evidence "of mercy to the insurrectionists," an idea that is not entirely insupportable. On the other hand, it should be borne in mind that Gabriel's plot

[48] Jefferson to Robert Pleasants, August 27, 1796.

[49] James Monroe to Jefferson, November 17, 1801; Jefferson to James Monroe, November 24, 1801.

[50] The letter has, for example, been cited by Dumas Malone, *Jefferson and His Time*, 6 vols. (Boston, MA: Little, Brown, 1962), vol. III, *Jefferson and the Ordeal of Liberty*, p. 480.

was discovered before it could be carried out, and that there were no white casualties as a result of the conspiracy. Furthermore, deportation to the West Indies was by no means a lenient punishment. Conditions on sugar plantations in the Indies were usually regarded as far more brutal than conditions in Virginia.

A year later, in 1802, Jefferson's opinion on Afro-American resettlement seemed to be shifting, and he wrote to Rufus King, apparently more convinced that emancipated slaves might be settled in Africa as indentured servants, after the pattern of European immigrants coming to the United States "if the regulations of the place would permit these emigrants to dispose of themselves, as the Germans & others do who come to this country poor." It might be possible that "provision for the settlement of emancipated negroes might perhaps be obtainable nearer home than Africa, yet it is desirable that we should be free to expatriate this description of people also to the colony of Sierra Leone, if considerations respecting either themselves or us should render it more expedient."[51]

An effort at colonization in Sierra Leone was later undertaken by Paul Cuffe, a Quaker merchant of African and American Indian parentage, who managed in 1816 to settle thirty-eight African American pioneers in that West African British colony. This was followed by the effort at African colonization undertaken by the Society for the Colonization of Free People of Color of America, founded on December 26, 1816, which established an American colony at Cape Mesurado the following year that was later incorporated into Liberia. Jefferson never joined this American Colonization Society, as it was usually called, but his interest in colonization persisted for many years after its founding. He continued to believe in African or Haitian resettlement, although he recognized that such a solution might not be agreeable to most African Americans. The historian John Hope Franklin has provided the most succinct summation of the Society's objectives, which were complicated and variable. While some of its supporters sincerely hoped it would be a means of encouraging universal emancipation, others viewed it simply as a means of getting rid of the Free Africans, while leaving the majority in slavery.[52]

Jefferson's hostility to the assimilation of free blacks and mulattoes born in the United States is as conspicuous as his lifelong tolerance of slavery, and his increasing support for it. His prospectus for the mass

[51] Jefferson to Rufus King, July 13, 1802.

[52] John Hope Franklin, *From Slavery to Freedom*, 7th edn. (New York: McGraw-Hill, 1994), p. 169.

resettlement of emancipated people was vague as to whether their eventual destination would be Africa or elsewhere. Regardless of where he intended to send them, the financing of their removal implied a big-government project on a scale beyond what one thinks of as "Jeffersonian." His reflections on deportation might be dismissed as a passing whimsy, if he had not let them stand for forty-five years.[53] The plan was among the most extensive and far-reaching exercises in government social engineering ever conceived in the United States.

He amplified these ideas in considerable detail in a letter of 1824 to the Unitarian minister, Jared Sparks, with reference to an "article on the African colonization of the people of color, to which you invite my attention." Jefferson detailed a proposal for combining emancipation with colonization, in which children born after a certain date were to be freed "after-born" and to be left "with their mothers, until their services are worth their maintenance, and then putting them to industrious occupations, until a proper age for deportation." He felt that, since the value of a newborn infant was so low, "say twelve dollars and fifty cents," slaveholders would yield them up gratis. This presupposition was worse than naïve: it was irrational, since it ignored the fact that every child produced by an African American mother must still be reared at her owner's expense for "a few years." Furthermore, that child was nascent collateral for her owner's future loans. A newborn infant represented the potential to acquire debt, and it is difficult to understand how this fact could have escaped the notice of one of America's most notorious debtors.

He imagined a purely hypothetical and abstract slaveholder, specifying neither a middling yeoman farmer with only seven slaves, nor a great landholder with over two hundred. He presumed that some or many slaveholders would be willing to maintain a slave child on his or her property for five to eight years, until it was old enough to leave its mother, and then willingly part with a property that over the same period would certainly have increased in value to something more than the initial "twelve dollars and fifty cents." Then the slaveholder would presumably experience no stresses, either humanitarian or economic, at separating the child from its mother or at parting with a little Topsy, who was daily

[53] Jefferson to Jared Sparks, February 4, 1824, refers to his "reflections on the subject five and forty years ago." Merrill Peterson, ed., *Thomas Jefferson, Writings* (New York: Literary Classics of the United States, 1984), p. 1485. Dumas Malone devotes a paragraph to this in Dumas Malone, *Jefferson and His Time*, 6 vols. (Boston, MA: Little, Brown, 1948), vol. I, *Jefferson the Virginian*.

increasing in value to the slaveholder. Neither the invisible hand of moral sentiments nor the presumably stronger hand of market forces would have left many slaveholders untouched on making such a decision.

In deciding on the fortune of an enslaved neonate, some speculation on slave futures would certainly have become a factor in appraising the value of that child. The closer a child came to maturity the more future value he or she would certainly have. Did it not occur to Jefferson that slaveholders and slave dealers might be just as inclined as holders of the old Continental currency to speculate in future prices? Jefferson's idea that slave children would be emancipated at birth for the presumably low market value of a newborn failed to take into account that American speculators – including himself – would be inclined to anticipate and to exploit the potential future prices of slave infants.

The Sparks letter or 1824 suggested that the destination of emancipated Americans would be Africa, where they might "introduce among the aborigines the arts of cultivated life." The deportees would become independent farmers in some foreign colony, as Jefferson had suggested in *Notes on Virginia*, making way for independent white farmers in America.

Jefferson estimated that his program, which would focus on the resettlement of children, would require only twenty-five years. He did not specify Africa, and indeed in the 1824 letter to Sparks he admitted that colonization, whether in Sierra Leone or in Mesurado, would be expensive. Possibly it might be financed by the sale of public lands. But he had already proposed a plan to give away public lands free to Virginian small farmers. Perhaps it would be better to settle the emancipated African Americans in one of the Western states or territories, as John Randolph did with his 400 slaves. Whatever the details of the project, he favored a massive government project of Negro removal, vastly more systematic and comprehensive than that advocated by the American Colonization Society, thirty years after publication of *Notes on Virginia*. Jefferson admitted that any national program of resettlement might involve, in addition to government expenditures, a "liberal construction" of the Constitution:

> I am aware that this subject involves some constitutional scruples. But a liberal construction, justified by the object, may go far, and an amendment of the Constitution, the whole length necessary. The separation of infants from their mothers, too, would produce some scruples of humanity. But this would be straining at a gnat, and swallowing a camel.[54]

[54] Jefferson to Jared Sparks, February 4, 1824.

Jefferson's employment of the biblical metaphor of the gnat and the camel cruelly transforms the meaning of Matthew 23:23–24, where Jesus' metaphor was directed at hypocrisy. The "scruple" or "gnat" to which Jefferson referred was more likely the constitutional scruple over "liberal construction," rather than the humanitarian scruple over snatching black children away from their mothers.[55] Jefferson's letters sometimes contained floating pronouns and unclear referents that can, despite his expertise with the pen, make his meanings difficult to discern. Therefore one must consider the probability that the "gnat" symbolized the separation of mothers from their children, and that the "camel" symbolized the unwanted presence of a free black population in the United States.

"Wolf by the ears" and "fire bell in the night" are two famous metaphors for the impending slavery crisis, written in the wake of the Missouri Compromise of 1820, that Jefferson employed in his letter of that year to John Holmes.[56] Jefferson's position on slavery in the territories was ambivalent long before 1820. Slavery already existed there at the time that Jefferson brought the Louisiana Territory into the United States, along with its French- and Spanish-speaking black and mulatto slaves. Although he proposed the legislation banning slavery from the territories, he questioned the power of Congress to exclude it. He opposed attempts to keep slavery out of Missouri, which he denounced as "a mere party trick." He declared that congressional attempts to keep slavery out of the West were a mere ploy of Federalists, whose real purpose was "rallying partisans to the principle of monarchism."[57]

Well in advance of Chief Justice Taney's dictum in the Dred Scott decision, Jefferson held that the Missouri Compromise was a violation of the Constitution. Hypocritical monarchists were "wasting Jeremiads on the miseries of slavery, as if we were for it." If they were sincere, they would be directing their efforts against it and uniting "their councils with ours in devising some reasonable and practical plan of getting rid of it." He did not reiterate the plan outlined in earlier notes or correspondence, but until his

[55] "Liberal construction" in ibid. The metaphor of the gnat and the camel is also in ibid., cf. King James Bible (Matthew 23:23–24): "Woe unto you, scribes and Pharisees, hypocrites! for ye pay tithe of mint and anise and cummin, and have omitted the weightier matters of the law, judgment, mercy, and faith: these ought ye to have done, and not to leave the other undone. Ye blind guides, which strain at a gnat, and swallow a camel."

[56] Jefferson to John Holmes, April 22, 1820.

[57] Jefferson to Charles Pinckney, September 30, 1820; Peterson, *Thomas Jefferson and the New Nation*, p. 996. John Chester Miller, *The Wolf by the Ears: Thomas Jefferson and Slavery* (New York: Meridian, 1980), p. 246.

death he believed that "the two races, equally free, cannot live in the same government." Most important was that the Union be preserved, and this made necessary the eradication of the Federalist Party. It was not slavery, but the exacerbation of partisanship that was "rendering desperate the experiment ... whether man is capable of self government."[58]

Jefferson's "*nunc dimittis* on slavery," as one historian called it, was a temporizing lamentation in a letter to James Heaton two months before his death. Prayer and patience were all he had to offer, until "time which outlives all things will outlive this evil."[59] Neither this letter nor the Sparks letter of two years earlier reiterated the proposal that ships be sent across the ocean to find white replacements. It made no mention of the terms on which they were to be imported, assuming that the original plan outlined in *Notes* was still operative. Even in 1785, he demonstrated some ambivalence concerning the mass importation of white immigrants. The proposal to send out ships to bring white immigrants to America as replacements for the presumably non-assimilable African Americans was contradicted later in the *Notes*, where he seemed uncertain about the process of Americanization.

We may perhaps assume that the plan he outlined to Rufus King in 1824 retained his idea of the 1780s that some unspecified agency would promote the sending of ships out to European nations to acquire white agricultural workers to take the place of the deported Africans. As for the expenses that might be incurred by such a massive program of resettlement both of white and black agricultural workers, Jefferson offered only the vaguest clues. One presumes that, in order to defray the costs of their transportation, the Europeans might be imported as indentured servants. One wonders what the status of children born to parents in this condition would be – an unhappy one for anyone in a land where all were presumably created equal. He did not address the problem of how such a massive influx of cheap labor would affect the economy, or how these lower-class white workers were to be integrated and absorbed into the population of American freeholders.

Of course, the Europeans need not necessarily be imported as indentured servants. They might come in as agricultural wage-earners, or as freeholders, and homesteaders, to be granted fee simple estates

[58] Jefferson to Charles Pinckney, September 30, 1820; Jefferson to William Short, April 13, 1820.

[59] Jefferson to James Heaton, 1826, is called his *nunc dimittis* by Peterson, ed., *Thomas Jefferson, Writings*, p. 1516.

immediately on arrival, but this Jefferson never clarified. With such an abundance of land in America, perhaps he might have considered the possibility that any government that imported immigrants might also find a means of helping them immediately establish homesteads. Jefferson reflected, as we have seen, on whether these imported European workers should be brought in as freeholders or as "Metayers" (sharecroppers). In either case, their importation and assimilation would imply some degree of government planning and assistance.[60]

Furthermore, Jefferson was not certain about the assimilability of all white ethnic groups. With his suspicions regarding Jews, Catholics, Quakers, and Germans, he seemed at times to be the father of American nativism, and anticipated ideas that became popular a century later. In the preferences that he tacitly showed for native black over white emigrant labor he anticipated the central point of Booker T. Washington's "Atlanta Exposition Address" of 1895, with its idea that native blacks were less of a threat to American manners and customs than white immigrants were. As Booker T. Washington, "the black Horatio Alger," said in that address:

> To those of the white race who look to the incoming of those of foreign birth and strange tongue and habits for the prosperity of the South, were I permitted, I would repeat what I have said to my own race: "Cast down your bucket where you are." Cast it down among the eight millions of Negroes whose habits you know, whose fidelity and love you have tested in days when to have proved treacherous meant the ruin of your fireside.

Jefferson in 1785 not only echoed Benjamin Franklin's hostility to unassimilated European immigrants, but he anticipated the cynically manipulated, and often overlooked, xenophobia of Booker T. Washington, who, with Machiavellian cunning, sought to exploit the ancient Jeffersonian prejudices concerning the cultural indigestibility of "those of foreign birth and strange tongue and habits," i.e. European immigrants. In the same year as Washington's "Atlanta Exposition Address," Thomas Bailey Aldrich, a white Anglo-Protestant supremacist, published his poem "Unguarded Gates," an amplification of ideas that had been less caustically expressed, but unmistakably present, in *Notes on Virginia*:

> Accents of menace alien to our air,
> Voices that once the Tower of Babel knew!
> O Liberty, white Goddess! is it well
> To leave the gates unguarded?

[60] Jefferson to Edward Bancroft, January 26, 1788.

Although Jefferson did not express his anxieties with equally picturesque language in *Notes on Virginia*, he used one of his favorite polemical devices, a propensity to express himself in terms of doubts rather than assertions, and to pose rhetorical questions, when he had, in fact, already made an *a priori* assumption. By this means he often conveyed an impression of scientific objectivity when he had already made up his mind. He displayed another of his favorite temptations, an inclination to play with mathematical algorithms more reminiscent of Pythagorean tropes than of demonstrable realities:

> Now let us suppose (for example only) that, in this state, we could double our numbers in one year by the importation of foreigners; and this is a greater accession than the most sanguine advocate for emigration has a right to expect. Then I say, beginning with a double stock, we shall attain any given degree of population only 27 years and 3 months sooner than if we proceed on our single stock. If we propose four millions and a half as a competent population for this state, we should be 54 1/2 years attaining it, could we at once double our numbers; and 81 3/4 years, if we rely on natural propagation, as may be seen by the following table ... But are there no inconveniences to be thrown into the scale against the advantage expected from a multiplication of numbers by the importation of foreigners?[61]

Here we have another of those characteristically Jeffersonian rhetorical questions complicated by a negative. At bottom, he feared that, "in proportion to their numbers," new arrivals from Europe would infuse "their spirit" into the laws and politics of the new nation "and bias its direction, and render it a heterogeneous, incoherent, distracted mass." And then he followed up with another of those rhetorical questions with which his *Notes on Virginia* abounds: "Is it not safer to wait with patience 27 years and three months longer, for the attainment of any degree of population desired, or expected? May not our government be more homogeneous, more peaceable, more durable?"

AFRICAN AMERICAN BLACKS AND EXPATRIATION

In the popular imagination, Jefferson's commitment to the rights of man, or his detestation for slavery, are sometimes illustrated by Jefferson's

[61] For more on the nativism of Franklin and Jefferson, see Peter Schrag, *Not Fit for Our Society: Nativism and Immigration* (Berkeley and Los Angeles: University of California Press, 2010), p. 3, and Jefferson, *Notes on Virginia*, p. 138.

advocacy in the 1770 case of *Howell v. Netherland*.[62] His youthful speech on behalf of his client, the mulatto Samuel Howell, challenged the legality of his servitude, but not the status of slavery or indenture. He was the lawyer for Howell, an escaped indentured servant, with an unspecified amount of black African ancestry, who sued for his freedom with Jefferson as his lawyer. The court records are confusing as to Howell's exact "racial type," but they record that Howell's grandmother was a mulatto, the offspring of a white woman and a "negro man." Howell's mother's degree of admixture is not given in the court record; we do not know whether her father was white, "negro," or mixed. We do not know whether Howell was more Caucasoid or more Africoid in appearance. A "runaway" advertisement in the August edition of the *Virginia Gazette* described him as a "mulatto servant man," but the term "mulatto" was inexact in the vernacular of the time, and might refer to a person who was half-white, one-quarter-white, or any other admixture of white and black. The advertisement described him as having "thin visage and sharp chin," which could indicate some European caste of features, but gives us no clue as to his skin color or hair texture. Jefferson provided a definition of mulatto in a letter to Francis Gray, written in 1815, but this letter is more confusing than helpful. The matter in his mind was defined in a Virginia law of 1792, which declared that every person who had one "negro" grandparent "shall be deemed a mulatto, and so every such person who shall have one fourth part or more of negro blood shall in like manner be deemed a mulatto." But this does not assist us in determining the facts of a forty-five-year-old case, or in determining how much European or African ancestry Howell may have possessed.[63]

The foregoing is important because Howell's appearance, combined with the fact that he was an indentured servant, not a slave, might have been a factor in determining the amount of sympathy Jefferson might have felt for him. Jefferson is known to have reacted negatively to the "veil of black" that covered Negro features, and he is known to have found them unattractive if they lacked "flowing

[62] As at December 31, 2015, references to the popular assumption of Jefferson's presumed abolitionism are common on the internet, e.g. Jefferson, quotations on "Slavery and Emancipation," at https://home.monticello.org, and the intelligent but typically inconclusive example of the deployment of *Howell v. Netherland* in popular history. See https://studiesinamericanhistory.wordpress.com/2012/07/26/howell-v-netherland/ This blog's position is supported by a disembodied reference to Gordon-Reed, *Hemingses of Monticello*, pp. 99–101.

[63] Jefferson to Francis Gray, March 4, 1815.

hair." In the court record, Jefferson referred to Howell twenty-six times as a "mulatto" and never as a "negro." He chose to present the case for Howell's freedom in terms of human rights and "the law of nature," to the neglect of an argument based on the laws of the colony of Virginia:

> Under the law of nature, all men are born free, every one comes into the world with a right to his own person, which includes the liberty of moving and using it at his own will. This is what is called personal liberty, and is given him by the author of nature, because necessary for his own sustenance.[64]

Nice words, but even the most callow young lawyer could not seriously have expected such an argument to have been entertained by the court. Its logic, if pursued, would have entitled not only indentured servants, but every slave in the colony, including Jefferson's own, to immediate freedom. Jefferson's argument unnecessarily reached beyond the legitimate claims of his client to have his indenture terminated. He jeopardized the case with his philosophical meandering, stubbornly making a controversial point that struck at the foundations of the entire institution of slavery and challenged the entire slave code. Obviously, this provided him a degree of moral and intellectual satisfaction, but it was a *beau geste*, an elegant but futile gesture. It could not, and did not, have the least effect on the institution of slavery in Virginia, nor did it result in the termination of Howell's servitude. Howell remained an indentured servant, and Jefferson remained a slave owner, although Howell subsequently ran away – it has been speculated "no doubt aided by the money given to him by his defeated lawyer."[65]

Two years later, Jefferson represented another indentured servant, George Manly, whose exact racial heritage also remains unknown. The son of a free woman of color, he was held in servitude three years past the legally prescribed expiration date of his indenture. According to law, the product of a mixed union, if male, was supposed to serve until the age of 31. Here, as in the case of Howell, the legal record is unclear as to Manly's somatic-norm features. For all we know, he could have been light

[64] Argument in the case of *Howell v. Netherland*, in Paul Leicester Ford, ed., *The Works of Thomas Jefferson* (New York: Knickerbocker Press, 1904), vol. I.

[65] Annette Gordon-Reed offers this speculation in *Hemingses of Monticello*, p. 100. Also see Annette Gordon-Reed, "Logic and Experience: Thomas Jefferson's Life in the Law" in Winthrop Jordan, ed., *Slavery and the American South* (Jackson: University Press of Mississippi, 2003). It has long been known that Jefferson voluntarily accepted the case *pro-bono*; see Malone, *Jefferson the Virginian*, pp. 121–122.

brown in complexion, with hazel eyes and wavy hair, or his white ancestry may have been hidden beneath the blackness of his visage. We do know, though, that Jefferson was unsuccessful in pleading Manly's case. Manly was employed at Monticello after eventually gaining his freedom. The point is that while both the Howell and the Manly cases provide evidence of Jefferson's ability to sympathize with at least two individuals of mixed African ancestry, the cases are ambiguous concerning his attitudes towards unadulterated Africans and are only indirectly related to the problem of slavery.[66]

The more influential of the critical studies of Jefferson's attitudes towards slavery include, but are not limited to, those of Paul Finkelman and Henry Wiencek. These concede that Jefferson did, in fact, make early attempts at anti-slavery legislation, and that he did make pronouncements against slavery. But two points must be borne constantly in mind – the practical and the intellectual. First, his stated position against slavery was never enforced by a practice of emancipation. Second, his ideological opposition to slavery was flimsy and inconstant. Finkelman believes that Jefferson's opposition was never very strong, and reacts huffily to charges that his judgments against Jefferson reflect presentism. Wiencek attempts to be less accusatory than Finkelman, but believes that Jefferson's emancipationism weakened with the passage of time, and raises the ire of Jefferson's defenders, a matter that is easily demonstrated from the hostile reviews given to his work by what one might call a Monticello mafia.[67]

AFRICAN DEPORTATION TO INFLATE SLAVE PRICES

Jefferson's June 1777 draft bill against the importation of slaves into Virginia was not a call for the immediate abolition of slavery. Although its complicated and legalistic wording did aim "to prevent more effectually the practice of holding persons in Slavery," it was more directly aimed at preventing the "importing them into this state" for the purpose of selling them. It provided in complicated language for the manumission of slaves brought into Virginia by the slave trade for the purpose of being sold, but

66 Paul Finkelman asserts that Howell appeared to be white, but does not document this contention in *Slavery and the Founders*, p. 144.

67 Paul Finkelman opines that Jefferson was never serious about antislavery, ibid. For a brief discussion of some hostile reactions to Wiencek's work, see the review essay on Henry Wiencek, *Master of the Mountain* (New York: Farrar, Straus & Giroux, 2012) by Jennifer Schuessler, "Some Scholars Reject Dark Portrait of Jefferson," *The New York Times* (November 26, 2012).

worked to protect the rights of slaveholders who otherwise brought their slaves into the state. Jefferson's bill also contained a fugitive slave clause that denied liberty to any "Slave absconding from the owner who resides in any of the thirteen united [sic] States of America."[68]

We have noted previously that the Atlantic slave trade worked against the interests of Virginians who wished to maintain high slave prices, while South Carolinians and Georgians wished to see prices decline. Thus, the opposition of Jefferson and other Virginians to the importation of slaves into Virginia had as much to do with economic interests as humanitarian concerns. Not only was Virginia a slave-producing state, but much of its credit and negotiable paper was based on slave property, and its citizens did not wish to see a deflation in slave prices. This would have led to difficulties for debtors like Jefferson, whose borrowing capacity depended on the perpetual inflation of slave prices. South Carolinians and Georgians, by contrast, were constantly clamoring for more slaves, desired a drop in slave prices, and lobbied for an extension of the Atlantic slave trade.

The economics of slavery, the suppression or maintenance of the international slave trade, and the role of government in retrieving lost slaves or compensating slaveholders were all fundamental constitutional issues in the early republic. Jefferson's bill to prevent the importation of slaves was a forerunner of the Constitution's language on the retrieval of fugitive slaves and the termination of the slave trade. But neither in Jefferson's bill of 1777, nor in his *Notes on Virginia* of 1785, Query VII, nor in any of his subsequent writings did he propose that the solution to the problem of slavery be relegated to the *laissez-faire* operation of market forces. Jefferson's proposal for the extirpation of American slavery implied massive governmental intervention in the domestic and international economies.

In Machiavellian language, Jefferson's draft bill of 1777 was deceptively worded as a bill "to prevent more effectually the practice of holding persons in Slavery and importing them into this state." What it really did was to punish slave traders by manumitting slaves brought into Virginia by the slave trade *for the purpose of being sold*. The bill would effectively control the supply, thereby sustaining the prices, of slaves, and also protect the rights of slaveholders who already held slaves "on the

[68] The text of the 1777 bill is in Philip B. Kurland and Ralph Lerner, eds., *The Founders Constitution*, 5 vols. (Indianapolis: Liberty Fund, 2001), vol. III, p. 278.

first day of this present [1779] session of Assembly."[69] The opposition of Jefferson and other Virginians to the slave trade had more to do with economic than humanitarian concerns, since Virginia was a slave-producing state, and its citizens did not wish to see a deflation in slave prices. Jefferson is generally characterized on popular television and by the class of chattering journalists as a noble abolitionist, whose humanitarianism was stymied by Georgia and South Carolina. In fact, he and his ilk profited handsomely from the prohibition on slave imports. This matter is discussed more fully in a later chapter.

Jefferson claimed that an amendment to this bill was introduced (passive voice), but it has never been located. The online repository Founders Online, National Archives, as modified June 29, 2016, reported, "If this emancipation amendment was reduced to writing, no manuscript or other record of it has yet come to light." The phantom amendment was printed nowhere but in the previously quoted passages on black deportation in *Notes on Virginia*, which made a vague reference to a bill to "emancipate all slaves born after passing the act. The bill reported by the revisers does not itself contain this proposition; but an amendment containing it was prepared, to be offered to the legislature whenever the bill should be taken up."[70]

Notes on Virginia is the only place where this amendment appears. Generations of American historians have repeated Jefferson's reference to this amendment, which he refers to in the passive voice. He refers to this bill and lost amendment again in his posthumously published *Autobiography*, as discussed by the editors of the Founders Online, National Archives edition. But all the bill actually did was to confirm the enslaved status of persons who were slaves at the time of the bill and to declare that "the descendants of the females of them" would inherit the status of slaves. Thus, the bill that was actually introduced did nothing to

[69] *The Founders Constitution,* vol. III, p. 278.

[70] "51. A Bill concerning Slaves, 18 June 1779," Founders Online: http://founders.archives.gov (ver. 2016-06-29). The National Archives edition of the bill notes that, in his *Autobiography*, Jefferson stated that:

> The bill on the subject of slaves was a mere digest of the existing laws respecting them, without any intimation of a plan for a future and general emancipation. It was thought better that this should be kept back, and attempted only by way of amendment, whenever the bill should be brought on. The principles of the amendment, however, were agreed on, that is to say, the freedom of all born after a certain day, and deportation at a proper age. But it was found that the public mind would not yet bear the proposition.

gradually emancipate slaves, and in fact provided for the perpetual replenishment and increase of slavery through the descendants of female slaves.

Jefferson's hostility to free African Americans born in the United States is more disturbing than his lifelong ownership of slaves and the decline in his supposed commitment to general emancipation. In the process of assessing the native abilities of black people in general, Jefferson said, "It would be unfair to follow them to Africa for this investigation." Apparently he spoke metaphorically, as any literal effort to "follow them" to Africa would have implied a Baconian process of collecting evidence, and there is no indication that he ever intended actually undertaking a trip to Africa in order to make first-hand observations. Perhaps he meant to indicate that what he had read of native African abilities had convinced him that Africans were unfairly treated in travellers' accounts. He was selective in accepting such accounts, and those he had read of Meso-American civilization he considered unreliable. As far as accounts of African peoples were concerned, some were available to him, but these he did not consider sufficient to provide a fair appraisal of African abilities.

Jefferson's fairly detailed prospectus for the cruel uprooting and deportation of emancipated slaves was vague on the particulars of their eventual destination, but, wherever he intended to send them, the financing of such an elaborate plan of big-government spending would have undermined the fundamental principle of Jeffersonian economics.[71]

Colonization, Jefferson's solution to the problem of racial slavery, was unequivocally "mercantilist," in the broadest sense, and no more extreme violation of *laissez-faire* is imaginable. The self-evident solution showed no confidence in the mysticism of Jefferson's pet French economist, Jean-Baptiste Say.[72] It necessitated big government and contained the elaborate complication of replacing the departing black labor force with white immigrants. Nothing would be left to chance or to the mechanism of market forces. This was an astonishing proposal for a man who loathed government spending and who viewed bureaucracies with horror, not to mention the negative attitudes towards white immigrants expressed in *Notes on Virginia*, Query VIII. Jefferson repeated this linkage of

71 Jefferson to Jared Sparks, February 4, 1824, refers to his "reflections on the subject five and forty years ago." Peterson, ed., *Thomas Jefferson, Writings*, p. 1485. For Peter Onuf's neo-Garveyite position that Jefferson's deportation scheme was ultimately benevolent, see the numerous index references in his *Jefferson's Empire*.

72 Jefferson to John Norvell, Washington, June 11, 1807.

emancipation with colonization at several points in his lifetime, most significantly in the previously cited letter to Jared Sparks in 1824.

ORDINARY WHITE FOLK, "THE RUBBISH," THE "PANDERS OF VICE"

Jefferson inherited a traditional country gentleman's disregard for common urban wage-earners, and a belief that "cultivators of the earth are the most virtuous and independant citizens."[73] One finds little admiration among his class for Adam Smith's "butcher, the brewer, or the baker," for Ben Franklin's "leather aprons," or, as Shakespeare once called them, the "crew of patches, rude mechanicals, that work for bread upon Athenian stalls." Secretly and hypocritically he would have endorsed Edmund Burke's position in *Reflections on the Revolution in France*:

> The occupation of a hair-dresser, or of a working tallow-chandler, cannot be a matter of honour to any person—to say nothing of a number of other more servile employments. Such descriptions of men ought not to suffer oppression from the state; but the state suffers oppression, if such as they, either individually or collectively are permitted to rule. In this you think you are combating prejudice, but you are at war with nature.[74]

Jefferson actually considered the class of artisans, or "artificers" as he called them, a present danger to the republic, saying, "I consider the class of artificers as the panders of vice, and the instruments by which the liberties of a country are generally overturned." His use of the term "artificer," as opposed to "artisan," in this instance seems slightly pejorative, that is to say, a venture into Burkean, or even Hobbesian, semantics. Although he sometimes made tolerant or even appreciative statements about industrial workers, he never completely overcame his contempt for the urban working class, and the hostility he consistently expressed in easily identifiable statements.

Because artisans as a class were corrupt, he famously said that it would be "better to carry provisions and materials to workmen" in Europe rather "than bring them to America and with them their manners and principles." "While we have land to labour then, let us never wish to see our citizens occupied at a workbench, or twirling a distaff. Carpenters,

[73] Nancy Isenberg, *White Trash: The 400-Year Untold History of Class in America* (New York: Viking, 2016); Jefferson, *Notes on Virginia*, Query XXII, p. 205.

[74] Edmund Burke, *Reflections on the Revolution in France* (London: J. M. Dent & Sons, 1910 [1790]), p. 47.

masons, smiths, are wanting in husbandry." Later, on overseeing the construction of the University of Virginia, he complained that "The dilatoriness of the workmen gives me constant trouble. It has already brought into doubt the completion this year of the building begun, which obliges me to be with them every other day."[75]

Jefferson showed little regard for the artisans or "artificers" who made the machines for which he took credit. A fascinating example was his frustrating relationship with Peter Spurck, who did the actual work on his "Great Clock." Although he was dissatisfied with Spurck's performance, he apparently was unable to identify exactly where Spurck went wrong, or to correct the problem.[76] His correspondence contains more than one revelation that he looked on artisans – including the blacksmith who made his moldboard plough, as well as the technician who constructed the Great Clock of Monticello – with condescension, if not contempt. Although he repeatedly expressed his distaste for monarchy and aristocracy, he never romanticized the stable boy or the milkmaid, nor did he waste much praise on the shoemaker or the weaver. He seldom used the term "democracy" and rarely took pains to identify himself with it.

He preferred to call his ideology not democracy, but republicanism, and he was not an egalitarian, but a snob. It takes one to know one, and Alexander Hamilton, an insufferable snob himself, knew his subject well:

> Mr. Jefferson has hitherto been distinguished as the quiet modest, retiring philosopher—as the plain simple unambitious republican ... But there is always "a first time," when characters studious of artful disguises are unveiled; When the vizor of stoicism is plucked from the brow of the Epicurean; when the plain garb of Quaker simplicity is stripped from the concealed voluptuary; when Cæsar coyley refusing the proffered diadem, is seen to be Cæsar rejecting the trappings, but tenaciously grasping the substance of imperial domination.[77]

Jefferson's public declaration that "all men are created equal" cannot be understood outside the context of 1776. He intended to repudiate the "artificial aristocracy" represented by King George, but not to abdicate his own class entitlements as one of the "natural aristoi." Michal Jan Rozbicki usefully reminds us that the vocabulary of liberty and equality held entirely different meanings in the eighteenth century from those they

[75] Jefferson to Joseph C. Cabell, October 24, 1817.

[76] Sylvio A. Bedini, *Thomas Jefferson: Statesman of Science* (New York: Macmillan, 1990), pp. 243–244.

[77] Alexander Hamilton, *Catullus* No. III, for the *Gazette of the United States*, Philadelphia (September 29, 1792). Harold Coffin Syrett, ed., *The Papers of Alexander Hamilton* (New York: Columbia University Press, 1962), vol. XII, pp. 498–506.

do today. The Founders of the Republic and the signers of the Constitution had no intention of placing farmhands, milkmaids, and "persons bound to service" on the same political footing as John Hancock of Beacon Hill or John Taylor of Caroline. Jefferson recognized a gap of education and culture between himself and the ordinary American, as did his contemporaries, whether urban or agricultural. The recent work of Nancy Isenberg, previously alluded to, reinforces the importance of class distinctions in America that were by no means eradicated by the Revolution.

THE NOBLESSE OBLIGE OF A NATURAL ARISTOCRAT

Such scholars as Claude Bowers, Arthur M. Schlesinger, Jr., and Richard Hofstadter studiously ignored the elitist Jefferson, presenting him as the great democratic egalitarian, but his displays of democratic feeling were never entirely egalitarian. He showed some concern for ordinary maritime workers when he correctly spoke out against the Royal Navy's impressment of Americans before and during the War of 1812, but this outrage merely reflected his constant hostility to Britain, rather than any concern for the working condition of ordinary seamen. Sailors in the Royal Navy were treated "worse than Negroes, or even dogs," as George Washington's English uncle observed. The condition of American seamen was a political issue, to excite the patriotic ardor of the citizenry and charge up anti-British sentiment when useful, but throughout Jefferson's lifetime American sailors were just as cruelly treated. He viewed British impressment as a challenge to national honor, but there is no record of Jefferson's concern for sailors extending to individual rights of sailors everywhere. Working conditions in the Royal Navy and the US Navy need not be worse than on a Virginia tobacco plantation, from an African American perspective, and involuntary servitude in the Royal Navy was hardly the worst of all possible fates. While Jefferson was president of the Senate, a bill providing for the hospitalization of wounded sailors was passed, and John Adams signed it, but there is no record of either having paid much attention to the living and working conditions of sailors on American vessels.[78]

[78] For African American self-emancipation in the early republic, and discussion of voluntary and involuntary service in the British military, see Alan Taylor, *The Internal Enemy: Slavery and War in Virginia, 1772–1832* (New York: Norton, 2013). Richard Henry Dana, *Two Years before the Mast* (New York: Harper and Brothers, 1840),

"Hamilton schemed to get the children into factories; Jefferson planned school systems," wrote Richard Hofstadter, but African American children sweating in the mills of Monticello were invisible in the liberal historians' mythology. Hofstadter's blindness was due neither to racism nor to the presentism of 1948, for he was as disturbed by the inconsistencies of Jefferson's equality doctrine as were most liberals of his era. But he forgot that Hamilton went to work "at a tender age," while Jefferson was the pet of private tutors. Hofstadter was simply reiterating the New Deal's doctrine that "Jeffersonian ends" were democratic and contained the seeds of a later "age of reform," and that its fruits were eventually harvested in the Progressive Movement, child labor reform, public school systems, and the New Deal. Hofstadter wrote *The American Political Tradition* in the decade before the history profession had responded to the *Brown v. Board of Education* decision and the ensuing escalation of the Civil Rights movement. Ralph Ellison was writing *Invisible Man*, and also invisible were the shadows of black children laboring in the darkness of Jefferson's forge.

FROM PLATO TO POPPER: JEFFERSONIAN EUGENICS

Jefferson, putatively a founder of the American libertarian tradition, was a defender of racial purity and a pioneering advocate of eugenics. Supposedly a foe of such an anti-democratic state as that proposed in Plato's *Republic*, which the philosopher Karl Popper attacked in his classic *The Open Society and Its Enemies from Plato to Marx*, Jefferson clearly made Plato a villain, perhaps because Plato was also the author of the *Crito*, which proposed an unacceptable theory of citizenship, and an apologist for the concept of the organic state, an idea later defended in the writings of John C. Calhoun. In Popper's eyes, and presumably Jefferson's, Plato was a progenitor of and apologist for a totalitarian state under a philosopher king, an idea just as abhorrent to Jefferson as any other monarchy. The tradition of anti-Platonism endures in admirers of Popper and in the Austrian School economics of Ludwig von Mises.[79]

describing Dana's experiences as a seaman between 1834 and 1836, reveals that the miserable conditions of workers at sea extended throughout and beyond Jefferson's lifetime.

79 Karl Popper, *The Open Society and Its Enemies from Plato to Marx*, 5th edn., revised (Princeton University Press, 1961), vol I, p. 51. Von Mises says, "Plato was anxious to find a tyrant who would use his power for the realization of the Platonic ideal state. The question whether other people would like what he himself had in store for them never

On the one hand, Jefferson shared the modern libertarian abhorrence of the organic state in its Platonic form and anticipated Popper's abhorrence for it in its Marxist form. But Jefferson's vacillation on slavery and consistency on race cannot be reconciled with any theory of an open society. Furthermore, he embraced human eugenics in one of the more troubling passages in *Notes on Virginia.* The man whose plantation encouraged racial amalgamation argued for keeping human lineages racially pure along lines that Popper would have found dangerously close to Plato's theory of eugenics:

> The circumstance of superior beauty is thought worthy of attention in the propagation of our horses, dogs, and other domestic animals; why not in that of man?[80]

Here was another of Jefferson's moral and ideological contradictions, expressed in the form of a rhetorical question, although Jefferson had already answered it with his opinion that, after several generations of crossing merino sheep with sheep of inferior stock, the inferior stock would become as good as the pure merino.[81] Still, there should have been no place in Jeffersonian libertarianism for a Platonic scheme of human breeding. Popper specifically targeted, in *The Open Society*, Plato's concept of eugenics, with its "demands that the same principles be applied to the breeding of the master race as are applied by an experienced breeder to dogs, horses or birds."[82] Although the Jeffersonian republic would have banished Plato, Jefferson would have accepted one of its most anti-libertarian features, the enforcement of what Jefferson elsewhere called natural aristocracy. While Jefferson is rightly remembered for his anti-statism, he is also remembered for the inconsistently aristocratic notions in his thought. His utopia was not remote from Plato's

occurred to Plato." Von Mises remarks of Lenin that he was "as great a stranger to the work of the bourgeoisie as a Hottentot to the work of an explorer taking geographical measurements": Ludwig von Mises, *The Ultimate Foundation of Economic Science: An Essay on Method* (New York: Van Nostrand, 1962), p. 95. Friedrich Hayek, another Austrian School thinker, supported Popper's linkage of liberal democracy with free market theory. Conservative philosopher Leo Strauss notably sought to reconcile his high regard for Plato with his celebration of individual freedom. Murray N. Rothbard, a von Mises disciple, comments negatively on Popper's analysis in his *An Austrian Perspective on the History of Economic Thought* (Cheltenham: Edward Elgar, 1995), p. 508.

80 Jefferson, *Notes on Virginia*, Query XIV, p. 176.

81 Jefferson to William Thornton, June 27, 1810.

82 Popper, *The Open Society and Its Enemies*, vol. I, p. 51.

when it came to the question of the cultivation of human hierarchies and the breeding of "natural aristocrats."

I am not certain that Jefferson, despite his superb mental endowments and boundless intellectual energy, ever reflected very profoundly on the source of rights and liberties. They simply came from God. The egalitarian author of the Declaration sometimes seemed to be a different person from the author of *Notes on Virginia*, who believed in human hierarchies. Both personae were alike, however, in their tendency to "feign hypotheses," to pontificate on Nature, and to beg theological questions by enthusiastic invocations of the will of God. Jefferson revealed in the *Notes* that he had postponed judgment on the supposedly "self-evident" truth of the Declaration that "all men are created equal." As we have seen, his notions were revealed to be aristocratic when he wrote to John Adams decades later and admitted the existence of a natural aristocracy. We may presume that his ideas on human equality were always more complicated than he was comfortable admitting, either in the Declaration of 1776 or in the *Notes* of 1785.

9

Education, Religion, and Social Control

RELIGION IN THE NATION'S FOUNDATION DOCUMENT

Jefferson recorded a rumor in his *Anas* that the "old fox," George Washington, when under clerical pressure "to declare publicly whether he was a Christian or not," had evaded the issue. Jefferson recorded the rumor – "Dr. Rush tells me that he had it from Asa Green" – in his "private papers" for all future generations to read, along with his own comment, "the old fox was too cunning for them." According to Jefferson and his informants, Washington's public statements contained no affirmations of Jesus' divinity, only vague references to "the benign influence of the Christian religion." Jefferson invoked the additional testimony of Gouverneur Morris, "who pretended to be in his secrets & believed himself to be so, has often told me that Genl. Washington believed no more of that system than he himself did." Jefferson, who questioned Washington's acuteness when convenient in the *Anas*, portrayed him here as at least clever enough to share Jefferson's own heterodoxy.[1]

Jefferson is supposed to have remarked that George Washington "has divines constantly about him because he thinks it right to keep up

[1] Joanne B. Freeman, "Slander, Poison, Whispers, and Fame: Jefferson's 'Anas' and Political Gossip in the Early Republic," *Journal of the Early Republic*, 15, no. 1 (spring, 1995), 25–57. Thomas Jefferson Randolph first published Jefferson's "Notes on a Conversation with Benjamin Rush, 1 February 1800" in *The Memoirs, Correspondence and Private Papers of Thomas Jefferson* (Charlottesville, VA, 1829). The editors at Founders Online report that the accuracy of Jefferson's record of the incident was immediately challenged by Ashbel Green, who had a long relationship with Rush. See the review of "Jefferson's Papers" in *The Christian Advocate*, 9 (January, 1831). Also see *The Life of Ashbel Green…, Written by Himself…* (New York: Robert Carter & Brothers, 1849), p. 156.

appearances but is an unbeliever."[2] Jefferson, author of the doctrine of "separation of church and state," could also keep up appearances. Speaking of "the benign influence of the Christian religion" in his First Inaugural Address, Jefferson deftly intertwined religion and politics in a lengthy sentence that terminated in one of his characteristic rhetorical questions:

> Enlightened by a benign religion, professed, indeed, and practiced in various forms, yet all of them inculcating honesty, truth, temperance, gratitude, and the love of man; acknowledging and adoring an overruling Providence, which by all its dispensations proves that it delights in the happiness of man here and his greater happiness hereafter – with all these blessings, what more is necessary to make us a happy and a prosperous people?

In this instance, Jefferson blandly invoked an ecumenical civil religion that unobtrusively, but unmistakably, mingled Christianity with the affairs of state, fortifying a striking implication of his *Notes on Virginia* that the various competing religions of the Republic promoted social and political stability, and were "all sufficient to preserve peace and order." Many of the Founders shared his views on the utility of this amorphous religiosity, although James Madison, as we shall presently see, considered religion an undependable guardian of domestic tranquillity, if not an outright threat to it.[3]

For better or for worse, Jefferson had placed religion at the beginning of the nation's narrative by invoking nature's God in the Declaration of Independence. A year earlier, he had referred to "the divine Author of our existence," as he justified "taking up arms," and in the Declaration he

[2] Joshua Brookes attributes these words to Jefferson in his journal, which is preserved at the New York Historical Society. The excerpt was published in R. W. G. Vail, "A Dinner at Mount Vernon, from the Unpublished Journal of Joshua Brookes (1773–1859)," *New York Historical Society Quarterly* (April, 1947); Brookes quotes Jefferson on p. 82. Also see the testimony of Oney (Ona) Judge that Washington prayed seldom, if at all, in "Washington's Runaway Slave," published in the abolitionist newspaper *The Liberator*, Boston (August 22, 1845); the Reverend T. H. Adams' interview of Oney Judge, who ran away from the household of President George Washington in 1796, is reprinted in the *Encyclopedia Virginia* online at www.encyclopediavirginia.org/_Washington_s_Runaway_Slave_The_Liberator_August_22_1845

[3] For a standard definition of "civil religion," see Robert Neelly Bellah, *The Broken Covenant: American Civil Religion in Time of Trial* (New York: Seabury Press, 1975). Eminently useful is Johann N. Neem, "A Republican Reformation" in Francis D. Cogliano, ed., *A Companion to Thomas Jefferson* (Malden, MA: Wiley-Blackwell, 2012), pp. 91–109. Also see William G. McLoughlin, *Revivals, Awakenings, and Reform: An Essay on Religion and Social Change in America, 1607–1977* (University of Chicago Press, 1978).

called on the Creator as he again justified the spilling of blood.[4] He mingled oil with water in his religion and politics, for he spoke of the divine right to violence in founding his country, but famously called for the separation of church and state after becoming its president. In his First Inaugural Address he spoke of "acknoleging & adoring an over-ruling providence," but he excluded religion from public ceremony with his later dictum that the Constitution creates "a wall of separation between church and state." And even there matters did not end, for within a few years, after so eloquently defending the sanctity of individual conscience, he defended the constitutional sovereignty of the states in matters of religious establishment. He equivocated and temporized on the idea of the nation's relationship to religious influence and authority. He implied that his own anti-Trinitarian version of "true religion" could justify war and function as a bulwark of true republicanism. He was a fellow traveller of Benjamin Rush, who wrote to Jeremy Belknap in 1791, "Republicanism is a part of the truth of Christianity."[5]

Despite the benign smile he cast on American religion in his first presidential speech, Jefferson privately expressed, as we shall see, hostility towards almost every established religious doctrine, including Catholicism, Quakerism, Protestantism, and Talmudic Judaism. The Inaugural Address made only a vague ecumenical reference to an amorphous religion that he believed conducive to a state of happiness and prosperity. It was a bland invocation of what historians call "civil

[4] The philosopher Matthew Stewart, Ph.D., Cantab., asserts in his *Nature's God: The Heretical Origins of the American Republic* (New York: Norton, 2014) that the "Nature's God" invoked in the Declaration of Independence "properly belongs to the radical philosophical religion of Deism," p. 7, and says on p. 5 that the deism of "America's revolutionary deists ... is in fact functionally indistinguishable from what we would now call 'pantheism'." He does not note Jefferson's sometimes pejorative use of the term "deism," as in Jefferson to Charles Thomson, January 9, 1816, mentioned elsewhere in the present text.

[5] Benjamin Rush to Jeremy Belknap, June 6, 1791, *Collections of the Massachusetts Historical Society*, 6th series (Boston, MA, 1841), vol. I, p. 504, quoted in F. Forrester Church, introduction to Thomas Jefferson, *The Jefferson Bible: The Life and Morals of Jesus of Nazareth* (Boston, MA: Beacon, 1989), p. 8. Cf. Jefferson's First Inaugural Address, with its references to religion in the republic. During the War of 1812, Jefferson wrote in the third person to justify "a war so palpably supported by reason. he supposes indeed that true religion and well informed reason will ever be in unison in the hands of candid interpretation" (Jefferson to Peter H. Wendover (Final State), March 13, 1815). He spoke of "sublime doctrines of philanthropism; and deism taught us by Jesus of Nazareth in which all agree, constitute true religion," in Jefferson to John Adams, May 5, 1817.

religion" by a man who had been accused of "atheism."[6] In the months during the bitter presidential contest of 1800, his opponents had recklessly made the charge. One editorial cartoon, which was more striking for its vividness than its logic, depicted Jefferson kneeling at the altar of despotism before the smoldering works of the supposed "atheists," William Godwin and Thomas Paine. An American eagle hovered above him with the United States Constitution in its grasp, while the all-seeing eye of God looked down from heaven.[7]

Did Jefferson accept the deism – some called it the "atheism" – of William Godwin or Thomas Paine? Atheism was not defined simply as denying the existence of God: the term "atheism" was applied to every variety of heresy or unpopular belief, after the rhetorical whimsy or defamatory intent of various authors. Jefferson was as guilty as anyone of recklessly throwing around the charge of "atheism," and he listed the various beliefs defined as "heresy" by the Protestant churches in his "Notes on Heresy," October 11 – December 9, 1776. He wrote that John Calvin was "indeed an atheist," with reference to Protestantism's foundational theologian. Jefferson knew that Calvin's ideas ran deep in American religion, and that both the Massachusetts Puritans and the Virginia Anglicans had accepted various transmogrifications of his doctrine of salvation. Despite the impact of Wesleyan reforms on the masses, and the effects of deism in intellectual circles, Calvinism remained at the core of American Protestantism.

And atheism was less a theological category than a term of opprobrium. The Cambridge Platonist Henry More deployed "atheism" rhetorically in 1660 as a synonym for heresy, denouncing the "swarms of atheistical spirits" whose existence was as axiomatic as it was dangerous. One person's atheism was often another's deism, and Percy Bysshe Shelley was being intentionally provocative when he used atheism as a synonym for

[6] For a working historiography of Jefferson and "civil religion," see Neem, "A Republican Reformation," pp. 107–109. There is much noteworthy in Arthur Scherr, "Thomas Jefferson versus the Historians: Christianity, Atheistic Morality, and the Afterlife," *Church History*, 83, no. 1 (March, 2014), 60–109. Charles B. Sanford, *The Religious Life of Thomas Jefferson* (Charlottesville, VA: University of Virginia Press, 1984). An argument that Jefferson did not believe in the immortality of the soul and a survey of related scholarship are in M. Andrew Holowchak, "Did Thomas Jefferson Believe in the Afterlife – or Was He a Full-Fledged Materialist?" at http://historynewsnetwork.org/article/160091#sthash.3Ys2ni67.dpuf (ver. 2018-10-03).

[7] "The Providential Detection," etching by an unknown artist, ca. 1800, The Library Company of Philadelphia. Also see James H. Hutson, with a foreword by Jaroslav Pelikan, *Religion and the Founding of the American Republic*, Exhibition Catalog (Washington, DC: Library of Congress, 1998).

deism and was "sent down" from Oxford, along with his friend, Thomas Jefferson Hogg, for publishing *The Necessity of Atheism*. Thomas Paine was famously and unfairly called "the filthy little atheist" in a historical work by Theodore Roosevelt, who knew full well that Paine was an avowed and exemplary deist.[8] Such intellectually refined categories as deism, theism, Arianism, Arminianism, Romishness, and atheism were terms of spite and as often employed for their emotional effects as for their theological denotations. Jefferson's enemies would have felt vindicated had they known that he once advised his nephew, Peter Carr, to "Question with boldness even the existence of a god; because if there be one he must approve of the homage of reason more than that of blindfolded fear."[9]

STATUTE OF VIRGINIA FOR RELIGIOUS FREEDOM

When he took his first presidential oath of office, it was in the aftermath of a vitriolic campaign in which he had been accused of the bloodthirsty Jacobin variety of atheism. His tribute to America's benign religious influences in his First Inaugural Address can be viewed in that context. Subsequently, in his First Annual Message to Congress, Jefferson publicly thanked God, "the beneficent Being who has been pleased to breathe into them [our people] the spirit of conciliation and forgiveness," adding "we are bound with peculiar gratitude to be thankful to him that our own peace has been preserved through so perilous a season," a season in which Jefferson was being accused of atheism. In addition to invoking a deity, he mentioned religion or religious tolerance several more times, alluding to the "enlightened and benign" forms of American religion, and suggesting that the time had come for godly persons to bury their religious hatchets.[10]

[8] With respect to the meaning of atheism, Henry More defined it in his *Theological Works* (1708), Book 2, Chapter 5, p. 27, as "those belonging to the Kingdom of Darkness, who either directly deny God, or at least particular Providence." Roosevelt's false attribution of that term to Paine is in Theodore Roosevelt, *Gouverneur Morris*, 1st edn. (Boston and New York: Houghton Mifflin, 1882), p. 289.

[9] Philosophy professor Gary Guting of Columbia University deploys the term "soft atheism" in *The New York Times* (May 15, 2014). The term generated 61,000 Google results on June 10, 2016. Thomas Jefferson to Peter Carr, August 10, 1787. Roy Porter, ed., *The Cambridge History of Science* (Cambridge University Press, 2003), vol. IV, *The Eighteenth Century*, p. 761. See John P. Clayton, "Thomas Jefferson and the Study of Religion" in John P. Clayton, *Religions, Reasons and Gods: Essays in the Cross-cultural Philosophy of Religion* (Cambridge University Press, 2006), pp. 16–57.

[10] Jefferson, "First Annual Message to Congress," December 8, 1801, first paragraph, reprinted in Merrill Peterson, ed., *Thomas Jefferson, Writings* (New York: Literary Classics of the United States, 1984), pp. 501–509.

Religious toleration has come to be considered one of the defining features of the Age of Reason. It is purely coincidental, but significant, that Jefferson's Bill for Establishing Religious Freedom was being debated in Virginia the same year that Immanuel Kant gushed excessively over the relative toleration that he ascribed to Frederick II of Prussia. Kant spuriously, but specifically, defined the epoch as "the age of the enlightenment, or the century of Frederick," thus fortifying the myth of the "Enlightened Despot." He viewed Frederick against the historical background of murder, famine, and destitution that swept over Germany in the preceding century.[11] Princes and prelates like Gustavus Adolphus, Cardinal Richelieu, and other absolutists had endowed the continent with memories of a Thirty Years War that ostensibly had pivoted on mutual hatreds between Catholics and Protestants, but had eventually made Catholics the bedfellows of Protestants, and Protestants the allies of Muslims. The British Isles experienced more than a century of religious despotisms, which included the pillage of the monasteries, the reign of Bloody Mary, the Puritan dictatorship of Oliver Cromwell, and the Glorious Revolution of 1688, to replace the Catholic King James II with the Protestant sovereigns, William and Mary.

By the late eighteenth century, Europeans and Americans had sought for, and sometimes found, better justifications than religion for murdering one another. To be sure, Massachusetts' intellectuals hanged a few witches after the nominal beginning of the Enlightenment in 1687, but they later cooled on the idea. The Long Eighteenth Century was to be an age of more reasonable violence, as European and American *philosophes* accepted religious freedom as an enlightened ideal. Kant and Voltaire extended the Enlightenment view of religious toleration farther than Milton had in his *Areopagitica*, or Locke in his *Letter Concerning Toleration*. So would Thomas Paine, although his revolutionary effusion, *Common Sense*, employed messianic, rhetorical, and biblical arguments leading to a justification for violence. Kant was optimistic in 1784 as to the "clear signs" that the infantilism of religious intolerance was gradually

[11] Immanuel Kant, "Beantwortung der Frage: Was ist Aufklärung?" *Berlinische Monatsschrift*, 4, no. 12 (December, 1784), 481–494. Kant is thought to have been agnostic, but also see Alan Wood's argument for "Kant's Deism" in P. Rossi and M. Wreen (eds.), *Kant's Philosophy of Religion Re-examined* (Bloomington: Indiana University Press, 1991); a counter-argument is Stephen Palmquist's "Kant's Theistic Solution"; see the PhilPapers Foundation Centre for Digital Philosophy, University of Western Ontario, https://philpapers.org/rec/PALTTP

diminishing, but Christian soldiers, Islamic jihadists, and other Chosen Peoples have continued marching off to war with prayers and religious slogans down to the present day.[12]

As a result of Madison's legislative skill, the Statute of Virginia for Establishing Religious Freedom, one of the particulars Jefferson dictated for his epitaph, was enacted on January 19, 1786, while its author was in Paris. John Ragosta notes that the statute had undergone some minor amendments that annoyed Jefferson, but his preamble was left intact, as was its essential resolution. Its most important result was that taxpayers would no longer be responsible for the maintenance of the Episcopal clergy.[13] By contrast, Massachusetts maintained its established Congregational church for another half century, despite the decline of Puritanism and the drift of many of its elite members, such as John Adams, towards Unitarian doctrines.

Three-fourths of the wording of Jefferson's Bill for Establishing Religious Freedom as drafted in 1779 was a discursive preamble filled with aggressive assertions about the nature of religion and assumptions about the relationship between God and man. Its author boldly professed to know

[12] I date the Enlightenment from 1687, with the publication of Newton's *Principia*. See J. B. Shank, "Introduction" and "Coda" to *The Newton Wars and the Beginning of the French Enlightenment* (University of Chicago Press, 2008). A roughly concurrent date is the Glorious Revolution of 1688, to which one might add the publication of Locke's *Two Treatises of Government*, 1689. For religion in the American Revolution, see James P. Byrd, *Sacred Scripture, Sacred War: The Bible and the American Revolution* (Oxford University Press, 2013); Thomas S. Kidd, *God of Liberty: A Religious History of the American Revolution* (New York: Basic Books, 2012).

[13] John A. Ragosta notes that an attempt to delete Jefferson's preamble and insert Christocentric language was made. See Ragosta, "Virginia Statute for Establishing Religious Freedom" in *Encyclopedia of Virginia*, at www.encyclopediavirginia.org/Virginia_Statute_for_Establishing_Religious_Freedom_1786 Ragosta says that this attempt to delete the preamble, "a ringing declaration of Enlightenment philosophy, was soundly defeated (48–99), and the bill passed with an overwhelming majority. The more conservative Senate also sought to remove the preamble, but Madison stood firm, and ultimately the bill passed with minor modifications. The Virginia Statute for Establishing Religious Freedom was signed and became law on January 19, 1786." Also see Ragosta, *Religious Freedom: Jefferson's Legacy, America's Creed* (Charlottesville, VA: University of Virginia Press, 2013), p. 90; and Ragosta, "The Virginia Statute for Religious Freedom" in Cogliano, ed., *A Companion to Thomas Jefferson*. Identified on his tombstone as "The Statute of Virginia for Religious Freedom," the text of reference is "82, A Bill for Establishing Religious Freedom, 18 June 1779," in Julian P. Boyd, *The Papers of Thomas Jefferson* (Princeton University Press, 1950), vol. I, pp. 545–553.

the plan of the holy author of our religion, who being lord both of body and mind, yet chose not to propagate it by coercions on either, as was in his Almighty power to do, but to extend it by its influence on reason alone.[14]

The preamble of the bill contained the loftily confident declaration "that truth is great and will prevail if left to herself," and truth had nothing to fear unless "disarmed of her natural weapons, free argument and debate." This was followed by the substance towards which all this rhetoric was driving, the resolve that "no man shall be compelled to frequent or support any religious worship, place, or ministry whatsoever," or be punished in any way, or persecuted for his religious beliefs. While the resolution acknowledged that its framers had no power over any future assemblies, which might revoke it, it declared that any attempt to repeal or to narrow the bill would be "an infringement of natural right." The bill terminated with a declaration that the rights it asserted were "the natural rights of mankind" and that it defended freedom of individual conscience in matters of religion, and then self-referentially endowed itself with divine authority and rendered itself, by the laws of nature, irrevocable.

Jefferson's yoking together of religious freedom with such ironclad rationalism had a doctrinaire ring. His announcement that the Almighty had chosen to propagate religion by reason alone was a bold theological assertion, not a universally accepted axiom. The idea was common enough in the writings of his radical contemporaries, but would have been rejected by many Christians, both liberal and conservative. In this particular document, Jefferson appealed to reason alone, not to the revelations of the Bible, and not to the sentiments of the human heart. By contrast, he would imply elsewhere that he thought of religion as having its basis in a social instinct, or a moral sense. In 1779, however, his writing bore at least a superficial similarity to such landmarks of rationalistic religion as Charles Blount's *The Oracles of Reason* (1693). Eventually Jefferson's library also contained a copy of Ethan Allen's similar, though intellectually less authoritative, 1784 publication, *Reason the Only Oracle of Man*.[15]

[14] "Catalogue of Bills Prepared by the Committee of Revisors, 1–5 June 1779," Founders Online. "82, A Bill for Establishing Religious Freedom, 18 June 1779," Founders Online.

[15] Stewart, *Nature's God*, p. 25, mentions Jefferson's ownership of Ethan Allen, *Reason, the Only Oracle of Man: Or, A Compendious System of Natural Religion* (1784), and discusses its possible influence on Jefferson.

He vacillated on whether reason is the only source of moral knowledge and whether God had intended the propagation of religion by "reason alone," referring several times in *Notes on Virginia* to humanity's common "moral sense." In an 1817 letter to Adams he wrote of "the moral precepts, innate in man."[16] Like many of his contemporaries, he was influenced by Francis Hutcheson's *A System of Moral Philosophy* and Lord Kames' *Essays on the Principles of Morality and Natural Religion*, both of which advanced the thesis that mankind was endowed not only with rationality, but with moral instincts that were the basis of mankind's social existence. The theological rationalism of the preamble of the Virginia Statute did not reflect a consensus on religious doctrine. Most members of the legislature were conventional Episcopalians who professed beliefs based on the Bible, and not on reason alone. The theological refinements of the preamble were of minor importance to the Virginia legislature. Yawning, they dipped their pens and signed away the obnoxious tradition of tax support for churches and clergy.

RELIGION IN NOTES ON VIRGINIA

In *Notes on Virginia*, Jefferson was less concerned with advancing a rationalist theology than with presenting an eloquent argument for religious toleration. He reformulated what he had averred in 1779, his conviction that "Reason and free enquiry," if given free rein, would support "the true religion, by bringing every false one to their tribunal, to the test of their investigation." As in the fields of medicine, astronomy, and physics, the progress of reason naturally led to the improvement of religion and morality. "Had not free enquiry been indulged, at the era of the reformation, the corruptions of Christianity could not have been purged away." The purpose of his discourse in the *Notes* was not, however, to laud the Protestant Reformation, but to present a case for religious tolerance.

He began Query IX of *Notes on Virginia* with a brief sketch of the differences and similarities between the religious histories of New England and Virginia, noting that both had punished non-conformists, and that both had passed oppressive laws "making it penal in parents to refuse to

[16] Jefferson to John Adams, May 5, 1817. Jefferson recommended as the basis of a legal education Francis Hutcheson's *A System of Moral Philosophy, in Three Books* (London, 1755) and Lord Kames' *Essays on the Principles of Morality and Natural Religion* (1751).

have their children baptized," and prohibiting the assembly of Quakers, or even keeping books which supported their tenets. These and other oppressive religious laws had generally fallen into disuse by 1776, and, as Jefferson noted, the Virginia legislature had declared in May of that year that "the exercise of religion should be free." Then in October it had permanently repealed all acts of Parliament "which had rendered criminal the maintaining any opinions in matters of religion, the forbearing to repair to church, and the exercising any mode of worship; and suspended the laws giving salaries to the clergy."

Query IX of the *Notes* did not provide a thorough contextualizing of the Bill for Establishing Religious Freedom, but it did reveal the oppressiveness of the residual laws that it abrogated. Statutes remained on the books, stripping away many of their legal rights "if a person brought up in the Christian religion denies the being of a God, or the Trinity, or asserts there are more gods than one, or denies the Christian religion to be true, or the scriptures to be of divine authority." His own "Unitarianism" was technically against the law, and he could have been punished "by incapacity to hold any office or employment ecclesiastical, civil, or military." By the time he left France, the Virginia legislature had passed the bill, and he was circulating copies of the statute as he had originally drafted it. Along with the several reasonable and eloquent pages in Query IX of the *Notes*, it established Jefferson's reputation as a champion of religious Enlightenment by Kant's definition, as he called for the complete repeal of all laws against heresy and the punishments associated with it. The rights of conscience were natural and inalienable, he asserted once again, and not to be abridged by government. Crimes of religious inquiry, if such could be said to exist, were no business of the state.

> We are answerable for them to our God. The legitimate powers of government extend to such acts only as they are injurious to others. But it does me no injury for my neighbour to say there are twenty Gods, or no God. It neither picks my pocket nor breaks my leg.[17]

EDUCATIONAL WINNOWING, THE ELITE AND THE RUBBISH

Religion, although a matter of conscience, was nonetheless necessary for the proper formation of the children of all classes. It must teach the

[17] Thomas Jefferson, *Notes on the State of Virginia*, ed. David Waldstreicher (Boston, MA: Bedford Books, 2002), Query XVII, p. 192.

children of the poor to understand that their happiness does not depend on their "condition of life." By the time of Jefferson's death, a young boy in Maryland named Frederick Douglass would be wondering about his "condition in life." He was asking why God had made him a slave, while white boys were free to pursue their happiness. Jefferson might have informed enslaved children like Frederick "that happiness does not depend on the condition of life in which chance has placed them." He might have offered the same consolation to "Free African" youth, like George T. Downing and Alexander Crummell, as they were hooted and harassed on their way to the African Free School in New York's Five Points district.[18]

To several friends, Jefferson privately communicated his own version of Christianity, which was stripped of the rites, ceremonies, rituals, priestcraft, mummery, chanting, and pageantry associated with the Church of Rome. The Anglican Church in which he was brought up had redefined or "Englished" some of the sacramental rituals of medieval Catholicism before he was born. After the American Revolution, it underwent further reforms and renamed itself the Episcopal Church. It seems that Jefferson attended the Episcopal Church throughout his life, was married in it, and had his children baptized in it. Probably there was no handy Unitarian congregation in his part of Virginia, or it may be that his association with the Episcopal Church signified a pragmatic need to convey an image of religious orthodoxy. Most likely, it reflected a father's desire to socialize his daughters within a traditional religious community.[19] There is no evidence that Jefferson was overly sentimental regarding the sacraments, relics, holy shrines, pilgrimages, or any of the traditions of Anglican Christianity. Over the years, he abandoned many of the doctrines of the Episcopal Church and eventually considered himself a Christian precisely because he rejected "The immaculate conception of Jesus, His deification, the creation of the world by Him, His miraculous powers, His resurrection and visible ascension, His corporeal presence in the Eucharist, the

[18] Ibid., p. 183. For African American schoolchildren in New York, see William J. Simmons, *Men of Mark* (Cleveland, 1887), p. 1004.

[19] George Harmon Knoles, "The Religious Ideas of Thomas Jefferson," *The Mississippi Valley Historical Review*, 30, no. 2 (September, 1943), 187–204. Marshall Smelser, *The Democratic Republic, 1801–1815* (New York: HarperCollins, 1968), pp. 7–8. Merrill D. Peterson and Robert C. Vaughan, *The Virginia Statute for Religious Freedom: Its Evolution and Consequences in American History*, Virginia Foundation for the Humanities and Public Policy (Cambridge University Press, 1988).

Trinity, original sin, atonement, regeneration, election, orders of Hierarchy, etc."[20]

Religion was important in his theory of education for citizenship, but he was uncertain about the utility of the unedited Bible as a means of teaching civil religion and republican ethics. He thought the religious instruction of children and other simple folk should be carefully guided, and since he knew that scripture could be confusing, he said the following under Query XIV, *Notes on Virginia*:

> Instead therefore of putting the Bible and Testament into the hands of the children, at an age when their judgments are not sufficiently matured for religious enquiries, their memories may here be stored with the most useful facts from Grecian, Roman, European and American history, such as, when further developed as their judgments advance in strength, may teach them how to work out their own greatest happiness, by shewing them that it does not depend on the condition of life in which chance has placed them, but is always the result of a good conscience, good health, occupation, and freedom in all just pursuits.

Support for public schools was to be provided "out of the public treasury," and his proposal initially met with resistance, because it would place on the wealthy the burden of educating the poor, and the wealthy class "were unwilling to incur that burthen."[21] The state of Virginia eventually passed a similar act.[22] His plan might be seen as proto-socialistic, and in violation of libertarian free market principles, but Jefferson was willing to swallow this camel as necessary for stable republican government, and later, as president, he even proposed a "national establishment for education."[23] He clearly viewed literacy as a component of republican citizenship, and in a letter to Du Pont de Nemours he cautiously raised the rhetorical question of eventually limiting the franchise to those who could read. Early in his public life, he promoted an education bill in the Virginia legislature, and in the *Notes* he supported public education at the local level, where "the great mass" should receive three years of education at public expense. This proposal included a process of winnowing, and every year a "visitor" should select from each class "the boy of best genius, in the school, of those whose parents are

[20] Jefferson to William Short, October 31, 1819.

[21] Thomas Jefferson: *Autobiography*, January 6 – July 29, 1821, January 6, 1821, Founders Online.

[22] Jefferson, "A Bill for the More General Diffusion of Knowledge, 18 June 1779." See note to this document at Founders Online.

[23] "Sixth Annual Message to Congress," December 2, 1806, in Peterson, ed., *Thomas Jefferson, Writings*, p. 531.

too poor to give them further education," and forward him to a grammar school for six years of study in Greek, Latin, and mathematics, to be followed by a second cut. "By these means twenty of the best geniuses will be raked from the rubbish annually."[24]

Virginia's white children, including the "rubbish," should be instructed in "reading, writing, and common arithmetic," but there would be an early process of filtering, beginning at the third grade, "turning out ten annually of superior genius," and, after six years of grammar school, selecting "ten others of still superior parts," who would go on to the College of William and Mary.[25] In contrast to Benjamin Franklin, he insisted on the continuing importance of Greek and Latin from an early age, at least for the white elite. Jefferson's public schools would prepare poor white children for "the condition of life in which chance has placed them." It must be "chance" that had placed "the great mass of the people" among the "rubbish," certainly not "their Creator," for God had created all men equal.

If "rubbish" was an unfortunate choice of words, it was also a revealing "pre-Freudian slip," for there are other indications in his writing that Jefferson had no high regard for what he called "the mass," white or black, male or female. His detestation for Alexander Hamilton, who had lifted himself from precarious and perhaps disreputable origins, and dared to think of himself as Jefferson's equal, was an illustration of this. Jefferson entertained ideas of natural inequity long before his 1813 letter to John Adams on that subject, which I discuss elsewhere. Jefferson's plans for public education referred specifically to boys and overlooked girls. It did not entertain Abigail Adams' idea that African children might be educated in the same classrooms as whites.[26] His proposal contained a mechanism to compensate for the fact that rich whites and poor whites are not born or "created" on an equal footing. It acknowledged that "we hope to avail the state of those talents which nature has sown as liberally among the poor as the rich, but which perish without use, if not sought for

[24] Jefferson to Pierre Samuel Du Pont de Nemours, April 24, 1816. Jefferson, *Notes on Virginia*, p. 183.

[25] This was the plan outlined in *Notes on Virginia*. Jefferson preferred to educate the students of "superior parts" within Virginia instead of sending them out of state, although other Virginians, notably James Madison, had been educated outside Virginia, graduating from Princeton in 1771. It is generally assumed that white girls as well as white boys would be educated up to the third grade, although the bill made no specific mention of girls.

[26] Abigail Adams to John Adams, February 13, 1797.

and cultivated." To his credit, he therefore acknowledged the need for the state to intervene with a program of affirmative action on behalf of poor white youth.

RELIGION AT THE UNIVERSITY OF VIRGINIA

He gave "Theology and Ecclesiastical history" an important place in his projected body of studies for the University of Virginia, although he rightly expressed dissatisfaction with curricula that laid too much stress on theology professorships to the disadvantage of natural sciences, technologies, and mathematics. Two constant but contradictory themes are present in all his discussions of religion – an opposition to sectarian indoctrination and a commitment to his conception of a "Unitarian," non-Calvinistic Christianity to ensure the health of the republic. But while his preference was for non-Trinitarian doctrines, he intended that the University of Virginia would make religious instruction available to and implicitly compulsory for adherents of all religious sects. A meeting of the University of Virginia Board of Visitors in October 1824, attended by Jefferson and Madison, resolved that:

> Should the religious sects of this state, or any of them, according to the invitation held out to them, establish within, or adjacent to, the precinct of the University, schools for instruction in the religion of their sect, the students of the University will be free, and expected to attend religious worship at the establishment of their respective sects, in the morning, and in time to meet their school in the University at it's stated hour.[27]

The ambiguous language of the resolution seemed to imply that students would be required to attend religious services, albeit those of their preference. The university also had rules forbidding the use of "any spirituous or vinous liquors" and the keeping of arms of any kind, "or gunpowder, or any weapon," including even a stick. Also forbidden was "the use of tobacco, either for smoking or chewing." The University of Virginia today provides a smoke-free environment and also specifies, as of this writing, that "The possession, storage, or use of any weapon by any university student, faculty, employee, trainee, or volunteer, except a law-enforcement officer, on university property is prohibited." Jefferson

[27] Jefferson Papers, Jefferson, Thomas, October 4, 1824, "Meeting Minutes of University of Virginia Board of Visitors, 4–5 October, 1824, 4 October 1824," Founders Online: https://founders.archives.gov/?q=%22Should%20the%20religious%20sects%20of%20this%20state%22&s=1511311111&r=1

expressed dismay in a letter of 1826 that in the student body "we have still about a dozen bad subjects, who game and drink under such cautions as to render detection very difficult."[28]

The University of Virginia offered its students freedom of religion, but not necessarily freedom from religion. Such liberty would have been outside its character as an institution dedicated to the shaping of morals for the young citizens of a republic. Furthermore, the university would play a role in the development of an educated clergy. In his 1814 letter to Peter Carr, Jefferson proposed what we would today call a Graduate School of Theology, although in the report of 1818, which he signed, he and his board refrained from proposing that the university install a professor of divinity. This abnegation was in conformity with the principles of the institution, which placed all religions on an equal footing and sought to avoid any jealousies that might arise from the appointment of a professor confessing an affinity to any of the various competing American denominations. It was clear, however, that some professor on the faculty must be charged with the responsibility of furnishing the moral aspects of religious belief:

> we have proposed no professor of Divinity; and tho rather, as the proofs of the being of a god, the creator, preserver, & supreme ruler of the universe, the author of all the relations of morality, & of the laws & obligations these infer, will be within the province of the professor of ethics; to which adding the developments of these moral obligations, of those in which all sects agree with a knolege of the languages, Hebrew, Greek and Latin, a basis will be formed common to all sects.[29]

"The proofs of the being of a god" were considered an essential part of the ethical instruction of the young men enrolled in the university. It was to be "inferred" that society must be based on some form of theism, that common elements of religion were assumed to be shared by all the sects represented among the students. It was further assumed that these sects shared a common tradition grounded in Hebrew, Greek, and Latin texts, containing the intersectarian, non-denominational ethics that ought to be

[28] Policy Directory, University of Virginia, SEC-028: No Smoking or Vaping; SEC-030: Regulation of Weapons, Fireworks, and Explosives, at http://uvapolicy.virginia.edu/ Jefferson to Robert Barraud Taylor, May 16, 1826.

[29] N. F. Cabell, ed., *Early History of the University of Virginia: as contained in the letters of Thomas Jefferson and Joseph C. Cabell, hitherto unpublished; with an appendix consisting of Mr. Jefferson's bill for a complete system of education, and other illustrative documents; and an introduction comprising a brief historical sketch of the university, and a biographical notice of Joseph C. Cabell* (Richmond, VA: J. W. Randolph, 1856), p. 441. Available online in the Hathi Trust Digital Library.

inculcated in all students. The Board of Commissioners shared the functionalist views of Jefferson, Franklin, Adams, and Rush that a core of Christian morality, presumed to be "common to all sects," would fortify law and order in a republic.

RELIGIOUS INSTRUCTION OF THE INDIANS

Jefferson's belief that the unedited Bible should be kept out of the hands of children applied as well to other unsophisticated people, and so he performed an act of benevolent censorship. With scissors and paste, he carefully selected excerpts from the New Testament, which he called *The Life and Morals of Jesus of Nazareth*. It is sometimes called *The Jefferson Bible*, although he never gave it that name. It was worse than bowdlerization: he pontifically excised from the Gospels whatever he considered improper, false, heretical, or disagreeable, and he arbitrarily rejected as falsification and heresy everything with which he did not agree. Its 1804 subtitle was *Being an Abridgement of the New Testament for the Use of the Indians, Unembarrassed with Matters of Fact or Faith beyond the Level of their Comprehensions*.

Presumably he intended that Cherokee children would read his edition of Jesus' teachings along with Defoe's *Robinson Crusoe*, which he also recommended.[30] His program for Indian education included a religious component, and most American educational programs for Indian peoples at the time presumed that Christianity and civilization advanced hand in hand.[31] Congress set aside funds for land grants to missionary communities such as the one established by David Zeisberger in Goshen, Ohio, requiring that "All converts must worship one God, but the one and only true God, who made us all creatures, and came into this world in order to save sinners; to him alone we pray." In 1803 Congress established a *Treaty Between the United States of America and the Kaskaskia Tribe of Indians*:

And whereas, The greater part of the said tribe have been baptised and received into the Catholic church to which they are much attached, the United States will give annually for seven years one hundred dollars towards the support of a priest of that religion, who will engage to perform for the said tribe the duties of his office

[30] For Jefferson's delight that Cherokees were reading *Robinson Crusoe*, see Jefferson to Governor James Jay, April 7, 1809.

[31] Anthony F. C. Wallace, *Jefferson and the Indians: The Tragic Fate of the First Americans* (Cambridge, MA: Belknap Press, 2001), pp. 161–205.

and also to instruct as many of their children as possible in the rudiments of literature. And the United States will further give the sum of three hundred dollars to assist the said tribe in the erection of a church.[32]

Certainly it was neither Jefferson's initiative, nor was it his preference, that government monies be used for the support of a Catholic mission to the Indians. It is, however, a significant indication of Jefferson's pragmatism and judicious compromise that the treaty was passed under his presidency and in the year following his famous and endlessly referenced position paper addressed to the Danbury clergy in which he coined the historic phrase "separation of church and state."

MENTAL AND MORAL EDUCATION OF BLACK YOUTH

Jefferson gave no evidence of caring whether African American children such as Phillis Wheatley, Ira Aldridge, or Alexander Crummell ever learned to read; they were simply invisible. Black education was mentioned only in connection with the African colonization fantasy of *Notes on Virginia*. For those Africans "destined to be free," he offered only the proposal that they be concentrated in lagers at an early age and prepared for deportation to some unspecified destination. They were to be separated from their parents at an unspecified early age, then "brought up, at the public expence ... till the females should be eighteen, and the males twenty-one years of age, when they should be colonized to such place as the circumstances of the time should render most proper."

Some authors have sought to find greater promise in the fragment of a letter he wrote to Robert Pleasants in 1796, which is vague and equivocal. Since Pleasants' own letter no longer exists, it is impossible to fully contextualize Jefferson's, but Pleasants apparently made some sort of proposal for the education of slaves, and Jefferson referred him to the revised code printed in 1784, including his own Bill for the More General Diffusion of Knowledge:

Permit me therefore to suggest to you the substitution of that as a more general and certain means of providing for the instruction of the slaves, and more desireable as they would in the course of it be mixed with those of free condition. Whether, for

[32] Treaty with the Kaskaskia, August 13, 1803. | 7 Stat., 78. | Proclamation, December 23, 1803. In Charles J. Kappler, ed., *Indian Affairs: Laws and Treaties*, vol. II (Washington, DC: Government Printing Office, 1904).

their happiness, it should extend beyond those destined to be free, is questionable. Ignorance and despotism seem made for each other.[33]

Jefferson makes characteristic use of floating pronouns, where he says that slaves might "in the course of *it* be mixed with *those* of free condition." The letter is ambiguous, and historian Henry Wiencek finds it evasive and misleading. The most generous interpretation of Jefferson's words does not lead to any suggestion that he was thinking of racially mixed schools. But his intentions are as undefined as his scheme outlined elsewhere for bringing in German immigrants to "settle them and my slaves on farms of fifty acres each, intermingled, and place all on the footing of the Metayers (Medictani) of Europe."[34]

Jefferson's writing style often made use of crafty equivocations, vague pronoun references, and rhetorical questions that left his meanings difficult to decipher. Much is left to the imagination in a letter such as the one to Pleasants, where he may have been expressing a candid ambivalence, although it is more likely that he was being carefully evasive. It is probable that Jefferson, ever aware of his image in the minds of contemporaries and posterity, wished to appear open to black education, although he was hardly promoting it. He had the mulatto, James Hemings, trained as a French cook, but we do not know anything more about his education. Professors Annette Gordon-Reed and Peter Onuf observe that "When they were ten or twelve, Jefferson put his three sons in apprenticeships" at Poplar Forest as woodworkers. The sons to whom the authors refer are presumed to be his offspring by Sally Hemings, and the professors feel that Jefferson "no doubt ... took a hands-on approach to overseeing their work."[35]

John Jay, Alexander Hamilton, and others made concrete, if minimal, efforts through the New York Manumission Society to provide for the education of black children. There George T. Downing, of mixed ancestry, and Alexander Crummell, of pure African ancestry, began the study of Latin and algebra. In Pennsylvania Benjamin Franklin also endorsed the idea that, since America was plagued with the curse of an ineradicable black presence, and since not all Africans were doomed to perpetual

[33] Jefferson to Robert Pleasants, August 27, 1796. This bill, which he originally drafted in 1779, is discussed in his *Autobiography*, January 6 – July 29, 1821, January 6, 1821, in Peterson, ed., *Thomas Jefferson, Writings*, p. 44.

[34] Jefferson mentions "mixing" in his letter to Robert Pleasants, August 27, 1796, as well as in Jefferson to Edward Bancroft, January 26, 1788.

[35] Annette Gordon-Reed and Peter S. Onuf, *"Most Blessed of the Patriarchs": Thomas Jefferson and the Empire of the Imagination* (New York: Liveright, 2017), p. 15.

slavery, it would be best to make some provisions, however meager, for the education of black children, at least at a basic level. In 1824, the Marquis de Lafayette visited New York's African Free School and was formally welcomed in an address by 11-year-old James McCune Smith. Lafayette responded with "Thank you, my dear child." If he mentioned this to Jefferson, there is no evidence that he saw any applications to the African American children who labored in his mills. [36]

REJECTION OF TRINITARIANISM

The concept of "Nature's God" that Jefferson wrote into the Declaration of Independence was linked to his attempt to reconcile what he believed to be original Christianity with the seventeenth-century mechanism of Newton and the reputed deism of Locke and numerous other authors. Jefferson examined the early church fathers to support what might be called his "Arianism," the idea that Jesus was a purely mortal man and a great moral teacher.[37] In his dialogue with Adams, he sought to intellectually justify this position by referencing St. Matthew, Origen, Thomas Aquinas, and even Pierre Daniel Huet, a Jesuit theologian, in support of his ramblings. The strongest influence was Joseph Priestley, but Jefferson opportunistically appropriated even Roman Catholic theology in order to humanize Jesus.[38]

Jefferson never called himself a deist, a term that then, as now, had multiple meanings.[39] He identified himself as "Anti-Trinitarian,"

[36] *A complete history of the Marquis de Lafayette, major-general in the American army in the war of the revolution. Embracing an account of his tour through the United States, to the time of his departure, September, 1825. By an officer in the late army* (Columbus: J. & H. Miller, 1858).

[37] Whether or not Jefferson was an "Arian" depends on how the term is defined. Jefferson meets the definition in the sense that he asserted that Jesus was purely a mortal man with no special pretensions to divinity. Joseph Priestley offered contrary explorations of the term "Arian" in his *An history of early opinions concerning Jesus Christ: compiled from original writers, proving that the Christian church was at first Unitarian* (1786), vol. I.

[38] One definition of Arianism is the belief that Jesus was a mortal man, but this was not the definition that Priestley used in his attack on that doctrine, and there is no evidence that Jefferson would have called himself an Arianist, although some orthodox theologians might have accused him of that heresy.

[39] Peter Onuf notes that Jefferson never called himself a deist in "Thomas Jefferson and Deism," *History Now: The Journal of the Gilder Lehman Institute*: www.gilderlehrman.org/history-by-era/age-jefferson-and-madisonreligion/essays/thomas-jefferson-and-deism Peter Gay, *Deism: An Anthology* (Princeton, NJ: Van Nostrand, 1968), p. 140. Also see Peter Gay's two-volume *The Enlightenment: An Interpretation*

sometimes employing the term "Unitarian" as a synonym.[40] He rejected the doctrine of the Holy Trinity and despised the Christology of Luther, Augustine, and St. Paul, and he rejected "the Platonic mysticisms that three are one, & one is three." Privately, he wrote to Adams in 1813, "it is too late in the day for men of sincerity to pretend they believe in the Platonic mysticisms that three are one, & one is three; & yet the one is not three, and the three are not one."[41] He was open with Adams, Rush, and Joseph Priestley when it came to declaring his principles in religion but non-committal with others. He wrote to Adams, late in life, predicting that "the day will come when the mystical generation of Jesus, by the supreme being as his father in the womb of a virgin will be classed with the fable of the generation of Minerva in the brain of Jupiter."[42]

The Trinitarian tenets of the Anglican Church were expressed in the Nicene Creed, the Apostles Creed, and the Athanasian Creed; Jefferson and Adams specifically rejected the Athanasian as completely unintelligible. *The Book of Common Prayer* of the Anglican Church, as authorized in 1662, considered all three as necessary to express the essential statements of Christian belief, to wit, the assertions that Jesus was divine, that he was born of a virgin, that he died on the cross, rose from the dead, and had a mystical relationship to the Father and the Holy Ghost. Most delegates to the Continental Congress would have been able to recite the Apostles Creed, but by 1776 Adams, Jefferson, and Franklin had rejected all three creeds, along with the belief in Jesus' redemption of mankind by his suffering on the Cross.

By 1773, both Adams and Jefferson knew Joseph Priestley's *History of the Corruptions of Christianity*. Jefferson alluded to it in a letter of 1803 to Benjamin Rush, explaining that his views on Christianity were "the result of a life of enquiry & reflection, and very different from that Anti-Christian system, imputed to me by those who know nothing of my opinions. to the corruptions of Christianity, I am indeed opposed; but not to the genuine precepts of Jesus himself."[43] Jefferson shared with Adams on April 11, 1823 his opinion that "the greatest enemies to the doctrines of Jesus are those calling themselves the expositors of them, who

(New York: Norton, 1966, 1969). See, for example, Jefferson to John Adams, March 10, 1823. For denunciation of Calvin, see Jefferson to John Adams, April 11, 1823.

40 Jefferson to John Adams, August 22, 1813.

41 Ibid.

42 Jefferson to John Adams, April 11, 1823.

43 Jefferson to Benjamin Rush, April 21, 1803.

have perverted them for the structure of a system of fancy absolutely incomprehensible, and without any foundation in his genuine words."[44]

Jefferson viewed Jesus somewhat as a Chinese intellectual might have viewed Confucius – a historically significant moralist and philosopher, but not a personification of God.[45] Jefferson saw religion as almost synonymous with moralism, and was impatient with other varieties of religious experience such as ecstasy, enthusiasm, and spirit possession. His definition of religion was solipsistic, and severely limited to what in his opinion religion ought to be – a rational system of morality, devoid of mysticism, totems, incantations, shrines, icons, litanies, and superstitions. The God that Jefferson created for deployment in the lengthy and tendentious preamble to his Statute for Establishing Religious Freedom was an affirmation of his own singular and controversial ideas, and yet, thanks partly to Madison's organizational genius, the Virginia legislature approved what he offered, and what many would call deism.[46]

If Jefferson did not call himself a deist, he was completely unabashed about calling Jesus one, and while he rejected the divinity of Christ, he showed no hesitancy in calling himself a Christian. Jefferson called himself "a Christian, in the only sense in which he [Christ] wished any one to be; sincerely attached to his doctrines, in preference to all others; ascribing to himself every human excellence, & believing he never claimed any other."[47] In a letter to Adams on May 5, 1817, he wrote of "the sublime doctrines of philanthropism and deism taught us by Jesus of Nazareth."[48] His complicated and variable use of the term "deism" over the years can be seen in his communications with John Adams, Joseph Priestley, and Benjamin Rush. He wrote a letter to Adams on April 9, 1803, which Adams quoted back to him in 1813, describing Jefferson's communications with Priestley and Rush.

44 The following exchange between Jefferson and Adams makes clear and specific their mutual rejection of the doctrine of the Trinity: Jefferson to John Adams, August 22, 1813; John Adams to Jefferson, September 14, 1813.

45 Dave Wang, "Ideas from the East: American Founders and Chinese Wisdoms," *Virginia Review of Asian Studies*, 18 (2016), 192–198, discusses possible Confucian influences on Jefferson. A few of Jefferson's correspondents mention Confucius, but Jefferson's letters show no reaction to their ideas.

46 Jefferson to William Short, August 4, 1820.

47 Jefferson to Benjamin Rush, April 21, 1803.

48 Onuf, "Thomas Jefferson and Deism," is on safe ground in stating that "Jefferson never called himself a deist," at least not in his writings, as the definitive edition currently stands. As already mentioned, he preferred the term Unitarian to deist in characterizing his religious hopes and preferences. See Jefferson to John Adams, August 22, 1813.

Jefferson had announced his intention in 1803 to send Rush a letter outlining "my View of the Christian System," which he eventually did. But the letter from Jefferson to Rush from which Adams quoted was not identical to the letter Jefferson wrote to Rush on April 21, 1803. In this missive he enclosed the outline alluded to, calling it a "Syllabus" on the doctrines of Jesus, with the caveat that it should be treated as private. It is difficult to say why the man who had expressed unconventional religious ideas so openly in the Declaration of Independence, the Virginia Statute, and *Notes on Virginia* should wish to suppress his relatively innocuous letters on matters of religion written to Priestley.[49]

Sometimes he used the term "deist" almost pejoratively, as when he referred to the "degraded state" of the "deism and ethics of the Jews" of the first century. He proclaimed that Jesus was a better teacher than Moses, who "had bound the Jews to many idle ceremonies, mummeries & observances of no effect towards producing the social utilities which constitute the essence of virtue."[50] In a letter to Adams of 1813, Jefferson asserted that Jesus "endeavoured to bring them [the Jewish people] to the Principles of a pure Deism, and juster Notions of the Attributes of God," but those words appear neither in the "Syllabus" of 1803 nor in the letter to Rush containing it. They do appear in a letter from Jefferson to Priestley on April 9, 1803. In the "Syllabus," he mentions the religion of "the Jews," saying, "Their system was Deism, that is, the belief of one only god. but their ideas of him, & of his attributes, were degrading & injurious." Deism in this instance was nothing more than a synonym for monotheism and was used, if not pejoratively, at least in a negative context. He gave the term a more negative connotation when writing to Charles Thomson on January 9, 1816, of "the vicious ethics and deism of the Jews." But in a later missive to Adams in May of 1817 he used the term "deism" positively, alluding to "the sublime doctrines of philanthropism and deism taught us by Jesus of Nazareth."[51]

[49] His secrecy concerning the Kentucky Resolution is discussed elsewhere in this volume. His attempt to suppress his letters to Priestley concerning religion are discussed in F. Forrester Church's introduction to the Beacon Press edition of *The Jefferson Bible* (see note 5 above, this chapter).

[50] Jefferson to William Short, August 4, 1820.

[51] Jefferson to John Adams, May 5, 1817. John Adams to Jefferson, July 16, 1813, quotes two of Jefferson's letters, that of March 21, 1801, and that of April 9, 1803, in which Jefferson planned to send Rush his "View of the Christian System." Compare Jefferson to Rush, April 21, 1803, which is reprinted in Peterson, ed., *Thomas Jefferson, Writings*, along with its enclosure, "Syllabus of an Estimate of the Merit of the Doctrines of Jesus, Compared with Those of Others," pp. 1122–1126.

Jefferson made a disturbing reference to what he saw as the ethnic otherness of the Jewish people in a letter to Lafayette of 1817, where he managed in two brief sentences to impugn the patriotism of Catholics and Jews, and Quakers:

Dispersed, as the Jews, they still form, as those do, one nation, foreign to the land they live in. They are Protestant Jesuits, implicitly devoted to the will of their superior, and forgetting all duties to their country in the execution of the policy of their order.[52]

He defined the ancient Jews as deists, but did he mean to include modern Jews in his prediction that every young man then living in America would "die an Unitarian?" There is little in his writings that might be called ethnic anti-Semitism in a modern sense, although it is true that in a letter to John Taylor of June 1, 1798 he used the Jewish "peculiarity of character" as a trope for inevitable divisions within a society, but this pejorative remark was not intended to incite hatred against Jewish people. The letter to Taylor is so exceedingly garbled and so filled with Jefferson's characteristic use of pronouns with imprecise referents that we must use our imagination to unravel his meaning. Religious anti-Semitism occasionally appears, as in the letter he wrote to Joseph Priestley that refers disparagingly to the "deism and ethics of the Jews" at the time of Jesus Christ.[53] He disparages the Talmud but reveals no systematic effort at Talmudic studies, which would have been difficult in any case, as he did not know Hebrew.

Choosing to accept whatever negative interpretations of the Talmud were at hand, he showed a cavalier disregard for scientific method, as understood by his contemporaries, but this was typical of Jefferson when dealing with all matters of race, religion, and ethnicity. In this case he cited a secondary reference to a translation of the German scholar Johann Jakob Brucker, whose opinions, as expressed in Jefferson's approved translation by William Enfield, were unquestionably anti-Semitic. Jefferson endorsed the application of the term "wretched depravity" to Talmudic teachings and perpetuated anti-Semitic stereotypes. His letter to Charles Thomson, speaking of "the vicious ethics and deism of the

[52] Jefferson to Lafayette, Monticello, May 14, 1817.

[53] Jefferson to Dr. Joseph Priestley, April 9, 1803. Gerd Korman, "Jews as a Changing People of the Talmud: An American Exploration," Cornell University ILR School (February 1, 2001); "Shavuot, Jewish Ethics, and a Rebuttal of Thomas Jefferson." Posted by Deborah Fishman on May 22, 2012, at the Avi Chai Foundation Blog, https://avichai.org/2012/05/shavuot-jewish-ethics-and-a-rebuttal-of-thomas-jefferson/

Jews," and his letter to William Short, saying that Jesus reformed "the depraved religion of his country," and his references to the Jewish priesthood as a "bloodthirsty race" were all negative. Jefferson was not a racial anti-Semite, but his references to Jewish religion consistently contained unsupported judgments expressed in disturbing language that would be unacceptable by "present" standards. To his credit, he expressed his disgust and hostility to the "British code," with its discriminatory "laws made for the Jews alone."[54]

QUAKERS

Jefferson's position on Quakers was ambivalent. In *Notes on Virginia* Query XVII, he condemned the unjustness of colonial anti-Quaker laws, but he later expressed concerns about the patriotism of Quakers during the War of 1812. He retrospectively described the ancient anti-Quaker policies of Walter Raleigh as "cruelly intolerant," but he nonetheless made it clear that he considered the sect undependable. They were, he felt, too readily inclined to accept policies of the Anglocentric mother church. He questioned the sincerity of their pacifism in times of war, suggesting that it was opportunistic and merely an expression of their essential Anglocentrism. Here, as in other instances, Jefferson demonstrated a penchant for helping his opponents up with his left hand after knocking them down with his right, for in another context he professed that he knew Quakers whose patriotism was impeccable. But he questioned outright whether Quakers, as Anglophilic pacifists, were in a position to discharge their republican responsibilities. This seems unjustly demanding for a person who never shouldered arms in any American war.[55]

[54] Jefferson to John Adams, October 12, 1813, reprinted in Peterson, ed., *Thomas Jefferson, Writings*, pp. 1301–1302. Jefferson to Charles Thomson, January 9, 1816, reprinted ibid., p. 1373. Jefferson to William Short, August 4, 1820, reprinted ibid., p. 1437. Jefferson to William Short, October 31, 1819, reprinted ibid., p. 1431. Jefferson to John Taylor, June 1, 1798, reprinted ibid., p. 1050. Jefferson's reference to anti-Semitic legislation in Britain is in *Reports of Cases in the General Court of Virginia* (Buffalo: William S. Hein, 1981), p. 94. Quoted in Willard S. Randall, *Thomas Jefferson: A Life* (New York: Henry Holt, 1993), p. 136.

[55] Jefferson was not intolerant of the Quaker faith, although unjustly critical of Quaker pacifism, considering that he never shouldered arms himself. He spoke out against Walter Raleigh's anti-Quaker policies as "cruelly intolerant." Jefferson to Lafayette, Monticello, May 14, 1817. Jefferson to Samuel Kercheval, Monticello, January 19, 1810.

The Quakers here have taken sides against their own government, not on their profession of peace, for they saw that peace was our object also; but from devotion to the views of the mother society. In 1797–8, when an administration sought war with France, the Quakers were the most clamorous for war. Their principle of peace, as a secondary one, yielded to the primary one of adherence to the Friends in England, and what was patriotism in the original, became treason in the copy.[56]

RELIGION AND THE DECLARATION'S COMMITTEE MEMBERS

The original draft of the Declaration of Independence included no references to any God, as Pauline Maier notes.[57] Three members of the Declaration drafting committee, Benjamin Franklin, John Adams, and Thomas Jefferson, were "unitarian." Robert Livingston, the youngest member of the committee, was Episcopalian and later a prominent freemason. He did not sign the Declaration, although he sent his cousin, Philip Livingston, to sign in his place; but if Robert contributed to the drafting, no record of such has survived. Roger Sherman, born in 1721, was a delegate from Connecticut and the only member of the Committee to sign the Declaration of Independence, the Articles of Confederation, and the Constitution. He was the product of Puritan upbringing in Massachusetts and had two brothers who became Congregationalist ministers. According to his biographer, Mark David Hall, Sherman was "profoundly versed in theology," as well as in mathematics and other areas. Sherman was apparently the strictest Christian on the committee, and once protested against a resolution of Congress to convene on a Sunday out of "regard for the commands of his Maker." It is unlikely he would have expressed any quibbles with the document's term "Nature's God," although Matthew Stewart argues that the reference might have had "deistic" or even "pantheistic" implications. Congregationalists of Sherman's generation were more likely to make references to "law of nature" and natural rights than their Puritan progenitors.[58]

[56] Jefferson to William Baldwin (draft), January 19, 1810.

[57] Pauline Maier, *American Scripture* (New York: Knopf, 1997), p. 186. Also see Garry Wills, *Inventing America: Jefferson's Declaration of Independence* (New York: Doubleday, 1978), pp. 13, 19. On Livingston, see Derek H. Davis, *Religion and the Continental Congress, 1774–1789: Contributions to Original Intent* (Oxford University Press, 2000), p. 98.

[58] Mark David Hall says "Puritans were less likely to make natural rights arguments than later Calvinists," in *Roger Sherman and the Creation of America* (Oxford University Press, 2013), p. 19. Stewart, in his *Nature's God* cited above, asserts that nature's God usually implies deism, as noted on pp. 5 and 7 there.

Franklin was never shy about public demonstrations of his religion, or his deviation from conventional Protestantism. Probably all the members of the drafting committee shared Franklin's position on prayer, which was "I had still an opinion of its propriety, and of its utility when rightly conducted."[59] In his *Autobiography* he asserted that, by middle age, his daily morning ritual was to "Rise, wash, and address *Powerful Goodness*."[60] Franklin was a product of the Massachusetts established church, which he identified in his *Autobiography* as Presbyterian. It was, in fact, the Congregationalist church of his father and Cotton Mather, but apparently in Franklin's mind the two denominations were indistinguishable. The founders of his native Boston came to America to establish a theocracy, in part because they considered the Churches of England and Holland too lax. He taught himself to read at an early age, from Cotton Mather's *Essays to do Good*. According to his *Autobiography*, he rejected divine atonement as early as 1728, but he retained Mather's ideas of the Christian's duty to perform community service.[61]

Franklin would have not have raised an eyebrow at the reference to the "Nature's God" invoked in the Declaration. Jefferson's autobiography portrays him as sarcastic and avuncular. Religiously ecumenical in his old age, Franklin had flirted with polytheism in his youth, having suspected that multiple universes might be the creations of several Gods.[62] At 20, he

[59] Jefferson, Notes on Heresy, October 11 – December 9, 1776. Their unequivocal rejection of the doctrine of the Trinity is made clear in Jefferson to John Adams, August 22, 1813; John Adams to Jefferson, September 14, 1813; Jefferson to John Adams, August 22, 1813; John Adams to Jefferson, September 14, 1813. The definitive edition of Franklin's *Autobiography* is Leo LeMay, ed., *Benjamin Franklin's Autobiography: An Authoritative Text, Backgrounds, Criticism* (New York: Norton, 1986), p. 65.

[60] In his *Dissertation on Liberty and Necessity, Pleasure and Pain* (London, 1725), Franklin offered two arguments for determinism: one for mechanical necessity in the universe of a clockmaker God, and a second that human reactions to biological stimuli were irresistible. Centuries later Pavlov "rediscovered" Franklin's second variety of determinism with his demonstration that a dog can be conditioned to involuntarily salivate at the ringing of a bell. For invocation of "Powerful Goodness," see LeMay, ed., *Benjamin Franklin's Autobiography*, Chapter 9.

[61] Strict Calvinist congregations were called Congregationalist in New England and Presbyterian in Scotland. The fact that Franklin used the terms interchangeably indicates how meaningless the doctrinal differences were between the two. See *Autobiography* (New York: Norton, 1986), p. 65, and Lemay's note on the same page.

[62] Benjamin Franklin, "Articles of Belief and Acts of Religion," private memorandum, November 20, 1728. Edmund S. Morgan, *Benjamin Franklin* (Yale University Press, 2002), p. 19, takes Franklin's youthful statement at face value. Kerry Walters, *Benjamin Franklin and His Gods: Beyond Providence and Polytheism* (Chicago: University of Illinois Press, 1999), finds the statement indigestible and reasons that a literally polytheistic reading cannot be correct.

penned a sneeringly brilliant essay that toyed almost irreverently with Calvinistic determinism and Newton's "watchmaker." But even after his rejection of Calvinism, he almost emptied his pockets into the collection plate of the Calvinist George Whitefield while listening to one of his sermons. He tended in his later years towards flexibility and tolerance on matters of doctrine, and hedged his bets by dropping his silver into a variety of church coffers. If the city of Philadelphia had possessed a shrine dedicated to the unknown God of the Areopagus, he would probably have burnt incense at that altar as well.[63]

Franklin shared Jefferson's view of an intervening God, who, if he was a watchmaker, must have been like Newton's deity, an intervening watchmaker who adjusted his mechanism from time to time, and a "Providence that takes Cognizance of, guards and guides and may favour particular Persons." In a letter addressed to an unknown recipient – possibly Thomas Paine – which dismissed the role of divine intervention in human affairs, Franklin wrote, "You strike at the Foundation of all Religion." In Franklin's view, this variety of deism provided "no Motive to Worship a Deity, to fear its Displeasure, or to pray for its Protection."[64] Franklin's religion, like Jefferson's, was a means of social control, an attitude that is less startling to discover in the pompous, officious John Adams than in such icons of liberalism as Franklin and Jefferson.[65] But all three made their positions clear, and Franklin, who had no aversion to mixing religion with affairs of state, wrote pessimistically in the same letter, "If Men are so wicked as we now see them with Religion what would they be if without it?"[66]

[63] St. Paul might be ironically identified as the pragmatic founder of Christian syncretism, when he told the pagans that in their worship of the "unknown God" they were actually and unbeknownst to themselves worshipping Yahweh (Acts 17:23).

[64] Benjamin Franklin to ——— [presumably to Thomas Paine], [December 13, 1757], Leonard W. Labaree, ed., *The Papers of Benjamin Franklin* (New Haven, CT: Yale University Press, 1963). The editors give six possible dates, ranging from 1751 to 1787. Despite conjecture that the letter was addressed to Thomas Paine, the editorial note discusses problems of identifying the recipient. Walter Isaacson, in *Benjamin Franklin: An American Life* (New York: Simon and Schuster, 2003), finds the date July 3, 1786 "likely" and believes that it was sent to Thomas Paine. Regardless of when the letter was written and whether it was addressed to Paine, it justifies religion as a means of controlling the behavior of "weak and ignorant Men and Women." If Franklin subscribed to such ideas about the social benefits of religion, then his views were similar to Thomas Jefferson's.

[65] See John Adams to Jefferson, September 14, 1813. Jefferson to Benjamin Waterhouse, June 26, 1822.

[66] Benjamin Franklin, presumably to Thomas Paine, December 13, 1757.

Unlike Jefferson, Adams made no objection to religious taxation, but Adams was doctrinally, if not ecclesiastically, "Unitarian," and his letters to Jefferson made disrespectful comments on the Athanasian Creed.[67] He expressed doubts concerning the divinity of Christ as early as 1755 and by 1756 he dismissed the "mystery" of divine atonement, writing in the margin of his diary, "Thus mystery is made a convenient Cover for absurdity." He decided not to pursue a career as a clergyman, giving as his reason, "a Spirit of Dogmatism and Bigotry in Clergy and Laity."[68] Adams recorded his anti-Trinitarianism in the fall of 1776 not long after the Declaration was drafted. His "unitarianism" was indistinguishable from the watered-down Calvinism that would eventually become tacitly acceptable to the Massachusetts Congregational establishment and eventually at Harvard. In contrast to the Episcopal Church in Virginia, the Congregational Church of Massachusetts would continue to receive state support until 1834. Historian John D. Cushing, in an article on Disestablishment in Massachusetts, ends with the wry observation that "more than half a century after achieving political independence, Massachusetts recovered the full measure of Religious Freedom granted by the royal charter of 1692 but compromised in the [Massachusetts] Constitutional Convention of 1780."[69]

The Framers of the United States Constitution were loath to intrude into the state religious establishments already in existence, which led them to legislate that "Congress shall make no law respecting an establishment of religion." This did not seem to bother a man like Adams, who, although rejecting the conservative Congregationalism that dominated his local community, continued to pay his Massachusetts state taxes, which went

[67] Adams expresses his opinion on religious taxation in a letter to Mercy Otis Warren, August 8, 1807: "Every Man is at Liberty to apply his Taxes to the Support of his own Church and Minister. Taxes however they are obliged to pay." Adams' encounters with the Athanasian Creed are described in "Harvard and Worcester, 1751–1755] [from the Diary of John Adams]" at Founders Online. Also see John Quincy Adams to John Adams from January 5, 1816: "I plainly perceive that you are not to be converted, even by the eloquence of Massillon, to the Athanasian Creed." Also see John Adams to Thomas Jefferson, July 13, 1813: "I have never read reasoning more absurd, sophistry more gross, in proof of the Athanasian creed, or transubstantiation, than the subtle labors of Helvetius and Rousseau to demonstrate the natural equality of mankind. Jus cuique, the golden rule, do as you would be done by, is all the equality that can be supported or defended by reason or common sense."

[68] John Adams, *The Works of John Adams* (Altenmünster: Jazzybee Verlag, 2015), vol. I, *The Life of John Adams*, p. 25.

[69] John D. Cushing, "Notes on Disestablishment in Massachusetts, 1780–1833," *The William and Mary Quarterly*, 26, no. 2 (April, 1969), 169–190.

to the support of the churches. He thought that everyone should be required to pay taxes for the support of churches, although "Every man is at liberty to apply his taxes to the support of his own church and minister."

In his *Common Sense*, published several months prior to the Declaration of Independence, Thomas Paine invoked the name of God prominently. Like the visionary poet and engraver, William Blake, he was thoroughly bourgeois. Neither of them knew Latin or Greek, and Bernard Bailyn might have called Blake what he did call Paine – an "ignoramus."[70] Both their cases show the rise of a class of literate persons with only a smattering of classics or formal theology but whose ideas of God and religion were influenced by exposure to a wide range of reading in English. Emanuel Swedenborg, who influenced Blake, was a "natural philosopher," and as impressive a scientist as Jefferson, but he found the rationalist version of natural religion untenable.[71] William Blake proclaimed "there is no natural religion" and parodied nature's man as a hairy beast. His demonic idol, Urizen (Your Reason), was like King George, a "wrathful Prince," who was "sickened to see ... That no flesh nor spirit could keep His iron laws one moment." Blake's prophetic poem "America" celebrated emotional energies in

> Souls of warlike men who rise in silent night,
> Meet on the coast glowing with blood from Albion's fiery Prince.
> Washington, Franklin, Paine, and Warren, Gates, Hancock, and Green:
> Washington spoke: 'Friends of America! look over the Atlantic sea;
> A bended bow is lifted in Heaven, and a heavy iron chain
> Descends, link by link, from Albion's cliffs across the sea, to bind
> Brothers and sons of America; till our faces pale and yellow ...
> ... a terrible blast swept over the heaving sea:
> The eastern cloud rent: on his cliffs stood Albion's wrathful Prince.

EVANGELICAL ENTHUSIASM

Blake strangely left Jefferson out of his prophetic book, and Jefferson took no greater note of William Blake. There was no reason Jefferson should

[70] Bernard Bailyn, *Faces of Revolution: Personalities and Themes in the Struggle for American Independence* (New York: Knopf, 1992), p. 82.

[71] Mark Schorer, "Swedenborg and Blake," *Modern Philology*, 36, no. 2 (November, 1938), 157–178. See Ralph Waldo Emerson, *Swedenborg: Or, the Mystic* (New York: Library of America, 1983). J. G. Herder, "Emanuel Swedenborg," see https://en.wikisource.org/wiki/1911_Encyclop%C3%A6dia_Britannica/Swedenborg,_Emanuel

have been aware of an idiosyncratic London engraver, but he might have shown greater awareness of the trends in American Protestantism from the time of the Revolution to the 1820s which were softening traditional Calvinism and serving as a more emotional alternative to the rational deism of Rush and Priestley. Unitarianism was not destined to be the religion of the masses. The rising religious movements were "evangelical," a mixture of the fecund and sweaty enthusiasm of the camp meeting with the cold-water preachments of a residual Calvinism. This undeniable reality was far too irrational for Thomas Jefferson, with his vain hope that rational "Unitarianism" would soon permeate the consciousness of ordinary citizens. The God most Americans worshipped was living in the awakenings, revivals, and reforms from the 1740s to the 1820s. Some revivalists presented God as the wrathful Calvinistic demon of Jonathan Edwards; others saw Him in the milder vision of George Whitefield, and the even milder presentation of Charles Wesley. During Jefferson's eighty-three years, William Gerald McLoughlin's oxymoron "Arminianized Calvinism" might be the best way to describe the American Protestantism that was evolving. Of course, many rural Americans had no church, and even the converted did not always adhere to the codes of behavior that the circuit rider preached. Very few concerned themselves with the elite theology of Jefferson, who was loftily removed from the enthusiastic revival of the 1820s called the Second Great Awakening.[72]

Jefferson made the aforementioned prediction in a letter of June 26, 1822 to Benjamin Waterhouse that every young man now living in the United States would probably "die an Unitarian." He reiterated this prediction in a letter to Thomas Cooper on November 2, 1822. He was probably correct if he meant that few Christians would be obsessed with Trinitarian mysteries, but wrong if he believed that they would affiliate formally with Unitarian congregations, for this was the era of dynamic Calvinistic renewal. In 1825, the last full year of Jefferson's life, the reform Calvinist, Charles Grandison Finney, was beginning a crusade that would

[72] "Arminianized Calvinism" is the intentional oxymoron used by William G. McLoughlin, ed., *The American Evangelicals, 1800–1900* (New York: Harper Torchbooks, 1968), p. 10. The term alludes to the influences of Dutch theologian Jacobus Arminius (1560–1609), whose teaching was seen as modifying strict Calvinism by leaving open the agency of free will. McLoughlin refers to Whitefield's "alleged Calvinism" and emphasizes his focus on a benevolent and approachable God in *Revivals, Awakenings, and Reform*, pp. 61–62. In 1741, the erudite Jonathan Edwards was preaching immediately after and probably in response to the 1740 tour of Oxford-educated George Whitefield and the Unitarian-leaning heretics of his day.

make him not only a rekindler of evangelical Protestant fires, but an early champion of numerous social reforms. He was an advocate of women's education, founding Oberlin College in Ohio, where men and women, black and white, could be educated together. His Calvinism aimed at the abolition of slavery, and he argued that the abandonment of slaveholding was no less evidence of a true conversion than the abandonment of rum-selling.[73]

Charles Grandison Finney's brand of revivalism, on the rise during Jefferson's final years, far exceeded the limitations of Jeffersonian democracy and civic religion.[74] The irony embodied in the rise of Finney was that he blended his traditional Calvinist doctrine of salvation through faith with a radical social activism and a program of good works for the betterment of society. It did not occur to Jefferson that the revitalized Calvinistic Protestantism of someone like Finney might carry the day in America and promote a reform agenda more progressive than his own disembodied "unitarianism." All the signs that enthusiastic religion was thriving should have been evident to an astute observer. Jeffersonian logic did not anticipate the oxymoron of "arminianized Calvinism."[75] The populist form of Calvinism in the 1820s was often characterized by a frenzied emotionalism that swept over upstate New York and had its counterparts in the Virginia countryside. But Jefferson, despite his powerful intellect and self-conscious erudition, was not the most astute social scientist. In religious studies as in other areas, Jefferson was a rationalist, predicting the future of American religion on the basis of what he held to be self-evident. A true Baconian should have based his "natural history" of American religion on the evidence of his senses.

JESUS AND SOCRATES

Jefferson dealt with Jesus just as he dealt with Socrates. He was convinced that he understood Socrates better than Plato, who was the father of lies insofar as the personality or teachings of Socrates were concerned. Only Xenophon preserved the true Socrates. He did not explain why he thought Plato wrong and Xenophon right; perhaps he held this truth to be self-

[73] Reverend Charles G. Finney, *Lectures on Revivals of Religion* (New York, Chicago, Toronto: Fleming H. Revell Company, 1868), Lecture XV, "Hindrances to Revivals," p. 282.

[74] For an alternative view, see Onuf, "Thomas Jefferson and Deism."

[75] McLoughlin, *The American Evangelicals*, p. 10.

evident. And equally self-evident was the postulate that Platonists had sought to "legitimate corruptions" by suppressing the pure thoughts of "primitive Christians."[76] Jefferson claimed to have separated the truth of the Gospels from the dross. The rest of the Bible, the parts that lacked his imprimatur, had been defiled by a "band of dupes and impostors, Paul was the great Coryphaeus, and first corruptor of the doctrines of Jesus." Jefferson's flaunting of the Greek word "Coryphaeus" was significant. It referred to the leader of the chorus in Greek drama, the person who intoned its responses. Jefferson deployed the term pejoratively, possibly thinking of the meaningless croaking of the chorus in Aristophanes' drama *The Frogs*.

St. Paul was widely interpreted as having endowed Christianity with the doctrine that the soul was saved not by good works, but by faith. Paul had written in Philippians 2:12: "work out your own salvation with fear and trembling. For it is God which worketh in you both to will and to do of His good pleasure." This had led many theologians to the idea that free will did not exist, and virtue was no more than the response of the soul to God's irresistible grace. Jefferson's compilation from the Bible emphasized "good works" and ignored those sections of the New Testament that stressed grace, worship, ritual, vicarious atonement, and salvation through faith. He was theologically closer to Aquinas, with his doctrine of justification by works, than to Paul, Augustine, and Luther, with their doctrines of justification by faith. It was this doctrine of salvation by faith that he found so offensive in the teaching of St. Paul. As for mainstream American Christianity, so indebted to Luther and Calvin, Jefferson was completely in opposition to it. In his letter to Adams, March 10, 1823, he managed to unite his anti-Calvinism with his hostility to the Books of Moses and most of the Old Testament. "Calvin's character of this Supreme Being seems chiefly copied from that of the Jews. But the reformation of these blasphemous attributes, and substitution of those more worthy, pure, and sublime, seems to have been the chief object of Jesus in His discourses to the Jews." And, as noted elsewhere, Jefferson called Calvin an "atheist."[77]

He dismissed, *a priori*, almost the entire discourse of salvation by faith associated with the teachings of Paul, Augustine, Luther, and Calvin.

[76] Jefferson to John Adams, October 13, 1813.

[77] Jefferson to John Adams, April 11, 1823. He also attacked Calvin in Jefferson to Thomas Cooper, November 2, 1822, and Jefferson to Jefferson, April 11, 1823, a letter essentially the same as Jefferson to John Adams of the same date (April 11, 1823).

It was perfectly legitimate for Jefferson to reject this doctrine, central to the Anglican Church and its Puritan and Wesleyan offshoots, but he should not have been surprised that he was pursued by accusations of "atheism." The language of his prologue in the Virginia Statute for Establishing Religious Freedom was an attack on "fallible and uninspired men" who had "established and maintained false religions over the greatest part of the world and through all time." It became evident when he was elected in 1800 that most people cared very little about whether Jefferson believed in the biblical deluge, or what he thought of Luther's position on transubstantiation.

Plato's Socrates, who owed a sacrificial cock to Asclepius, or Aquinas' Jesus "observing the law completely" at Passover as he "reclined with his brothers," were not only useless, but must be expunged from the moral universe of Thomas Jefferson.[78] He pontificated that certain words could not have issued from the mouth of Jesus Christ or Socrates simply because, in his view, such words would have been out of character for either of them, thus committing the logical fallacy of "begging the question." Jefferson's republican rationalism embodied a fastidious distaste for ritualistic piety and mummery. He would give his *nihil obstat* only to Jesus' "true" teachings. Just as he thought the Bible should be kept out of the hands of children, he felt it should be dispensed in moderation to the Indians, whom he officially addressed as "my children."[79]

METHODOLOGY IN THE LIFE AND MORALS OF JESUS

In the cut-and-paste job he called *The Life and Morals of Jesus* Jefferson ignored even the most obvious conventions of textual editing. Long before he began work on his *Life and Morals*, numerous scholars were applying the methods of classical scholarship to the Bible. Jefferson provided no discussion of methods, either textual or contextual, just as he gave no

[78] According to David White, *Myth and Metaphysics in Plato's Phaedo* (Plainsboro, NY: Associated University Presses, 1989), p. 275, Socrates was at least paying lip-service to the religious practices of the day. Jefferson might have ignored this anecdote due to his contempt for Plato's accounts of Socrates' life and character. But Xenophon, whom Jefferson admired, is believed to have seen Socrates as conventionally pious where sacrifice and ritual are concerned. See Robin Waterfield, *Why Socrates Died: Dispelling the Myths* (New York: Norton, 2009), pp. 39, 41. Donald R. Morrison, "Socrates" in Mary Louise Gill and Pierre Pellegrin, eds., *A Companion to Ancient Philosophy* (Blackwell: London, 2006), p. 116.

[79] Owen Edwards, "How Thomas Jefferson Created His Own Bible," *Smithsonian Magazine* (January, 2012).

reason for his global rejection of Paul's epistles. His biblical analysis was not completely unscholarly, however. He had as his guide Joseph Priestley's *History of Corruptions* that addressed the Bible with critical tools borrowed from philology and literary criticism, and Jefferson seems to have swallowed Priestley whole. This learned and systematic work provided all the tools Jefferson needed to strip the Gospels of their superstitious trappings and discover their core of rational moralism. He pared them down to a universal golden rule, rejecting the observable evidence that religion has historically addressed a much more complicated spectrum of human needs.

Adams queried Jefferson on bibliography and methods, asking if he was aware of the speculations of "Goethens," without belaboring the point that Goethe knew Hebrew, as well as Greek. Jefferson seemed irritated when Adams reminded him of the utility of Hebrew. As for Goethe's theology, he responded with a curt "Never." Kevin Hayes points out that he possessed an illustrated edition of Goethe's *Faust*, but offers no speculations on whether he perused the philosophical content of Part II, so closely in accord with his own belief in the redemptive power of good works.[80] Goethe, like Blake, was fascinated with the theodicy of the Book of Job, with Satan's eternal damnation, and with other matters that captivated the incipient "Romantic movement." But the God of the romantics held little attraction for Jefferson, and the American discovery of German letters was to be left to the later romantics, including Ralph Waldo Emerson, Margaret Fuller, and George Bancroft.

The recurrent theme in Jefferson's selections was Jesus' disputes with the Pharisees, and his confutation of their extreme legalism. The Sermon on the Mount, which Jefferson venerated and included in his testament, contains Jesus' admonition to observe the law even more rigorously than the Pharisees. Jefferson's reading of the Beatitudes removes them from the context of the Book of Matthew and the rest of the content of the Sermon of the Mount, retaining its moralism but rejecting its reference to Jewish piety. As for the moral teaching of the Sermon, there is nothing in it that

80 Adams drew attention to Goethe in John Adams to Jefferson, November 14, 1813. Kevin Hayes remarks on the copy of Goethe's *Faust* in Jefferson's library; Jefferson's response to Adams was on January 24, 1814. Jefferson's remarks on the work of David Levi, a Jewish scholar of Hebrew, are revealing: "I have lately been amusing myself with Levi's book, in answer to Dr. Priestley. It is a curious and tough work. His style is inelegant and incorrect, harsh and petulant and finally, he avails himself all his advantage over his adversaries by his superior knowledge of the Hebrew." Jefferson's reference to Hebrew itself seems rather petulant in this letter to John Adams, April 8, 1816.

cannot be found in that very Talmud that Jefferson dismissed as totally devoid of moral teaching, a claim he made despite his lack of Hebrew, and apparently having made minimal effort to discover what the Talmud contains.[81]

RELIGION AND SOCIAL CONTROL

Jefferson, like Franklin, accepted that religion could give stability to society. By contrast, James Madison wrote that religion, whether "enthusiastic" or "civil," could neither be relied on as a means of social control, nor accepted as a foundation of government. In his appraisal of the "Vices of the Political System of the United States," drafted in April of 1787 and privately circulated to the Constitutional Convention that opened in Philadelphia the following month, he questioned whether religion could inspire law and order, or discourage a government "from unjust violations of the rights and interests of the minority, or of individuals":

> The conduct of every popular assembly acting on oath, the strongest of religious Ties, proves that individuals join without remorse in acts, against which their consciences would revolt if proposed to them under the like sanction, separately in their closets. When, indeed, Religion is kindled into enthusiasm, its force like that of other passions is increased by the sympathy of a multitude. But enthusiasm is only a temporary state of religion, and while it lasts will hardly be seen with pleasure at the helm of Government. Besides as religion in its coolest state is not infallible, it may become a motive to oppression as well as a restraint from injustice.[82]

Madison knew that religion had a history of releasing the volatile emotions of crowds and stimulating societies to acts of injustice. Jefferson stubbornly insisted that natural religion should be rational and thus equivalent to morality. Madison might have conceded as much, but he knew that historically religion had sometimes run counter to both reason and morals, manifesting itself as mob rule. He granted that religion

[81] See www.sacred-texts.com/jud/rio/rio10.htm for Talmudic parallels in the Sermon on the Mount. In that same vein, also see http://jdstone.org/cr/files/thesermononthemount.html For Jefferson's negative impressions of and reliance on secondary sources for information on the Talmud, see Jefferson to John Adams, October 12, 1813. Jefferson had read *The History of Philosophy, from the Earliest Times to the Beginning of the Present Century: Drawn up from Brucker's Historia critica philosophiae* by William Enfield, LL.D. (London: J. Johnson, 1791).

[82] Madison expressed profound disagreement with Jefferson's opinion on religion as a form of social control in letters to Jefferson (October 24 and November 1, 1787). His public statement to the same effect, "Vices of the Political System of the United States," drafted in April of 1787, had already been delivered to the Constitutional Convention.

was not always linked to the enthusiastic passions of a multitude, but nonetheless, "Even in its coolest state it has been much oftener a motive to oppression than a restraint from it." Jefferson fancied, as did Benjamin Franklin, that religion placed moral restraints on peoples and governments.[83] Madison had a more empiricist and historically based perception of religion. Like Voltaire, he could see that religion had never stopped anyone from taking slaves, exterminating tribes, or treating women as the spoils of war. Madison's historical memory never excluded the ancient atrocities of Joshua at the sack of Jericho, the examples of the feuding Greek democracies, or the horrors of the Thirty Years War. Whatever his evidence or reasoning, Madison rejected the idea that the American or any other government could depend on religion as the foundation of its political ethic.

"SUSCEPTIBLE OF MUCH IMPROVEMENT"

Jefferson's position was stable, if optimistic, and it remained consistent with what he expressed at the age of 63 in a letter to Du Pont de Nemours:

> enlighten the people generally, and tyranny and oppressions of body & mind will vanish like evil spirits at the dawn of day. altho' I do not, with some enthusiasts, believe that the human condition will ever advance to such a state of perfection as that there shall no longer be pain or vice in the world, yet I believe it susceptible of much improvement, and, most of all, in matters of government and religion.[84]

Jefferson was still enough of a child of his age to believe that education and religion should work in tandem for the improvement of society, but he did not believe that the human condition could be perfected. He wrote Bishop James Madison, cousin of the other James Madison and president of the College of William and Mary, to comment on the third volume of *The Anti-Christian and Anti-Social Conspiracy: An Extract from the French of the Abbé Barruel*. The book explicated its Jesuit author's paranoid attitudes towards freemasonry and the Illuminati, and Jefferson, although he belonged to neither, considered Barruel's ideas "perfectly the ravings of a Bedlamite." He confessed that the work "gives me the first idea I ever had of Illuminatism." The book contained quotations from Spartacus Weishaupt (which he misspelled "Wishaupt" – he and Adams had difficulty with German names). He wrote:

83 Benjamin Franklin to ——— [presumably to Thomas Paine]. See note 64 above in this chapter.
84 Jefferson to Pierre Samuel Du Pont de Nemours, April 24, 1816.

Wishaupt seems to be an enthusiastic Philanthropist. He is among those (as you know the excellent Price and Priestley are) who believe in the indefinite perfectibility of man. He thinks he may in time be rendered so perfect that he will be able to govern himself in every circumstance so as to injure none, to do all the good he can do to leave government over him, & of course to render political government useless.[85]

There was a point of overlap between Jefferson and the Illuminati, and that was their common belief that the object of Jesus Christ was "simply to reinstate natural religion & by diffusing the light of his morality to teach us to govern ourselves." Jefferson was put off by the anti-masonic content of Barruel's book and felt it represented his fears of "spreading of information, reason, & natural morality among men." Jefferson expressed considerable interest in Weishaupt, but felt that the latter's experiences in Bavaria "under the tyranny of a despot and priests ... has given an air of mystery to his views." Although Jefferson was not entirely opposed to the ideas of Weishaupt, he never quite divested himself of an emotional need for the traditional Protestant God, for he was old-fashioned enough to require a God who meted out justice either in this world or possibly even the next.

"I tremble for my country," he wrote on reflecting that the republic might suffer divine retribution in this world for its collective guilt, but what of retribution against the individual sinner in the next? One of his assertions about ancient Judaism was that it contained no belief in the immortality of the soul or in rewards or punishments after death. He wrote:

Moses had either not believed in a future state of existence, or had not thought it essential to be explicitly taught to his people. Jesus inculcated that doctrine with emphasis and precision.[86]

Voltaire and other examiners of Christianity disagreed with him, remarking that Jesus preserved and inculcated the Jewish belief in an afterlife.[87] Jefferson might have recalled that Jesus' parable of Lazarus and Dives presupposed that Jesus and his Jewish contemporaries shared a traditional belief in the doctrine of saved and lost souls. Jewish tradition

[85] For an explanation of the Illuminati, see Alan V. Briceland, "The Philadelphia *Aurora*, the New England Illuminati, and the Election of 1800," *The Pennsylvania Magazine of History and Biography*, 100 (1976), 3–36.

[86] Jefferson to William Short, August 4, 1820.

[87] Voltaire, *L'Opinion en alphabet*, ed. Louis Moland, Œuvres complètes de Voltaire (Paris: Garnier, 1877–85 [1752]), vol. XVII, p. 20: "Enfin, les pharisiens et les esséniens, chez les Juifs, admirent [paid homage to] la créance d'un enfer à leur mode [after their fashion]: ce dogme avait déjà passé des Grecs aux Romains, et fut adopté par les chrétiens."

had referred to the blessed as dwelling after death in the bosom of Abraham. The apocryphal second Book of Maccabees referred to praying for the souls of the dead. Jefferson's occasional intimations of immortality had to be reconciled with his identification of himself in a letter to William Short as an Epicurean. Epicurus had denied the existence of a soul separate from the body and also rejected the principle of an afterlife. Jefferson enlisted Epicurus to support his thinking that God and the material universe were coeval, but Epicurus' doctrine that the human soul is material and perishable was inconveniently opposed to another of Jefferson's pet queries: if, in fact, the human soul was merely mortal, why should one fear God's eternal displeasure?[88]

If there was to be a judgment after death, then "we have nothing to fear," he wrote to Adams, with apparent confidence, in that same 1820 letter of March 14, "for we have, willingly, done injury to no man." This placed him on the side of those theologians who held that justification in the eyes of God is dependent upon one's actions, rather than faith alone. Eternal punishments and rewards must ultimately be based on how one dealt with one's fellows. This seeming adherence to the doctrine of works placed him on the side of Aquinas and the Catholic theologians, rather than on the side of Luther and Calvin. His "Unitarian" theology had led him away from the Protestant doctrines of his Anglican upbringing and towards the medieval in the doctrine that salvation was the reward for one's good deeds. But Jefferson left behind no written evidence of an unequivocal belief in eternal rewards and punishments.

To friends in hours of bereavement, he offered consoling reflections on at least the possibility of an afterlife. In a letter to John Page on the occasion of the death of his daughter, Maria Eppes, in 1804, he wrote in equivocal

[88] "As you say of yourself, I too am an Epicurian. I consider the genuine (not the imputed) doctrines of Epicurus as containing everything rational in moral philosophy which Greece and Rome have left us," Jefferson to William Short, Monticello, October 31, 1819. The term "epicurianism" in its pejorative sense was applied to Jefferson by Representative William Loughton Smith of South Carolina in 1792, cited in Dumas Malone, *Jefferson and His Time*, 6 vols. (Boston, MA: Little, Brown, 1951), vol. II, *Jefferson and the Rights of Man*, p. 474. For Lucretius see Stephen Greenblatt, *The Swerve: How the World Became Modern* (New York: Norton, 2011). For Jefferson's invocation of Thomas Aquinas and Francis Toleta, see Jefferson to John Adams, April 11, 1823. Jefferson quoted approvingly an opinion attributed to St. Thomas Aquinas in a mammoth 1599 work on his *Summa Theologica* by the Jesuit theologian Cardinal Franciscus de Toledo, sometimes referred to as Franciscus Toletus, although Jefferson referred to him as Toleto or Toleta. He provided no explanation as to why he relied on Toledo's interpretation. Cardinal Toleto appears in various documents spelled "Toleto," or "Toleta," or "Tolet."

terms of a hope "to rise in the midst of friends we have lost . . . But whatever is to be our destiny, wisdom, as well as duty, dictates that we should acquiesce."[89] Based on such evidence as his letter to John Adams at the time of Abigail's demise, Annette Gordon-Reed and Peter Onuf express an intimation that Jefferson believed in an afterlife.[90] His kindly words of consolation revealed a hope of an Elysium in which, at least metaphorically, loving souls might be reunited. Other scholars have found Jefferson's position to be more shifting and ambiguous.

Based solely on his writings one cannot dismiss the positions of such historians as Charles B. Sanford and M. Andrew Holowchak, who observe that "Jefferson unequivocally commits himself to materialism." He wrote that thought, will, and action were properties of the body just "as that of magnetism is to the Needle, or of elasticity to the spring," and the quality called mind dissipates "on dissolution of the material organ." There is, of course, no way of knowing exactly what anyone "believes" about the nature of God or the doctrine of salvation, it is possible only to hear or to read their words. On March 14, 1820, at the age of 77, he wrote to John Adams "that nobody supposes that the magnetism or elasticity retire to hold a substantive and distinct existence" if the steel containing them is destroyed:[91]

> when once we quit the basis of sensation all is in the wind. to talk of immaterial existences is to talk of nothings. to say that the human soul, angels, god, are immaterial, is to say they are nothings, or that there is no god, no angels, no soul. I cannot reason otherwise.[92]

But the speculations of these sentences tax our powers of exegesis. He wrote to Adams more than once in 1820 concerning the mysteries of an afterlife and the immortality of the soul, describing them as matters "which may indeed be, but of which I have no evidence," and pretended

89 Jefferson to Governor John Page, June 25, 1804. I failed to locate this letter either in the 1904 Ford edition or at Founders Online. Following Professor John B. Boles' endnote, I located it in A. E. Bergh, ed., *The Writings of Thomas Jefferson* (Washington, DC: The Thomas Jefferson Memorial Association, 1907), vol. XI, online edn. at www.constitution.org/tj/jeff11.txt

90 Gordon-Reed and Onuf, *"Most Blessed of the Patriarchs,"* p. 310. They cite Jefferson to John Adams, November 13, 1818.

91 Jefferson to Adams, March 14, 1820. Sanford, *The Religious Life of Thomas Jefferson*, p. 149. Holowchak, "Did Thomas Jefferson Believe in the Afterlife?" For the contrasting view shared by Annette Gordon-Reed and Peter Onuf, see their *"Most Blessed of the Patriarchs,"* p. 310.

92 Jefferson to John Adams, August 15, 1820, is speculative and indefinite. The letter reveals an uncertainty as to whether the soul is immortal.

that in such matters he had "little indulged" himself. This was pure rhetoric, contradicted by the fact that these same letters were evidence of a lifetime devoted to reading and reflection on these themes. His summary statement was that it required undue mental contortion to believe in "an existence called Spirit, of which we have neither evidence nor idea." "Perhaps," he concluded, and only "perhaps," he and his friend would "know ere long" the answer to the "incomprehensibility" of how their material bodies were "endowed with thought." Never in his correspondence did Jefferson reveal a perfect "faith" in the immortality of the soul; on the contrary, he repeatedly revealed a profound chasm of doubt concerning its mortality.[93]

MATERIALISM, EPICURUS, AQUINAS, AND TOLEDO

As a "materialist," Jefferson separated himself from the teachings of Jesus in at least one essential respect. "It is not to be understood that I am with him in all his doctrines," he wrote to his intimate correspondent, William Short. "I am a Materialist; he takes the side of spiritualism."[94] Jefferson asserted that Jesus was a spiritualist, but, as we have seen, he also asserted that the early fathers of the church "generally, if not universally were materialists." At some point Jefferson must have applied his almost limitless powers of imagination to reconciling the two ideas. We cannot retrieve any writings in which he attempted to square the circle of his Epicurean materialism with his Christian moralism, and it would be fascinating to see how he reconciled his ambivalence concerning the reality of an afterlife with his idea of religion as a necessary instrument of social control.

It was not only that God had always co-existed with the intellectual Logos of St. John the Evangelist, but the material world had also existed "*ab aeterno.*" Jefferson enlisted the third-century theologians Tertullian and Origen, the latter an extremist renowned for castrating himself, and went so far as to invoke Roman Catholic commentators such as the Jesuit

93 My reading of the letters to John Adams of March 15 and August 15, 1820, reveal no certainty in Jefferson's mind as to the immortality of the soul. These letters, taken together with the one addressed to Thomas Cooper, August 20, 1820, are speculative and open.

94 Jefferson to William Short, April 13, 1820. Jefferson to François Adriaan Van der Kemp, February 9, 1818, cites Aquinas in connection with the idea that God willed the creation of the world from all eternity. Jefferson to John Adams, April 11, 1823, mentions Toleto (Francisco Toledo) and St. Thomas Aquinas.

Bishop of Soissons, Pierre Daniel Huet, to the effect that God's nature was "*spiritus etiam corporis.*" In his old age, Jefferson conveniently employed obscure papist commentaries to refute Protestant theologians, reviling Calvin's characterization of a God "chiefly copied from that of the Jews," and rejecting both Calvinism and Orthodox Judaism as "blasphemous." Jefferson invented a place for himself in a tradition that he saw stretching from the pagans Epicurus and Lucretius to the Roman Catholic Aquinas. He saw in his blending of pagan with papist doctrines the basis for his own avowed materialism. To say that God was a disembodied spirit was, in his view, to remove him from reality; it was either a blasphemy or a denial of his existence. Jefferson was turning to and citing not only Aquinas, but the Catholic Cardinal Toleta's (or Toleto, or Francisco, or Franciscus, de Toledo) commentaries on Aquinas, showing himself to have a mind that was open to Roman Catholic doctrine – at least insofar as he could enlist it in support of materialism. He was ecumenical enough to cite Catholic theologians if he could use their dogma to undermine America's dominant Calvinism.[95]

In sum, Jefferson claimed no certainty regarding the Christian doctrine of the afterlife or the immortality of a non-material soul. In his youth he tried to puzzle out the question, and, in a letter to an unidentified recipient, he did not specifically reject the idea of a soul existing separate from the body, but his words were equivocal: "We are generally taught that the soul leaves the body at the instant of death, that is, at the instant in which the organs of the body cease totally to perform their functions."[96] In mid life, he found the immortality of the soul to be an unassailable problem, which he addressed in a letter to Isaac Story, December 5, 1801, with irony and eloquence:

> the laws of nature have withheld from us the means of physical knowlege of the country of spirits and revelation has, for reasons unknown to us, chosen to leave us in the dark as we were. when I was young I was fond of the speculations which seemed to promise some insight into that hidden country, but observing at length that they left me in the same ignorance in which they had found me, I have for very many years ceased to read or to think concerning them, and have reposed my head on that pillow of ignorance which a benevolent creator has made so soft for us, knowing how much we should be forced to use it.

[95] Jefferson to John Adams, April 11, 1823. Jefferson's religious pragmatism and evolution are briefly presented in Smelser, *The Democratic Republic*, pp. 7–8.

[96] Jefferson to unidentified recipient, July 26, 1764.

In later writings he avowed to Adams his convictions regarding the researches of Priestley, who thought that the early Christians had not entertained any theory either of predestination or of the immortality of the soul.[97] He called himself an Epicurean and a materialist. Epicurus was supposed to have written, in his *Letter to Menoeceus*, "when death is come, we are not ... and the dead exist no longer." In addition to his fondness for Epicurus, Jefferson showed an abiding interest in Lucretius, another proponent of materialism, *and* he had numerous copies of his *De rerum natura* in his libraries.[98] Late in life, Jefferson associated spiritualism with "fanaticism" and with royalism (in a letter to Thomas Cooper, August 14, 1820), although the connections were not explicitly stated. He asserted that monarchists encouraged fanaticism as a variety of irrationality necessary to their ambitions: "Presbyterians indeed, the Loyalists and Loyolists, of our country, spare no pains to keep it up." He referred to "the heresy of spiritualism," but seemed confident that such "fanaticism is vanishing with us." He cited Locke as to the materiality of the soul, but also averred that "the fathers of the church, of the three first centuries, generally, if not universally materialists, extend[ed] it even to the creator himself."[99]

Jefferson expressed the strongest of doubts on the immortality of the soul very late in life, in a letter of January 11, 1825 to François Adriaan Van der Kemp. He could not resist a swipe at "the Athanasians," but he was not attacking their Trinitarianism. It was their insistence on the idea of an immaterial soul that could be detached from the body at death and continue to exist independently of it. He had been reading a book by Jean-Pierre Flourens, the pioneer physiologist, whose researches had convinced Jefferson that human consciousness was located in the cerebrum. He discussed Flourens' researches briefly and made many sarcastic comments. He had written three days earlier to John Adams stating his opinions more succinctly, but making it obvious he considered the new field of brain science more convincing than any received dogma on the immortality of the soul:

> Cabanis had proved, from the anatomical structure of certain portions of the human frame, that they might be capable of recieving from the Creator the faculty of thinking. Flourens proves that the cerebrum is the thinking organ, and that life and health may continue, and the animal be entirely without thought, if

[97] Jefferson to John Adams, August 22, 1813.

[98] https://en.wikipedia.org/wiki/De_rerum_natura

[99] Jefferson to Thomas Cooper, August 14, 1820.

deprived of that organ. I wish to see what the spiritualists will say to this. whether, in this state, the soul remains in the body deprived of it's essence of thought, or whether it leaves it as in death and where it goes?[100]

The Cabanis to whom he referred was Pierre Jean Georges Cabanis, a French materialist who believed that the brain was the organ of thought. Once again he concluded with one of his hypothetical questions indicating that he had already come close to an answer. Proofs for existence of the soul after death seemed unlikely.

FIRST AMENDMENT TO THE BILL OF RIGHTS

Jefferson, who was in France during the Constitutional Convention, was one of those who persuaded Madison to draft the First Amendment. There was a copycat quality about the American Bill of Rights. The thinking was that since England had a Bill of Rights, including the right of every *Protestant* to bear arms, the United States ought to have a Bill of Rights, as well. Madison did not see the necessity of a Bill of Rights, but diplomatically succumbed to pressure. Jefferson's words concerning the First Amendment are far removed from their original intent. The First Amendment took a neutral stance on religious liberty and preserved the traditional rights of the several states to violate the consciences of individuals within their borders.

Since Jefferson was not the actual framer of the Bill of Rights, or any other part of the Constitution, it is ironic that his pronouncement on the "wall of separation between church and state" eventually became an ever-present quasi-constitutional doctrine in the minds of most Americans who bother to think about the question of religion in public life. Jefferson's hostility to conventional Protestantism, with its doctrines of vicarious atonement and the divinity of Jesus Christ, are well known to us today. Jefferson made clear that he considered almost every aspect of *conventional* Christianity and Judaism to be little more than superstition. He asserted that religion should consist primarily of a moral code and implied the existence of a God who agreed with his own notions of justice, and would reward good and punish evil, both in the secular and in the eternal world.[101]

100 Jefferson to John Adams, January 8, 1825.

101 Jefferson to Benjamin Rush, April 21, 1803; Jefferson to Doctor Benjamin Waterhouse, Monticello, June 26, 1822.

PUBLIC AND CEREMONIAL RELIGION: NEHEMIAH DODGE, DANBURY BAPTISTS, AND SAMUEL MILLER

In 1802, less than a year after demonstrating that he was not an atheist, with public references to a "beneficent Being," Jefferson denied the request of a committee representing the Baptist Association of Danbury, Connecticut, that he officially proclaim a national day of thanksgiving. It was here that Jefferson made his most famous pronouncement on church and state separation. Probably unawares, the Baptists had provided Jefferson with an opportunity that he had "long wished to find" to articulate a principle that was close to his heart and was to leave an indelible mark on American constitutional history. At least that was what he claimed in a letter to Levi Lincoln, his Attorney General.[102] Jefferson was lying in wait when the Danbury Baptist Association asked him to set aside a national day dedicated to religious purposes, and one wonders if they realized the controversy they were opening. Jefferson's Virginia Statute for Establishing Religious Freedom provided no warnings that he desired any religious confrontations. It seemed to represent little more than a healthy and reasonable disestablishmentarianism. As of this writing, the Library of Congress website notes that "Throughout his administration Jefferson permitted church services in executive branch buildings."[103] But Jefferson's private goals must have differed dramatically from what his public behavior indicated. He seemingly desired to pull the props from under any presidential endorsement of orthodox priestcraft.

His famous response to the Danbury Clergy contained the still-controversial phrase "separation between church and state." He asserted "that religion is a matter which lies solely between man and his God." Then he offered an exceedingly loose interpretation of the constitutional clause, "Congress shall make no law respecting an establishment of religion, or prohibiting the free exercise thereof." He constructed these words broadly as meaning that the American people had built "a wall of separation between church and state." But in a strict, literal sense, the Constitution had built no such wall; it had merely restricted the law-

[102] Jefferson to Levi Lincoln, January 21, 1802. Also see Leonard Levy, *Jefferson and Civil Liberties* (Cambridge, MA: Harvard University Press, 1963), pp. 7–8.

[103] Religion and the Founding of the American Republic, Religion and the Federal Government, Part 2, Exhibitions (Library of Congress) available at: www.loc.gov/exhibits/religion/rel06-2.html

making powers of the national Congress, without placing any constraints on the states in matters of religious establishment.[104]

Jefferson's Danbury letter came close to undermining not only his signal position on states' rights, but also his dogma on strict construction. He declared in favor of the idea that the Constitution is an expression of the "supreme will of the nation." Yet he referred to the Constitution not only as an expression of the national will, but as a statement "in behalf of the rights of conscience." This seemingly placed a distance between himself and others who suggested that the Constitution was a mere compact between the states. He took a position that would later be iterated by Andrew Jackson, that the Constitution was a creation of the people and acted on them collectively, without the intervening medium of the states. This was contrary to the state sovereignty position that Jefferson had asserted on other notable occasions. Jefferson's position usually resembled that of his beloved enemy, Patrick Henry, who had claimed that the constitutional Framers should have used the phrase "We the States," and not "We the People." Asserting the sovereignty of the people over the states was a curious position for the author of the Kentucky Resolution of 1798, who had implied that the Constitution created neither a consolidated republic nor a perpetual nation, but only a dissolvable pact between the states. Now, in the Danbury Baptist letter, he called the Constitution an "expression of the supreme will of the nation."[105]

In the Danbury letter, Jefferson asserted, as Andrew Jackson later would, the prerogative of the executive branch to interpret, as well as to enforce, the Constitution. Secondly, he introduced a matter conspicuously absent from the First Amendment's religion clause, the issue of individual conscience. In effect, the Danbury letter placed the federal government in the broadly constructed role of protecting individual conscience. The Constitution, he asserted, expressed the national will and existed "to restore to man all his natural rights, convinced he has no natural right in opposition to his social duties."[106] The assertion that the

[104] Jefferson to Messrs. Nehemiah Dodge, Ephraim Robbins, and Stephen S. Nelson, a Committee of the Danbury Baptist Association, in the State of Connecticut, Washington, January 1, 1802. Neem, "A Republican Reformation," pp. 91–109, discusses the context of the Address to the Danbury Clergy and some editorial problems.

[105] Patrick Henry, speeches in the Virginia Convention, June 4–5, 1788. Thomas Jefferson, Kentucky Resolution, November 16, 1798. In Richard Hofstadter, *Great Issues in American History, From the Revolution to the Civil War* (New York: Vintage, 1958), pp. 119–124, 176–182.

[106] Andrew Jackson, "Proclamation to the People of South Carolina," December 12, 1832. The discussion of Thomas Jefferson as a nationalist by Brian Steele, *Thomas Jefferson*

Constitution had a direct relationship to the individual implied that it superseded even the rights of those several states that still insisted, in 1801, on their establishmentarian prerogatives.

Although this Jeffersonian interpretation of the Constitution limited the power of the federal government to establish religion, it indirectly implied that the federal Constitution protected the individual from religious burdens imposed by state and local authorities, as well as by the national government. According to Jefferson's radically broad and extremely loose construction, the federal Constitution protected the individual from any intrusion by government, whether national or local, into matters of religious conscience in any way. His pronouncement on church–state separation partially accounts for the continuing willingness of American liberals, progressives, Quakers, Reform Jews, and Unitarians to overcome their distaste for his libertarian political doctrines and their abhorrence at his apparent engagement in an unequal sexual relationship with a teenager.

Jefferson told Levi Lincoln he was seeking a test case, but were the Danbury Baptists also looking for a test case? Probably not; they were expecting a bland ecumenical endorsement of the vague civil religion that Jefferson had approved in his First Inaugural Address. They expected that he would behave no differently from Washington and Adams, who had obviously considered public religious observances appropriate. And neither of the first two presidents had seen any harm in making blandly pietistic public pronouncements. Civil religion in America under the Unitarians, Washington, and Adams had implied a reverence for law and order, common decency, and the Golden Rule. Their civil religion was a simple acknowledgement of "Nature and Nature's God," and implied nothing more presumptuous than a hope that God would bless America so long as the republic remained true to the dictates of nature and of conscience.

The Danbury request, although it came from Baptists, was not sectarian. It contained no implication of institutionalized worship or evangelical manifestations of pietism. More to the point, it did not suggest any violation of the Constitution. Strictly speaking, the clergymen's request

and American Nationhood (Cambridge University Press, 2012), takes a somewhat different approach from my own, giving lesser significance to the importance of Patrick Henry and overlooking the irascible and unpredictable anti-localism and nationalism of Andrew Jackson's position during the South Carolina crisis. Abe Lincoln, of course, made brilliant use of Jackson's reasoning.

would have had to call for Congress to make a law interfering with the states' prerogative to establish religious practices in order to be unconstitutional. But Jefferson inferred that even a non-legislative proclamation would violate the Constitution. A simple announcement by the president would compromise the rights of individual conscience and contradict "the progress of those sentiments which tend to restore to man all his natural rights." The First Amendment did not address any of these noble and enlightened issues. It limited the powers of Congress to pass laws, but not the powers of the president to make non-binding pious proclamations, such as those he had previously made on state occasions.

The First Amendment had nothing to do with the executive branch, although Jefferson's reading of it involved placing limitations on the executive.[107] Strictly constructed, the First Amendment merely placed limitations on Congress' legislative powers. Thus, compliance with the Danbury request need not necessarily have been interpreted as a constitutional issue at all, since it dealt neither with the legislative powers of Congress, nor with the executive power of the president to enforce a law. Furthermore, individual conscience was not a constitutional matter. The Constitution was no more concerned with the religious conscience of a white Baptist clergyman in Connecticut than it was with the life, liberty, or property of a Monticello slave.

Jefferson's response in 1802 to the Danbury request must be contrasted with his 1808 response to a similar request. In the Danbury letter, Jefferson had engaged in broad construction, but, by contrast, he used strict construction and introduced a more proper constitutional issue when he addressed a letter to the Reverend Samuel Miller on January 23, 1808. Miller, like the Danbury Baptists, had suggested that the president set aside a day of fasting and prayer, and Jefferson again responded in the negative. But his strict constructionist reasoning in this letter was strikingly different from his loose constructionist argument in the Danbury letter of 1802. The Danbury letter argued for freedom of conscience and individual rights. The letter to Miller, in glaring contrast, completely avoided the matter of individual conscience and presented not only a constitutional argument in general, *but a states–rights argument in particular*.

The government in Washington was "prohibited by the Constitution from meddling with religious institutions, their doctrines, discipline, or

[107] For another view, see Daniel Jacob Hemel of the Yale University Law School, "Executive Action and the First Amendment's First Word," *Pepperdine Law Review*, 40 (2013).

exercises" on two grounds. The first of these was "the provision that no law shall be made respecting the establishment, or free exercise, of religion." This was the provision on which Jefferson had based his argument of 1802. But in this instance, he produced a different argument, based on the Tenth Amendment, the constitutional provision "which reserves to the states the powers not delegated to the U.S." It was a strict constructionist argument in that "Certainly no power to prescribe any religious exercise, or to assume authority in religious discipline, has been delegated to the general government." Thus, the power to set aside a day of religious observance must "rest with the states, as far as it can be in any human authority." By this logic, he continued in the same letter to Miller, it was not acceptable for the president even to "recommend, not prescribe a day of fasting & prayer. That is, that I should indirectly assume to the U.S. an authority over religious exercises which the Constitution has directly precluded them from."

A presidential recommendation would carry authority and imply a sanction "by some penalty on those who disregard it; not indeed of fine and imprisonment, but of some degree of proscription perhaps in public opinion." He followed up with one of his characteristic rhetorical questions: "And does the change in the nature of the penalty make the recommendation the less a law of conduct for those to whom it is directed?" He was far too cautious to assert that his recommendation of a day of prayer would expose those who ignored it to public abuse, but, on the other hand, he mildly chided, he did not think it would be in "the interest of religion" for any religious body to invite the civil magistrate to become involved in the implicit propagation of religious doctrine. This would be tantamount to investing the national government "with the power of effecting a uniformity" of time or content of religious observances. The letter to Miller seemingly backed away from the letter to the Danbury clergy, which implied an executive power to protect the people even from the states in matters of religious conscience.

The Constitution neither limited nor bestowed powers on the president regarding religious rites, although previous executives may have seemed to set precedents in this regard. Jefferson recognized that the Constitution did not interfere in the question of whether the several states had a right to fix public religious observations. But he felt "that what might be a right in a state government, was a violation of that right when assumed by another" government. That is to say, although the states had powers to violate the conscience of the individual, the federal government did not. In any case, he told Miller he would act according to the dictates of his own reasoning, which told him "that civil powers alone have been given to the President of the U. S. and no authority to direct the religious exercises of his constituents."

Strictly constructed, the First Amendment did not speak to the issue of presidential powers at all: it merely placed restrictions on the law-making powers of Congress. Secondly, it did not address the individual rights of citizens of the United States in matters of conscience or anything else. The Constitution did not guarantee the slave's right to life, liberty, or the pursuit of happiness. The First Amendment did not guarantee the white citizen's rights with respect to an establishment of religion, or even restricting the free exercise thereof. The Constitution merely prohibited Congress from passing a law limiting the freedom of exercise of religion. It did not address the rights of Virginia or Massachusetts in this regard. Jefferson's letter to Miller adhered to the strict interpretation of the Constitution, and implied that any rights related to religious conscience existed purely at the whim of the states.

In the reasoning of present-day Christian conservative Rick Santorum, the separation of church and state, far from being a fundamental American doctrine, is downright disgusting.[108] Alan Keyes and other Christian conservatives are as fond of reminding us of Jefferson's religious rhetoric in the Declaration as they are of reminding us that the separation of church and state does not appear in the Constitution.[109] They are correct in pointing out that the Bill of Rights contains no separation clause; in fact, the First Amendment ignores freedom of conscience altogether and preserves the right of the states to tax in support of the churches. The Constitution's abdication of any moral responsibility to

[108] Commenting on presidential candidate John F. Kennedy's statement "I believe in an America where the separation of church and state is absolute" in a 1960 address to the Greater Houston Ministerial Association, Senator Rick Santorum said, "I had the opportunity to read the speech, and I almost threw up," *The Washington Post* (February 26, 2012).

[109] Alan Keyes, organizational website, RenewAmerica.us, "On The Issues," August 3, 2004, at www.ontheissues.org/Celeb/Alan_Keyes_Civil_Rights.htm, or see the 2008 Senate campaign website, www.alankeyes.com, "Issues," October 1, 2007:

> School prayer is constitutional. The doctrine of "separation of church and state" is a misinterpretation of the Constitution. The First Amendment prohibition of established religion aims at forbidding all government-sponsored coercion of religious conscience. It does not forbid all religious influence upon politics or society. The free exercise of religion means nothing if, in connection with the ordinary events and circumstances of life, individuals are forbidden to act upon their religious faith.

Source: www.keyes2000.org/issues/religionschoolprayer.html (January 7, 1999).

protect freedom of conscience was in deference to colonial tradition. It was no secret that Puritan Massachusetts had been established by fanatics, who discriminated against Quakers and other heretics. The Mayflower Compact swore allegiance to "our dread sovereign lord, King James" and undertook the "advancement of our Christian faith and honor of our king and country."

The Puritan colony of Massachusetts is forever associated with missionary zeal, moral uprightness, and a Protestant ethic. By contrast, the Cavalier colony of Jamestown, largely due to the report of its founder, Captain John Smith, is remembered for its cut-throats, idlers, and fops, and among them at least one cannibal, who pickled and ate his wife. The more positive aspect of Virginia's foundation legend is that it was relatively innocent of any theocratic mission, for the most part ignoring Quakers, and suffering maypoles to stand. Executions for witchcraft were rare and remarkable, and if they occurred at all Jefferson said he was not aware of them.[110] In obeisance to the diversity of founding traditions, religious backgrounds, and the existing legal codes of the several colonies, the Bill of Rights neither fortified nor denied any state prerogatives "respecting an establishment of religion."

Jefferson's claim in his letters to Joseph Priestley, John Adams, and Benjamin Rush that he knew something about the character of Jesus reinforced his political theory. His assertion that Jesus was not divine was useful to his theory of the wall of separation between church and state. He had already leapt that wall in the Declaration of Independence. But if Jefferson's God was an abstract natural force embodied in the material world, and Jesus was only a great moral teacher, then sending a bowdlerized Testament to the Indians was not a violation of the separation principle. Christian conservatives are fond of reminding us that the Declaration of Independence presupposes the existence of God, and that it invokes God in the act of creating the nation. They are correct, but if Jefferson's God was a watchmaker, he was something more than a disinterested mechanic, disinterested in his universe or its moral laws. He was a just being, righteous in his wrath, who might some day punish the entire nation for the slaveholder's peculiar crimes. In *Notes on Virginia* Jefferson accordingly raised the following rhetorical question:

110 See Monica C. Witkowski and Caitlin Newman, "Witchcraft in Colonial Virginia" in *Encyclopedia Virginia*, www.encyclopediavirginia.org: "English law prescribed harsh punishments for witchcraft, the most extreme being 'paines of deathe,' but no person accused of the crime in colonial Virginia was executed. By comparison, in the Massachusetts Bay Colony, nineteen so-called witches were executed in 1692 alone."

And can the liberties of a nation be thought secure when we have removed their only firm basis, a conviction in the minds of the people that these liberties are of the gift of God? That they are not to be violated but with his wrath? Indeed I tremble for my country when I reflect that God is just.[111]

Jeffersonian religion obviously demanded a God of wrath and vengeance, but not necessarily the immortality of the soul. He raised two questions – trickster-ish ones at that, for they issue from the same pen that is so famously associated with the doctrine of the separation of church and state. To say that "the only firm basis" of civil liberties was a religious "conviction in the minds of the people" was to imply, as Franklin had, that religion was central to the social order. The rhetorical questions may have equivocated on whether religion is essential to the preservation of "liberties," but they nonetheless implied that the "only firm basis" for securing liberties was a conviction in the minds of the populace of the existence of a righteous and impatient God, whose wrathful hand periodically shook the clockwork of the universe.

Would God inflict his punishments on miscreant individuals in an afterlife, or would he punish entire nations in the here and now, when his patience ran out? Voltaire had said that "If there were no God, it would have been necessary to invent him," in order to check the power of tyrants. Franklin thought God was necessary in order to check the impulses of Everyman. Regardless of what questions the two iconic American *philosophes*, Jefferson and Franklin, might pose about the nature of God, they found it necessary and convenient to invoke him, at least rhetorically. Certain questions remained open: would this Old Testament God of wrath and vengeance punish the individual in this world, or in an afterlife? Would he punish only the wayward individual, or would He visit his judgments on the entire nation collectively when his patience ran out?

Jefferson's political ethos was inseparable from a premonition that Providence was likely to reward the good and punish the wicked. He knew evil when he saw it, and reflected that God might recognize it as well. Whether he literally feared the possibility of a divine intervention on behalf of the slave is difficult to say. "Considering numbers, nature and natural means only," a slave insurrection was possible, and if one should "become probable by supernatural interference! The Almighty has no attribute that can take sides with us in such a contest."[112] Whether or not Jefferson should be taken literally in these semi-mystical meanderings

111 Jefferson, *Notes on Virginia*, p. 185.
112 Jefferson, *Notes on Virginia*, pp. 195–196.

cannot be ascertained, but it is certain that he had no more scruples than Abraham Lincoln would about mixing religious rhetoric into his discourse on slavery, liberty, and the state.

Lincoln's Second Inaugural Address recycled Jefferson's fears in a famous jeremiad foreboding that "every drop of blood drawn with the lash shall be paid by another drawn with the sword." This address averred that "this mighty scourge of war" was the result of divine justice. Lincoln's was not the theodicy of the Book of Job, where the workings of Providence were beyond mere human understanding. His was not the doctrine of William Blake, Swedenborg, or the Quakers, in which acts of God were beyond the measure of Newtonian reason and natural religion.[113] Lincoln was adopting a Jeffersonian logic in which a nation "conceived in liberty" was subject to "the Laws of Nature and Nature's God." His address was an admonition that national tribulations were manifestations of divine justice, and a proof that "the judgments of the Lord are true and righteous altogether."

Did Jefferson "believe" that his God would visit divine justice on slaveholders in this world, or in the next? He seemingly trembled more for his country in this world than he did for his soul in the hereafter, for, as we have seen, he doubted whether he, or any other creature, actually had an immortal soul. Flourens' experiments on lobotomized pigeons rendered immortality a matter on which he could express uncertainty. And even if he had an immortal soul, and even if slaveholding was a sin, his culpability was merely part of the nation's collective guilt. It had been forced on him against his will, and we have seen how he boasted to John Adams that he had "willingly done injury to no man." God's judgment might be inflicted on all the citizens of a nation that tolerated slavery, for God "maketh His sun to rise on the evil and on the good, and sendeth rain on the just and on the unjust," but it was not certain that any individual slaveholder would suffer the eternal fires of hell.[114]

[113] Northrup Frye, *Fearful Symmetry: A Study of William Blake* (Princeton University Press, 1947), p. 161, for Blake's war with deism, and Newton. Also see Mark Schorer, *William Blake: The Politics of Vision* (New York: H. Holt and Co., 1946) for "The Case against Locke."

[114] The quoted verse, Matthew 5:45 (King James Bible), is in Jefferson's pastiche of *The Life and Morals of Jesus of Nazareth* (see note 5 above).

10

Women and the Count of Monticello

When Jefferson wrote in the Declaration of Independence that "All men are created equal," it was no mere instance of synecdoche (or any literary device that uses one word to represent a greater whole). He did not intend to write, as one might write in the twenty-first century, "all men and women are created equal." His reference to "all men" should not be shifted into the category of what used to be called "non-specific gender." It was neither an innocent slip of the pen nor an accident of contemporary vernacular diction. He wrote "men" meaning "men," without considering the word as an inclusive metaphor, and there was no tacit understanding that it encompassed women in the fullest cultural or political sense. Abigail Adams' noteworthy "Remember the ladies" injunction did not affect the deliberations of the Continental Congress. The "common sense" of the time and place dictated that women were to be kept out of men's affairs and, in Jefferson's words, "excluded from their deliberations."

Not that he would have reduced women to domestic animals or barefoot menials. He was fascinated by quick, witty, and perceptive women, as were many of his contemporaries. He fancied himself a champion of the legendary equality of Anglo-Saxon womanhood, which was already evident in English towns of the fourteenth century. So many enterprising women operated businesses and industries in Chaucer's England that scholars have had difficulty saying which of them might have been the model for the *Canterbury Tales*' Wife of Bath. By the eighteenth century, British society was more egalitarian in most respects, including gender, than the rest of Europe, and this was acknowledged on the Continent, as in the declaration of one heroine, "I am an English woman born to Freedom," in

Mozart's opera *Die Entführung aus dem Serail*. Egalitarian notions, including those affecting women, were rapidly developing in the West, but especially in English-speaking cultures.[1] Jefferson showed that he had assimilated at least the common rhetoric in his *Notes on Virginia*, which disparagingly compared the barbarous condition of Native American women to the supposed elevation of women under civilization:

> The women are submitted to unjust drudgery. This I believe is the case with every barbarous people. With such, force is law. The stronger sex therefore imposes on the weaker. It is civilization alone which replaces women in the enjoyment of their natural equality. That first teaches us to subdue the selfish passions, and to respect those rights in others which we value in ourselves. Were we in equal barbarism, our females would be equal drudges.[2]

He made these comparisons thoughtlessly, and his allusion to "natural equality" was careless, for that nebulous phrase had a very restricted meaning in his world. His thoughts on women revealed a mélange of contradictory emotions, but on the role of women in political discourse he was clear. He exchanged serious letters with Abigail Adams in which they disagreed frankly and sharply over Shays' Rebellion in her state of Massachusetts. By contrast, he wrote some months later to Angelica Schuyler Church advising her not to concern herself with the agitation in her native state over the new constitution: "The tender breasts of ladies were not formed for political convulsion; and the French ladies miscalculate much their own happiness when they wander from the true field of their influence into that of politicks."[3] Annette Gordon-Reed notes that Jefferson showed no support for women in public office, elected or appointed. She notes that when Secretary of the Treasury Albert Gallatin suggested hiring women in government offices during the second Jefferson administration, "President Jefferson, taking his role as the symbol of the nation to heart, replied, 'The appointment of a woman to office is an innovation for which the public is not prepared,

[1] John Matthews Manly, *Some New Light on Chaucer* (New York: H. Holt and Co., 1926). Hope Phyllis Weissman, "Why Chaucer's Wife Is from Bath," *The Chaucer Review*, 15, no. 1 (summer, 1980), 11–36. John A. Garraty comments on the feminist element in Mozart's *Die Entführung aus dem Serail* in his textbook, *The American Nation: A History of the United States to 1877*, 7th edn. (New York: HarperCollins, 1991), vol. I, p. 95.

[2] Thomas Jefferson, *Notes on the State of Virginia*, ed. David Waldstreicher (Boston, MA: Bedford Books, 2002), p. 122.

[3] Abigail Adams to Jefferson, January 29, 1787; Jefferson to Abigail Adams, February 22, 1787. Jefferson to Angelica Schuyler Church, September 21, 1788.

nor am I.'"[4] Even in the purely social sphere, Jefferson placed limitations on women's activities, offering spurious biological reasoning regarding what he called the "weaker" sex, as he penned his objections even to women dancing after marriage in a letter to Nathaniel Burwell: "The French rule is wise, that no lady dances after marriage. This is founded in solid physical reasons, gestation and nursing leaving little time to a married lady when this exercise can be either safe or innocent."[5]

Respecting the "unjust drudgery" endured by "barbarous people," he seemed unmindful of the drudgery experienced by white women of his own frontier Virginia, and of course he gave no thought to the black women and girls on his plantations. The fortunes of working women were hard, and even women of the upper classes usually worked as vigorously as their ages, health, and strength allowed. In many cases, the burdens of childbearing were onerous and, in all cases, potentially life-threatening. The Gospel of St. John 16:21 has Jesus say of a woman that "as soon as she is delivered of the child, she remembereth no more the anguish, for joy that a man is born into the world." In fact, circumstances did not always lead to joy. Even if a woman survived the delivery of her infant, most children did not live long, and the woman was frequently crippled by physical pain, and enduring depression, or both.

As for his application of the phrase "natural equality" in the passage above, we need only recall the difficulty of defining that term to which historians such as Rozbicki, Valsania, and others have alluded. In every historical context, "equality" is a nebulous concept, but Jefferson's conception of gender equality was firmly imbedded in the more traditional, rather than the more radical, notions of his times, and paid no heed to views of such eighteenth-century feminists as Mary Wollstonecraft or Olympe de Gouges. In fairness to Jefferson, it should be admitted that neither of these bourgeois authors wrote an exposé of the drudgery that women laborers experienced, either in agricultural communities or in Europe's nascent industrial sweatshops.[6]

[4] Annette Gordon-Reed, "Female Trouble," *New York Review of Books* (February 8, 2018), p. 12.

[5] Jefferson to Nathaniel Burwell, March 14, 1818, reprinted in Merrill Peterson, ed., *Thomas Jefferson, Writings* (New York: Literary Classics of the United States, 1984), p. 1411.

[6] Olympe de Gouges (1748–93) was the author of the *Déclaration des droits de la femme et de la citoyenne* (Paris, 1791). The pamphlet was the work of a royalist, dedicated to Marie Antoinette, and by no means a manifesto on the rights of common women laborers. De Gouges was one of the many women guillotined during the French Revolutionary Reign of Terror.

ATTITUDES TO WHITE WOMEN

We have previously mentioned the cruel punishments delivered to white women who had affairs with black men in Jefferson's reformed Virginia Code. His Bill for Proportioning Crimes and Punishments offered telling commentary on the sexual morality of women. His revisions were submitted nine years after his challenge to the law regarding indentured servitude. Merrill Peterson's edition of the *Writings* reproduces the text, along with Jefferson's brilliantly erudite scholarly apparatus. But while Jefferson's footnotes, commentary, citation of British precedents, and lengthy Latin quotations reveal the impressive depths of his legal scholarship, they are frustrating to modern readers, due to the author's reticence with respect to his own opinions regarding certain of the bill's most startling provisions: "Whoever shall be guilty of rape, *polygamy*, or sodomy with man or woman, shall be punished; if a man, by castration, a woman by boring through the cartilage of her nose a hole of one half inch in diameter at the least." The crime of "buggery" was to be punished by castration.[7]

A woman who deviated from the sexual norms was, at least theoretically, to be punished with disfigurement, and a man by castration. Dumas Malone correctly places the brutal language of Jefferson's bill within the context of his intention to actually soften the existing Code, and his desire to purge it of needlessly vindictive and traditionally cruel provisions.[8] Even in its revised form the Code retains its traditional harshness and seems hardly in accord with our cherished notions of the Age of Enlightenment. The Bill of Rights' abolition of "cruel and unusual punishment" certainly reflects more correctly the intentions of Jefferson, Madison, and others of the Founders. Nonetheless, Jefferson's attitudes to women in this code of punishments contained vestiges of medieval thinking.

[7] Dumas Malone, *Jefferson and His Time*, 6 vols. (Boston, MA: Little, Brown, 1948), vol. I, *Jefferson the Virginian*, p. 272. Also see Thomas Jefferson, "64. A Bill for Proportioning Crimes and Punishments in Cases Heretofore Capital, 18 June 1779" in Julian P. Boyd, *The Papers of Thomas Jefferson* (Princeton University Press, 1950), vol. II, pp. 492–507. The text of the Bill is also reproduced in Peterson, ed., *Thomas Jefferson, Writings*, pp. 349–364. Also see www.monticello.org/site/research-and-collections/bill-64 Also see Malone, *Jefferson the Virginian*, p. 272. A footnote to the document cites the following definition: "Sodomy is a carnal copulation against nature, to wit, of man or woman in the same sex, or of either of them with beasts."

[8] Malone, *Jefferson the Virginian*, pp. 269–273.

Despite his touching on serious ideas in his correspondence with Abigail Adams, and presumably with his hostesses in the salons of Paris, he did not believe that women should trouble their heads with politics. To some extent this attitude derived from his discomfort with women in any role outside the roles of lover, housewife, or mother. There was, however, an additional reason women could not participate either in a democratic or in a republican assembly, and the objection he raised was not purely mechanical. Nor was it based on any presumed intellectual inability of women to participate in public affairs: his objections were of a more primal sort. Even in a representative or republican democracy he pontificated on the exclusion of "Women, who, to prevent depravation of morals and ambiguity of issue, could not mix promiscuously in the public meetings of men."[9]

While the term "promiscuous" need not necessarily be interpreted in today's sense of indiscriminate carnality, it carried at least a double entendre in Jefferson's day, denoting a lack of discrimination, or vulgarity, and disorderly behavior. Furthermore, when used within such close proximity to the phrase "ambiguity of issue," there was a detectable innuendo. He was certainly aware that his words referred obliquely to sexuality and reproduction. The implication was that participation in political meetings would lead women to a social promiscuity, resulting inevitably in the birth of children of questionable paternity. To modern ears, such an idea is annoying, but even more disturbing is Jefferson's advocacy of lessening the penalty for sexual crimes.[10]

He disassociated his attitudes towards aristocratic women from attitudes towards those who must work for a living. Following his tour of Germany and the Rhine valley in 1788, he was quick to criticize European cultures where he saw women consigned to drudgery, and he demonstrated his usual genius for detecting motes in the eyes of others:

> The women here, as in Germany, do all sorts of work. While one considers them as useful and rational companions, one cannot forget that they are also objects of our pleasures. Nor can they ever forget it. While employed in dirt and drudgery some tag of a ribbon, some ring or bit of bracelet, earbob or necklace, or something of that kind will shew that the desire of pleasing is never suspended in them. How valuable is that state of society which allots to them internal emploiments only, and external to the men. They are formed by nature for attentions and not for hard labour. A woman never forgets one of the numerous train of little offices which belong to her; a man forgets often.

[9] Jefferson to Samuel Kercheval, September 5, 1816.

[10] Jefferson to James Madison, December 15, 1786. Also see Malone, *Jefferson the Virginian*, p. 272.

Within one sentence he referred to women as "useful," and then as "rational companions," and then finally as "objects of our pleasures." For the previous three years, he had been distributing *Notes on Virginia*, with its reference to the civilization "which replaces women in the enjoyment of their natural equality," and lamenting the barbarous treatment of Native American women. As previously, he overlooked that many women in Virginia were "employed in dirt and drudgery." By contrast, he was currently keeping in his Paris household one charming young mulatto girl, apparently "formed by nature for attentions and not for hard labour," and possibly as the object of his pleasure.

WHITE WOMEN IN JEFFERSON'S DOMESTIC LIFE

Jefferson was married in 1772, at the age of 29, to Martha Wayles Skelton, born in 1748. She was refined, educated, literate, and musical: she played the piano and participated in the concerts at Monticello during the Revolutionary War. The number of pregnancies she may have endured is uncertain, but we know that she had six children during her ten-year marriage to Jefferson, three of them dying in infancy. Her health apparently declined with each pregnancy, and she died shortly after giving birth in 1782 to her seventh child, Lucy Elizabeth, who survived until the age of 2. According to legend, Martha on her deathbed secured Jefferson's promise not to remarry, presumably in order to prevent her surviving children from being subjected to a stepmother and to competition with her children.[11]

She had been married previously, in 1766, to Bathurst Skelton, and gave birth to a son, John, in 1767. Bathurst died the following year of a sudden illness, and John died of a fever a few years later, in June of 1771. Inadvertently, Jefferson left a hint that he might initially have found Martha's previous sexual experience intimidating. Historian Jack McLaughlin wonders whether he:

> was guilty of a mental slip when he identified her on their wedding license, written in his own hand, as a 'spinster.' The word was crossed out and above it, in another hand, the word "widow" was inserted. It was not the kind of error a lawyer, particularly a Thomas Jefferson, would normally make, and it suggests that he would have preferred that his wife had not been married before.[12]

[11] Annette Gordon-Reed discusses Martha's death and Jefferson's promise not to remarry in *The Hemingses of Monticello* (New York: Norton, 2008), pp. 144ff.

[12] Jack McLaughlin, *Jefferson and Monticello: The Biography of a Builder* (New York: Henry Holt, 1990).

The era placed great cultural and sentimental value on marrying a virgin, but sometimes placed an even greater, and more practical, value on marriage to a wealthy widow. When Jefferson married Martha he already had over fifty slaves, and he multiplied his slaveholdings when he married Martha, with her dowry of a hundred enslaved people.

John Adams, the sole non-slaveholder among the first four presidents, seems to have been the only one to spend his wedding night with a virginal white woman. No presumption of male premarital celibacy existed in those days. One recalls Benjamin Franklin's observation on the use of "venery" for reasons of health. His admitted premarital escapades, and the ambiguity of his post-marital relationships, not to mention his common-law marriage to Sarah, who never secured a divorce from her first husband, have not gone unnoticed. She was an economic asset and an excellent business partner, who defended his interests during Franklin's lengthy sojourn in London, where he sustained a nebulous relationship with Margaret Stevenson. Gouverneur Morris married a "woman with a past" once tried for the infanticide of a child that might have been her own and possibly conceived with Richard Randolph, her brother-in-law. This was Ann "Nancy" Randolph, related both by ties of sanguinity and by marriage to the Jeffersons.[13]

Jefferson was a kindly and solicitous father to his daughters, providing for their education in the arts and letters, although it must have pained him that his only son died in infancy. He wrote tellingly in a letter to Baron Riedesel, offering his sincere condolences when the baroness gave birth to a daughter and not a son. He placed his daughters in a convent school during the years in Paris, and he advised his older daughter, Martha, whom he called Patsy, to study French, music, drawing, and English spelling, in his letter of November 28, 1783. Later in life, she offered him advice on personal finances, but he seemed unable to benefit from her acumen. She eventually married Thomas Mann Randolph, her third cousin, but left him intermittently to play the role of Jefferson's first lady during his residency at the president's house. She had become estranged from her husband, a drunkard and a madman, and, at the time of Jefferson's death, she was mistress of Monticello.

Randolph's death occurred less than two years after Jefferson's, and Patsy, being left with very meager resources, was forced to sell Monticello in 1834. Certainly she could have used any monies she might have gained

[13] Cynthia A. Kierner, *Scandal at Bizarre: Rumor and Reputation in Jefferson's America* (Charlottesville, VA: University of Virginia Press, 2004).

from putting the Hemingses on the market, but she respected her father's wish to emancipate Sally's children, Madison and Eston. This suggests as well some revulsion at the idea of selling her own flesh and blood, especially since they were almost as white as she. Sally could depend on her children for support, but Patsy could not. Like Dolley Madison, she found herself teetering on the edge of poverty in her final years, until she was saved from destitution by grants from the state legislatures of South Carolina and Louisiana, apparently disinclined to send to the poor house the daughter of the author of the Declaration of Independence.

Given Jefferson's closeness to and emotional dependence on Patsy, it is tempting to compare his relationship with her to the often discussed relationship between Aaron Burr and his daughter, Theodosia. Historian Nancy Isenberg, noting Burr's admiration for Mary Wollstonecraft's *Vindication of the Rights of Woman* (1792), describes the extraordinary education that he provided to Theodosia, and comments on the elevated level of their correspondence. In reading Isenberg one becomes instantaneously aware that we know much more about Burr's wife than we do about Jefferson's, and it also becomes clear that Burr was not intimidated by women who were experienced in the world of men and moved easily within it. Burr was, admittedly, as psycho-historian Arnold A. Rogow observes, "a rarity in his day," and Thomas Jefferson, as Jon Kukla has observed, was not.[14] Rogow observes that Aaron Burr had views about the role of women "that did not fall short of those associated with modern feminism."[15]

Throughout his long life, Jefferson found it difficult to separate "objects of our pleasures," that is women, from their domestic functions or corporeal attributes. It was a convention of seventeenth- and eighteenth-century English letters that women were frequently referred to as

[14] Arnold Rogow, *A Fatal Friendship: Alexander Hamilton and Aaron Burr* (New York: Hill and Wang, 1999), p. 91. Nancy Isenberg, *Fallen Founder: The Life of Aaron Burr* (New York: Penguin Books, 2007), pp. 65–67; also see index. Jon Kukla, *Mister Jefferson's Women* (New York: Vintage, 2008), is an accurate, but selective, analysis of Jefferson's intellectual interactions with women. For more on Jefferson's relationship to his older daughter, "Patsy," see Billy Wayson, *Martha Jefferson Randolph: Republican Daughter and Plantation Mistress* (Chapel Hill: University of North Carolina Press, 2012).

[15] See the review by Stacy Schiffoct, *The New York Times* Sunday Book Review, 14 (2007). For a more recent study, see Virginia Scharff, *The Women Jefferson Loved* (New York: HarperCollins, 2010). For Jefferson's ambiguous relationship to Angelica Church, see William Howard Adams, *The Paris Years of Thomas Jefferson* (New Haven, CT: Yale University Press, 1997).

"the Sex," with a capital letter.[16] Such usage seemed to suggest that sex was a characteristic peculiar to women, or at least that women were more subject to the forces of sexuality than men. Taken as a whole, Jefferson's writings to and about women reveal a nervous ambivalence. While he was generally suspicious of the intellects of women, he was obviously attracted to women who could be "rational companions," and he corresponded appreciatively with several bright women, notably Abigail Adams, Angelica Church, Mercy Otis Warren, and Madame de Staël. The most important of his intellectual relationships with a woman was that which developed between him and Maria Cosway, an Italian-English artist seventeen years his junior during his residency in Paris.

JEFFERSON'S WERTHER, MATE-SHARING, AND THE COSWAYS

Beginning while he was minister to France, and continuing intermittently for many years afterward, Jefferson maintained a friendship with Maria Cosway, a popular hostess, fully fluent in French, Italian, and English, a musician, and an accomplished artist. She was also married, and the ambiguous nature of Jefferson's relationship to the Cosways has led to considerable speculation among scholars. It seems doubtful Maria was so vacuous as she has been portrayed by Jon Meacham. Another historian, Andrew Burstein, has endowed her portrait with greater nuance. Fawn Brodie suspected that the relationship may have been successfully consummated, but there can be no certainty. E. M. Halliday suggests that Cosway thought fondly of Jefferson, but saw him as a perplexing and irresolute American provincial.

In the correspondence between the two we see a pattern that is present in Jefferson's bilingual communications. Regardless of the language in which he received a letter, he usually responded in English. Several times, she wrote to him in Italian, but Jefferson never responded to her with a letter entirely in that language. It is probable that he was able to make sense of her letters, as Romance languages share some similarities, and his French reading ability was good. While crossing the Atlantic he had worked through a bilingual French–Spanish edition of *Don Quixote* (see

[16] Some examples of "the Sex" as a synonym for the female sex are to be found in the *Oxford English Dictionary*, definition 1, section e. Additional examples are in Joseph Addison and Richard Steel, *Spectator*, no. 81; Joseph Addison, *Spectator*, no. 98; Joseph Addison, *The Freeholder*, no. 38; Samuel Johnson, *The Rambler*, no. 39. Jefferson to George Washington, December 4, 1788. In the late twentieth century, many English speakers attempted to divorce the concept of gender from genitalia.

Chapter 1 note 1 above). It seems likely that he and Cosway may have engaged in occasional badinage in Italian, with her doing most of the talking, but if Jefferson was reticent when it came to writing in French, he was even more bashful when it came to Italian.

Maria seemed sometimes to be testing his linguistic abilities. In September 1786, she playfully asked why she was writing him in English, a language that did not belong to her, "una lingua che non m'appartiene," when she could write in her own, "which you understand so well," and switched to Italian midway through. A month later she began a letter in English, then switched to Italian, asking rhetorically, "But what am I doing, that I write so much English when I can write in my own language, and become a little less involved?" The desire to be more or less "involved" by either party in a relationship of this sort can be ambiguous whether or not language is a barrier, but in any case, and with few exceptions, Maria's letters to Jefferson were in English.

On September 18, 1786, shortly after they met, while they were walking in the Cours-la-Reine, a public garden along the River Seine (possibly it was their first promenade alone), Jefferson suffered the embarrassment of a broken wrist, to which he alluded several times in their correspondence. The 43-year-old, perhaps in an attempt to impress the much younger woman, had apparently attempted to leap a fence and suffered a fall. The incident left Maria "more uneasy than I can express," and she attempted to visit him two days later, starting out for his house along with her husband, who killed the project by "forgetting the hours," so that they started out too late "and we were forced to turn back" due to a previous engagement, as they were expected "to be at St. Cloud to dine with the Duchess of Kingston." She and her husband would come to see him the following morning, "if nothing happened to prevent it."[17]

Jefferson kept up the correspondence during her absences from Paris, and his own. In the course of his Rheinland tour of 1788 he described to her a visit to a gallery of paintings in Düsseldorf which he called "sublime, particularly the room of Van der Werff," making brief mention of one of its paintings in a letter that some historians have found significant:

[17] Descriptions of the injury are located at the website of the Jefferson Encyclopedia (www.monticello.org/site/research-and-collections/tje), where documents cited are Jefferson's account-book reference to paying two surgeons on September 18, 1786, and a letter dated September 20, 1786. L. G. Le Veillard to William Temple Franklin: "20 7bre. Day before yesterday, Mr. Jefferson dislocated his right wrist when attempting to jump over a fence in the Petit Cours." Also see Maria Cosway to Jefferson, September 20, 1786.

At Dusseldorp [Düsseldorf] I wished for you much. I surely never saw so precious a collection of paintings. Above all things those of Van der Werff affected me the most. His picture of Sarah delivering Agar to Abraham is delicious. I would have agreed to have been Abraham though the consequence would have been that I should have been dead five or six thousand years.[18]

Fawn Brodie and E. M. Halliday have offered incisive commentary on Van der Werff's painting, "Sarah Delivering Hagar to Abraham," which was one of the few references that Jefferson made to German artistic or intellectual life during this tour of the Rheinland. We are dependent on his letters to Cosway for some of the few glimpses we have of Jefferson's emotional and aesthetic experiences during his tour. Brodie and Halliday point out that Jefferson's visit to the Düsseldorf Museum and his viewing of Van der Werff's painting, and the fact that he reported the visit to Maria Cosway, offer clues to his relationship with Sally Hemings, to Cosway, and to his deceased wife, Martha. Just as Sarah had delivered her servant Hagar to Abraham, so too had Martha "delivered" Sally to him.[19]

He wandered about in the land of thinkers and poets like some gloomy figure from a Caspar Friedrich painting, contemplating the ruins of castles, particularly the Schloss at Heidelberg. In his travel notes he called it "the most noble ruin I have ever seen," and he wrote Cosway, saying, "Heidelbourg would stand well along side the pyramids of Egypt. It is certainly the most magnificent ruin after those left us by the antients."[20] His commentary is tantalizing, for it contrasts with what is usually perceived as his theory of architecture and his architectural tastes. The latter revealed a preference for the chaste Palladian style of Monticello and the University of Virginia rotunda. The jumbled eclectic castle, with its jarring combinations of Roman, medieval, and baroque elements, egregiously violated the rational principles of classicism. His fascination with it reveals that he stood with other Enlightenment intellectuals at the juncture of classicism and romanticism.

During the days of poking about in the ruined castles of Hanau and Heidelberg, and writing letters to Maria Cosway, he revealed a romantic temperament that invites comparison with the frustrated protagonist of Goethe's epistolary novel, *Werther*. These letters have an unmistakable tone of maladroit flirtation and awkward seductiveness, suggestive of an

[18] Jefferson to Maria Cosway, April 24, 1788.

[19] Fawn Brodie, *Thomas Jefferson: An Intimate History* (New York: Norton, 1974), pp. 230–231. E. M. Halliday, *Understanding Thomas Jefferson* (New York: HarperCollins, 2001), Chapter 8.

[20] Jefferson to Maria Cosway, January 24, 1789.

adulterous longing that is commonly presumed to have gone unfulfilled. The letters reveal a capacity for self-deprecation uncharacteristic of Jefferson, as on the occasion noted elsewhere here in the letter to Cosway, when he compares his emotions to those of an orangutan. But the *Sturm und Drang* of his presumably unconsummated passion is usually more gently expressed and sometimes approaches, if it does not duplicate, the tone of Goethe's *Werther*, the story of a young man who commits suicide over his unrequited love with a married woman.[21]

Like Werther's letters, Jefferson's were irresolute and uncertain missives that the poor woman sometimes found puzzling. Jefferson was well acquainted with Rousseau's epistolary novel on a related theme, *Julie ou La nouvelle Héloïse*, a story of premarital sex and unconsummated adultery that was placed on the Catholic Index. His admiration for *Héloïse* is documented, and, although he never mentions Goethe's immensely popular novel, it is inconceivable that he could have been ignorant of the "Werther fever" that swept Europe, and generated numerous copycat suicides, not to mention several imitations, satires, and parodies. Jefferson's letters to Cosway invite comparison to the passionate epistolary effusions of both literary events, although the parallel is not commonly drawn. There are numerous analyses of this correspondence, notably that of Jon Meacham, who thinks that Cosway was too vacuous to appreciate Jefferson, and that of E. M. Halliday, who intimates that Jefferson was too much the Puritanical American bumpkin to handle his own feelings.

Contemplating the unhappy possibility of a mate-sharing relationship with the Cosways, it is almost impossible that Jefferson would have been unaware of his similarity to the protagonist of Goethe's *Werther*. The parallels to his own romantic episode were self-evident. He once recommended Rousseau's *Héloïse* to Robert Skipwith in 1771. He also recommended *Émile et Sophie*, Rousseau's sequel to *Émile*, under its English title *Emilius and Sophia*. Jefferson wrote to Maria of a contest between his head and his heart reminiscent of Goethe's "Zwei Seelen wohnen, ach! in meiner Brust" ("Two souls dwell, alas! in my breast"). He concluded this celebrated "Heart and Head Letter" with a request that she remember him "in the most friendly terms to Mr. Cosway." He may have been dimly aware that his attempt to maintain an ambiguous relationship with a married woman and at the same time to maintain the illusion of friendship with her husband was a real-world cognate to Werther's frustration. Like Charlotte, the object of Werther's passion,

[21] Ibid.

Maria was obviously tempted by Jefferson's approaches, but how far either of them was willing to proceed with the affair is a matter of conjecture. There is no incontrovertible evidence that Jefferson ever consummated any sexual relationship with any woman after his wife's decease, but there seems to be less doubt that in this instance he did "covet his neighbor's wife."[22]

Jefferson was the emblematic American "innocent abroad," and the sophisticated, polyglot Maria Cosway was considerably more cosmopolitan than his departed wife. Little as we know of Jefferson's relationship to Maria, we have at hand more information on his romance with her than on his romance with Martha Jefferson. No letters between him and his wife survive. Certainly there is nothing so intimate as the effusion of the "Heart and Head Letter" he sent to Maria early in their relationship, a few weeks after the fence-leaping incident. This document, faltering but elegant and suffused with passion, has received much comment, despite the understandable vagueness of its expectations. Fawn Brodie has provided a creative exegesis in which she envisions "thinly disguised in this letter, Jefferson's fantasy that the Cosways will visit America, that her husband will die and Maria will be left to be cherished and comforted at 'our own dear Monticello.'"[23]

COUNT ALMAVIVA AND THE COUNT OF MONTICELLO, AN "INCONSTANT LORD"

Jefferson should have been squirming in his seat throughout the performance of Beaumarchais' dark comedy, *Le Mariage de Figaro*, in August of 1786.[24] The author of the Declaration of Independence was indulging in radical chic when he viewed the sixteenth Paris performance of this Juvenalian satire on the residual practice of *droit de seigneur*, sometimes called the "right of the first night," or *jus primae noctis*, the medieval entitlement of the lord of a manor to violate a bride on the night of her wedding. The play's pompous but bumbling villain, Count Almaviva,

[22] Fence-leaping incident described in Merrill Peterson, *Thomas Jefferson and the New Nation* (Oxford University Press, 1970), p. 349. "Zwei Seelen": cf. Chapter 6 note 34 above. The "Heart and Head Letter" of October 12, 1786, has commanded a great deal of attention from almost every biographer or commentator. It would be an endless and unnecessary task to list and recount the myriad speculations on whether or not Jefferson and Maria Cosway ever experienced bodily sexual contact.

[23] Brodie, *Thomas Jefferson*, p. 211.

[24] William Howard Adams, *Paris Years*, p. 71.

attempts to seduce Susanna, the fiancée of his servant, Figaro. It is a bitter comedy of errors, in which the lord of the manor is made to appear ridiculous, and the hero, Figaro, delivers a famous declamation on the equality of all men. Jefferson was aware of Mozart's highly successful operatic adaptation, *Le Nozze di Figaro*, with his librettist, Lorenzo Da Ponte, which had opened in Vienna three months earlier, and Jefferson eventually acquired music from their *Don Giovanni*, which likewise handled themes of rape, seduction, betrayal, and class conflict.[25] The Paris censors were shocked by the anti-aristocratic themes of *Figaro* but eventually lifted their interdiction, apparently at the insistence of Marie Antoinette. Jefferson recorded no discomfort, and no reflection on these themes, although the dynamics were poignantly reminiscent of the situation in his Parisian household, with its servants, James Hemings and his sister, Sally.

Count Almaviva and the Count of Monticello shared elements of seigneurial culture, if Jefferson's recent biographers are correct, for it is certain that a sexual relationship leading to mulatto offspring existed between the Jefferson family and the Monticello slave, Sally Hemings. Most students of the matter believe it probable that the father of at least some of Sally's quadroon children was Thomas Jefferson himself. The proximity of *Figaro*'s theme to the custom of his own country must have occurred to him, with a nubile, wavy-haired, nearly white teenager among his house servants. The practice of using African American women, particularly light-brown ones, for sexual purposes is inextricable from the history of the American South, although concubinage was not an aspect of local culture that Jefferson directly addressed in his revision of the Virginia Code. Some years earlier he had weakened that code's provisions concerning rape because of "the temptation women would be under to make it the instrument of vengeance against an inconstant lover." The usually fastidious biographer, Dumas Malone, made a fortuitously titillating slip of the pen when he incorrectly transcribed an extract from one of Jefferson's letters, inadvertently substituting for "inconstant lover" the more provocative words "inconstant lord."[26]

25 Lorenzo Da Ponte eventually migrated to the United States, where he became the French tutor of Clement Clarke Moore, author of the poem "A Visit from St. Nicholas," or "The Night Before Christmas." Moore's authorship of that work has also been attributed to Clement Clare, as noted elsewhere in this volume, but Moore's denunciation of *Notes on Virginia* is uncontested, stating that Jefferson's book "debases the negro to an order of creatures lower than those who have a fairer skin and thinner lips."

26 Annette Gordon-Reed, *Thomas Jefferson and Sally Hemings: An American Controversy* (Charlottesville, VA: University of Virginia Press, 1997). Also see Annette Gordon-Reed,

Jefferson and Marie Antoinette may never have sat in the same audience, but it is said that she attended numerous performances. The "inconstant lord" and clever trickster who was the author of the ambiguous words "all men are created equal" understandably spent his time among the aristocracy, not the "Canaille of Paris." Attendance at the Beaumarchais drama, even if one did not understand every word, was just the thing to do. It is understandable that he would relish the fashionable self-disparagement of the upper classes by that same aristocracy. In any case, the queen was known for her sentimental attitudes towards peasants, and she was criticized by some contemporaries for reveling in the drama's lambasting of her own caste.[27] The shared interest of Jefferson and the queen would represent one among many instances of the controlling irony of Jefferson's life. The young dandy in powdered wig and fluffy jabot in the 1786 portrait by Mather Brown would write approvingly of the deposition and humiliation of the French aristocracy, and especially Marie Antoinette.[28]

"You will learn to speak [French] better from women and children in three months, than from men in a year," he wrote to Thomas Mann Randolph. To another correspondent, the Reverend James Madison, he described a conversation with a poor Frenchwoman, whom he casually encountered while walking in the country. "Wishing to know the

"Thomas Jefferson and Sally Hemings: A Brief Account," at the Monticello website, https://home.monticello.org/ M. Andrew Holowchak, *Framing a Legend: Exposing the Distorted History of Thomas Jefferson and Sally Hemings* (Amherst, NY: Prometheus Books, 2013), challenges Annette Gordon-Reed, Fawn Brodie, and Andrew Brustein, placing great weight on two spurious arguments: that Jefferson would have found the idea of sex with an almost white mulatto repugnant, and that to have had sex with her would have violated his sense of right and wrong. Dumas Malone, through apparent inadvertence, placed this text in the context of *droit de seigneur*, accidentally substituting, as mentioned, the provocative words "inconstant lord" for "inconstant lover." Compare Jefferson to James Madison, December 15, 1786, with Malone, *Jefferson the Virginian*, p. 272. Malone incorrectly quotes "inconstant lord," cf. Boyd and the Library of Congress manuscript of the original. This was an error in the Ford edition of the *Works of Thomas Jefferson* (1904), which dated the letter December 15, 1786; Malone, *Jefferson the Virginian*, p. 272. Boyd's edition dates the letter December 16, 1786, and corrects the text. The original can be verified in The Thomas Jefferson Papers, online edition, Library of Congress.

[27] Blog, https://tyntyn50.wordpress.com/2015/10/12/the-opera/: "The play opened at the Théatre Odéon in Paris on April 27, 1784, and ran for sixty consecutive performances. Marie Antoinette is reported to have attended every one of them."

[28] The Mather Brown portrait, the only painting of Jefferson from the period of his Paris sojourn, does not resemble portraits from later life. William Short felt it did not resemble him. See William Short to John Trumbull, September 10, 1788, in a note to Thomas Jefferson from John Trumbull, December 19, 1788, Founders Online.

condition of the laboring poor," and needing directions along the road, he entered into conversation with her as to "her vocation, condition and circumstances." She told him she was a day laborer with two children to maintain, and a rent she could barely manage. Often she could get no employment "and of course was without bread." Since she had served him as a guide, he gave her 24 sous on parting. "She burst into tears of a gratitude which I could perceive was unfeigned because she was unable to utter a word. She had probably never before received so great an aid." As he continued his walk he reflected on the "unequal division of property which occasions the numberless instances of wretchedness which I had observed in this country and is to be observed all over Europe."[29]

As for the matter of *droit de seigneur*, his presumed relations with Sally Hemings are implicitly addressed within today's imbalance-of-power discourse, in which any suspicion of an unequal power relationship leads to accusations of a sexual offense. Few of his contemporaries would have thought along such lines, for nowhere in the Bible or the Code of Hammurabi, or in his ancient Saxon documents, would Jefferson have discovered much discussion of the sexual abuse of a "servant." In an age of arranged marriages, forced marriages, and marriages of convenience, few people experienced sexuality completely free of emotional or societal duress. Harriet Jacobs and Sally Hemings may have achieved better bargains than many of their contemporaries, regardless of race and class, or gender.[30]

SALLY HEMINGS AND THE SCHOLARS

Since the publication of a study conducted by geneticists on living descendants of Jefferson and the Hemingses, even some very cautious historians have accepted Madison Hemings' statement that Sally named Jefferson as his father.[31] Fawn Brodie expressed a reasonable suspicion that the

[29] Jefferson to Thomas Mann Randolph, July 6, 1787. Jefferson to the Reverend James Madison, October 1, 1785.

[30] Annette Gordon-Reed has speculated that Sally was occasionally able to set some conditions in her relationship to Jefferson. See, for example, Gordon-Reed, *Hemingses of Monticello*, p. 348. One scholar has suggested that Sally's mother, Betty (Elizabeth), having been able to make the most of her alleged relationship as concubine to the widower John Wayles (father of Jefferson's wife, Martha), may have been seeking to secure her daughter's interests by encouraging or promoting a relationship with Jefferson. See Halliday, *Understanding Thomas Jefferson*, p. 98.

[31] Eugene A. Foster, et al., "Jefferson Fathered Slave's Last Child," *Nature* (November 5, 1998), 27–28. Eliot Marshall, "Which Jefferson Was the Father?" *Science*, 283, no. 5399 (January 8, 1999), 153–155, makes the point that the DNA evidence establishes only that

Jefferson family destroyed long ago all evidence that might have clarified Jefferson's relationship to Sally Hemings. It is known that she and her children had a special relationship to him, and that their lives were different from those of most slaves. Research into the family DNA has established that at least some of the Hemings children were descended from a male member of the Jefferson family. Although Jefferson had a brother, Randolph, who might have been the culprit, the Jefferson family never in the past assigned paternity to him, but firmly took the position that Sally's children were fathered by Jefferson's nephew, Peter Carr.[32]

Annette Gordon-Reed has executed a posthumous paternity suit that gives substance to contemporary reports of Jefferson's keeping a slave concubine. The tradition of miscegenation in the American South provides further confirmation. Using the testimony of contemporary witnesses, and confirming the findings of Jefferson's chief biographer and apologist, Dumas Malone, who revealed that Jefferson was always present at Monticello when Sally Hemings' children were conceived, Gordon-Reed convinces many biographers and historians of Jefferson's paternity, and the DNA evidence is, in the present author's view, mere "icing on the cake."

Jefferson's character is the strongest argument that he was among the founders of the segregation–miscegenation tradition of Strom Thurmond.[33] He was opportunistic, flexible, and shifty on many issues, both in theory and in practice. Presenting himself to the world as a champion of the simple life, he was a self-confessed Epicurean, both in the popular and in the philosophical sense. He wore a powdered peruke and

one of the male members of the Jefferson family was the father of the Hemings children. The evidence does, however, indisputably show the falsity of the Jefferson family's story that the father was Peter Carr.

32 Foster, et al., "Jefferson Fathered Slave's Last Child," detail the results of a genetic study, concluding that "a Jefferson male" – although not necessarily Thomas Jefferson – fathered Eston Hemings. In January of 2000 the Thomas Jefferson Foundation, which has owned and operated Monticello since 1923, released the findings of an investigation, concluding that Thomas Jefferson was probably the father of Sally Hemings' children. The descendant of Eston Hemings Jefferson did have the Field Jefferson haplotype. The Carr haplotypes differed markedly from those of the descendants of Field Jefferson. See article at Encyclopedia Virginia (www.encyclopediavirginia.org/Hemings_Sally_1773-1835#start_entry).

33 Senator Strom Thurmond, the South Carolina segregationist, died in 2003, and it was afterwards revealed that he secretly had a mulatto daughter, Essie Mae Washington-Williams (1925–2013), the result of an affair with a 16-year-old servant.

rode in a liveried carriage attended by slaves.[34] He flagrantly demonstrated how to convert debt into a blessing while constantly prating on the evils of indebtedness. After pretending to advocate abolition for almost fifty years, he finally supported the extension of slavery into the unsettled territories of the American West. The strongest evidence is Jefferson's Machiavellian character, revealed not only in his pragmatic inconstancy, but in ideological flexibility.

Some historians have asserted that no one who made such disparaging remarks concerning the appearance and body odor of Negroes could possibly have shared his bed with a black woman. In fact, white Virginians who shared his opinions were habitually suckling from the breasts, bathing in the sweat, and inhaling the breath of, and swapping saliva and sharing sexual secretions with, Negroes. Jefferson's plans to rid America of the black genetic presence were already too late when he presented his deportation plan to the Virginia legislature, and even less workable by the time they were published in his *Notes on Virginia.* Despite his call for selective breeding, the culture of Southern white males was as Negrophiliac as it was Negrophobic. Although many white males made pejorative remarks about the appearance of black women, they were constantly generating a population of mulattoes, quadroons, and octoroons, many of whom were sexually desirable "high yellow" women. Elizabeth Hemings, Sally's mother, who was described by contemporaries as "very fair," was allegedly the concubine of John Wayles, a widower, whose legitimate daughter, Martha, became Jefferson's wife, which would have made Sally his sister-in-law.

Whoever her father was, Sally's genetic heritage was more European than African, and contemporaries described her as "very fair." As such, she could have met Jefferson's standards of beauty, and she may even have resembled her presumed half-sister, Martha. A 39-year-old, white male widower, although claiming to be repulsed by black skin, could have been tempted by the proximity of an almost-white teenage girl, brought up among cultured Euro-Americans. After spending her adolescence in Paris, she may have become more cosmopolitan than Martha had been. She would have known a few French phrases, possibly could hum an air by Handel, and her literary sensitivity would have encompassed at least the metaphors of the twenty-third psalm. Quite possibly, Jefferson brought

[34] Jefferson describes his pursuits as "epicurianism" to John Adams in a letter, June 27, 1813.

her to Paris to provide her with some of the cultural attributes of bourgeois white women. Thus, Fawn Brodie and Barbara Chase-Riboud do not reject the conceivability of an emotional attachment between Jefferson and Sally Hemings. If such a tie did exist, perhaps it provided Sally herself some comfort, despite the anxiety and torment that accompanied a slave woman's condition.[35]

After Martha died in 1782, it is certainly possible that Jefferson remained as celibate as a Roman Catholic priest, but that would have been inconsistent with his cultural background. Eighteenth-century males believed they should "use venery in moderation for reasons of health." John Hartwell Cocke was making such a contemporary assumption when he stated as fact that Sally Hemings was Jefferson's concubine.[36] Jefferson's descendants never denied that some Jefferson male was responsible for the gray-eyed, red-haired children in their biogenetic family. Jefferson's grandson, Thomas Jefferson Randolph, famously claimed that Thomas Jefferson's nephew, Peter Carr, fathered Sally's children, but DNA tests conducted in 1998 revealed that this was impossible. The tests demonstrated that no Carr family ancestry existed in the Hemings' line, and that the Jefferson family legend was untrue.[37] The same tests revealed several mixed descendants of the Jefferson line, and Thomas Jefferson seems to be the most likely progenitor.[38]

[35] The discussion of such a relationship is appropriately left to the novelist Barbara Chase-Riboud, who handles it brilliantly in her *Sally Hemings: A Novel* (New York: Viking Press, 1979), with which she single-handedly resuscitated the controversy of Jefferson's presumed liaison with her. Also see the "Afterword" to the Chicago Press, 2009 edition. Particularly noteworthy in this genre is William Wells Brown, *Clotel, Or the President's Daughter: A Narrative of Slave Life in the United States* (London: Partridge and Oakey, 1853). The author of this novel was a fair-skinned quadroon who had escaped from slavery and pursued a career as an abolitionist, public speaker, barber, banker, dentist, and physician in the United States, England, and France.

[36] See journal of John Hartwell Cocke, January 26, 1853; April 23, 1853, quoted in Gordon-Reed, *Thomas Jefferson and Sally Hemings*.

[37] James Parton, *Life of Thomas Jefferson, Third President of the United States* (Boston, MA: J. R. Osgood and Company, 1874), pp. 569–570. As previously noted, the DNA studies of Eugene A. Foster et al. and Eliot Marshall prove conclusively that Carr could not have been the father. See note 31 above. There is copious material on the Hemings controversy at Monticello.org., especially at www.monticello.org/site/plantation-and-slavery/jefferson-hemings

[38] *Nature* (November 5, 1998); *Science News* (December 12, 1998). *Report of the Research Committee on Thomas Jefferson and Sally Hemings*, Monticello, January, 2000.

APES, MISCEGENATION, AND THE MISSING LINK

Jefferson had suggested that blacks were the link between whites and apes by his assertion that black males sought to mate with white females just as orangutans sought to mate with black females. He offered no evidence for either hypothesis: no evidence that black men feel any extraordinary attraction for white women; no evidence that any species of ape feels any preference for any human woman over members of its own species. He did not suggest the possibility that apes might find white women equally as attractive as they supposedly found black women, or even more so. But that was not as amazing as his neglect of the more easily demonstrable certainty that white men are attracted to black women.

Jefferson compared his own sexual impulses to those of "a mere Oranootan" (orangutan) in a letter to Maria Cosway of January 14, 1789, as E. M. Halliday notes with relish.[39] He was suggesting that it was some apish atavism that was drawing him to a white woman. Jefferson asserted, as if it were common knowledge or a self-evident fact, that black men prefer to mate with white women, "declared by their preference of them, as uniformly as is the preference of the Oranootan for the black women over those of his own species." Here is another example of how the *Notes on Viriginia* were based on "self-evident" truths rather than supposedly "Baconian" inductions from assembled data. This statement is all the more curious since he knew nothing about orangutans, and all the empirical evidence indicated that miscegenation in Virginia was "uniformly" the result of white males copulating with African women. Slavery was the cause of miscegenation, not its cure, and Jefferson's ideas on eugenics flew in the face of all evidence.

He was correct in assuming that the values of white supremacy encouraged biogenetic mixing of the races. Pressures to have lighter-skinned children have not been absent in American history. The slave narrative of Harriet Jacobs, published under the pseudonym Linda Brent, describes the predicament of a woman of mixed ancestry who selects a white companion aware of the disadvantages of having children with a black man. The black sociologist Sutton Griggs, writing in the early decades of the twentieth century, advanced the uncomfortable theory that black women were under considerable pressure to have lighter-skinned children. The theory cannot be dismissed out of hand. The dynamics of these social pressures may have persisted into the era of Sutton Griggs, and probably even into the twenty-

[39] Halliday, *Understanding Thomas Jefferson*, p. 107.

first century. There seems to be evidence within living memory, when one recalls the case of Carrie Butler, a young servant girl of 16, who conceived a child by the infamous segregationist Senator Strom Thurmond.[40] Halliday notes that Sally Hemings, a young and helpless teenager, might resign herself to the reality that the life chances of her children might be less onerous if they were the light-skinned offspring of a powerful and wealthy white male, who should have been "preferred" by any sane woman.[41]

We have shown, then, that black people may have seen the uncomfortable advantage of their children's being spared dark complexions, but also how Jefferson made a scientific or empirical error when he claimed that the source of American miscegenation was the fatal attraction of black men towards white women, despite the contradictory evidence. In addition to that, he "feigned the hypothesis" of an orangutan preference for human women over the females of its own species. Setting aside the moral–aesthetic bizarreness of this comparison, and the aforementioned non-empirical hypothesis of his declaration, the statement contained the formal flaw of "begging the question," a breakdown of the Aristotelian logic he had supposedly mastered as a schoolboy. Jefferson stated as axiomatic a preference that was neither evident nor demonstrable. And it bears repetition that he had collected no data and had never studied the sexual behavior of any anthropoid ape. How then could he pontificate that a species whose habitat was limited to Asia displayed a "uniform" preference for human females in Africa, a continent where that species had never been observed?

Jefferson was aware that white women occasionally showed sexual interest in black boys and men. His involvement with the Howell case would have heightened that awareness, and he was involved in the rewriting of Virginia laws to repress and punish that interest. William Wells Brown's slave narrative recalled an incident that occurred in 1823, during

[40] *Incidents in the Life of a Slave Girl*, ed. L. Maria Child (Boston, MA: Published for the Author, 1861) is the narrative of Harriet Ann Jacobs, under the pseudonym Linda Brent. "Thurmond's Family 'Acknowledges' Black Woman's Claim as Daughter," Fox News, Associated Press, December 17, 2003.

[41] Halliday, *Understanding Thomas Jefferson*, p. 98. Sutton Griggs, an amateur black sociologist, issued a dire warning that black women were tempted to select white men as fathers for their children in order to improve their chances for success in a color-oriented society. In this view, racial segregation had the counter-intuitive effect of promoting miscegenation. See Sutton Griggs, *Wisdom's Call* (1911), *Life's Demands or According to Law* (1916), and *Guide to Racial Greatness* (1923). See Harriet Jacobs, *Incidents in the Life of a Slave Girl*, ed. L. Maria Child (Boston, MA: Published for the Author, 1861).

Jefferson's later years, indicating the prurient interest of a white slave mistress in the bodies of young black males. Brown describes how he and fifteen other black boys were ordered to impress their "old mistress":

> My master's brother lost his wife, she leaving an infant son a few months old, whom my mistress took to bring up. When this boy became old enough to need a playmate to watch over him, mistress called the young slaves together, to select one for the purpose. We were all ordered to run, jump, wrestle, turn somersets, walk on our hands, and go through the various gymnastic exercises that the imagination of our brain could invent, or the strength and activity of our limbs could endure. The selection was to be an important one, both to the mistress and the slave. Whoever should gain the place was in the future to become a house servant; the ash-cake thrown aside, that unmentionable garment that buttons around the neck, which we all wore, and nothing else, was to give way to the whole suit of tow linen. Every one of us joined heartily in the contest, while old mistress sat on the piazza, watching our every movement – some fifteen of us, each dressed in his one garment, sometimes standing on our heads with feet in the air – still the lady looked on.[42]

Brown narrated the episode in such a way as to suggest that the "old mistress" was not merely indifferent to conventions of Victorian modesty, but that she "looked on" with interest in the young boys' display. It was not necessary to call on the boys to perform in such a manner, and Brown had his reasons for his recording the episode. His likely purpose was not only to raise the question of prurient curiosity on the part of the old mistress, but to illustrate the vulnerability of black boys to the sexual unpredictability of white women. Brown makes no direct accusation as to whether the behavior of his mistress was motivated by sexual curiosity or pedophilic voyeurism. He simply suggests the possibility of a conscious sexual interest in black boys on the part of one white woman, who could boast "that the best blood of the South coursed through her veins."

Jefferson could not have avoided a disquieting, subliminal awareness that most women find vigorous, frolicsome, and mirthful boys attractive. Only the strictest enforcement of social control can thwart the call of the wild. As many a father of adolescent daughters discovers to his dismay, teenage girls are perversely attracted to young lads who are frisky, funny, acrobatic, mischievous, and hyperactive. Heterosexual women, regardless of age, race, or social class, like athletic boys who look good when they take their shirts off and display strong white teeth when they laugh.

[42] William Wells Brown, *The Black Man, His Antecedents, His Genius, and His Achievements* (Boston, MA: Thomas Hamilton, 1863), p. 11.

Presumably, Jefferson, like most fathers of nubile girls, was horrified by the suspicion that young white women were sexually excited at the sight of handsome, sportive, young men of any race. As the father of teenage girls, he was perfectly aware that any adolescent woman could glance appreciatively at a half-nude prime field hand, with black skin gleaming in the sun.

Slavery did not protect society from miscegenation, but it reduced the incentives for white girls to approach black boys, and increased the hazards if they did so. John Quincy Adams, like most white males, was not particularly disturbed by miscegenation between white men and black women. But the thought of a white woman in the arms of a black man was both titillating and repugnant to him. He imagined what Shakespeare imagined, and what a Venetian father might imagine, at the thought of his daughter making the beast of two backs with a blackamoor. Adams' description amounted almost to an exercise in self-titillating masochism:

> My objection to the character of Desdemona arises not from what Iago, or Roderigo, or Brabantio, or Othello says of her; but from what she herself *does*. She absconds, from her father's house, in the dead of night, to marry a black-a-moor; she breaks a father's heart, and covers his noble house with shame, to gratify—what—pure love, like that of Juliet or Miranda! No! unnatural passion! it cannot be named with delicacy.[43]

Annette Gordon-Reed is not the first American historian to descant perceptively on what one might call the "Desdemona syndrome," but her prime interest is with a beautiful quadroon in the arms of Thomas Jefferson, while Quincy was torturing himself with the image of a young white girl in the arms of a "blackamoor." Quincy's problem was not limited to miscegenation, nor even to the problem of white women being attracted to black men.[44] It also encompassed the theme of

[43] Mrs Abigail Adams Smith, *Correspondence of Miss Adams, Daughter of John Adams, Second President of the United States, Edited by her Daughter* (New York, London: Wiley and Putnam, 1842), vol. II, p. 168.

[44] Gordon-Reed, *Hemingses of Monticello*, pp. 195–196. Paul E. Teed, *John Quincy Adams: Yankee Nationalist* (New York: Nova Science, 2011), p. 138. William Jerry MacLean, "Othello Scorned: The Racial Thought of John Quincy Adams," *Journal of the Early Republic*, 4, no. 2 (summer, 1984), 143–160. Elise Lemire, *"Miscegenation": Making Race in America* (Philadelphia, PA: University of Pennsylvania Press, 2009), pp. 98, 99, 168. Werner Sollors, *Interracialism: Black–White Intermarriage in American History, Literature, and Law* (Oxford University Press, 2000), pp. 358–361. Yoriko Ishida, *Modern and Postmodern Narratives of Race, Gender, and Identity: The Descendants of Thomas Jefferson and*

a daughter's "unnatural" resistance to her father's protective love, a theme that occurs elsewhere in Shakespeare. Freudians have found it in *King Lear*, and it is a sub-plot in *The Merchant of Venice*, where a Jewish daughter breaks her father's heart by eloping with a gentile. Critics often make the obvious comparison between *King Lear* and the tragic father protagonist of Honoré de Balzac's novel, *Père Goriot*. Slavery might ease the fears of white parents with respect to their daughters' sexual vulnerability, but paradoxically it increased the likelihood of biogenetic mixture, since white boys were permitted, and even encouraged, to have sex with black women, whose daughters became increasingly white with every generation. Still, slavery was an effective device employed by white communities to protect pubescent white girls from their own libidinous curiosity, and discourage them from making advances to black boys.

L'AMOUR ET L'OCCIDENT

Jefferson's relationship with Sally Hemings is symbolic of deeper problems, both moral and intellectual, that are not peculiar to American culture, but pervasive in the Western world. It is interesting to speculate as to whether their relationship was based on love or on exploitation. Oh, sweet mystery of life! It requires the genius of a Fawn Brodie or a Barbara Chase-Riboud to sketch the contours of any possible romance between Thomas Jefferson and Sally Hemings. Lucia Stanton, Annette Gordon-Reed, and others have addressed the Jefferson family history with majesty and force, and I have little to add. The narrative of Harriet Jacobs suggests that both romantic and fortuitous connections sometimes allowed a black woman to wrest limited degrees of self-determination from slave culture. E. M. Halliday has delicately suggested that Sally's relationship to Master Tom might have been a means to a very constricted empowerment, under the cruel circumstances of contemporary manners and customs.[45]

Human sexuality writhes between the sordid and the sublime. Garry Wills once clumsily suggested that Jefferson's attitude towards Sally Hemings was that of a patron to a "prostitute." Given the length and

Sally Hemings (New York: Peter Lang, 2010), p. 59. Paul F. Boller, Jr., "The American Presidents and Shakespeare," in Boller, *Essays on the Presidents: Principles and Politics* (Fort Worth, TX: TCU Press, 2013), pp. 193–208.

45 Halliday, *Understanding Thomas Jefferson*, p. 98, suggests that Sally seduced Tom at her mother's suggestion.

intimacy of the relationship between the Hemings and the Jefferson families, the assertion seems inappropriate. Annette Gordon-Reed's simmering reaction was that "There are, in fact, levels of male–female attachment that exist between being a trick and her John and being the equivalent of Tristan and Iseut."[46] Gordon-Reed's reference to Tristan and Iseut induces further complications, since the protagonists of that legend are immersed in anti-social behavior based on adultery, deceit, and even perjury, matters that Wagner may have transfigured, but Tennyson refused to ignore. We know nothing of Sally or what sort of companionship she might have been capable of offering her master. Due mainly to Jefferson's own reticence, there may never be additional evidence from which historians can extrapolate the narratives of his relationships to Sally Hemings, Maria Cosway, or Martha Wayles Skelton Jefferson.

[46] Gordon-Reed, *Thomas Jefferson and Sally Hemings*, p. 170. My observations on the "Victorian" reception of the legend of Tristan and Isolde are from a work in progress, partially inspired by Henry Adams' commentary on the legend. In addition to being Thomas Jefferson's most celebrated biographer, Adams was also a medievalist.

11

Debt, Deference, and Consumption

FAMILIAR DEBT AND DEFERENTIAL DEMOCRACY

In *Federalist* 10, Madison recognized various interests dividing the propertied classes: "A landed interest, a manufacturing interest, a mercantile interest, a moneyed interest, with many lesser interests," but not the slaveholding interest that had divided the Constitutional Convention in 1787 and forced compromises that included a limit on the duration of the slave trade, an innocuously worded fugitive slave law, and a three-fifths compromise on slave representation. The "landed interest," with which he and Jefferson and his Democratic Republican Party passionately identified, was split between those who opposed the Atlantic slave trade and those who wished to see it thrive. The Federalist Party also included a landed interest, embodied in John Adams, who during his presidency escaped for extended periods to his Braintree Massachusetts farm and, according to Edmund S. Morgan, "allowed his enemies to gain control of national affairs, while he managed the corn and potatoes." Adams was a Federalist who detested banks and was hostile to the "mercantile interest," but Jefferson always thought he detected in him a "squinting" at monarchy and a desire to make the American constitutional system resemble that of Great Britain. Jefferson habitually referred to the Federalists as "Anglomen" and "Monarchists."

But the Republican Party harbored its own aristocratic ideals, within the framework of what historians have called "deference democracy," the idea that government was not to be a mirror but a filter of public opinion, and that gentlemen of property and standing were likely to emerge as the best representatives of local values, and that their virtues would naturally be recognized by local communities.[1] This widespread deference was by no means confined to the Republicans or to the agrarian South. Jefferson opined in a letter to John Adams that it was even stronger in Massachusetts than it was in Virginia:

> From what I have seen of Massachusetts and Connecticut myself, and still more from what I have heard, and the character given of the former by yourself, (volume I, page III,) who know them so much better, there seems to be in those two States a traditionary reverence for certain families, which has rendered the offices of the government nearly hereditary in those families.[2]

Regardless of regional manifestations, the party must smooth over the factionalism described in *Federalist* 10 between "those who hold and those who are without property," while maintaining the social superiority of Jefferson's "natural aristoi" over small farmers, artisans, and "persons

[1] The concept of "deference democracy" is explored by William F. Willingham in "Deference Democracy and Town Government in Windham, Connecticut, 1755 to 1786," *The William and Mary Quarterly*, 30, no. 3 (July, 1973), 401–422. Nancy Isenberg perceptively notes the "expectations of deference" within Jefferson's Virginia in her *White Trash: The 400-Year Untold History of Class in America* (New York: Viking, 2016), p. 99. Also see Kenneth A. Lockridge, *A New England Town, The First Hundred Years: Dedham, Massachusetts, 1636–1736* (New York: Norton, 1970); Michael Zuckerman, *Peaceable Kingdoms: New England Towns in the Eighteenth Century* (New York: Knopf, 1970); Charles S. Grant, *Democracy in the Connecticut Frontier Town of Kent* (New York: Norton, 1961). Michael G. Kammen, ed., *Politics and Society in Colonial America: Democracy or Deference?* (New York: International Thomson, 1967); and Stanley N. Katz, ed., *Colonial America: Essays in Politics and Social Development* (New York: Knopf, 1971). I must thank Peter Onuf for focusing my attention on questions of deference and the "genteel ethos" in the works of Michael Rozbicki. See Michal Rozbicki, *The Complete Colonial Gentleman: Cultural Legitimacy in Colonial Virginia* (Charlottesville, VA: University of Virginia Press, 1998) and Rozbicki, *Culture and Liberty in the Age of the American Revolution* (Charlottesville, VA: University of Virginia Press, 2011). Rozbicki does not push his gentility thesis so radically as I do. "Deference" is introduced, but not thoroughly discussed, in Gordon Wood's *The Radicalism of the American Revolution* (New York: Vintage, 1991), pp. 56. 63, 85, 88, 145, 153, 154, 171, 225. "Deferential relations" in Daniel Shays' Massachusetts are discussed in John L. Brooke, *The Heart of the Commonwealth: Society and Political Culture in Worcester Massachusetts, 1713–1861* (Cambridge University Press, 1989). See especially Chapter 2 there. Also see Willingham, "Deference Democracy," 401–402, and Jack P. Greene, "Changing Interpretations of Early American Politics" in Ray Allen Billington, ed., *The Reinterpretation of Early American History: Essays in Honor of John Edwin Pomfret* (San Marino, CA: Huntington Library, 1966), p. 173.

[2] Jefferson to John Adams, October 28, 1813. Jefferson refers here to John Adams, *A Defense of the Constitutions of Government of the United States of America, against the Attack of M. Turgot, in his Letter to Dr. Price, 22 March, 1778* (London: C. Dilly, 1787).

bound to service." Although the Jeffersonian democrats constantly brandished an egalitarian rhetoric, their subliminal intent was to maintain control over the hearts and minds of the yeomanry, especially those in the South, who admired and emulated them. The lower class had habits of deference towards big planters, in an economy that was largely based on barter and credit and was deficient in both hard money and paper currency.

Before and after the Revolution, many Americans saw the need for a stable and standardized monetary system, but this was not met by the so-called "Continental currency." Since the Continental Congress had neither gold nor silver to finance the Revolutionary War, nor the power of taxation, it created fiat money, which was eventually "not worth a Continental." Lacking the power to tax, Congress had no choice but to issue rapidly inflating bills in order for George Washington to supply his troops. At its very inception, the new nation necessarily practiced deficit spending in order to fund the "fiscal military state," but after the war there was no standing army and the Jeffersonians revealed an abhorrence for military spending, as well as all other government spending. Jefferson was neither in Congress nor in the Army during the war, and thus had no responsibility for paying soldiers or for creating the paper currency with which to pay them. Unlike George Washington, he had no incentive to overcome the visceral hatred of the planter class for levying taxes and creating paper money.[3]

The United States government had little financial credibility until Washington and Hamilton, with Jefferson and Madison's support, restructured the debt to the benefit of wartime creditors. Economic historians disagree on whether wartime inflation retarded or benefitted the public interest in general, but it is well known that Jefferson's debt increased during the war, and that he not only developed, as did many Virginia planters, a sense of moral outrage towards the Continental currency, but also maintained the traditional hostility of his class towards a strong central government, especially one that promoted a national bank and issued a paper currency. If he believed that all financial transactions should ideally be transacted in specie, this was incongruent with the fact that he never possessed very much of it.

[3] William Appleman Williams, *The Contours of American History* (Chicago: Quadrangle Books, 1966), more than once refers to Jefferson's medieval atavism and "hankering after the physiocrat's feudal utopia," pp. 152–155.

The position of the Democratic–Republicans on national debt and banking involved more than matters of mere political economy: they disclosed a clash between competing elitist traditions. Jefferson's class would prefer that small farmers come to them, rather than to a bank, when seeking endorsement of a note, asking for credit, or borrowing a mule, an ox, or a slave. Keeping credit out of banking institutions and confining it to personal relationships between patrician lenders and plebeian borrowers would reinforce the patterns of dependency and "deference democracy" so important to the maintenance of Jefferson's seigniorial position in his local community. Thus, the debates over American financial institutions involved much more than the ostensible economic and constitutional agenda: they involved the gravitas and social position of Mr. Jefferson when he borrowed money on his slaves or endorsed notes for relatives.

In theory, at least, banks issued money based on precious metals, and their patrons wrote checks, backed by the gold in their vaults. Jefferson's financial transactions used land and slaves as collateral. His relation to debt presented a dramatic contradiction between his political faith and his private practice. In government he was obsessed with reducing debt and maintaining the treasury's gold and silver reserves; in his personal affairs he ran up debt and had no interest in hoarding precious metals. But if land and slaves were money, they were undependable as a means of storing wealth, while they functioned well as the basis for his medium of exchange. He successfully maintained his ability to consume by issuing paper based on the futures of his slaves. But he was perpetually in debt, a problem that began before the Revolution and was tied to the limits of the colonial money supply. Although economic historians Jonathan Hughes and Louis P. Cain are impressed by colonial America's ingenuity in creating what amounted to a system of paper currency in the form of bills of credit, Jefferson did not benefit from the system.[4]

It is worthy of note that the Declaration of Independence made no mention of the real or imagined problems of money supply, banking, finance, or any other commercial grievances. Historians Samuel Eliot Morison and Henry Steele Commager discussed the repressive monetary

[4] Hughes and Cain pose the rhetorical question as to whether or not there was a colonial money shortage. Benjamin Franklin felt the answer was a definite yes, but Hughes and Cain make a case for money equivalents in various forms of financial paper and argue that "The product of colonial monetary genius [was] the invention of paper money" in their *American Economic History* (New York: HarperCollins, 1994), pp. 69–77.

policies of Great Britain towards the colonies, but found few signs in the historical record that these policies generated much rhetorical response. Carl Van Doren explains this deficiency with the argument that "Economics had not yet evolved a language that was authoritative and equally understood ... Their rich and lofty political eloquence clouded their economic realism." More recently, Staughton Lynd and David Waldstreicher have provided evidence to support the logic that commercial and financial issues had to be among the catalysts of the American Revolution.[5]

Another money-related factor was observed by Benjamin Franklin, who noted that colonial Americans were eager to spend money on luxuries, even to the point of "conspicuous consumption." T. H. Breen describes America's pre-Revolutionary consumer economy and notes, in passing, the irony that the American colonies experienced economic depression after the French–Indian War. Americans lost consumers when "The withdrawal of so many British troops from the American theater of war depressed local commerce, for without the soldiers ... the demand for goods and services decreased quite rapidly." After the Revolution, Jefferson extolled the benefits of consumerism, writing in 1784 to George Washington, "Our citizens have too full a taste of the comforts furnished by the arts and manufactures to be debarred the use of them." The purpose of this letter was to express support for "opening the upper waters of the Ohio and Patowmac," one of Washington's favorite schemes, and seemed to be thinking in terms of markets for the "workshops of Europe" without mention of credit or money supply.[6]

The American Revolution abolished the disadvantageous aspects of British mercantilism, but it established a mercantilism of its own, because

[5] Samuel Eliot Morison and Henry Steele Commager, *The Growth of the American Republic* (Oxford University Press, 1958), vol. I, pp. 100–106. Carl Van Doren, *Benjamin Franklin* (New York: Penguin, 1991 [1938]), p. 361. Staughton Lynd and David Waldstreicher, "Free Trade, Sovereignty, and Slavery: Toward an Economic Interpretation of American Independence," *The William and Mary Quarterly*, 68, no. 4 (October, 2011), 597–630, treat economic issues and a survey of literature on money and banking. Also see Lynd and Waldstreicher, "Reflections on Economic Interpretation, Slavery, the People Out of Doors, and Top Down versus Bottom Up," *The William and Mary Quarterly*, 68, no. 4 (October, 2011), 649–656.

[6] Benjamin Franklin, *A Modest Enquiry into the Nature and Necessity of a Paper-Currency* (Philadelphia: Printed and Sold at the New Printing-Office, near the Market, 1729). T. H. Breen, *The Marketplace of Revolution, How Consumer Politics Shaped American Independence* (Oxford University Press, 2004), p. 204. Note undeveloped reference to "conspicuous consumption," p. 47. Jefferson to George Washington, March 15, 1784.

mercantilism may be defined in more than one way, both in the monetary sense and in the protectionist sense. In the monetary sense, Virginia had no capacity for hoarding or issuing currency based on precious metals, but it did have the power to protect the domestic market in slaves. Jefferson was opposed to protectionism before the Revolution in his *Summary View of the Rights of British America* when he protested against mercantilist restrictions on industrial production. But he did not treat the mercantilist restrictions on banking, finance, and money supply. Jefferson praised Adam Smith's *The Wealth of Nations*, which attacked both the monetarist and protectionist aspects of mercantilism and slavery as well. He agreed with Smith that gold and silver are not identical with wealth, and like Smith he opposed the mercantilist policy that had as its primary goal the accumulation of precious metals in the national treasury, a policy that inhibited American commerce and industry, and he accepted Smith's general opposition to paper money. Jefferson's guardedly high opinion of *The Wealth of Nations* appeared to be due to his endorsement of its *laissez-faire* values, but he also expressed mild reservations, for reasons that may be partially explained by Smith's hedging on the usefulness of a paper currency.[7]

William Appleman Williams was not being perversely imaginative when he described the economy of Jefferson's post-Revolutionary Virginia as mercantilist. It was not so in the monetary sense, for Virginia's government did not maintain a bank that hoarded precious metals, but it was mercantilist in the protectionist sense, as it worked to give its citizens a monopoly on the slave trade by keeping it domestic. Williams associated Jefferson with mercantilism because Virginians encouraged the hoarding of slave property and recognized that slaves had a fiscal as well as an industrial value. Financial paper based on land and slaveholdings had a monetary function before, during, and after the Revolution. Jefferson's sentimental attachment to this system of credit and trade was as real as the attachment of any British mercantilist to the sentimental power of gold and silver. Williams made the sarcastic observation that Jefferson's "entire career can be understood as the attempt of a physiocrat to use mercantilist means to realize his feudal utopia."[8]

[7] With respect to political economy, Jefferson wrote to John Norvell, June 11, 1807, "Smith's Wealth of Nations is the best book to be read, unless Say's Political Economy can be had, which treats the same subjects on the same principles, but in a shorter compass and more lucid manner. But I believe this work has not been translated into our language." Smith's toleration for paper currency in Pennsylvania is discussed later in this chapter.

[8] Williams, *Contours of American History*, p. 154.

JEFFERSONIAN FINANCE: THE NEGRO RESERVE SYSTEM

By the time Jefferson was Secretary of State, his friend John Taylor was one the most articulate and systematic apologists for the culture that Madison had called "the farming interest." The variety of "agrarianism" associated with Taylor is not to be confused with the "agrarianism" advocated by Thomas Paine, which was actually a form of socialism: his program resembled the ancient Roman "Lex Sempronia Agraria," government redistribution of wealth in the form of land (see above, Chapter 3, note 16). Taylor opposed "equalising property by agrarian laws," and his works employed the term "agrarianism" in a sneering and pejorative sense. Sharing with Jefferson a moral advocacy of economic self-sufficiency and minimal government, Taylor was the author of several learned treatises, among them *An Enquiry into the Principles and Tendency of Certain Public Measures*, a copy of which he sent to Jefferson at Jefferson's request. He ridiculed the concept of "natural aristocracy," not knowing that Jefferson was to endorse the ideal many years later, and he advocated local and popular government.

The *Inquiry* was erudite, acerbic, and polemical. It intermittently associated bankers with monarchy, aristocracy, and tyranny, a tendency that was omnipresent in Jefferson's thinking as well. Taylor acknowledged in a later work the existence of a "really useful capitalist class, as consumers, as giving value to productions, as encouraging industry, and as extending comforts," but asserted that "capitalists or consumers created by exclusive privileges or fraudulent laws of any kind, are, unexceptionably, drones with stings." Of course, his own class was protected by the laws that made men, women, and children his slaves for life. While he paid lip-service to an egalitarian form of agrarianism, the historians Manning Dauer and Hans Hammond note that it was "agrarianism to be in the hands of an aristocratic leadership." Not surprisingly, Taylor viewed Hamilton's financial policies as a conspiracy to destroy the libertarian and democratic achievements of the Revolution and erect a "modern species of aristocracy."[9]

Before the Revolution, specie was rare in the colonies, because the monetary aspect of British mercantilism was, by definition, the hoarding

[9] John Taylor, *An Enquiry into the Principles and Tendency of Certain Public Measures* (Philadelphia: Thomas Dobson, 1794). John Taylor, *Tyranny Unmasked* (Liberty Fund, 1992 [1822]), p. 164; see http://oll.libertyfund.org/titles/taylor-tyranny-unmasked Manning J. Dauer and Hans Hammond, "John Taylor: Democrat or Aristocrat?" *The Journal of Politics*, 6 (1944), 381–403.

of gold and silver inside the mother country, which prohibited the circulation of British coins in the colonies, and, to make matters worse, Parliament eventually prohibited the printing of paper money. Business transactions in the colonies were conducted largely on the basis of promissory notes and bills of credit drawn on real estate and other forms of property, sometimes on tobacco stored in British warehouses, sometimes on slaves yet to be unloaded from the bellies of slave ships. The shortage of gold and silver coins in the pre-Revolutionary economy inflated consumer prices and angered the commercial classes, who bought and sold not only commodities, but the indentures of servants, white and black. Southern planters bought and sold bills of credit based on real estate and the bodies of African American slaves.

The traditional hostility of Jefferson's class to financiers, to paper money, and to commercial banking was passed on to subsequent generations, and it inflamed the notorious bank war of the Jackson administration. Its echoes continued to be heard in the feverish rhetoric of gold bugs in later epochs. An emotional, almost superstitious, faith in hard money was one of the roots of Jefferson's opposition to Washington's financial reforms. Jefferson's failure to feel positively about these reforms was not due to naïveté or any deficiency in powers of comprehension. Nor is it to be explained by recycling the simplistic cliché that he was a sentimental agrarian. In fact, he was a floundering industrialist, with his nailery and brick factory, and his experiments with the exploitation of child labor. Jefferson was far too pragmatic to categorically exclude manufacturing and commerce from his vision of America's future.

Virginia's pre-Revolutionary system of exchange did not work to Jefferson's advantage, but after the Revolution he opposed a national banking system that might have mitigated those economic embarrassments that plagued him for the rest of his life. Nonetheless, he was rigid in his views on banking, for, like John Taylor, he viewed the banking and financial sectors as parasitical and found it impossible to accept that they made any contribution to the nation's wealth. He was deaf to the argument that financiers, operating in tandem with the central government, had the potential to create economic stability and minimize risk. In his view, finance was not a legitimate profession, but the essence of corruption, a direct assault on all notions of political and economic liberty. This being the case, governments that became involved in banking and finance were *de facto* corrupt. His superstitious veneration for the abstract ideal of free trade and his distaste for the culture of eighteenth-century commercialism were profound.[10]

After the Revolution, Virginia had nothing approximating a free market economy. "Slavery," wrote the historian William Appleman Williams, "developed within the logic and politics of English mercantilism," and it was "the mainspring of Virginia society." Slavery was "the frayed and raveled end of the strand of mercantile economic theory which stressed the importance of a large, cheap, and controlled labor force that could produce a staple surplus for profit."[11] If one accepts Williams' unconventional – and perhaps tongue-in-cheek – definition, Jefferson and his Virginia compatriots sought a controlled market. Despite Jefferson's lip-service to Adam Smith and enthusiasm for J. B. Say, he was not a "free trader" but a "mercantilist," who sought to maintain a protected economy. The United States Constitution was protectionist with respect to "persons bound to service" and the Atlantic slave trade. It did not establish a *laissez-faire* economic system, but one that specifically protected a slave-based mode of production. The Constitution protected the slave-based financial system of the plantation South and its deference democracy. The Constitution could never have been ratified without protecting the interests of Virginia, the largest, richest, and most powerful state in the Union. The Constitution yielded to Virginia's interests by calling for an eventual ban on the importation of slaves after twenty years. This was, in effect, the promise of an eventual monopoly on the slave trade to the advantage of states that produced a slave surplus. While the Constitution did not grant Virginia a "mercantilist" monopoly in the same sense that England had once given one to the Royal African Company, it was mercantilist in that it cemented together a national economy in which Virginia's slave exportations would play an essential role.

THE SLAVERY BILL OF 1779 AND ITS PHANTOM AMENDMENT

In 1778 Jefferson introduced a law banning the importation of slaves into Virginia. In 1784 he also proposed a prohibition on slavery in the territories, but, twenty years later, he purchased the Louisiana Territory,

[10] Claudio J. Katz, "Thomas Jefferson's Liberal Anticapitalism," *American Journal of Poitical Science*, 47, no. 1 (January, 2003), 1–17, surveys much literature on Jefferson's attitudes to commercialism.

[11] Williams, *Contours of American History*, defines mercantilism very broadly, and non-traditionally, in terms of Virginia's efforts at protectionist regulation of the economy, pp. 40, 78.

which already contained a substantial slave population. It is estimated that, although he never had more than 200 slaves at a time, almost 600 passed through his hands in his lifetime. All but seven of these he either transferred to others as property or sold to cover debt. Merrill Peterson collected some of Jefferson's positions on slavery, emancipation, and expatriation, including his often-cited opinions in *Notes on Virginia*. Peter Onuf, Ari Helo, and numerous others, before and since, have discussed the moral issues involved in Jefferson's musings on the possibility of the forced expulsion of slaves from Virginia and resettlement elsewhere.[12]

In *Notes on Virginia*, Query XIV Jefferson referred to a bill revising the Virginia Code, including a plan "to emancipate all slaves born after passing the act." He allowed that the bill did "not itself contain this proposition," but averred that "an amendment containing it was prepared, to be offered to the legislature whenever the bill should be taken up." He also referred to this bill in his posthumously published *Autobiography*. But this so-called emancipation provision has never been located by historians.[13] The actual bill authored by Jefferson, and printed in the Boyd edition of his *Papers*, and the one actually passed on December 5, 1785, accomplished something quite different from encouraging emancipation: what it actually did was to confirm the enslaved status of all persons who were slaves at the time, and to declare that "the descendants of the females of them" would inherit the status of slaves. Thus, the bill did nothing to gradually emancipate slavery, and in fact provided for its perpetual replenishment and increase through the descendants of the female slaves. Furthermore, the bill declared that any free Africans or mulattoes entering Virginia must leave within a year. It even went so far as to declare:

12 Merrill Peterson, in the Library of America edition of Jefferson's *Writings*, brings together several documents that illustrate Jefferson's evolving positions on slavery, and the index to that volume offers a convenient, although necessarily incomplete, introduction. Jefferson's moral positions regarding slavery and deportation are staunchly defended in Ari Helo, *Thomas Jefferson's Ethics and the Politics of Human Progress: The Morality of a Slaveholder* (Cambridge University Press, 2013). Peter Onuf, *Jefferson's Empire* (Charlottesville, VA: University of Virginia Press, 2000), contains several index references under "colonization."

13 See note to "A Bill concerning Slaves, 18 June 1779," Founders Online, last modified April 12, 2018. The editors say, "If this emancipation amendment was reduced to writing, no manuscript or other record of it has yet come to light; in the more detailed account of this suppressed amendment as given in *Notes on Virginia*, TJ indicated that such an amendment had been reduced to writing."

> If any white woman shall have a child by a negro or mulatto, she and her child shall depart the commonwealth within one year thereafter. If they fail so to do, the woman shall be out of the protection of the laws, and the child shall be bound out by the Aldermen of the county, in like manner as poor orphans are by law directed to be, and within one year after its term of service expired shall depart the commonwealth, or on failure so to do, shall be out of the protection of the laws.

Since the law guaranteed the perpetual enslavement of the descendants of all living female slaves residing in the state, the passage of this bill, with or without the clauses of its missing amendment, could have done nothing to weaken slavery in Virginia or to hasten its demise. Its practical effect was to bar importation of any new slaves, since any slaves imported after the passage of the bill were declared free. "But if they shall not depart the commonwealth within one year thereafter they shall be out of the protection of the laws." The law, incidentally, placed severe restrictions on the civil rights and liberties of every "negro or mulatto," whether slave or free, including the right to testify in court, the rights to free speech and assembly, and the right to keep and bear arms.

The effect of the law was to discourage, directly and indirectly, the importation of slave property into Virginia with the object of sale. An increase in the market supply of slaves would have had the effect of lowering demand, with the result of lowering slave prices. Since Virginia was not a center of banking and finance, paper transactions within the state (as noted above) were usually based on promissory notes drafted on the basis of land and slaves, where Jefferson and other wealthy Virginians were known to invest their wealth. Deflation of the price of slaves was not in the interest of a credit system based on slavery and lands that derived their value from the labor of slaves.

PLANTER ARISTOCRATS AND DEFERENCE DEMOCRACY

Jefferson, Taylor, and others, while denouncing the Federalists as aristocrats, were clinging to an ancient patriarchal system that was as elitist as it was parochial. Jefferson would eventually grasp what Washington and Hamilton had already grasped. The American Empire was destined to become a rival to the British Empire, and would require a centralized fiscal military administration. A provincial economy in which small farmers would obtain credit not from banks in distant cities but from wealthy patricians in their local neighborhoods might be functional under a social and economic structure limited to a provincial network of communes numbering no more than 100 freeholds, but it was completely irrational for a continental empire.

The planter aristocrats, although they were Southern patricians, shared the resentments of poor white debtors of all regions towards the Northeastern elites. George Washington was something of a hybrid, an entrepreneur who grew wheat, invested in a newly patented milling technology, produced 278,000 pounds of flour a year, and built one of America's largest distilleries. For Jefferson's taste, Washington was much too comfortable with the party of commerce.[14] Jefferson was perennially a member of the debtor class, and therefore not entirely hypocritical in exploiting the proletarian detestation for creditors that he shared with middling farmers like Daniel Shays. He could even muster a sense of solidarity with "the yeomanry of the city" in Philadelphia, as well as with the agrarian malcontents of Western Pennsylvania.[15] The party of Jefferson was quietly ready to exploit the Democratic Republican clubs that flocked to the standard of Citizen Genêt, and to side with the Whiskey Rebels, whom George Washington dispersed with that same "well armed militia" guaranteed by the Second Amendment.

While it is true that American society became increasingly egalitarian from the time of the Revolution to the symbolic day of Jackson's boisterous inauguration a half-century later, patterns of deferential democracy survived, especially in Southern culture, up to and even after the Civil War. Veterans of the Army of Northern Virginia revealed their nostalgia and fond admiration for the patrician-equestrian class by whimsical, half-serious references to their elegant, handsome, and aristocratic Robert E. Lee as "Marse Robert."[16] The nature of white populism in every region of the country was that many poor whites hated slaves without hating slavery. Ironically, slavery provided emotional compensation to the white *sans culottes*, who possessed no capital in the form of slaves and had no hopes of ever owning a slave, heedless of the fact that slavery could only result in depressing the price of poor white labor. A populist mob would

[14] For an appreciative discussion of Washington's business vision, see Joel Achenbach, *The Grand Idea: George Washington's Potomac and the Race to the West* (New York: Simon and Schuster, 2004). Also see Edward G. Lengel, *First Entrepreneur: How George Washington Built His – and the Nation's – Prosperity* (Boston, MA: Da Capo Press, 2016).

[15] Jefferson used the term "yeoman" to refer to urban as well as rural populations. Jefferson to James Monroe, Philadelphia, May 5, 1793.

[16] I thank Professor Marc Neely for bringing to my attention a soldier's memoir by Robert Stiles (1836–1905) entitled *Four Years under Marse Robert* (New York: Neale Publishing, 1903).

lynch the abolitionist editor Elijah Lovejoy in 1837, and the yeomen of the South would ignore the class issues raised by the abolitionist *qua* racist, Hinton Rowan Helper, twenty years thereafter. Shoeless Confederates would subserviently bow to the Jeffersonian patrician they called "Marse Bob" and hurl their bodies into the kamikaze attack called "Pickett's Charge."[17] Slavery was maintained not by the economic interests of a homogenous slaveholding class, but by a culture of white supremacy that permeated every level of society. American populism's tendency towards a self-destructive paranoia was illustrated in the willingness of poor whites to undermine their own class interests by defending slavery.

What began as Lincoln's war to preserve slavery within the Union became a war to end slavery, and to transmute the Jeffersonian canard that "all men are created equal." At the helm of a Hamiltonian military-industrial complex, Lincoln formed an abolitionist government, revised the Constitution, overthrew the Jeffersonian patricians, and effectively created the Second American Republic. One cannot ignore the irony that Dwight D. Eisenhower, a century later, although warning of the military-industrial complex, would utilize the powers invested in him by that same military-industrial complex to further advance Lincoln's pronouncements on racial equality. Eventually a military-industrial empire with powerful executives like Roosevelt and Eisenhower – even more powerful than Hamilton had anticipated – would inherit the vigorous, centralized, nationalistic government that Jefferson had inadvertently helped create, and use it to chip away at the ideals of racial inequality that Jefferson handed down to Chief Justice Taney.

Jefferson's personal economics compelled him to make pragmatic adjustments in his understanding of the laws of nature and nature's God, so that he could never free his slaves. The contrast between Jefferson's philosophical preachments and his practical temporizing should no longer be a matter of controversy, necessary as it is to reiterate this contradiction. He consciously and unconsciously flailed at, and attempted to reconcile, the contradictions that were the body and soul of the world he not only inherited, but also helped to shape. The forces of history, the methods of science, and the proddings of conscience must be perpetually balanced against the exigencies of the hour. He believed that

[17] While there was neither a shoe factory nor a shoe warehouse in Gettysburg, the Confederate rank and file were ill-provisioned and indeed in need of footwear. In his memoirs, Major-General Henry Heth reported sending a scouting party in search of shoes: http://encyclopediaVirginia.org/shoes_at_gettysburg

"the earth belongs in usufruct to the living," but was incapable of grappling with slavery, the question of the hour, and afraid to seize the liberty to change the world in which he lived. Even in the Declaration, he had acknowledged that it was human nature to temporize. This self-acknowledged human trait made Jefferson, no less than other human beings, "more disposed to suffer while evils are sufferable than to right themselves by abolishing the forms to which they are accustomed." These, his own words, revealed the soul of a man who, as Hamilton justly observed, was "as likely as any man I know to temporize." Jefferson's position on slavery amounted to fifty years of temporizing, consoling himself with the thought that "time, which outlives all things, will outlive this evil too."[18]

SLAVE-TRADING CONSIDERED DISHONORABLE

Jefferson has been described as "a man who sold numerous slaves to support his extravagant life-style," but, for more than one reason, Jefferson did not feel comfortable about selling slaves.[19] In Virginia, as in ancient Rome, it was not uncommon for patricians to imagine a tremendous moral and social gulf between those who owned slaves and those who traded in them. While individual slave owners might have few inhibitions concerning the arbitrary and capricious exploitation of slaves for venal, sexual, or sadistic purposes, it was generally presumed that a kind master was morally superior to a brutal one. There was a tacit assumption that the ideal master ought to view his slaves as children, subject to his severity, but entitled to his kindness. By contrast, the slave trader was often stereotyped as the lowest form of shopkeeper in a society that sentimentalized the virtues of its aristocracy and sneered at the unpolished, money-grubbing merchant class.[20]

[18] Jefferson to James Heaton, Monticello, May 20, 1826. Also see Paul Finkelman. "Thomas Jefferson and Antislavery: The Myth Goes On," *The Virginia Magazine of History and Biography*, 102, no. 2 (April, 1994), 193–228. Merrill Peterson creatively employed the *nunc dimittis* trope of St. Jerome's Latin Vulgate in his edition: Merrill Peterson, ed., *Thomas Jefferson, Writings* (New York: Literary Classics of the United States, 1984).

[19] The harsh portrayal of Jefferson in Paul Finkelman, *Slavery and the Founders: Race and Liberty in the Age of Jefferson*, 2nd edn. (Armonk, NY: M. E. Sharpe, 2001), p. 250 note 123, contrasts sharply with the sympathetic portrait of Jefferson in Lucia Stanton, *Slavery at Monticello* (Charlottesville, VA: Thomas Jefferson Memorial Foundation, 1996), p. 13.

[20] Thomas Wiedemann, *Greek and Roman Slavery* (Baltimore: Johns Hopkins University Press, 1981), Chapters 1 and 5 are especially useful. Moses Finley, *Aspects of Antiquity: Discoveries and Controversies* (New York: Viking, 1968); Moses Finley, *Ancient Slavery and Modern Ideology*, expanded edn. (Princeton, NJ: Markus Wiener, 1998).

Jefferson referred to his slaves as members of an extended family, and he had described at least the international slave trade in terms of "waging cruel warfare against human nature itself" by transporting people "against their wills." The paternalistic, "seigniorial" or patriarchal concept of slave ownership among the Romans was not unknown to American slaveholders. Jefferson and his class emulated the Romans, but Jefferson liked to think that Americans exceeded them in republican virtue and patrician honor. There were few true patricians in early colonial America, but by the end of the French–Indian War the South had a rising class of country squires who, as they ascended in wealth, comfort, and social rank, viewed themselves as benevolent patriarchs, not as heartless dealers in human flesh. A controversy over the existence of benevolent seigniorialism came to dominate the rhetoric of both abolitionists and apologists for slavery, reaching its culmination by the mid nineteenth century in Harriet Beecher Stowe's *Uncle Tom's Cabin.* Almost a century before Harriet Beecher Stowe had begun to make the distinction between the apparently righteous slaveholder and the obviously nefarious slave trader, the distinction was already becoming part of American folklore. Slaveholders from the time of Thomas Jefferson to that of Jefferson Davis spoke of their slaves as "my people," telling themselves and anyone who would listen that they viewed their colored servants as dependants and wards.[21]

The historian Michael Tadman has discussed this "my family" mythology and illustrated how "white southern propagandists pretended that the trade was of only marginal importance and that slave traders were social outcasts." Stowe did not find it necessary to confront the myth with a systematic argument; she simply illustrated how even a kind-hearted master might be forced to sell an occasional slave, thus becoming, in effect, a slave trader by delivering his faithful servant into the hands of a heartless profiteer. Jefferson's financial embarrassments made his involvement with slavery not that of a genteel *paterfamilias*, but that of a crude jostler in a singularly unpleasant marketplace. Jefferson was sincerely concerned about the subsistence, if not the happiness of his slaves, since their survival

[21] For Jefferson on the "my family" myth, see Stanton, *Slavery at Monticello*, p. 13. Michael Tadman, "The Reputation of the Slave Trader in Southern History and the Social Memory of the South," *American Nineteenth Century History*, 8, no. 3 (September, 2007), 247–271. Also see Michael Tadman's chapter, "The Interregional Slave Trade in the History and Myth-Making of the U.S. South" in Walter Johnson, ed., *The Chattel Principle: Internal Slave Trades in the Americas* (New Haven, CT: Yale University Press, 2004), pp. 117–142.

had both material and symbolic value. To some of them, he seems to have been closely bonded, and, with all due respect to Stanley Elkins, it would be absurd to compare Monticello to a Nazi death camp. Indeed, maintaining the stability of a plantation's culture was obviously in the interests of ordinary field hands, who worked hard in order to prevent their families from being split up and sold off. But hard as Jefferson's people worked, and whether they worked in industry or agriculture, what they produced was not in the long run sufficient to sustain their master's needs, and barely sufficient to keep the plantations in operation.[22]

LOVE, HONOR, AND THE WAYLES' SLAVE-TRADING DEBT

Falling in love with an Atlantic slave-trader's daughter was probably a matter of both the heart and the head, and a good marriage always requires both. In 1772 Jefferson married Martha Wayles Skelton, an apparently wealthy young widow of 23, and when Martha's father, John Wayles, died a year after their marriage, Jefferson increased his property in land and slaves, because under the legal codes of the time husbands acquired title to their wives' property. The estate was divided between Martha and her sisters, and her share of the inheritance amounted to 11,000 acres and 135 slaves. Jefferson also became one of the executors of the estate, which at the time of Wayles' death could be estimated at £30,000, but there were liens on the properties amounting to £11,000 owed to Wayles' English creditors, plus an additional £6,000 debt, resulting from a disastrous Atlantic slave-trading venture, in which most of the human cargo was lost.

The last left Jefferson at least indirectly entangled in the Atlantic slave trade, although, as he put it, he was not morally obliged to pay for that loss, since "we have not the property." But it was not only the human cargo that was "under water."[23] The value of the lands included in the

[22] Cf. Elkins' brilliant but flawed study, which is based on the fundamental error that all slavery experiences were comparable to prisons or to death camps. Conditions for slaves in Virginia were superior to those of slaves in the sugar plantations of Surinam or the rice swamps of Louisiana, which often were death camps. Michael Tadman, "The Demographic Cost of Sugar: Debates on Slave Societies and Natural Increase in the Americas," *The American Historical Review*, 105, no. 5 (December, 2000), 1534–1575, surveys literature comparing conditions on tobacco plantations with those on sugar plantations.

[23] My starting-point for exploring the Wayles debt is Herbert Sloan, *Principle and Interest: Thomas Jefferson and the Problem of Debt* (New York: Oxford University Press, 1995), pp. 13–49. Sloan acknowledges a debt to Steven Harold Hochman, "Thomas Jefferson:

estate depreciated during the Revolution, and those that were sold in an attempt to pay off the creditors brought only a portion of their estimated value. Limitations on the money supply in the Virginia economy of 1774 induced him to accept bonds in payment, which was unwise, because the London creditors were unwilling to accept them in lieu of pounds sterling. In the meantime, not only were the bonds losing value, but, due to Virginia's legal tender laws, he was forced to accept worthless currency in exchange for some of them. Jefferson might have been willing to leave the estate intact and postpone taking possession of his portion of it until all liens were paid off, but negotiations with Martha's half-sisters and their husbands may have been a source of pressure.

Jefferson probably had moral reservations about increasing his holdings in slaves, given his simultaneous expression of antislavery sentiments that same year (1774) in the *Summary View*, but his new bride may have pressured him to retain her dowry for sentimental as well as for financial reasons. Whatever the justification, he increased his slaveholdings and became vicariously entangled in the Atlantic slave trade, involving a cargo of black people lost at sea but blaming King George for "captivating & carrying them into slavery in another hemisphere or to incur miserable death in their transportation thither." He was as morally involved in the Atlantic slave trade as King George. Although his wish to free his slaves was, no doubt, sincere, he remained, like it or not, a slaveholder, and became effectively a slave trader.

Jefferson must have felt honor bound in 1818 when he made the ill-advised, and ultimately disastrous, error of endorsing a note for Wilson

A Personal Financial Biography" (Ph.D. diss., University of Virginia, 1987), as "confirming what readers have derived from Malone, esp. vol. I [*Jefferson the Virginian*], pp. 435–446; vol. III [*Jefferson and the Ordeal of Liberty*], pp. 529–530; vol. VI [*The Sage of Monticello*], pp. 505–512." These I consulted, along with the documents in Julian P. Boyd's edition of *The Papers of Thomas Jefferson* (Princeton University Press, 1958), vol. XV. Jefferson's sympathetic biographers agree with Jon Meacham's assessment in his *Thomas Jefferson and the Art of Power* (New York: Random House, 2012), p. 70, that Jefferson's economic woes originated in debts "initially inherited from his wife's father." See "Sales of Slaves Imported in *The Prince of Wales*" (September–December 1772) at Founders Online. Also see the Editorial Note, "The Debt to Farell & Jones and the Slave Ship," at Founders Online https://founders.archives.gov/documents/Jefferson/01-15-02-0620-0001 Also see Dumas Malone, "Long Note on Jefferson's Debts" in his *Jefferson and His Time*, 6 vols. (Boston, MA: Little, Brown, 1948), vol. III, *Jefferson and the Ordeal of Liberty*, pp. 529–530. Sloan, *Principle and Interest*, offers a summary of Jefferson's financial history. A detailed summary of Wayles' finances can be traced through the extensive footnote references in Annette Gordon-Read, *The Hemingses of Monticello* (New York: Norton, 2008).

Cary Nicholas, the father-in-law of his grandson, Jeff Randolph. All finance is ultimately a confidence game, and all business must be contracted on some element of trust. Being willing and able to stand behind the debts of a family merger reinforced the self-image and local prestige of a planter like Jefferson, but undermined his financial security. When confidence is not placed in banks, then finance must rely on sentimental factors such as interlocking friendly and familial relationships and a personal sense of honor.[24] Jefferson lived by a code of honor that led him to denounce slavery while entering deeper into slavery-related debt. His code of honor, his sense of noble obligations, and his position as a *paterfamilias* practically forced him to extend credit to a member of his extended family.

Jefferson's economic difficulties originated in a knowing involvement in a business that he putatively despised and in the assumption of excessive debt, a not uncommon variety of American foolishness. He and his in-laws decided to divide the highly burdened estate immediately, and before the British creditors had been paid. Through what some might describe as excessive optimism, or what others might call a lack of finesse in accounting, Jefferson had allowed his portion of the Wayles estate to be merged with his prior holdings. Under the laws existing in 1774, he now shared in the debt that encumbered his wife's inheritance. If he had patiently insisted that the estate remain undivided, or simply allowed his in-laws to have it all, Jefferson would have acquired none of Wayles' obligations. In the end, he might have been better off than his in-laws, but he chose to divide the estate with them, and, by doing so, Jefferson went into debt to acquire property that was as much a liability as an asset. His original hope was to pay off the debt by selling the agricultural proceeds of all the lands, but this was a poor strategy, if we are to believe the opinions of George Mason and other planters among his peers. Jefferson soon came to realize as much, and proceeded to a second plan of selling off a portion of the estate. This turned out to be a disastrous decision in the politicized and volatile economic climate of January 1774.[25]

Financial geniuses like Benjamin Franklin and George Washington might "get along swimmingly" while others were going under. Paying

[24] Jefferson's loan to Wilson Cary Nicholas is described in Sloan, *Principle and Interest*, pp. 219–220.

[25] George Mason wrote to George Washington, December 1773, that it was unwise to rely on agricultural proceeds, rather than selling off lands and slaves as a means of paying off debt. Cited in Sloan, *Principle and Interest*, p. 16.

off the debts was a matter of principle for Jefferson, and he was forced immediately to sell a portion of the Wayles lands and, by degrees, many of the slaves. Here he made his second bad decision, for he accepted payment in risky bonds.[26] Somehow his British creditors discovered this as soon as he had done it. Apparently having a better sense of business premonition than Jefferson, they refused to accept these bonds, which eventually proved worthless, preferring that Jefferson accept the responsibility himself. Jefferson was now left with the debts that had formerly been Wayles' and must rely on his creditors, and on the nearly worthless bonds, in order to balance his books. While in every technical respect he was still a large landowner, he was also a member of the debtor class. He could go even deeper into debt, if he so chose – an arrangement with which his creditors seem to have been perpetually contented. By the time he drafted the Declaration, he had already lost a significant portion of the Wayles land holdings, and he had been forced to sell fifty slaves.

Jefferson's public economic philosophy of righteous self-sufficiency concealed his dependency on slavery debt inherited from Wayles' slave-trading disaster, and his conspicuous enjoyment of the blessings of debt. While he demonstrated little success in the accumulation and preservation of liquefiable assets, or in paying off his debts, he showed an excellent capacity at acquiring debt, retaining his property, and managing to live well. Jefferson conveniently ignored Virginia's domestic slave trade when he wrote, in *Notes on Virginia*, "We never had an interior trade of any importance."[27] The domestic trade was important, although difficult to estimate in terms of how much wealth it contributed to the gross domestic product. In the life of a floundering farmer like Jefferson, who was constantly teetering on the brink of bankruptcy, it was a controlling factor. The domestic trade was also significant as a political issue, for it benefitted those states that desired lowered slave prices, but undermined Jefferson's Virginia, where the economy depended on higher slave prices. The lines of the Declaration concerning the Atlantic slave trade were perceived as self-serving. The issue of Virginia's opposition to the Atlantic slave trade and

[26] At this point no historian has determined whether Jefferson should have accepted these bonds, but his willingness to accept risk seems to be part of a life-long pattern. Monticello .org notes that Jefferson endorsed a $20,000 note for his relative by marriage, Wilson Cary Nicholas, whose daughter was married to Jefferson's grandson, Thomas Jefferson Randolph, a land speculator, who lost heavily in the panic of 1819. Sloan describes the Nicholas dealings in *Principle and Interest*, pp. 219–220.

[27] Thomas Jefferson, *Notes on the State of Virginia*, ed. David Waldstreicher (Boston, MA: Bedford Books, 2002), Query XIX, p. 196.

South Carolina's support of it recurred at the Constitutional convention, and the same battle of interests occurred.[28]

Selling slaves may have been repugnant to Jefferson for two reasons. Not only did it provide public evidence that his business affairs were not going well, but, more subtly, it made him, if only in the most technical sense, a slave trader. Jefferson did not want to be a trader; he detested traders of every sort, but especially slave traders. He saw himself as an honest farmer. In 1820 he expressed "scruples about selling negroes but for delinquency, or on their own request." It was, of course, at the arbitrary whim of the slaveholder that "delinquency" was to be defined. But Jefferson consoled himself with the justification that his slave-selling was benevolent. Lucia Stanton writes that he once "reluctantly" sold a slave in order that the latter might remain with his wife, who was being forced to leave Monticello with her master. He prided himself on his willingness to "indulge" his slaves' desire to maintain slave marriages that had been made "reasonably," and even those that in his opinion had been made "imprudently." Paul Finkelman, on the other hand, notes that Jefferson sold many slaves.[29]

Jefferson's moral aversion to selling lands and slaves was widely shared, and besides it was a strategy of doubtful effectiveness, as his daughter Martha counseled him and as George Mason believed.[30] Aside from the moral question, slave property was difficult to liquefy, but why sell them? He could always borrow money on his slaveholdings, and his creditors were contented with such an arrangement. He speculated in slaves almost as if they were tulip bulbs, but while he felt that it was wrong to own slaves, and unseemly to trade in them, he sometimes felt compelled to do both, consoling himself with the idea that his involvement in slavery was only temporary. "I am miserable till I shall owe not

28 Adrienne Koch, ed., *Notes on the Debates on the Federal Convention of 1787, Reported by James Madison* (New York: Norton, 1987 [1966]), p. 505. One should be skeptical about the myth that everyone in America profited from the Atlantic slave trade with the exception of Virginia. While a topic of discussion not only at the drafting of the Declaration, but also of the Constitution, was the opposition of Georgia and South Carolina to sinking the Atlantic slave trade, the merchants of Norfolk, no less than those of Boston, Charleston, and New York, were involved in the international commerce.

29 Stanton, *Slavery at Monticello*, pp. 13–14. Reprinted from Peter Onuf, ed., *Jeffersonian Legacies* (Charlottesville, VA: University of Virginia Press, 1993), pp. 147–180. Jefferson's desire to ameliorate the nature and to improve the condition of "his people" is a constant theme in Stanton's sympathetic works, but Paul Finkelman is impatient with such a view in his *Slavery and the Founders*.

30 George Mason to George Washington in Sloan, *Principle and Interest*, p. 15.

a shilling: the moment that shall be the case, I shall feel myself at liberty to do something for the comfort of my slaves," he wrote in his daybook in 1786. Fifty years later, he was still miserable, for the enlightened despot of Monticello was deeper than ever in debt. And over the years, he was tormented as much by the self-inflicted necessity of slave-dealing as by that of slave ownership in general. His desire to be a kind master was undoubtedly sincere, but the idea was an oxymoron. He regretted the necessity of being a slave merchant; the practice did not accord with his self-image. Why should we question the sincerity of such regrets any more than we question the sincerity of the obese person who sobs miserably into his hot fudge sundae?[31]

His *Notes on Virginia* never addressed the importance of slavery to the Southern economy at any level. The statements of George Mason and his daughter Martha lend credibility to the controversial findings of Engerman and Fogel that income from slave labor was not an efficient means of rapidly increasing capital.[32] It is clear the value of Jefferson's slaves may have meant less to him as a source of agricultural profit than as collateral for loans. Slaves were a means of storing wealth, if not quite as good as gold. For while paper currency of any sort, whether money or bonds, had a bad habit of losing value, slaves were investments that could hold their worth. Madison noted the following remark by Charles Pinckney: "South Carolina and Georgia cannot do without slaves. As to Virginia, she will gain by stopping the importations."[33] While Jefferson shared Madison's aversion to acknowledging the importance of slavery to the Republic, he could never deny the point that Virginia was a slave-producing state, and that he stood to profit from rising prices due to both the interstate commerce in slaves and the closing of the international slave trade. Both led to an escalation in the price of slaves, and he did not need

[31] Lucia Stanton, *Free Some Day: The African-American Families of Monticello* (Charlottesville, VA: The Thomas Jefferson Foundation, 2000), p. 56.

[32] Statements by Martha Jefferson Randolph and George Mason as noted in Sloan, *Principle and Interest*, pp. 15, 16, 254. Engerman and Fogel argued, in *Time on the Cross: The Economics of American Negro Slavery* (New York: Norton, 1974), "over the course of a lifetime a slave field hand received approximately ninety percent of the income produced," pp. 5–6. This figure, while debatable, lends credence to George Mason and Martha Jefferson Randolph's opinions, discussed elsewhere, that reliance on plantation surpluses as a means of sinking debt was an ill-considered strategy.

[33] Tuesday, August 21, 1787, Mr. Pinckney, in Koch, ed., *Notes on the Debates*, p. 505. Also see David Ramsey to Benjamin Lincoln, January 20, 1788, in Bernard Bailyn, *The Debate on the Constitution* (New York: Library of America, 1993), Part 2, *January to August 1788*, p. 117. George Mason and James Madison debate the Slave Trade Clause in Bailyn, *Debate*, Part 2, p. 706.

to engage directly in slave-trading to realize a capital gain from this escalation of prices.

Jefferson's medium of exchange currency was the "Negro Reserve Note," backed by the "Negro Reserve System," and Jefferson never needed a bank, so long as he could issue his own paper, based on his holdings. Even if these were heavily mortgaged, they were associated with his good name, his political status, and his hereditary patrician status within the Southern seigniorial system. These were all the collateral he required. A bank located in Philadelphia and issuing paper money, especially good paper money, would have undermined the pattern of obligations and social hierarchy on which Virginia's economic culture was based. The more debt he acquired, the more capable he was of maintaining his slaves, the symbols of wealth which served as a means of increasing his debt.

Jefferson's household economy was ostensibly focused on the impossible task of obliterating his debt with the proceeds of farming. His daughter, Martha, reminded him that this strategy had been tried by others and had proven generally to be impractical.[34] His financial difficulties over the entire sixty years of his adult life stemmed in part from his unwillingness to see himself, or to have others see him, as a seller of slaves. When forced to sell off his holdings, he would seek first to sell lands rather than slaves. Confronted with the latter distasteful option, he consoled himself on one occasion with the reasoning that he had sold them to his grandson, Francis Eppes, so that at least they remained in the family. But even if he did not sell slaves outright, he continued to borrow money, using their bodies as collateral, or, as we might say in the early twenty-first century, making every slave into a precursor of the ATM machine.[35]

Jefferson intoned an everlasting jeremiad on the virtue of balanced budgets but privately demonstrated, for future generations, the pragmatic benefits of living on debt. His family name, his web of friends, his ability to dispense political largesse, and his ability to generate confidence all contributed to his ability to pile debt on top of debt. Added to this, Jefferson knew the art of winning by the successful manipulation of status symbols. His ability to host excellent dinners, to serve fine wines, to own beautiful

[34] Martha Randolph to Jefferson, January 16, 1808, cited in Sloan, *Principle and Interest*, pp. 15, 254.

[35] In 1821, he transmitted several slaves to his grandson, Francis Eppes. See Merrill Peterson, *Thomas Jefferson and the New Nation* (Oxford University Press, 1970), p. 992.

horses, to maintain lovely gardens, to display scientific specimens in his entry hall, were not financial burdens but economic assets. His carefully managed spending created an impression of greater wealth than he actually possessed. His ability to impress an admiring world with his beautiful home and his hundreds of slaves instilled confidence in lenders. His spending habits demonstrated something more than vanity: they showed a shrewd understanding of the value of conspicuous consumption.

WEBER'S PROTESTANT ETHIC, VEBLEN'S CONSPICUOUS CONSUMPTION

If Max Weber was right, then Thomas Jefferson was wrong. If the proof of the American business mentality is the accumulation of unencumbered wealth, as Weber maintained in *The Protestant Ethic and the Spirit of Capitalism*, then Jefferson did very poorly. Only his public image and his artful dealing kept him out of debtors' prison. Even his admirers at the Monticello foundation admit that "it was his reputation in large part that kept creditors at bay." The observation shared by Dumas Malone, Julian P. Boyd, Stephen Harold Hochman, and Herbert Sloan that Jefferson kept detailed records is incontestable, but his bookkeeping was a magnificent sophistry. Resources on Jefferson's finances are becoming more accessible to researchers through electronic media, and new light may yet be shed on them, but it seems clear that his difficulties did not result from financial naïveté or from wastrel habits. He made imprudent financial decisions at several crucial junctures, and some of his difficulties originated on January 1, 1772, the day of his marriage. This is not to imply that Jefferson stood outside the ethos of consumption.[36]

We have seen Jefferson's encouragement of consumption in the aforementioned 1784 letter to George Washington, where he discussed commerce, presumably with European workshops, and with no mention of money supply, a dominant interest in the mind of Washington, as it had

[36] Sloan, *Principle and Interest*, p. 22. Malone, *Jefferson and the Ordeal of Liberty*, p. 6. As of February 14, 2015, the Monticello Foundation offered a brief online discussion of Jefferson's debt: www.monticello.org/site/research-and-collections/debt

Henry Wiencek, personal communication to Wilson J. Moses, February 26, 2014, wrote, "I do think he was a financial genius, and [Billy] Wayson agrees with me on this. As I've said, Jefferson adeptly found new sources of credit and re-financing. One of his creditors said he would never call a debt on the Author of the Declaration." This creditor was cited in Hochman, "Thomas Jefferson: A Personal Financial Biography." I wish to thank Henry Wiencek for bringing this page to my attention. Monticello.org says, "it was his reputation in large part that kept creditors at bay."

been many years earlier in a treatise by the precocious Benjamin Franklin, *A Modest Enquiry into the Nature and Necessity of a Paper-Currency*, where he extolled paper money as a stimulant to commerce and consumption. After getting a footing in Philadelphia, Franklin visited old friends in his native Boston, where the talk soon naturally turned to money, always an interesting topic, but especially so in the inconsistent colonial financial environment of 1724. One of the journeymen asked him what sort of money they had in Philadelphia, and "I produc'd a handful of silver, and spread it before them, which was a kind of raree-show they had not been us'd to, paper being the money of Boston." Eighteenth-century Americans tended to use foreign specie, such as bits of the famous Spanish "pieces of eight," as substitutes for British coins.[37]

Benjamin Franklin was the centerfold illustration in Max Weber's brilliant, but flawed, work *The Protestant Ethic and the Spirit of Capitalism*. In fact, Weber admitted that he was not a Protestant, but "a colorless deist." But Weber's title related both to the Protestant work ethic and to the capitalist spirit, which Franklin inherited from Puritanism's putative asceticism that supposedly results in capital accumulation and reinvestment. Weber made much of Franklin's Puritan upbringing, and his preachments of asceticism and parsimony, and rightly attributed Franklin's Puritan values to the influences of his father, Josiah Franklin, but he was unaware, as most people are, of a strong bond that existed between Franklin and Cotton Mather, or the fact that, as a child, Franklin read "Dr. Mather's *Essays to Do Good*, which perhaps gave me a Turn of thinking that had an influence on some of the principal future events of my life." Franklin would have encountered Mather's opinion that "there is no popish nation but would, by embracing the protestant religion ... double its wealth immediately."

Weber reduced Franklin's voice to the persona that spoke in his 1748 essay, *Advice to a Young Tradesman*, and quoted such maxims as "Remember that TIME is Money," as if Franklin had no other goal than the accumulation of money as an end in itself. Weber correctly recognized Franklin's enjoyment of steadily increasing his capital, but he fixated on Franklin' "success books," to the neglect of his *Autobiography*, and overlooked the fact that Franklin lived very well. In his London club, Franklin

[37] Franklin, *A Modest Enquiry*. Franklin also discusses paper money in Leo LeMay, ed., *Benjamin Franklin's Autobiography: An Authoritative Text, Backgrounds, Criticism* (New York: Norton, 1986), pp. 53–54. Jefferson to George Washington, March 15, 1784.

was an exemplary consumer of good food and conversation. He also established that tradition of American philanthropy that found expression in his imitator and fellow Pennsylvanian, Andrew Carnegie. Weber was seemingly unaware that Cotton Mather had supported a Massachusetts paper currency, and that Franklin's *Nature and Necessity of a Paper-Currency* had advocated an increased money supply and luxury spending. Franklin also confessed that he made out handsomely by printing paper money.[38]

Jefferson lived by the consumerism that Franklin advocated, rather than the asceticism that Poor Richard preached, but he was less attentive than Adam Smith had been to Franklin's defense of paper currency. Jefferson may have been aware of the friendship between Hume, Smith, and Franklin, and he may even have suspected Franklin's influence on Smith's decision to write somewhat sympathetically with regard to Pennsylvania's paper currency. Weber did not mention Adam Smith's or David Hume's economic writings. Farley Grubb, a University of Chicago-trained economist, and professor of economics at the University of Delaware, summarizes Franklin's relationship to money and banking in the late colonial period and notes that "In 1765, in response to Lord Grenville's challenge to come up with some palatable way for the British to increase taxes on the colonists to help pay for the Seven Years War, Franklin writes up a proposal for a North-America-wide universal paper currency modeled on Pennsylvania's land bank system." Jefferson, despite his friendship with Franklin, and his attempt to claim Franklin's scientific mantle, turned a deaf ear to Franklin's Federalist strategies for increasing money supply and stability and for a national banking system.[39]

[38] Max Weber, *The Protestant Ethic and the Spirit of Capitalism* (New York: Charles Scribner's Sons, repr. 1904–5 [1858]), pp. 47–78. Franklin cites Mather's *Essays to Do Good* (London, 1816) in his *Autobiography*, and again in speaking of Mather's influences in Benjamin Franklin to Samuel Mather, May 12, 1784. Carnegie cited Franklin several times in his *Autobiography* (London: John Constable & Co., 1920): "One truth I see. Franklin was right. 'The highest worship of God is service to Man,'" p. 285, and "'The highest worship of God is service to man.' At least, I feel so with Luther and Franklin," p. 340. David Hume describes the disadvantages of the Stuart dynasty as including the Roman Catholic religion, and avers the Hanoverian advantages, i.e. "Trade and manufactures, and agriculture, have encreased." See David Hume, *Essays and Treatises on Several Subjects in Two Volumes; Vol. I. Containing Essays Moral, Political, and Literary, A New Edition* (London: T. Cadell; Edinburgh: A. Kincaid and A. Donaldson, 1762), p. 509.

[39] Adam Smith, *The Wealth of Nations*, 2 vols. (Oxford University Press, 1976), pp. 326, 820, 940. Farley Grubb, "Benjamin Franklin and the Birth of a Paper Money Economy," based on a lecture given by Professor Grubb on March 30, 2006, at the Federal Reserve

If Thorstein Veblen was right, then Jefferson exemplified "conspicuous consumption" far better than Franklin exemplified Weber's "Protestant ethic." Thorstein Veblen's *The Theory of the Leisure Class* provides a framework for understanding Jefferson's complicated relationship to his wealth in slaves, based as it was on the primal exploitative instincts that Veblen attributed to the "leisure class." Monticello also provides illustrations for Veblen's coined phrase "vicarious consumption of leisure," to indicate that the wives, children, and servants of the wealthy are also consumers of leisure. In Veblen's system, the upper classes derive virtue, dignity, and status from their idleness. The lower classes are industrial workers, farmers, servants, and slaves who must work, and therefore they have lesser virtue, because work, as Veblen points out with his beautiful sarcasm, is from the dawn of history less honorable than leisure and "exploit." Manly exploits such as hunting, warfare, and sport conferred status, Veblen averred, as did such material symbols of wealth as horses and landed estates. But what truly conferred status, he added with irony, was the ability to exploit labor and consume leisure. Women, said Veblen, constituted the first working class, and it was this fact in the collective consciousness of the human race that degraded labor and conferred on men their status as the primal leisure class.

Peasant women in Europe and Indian women in America were exploited, as Jefferson noted, and he should have observed that in Virginia, too, much of servile labor was performed by women. At Monticello, drudgery was consigned to slaves, men and women alike. White males of Virginia's cavalier class stereotypically enjoyed leisure, sport, and warfare. Jefferson's pacifistic behavior was among the reasons Theodore Roosevelt wrote so critically of him. The militant antebellum South might have furnished Veblen with much material to support his thesis, but he might have found Jefferson an interesting paradox. Jefferson, Madison, and Patrick Henry enjoyed status of the leisure class, despite having no military exploits, in contrast to George Washington, Andrew Jackson, and the Lee family. But Jefferson possessed the essential attribute of the cavalier class that Veblen described, the ability to consume, as Jefferson said in his previously mentioned letter to Washington, "the comforts furnished by the arts and manufactures," and he also participated in what Veblen called "the conspicuous consumption of leisure."

Bank of Philadelphia and under the auspices of the Library Company of Philadelphia: www.philadelphiafed.org/-/media/publications/economic-education/ben-Franklin-and-paper-money-economy.pdf

Jefferson was not foolishly extravagant: he made no attempt to emulate the conspicuous consumption of the British aristocracy. His British social analogue in 1808, when he returned from Washington to Monticello, would have been situated in the hierarchy at the level of Jane Austen's Mr. Bennett, a gentleman, to be sure, but not controlling the wealth of a Mr. Darcy. Both Bennett and Darcy were of the British leisure class, but neither was at its apex; they occupied different ranks within the British gentry, in any analysis based purely on wealth. In terms of class structure, both were *sine nobilitate*. Jefferson lived the comfortable life of the gentry class, but did not attempt to emulate the life of a Darcy. The elegance of his lifestyle consisted in his library, his love of music, and his life in letters, but he was not profligate. Monticello is a handsome mansion, but not a princely palace. Bernard Bailyn notes that there was "no possible correspondence" between eighteenth-century American mansions and the country estates of the British nobility. But one factor that an American like Jefferson added to his social status was the retention and display of numerous slaves.[40]

But Jefferson could compete with both Mr. Bennett and Mr. Darcy in one respect, "the vicarious consumption of leisure," as Veblen would have noticed. The leisure class is obliged to display their wealth through proxies – usually their wives and children, who are honorary members of the leisure class, but favored slaves may also serve this function. Idleness in women was a trait that Jefferson cultivated in his daughters, as his letters notoriously indicate. The maintenance of teenaged Sally Hemings and her brother, while in Paris, was also a display of his wealth and status. The self-portrait of devoted fatherhood that he paints in letters to his daughters is charmingly similar to the character of Jane Austen's doting Mr. Bennett. Jefferson saw it as a duty to preserve both married and unmarried women of his class from drudgery. The relative leisure of his women was a primary status symbol for a country squire in the England or America of the early nineteenth century.

American plantation society mingled a patrician aesthetic with a Protestant ethic; thus, the master must simultaneously be the enterprising frontier farmer and the patrician consumer of status symbols.

40 Bernard Bailyn, *To Begin the World Anew: The Genius and Ambiguities of the American Founders* (New York: Knopf, 2003), p. 12. *Sine nobilitate* (without nobility) or "s.nob." According to an apparently discredited folk etymology, it was an abbreviation affixed to the names of commoners in one of the British boarding schools to distinguish upstarts from the nobility.

Jefferson in his daily routine conformed quite admirably to the Protestant work ethic, but he never neglected the role of the gentleman of leisure, and always made time for such pursuits as chamber music, horsemanship, wine-tasting, and letter writing.[41] Jefferson conspicuously consumed leisure, and so did some of his slaves. The majority of them labored in his shops and fields, but he displayed his wealth by maintaining James Hemings, his Paris-trained cook. A few menials on the great estates of Europe and America might wear powdered wigs and fine livery, or perhaps be displayed as the winsome *Kammermohr*, who served chocolate to the guests on a silver tray, but on Virginia's small farms, the wives and children of ordinary yeomen worked in the fields with their slaves, and had to "tote that barge and lift that bale."

The twentieth-century African American exhorter Malcolm X was mistaken when, in one of his stirring orations, he generated a popular myth of class division between "house Negroes" who identified with their masters' interests and "field Negroes" who did not. Malcolm X was probably right in thinking that if the master's house caught fire, the house Negro would "fight harder to save it than the master himself," but was it true that the field Negro "would pray for a wind to come along and fan the breeze?" Common field hands were the ones most likely to suffer if the master suffered economic misfortune. They might be sold away from their friends and families, and Malcolm admitted himself that "house Negroes" were very few. Slaves who worked only as butlers, chambermaids, and chefs were an economic extravagance that only a few planters could afford. Jefferson, as a great planter, gained status from displaying a few slaves who were free from drudgery, as were the Hemingses, who apparently did not experience the worst conditions known to field hands under a low-class slave-driver like Simon Legree.[42]

Steven Harold Hochman argues that Jefferson's perpetual debt was more the result of mismanagement than profligacy.[43] True, he set a nice table, and even the Hessian prisoners of war were handsomely entertained at Monticello, dancing, playing chamber music, and savoring good wines, but Monticello was no Versailles, and Jefferson made no attempt to rival the spending patterns of contemporary European nobles. If we accept the findings of the current scholarship, we must believe that his personal

41 Jefferson to Dr. Thomas Cooper, October 7, 1814.

42 Annette Gordon-Reed, *The Hemingses of Monticello* (New York: Norton, 2008), pp. 617–618.

43 Hochman, "Thomas Jefferson: A Personal Financial Biography."

economic difficulties derived less from conspicuous consumption than from an inability to solve the problem of revenue, although he made reasonable attempts to address that problem. In addition, he was motivated to lend money, out of his patrician's sense of affable "condescension" (in the positive, eighteenth-century sense of the word), his devotion to friends and family, and his personal code of honor, but his generosity exceeded his good judgment.

Although Jefferson was on the verge of bankruptcy when he died in 1826, he does not seem to have lacked a genius for accounting. His farm book reveals a marvelous fixation on detail, but his real skill was not the balancing of budgets: it was the piling of debt on top of debt. He was not terribly obsessed with increasing his amount of unencumbered capital, and, despite his public horror of debt, privately he was a genius at understanding the power of deficit spending and the possibilities of living well on debt. Thus, in his private economy he was a pragmatist, displaying a refinement of policy that contradicted his public image. In his agrarian economics, as in his antislavery rhetoric, he was not an ideologue, but a temporizer and a moderate.

Jefferson's individual trajectory did not parallel the flourishing of the American economy, which despite its turbulence and uncertainty burgeoned magnificently during his lifetime. He started life with greater resources than George Washington, and never had the numerous conflicting obligations and political distractions, such as running a plantation while leading an army, but he ended up poorer. Some historians have excused Jefferson's economic collapse by saying that he lived too long. Presumably Washington might have suffered equally to Jefferson if he had lived another twenty years, to experience the crash of 1819, but there were fluctuations in the American economy during Washington's lifetime; he was simply a better manager of capital. It is true that Jefferson was hurt by the panic of 1819. During the first two decades of the nineteenth century, bankers were eager to lend money in support of land speculation in the West, and expansion of the money supply was inflationary. Deflationary correctives, undertaken by the Bank of the United States, caused the panic of 1819, which hurt Jefferson and soured Andrew Jackson permanently on banks. But Jackson recovered, and it seems that Jefferson, a brilliant lawyer, and the heir to two fortunes, a man with tremendous prestige and political influence, could have managed to live well and still multiply his capital.

Despite his ridicule of Hamilton's claim that a debt could be a blessing, Jefferson's life demonstrated that a variety of truth could be extracted from that maxim. The truth that existed on the pragmatic level was that he was able to live well, but on a moral level his debt thwarted an act of benevolence that would have rounded out his historical image. He had claimed that he sought to liberate his slaves with provision for their welfare after emancipation. The final mark of Jefferson's success as a farmer, and the proof of his benevolence and patrician status, would have been to free his slaves, but this he could never do. Slaves served not only as agricultural workers, but also as collateral for debts, and, rather than freeing them, he must use them to increase his debt. In theory, he was simultaneously trying to pay off the debt on his heavily mortgaged people while continually borrowing money on them, a practice that not only compounded the problem but was, by his own standard, morally wrong.

If Jefferson had actually been inclined towards Parisian cosmopolitanism, as Henry Adams fancied, or had he been the abolitionist he pretended to be, he might have liberated his slaves and moved to a city. In a heaven exceeding his reach, his grasp, and even his desire, he might have been able to live a life approximating what he had known in Paris. In Philadelphia, for example, he could have enjoyed lectures, music, and theatre. The sophisticated conversation he so cherished would have been sustained by his Philosophical Society, or by a "Junto Club and Lending Library" such as the one Franklin established in his youth.[44] Becoming the cosmopolite that Henry Adams imagined would have involved more than a drastic and uncomfortable cultural shift, however: it would have involved an extraordinary financial triumph exceeding his powers, although achieved by some of his contemporaries.

Jefferson was disappointed in one social aspiration: he was incapable of the *beau geste* of freeing his slaves, as did the more solvent Washington, and John Randolph of Roanoke, and Edward Coles. These others were in vastly superior positions to demonstrate their abolitionism with wealth. Jefferson could not afford to achieve the status of a humanitarian by anticipating the experiment that Robert E. Lee would later conduct, educating a number of slaves and colonizing them in Africa.[45] Although he died without having to face the humiliation of liquidating his slave property, Jefferson was never able to achieve the status of emancipator. Horatio Gates made arrangements for the gradual emancipation of his

[44] Henry Adams, *History of the United States during the Administrations of Thomas Jefferson* (New York: Library of America, 1986 [1890]), p. 98.

[45] Bell Irvin Wiley, *Slaves No More: Letters from Liberia, 1833–1869* (Lexington, KY: University Press of Kentucky, 1980).

slaves in 1790, at the urging of John Adams, and finally had at least that one thing in common with his ancient enemy, George Washington, who also declared that his slaves should eventually be freed.[46] John Randolph of Roanoke would free his on his deathbed, seven years after Jefferson's own demise. There were few abolitionists among the planter class, and even fewer able to demonstrate simultaneously their business acumen and their humanitarianism.

Thorstein Veblen would have described the few Hemings slaves, who were relieved from drudgery, not only as wealth symbols, like the mansion, library, wine cellar, clocks, and mammoth bones, but also as "vicarious consumers of leisure." Jefferson was wealthy enough to maintain several slaves whose labor was not strenuous and whose activities produced no great profit, most notably Betty Hemings and her children. He brought two of them to Paris with him: James, to be trained as a cook, and Sally, as a travelling companion for his daughter, Polly. But Polly was soon placed in a convent, which lends credence to Abigail Adams' questioning what usefulness Sally might have in the Jefferson household. Professor Annette Gordon-Reed's exhaustive research has turned up no evidence that Sally's labors, either in France or in America, were economically profitable to Jefferson in any conventional sense. The typical slaveholder never brought two young mulatto house servants to Paris. A typical slaveholder kept between seven and twenty slaves, usually semi-skilled laborers of both sexes, who could plough a field in the morning, pitch manure in the afternoon, and shuck corn in the evening. Enslaved teenagers had to do meaningful work, and the yeoman slave owner neither desired a French cook nor had the resources to maintain one. Along with his wife and children, he might even work alongside his slaves in the fields when the seasonal cycles of farming demanded it.

Joseph Pieper, in *Leisure: The Basis of Culture*, gives to the term "leisure" a dignity encompassing the higher aspirations of Western civilization, and in Jefferson's case a distinction must be drawn between

[46] Some abolitionist sources related that Gates freed his slaves outright; historian Paul Nelson contends that he sold them "to John Mark, a close friend," under the stipulation that "six older Negroes be freed after five years' service and eleven younger ones upon reaching the age of twenty-eight": Paul David Nelson, *General Horatio Gates: A Biography* (Baton Rouge: Louisiana State University Press, 1976), pp. 287–288. Julia Lipkins, Reference Archivist, Manuscript Department, New York Historical Society, questions an account in *The Anti-Slavery Record* 3 (1838) claiming that Gates "summoned his numerous family and slaves about him, and amidst their tears of affection and gratitude, gave them their freedom" – http://blog.nyhistory.org/horatio-gates-samuel-washington-and-americas-original-sin/

leisure and idleness. Leisure, in the sense that Veblen employed the term, includes time devoted to managerial tasks, manly sport, and positively sanctioned elite intellectual activities. Jefferson's leisure represented not only the exploitative and wasteful functions that Veblen satirized, it also encompassed the positive meanings attributed by Pieper. He was simultaneously a man of leisure and a hard worker, but the labor he performed was the labor reserved for a leisure class; it did not involve drudgery, and therefore conferred status. In a famous letter to Tadeusz Kościuszko, Jefferson wrote, at the age of 67, "My mornings are devoted to correspondence. From breakfast to dinner, I am in my shops, my garden, or on horseback among my farms; from dinner to dark, I give to society and recreation with my neighbors and friends; and from candle light to early bed-time, I read." His time was devoted to management tasks, to creativity, to cultured and civilized pursuits having an aesthetic and intellectual value, activities regarded in the occidental tradition as conferring esteem.[47]

TAKING CARE OF BUSINESS, "ROUGH ESTIMATES BY MY HEAD"

Incredibly, Jefferson, the gifted mathematician, who calculated with such finesse the amount of whiteness in the blood of a mulatto, seems to have based his White House finances on "rough estimates by my head."[48] Despite his reputation for precise record-keeping and mathematical acuity, President Jefferson apparently operated on the basis of optimism rather than reality. Jefferson's legendary bookkeeping acumen was like the exquisite calculations of cycles and epicycles that medieval mathematicians employed to make the sun revolve around the earth. But it was no more potent than the legendary Papal Bull against the comet. It is an established fact that only the most refined sensibilities can appreciate the "music of the spheres," and the cognoscenti are still impressed by Jefferson's magnificent fiddling. He almost succeeded in making the world revolve around Monticello and getting the Virginia legislature to dance on the head of a pin.

His attempt to persuade the legislature to set up a lottery for his benefit seems somewhat embarrassing for a man who seemed so committed to

[47] Jefferson to Thaddeus Kosciusko, February 26, 1810. Joseph Pieper, *Leisure: The Basis of Culture*, trans. Alexander Dru, with an introduction by T. S. Eliot (New York: Random House, 1952). (Originally *Muße und Kult* (Munich: Kösel-Verlag, 1948).) The work, as its title implies, counterbalances Veblen's satirical *Theory of the Leisure Class*.

[48] Jefferson to George Jefferson, December 24, 1808.

laissez-faire economics. Gaye Wilson's article in the *Colonial Williamsburg Journal* describes his desperate attempt to manipulate the Virginia state legislature during the last year of his life.[49] It is another example of Jefferson's opportunism. The wall of the separation between business and the state was no more concrete than his other celebrated wall of separation. At one point, efforts for his relief were organized not only in Virginia, but in Philadelphia and Baltimore. Even the mayor of New York, Philip Hone, became involved in efforts to assist him, but the amount of $16,500 eventually raised was to defray debts amounting to over $100,000, and was not sufficient to bail out the author of the Declaration of Independence.

In December of 1808, as the date of his departure from Washington impended, he confessed in a panicky and embarrassed letter to George Jefferson that he had failed to keep his expenses within the limits of his income. He was asking for help in finding funds to repay debts incurred during his presidency, and seeking George's friendly offices in negotiating with a bank in Richmond for funds to be advanced on the basis of his continuing optimism. "My resources for repaiment within that time will be my crop of tobo. of this year." Bearing in mind that all planters must speculate against the future, one recognizes the shakiness of his reliance on a strategy that had failed him many times in the past. One is again reminded of the contrast with George Washington, known for his strict attention to business. Historian Edward G. Lengel notes that he had to make Valley Forge "a hub of commerce" while managing from a distance the affairs of Mount Vernon, and all this in the midst of currency depreciation.[50]

Depending on how one defines the terms, Jefferson may be called a financial incompetent, a fiscal genius, or a crafty embezzler. As he floundered on "the boisterous seas of [economic] liberty," his ownership of the Declaration was something of a life preserver. Steven Hochman says that "While Jefferson often failed to pay his debts on time, creditors rarely complained. Generally, a warm letter would be sent to him, as from Leroy and Bayard in 1822, granting more time 'to the author of the Declaration of Independence.'"[51] Hochman's statement was generously formulated,

49 Gaye Wilson, "Monticello Was among the Prizes in a Lottery for a Ruined Jefferson's Relief," *Colonial Williamsburg Journal* (winter, 10).

50 Jefferson to George Jefferson, December 24, 1808. On George Washington's fastidious attention to financial details, see Lengel, *First Entrepreneur*, pp. 126–127, 143–146, 156, and Achenbach, *The Grand Idea*.

51 Hochman, "Thomas Jefferson: A Personal Financial Biography," pp. 287–288. I wish to thank Henry Wiencek for bringing these pages to my attention.

for Jefferson did not simply postpone payment on his debts; in the end, he failed to pay them, leaving his heirs a financial burden that his grandson, Thomas Jefferson Randolph, reported to be $100,000. It was not until Randolph's death and the settlement of his estate in 1878 that all debts were finally paid. His heirs bore only a portion of the suffering caused by his talent for borrowing: the other victims were the slaves who constituted the bulk of his capital, and whose families and communities had to be liquidated at the time of his demise.

In his final years, Jefferson's creditors, living and dead, included such long-term allies and political sympathizers as William Short, Tadeusz Kościuszko, and Phillip Mazzei. These latter three had entrusted funds to his care, listening to his arguments that American banks were untrustworthy; he offered the assurance that he would repay them with interest. He was able to repay Short and Kościuszko, but only after the sale of his library to Congress, and the funds Kościuszko had given to Jefferson for the emancipation of his slaves were put to other purposes. His resolution of the Mazzei debt involved additional borrowing. Jefferson's indebtedness has been visited many times in secondary literature, where even a historian so kindly disposed towards him as Herbert Sloan is compelled, in tones of dismay, to take recourse to such language as "Jefferson should have known better," and "The sensible course of action would have been ..."[52] Jefferson could engage in such whimsies as using calculus to design a plough, but basic household arithmetic seemed to elude his grasp.

POTLATCH CEREMONY OR GOVERNMENT BAIL-OUT?

Financial dealings often involve an expertise at public relations, and in that realm Jefferson's financial genius was as mountainous as his debt. His ability to generate funds was evidenced in his negotiating the sale of his library to Congress, which amounted to asking for a congressional bail-out. Congress purchased his books for $23,950, at a time when that was a considerable sum. He made the subtle offer in September 1814, and Congress bailed him out in January 1815. It would have been a wonderful gesture to donate his library to Congress. Along with the emancipation of his slaves, the donation would have solidified forever his position as a philanthropist. It would have been the ultimate "potlatch ceremony," the act of public generosity demonstrating his benevolence and public-spiritedness (see below). This manipulation has some symbolic

[52] Sloan, *Principle and Interest*, p. 219.

significance for the interpretation of his and the nation's economic policies. Furthermore, his "donation" of his library to Congress is not to be mistaken for what Franz Boas observed as a potlatch ceremony. This is the Native American ritual in which one demonstrates one's social status through the conspicuous impoverishment of oneself by giving away all worldly goods. This ritual has parallels of course in medieval Christianity, in which many saints demonstrated their penitence by giving all their goods to the poor and taking up the religious life. It also has parallels in the Republican tradition of disinterested sacrifice to one's nation.[53] But Thomas Jefferson had no unencumbered debt to sacrifice in either the Christian or the Republican tradition. He sold his books to Congress more out of necessity than public spirit and, once again, was a melancholy optimist, whose public virtues were less the result of civic virtue than of business exigency. In this regard it might be mentioned that King George III assembled a splendid library which, upon his death, was given by King George IV to the British nation.

Jefferson's public anxiety over balanced budgets probably derived from his private anxieties over his personal private debt. His perpetual embarrassment over borrowing, his necessary compounding of his debt, is an inescapable contradiction. An ironist is tempted to surmise that Jefferson's private incompetency was the historical root of America's conservative economic theory. Americans are notorious for the constant preachment of balanced budgets while practicing the most irresponsible amassment of debt. In theory, Jefferson was opposed to taxation, and yet he proposed policies, such as establishing an American military presence in the Muslim world, that, if seriously pursued, would have necessitated tremendous expenditures. He took on the expense of acquiring a vast land empire extending to the Rockies, at a bargain price to be sure, but at the cost of increasing the national debt. His proposal for the massive deportation of the African population and its replacement with European workers would have involved colossal expenses, and possibly a "liberal construction" of the Constitution.

Thomas Jefferson was the founder of the tradition that prefigured Reaganomics, to wit, preaching balanced budgets as a moral principle while actually increasing the national debt. Jefferson never acknowledged that the ideas he proposed, such as the military acquisition of Canada,

[53] Cf. martyrdom of Lincoln and Kennedy. Harriet Beecher Stowe specifically made Lincoln into another Christ. See Wilson J. Moses, *Black Messiahs and Uncle Toms: Social and Literary Manipulations of a Religious Myth* (Philadelphia, PA: University of Pennsylvania Press, 1993).

would involve tremendous public spending and could not be accomplished without increasing sources of revenue. His restrained but remarkable praise for the "Agrarian Justice" of Thomas Paine implied the creation of a social welfare system, destined to be both expensive and proto-socialistic. And his planned deportation of the Americanized Africans would have rivaled the most massive and brutal ethnic cleansing projects of the twentieth century. It is an easy thing to preach small governments and balanced budgets; it is another matter to finance the building and maintenance of an imperial hegemony. "Hamiltonian means towards Jeffersonian ends" is the now familiar bromide, coined by Herbert Croly and Theodore Roosevelt in 1912. The slogan might ironically have been applied by President Jefferson himself.

CONCLUSION

The historian Joseph Ellis has opined that Jefferson "never fully grasped his economic predicament," but that idea is not sustainable. He was a fastidious accountant, who kept track of every penny. Other historians are convinced that Jefferson realized from the beginning that he was in trouble.[54] In attempts to address his monetary problems, he speculated in land and undertook industrial experiments. He experimented ingeniously with agricultural improvements, hoping to increase productivity, and he was obsessed with farming science on both a theoretical and a practical level, but his proceeds from farming were never sufficient to make ends meet. He was a frontier improviser and inventor, as were most men of his status at that time. He showed openness to the importation of foreign farm machinery and an eagerness to introduce European farm products into America. He designed a plough that apparently functioned impressively, although it would be an exaggeration to claim that he ever made an innovation of such revolutionary magnitude as Whitney's cotton gin or McCormick's later threshing machine. George Washington's undertakings as an innovative farmer were equally impressive, and, whether through circumstances, perspicacity, or pure luck, were ultimately more successful.

Herbert Sloan's position is more tenable than Ellis', although he too suggests that Jefferson did not grasp his predicament. But he offers

[54] Joseph Ellis, *American Sphinx: The Character of Thomas Jefferson* (New York: Knopf, 1997), pp. 137–139. Cf. Sloan's "he should have known better," *Principle and Interest*, p. 218.

a somewhat convincing comparison to Mme. Ranevskaya, Anton Chekov's protagonist in *The Cherry Orchard*. On one level, Chekov's fictive symbol of aristocratic carelessness is reminiscent of Jefferson, for she was somewhat like him – elegant, attractive, sentimental, and temporizing. But that was in another country, and besides the lady never lived.[55] Unlike Mme. Ranevskaya, who seems incapable of comprehending the impending crisis, for herself, for her class, or for her nation, Jefferson heard his "fire bell in the night." The nightmare of his personal economic and moral problems was constantly with him, and he knew that his difficulties presaged a crisis for his class and the nation as a whole. A man obsessed with bookkeeping must have grasped his predicament, and one prone to headaches must have experienced some sleepless nights.

Jefferson's wealth lay not in unencumbered capital, not in reserves of specie, but in his ability to inspire confidence and generate paper money. He was the man of the shrewd, penetrating, alluring smile, the comely, fur-collared philosopher king revealed in the Rembrandt Peale portrait of 1805. He far less resembles Chekov's dreamy heroine of *The Cherry Orchard* than he does the dynamic Frank Cowperwood, protagonist of Theodore Dreiser's *Trilogy of Desire*. Cowperwood's wealth consisted of an intellectual construct, based on the dynamic magnetism of his personality and the confidence he inspired in the members of every class. The goal of Jefferson's personal economy was to accumulate mountains of debt and to enjoy the prestige that accrues to Veblen's leisure class by virtue of their ability to consume leisure and luxury. His hostility to debt in the public sector derived not from any thrifty Protestant ethic but from a patrician's hostility to the merchant culture and to a commercial class that he viewed as having no virtues and having "no country."[56]

It was poor business judgment, not extravagant lifestyle, that led to Jefferson's perpetual indebtedness, that and a code of honor that led him to assume excessive risk. Monticello's slaves bore the burden of Jefferson's code of honor. They were the children of Sisyphus, perpetually engaged in the endless task of paying off a constantly growing debt. More than that: they were the very collateral for that debt. Those slaves who understood

55 Sloan, *Principle and Interest*, p. 41. He makes an apt reference on p. 20 to the character Mr. Micawber, who goes to debtors' prison in Charles Dickens' *David Copperfield*, famous for two quotations: "something will turn up" and "Annual income twenty pounds, annual expenditure nineteen nineteen six, result happiness. Annual income twenty pounds, annual expenditure twenty pounds ought and six, result misery."

56 "But merchants have no country ... least virtuous," Jefferson to Horatio G. Spafford, March 17, 1814.

such things lived with the knowledge that their market value was increasing, and that they could be sold away from their homes, friends, and families. Jefferson's public policy was to sermonize and fret constantly over debt, while his private policy depended on multiplying his debts, with no real interest in eradicating them. Ultimately his legacy was a burden to his family, who worked to pay them off in the name of family honor. His cleverly cultivated reputation for parsimony was a splendid camouflage for his position as America's most magnificent debtor. He had profited from Ben Franklin's lesson that the public display of industry facilitated the acquisition of debt. He set a pattern for subsequent generations of Americans who enshrine Weber's Protestant ethic, but practice Veblen's conspicuous consumption.

12

Defining the Presidency

"His mind was great and powerful," was Jefferson's considered assessment of George Washington, but there was a sting in the tail. "His mind was great and powerful, without being of the very first order; his penetration strong, tho' not so acute as that of a Newton, Bacon or Locke." Jefferson once flaunted the maxim of Horace, *"Mutato nomine, de te fabula narratur,"* meaning, "Change the name, and the fable applies to you."[1] The maxim appears apt, for neither Washington not Jefferson possessed the mind of an Isaac Newton, or composed treatises like those of Bacon or Locke. But Dumas Malone may have been overly rigorous in denying him the status of a "political philosopher," for the Declaration of Independence, and other Jeffersonian positions, have profoundly affected the subsequent development of political philosophy, although few Americans either in 1776 or today would be able to say who drafted the Declaration of Independence. Even fewer would have any idea as to whether George Washington was among its signatories.[2]

Jefferson was given no more than Washington to publishing philosophical discourses, and in private he was a raconteur, not a lecturer. He did not engage noticeably in the debates leading up to Richard Henry Lee's

[1] The Horace quotation is from Jefferson to Martin Van Buren, June 29, 1824.

[2] Dumas Malone called Jefferson "a philosophical statesman rather than a political philosopher" in *The Concise Dictionary of American Biography* (New York: Charles Scribner's Sons, 1964), p. 469. Robert M. S. McDonald, "Thomas Jefferson's Changing Reputation as Author of the Declaration of Independence: The First Fifty Years," *Journal of the Early Republic*, 19, no. 2 (summer, 1999), 169–195. Philip F. Detweiler, "The Changing Reputation of the Declaration of Independence: The First Fifty Years," *The William and Mary Quarterly*, 19, no. 4 (October, 1962), 557–574.

independence resolution, and in Paris, during the drafting of the "Declaration of the Rights of Man," he was as reticent as he had been in Philadelphia. He avoided conversations that might lead to open controversy or potential confrontations, and he might have applied to himself the hyperbolic observation he made respecting Washington and Franklin: "I have never heard either of them speak ten minutes at a time."[3] Only in private letters and the mental sanctuary of an unpublished biography did Jefferson reveal his hypersensitivity, his vanity, and his long-held grudges with a smoldering vindictiveness that the pages still exude. Subtly he implied that Washington bordered on senility from the moment he took office. George Washington, at 57, was younger at his first inauguration than Jefferson, who was 58 at his. It is difficult to remember this when reading Mercy Otis Warren's 1805 *Progress of the American Revolution*, a work dedicated to the Jeffersonian assertion that Washington commenced his administration as the doddering and credulous victim of Alexander Hamilton.[4]

Jefferson's *Anas* and *Autobiography* comprised secret musings that Jefferson dedicated to driving stakes through the hearts of corpses that he mistook for vampires, and in doing so he deliberately left to posterity a condescending and pejorative view of Washington.[5] The volume was not published until after Jefferson's death, for, while he was obsessed with

[3] Thomas Jefferson, *Autobiography*, in Merrill Peterson, ed., *Thomas Jefferson, Writings* (New York: Literary Classics of the United States, 1984), p. 53.

[4] Mercy Otis Warren, *History of the Rise, Progress and Termination of the American Revolution*, 2 vols. (Boston, MA: Manning and Loring, 1805). Stuart Leibiger, *Founding Friendship: George Washington and James Madison, and the Creation of the American Republic* (Charlottesville, VA: University of Virginia Press, 1999). Garry Wills, *Cincinnatus: George Washington and the Enlightenment* (New York: Doubleday, 1984), does not slight Washington's intellectual abilities; see esp. pp. 90–97. Thomas Fleming, *The Great Divide: The Conflict between Washington and Jefferson that Defined a Nation* (Boston, MA: De Capo Press, 2015), emphasizes Washington's intellectual strengths and political acumen.

[5] Thomas Jefferson Randolph posthumously gave the name "Anas" to Jefferson's "Explanations of the three volumes bound in marbled paper" which included Jefferson's notes on "secret communications while in the office of the state." "Anas" is defined by the *Oxford English Dictionary* as a "collection of memorable sayings or tabletalk, anecdotes, bits of information or gossip about persons." See the one-page entry, "Thomas Jefferson's Explanations of the Three Volumes Bound in Marbled Paper (the so-called 'Anas'), 4 February 1818," Founders Online, at https://founders.archives.gov/documents/Jefferson/03-12-02-0343-0002 (hereafter "Thomas Jefferson's Explanations"). Original source: Charles T. Cullen, ed., *The Papers of Thomas Jefferson* (Princeton University Press, 1986), vol. XXII, *6 August 1791 – 31 December 1791*, pp. 33–38. Also see "Editorial Note: The 'Anas'" at https://founders.archives.gov/?q=%25E2%2580%259CEditorial%20Note%253A%20The%20%25E2%2580%2598Anas&s=1111311111&sa=&r=1&sr

future interpretations of his legacy, he was squeamish about circulating volatile opinions during his lifetime. His *modus operandi* was to publish his more strident opinions anonymously, as in the aforementioned Kentucky Resolution, or through proxies like Phillip Freneau, editor of his party's mouthpiece, the *National Gazette*. Often in communication with his trusted confidant, James Madison, he literally wrote in code.[6] Publicly, he displayed a Don Giovannesque hospitality, plying his dinner guests with fine wines and chamber music, and regaling them with his dazzlingly brilliant conversation. In private, Jefferson impressed everyone with the potency and charm of his intellect, but he was judicious and selective about displaying it publicly.

Astonishingly, the perpetually indebted Jefferson questioned Washington's economic sense, stating that he was "Unversed in financial projects & calculations, & budgets."[7] The proposition is risible, when we reflect that Mount Vernon was a booming enterprise and Washington died one of the wealthiest men in America. In his *Anas* Jefferson planted the idea that disagreements on economic policy between himself and the first president stemmed from Washington's naïveté and the infernal manipulations of Hamilton. He attributed Hamilton's economic and political thought to the serpent of monarchism writhing within his bosom. This notion, carefully left to germinate in darkness and independently supplemented in the crafty account of Mercy Otis Warren, has influenced standard narratives of American history. Recent scholarship argues forcefully and convincingly that Washington's economic ideas were his own.

Obsessed with his own economic and political superstitions, Jefferson eventually called Washington's administration a "reign of witches," pretending not to understand the political and economic thinking of a president he described as the credulous dupe of Hamilton's guile and the victim of mental atrophy:

> From the moment, where they end, of my retiring from the administration, the federalists got unchecked hold of Genl. Washington. His memory was already sensibly impaired by age, the firm tone of mind for which he had been remarkable, was beginning to relax, it's energy was abated; a listlessness of labor, a desire for

[6] Jefferson's cipher machine was among his ingenious inventions. Silvio Bedini describes its development in his *Thomas Jefferson: Statesman of Science* (New York: Macmillan, 1990), pp. 233–243. Also see David Kahn, *The Codebreakers: The Story of Secret Writing* (New York: Macmillan, 1967).

[7] "Thomas Jefferson's Explanations."

tranquillity had crept on him, and a willingness to let others act and even think for him.[8]

The specter of monarchism constantly haunted Jefferson's imagination: his *Anas* and *Autobiography* are peppered with references to the phantoms of "monarchy," "royalism," and "the atrocious conspiracy of Kings against their people." In speaking of Washington's administration, the construct of his historical memory was that "the contests of that day were contests of principle, between the advocates of republican, and those of kingly government." Jefferson's obsessive anti-monarchism must not be mistaken for a democratic or egalitarian spirit, and it was not intellectually justifiable. Despite his lifelong pretense of *bonhomie*, Jefferson was a reverse snob, and despite his intellectual sophistication he was intellectually timid and conservative. Washington, despite his cold exterior, was of no less egalitarian a disposition, and although he only once travelled outside the United States, he was in many respects less provincial than Jefferson. His worldly knowledge was proven by his political acumen and his business success. Capable of undertaking a variety of commercial and agricultural enterprises and making them pay, he was able to dispense largess in the posthumous action of freeing his slaves. Jefferson's financial genius was in his extraordinary ability to amass debt on top of debt and to maintain an elegant lifestyle, leaving behind a mass of unpaid bills.

More realistic in terms of financial judgment than Jefferson, and also in political thinking, Washington shared with most of his contemporaries a belief that government, like all social institutions, exists to not so much protect the liberty as the security of the individual. Therefore, he wrote:

> there can be no hesitation I conceive in pronouncing one thing, that in all Societies, if the bond or cement is strong and interesting enough to hold the body together, the several parts should submit to the inconveniencies for the benefits which they derive from the conveniencies of the compact.[9]

Washington once struck Jefferson's allusion to "natural rights" from a draft of his message to Congress, and his life and his rhetoric revealed Washington's Hobbesian worldview. He was trained to his position by military habits and saw the necessity of sacrificing liberties in order to gain rights.[10]

[8] *Autobiography*, in Peterson, ed., *Thomas Jefferson, Writings*, p. 86; also see "Thomas Jefferson's Explanations."

[9] George Washington to James Madison, August 3, 1788.

[10] Washington to Alexander Hamilton, Newburgh [New York], April 22, 1783, speaks of rights as obtained through submission to inconveniences. For stricken language, see

The "conveniences of the compact" to which Washington referred was the entitlement to rights that the individual gains by yielding a portion of their freedom in order to gain the benefits of civil society. Tacitly he dismissed the libertarianism of Jefferson and Thomas Paine, in much the same way that Voltaire dismissed Rousseau, for he had no illusions about the man with the hoe, and he did not associate happiness with some hypothetical "state of nature" so much as with "the foundation of our Empire." When he spoke of "state of nature," it was seldom, and with a sense of foreboding:

> It is only in our United Character, as an Empire, that our Independance is acknowledged, that our power can be regarded or our Credit supported among foreign Nations—the Treaties of the European Powers with the United States of America will have no validity in a dissolution of the Union. We shall be left nearly in a state of Nature, or we may find by our own unhappy experience, that there is a natural and necessary progression, from the extreme of anarchy to the extreme of Tyranny; and that arbitrary power is most easily established on the ruins of Liberty abused to licentiousness.[11]

George Washington's dread of "liberty abused to licentiousness" had little to do with abstract theories. It is not likely that the thoughts of Thomas Hobbes, David Hume, or other royalists had anything to do with his political philosophy of strong government. Unlike Jefferson, he derived his thoughts on political economy not from solitary reflection, but from the practical experience of finding the ways and means to feed and clothe armies. He would not have expended much effort in discussing "natural rights," having experienced state of war. At Valley Forge, his job was not to "ensure" natural rights, but make certain his armies were not left in a state of Nature.[12]

editorial note, "From George Washington to the United States Senate and House of Representatives, 5 December 1793," at Founders Online: http://founders.archives.gov/documents/Washington/05-14-02-0313

11 George Washington to The States, June 8, 1783, Founders Online.

12 Discussions of rights seem to have been inextricable from discussions of property. Ayn Rand does a brilliant job of arguing that "without property no other rights are possible." See Ayn Rand, "Man's Rights" in *The Virtue of Selfishness* (New York: Signet, 1964), p. 94. She ignores Benjamin Franklin's assertion that property is "the Creature of public Convention," which is much closer to the views of Hobbes, Locke, and Adam Smith, all of whom see government as indispensable for the protection of property. For an alternative to Ayn Rand's discussion of the Enlightenment concept of rights in relation to property, see Staughton Lynd, *Intellectual Origins of American Radicalism* (New York: Vintage, 1968).

Artfully Jefferson avowed his confidence in the integrity of Washington's mind and the sincerity of his republicanism, but craftily he manured the seeds of doubt. Almost simultaneously he accused Washington of senility while invoking Washington's writings as proof of his mental alertness. He accused John Marshall of misusing the documents in composing Washington's biography in such a manner as to attribute to him royalist tendencies and monarchical distortions:

> Had Genl. Washington himself written from these materials a history of the period they embrace, it would have been a conspicuous monument of the integrity of his mind, the soundness of his judgment, and its powers of discernment between truth & falsehood; principles & pretensions. Facts indeed of his own writing & inditing, must be believed by all who knew him; and opinions, which were his own, merit veneration and respect; for few men have lived whose opinions were more unbiassed and correct ... Let no man believe that Genl. Washington ever intended that his papers should be used for the suicide of the cause.[13]

Privately, however, and with vulpine finesse, Jefferson suggested to Charles Pinckney that Washington had "squinted at" monarchy.[14] If, in one paragraph, he graciously absolved Washington of any latent tendencies to royalism, he was capable of casting doubt in another.

While most historians admit that the differences between Jefferson and Washington theoretically represent somewhat conflicting theories of government, many have recognized latent Federalist tendencies in Jefferson, giving confirmation to the opinion of Josiah Quincy that the Democratic Republican Party eventually "out-federalized the federalists."[15] In the course of two terms, Jefferson exercised authority with as much autonomy as George Washington, and more than King George III ever commanded.

He was the first president to concentrate power in the nation's new capital. Jefferson doubled the size of the empire, sent a naval squadron "to the shores of Tripoli," and enforced an international embargo. Although in his writings he frequently substituted the word "monarchist" for "Federalist," he was capable of admitting there was no contradiction

[13] "Thomas Jefferson's Explanations."

[14] "Washington has squinted at it [monarchy]," Jefferson to Charles Pinckney, Monticello, October 29, 1799.

[15] Fleming's *The Great Divide* provocatively highlights differences between Federalists and Democratic Republicans; Peter Onuf offers a chapter on the Federalist Jefferson in *The Mind of Thomas Jefferson* (Charlottesville, VA: University of Virginia Press, 2007), see especially Part 2. Richard Hofstadter, *The American Political Tradition* (New York: Knopf, 1948), offers a dialectical approach towards reconciliation, in which the negations are pragmatically resolved during the Madison administration.

between a principled republicanism and a pragmatic federalism, a matter he acknowledged in his Inaugural Addresses and in his *Autobiography*. As Hamilton predicted, he was pragmatically inclined to champion the same sort of vigorous government that he condemned in Federalists, when it was in the hands of himself or his friend Madison. He exercised executive power without undue scruples, and encroached directly and indirectly on the domains of the legislative and judiciary branches.

WASHINGTON ADMINISTRATION – DEBT, BANKING, AND CREDIT

Alexander Hamilton was every bit as Machiavellian as Jefferson, but not nearly so princely. He was ambitious, obnoxious, daring, and brilliant. On at least one occasion, he impressed George Washington as arrogant, but the general elevated him rapidly to the rank of lieutenant-colonel, and Hamilton suffered with the Continental Army through the brutal winter at Valley Forge. His abilities at organizing and provisioning the army were obvious to Washington, and he shrewdly appointed him the first Secretary of the United States Treasury. Within a few months, at the behest of Congress, Hamilton produced a Report on the Public Credit, proposing that the federal government assume responsibility for debts incurred by the United States during the war for independence. Those states such as Virginia that had already paid off at least portions of their debts were naturally irate. When Jefferson arrived at the capital to assume his position as first Secretary of State, he discovered that the infant Union was about to fall apart over this issue: "the parties being too much out of temper to do business together . . . threatened a secession and dissolution." Jefferson, ever calm, ever judicious, and, above all, ever gracious, was able to intervene on behalf of national unity and the Public Credit plan:

> Hamilton was in despair. as I was going to the President's one day, I met him in the street. he walked me backwards & forwards before the President's door for half an hour. he painted pathetically the temper into which the legislature had been wrought, the disgust of those who were called the Creditor states, the danger of the secession of their members, and the separation of the states. [16]

[16] "Thomas Jefferson's Explanations." Joseph J. Ellis describes "The Dinner" in *Feuding Brothers: The Revolutionary Generation* (New York: Knopf, 2000), pp. 48–80.

Elsewhere, he described the same encounter in even starker terms:

> His look was sombre, haggard, and dejected beyond description. Even his dress uncouth and neglected. He asked to speak with me. We stood in the street near the door. He opened the subject of the assumption of the state debts, the necessity of it in the general fiscal arrangement and it's indispensible necessity towards a preservation of the union.[17]

No doubt Jefferson was sincerely moved by Hamilton's distress, but he was obviously motivated by an apprehension of "the separation of the states" and the "dissolution of our Union at this incipient stage." He graciously offered to host a dinner in his home in mid June 1790. During the dinner, Jefferson took no part in the discussion "but an exhortatory one, because I was a stranger to the circumstances." Nonetheless, he and Madison removed the obstacles to the creation of a national debt. In exchange for the Federal assumption of debt, the South would be pacified with the relocation of the nation's capital from Philadelphia to the future District of Columbia. Over the years, Jefferson wrote dismissively of Hamilton's talk about "a public debt being a public blessing," pretending that the phrase violated the common sense, as well as the experience, of many debtors. Of course, Jefferson later benefitted from the national debt, which he utilized for the Louisiana Purchase and Madison for financing the War of 1812. But however necessary it might be, debt remained an evil, and as president he was to make a policy of cost-cutting, even when his cuts to the defense budget conflicted with such aims as securing New Orleans or invading the Barbary Coast. In 1790 Jefferson temporarily overcame his scruples about national debt, because "the preservation of the union, & of concord among the states was more important."[18]

At Washington's behest, Jefferson hosted another dinner, in April of 1791, which he described in a letter written in 1811 to Benjamin Rush. On this occasion, Hamilton behaved in a needlessly provocative manner, demonstrating that he "was not only a monarchist, but for a monarchy bottomed on corruption." As proof, Jefferson related an anecdote "for the truth of which I attest the God who made me." As Washington had asked Jefferson to invite John Adams as well, the vice president was duly invited.

[17] See "Jefferson's Account of the Bargain on the Assumption and Residence Bills," Founders Online.

[18] Jefferson recorded his street conversation with Hamilton in *Anas*: see "Thomas Jefferson's Explanations." Malone sets the date at ca. June 20, 1790, in Dumas Malone, *Jefferson and His Time*, 6 vols. (Boston, MA: Little, Brown, 1951), vol. II, *Jefferson and the Rights of Man*, "Chronology," p. xxvii.

After dinner, Adams, a punctilious elitist by reputation, made some remarks in praise of the British constitution, saying that if only it could be rid of its corruption and made more democratic, it "would be the most perfect constitution ever devised by the wit of man." Jefferson might have choked at this expression of egalitarian-populist sentiment coming from the proud and portly Adams, but he was appalled by Hamilton's sarcastic retort: "Purge it of its corruption, and give to its popular branch equality of representation, and it would become an impracticable government."[19]

That was bad enough, but Jefferson attested to Rush that what truly proved Hamilton's monarchist principles was his commentary on the portraits that Jefferson had had hung on his walls:

> among them were those of Bacon, Newton and Locke. Hamilton asked me who they were. I told him they were my trinity of the three greatest men the world had ever produced, naming them. He paused for some time: *"the greatest man,"* said he, *"that ever lived, was Julius Caesar."* Mr. Adams was honest as a politician, as well as a man; Hamilton honest as a man, but, as a politician, believing in the necessity of either force or corruption to govern men.[20]

Jefferson identified the British form of government as corrupt, not least of all because it had arisen in tandem with such economic institutions as the Bank of England, the Lords of Trade, Lloyds of London, the East India Company, and the entire panoply of private and governmental institutions and monopolies that had worked to the disadvantage of American elites before the Revolution. Hamilton's cynical response was that any government worthy of the name must have an economic structure similar to that of Great Britain.

Washington showed Machiavellian finesse in asking for Jefferson and Hamilton's advice on the constitutionality of the Bank of the United States. He was less interested in their arguments than with how a bank

[19] Malone describes and places this dinner in spring of 1791, ibid., p. 287; also see "Thomas Jefferson's Explanations" and A. E. Bergh, ed., *The Writings of Thomas Jefferson* (Washington, DC: The Thomas Jefferson Memorial Association, 1907), vol. I, p. 279. Adams' anti-democratic traits are discussed by Joseph J. Ellis in *Passionate Sage* (New York: Norton, 1993), pp. 128–130. Gordon Wood, *Revolutionary Characters* (New York: Penguin, 2006), pp. 175–202, presents Adams' attitudes on democracy as generally elitist, but nuanced and ambivalent. Edmund S. Morgan's treatment of Adams' anti-democratic and aristocratic notions are in his *The Meaning of Independence* (New York: Norton, 1978); Morgan asserts that Adams' first love was his farmstead, which suggests an "agrarian" affinity to Thomas Jefferson.

[20] J. G. A. Pocock considers Hamilton's "feelings" about Caesar to be "rich in moral ambiguity," in his *The Machiavellian Moment: Florentine Political Thought and the Atlantic Republican Tradition* (Princeton University Press, 2003), p. 429.

might become "the foundation of our Empire," making America into a Western power, a rival seat of the Anglo-Atlantic imperium. It was no rhetorical accident that, when laying the foundations of Washington, DC, he referred to the new capital as the "seat of empire."[21] Jefferson always underestimated Washington, who, with his usual political finesse, tricked him into mounting a purely legalistic objection to the bank, and Jefferson took the bait. His opinion was mired down in legalistic jargon about "the laws of *Mortmain* ... of *Alienage* ... of *Forfeiture and Escheat.*" Hamilton's smoother defense of the bank addressed a more direct set of issues, arguing not legalistically, but practically, that the general principle of financial regulation by the government was:

> inherent in the very definition of government and essential to every step of the progress to be made by that of the United States, namely that every power invested in a government is in its nature sovereign, and includes by force of the term a right to employ all the means requisite and fairly applicable to the attainment of the ends of such power.[22]

Hamilton shared Washington's strong feelings that a system of regulated finance was essential to the functioning of a government, and by implication any self-respecting government must have a central bank on the order of the Bank of England – that unless there were a Bank of the United States, its government would be second-rate. Hamilton gave a liberal construction to the Constitution's wording, which said that the government could do everything "necessary and proper" to carry out its functions. He said that in the ordinary, popular sense of the term "necessary" didn't really mean "necessary": it meant whatever was convenient – "*necessary* often means no more than *needful, requisite, incidental, useful,* or *conducive to.*" Ultimately Hamilton's justification of the bank lay not in the specious semantics, but in the fundamentally unassailable argument that a bank was essential to the imperial ambitions that he shared with Washington. Both men might have

[21] Washington referred to the new capital as the "seat of empire." See George Washington to Commissioners of the District of Columbia, August 28, 1799. He refers to America as "This rising Empire" in his last will and testament.

[22] As the reader will recall, this frequently cited and anthologized opinion of Alexander Hamilton on the constitutionality of the Bank of the United States was later the basis of Justice John Marshall's landmark opinion in *McCullough v. Maryland.* For a reminder as to the immense bibliography, I cite: Bray Hammond, *Banks and Politics in America from the Revolution to the Civil War* (Princeton University Press, 1957); G. Edward White, *The Marshall Court and Cultural Change, 1815–1835* (New York: Oxford University Press, 1988); Gerald Gunther, ed., *John Marshall's Defense of McCulloch v. Maryland* (Stanford University Press, 1969); Samuel J. Konefsky, *John Marshall and Alexander Hamilton, Architects of the American Constitution* (New York: Macmillan, 1964).

been thinking as Franklin had decades earlier, that the Anglo-American population was destined to exceed the population of England, and "the greatest Number of Englishmen will be on this Side the Water."[23]

The hostility of the Jeffersonian faction to the Bank of the United States was not founded on recondite debates over the original meaning of the Constitution. In coming years, Jefferson would prove amenable to "a liberal construction" when it could be "justified by the object."[24] The Jeffersonians' opposition grew out of the culture of their plantation-based and patrician economic interests. We have noted previously that Virginia aristocrats like Jefferson and Madison shared the hostilities of small farmers of Massachusetts and Pennsylvania towards the class of bankers and financiers. Democratic Republicans did not have to consciously guide the resentments of poor white debtors, which were rooted organically in hostility to the commercial class. Of course, the Republican Party included commercialists under its broad tent – petty businessmen, small farmers operating small rural whiskey distilleries, and floundering industrialists like Jefferson. But George Washington, the most impressive of all Virginia farmers, believed that the nation's commercial and industrial interests required a reliable system of banking and finance, which to his mind implied a central bank. It would require another century before people of every interest and both parties would show they could, when "necessary and proper," transcend their anti-governmental superstitions and recognize the necessity of a federally regulated system of banking.

THE GENÊT EPISODE AND WHISKEY TAX

The catalyst for Jefferson's breach with Washington's administration was the picaresque career of Citizen Edmond-Charles Genêt, France's Revolutionary ambassador to the United States. His reception by the populace as he progressed along the east coast in 1793 occasioned a slight relaxation of Jefferson's usual suspicion concerning the urban masses. The "yeomanry of the city" greeted the Frenchman with as much

[23] Benjamin Franklin, "Observations Concerning the Increase of Mankind," printed in [William Clarke], *Observations On the late and present Conduct of the French, with Regard to their Encroachments upon the British Colonies in North America ... To which is added, wrote by another Hand; Observations concerning the Increase of Mankind, Peopling of Countries, &c.* (Boston, MA: Printed and Sold by S. Kneeland in Queen-Street, 1755) at: https://founders.archives.gov/documents/Franklin/01-04-02-0080

[24] Jefferson used the phrase "a liberal construction, justified by the object" in Jefferson to Jared Sparks, February 4, 1824.

enthusiasm as did the farmers in the countryside, and he was greeted with a climate of festivity from Charleston to Philadelphia. Genêt, like the Girondiste government that he represented, misunderstood the complex emotions of the American people, whose suspicion of the national government was contradicted by a boundless hero-worship for its leader. Genêt arrived in the States with a fatal misunderstanding: he thought that he must report not to George Washington, but to the Congress, and he practically snubbed the president during the weeks following his arrival. Meanwhile, under Jefferson's minion, Philip Freneau, the *National Gazette* became, in the words of historian Marcus Daniel, "a quasi-official mouthpiece for Citizen Genêt and the French."[25]

Whether or not he initially encouraged Genêt's disregard for the president's policies, there can be no question as to where Jefferson's sympathies were. Shortly after Genêt's landing, Jefferson wrote to James Monroe, observing that the French ambassador's arrival was coeval with other advantageous events, rekindling "All the old spirit of 1776" in the newspapers from Charleston to Boston. Jefferson rejoiced that a French frigate had recently taken a British prize off the cape of Delaware and brought it into an American port, although the United States was officially neutral in the conflict between France and Britain. Despite later public opposition to Genêt's activities, Jefferson at the time privately expressed jubilation when the French ship arrived with her prize. "Upon her coming into sight, thousands and thousands of the yeomanry of the city crowded and covered the wharves." It was interesting that he regarded urban dwellers as fellow travellers and greeted with relish their enthusiastic republicanism. "Never before was such a crowd seen there; and when the British colors were seen reversed, and the French flying above them, they burst into peals of exultation."[26]

Genêt began a leisurely journey to the Philadelphia capital, progressing through Pennsylvania, where, "in the midst of perpetual fetes," he was met by adoring crowds calling themselves Democratic Republican Societies and proclaiming their allegiance to the French Revolution. These anti-Federalist, anti-taxation elements, although for the most part urban, were superficially related in their ideology to the rural farmers of Western Pennsylvania, who rose up against the Whiskey Tax in 1794, by which time Jefferson had already (in late December of 1793) resigned his

[25] Marcus Daniel, *Scandal and Civility: Journalism and the Birth of American Democracy* (Oxford University Press, 2008), p. 107.

[26] Jefferson to James Monroe, Philadelphia, May 5, 1793.

position in Washington's cabinet, arguably due to vexation or embarrassment over the Genêt affair.[27]

Oddly enough, American farmers, inflamed with republican sentiments, viewed themselves as comrades of the mobs of Paris. Just as oddly, Virginia planters sympathized with Robespierre and the Committee of Public Safety. Jefferson offered little support to Genêt after the Jacobins replaced the Montagnards, took control of the French government, and recalled Genêt in 1794, presumably *pour profiter d'un rendezvous avec Madame Guillotine.* Hamilton, who had previously urged that the French government recall Genêt, now encouraged Washington to grant him asylum. Jefferson would apparently have sent him back to France as one of his martyrs to the cause of liberty.[28] Jefferson's callous view of events in Paris were privately expressed on January 3, 1793, when he wrote from the safety of Philadelphia to William Short, who succeeded him as minister to France, with a bizarre mélange of passion and detachment:

> My own affections have been deeply wounded by some of the martyrs to this cause, but rather than it should have failed I would have seen half the earth desolated; were there but an Adam and an Eve left in every country, and left free, it would be better than as it now is.[29]

He later wrote, "I have no acquaintances left in France. Some were guillotined, some fled, some died, some are exiled."[30] It was the magnanimity of the Federalists, not the opportunistic friendship of the Jeffersonians, that ultimately saved Genêt's neck. Genêt's lack of diplomatic restraint had become counter-productive to the cause of the Jeffersonians. While, in April of 1793, Madison, Monroe, the Democratic Societies, and the *National Gazette* had at least passively encouraged the Frenchman in his delusion that he could ignore the

[27] David Waldstreicher, *In the Midst of Perpetual Fetes: The Making of American Nationalism* (Chapel Hill: University of North Carolina Press, 1997), pp. 133–136. Meade Minnigerode, *Jefferson, Friend of France, 1793: The Career of Edmond Charles Genêt* (New York, London: G. P. Putnam's Sons, 1928), pp. 188–189. Harlow Giles Unger, *Mr. President* (Philadelphia: De Capo Press, 2013), reveals a pro-Washingtonian, anti-Jeffersonian perspective.

[28] Ron Chernow, *Washington: A Life* (New York: Penguin, 2010), pp. 692–697, posits a continuity between the Genêt incident and the rise of the Democratic Republican Societies. For Hamilton's urging a recall, see Jon Meacham, *Thomas Jefferson and the Art of Power* (New York: Random House, 2012), p. 274; for his urging asylum, see Jason Ripper, *American Stories* (New York: M. E. Sharpe, 2008), p. 146.

[29] Jefferson to William Short, Philadelphia, January 3, 1793.

[30] Jefferson to Albert Gallatin, Monticello, April 11, 1816.

president and appeal directly to the American people, by July 5 Jefferson had come to view Genêt's activities with alarm. Writing to Monroe, he described Genêt as "Hotheaded, all imagination, no judgment, passionate, disrespectful and even indecent towards the P[resident] in his written as well as verbal communications." Madison advised Jefferson that Genêt's activities had become an embarrassment, and that his indiscretions unnecessarily exacerbated domestic party tensions.[31]

Years later, Genêt expressed the opinion that Jefferson had been duplicitous. Meade Minnigerode, Genêt's most interesting biographer, credited him with penning the following accusation to Jefferson. Minnegerode was vague about the document's source, and, if Jefferson ever received the letter, he did not retain a copy of this letter of July 4, 1797, although a toned-down summary of it is preserved in the Jefferson Papers. Minnegerode's translation reads:

> Sir, skillful in the art of deception, you continued to see me ... for according to my instructions, I told you everything, I consulted you about every thing ... Would to God, Sir, that rendering more justice to your talents you also had consecrated the rest of your life to the cult of the sciences ... France would perhaps have passed without suspension of movement from one energetic government to another energetic government; the blood of the Bourbons, banished like that of the Tarquins, would not have flowed from the scaffolds.[32]

The charge that Genêt consulted with Jefferson "about everything" may be somewhat inflated, as was the implicit charge that Jefferson was somehow responsible for the beheading of Louis XVI, but it is clear that

[31] There was more than one letter, e.g. James Madison to Jefferson, July 18, 1793, James Madison to Jefferson, August 5, 1793, and James Madison to Jefferson, August 27, 1793. The lengthiest letter was James Madison to Jefferson, September 2, 1793, with an attachment, Resolution on Franco-American Relations, [ca. August 27] 1793.

[32] A translation of this letter, in which Genêt disparages Jefferson's role in the American Revolution and reveals that he felt himself to have been actively encouraged by Jefferson, was published in 1928, identified only as "Translation of the duplicate of the letter written by Genêt to Jefferson on July 4, 1797. From the original in the Genêt papers, now published in full for the first time." It was printed in Minnigerode, *Jefferson, Friend of France*, pp. 420, 423, with references to the Genêt Papers in the Library of Congress and "Private Papers in the possession of his granddaughter." The document preserved at Founders Online is only a summary of this letter, entitled, "To Thomas Jefferson from Edmund Charles Genet, 4 July 1797, from Edmund Charles Genet [summary]." It does not preserve the accusatory tone of Minnegerode's translation, and the editors of the Jefferson Papers speculate that Jefferson never saw it. See: https://founders.archives.gov/?q=%22Stirred%20from%20his%20present%20tranquil%22&s=1511311111&r=1 Genêt's allusion to the Tarquins referred to Lucius Tarquinius Superbus, the legendary last king of Rome, who was exiled at the foundation of the Roman Republic.

Jefferson's attitude towards Genêt changed rapidly from glee to horror. In his letter to Madison of August, 11, 1793, Jefferson wrote, "I adhered to him as long as I could have a hope of getting him right ... Finding at length that the man was absolutely incorrigible, I saw the necessity of quitting a wreck which could not but sink all who should cling to it." The Genêt affair strengthened the bond between Jefferson and Madison, and destroyed what was left of Madison's partnership with Washington.[33] Otherwise the question of Jefferson's initial support for Genêt remains problematic. Conor Cruise O'Brien, a historian strongly disinclined to romanticize Jefferson, opined that Genêt required no "egging on," but Merrill Peterson, one of Jefferson's steadfast admirers, is more accusatory than the critical O'Brien. He writes, "It could not be denied that Jefferson had confided in Genêt, sympathized with his cause, egged him on, then tried to restrain him, and finally collaborated in his destruction."[34]

The Genêt affair showed that the common people were susceptible to manipulation, or, as Jefferson expressed it elsewhere, "fit tools for the designs of ambition," or willing subordinates to Jefferson's aristocratic republicans. Populist enthusiasms never posed a threat to the American ruling classes, neither in the case of Shays Rebellion, nor the Genêt affair, nor the Whiskey Rebellion. The masses of the people would invariably succumb to the democratic rhetoric of the Republicans and remain suspicious of the Federalists. The "yeomanry of the city" were, no less than the yeoman farmers, perfect tools in the hands of a Machiavellian Republican like Thomas Jefferson.

THE JAY TREATY AND SLAVE PROPERTY, 1795

A major controversy of Washington's tumultuous second term centered on the 1795 Jay Treaty. The pre-existing Treaty of Paris, in 1783, had left several matters unresolved, and Americans were angered at British non-compliance with other issues. At Washington's behest, Alexander Hamilton drafted a set of American demands, and asked John Jay to resign his position as Chief Justice of the United States and travel to

[33] Stuart Leibiger, *Founding Friendship: George Washington, James Madison, and the Creation of the American Republic* (Charlottesville, VA: University of Virginia Press, 1999), offers a detailed treatment of the declining friendship between Washington and Madison.

[34] Merrill Peterson, *Thomas Jefferson and the New Nation* (Oxford University Press, 1970), p. 507.

London to negotiate a new treaty. Jay's Treaty is an object of contumely to the present day because it failed to resolve the issues of the British stopping and searching American vessels, and the impressment of American seamen. Jeffersonians were ever ready to stir up as much turmoil as possible over impressment, despite their unwillingness to spend money on a navy and despite their contempt for seamen, as for all other members of the working class. Merchant capitalists in Northern cities sometimes viewed the issue of impressment with bland callousness.

The treaty did provide limited economic and military benefits, however. It restored some elements of trade as they had existed before the Revolution; it demanded and received British reparation for cargoes seized in 1793–94; it achieved the removal of British forts from the western frontier, and consequently opened up lands west of the Appalachians to further American settlement. The ability of American farmers to push westward was further enhanced by Spanish reaction to the Jay Treaty, which led Spain first to ease restrictions on American navigation of the Mississippi and subsequently to concede navigation rights via the 1795 Pinckney Treaty. American farmers were consequently relieved of the temptation to convert grain into whiskey, as they would now be enabled to ship grain by waterways and through the port of New Orleans. From the perspective of Jeffersonians, however, the Jay Treaty seemed a bad bargain, particularly as it had to do with British "carrying-away" of formerly enslaved persons.

The Treaty of Paris, which marked the official end of the Revolutionary War in 1783, had contained the infamous provision that the British would depart without "carrying away any negroes or other property of the American inhabitants." Benedict Arnold, Lord Dunmore, General Clinton, and other British commanders had liberated numerous slaves during the course of the Revolution.[35] Jay, a known abolitionist, had not insisted on compensation for the slaves, nor had he demanded their return. Hamilton notably addressed the moral issue of slavery in

[35] A PBS feature reveals the remarkable history of Charles Ball, an African American who fought in the US Navy in the War of 1812. "But for most American slaves, the options were limited to the British Navy. When the British fleet arrived in the Chesapeake Bay in March 1813, entire families of slaves made their way by canoe to the enemy ships." Within a narrative of African American patriotism, Jeffrey Bolster presents instances of African Americans who preferred Dartmoor Prison in England to service in the Royal Navy, but offers little discussion of those blacks who chose to fight against the United States in the War of 1812. See W. Jeffrey Bolster, *Black Jacks: African American Seamen in the Age of Sail* (Cambridge, MA: Harvard University Press, 1997), pp. 113, 114, 115.

a manner to which few have paid attention. His argument did more than simply deny the Jeffersonians' entitlement to compensation for their lost slaves: it denied the legality of Article 7 of the Treaty of Paris on moral grounds and declared it non-binding. The old treaty's provisions calling for the re-enslavement of those people who had joined the British Loyalists were fundamentally invalid, said Hamilton, because they contradicted the laws of God and "the law of nations." The return of slaves to American slaveholders would have been "an odious thing," Hamilton wrote to Washington. Two weeks later, writing publically as "Camillus," he further declared:

> In the interpretation of treaties, things odious or immoral are not to be presumed. The abandonment of negroes, who had been induced to quit their masters on the faith of official proclamation, promising them liberty, to fall again under the yoke of their masters, and into slavery, is as odious and immoral a thing as can be conceived. The general interests of humanity conspire with the obligation which Great Britain had contracted towards the negroes.[36]

Hamilton argued that if slaves were property, as the slaveholders claimed, then they became spoils of war as soon as the British took possession of them, and since they were persons, they became free as soon as the British declared them so. "Nothing in the laws of nations or in those of Great Britain will authorize the resumption [taking back] of liberty, once granted to a human being." Hamilton was far less concerned with the question of whether the British owed compensation for freed African Americans who had been evacuated with them in 1783 than he was with the question of whether the British ought to have evacuated the freed persons in the first place. Simply leaving them behind would have constituted an "abandonment" both "odious and immoral." One need not engage in the sentimentalization of Hamilton that makes him an "abolitionist" to appreciate that he chose to defend the Jay Treaty on moral grounds.

As a delegate to the Continental Congress, Hamilton should have been aware of the stricken passages of Jefferson's Declaration of Independence, attacking the king for inducing the African population "to rise in arms among us, and to purchase their freedom." Possibly there were a few members of Congress who blushed at the sophistry of those other lines, in which Jefferson, the son-in-law of slave trader John Wayles, blamed King George for the slave trade. More likely, Jefferson's own later

[36] "The Defence No. III, [29 July 1795]," Alexander Hamilton to George Washington, Cabinet Paper, July 9, 1795.

explanation was valid, that those lines were stricken "in complaisance to South Carolina and Georgia, who had never attempted to restrain the importation of slaves, and who, on the contrary, still wished to continue it." More importantly, Jefferson's entire attitude towards the British and slavery in the empire was deeply colored by his undignified flight from Monticello at the approach of Benedict Arnold, who freed some of Jefferson's own slaves.

Jefferson's draft Declaration's deleted passage on the slave trade should not be confused with abolitionist sentiments, for it also condemned the British emancipation and military enlistment of African Americans. We have seen in Chapter 4 above what Jeremy Bentham thought of the contradiction between professions of abolitionism and complaints about the British emancipation of slaves. In the summer of 1781, nineteen of Jefferson's slaves fled to enemy lines. Lucia Stanton has noted that at the time he described the actions of his slaves with such phrases as "fled to the enemy," "joined enemy," or "ran away," but in later correspondence he referred to them as "carried off by Cornwallis." Writing in 1788, he practically accused the British of genocide: "Had this been to give them freedom he would have done right, but it was to consign them to inevitable death from the small pox and putrid fever then raging in his camp." But the accusation that the British were killing the emancipated persons is contradicted by the Virginians' claim that the British absconded with them permanently.[37]

In his aforementioned correspondence with Washington, Hamilton toyed with the proposition that the British "proceedings in seducing away our negroes during the war were to the last degree infamous, and form an indelible stain on her [Great Britain's] annals." But he added that, once having attracted them away, "it would have been still more infamous to have surrendered them to their masters." But in the final draft of his "Defence" (see note 36 above), published, after Washington's perusal, in the *Argus* of July 22, 1795, Hamilton omitted any reference to the "infamy" of British actions. He took no pains to mention that Benedict Arnold, on his passage through Richmond, did not return the fugitive slaves of government officials, military personnel, or persons available for

[37] Jefferson makes this accusation in Jefferson to William Gordon, July 16, 1788. Lucia Stanton, *Free Some Day: The African-American Families of Monticello* (Charlottesville, VA: The Thomas Jefferson Foundation, 2000), pp. 53–57. Jefferson's Farm Book, p. 241, contains losses to the British and also catalogues the deaths of several slaves who became infected with lethal pestilences while with the British, as well as those who died as a result of diseases contracted while with the British.

service in the militia, but that he kindly made provisions for returning the slaves of widows and orphans.[38]

Amidst calls for Washington's impeachment and prayers for his death coming from both Republicans and Federalists, Jefferson worked both overtly and covertly to abort the Jay Treaty.[39] Jefferson did not choose to produce a literary exercise on the subject, and certainly not one centering on a defense of slavery. Peaceable and reserved by nature, and temperamentally disinclined to engage in public feuds, the author of the Declaration of Independence was, in this instance, not surprisingly reticent. He did write to Madison, urging him to enter the lists: "Hamilton is really a colossus to the anti-republican party," he wrote. "For God's sake take up your pen, and give a fundamental reply." But, as Henry Cabot Lodge noted, "Madison had no stomach for the fight, and prudently abstained."[40]

WASHINGTON'S PRESIDENCY AND THE QUESTION OF DISLOYALTY

While serving as Washington's Secretary of State, Jefferson's partisan efforts were independent, high-handed, and disloyal to the limits of legality. A likely misuse of funds was his employment of Philip Freneau as a "translator" in the State Department, while actually charging him with the handling of anti-Washington propaganda. Hiring a native speaker of French, the principal language of international diplomacy, was clearly justifiable, but many Federalists suspected that Freneau's real function was to produce the anti-Federalist newspaper *The National Gazette*.[41] Systematically disloyal to the Washington administration that employed him, Jefferson whispered about town that Washington had abandoned republican principles.

38 Benjamin Quarles, *The Negro in the American Revolution* (New York: Norton, 1961), p. 131. The full title of the *Argus* (a New York newspaper of some importance): *The Argus, or Greenleaf's New Daily Advertiser.*

39 Michael R. Beschloss, *Presidential Courage: Brave Leaders and How They Changed America 1789–1989* (New York: Simon and Schuster, 2007), p. 1, describes the furor in which "some wanted Washington impeached. Cartoons showed the President being marched to a guillotine. Even in the President's beloved Virginia, Revolutionary veterans raised glasses and cried, 'A speedy Death to General Washington!'"

40 Jefferson to James Madison, September 21, 1795. Henry Cabot Lodge, ed., *The Works of Alexander Hamilton* (New York: G. P. Putnam's Sons, 1904), vol. V, pp. 189–190.

41 Stanley Elkins and Eric McKittrick, *The Age of Federalism* (New York: Oxford University Press, 1993), pp. 239–240, 282ff.

In 1796, an anonymous and disparaging article revealing confidential proceedings of a cabinet meeting appeared in the *Philadelphia Aurora*, a newspaper operated by Benjamin Franklin's grandson, Benjamin Franklin Bache. Jefferson wrote an unsolicited denial of its authorship to Washington, who responded that he neither suspected Jefferson of its authorship nor had reason to believe any rumors of his disloyalty. The icy anger of Washington's response in his "Nero Letter" was palpable:

My answer invariably has been, that I had never discovered any thing in the conduct of Mr. Jefferson to raise suspicions, in my mind, of his insincerity ... nor did I believe until lately, that every act of my administration would be tortured, and the grossest, and most insidious misrepresentations of them be made (by giving one side only of a subject, and that too in such exaggerated and indecent terms as could scarcely be applied to a Nero; a notorious defaulter; or even to a common pick-pocket). But enough of this; I have already gone farther in the expression of my feelings, than I intended.[42]

The contradictions within so-called Jeffersonian democracy, with its mingled elements of proletarianism and elitism, were highlighted during the post-Revolutionary career of Thomas Paine. After his release from prison in France, largely through the agency of James Monroe, Paine denounced Washington, who he believed had abandoned him. He drafted a notorious attack on Washington in July of 1796, the summer in which Benjamin Franklin Bache's newspaper the *Aurora* attacked Washington repeatedly, with Jefferson's tacit endorsement. Jefferson was able to deny direct involvement in the attacks, and the supposedly decrepit Washington responded with his skillfully structured "Nero Letter." He would not have had to rely on rumors of Jefferson's duplicity, either before or after 1796. After resigning from Washington's cabinet in the wake of the Genêt affair, Jefferson privately showed Washington's thinly veiled suspicions to be more than valid, as he penned poisonous letters to Philip Mazzei, John Taylor, and Charles Pinckney attacking the president.[43] Joshua Brookes recorded in his unpublished journal, after visits to Mount Vernon in February and Monticello in August of 1799, that Jefferson delivered the following soliloquy:

George Washington is a hard master, very severe, a hard husband, a hard father, a hard governor. From his childhood he always ruled and ruled severely. He was first brought up to govern slaves, he then governed an army, then a nation. He

[42] George Washington to Jefferson, July 6, 1796.

[43] Jefferson to Philip Mazzei, Monticello, April 24, 1796; to John Taylor, Philadelphia, June 1, 1798; and to Charles Pinckney, October 29, 1799.

thinks hard of all, is despotic in every respect, he mistrusts every man, thinks every man a rogue and nothing but severity will do. He has no idea of people being left to themselves to act; he thinks that they cannot think and that they ought only to obey. As I lived near him and saw him every day, I thought I knew what was in his mind at that time, but afterwards I found that ideas were there that I had no conception of. If he had died when Congress met in New York, he would have been the greatest man that ever lived, but he is now losing his reputation daily. He is not the man he was, else he would not allow himself to be led as he does, or give his sanction to things he does sanction. He has divines constantly about him because he thinks it right to keep up appearances but is an unbeliever.[44]

WASHINGTON TO ADAMS TRANSITION

The election of 1796 in which Adams became president and Jefferson, as runner-up, became vice president involved no "presidential campaign" in the modern sense. The president was, of course, chosen by the Electoral College, which was to be a bulwark against the vulgar impulses of the populace. It would have seemed ridiculous for Jefferson, Adams, or any other presidential candidate in 1796 to make appeals for the votes of hired hands, indentured servants, or slaves in any district, urban or rural, for universal white male suffrage was still a thing of the future, and most citizens were not among the "natural aristoi" that comprised the wise, good, and just decision-makers in the Electoral College.

Adams' presidential style fluctuated dramatically between icy punctiliousness and dramatic irascibility. Although a Puritan at heart, he could indulge in ostentatious display, adopting a courtly formality while in office, and sometimes wearing a ceremonial sword on occasions of state. Some of Adams' sentiments resembled Jefferson's, as both of them believed the United States was destined to be an agricultural economy for the foreseeable future. But, like Jefferson, Adams recognized that "The Agriculture of this Country and its Commerce are wedded together, for better and for Worse, in sickness and in health. And both are equally interested in the Honor and Independence of the Country."[45] Nonetheless, at the dawn of the Revolution, Adams had written that "The Spirit of Commerce is mercenary and avaricious," and from time

[44] Joshua Brookes' journal, with its quotations from Jefferson's scathing assessment, is preserved at the New York Historical Society. The excerpt was published in R. W. G. Vail, "A Dinner at Mount Vernon, from the Unpublished Journal of Joshua Brookes (1773–1859)," *New York Historical Society Quarterly* (April, 1947).

[45] John Adams to George Conway, January 11, 1799.

to time he would warn of the dangers that a commercial spirit presented to republican morals:

> Virtue and Simplicity of Manners, are indispensably necessary in a Republic, among all orders and Degrees of Men. But there is So much Rascallity, so much Venality and Corruption, so much Avarice and Ambition, such a Rage for Profit and Commerce among all Ranks and Degrees of Men even in America, that I sometimes doubt whether there is public Virtue enough to support a Republic.[46]

As in the case of Jefferson, it was not commerce itself but the commercial culture that repelled Adams, and he wrote to Benjamin Rush in 1808 that "Commerce Luxury and Avarice have destroyed every Republican Government; England and France have try'd the Experiment, and neither of them could preserve it, for twelve years." The "mercenary spirit of commerce" had destroyed the republics of Holland, Switzerland, and Venice. "Commerce and Luxury and Dissipation had introduced Avarice among the Greeks" and made them susceptible to conquest by Philip of Macedonia and his son. These were the words of the provincial Braintree agrarian, whose homely philosophy placed him at odds with the "High Federalists," and till the end of his life he wrote passionately against the "rise & progress of banks, those enormous corrupters of the people."[47]

By the beginning of Adams' administration, the French Republic, righteously petulant when the United States refused to repay debts owed to the deposed monarchy for its aid in the American Revolution and angered by the Anglo-American trade provisions of the Jay Treaty, began to attack American shipping. By 1797 the United States was involved in a "quasi war" with France, which Adams sought to end by negotiation, although anti-French sentiment was perpetually rife among some members of his own Federalist Party. Adams sent three agents to France, who were greeted by three agents of the French government, identified in the diplomatic correspondence as X, Y, and Z, who demanded a bribe in order to arrange a meeting with the French Foreign Minister, Talleyrand. News of this led to an outpouring of anti-French sentiment in the United States, and Americans took up the cry, "millions for defense, but not one cent for tribute!"

The United States was not being singled out for exceptional treatment. Other nations normally paid bribes, ransoms, and duties to one another in

[46] John Adams to Mercy Otis Warren, January 8, 1776.
[47] John Adams to Theron Metcalf, September 8, 1822.

the normal course of eighteenth-century commerce. George Washington's government initiated in 1796, and Adams sent to the Senate for ratification in 1797, a treaty involving payment in goods and money to the so-called Barbary pirates. Jefferson had protested against the policy of paying tributes at least to weaker adversaries. As early as November 1784, Jefferson had posed to James Monroe one of his characteristic rhetorical questions: "Would it not be better to offer them [the Barbary pirates] an equal treaty? If they refuse, why not go to war with them?" In December of that same year he wrote to Horatio Gates, "Tribute or war is the usual alternative of these pirates. If we yield the former, it will require sums which our people will feel. Why not begin a navy then and decide on war? We cannot begin in a better cause nor against a weaker foe." Decades later, as president, Jefferson sent a naval squadron to subdue the Barbary pirates, but with mixed results.[48]

Christopher Hitchens made an argument tinged by "presentism" when he implied that Jefferson's military invasion of North Africa was an American crusade against Islam. There is not a shred of evidence that Jefferson conceived either himself or his country as being at war with the Muslim world, although Hitchens presents a subtly imaginative thesis:

> It seems likely that Jefferson decided from that moment on that he would make war upon the Barbary kingdoms as soon as he commanded American forces. His two least favorite institutions—enthroned monarchy and state-sponsored religion—were embodied in one target, and it may even be that his famous ambivalences about slavery were resolved somewhat when he saw it practiced by the Muslims.[49]

Jefferson and his predecessors avoided any language that might give the impression that the United States was engaged in a holy war. They presented the matter rather as conflict with pirates operating from rogue states. Tripoli's rulers had only limited control over the motley crews who conducted raids in the Mediterranean and wherever else they could on the high seas. Tripolitan anarchy was hardly a shining example, but a bizarre caricature of the weak, decentralized government that Jefferson claimed to admire. The region's internal disorganization was clearly illustrated

48 Jefferson to James Monroe, November 11, 1784; Jefferson to Horatio Gates, December 13, 1784.

49 Christopher Hitchens, "Jefferson Versus the Muslim Pirates," *City Journal* (spring, 2007). For a more nuanced view, see Frank Lambert, *The Barbary Wars: American Independence in the Atlantic World* (New York: Macmillan, 2005), p. 118: "Indeed in its Tripoli Treaty of 1797, the United States explicitly declared that it was not a Christian state ... Years later Madison reflected on the religious clause in the Tripoli Treaty ... For him the two sides were not, nor had they ever been, engaged in a holy war."

when William Eaton, a former army captain, and Lieutenant Presley O'Bannon, with 8 US Marines, 500 mercenaries, and various other disaffected locals, led a daring overland attack on the city of Derna and took it.

O'Bannon's success was due to the same factors of internal anarchy that facilitated Hernando Cortez's toppling the Aztec Empire some centuries earlier, although the American victory was not nearly as successful or far-reaching in its consequences. The pirates were not a governmental force, but a collection of squabbling brigands, and it was much easier for the local authorities to collect tribute than it was for them to control the predations of lone wolves. Jefferson could no more effectively police Mediterranean pirates than he could New England smugglers, and he was forced to pay a ransom of $60,000 to redeem American prisoners.[50] Jefferson set an American precedent for later Middle East policies, notably those of President Reagan and the second President Bush, in the paying of dollars to Middle Eastern brigands. When Jefferson began his policy of embargo and isolation in 1807, the US fleet withdrew from the Mediterranean, and the pirates resumed their predations. In fact, as historian Gerard W. Gawalt has pointed out, "it was not until the second war with Algiers, in 1815, that naval victories by Commodores William Bainbridge and Stephen Decatur led to treaties ending all tribute payments by the United States."[51]

A JEFFERSONIAN NAVY – ADAMS TO MONROE

Naval policy, military spending, foreign diplomacy, and Caribbean affairs under the Adams presidency were part of a continuum that would persist for several decades. Adams continued George Washington's construction of six frigates, including the famed USS *Constitution.* Jefferson did not follow through. For the defense of American harbors he advocated the use of small gunboats, which could be constructed for $5,000, rather than

[50] For a summary that responsibly avoids jingoistic fervor, see Peterson, *Thomas Jefferson and the New Nation*, pp. 799–800. By contrast, see Brian Kilmeade and Don Yaeger, *Thomas Jefferson and the Tripoli Pirates: The Forgotten War That Changed American History* (New York: Sentinel, 2015), a patriotic narrative that portrays the war as an unequivocal American triumph.

[51] Gerard W. Gawalt, "America and the Barbary Pirates ... An International Battle against an Unconventional Foe" (Source: Library of Congress website on April 10, 2008). Sam Dagher reported to *The Christian Science Monitor* on November 26, 2007, that "In some areas, hundreds of ex-Sunni insurgents and even a few Al Qaeda-linked fighters are on the US military's payroll as neighborhood guards."

frigates like the USS *Constitution*, which cost $302,000, a decision that was later denounced by Theodore Roosevelt, who called the embarrassments in the War of 1812 "a painfully ludicrous commentary on Jefferson's remarkable project of having our navy composed exclusively of such craft."[52] In his view, that made Jefferson "less fit to conduct the country in troublesome times than any president we ever had." In later years, particularly after the War of 1812, Jefferson arrived at a greater tolerance for the military and fiscal exigencies of the modern state. Initially, however, when Adams moved to strengthen naval defenses, Jefferson was not enthusiastic.

The British Navy, overwhelmingly superior to all others, was particularly obnoxious throughout the administrations of Washington, Adams, Jefferson, and Madison. Until the end of the Napoleonic wars, their need for manpower led them to the practice of impressing American seamen into the British Navy, and there was little the United States could do about it. Ironically, it was Southern Republicans who were particularly outraged at the continuing insult of the impressment of American citizens on the high seas, while (as mentioned above) Northern Federalists were often inclined to view impressment simply as a "cost of doing business."

As Jefferson awakened slowly to the French threat and Napoleon's dream of re-establishing the French Empire in the New World, he anticipated a new and different relation to the British Navy: "the day that France takes possession of N. Orleans fixes the sentence which is to restrain her forever within her low water mark. it seals the union of two nations who in conjunction can maintain exclusive possession of the ocean. from that moment we must marry ourselves to the British fleet & nation."[53] He would live to witness this marriage, hidden behind the Monroe doctrine. Not until the Spanish–American War did the United States prove itself capable of independently enforcing this doctrine. Theodore Roosevelt amplified it with the "big stick" of his imperialistic "Great White Fleet" and his "Roosevelt Corollary" when he announced

[52] Daniel Ruddy, *Theodore Roosevelt's History of the United States* (New York: Smithsonian Books, 2010), p. 84.

[53] Jefferson to Robert E. Livingston, April 18, 1802. John B. Boles, *Jefferson: Architect of American Liberty* (New York: Basic Books, 2017), p. 351, points out this letter was carried by Pierre Samuel Du Pont de Nemours, unsealed, to guarantee French awareness of the threat of an Anglo-American alliance. The device would have seemed unnecessary and perhaps even harmful, as Malone points out in his *Jefferson and His Time*, 6 vols. (Boston, MA: Little, Brown, 1970), vol. IV, *Jefferson the President, First Term 1801–1805*, p. 255.

in 1904 that the United States claimed international police power over all nations in the western hemisphere.

Madison inherited Jefferson's legacy of limited naval spending on the eve of the War of 1812, in which Washington, DC, was invaded and the White House was burned. This fiasco led to Theodore Roosevelt's comments on Jefferson's performance in the arena of national defense. He wrote of "the cowardly infamy of which the politicians of the stripe of Jefferson and Madison, and the people whom they represented, were guilty in not making ready, by sea and land, to protect their Capital," and declared "It was criminal folly for Jefferson, and his follower Madison, to neglect to give us a force either of regulars or of well-trained volunteers during the twelve years they had in which to prepare for the struggle that any one might see was inevitable."[54]

JOHN ADAMS AND THE FIRST AMENDMENT – THE ALIEN AND SEDITION ACTS

Adams' quasi-war with France in 1798 was often accompanied by paranoid rhetoric aimed at Jefferson and his party. Congress passed, and Adams signed, the Alien and Sedition Acts of 1798, which Washington in retirement supported. These acts placed restrictions on resident aliens and instituted penalties for activities broadly defined as disloyal. Benjamin Franklin's grandson, Benjamin Franklin Bache, founder of the *Philadelphia Aurora*, was imprisoned for libeling Adams, and died shortly after his release, a victim of the Philadelphia yellow-fever epidemic, at the age of 29. It was in this cycle of events that Jefferson wrote the Kentucky Resolution, in which he argued that the Constitution was a compact between the states; that individual state legislatures could declare laws passed by Congress unconstitutional; and that individual states could nullify acts of Congress. The Kentucky Resolution declared "that these and successive acts of the same character, unless arrested at the threshold, necessarily drive these States into revolution and blood."[55]

Jefferson was correct in his opinion that the Alien and Sedition Acts were a direct assault on First Amendment liberties and therefore unconstitutional. His other opinion, that the states could nullify acts of Congress or withdraw from the Union, was stoutly contested by Presidents Andrew

54 Theodore Roosevelt, *The War of 1812*, 3rd edn. (New York: G. P. Putnam's Sons, 1883).

55 Jefferson's Draft of the Kentucky Resolution as submitted to Madison (before October 4, 1798), in Founders Online.

Jackson and Abraham Lincoln. Theodore Roosevelt later accused, unjustly, that Jefferson used Madison's Resolution and his own Kentucky Resolution "as handles wherewith to guide seditious agitation —not that he believed in sedition, but because he considered it good party policy, for the moment to excite it."[56] Jefferson recognized, in fact, a real threat to the freedoms guaranteed by the First Amendment, and threatened nullification and secession, because they seemed at the time to be the only remedies available.

Jefferson, in all fairness, was not guilty of crying fire in a crowded theatre: he was responding to government excess, and insisting on the rule of Constitutional law. There was as yet no doctrine of "judicial review," and Jefferson was no worshipper of the Supreme Court, as the impeachment trial of Justice Samuel Chase would later reveal. Chase, who was impeached at Jefferson's instigation, had, in fact, supported the Alien and Sedition Acts. The *Marbury v. Madison* decision, asserting that the Supreme Court had the power to declare a law unconstitutional, lay five years in the future, and an appeal to the Supreme Court would hardly have occurred to Jefferson at the time.[57] The position taken by Jefferson's nemesis, Chief Justice John Marshall, on the Alien and Sedition Acts remains a matter of controversy. Historian Jean Edward Smith says that he openly criticized the acts as useless and "calculated to create unnecessary discontents and jealousies at a time when our very existence as a nation may depend on our union." He notes that Marshall also voted for the repeal of the Sedition Act in 1800. In any event, the remedy of judicial review was not yet a principle of American law, and Jefferson's Kentucky Resolution, while a disastrous precedent in terms of states' rights, expressed valid concerns with respect to the rights of the individual citizen.[58]

[56] Theodore Roosevelt, *Gouverneur Morris* (Cambridge, MA: The Riverside Press, 1892), p. 303.

[57] The signal instances in which the protections of the First Amendment seem to have been challenged are the Alien and Sedition Acts of 1798, the South Carolina Nullification Crisis of 1832, President Lincoln's suspension of habeas corpus in 1861, the Espionage Act of 1917, and the Patriot Act of 2001.

[58] Marshall's opposition to the Alien and Sedition Acts is accepted as true in William E. Nelson, *Marbury v. Madison* (Lawrence, KS: University Press of Kansas, 2000), p. 46. By contrast, some scholars entertain the possibility that Marshall may have collaborated in the Federalist document entitled "Report of the Minority on the Virginia Resolutions." See Gregg Costa, "John Marshall, the Sedition Act, and Free Speech in the Early Republic," *Texas Law Review* (March, 1999). Jean Edward Smith, *John Marshall: Definer of a Nation* (New York: Henry Holt, 1996), p. 6, sees Marshall as a staunch opponent of the Alien and Sedition Acts, and gives no credence to his alleged

JOHN ADAMS, JEFFERSON, AND HAITI

The Adams years witnessed the relatively benevolent stage of the Haitian Revolution led by Toussaint Louverture. The contrast between the attitudes of Presidents Adams and Jefferson towards Haiti is covered in the work of historian Ronald Johnson, who remarks on Jefferson's compulsive references to the blackness of Toussaint and his people, and notes that Adams felt no so such compulsion. While Jefferson's color references were not so conspicuously vicious as those of some of his contemporaries, they were unnecessary. Johnson makes it clear that Jefferson and his party undermined any attempts Adams made towards decent treatment of Haiti, and concludes his work with the observation that Adams and Toussaint "deserve historical commendation for their extraordinary engagement." It is clear that "After John Adams and Toussaint Louverture, the two nations never again shared an equal footing."[59]

Adams' great-grandson, Henry Adams, offered a surprisingly sympathetic treatment of Toussaint Louverture in his *History of the United States during the Administrations of Jefferson*. Whatever racism this Boston Brahmin may have expressed in other contexts, Henry Adams was nonetheless capable of visualizing Toussaint as a symbol of Enlightenment and Civilization.[60] White supremacy and Eurocentrism were presuppositions in Henry Adams' worldview, but these elements do not leap off the pages of his chapter on Toussaint in the *History of the Jefferson Administrations*. Henry Adams was among the earliest historians to stress the linkage between Toussaint's revolution and Napoleon's decision to abandon his ambitions in the Americas. Frustrated by his loss of a base in the Caribbean, Napoleon decided that he could not control Louisiana, and therefore decided to sell it to the United States.

The ultimate effect of the Haitian Revolution was to hand Jefferson the most important triumph of his political career, which was the Louisiana Purchase. Whatever the verdict of historians on Jefferson's role in American history, there can be no questioning of his importance in

involvement with the "Minority Report," which is not attributed to Marshall by the editors of his papers.

59 Ronald Angelo Johnson, *Diplomacy in Black and White: John Adams, Toussaint Louverture, and their Atlantic World Alliance* (Athens, GA: University of Georgia Press, 2014), pp. 31, 173, 184.

60 Henry Adams famously believed that the African Freedmen should not have been granted the vote, which was perfectly consistent with his belief that most Americans were incapable of intelligently exercising the franchise.

American territorial expansion. James K. Polk is the only American president whose administration accomplished a greater expansion of the United States as a contiguous empire. But Jefferson accomplished the greatest feat of his presidency only because he was able to profit from the victory of Toussaint. By seizing this opportunity, he magnified executive power by an act that pragmatically contradicted his abstract ideological commitment, an act that, as John Boles notes, he came to feel was irrepressible.[61] There is no evidence that Jefferson ever viewed Haiti as a potential ally, or that he viewed Toussaint as a kindred spirit. He probably never saw the words of William Wordsworth's sonnet "To Toussaint Louverture":[62]

> There's not a breathing of the common wind
> That will forget thee; thou hast great allies;
> Thy friends are exultations, agonies,
> And love, and man's unconquerable mind.

Jefferson was not "breathing of the common wind" with Toussaint. Possibly G. W. F. Hegel was impressed and inspired by it, according to Susan Buck-Morss. In her treatment of the reactions of the German philosopher, who is more frequently remembered for his white-supremacist attitudes than for his abstract sympathies for Haiti, she discloses the Age of Enlightenment's contradictions regarding human rights and freedoms. Progressive historians rightly allude to examples of European racism in the minds of Kant and Hegel. None of their pejoratives should be rendered harmless, but neither went so far as the extended defamatory rhetoric of Jefferson's *Notes on Virginia*, worse than anything to be found in Kant or Hegel. Buck-Morss performed a service, although she showed little interest in the reactions of Jefferson or the American Enlightenment to Haiti.[63]

[61] Seward's acquisition of Alaska involved the purchase of 663,268 square miles. The Louisiana Purchase amounted to 828,000 square miles. The bill to annex Texas was signed by Tyler and ratified by Texas on Polk's watch. The Texas–Mexican expansion under Polk added 1.2 million square miles to United States territory.

[62] Johnson, *Diplomacy in Black and White*, p. 179. Gordon S. Brown, *Toussaint's Clause: The Founding Fathers and the Haitian Revolution* (Jackson: University Press of Mississippi, 2005), pp. 194–195. William Wordsworth, *Poetical Works* (Oxford University Press, 1965), p. 242.

[63] Susan Buck-Morss, "Hegel and Haiti," *Critical Inquiry*, 26, no. 4 (summer, 2001), 832, is a rare instance of describing the stricken slave-trade clauses of the Declaration of Independence in the following simple manner: "Thomas Jefferson blamed black slavery on the British." Michael Rozbicki's *Culture and Liberty in the Age of the American Revolution* (Charlottesville, VA: University of Virginia Press, 2011), discussed elsewhere,

Toussaint's willingness to work with French planters might have led Jefferson to reconsider his theory that slaves' liberation would inevitably lead to a bloodbath. This had already been contradicted by his own slaves' actions when the British invaded Virginia. Several of the slaves at Monticello remained good and faithful servants and, according to legend, hid the family silver.[64] Jefferson's African American contemporary, Prince Hall, was inspired by the efforts of Toussaint to establish law and order and to keep the peace with the French. Perhaps aware that Toussaint had abetted the return of his white former overseer, whom he had assisted in fleeing the island at the start of the revolution, Hall wrote:

> Six years ago, in the French West Indies. Nothing but the snap of the whip was heard from morning to evening; hanging, broken on the wheel, burning, and all manner of torture inflicted on those unhappy people, for nothing else but to gratify their master's pride, wantonness and cruelty: but blessed be God, the scene is changed; they now confess that God hath no respect of persons, and therefore receive them as their friends, and treat them as brothers.[65]

Prince Hall spoke too optimistically. White resentments and black retaliations accelerated in the ensuing years, and Jeffersonian Republicans exploited fears generated by developments in Haiti against the Adams administration. By supporting a trade agreement with Haiti, the Adams government ran up against the white-supremacist sentiments in the United States. Quick to see how the slightest hint of Federalist sympathies for Haiti might be used against Adams and the Federalists, Jefferson wrote to Monroe: "A clause in a bill now under debate for opening commerce with Toussaint & his black subjects now in open rebellion against France, will be a circumstance of high aggravation to that country." When the Haitian minister arrived in Philadelphia with his mulatto wife, Republicans frothed at the mouth. Albert Gallatin, Republican congressman from Pennsylvania, whipped up racist sentiment against the clause in what is called his "Black Speech" of January 21, 1799. The slaveholding Republicans of the Southern United States,

does not include the Haitian Revolution's central role in the eighteenth-century discourse of liberty.

64 Accounts of the Monticello slaves' loyalty during the British invasion of Monticello are discussed by Fawn Brodie in *Thomas Jefferson: An Intimate History* (New York: Norton, 1974), p. 147. Also see James Adam Bear, ed., *Jefferson at Monticello: Recollections of a Monticello Slave and a Monticello Overseer* (Charlottesville, VA: University of Virginia Press, 1967), p. 8.

65 Prince Hall, *A Charge Delivered to the African Lodge, June, 24, 1797 at Menotomy* (Published by the Desire of the Members of said Lodge, 1797).

represented by Jefferson, while rabidly supportive of the French nation, which had abolished slavery, were barely able to veil their hostility towards "Toussaint & his black subjects."

ADAMS TO JEFFERSON TRANSITION

In 1800, the vote in the Electoral College produced a tie between Jefferson and Aaron Burr, and the Constitution provided that the House of Representatives must choose between the two. Alexander Hamilton, who hated Burr, used his influence to marshal support for Jefferson, who consequently succeeded to the presidency. Garry Wills' book *"Negro President": Jefferson and the Slave Power* points out the irony that Jefferson, a slaveholder, won the election over Adams, who never owned a slave, due largely to the representation of slaves in the census, and thus in the Electoral College. After the election of 1800 some of Jefferson's Federalist critics referred to him as "The Negro President," since his victory was due to twelve extra votes given to him by the slave presence in the census. Federalist newspapers, such as the *Mercury and New-England Palladium* of Boston, said (January 20, 1801) he had made his "ride into the temple of Liberty on the shoulders of slaves." The three-fifths clause increased Southern representation by one-third, and, but for the three-fifths clause, Jefferson would not have been elected.[66]

The brutal election and the rough transition from Adams' to Jefferson's administration have been recounted often. After his unceremonious departure from Washington, DC, on the eve of Jefferson's inauguration, Adams retired to the bucolic sanctuary of his farm in Braintree, Massachusetts, a retreat as dear to him as Monticello was to Jefferson.[67] Their communications were for some years disrupted by the rancor of the 1800 presidential contest, but their friendship was restored in 1811, partly through the good offices of Benjamin Rush, knowing of the mutual respect and admiration that persisted between them. Their subsequent exchange of letters expressed agreement on such matters as their anti-

[66] Garry Wills, *"Negro President": Jefferson and the Slave Power* (Boston, MA: Houghton Mifflin, 2003). Also see the transcript of Jack Rakove and Garry Wills, "A Slave to the System? Thomas Jefferson and Slavery," recorded on Monday, January 19, 2004, at the Hoover Institution, Stanford University: www.hoover.org/research/slave-system-thomas-jefferson-and-slavery

[67] As cited above in Morgan, *The Meaning of Independence*, pp. 6, 13, and McCullough, *John Adams* (New York: Simon and Schuster, 2001), pp. 508ff.

Trinitarianism, and their shared disdain for the culture of banking and commerce.

Adams left Washington in disgust, and Jefferson walked to his inauguration. The middle-aged president elect had become bashful about displaying his wealth, unlike the young man who had arrived as a delegate to the Continental Congress in 1776 with a company of servants and a coach and four. From now on he would be ostentatious in his pretentions of simplicity. Nonetheless, as Adams later noted, Jefferson carefully attended to those presidential rites that could consolidate his power, such as the formal open house, or levee. Adams later wrote to Benjamin Rush, "I held Levees once a week, that all my Time might not be wasted by idle visits. Jeffersons whole Eight years was a Levee."[68]

MARBURY V. MADISON AND THE PICKERING AND CHASE IMPEACHMENTS

Shortly before leaving office, John Adams appointed William Marbury to the office of Justice of the Peace for the District of Columbia, but the commission was never delivered. Marbury petitioned the Supreme Court to force Secretary of State James Madison to deliver his commission by a writ of mandamus. Chief Justice John Marshall refused, on the grounds that the Supreme Court had no jurisdiction. The Judiciary Act of 1789 appeared to give the court that authority, but Marshall said the act was unconstitutional. He did make the passing observation that Marbury was entitled to his commission, but that was merely an *obiter dictum*, an opinion that, however reasonable, had no force of law. Marbury got nothing, to Jefferson's satisfaction, but Marshall had defined the power of the Supreme Court to declare an act of Congress unconstitutional, and with this decision he established the principle of judicial review.

Jefferson expressed his strongest reservations about the powers of the Supreme Court in a letter to Spencer Roane in 1819, long after he had left the presidency. The purpose of the Constitution had been "to establish three departments, coordinate and independent, that they might check and balance one another," and it did not give the court "the right to prescribe rules for the government of the others; and to that one, too, which is unelected by, and independent of, the Union."[69] Jefferson had entered office in 1800 with a fundamental suspicion regarding the

68 John Adams to Benjamin Rush, December 25, 1811.
69 Jefferson to Spencer Roane, September 6, 1819.

Supreme Court as an institution. There is no doubt of his resentment and hostility towards Chief Justice Marshall, his distant cousin, who was born in a log cabin, fought in the Revolution, and published the aforementioned five-volume biography of George Washington that Jefferson detested. Jefferson wrote to Madison on March 25, 1810, disparaging Marshall's character and saying, "His twistifications in the case of Marbury, in that of Burr, & the late Yazoo case, shew how dexterously he can reconcile law to his personal biases."

Jefferson was never able to do anything about Marshall, who continued to write landmark opinions, and Marshall's support for the impeachment of John Pickering, although he had committed no "high crimes and misdemeanors," should have pleased Jefferson. Pickering was mentally ill, often drunk on duty, and given to profane outbursts. The impeachment trial of Supreme Court Associate Justice Samuel Chase, which has attracted the notice of novelists and biographers of Jefferson, is generally acknowledged to have been initiated purely on political grounds, and Chase had leveled an oblique but obvious attack on Jefferson in a charge to a Maryland grand jury. In a letter to Joseph Nicholson, a Republican Congressman from Maryland, Jefferson took umbrage at this, then posed some of his characteristic rhetorical questions:

> you must have heard of the extraordinary charge of Chace to the grand jury at Baltimore. ought this seditious & official attack on the principles of our constitution, and on the proceedings of a state, to go unpunished? and to whom so pointedly as yourself will the public look for the necessary measures? I ask these questions for your consideration. for myself, it is better that I should not interfere.[70]

Dumas Malone could find no additional evidence of Jefferson's interference, nor has anyone writing since him offered anything beyond the letter to Nicholson. Jefferson never backed up his accusation that Chase's behavior was "seditious," but unquestionably Chase's charge to the grand jury constituted an attack on democracy and on all the pretensions of Jefferson's party. Chase declaimed against universal suffrage as a danger to "property, and all security to personal liberty"; if it were permitted, "our republican constitution will sink into a mobocracy, the worst of all possible governments." Jefferson's letter to Nicholson was evidence of interference in a trial, although in it he absolved himself of interference.

[70] Jefferson to Joseph H. Nicholson, May 13, 1803. Descriptions of Chase's attacks on Republican Party ideology are not detailed in any of the recent Jefferson biographies but can, at least for the time being, be found at Wikipedia.

In the following year, however, Jefferson's conduct in the trial of Aaron Burr was obvious, unconcealed interference. That matter will be discussed later in this chapter against the background of Jefferson's thoughts and emotions concerning the future of Louisiana and the Western Territories.

LOUISIANA: SISTER REPUBLIC, OR EMPIRE FOR SLAVERY?

Jefferson was the prophetic forerunner of Manifest Destiny, the idea that America had a divine mandate to carry civilization westward. This was a notion that antedated not only his presidency, but even the War for American Independence. In 1726, Bishop Berkeley sounded the trumpet, "Westward the course of Empire takes its way."[71] Decades later, at the Constitutional Convention, Benjamin Franklin referred to the United States as an empire, and as early as 1755 he had even implied that British North America was destined to rival, and possibly usurp, the position of Britain. Dominance in commerce, manufacturing, politics, and banking of the Anglo-Atlantic Empire must ultimately fall to North America, where "there are suppos'd to be now upwards of One Million English Souls . . . This Million doubling, suppose but once in 25 Years, will in another Century be more than the People of England."[72]

Geographical expansion would dictate that the United States adopt the political and economic mechanisms necessary for the administration of a great empire, as, within fifty years of the Constitutional Convention, the agricultural capitalism of the South would be fatally threatened by the industrial capitalism and the commercial culture of the North, celebrated in Franklin's *The Way to Wealth*. In Jefferson's mind, the acquisition of Louisiana provided a wilderness so immense that every American might potentially realize the dream of owning an independent homestead. His fee simple empire would accord with the tradition of the Anglo-Saxon yeoman.[73]

71 George Berkeley, *Verses on the Prospect of Planting Arts and Learning in America* (London, 1726).

72 Franklin, *Observations Concerning the Increase of Mankind.*

73 An early application of the term "Yeoman and the Fee Simple Empire" was in a chapter by that title in Henry Nash Smith, *Virgin Land: The American West as Symbol and Myth* (Cambridge, MA: Harvard University Press, 1950), p. 133. An imaginative recycling of the empire metaphor in recent Jefferson studies comes from Peter S. Onuf in his *Jefferson's Empire* (Charlottesville, VA: University of Virginia Press, 2000), and more recently in the subtitle of Annette Gordon-Reed and Peter S. Onuf, *"Most Blessed of the Patriarchs": Thomas Jefferson and the Empire of the Imagination* (New York: Liveright, 2017).

The Louisiana Purchase was not among the accomplishments Jefferson dictated to be engraved on his tombstone, although it was the most important achievement of his political career. The New Yorker Robert Livingston, the ambassador in Paris during the negotiations, has never been accorded much recognition for the acquisition of this territory by the Virginia Republicans. James Monroe, who had been minister to France from 1794 to 1796, had the virtue of being a Virginian.[74] Jefferson commissioned the able and trustworthy Monroe to carry instructions to Livingston, who was not exactly mistrusted. As an old friend, a member of the Declaration's drafting committee, a fellow Democratic Republican, and an ideological comrade, Livingston had already proven to be a tough negotiator, having informed the French of "the ardor of some Americans to take it [Louisiana] by force." This reference to the military ardor of some Americans was most likely, as historian Roger Kennedy reasonably surmises, an allusion to the bellicosity of General Andrew Jackson, General Alexander Hamilton, and Colonel Aaron Burr.[75]

The purchase provided France with financial support for Napoleon's continuing wars on the European continent, not to mention his plans for an invasion of England. Some Americans preferred purchasing the territory, along with "the Floridas," more cheaply from Spain. Spanish pretentions to ownership seemed more valid than those of the French in the eyes of some legalists. The final agreement, overseen by Monroe, implied the right to extend American slavery into Louisiana, which suggests that Jefferson's belief that slavery should be allowed in the territories was insecure long before the 1820 Missouri Compromise.[76] Leading from behind, Jefferson let circumstances drag him into supporting the continuation and expansion of slavery. He had temporized for fifty years on the question of emancipation before he eventually resigned himself to the inevitability of its expansion and "confided himself childlike to the genius of his age."[77]

[74] Jefferson's handling of Livingston's negotiations is interpreted in Roger G. Kennedy, *Mr. Jefferson's Lost Cause: Land, Farmers, Slavery, and the Louisiana Purchase* (New York: Oxford University Press, 2003). Kennedy also suggests obliquely that he trusted Monroe's willingness to preserve slavery in Louisiana, in Kennedy, *The Louisiana Purchase*, at: www.common-place.org/vol-03/no-03/author/

Joseph Ellis shares my opinion that Jefferson and Madison begrudged Livingston any credit for the acquisition of Louisiana.

[75] Kennedy, *The Louisiana Purchase*.

[76] Ibid. Ron Chernow, *Alexander Hamilton* (New York: Penguin Press, 2004), p. 671.

[77] The quotation is from Ralph Waldo Emerson, "Self Reliance," in Emerson, *Essays and Lectures* (New York: Library of America, 1983), p. 260.

Hamilton attributed Jefferson's acquisition of Louisiana to "an accidental state of circumstances, and not to wise plans." It was blind luck, an accident resulting from the success of Toussaint, to whom Hamilton had given qualified and extremely limited support. No less Machiavellian than Jefferson, Hamilton viewed the purchase as a stunning political coup, an unearned reward for policies characterized by "feebleness and pusillanimity." Giving Jefferson little, if any, credit for the acquisition, Hamilton expressed a disdain matched only by his wonder at the inflated prestige of Jefferson's party in the eyes of a myopic American populace:

> This purchase has been made during the period of Mr. Jefferson's presidency and will, doubtless, give éclat to his administration. Every man, however, possessed of the least candor and reflection will readily acknowledge that the acquisition has been solely owing to a fortuitous concurrence of unforeseen and unexpected circumstances and not to any wise or vigorous measures on the part of the American government.[78]

This position was inherited by the neo-Hamiltonian historians, Theodore Roosevelt and Henry Cabot Lodge, but neither pounced on the opportunity to make an additional point. Jefferson had not promised Louisiana to the United States in perpetuity. He wrote to John C. Breckinridge containing ambivalent musings on the possibility that two nations, one on either side of the Mississippi, might eventually flourish as two independent confederacies. And why should Americans of the existing Atlantic confederation complain? The full populating even of the eastern territories seemed to be in the distant future. He mused that it might be proper "to give establishments to the Indians on the East side of the Mississippi, in exchange for their present country."[79] A year later he expressed in less equivocal terms to Joseph Priestley his serenity at the prospect of a future hiving-off of the Western territories:

> Whether we remain in one confederacy, or form into Atlantic and Mississippi confederacies, I believe not very important to the happiness of either part. Those of the western confederacy will be as much our children and descendants as those of the eastern, and I feel myself as much identified with that country, in future time, as with this; and did I now foresee a separation at some future day, yet I should feel the duty and the desire to promote the western interests as zealously as the eastern,

[78] [Alexander Hamilton,] "Purchase of Louisiana," *New York Evening Post* (July 5, 1803). Gautam Mukunda, interviewed on the C-Span program "After Words" by Richard Brookhiser, editor at *National Review*, asserts in his book *Indispensable: When Leaders Really Matter* that Jefferson was not indispensable to the Louisiana Purchase because most leaders would have done the same.

[79] Jefferson to John Breckinridge, August 12, 1803.

doing all the good. for both portions of our future family which should fall within my power.[80]

As he shared these musings with Breckinridge and Priestley, he seemed to think the future of Louisiana was tied only vaguely to that of the United States, and at first glance his indifference to the emergence of a sister republic in the West might have appeared sincere. Such a notion was not inconsistent with his ideology of small government and home rule. Then a disturbing development revealed his true emotions, when Aaron Burr was accused of plans to appropriate the trans-Mississippian territories. His letters to Breckinridge and Priestley had contained nothing but vague and equivocal hypotheses.

THE BURR TRIAL

President Jefferson was livid when he received news of a western conspiracy by Aaron Burr.[81] In 1804, while still serving as vice president, Burr was supposed to have approached Anthony Merry, British minister to the United States, with a proposal to detach Louisiana and re-establish British power in the Southwest. Whether or not his fury was justified, Jefferson's reaction has troubled even those inclined to understand it. Jefferson assumed the role of a prosecutor in the proceeding, declared Burr to be a traitor in advance of his trial, overlooked the constitutional "privilege" of habeas corpus, and ordered the military arrest of material witnesses to the trial. Dumas Malone thought Jefferson must have been aware that Burr had early abandoned any practical plans to separate Louisiana. The charges of treason were nonetheless based on the assumption that he had originally conspired to do so.[82]

[80] Jefferson to Joseph Priestley, Washington, January 29, 1804.

[81] Nancy Isenberg, *Fallen Founder: The Life of Aaron Burr* (New York: Penguin Books, 2007), covers Burr's trial and acquittal on treason charges intermittently, but see especially pp. 308–309, 323–363. Buckner F. Melton, Jr., *Aaron Burr: Conspiracy to Treason* (New York: John Wiley & Sons, 2002).

[82] John A. Garraty, *The American Nation: A History of the United States to 1877*, 7th edn. (New York: HarperCollins, 1991), vol. I, admits that Jefferson behaved only as any chief executive ought to behave in circumstances approximating treason, but feels the episode showed neither Jefferson nor Justice Marshall at their best. Dumas Malone offers a judicious and balanced interpretation, Dumas Malone, *Jefferson and His Time*, 6 vols. (Boston, MA: Little, Brown, 1974), vol. V, *Jefferson the President, Second Term 1805–1809*, pp. 294, 338, passim. Nancy Isenberg, in *Fallen Founder*, pp. 307–365, offers a subtle examination of Jefferson's motives.

People's lives often contradict their abstract principles, and there continued to be elasticity in Jefferson's thinking. His vagueness regarding the future of the West was evident as late as May 24, 1812, long after the Burr trial, when he wrote to John Jacob Astor regarding the latter's "enterprise for establishing a factory on the Columbia river, and a commerce thro' the line of that river and the Missouri." This was a project he had encouraged "with the assurance of every facility and protection which the government could properly afford." He toyed with the prospect of an independent entity on the Pacific:

> I considered as a great public acquisition the commencement of a settlement on that point of the western coast of America, and looked forward with gratification to the time when its descendants should have spread themselves through the whole length of that coast, covering it with free and independent Americans, unconnected with us but by the ties of blood and interest, and employing like us the rights of self-government.[83]

JEFFERSONIAN ECONOMIC POLICIES

"Hamilton on steroids" would be an anachronistic, but apt, appellation for Albert Gallatin, Jefferson's hyperactive Secretary of the Treasury. Gallatin, who had supported the Whiskey Rebellion, turned out to be a pragmatist who subordinated ideology to necessity. Madison retained him in office and, at Gallatin's advice, signed the charter for the Second Bank of the United States. In the final year of Jefferson's second term, Gallatin issued his *Report on Roads, Canals, Harbors, and Rivers*, which exceeded Hamilton's nationalistic federalism by far. Henry Adams and his student Henry Cabot Lodge recognized the irony of Gallatin's Hamiltonianism and, like Theodore Roosevelt, made much of Jefferson's and Madison's pragmatic adoption of Gallatin's policies.[84]

Jefferson's commitment to free trade was evident in the respect he paid to Adam Smith, and even more to Jean-Baptiste Say, but he was forced to

[83] Jefferson to John Jacob Astor, May 24, 1812.

[84] Henry Adams on Gallatin is generally positive in his *History of the United States during the Administrations of Thomas Jefferson* (New York: Library of America, 1986 [1890]); Gallatin is praised for his flexibility, e.g. p. 1034. Henry Cabot Lodge wrote a strongly positive biography of Gallatin for *Encyclopedia Britannica*. Theodore Roosevelt, who viewed the Jefferson–Madison era negatively, as previously noted, nonetheless ranked Gallatin's "services to our Treasury" just below Hamilton's in Theodore Roosevelt, *The Works of Theodore Roosevelt*, Memorial Edn., (New York: Charles Scribner's Sons, 1926), vol. VII, *Thomas Hart Benton/Gouverneur Morris*, p. 352.

depart from their principles by the exigencies of the times. At the height of the Napoleonic wars he preferred neutrality – not because he was a pacifist in principle, but because he lacked the navy to contest either the French or the British fleets. On becoming president he made a decision that was both practical and ideological, and reduced the size of the army to under 3,000, but he later called for dramatic increases.[85] Jefferson's opposition to military spending and his fear of maintaining a standing army was in accord with the founding principles of the Republic. Even if creating a fleet to rival the Royal Navy had been possible, such an undertaking would have required a policy of taxation and military spending repugnant to Jefferson and to American culture.

Without a drastic transformation of the American mind, the government could not have imposed taxation to build up the navy and put up any meaningful resistance to British impressment of American seamen. It could do nothing about the French practice of seizing American vessels that complied with other British demands. In order to avoid conflict for which the United States was unprepared, Jefferson took the drastic measure of pushing through Congress the Embargo Act of 1807 that prohibited all foreign trade. This meant, almost inevitably, that the second term of his administration was characterized by vigorous measures of dubious constitutionality, such as seizing cargoes without due process, and the enforcement of martial law on Lake Champlain. Such exercise of executive authority seemed inconsistent with Jefferson's libertarian, small-government principles.

It literally gave him headaches when forced to think of himself or his policies as despotic, for in his own mind he was always struggling to preserve republican government in the face of reactionary forces. Nonetheless, the means he used to enforce the act have been described by Forrest McDonald as "unconstitutional," and he was as a result faced with the threat of nullification coming from Massachusetts Federalists.[86] Leonard Levy found it ironic that the author of the Kentucky Resolution should be presented with a New York "Memorial and Remonstrance" against the Fifth Embargo Act. Even Jon Meacham calls the bill that Jefferson signed on December 7, 1807, "a projection of governmental power that surpassed even the hated Alien and Sedition Acts." Dumas

85 Leonard Levy, *Jefferson and Civil Liberties* (Cambridge, MA: Harvard University Press, 1963), p. 111.

86 Forrest McDonald on constitutionality, in McDonald, *The Presidency of Thomas Jefferson* (Lawrence, KS: University Press of Kansas, 1976), p. 149.

Malone justified Jefferson's vigorous executive activism by comparing it to Lincoln's exercise of power during the Civil War.[87]

Gallatin became Jefferson's enforcer in the embargo years, as Hamilton had been Washington's enforcer in the Whiskey Rebellion. Jefferson and Gallatin had become nationalists, and Jefferson wrote to him with a justification for "the most arbitrary powers," and proposing that Congress "should legalize all means which may be necessary to obtain its end."[88] Jefferson during his final term in office was accused of practically abdicating. He was beginning to show the signs of age and fatigue that he so paradoxically had attributed to the slightly younger Washington. He retired to his room with migraines, and Gallatin was left to defend the policy in a series of articles in the *National Intelligencer*. Although Gallatin had been initially opposed to it, his inner opinion was that "In every point of view, privation, suffering, revenue, effect on the enemy, politics at home, I prefer war to a permanent embargo" (by "permanent embargo" meaning of unspecified length).[89] The willingness of Gallatin to modify his republican creed, to assert federal authority, and, in the course of his career, to make adjustments on such matters as internal improvements and the necessity of a national bank earned him high praise from historians Henry Adams and Henry Cabot Lodge. John Quincy Adams supported the Embargo Act, and suffered a loss of popularity in New England.

POST-RETIREMENT LETTER TO JOHN B. COLVIN, 1810 EXECUTIVE PREROGATIVES

Henry Adams thought it "was hard to see how any President could be more federalist than Jefferson himself." He noted this without resorting to Josiah Quincy's wisecrack that the Republicans "out-federalized Federalism."[90] Adams' observation accorded with the prediction of

[87] For more on the embargo, see McDonald, ibid., p. 144. On constitutional scruples, see Levy, *Jefferson and Civil Liberties*, p. 211 note 43. Malone, *Jefferson the President, Second Term 1805–1809*, p. 389. Meacham, *Thomas Jefferson*, p. 430.

[88] Albert Gallatin to Jefferson, July 29, 1808, and August 11, 1808.

[89] Albert Gallatin to Jefferson, December 18, 1807. On Jefferson's headaches, see "Headaches" at https://home.monticello.org/. Forrest McDonald mentions this migraine, *The Presidency of Thomas Jefferson*, p. 147.

[90] Henry Adams, *History of the United States during the Administrations of Thomas Jefferson*, p. 354. Also see Charles W. McKenzie, *Party Government in the United States* (New York: Ronald Press Co., 1938), vol. II, p. 88; Hofstadter, *The American Political Tradition*, p. 42.

Hamilton that Jefferson, if elected president, would do nothing to diminish or erode executive power. Adams is echoed by other historians, most of whom accept the truism of Jefferson's First Inaugural Address, "we are all Federalists; we are all Republicans," observing that Jefferson and Madison carried out policies that they had previously opposed.

The argument can be extended into the Jacksonian era to make the case that the party styling itself the party of Jefferson became a defender of Federalist doctrine when Jackson reacted to the Nullification Crisis, saying that the Constitution "forms a government, not a league." In effect the Jeffersonians established the tradition of arguing against executive prerogative when the opposing party held the presidency but asserting executive prerogatives when they held it themselves. Within this tradition, Federalist, Democratic, Whig, or Republican presidents have all justified "vigorous government" in order, as Jefferson justified it, "to place our country in safety."

Jefferson made that often-cited statement related to the powers of the executive in his response to a letter of September 14, 1810, from John B. Colvin, who was ghost-writing a biography of James Wilkerson, justifying Wilkerson's role in the Aaron Burr Conspiracy. Colvin wrote to Jefferson asking:

> Are there not periods when, in free governments, it is necessary for officers in responsible stations to exercise an authority beyond the law—and, was not the time of Burr's treason such a period? Gen. Wilkinson goes to press with his memoirs this autumn, and intends them to be published by the next meeting of Congress.

Jefferson's response to Colvin was that the question proposed "is easy of solution in principle, but sometimes embarrassing in practice." The letter has been cited by those who accept the idea that the practical Jefferson, once in office, confirmed his inaugural principle that we are all Federalists, while others have suggested that Jefferson's philosophy was different before and after his presidency. In fact, as we have seen, he did not deny that the exigencies of the Napoleonic wars had necessitated flexibility in his doctrines. Historian Jeremy David Bailey defends Jefferson from the charge of inconsistency and concludes that "Jefferson advanced a doctrine of presidential prerogative that was both democratic and strong: the president, like the good officer, can transgress the details of the law in order to fulfill its purpose. And, because the president acts in constant agency on behalf of the people, he must." This perspective on "presidential prerogatives" is hardly irrational, but it is dangerous.[91]

Jefferson was neither power-hungry nor immoderate, and his use of loose construction did no permanent damage to the rule of law. In the hands of a demagogue, transgression of the law will always be justified as action "on behalf of the people." Jefferson's response to Colvin presented additional instances in which the rules of law might be transgressed – some of them related to civilian matters, some to military matters, some recalling actual historical events, others hypothetical. One of Jefferson's hypotheticals expressed in the same letter to Colvin was the following: "a ship at sea in distress for provisions meets another having abundance, yet refusing a supply; the law of self preservation authorizes the distressed to take a supply by force. in all these cases the unwritten laws of necessity, of self-preservation, & of the public safety controul the written laws of meum & tuum."[92] Such a categorical imperative would justify the action of any vessel in need, and might even encompass an act of piracy. According to this reasoning, a galley slave, no less than an admiral, would seem to be justified in stealing a loaf of bread, in accordance with the law of self-preservation.

Another hypothetical case made allusion to his purchase of Louisiana without prior constitutional authorization. An executive might have had an opportunity to purchase Florida in 1805, before a given expiration date, but congressional leaders might have opposed the purchase in an attempt to protract the proceeding beyond the expiration date. In this case the said executive would be justified in "transcending the law" in order to "secure the good of his country." Besides, the action, although in violation of the principle of strict construction, would not be clearly illegal or unconstitutional.

But his response to Colvin's query regarding "Burr's treason" was a matter of historical memory, and Jefferson justified his actions on the basis of "the state of the information, correct & incorrect." Whether or not these actions constituted constitutional breaches, Jefferson's response to Colvin indicated some scruples regarding the "risk" involved.

[91] Jefferson to John B. Colvin, September 20, 1810. Jeremy David Bailey, "Executive Prerogative and the 'Good Officer' in Thomas Jefferson's Letter to John B. Colvin," *Presidential Studies Quarterly*, 34, no. 4 (December, 2004), 732–754. Also see Eyler Robert Coates, Sr., "Objectivism and Thomas Jefferson: Seven Essays on the Philosophy of Ayn Rand" (1997), at http://eyler.freeservers.com/JeffWritings/otj61.htm

[92] Jefferson to John B. Colvin, September 20, 1810.

Nonetheless he had only done his duty in reacting to a perceived emergency, combining factors that:

> constituted a law of necessity & self preservation, and rendered the *salus populi* supreme over the written law. the officer who is called to act on this superior ground, does indeed risk himself on the justice of the controuling powers of the constitution, and his station makes it his duty to incur that risk.

It was incumbent on those who accepted great responsibilities to "risk themselves" on "great occasions" and to let public opinion decide later as to whether necessity legitimized their actions. The man who had insisted on the Bill of Rights had taken the "risk" of reaching beyond the law. The man who had protested the Alien and Sedition Acts, seemingly to the point of justifying rebellion, now maintained that, if he had stretched his executive powers, the extension had been necessary and proper.[93]

MADISON AND IDEOLOGY

The history of ideas contains pairings in which the supposed junior partner may at times be more intellectually impressive. Ferdinand and Isabella, Marx and Engels, Darwin and Huxley, Jefferson and Madison are noteworthy instances. In the opinion of their contemporary, Benjamin Stoddard, Madison was "but the puppet of Jefferson," yet this cannot be supported by a reading of the correspondence between the two men. For thirty years Madison was the most influential figure in American politics, beginning in 1787, when he convinced Washington to preside over the Constitutional Convention, and continuing until he left the presidency in 1817. He was the "true architect" of the embargo in the opinion of some historians.[94] He drafted the Virginia Resolution when he saw the need for a check on the law-making powers of Congress, and he edited Jefferson's more radical Kentucky Resolution. But he offered a moderate interpretation of both Resolutions, when consulted in the Secession Crisis of 1832, with reflections on the passage of time. His position as a senior statesman remained authoritative, from the time of his death in 1836 to the present, and "the last of the Fathers," rightly or wrongly, retains his title "Father of the Constitution," although, as Mary Sarah Bilder has argued, his central

[93] Jefferson to John B. Colvin, September 20, 1810.

[94] McDonald, *The Presidency of Thomas Jefferson*, pp. 139–144; Malone in *Jefferson the President, Second Term 1805–1809*, pp. 578, 619, 622.

ideas did not prevail at the Convention.[95] Nonetheless, with the posthumous circulation of his notes, he became the most magisterial of authorities with respect to the original intent of the Founding Fathers. Madison not only prodded Jefferson into timely action on the Louisiana Purchase, according to some historians: for better or for worse, he conceived of and implemented the Embargo Act, a crucial expansion of central government powers.[96]

Vigorous government, industrialism, and commercialism, once seen as high Federalist watchwords, were incorporated into Republican policy while Madison was in office. American industrialism was stimulated by the disruption of the Atlantic trade during Jefferson's embargo, and during the War of 1812. Both occurrences led Jefferson to revisit ideas on manufacturing that had seemed important to him in his *Summary View of the Rights of British America* of 1774, where historian Peter Onuf has correctly identified hints of Federalist ideology.[97] Prior to the embargo he wrote to Jean-Baptiste Say that "the best distribution of labour is supposed to be that which places the manufacturing hands alongside of the agricultural; so that the one part shall feed both." After the embargo came the war, and he wrote to John Jacob Astor that "in the present state of affairs between Gr. Britain & us, the government is justly jealous ... to exclude the use of British manufactures in these states & to promote the establishment of similar ones among ourselves."[98]

In the War of 1812, "Mr. Madison's War," Jefferson became a principal "War Hawk."[99] He had used that term disparagingly in 1798 directed at those who wanted war with France, but in 1812, ever hostile to England, he was eager to expand the American Empire by making a grab for Canada. To advance imperial ambitions, he was clever enough to exploit national pride with expressed indignation at the Royal Navy over the perennial issue of the impressment of American seamen. Jefferson, like most Virginia

[95] Mary Sarah Bilder, *Madison's Hand: Revising the Constitutional Convention* (Cambridge, MA: Harvard University Press, 2015).

[96] Forrest McDonald attributes the embargo to Madison in *The Presidency of Thomas Jefferson*, p. 144. Fleming, in *Louisiana Purchase* (New York: John Wiley & Sons, 2003), p. 100, presents Madison's efforts throughout as crucial to the Louisiana Purchase. Hofstadter uses Madison to exemplify "the Jeffersonians'" adoption of Federalist policies. Drew R. McCoy, *The Last of the Fathers: James Madison and the Republican Legacy* (Cambridge University Press, 1991). Peter Onuf, "Thomas Jefferson, Federalist" in his *The Mind of Thomas Jefferson*, pp. 83–98.

[97] Onuf, *The Mind of Thomas Jefferson*, pp. 88, 89, 94.

[98] Jefferson to John Jacob Astor, May 24, 1812.

[99] Jefferson to James Madison, Philadelphia, April 26, 1798, uses the term "War Hawk."

planters, had no direct ties or interests regarding American naval commerce or the issue of impressment. Transatlantic merchants took the cynical view that the impressment of American sailors or bribes to Arab pirates were simply a "cost of doing business," but the pacifist author of the embargo had become disillusioned with neutrality in the course of four years. Now he was prepared to attack the British juggernaut, although the nation was painfully unprepared. By the end of the war, Madison had learned from experience and was advocating a military build-up, as well as a protective tariff to support manufacturing and internal improvements, and he tolerated a national bank. In short, under his leadership, the Republican Party adopted a nationalism anticipating the "American System" of Henry Clay. In the meantime, in one of those curious and amusing reversals that characterize the ideology of American parties, the Federalists had become the bulwark of states' rights, nullification, and disunion.

It was no secret that the Federalists had met in Hartford, Connecticut, from December 1814 to early January 1815 with calls for amending the Constitution, threats of secession, and talk of making a separate peace with the British. Jefferson ridiculed the Hartford convention, saying "when they shall see, as they will see, that nothing is done there, they will let go their hold, and we shall have peace, on the status ante bellum ... New Hampshire and Vermont refuse to join the mutineers," and even Connecticut had reaffirmed "her duty to the federal Constitution." It was beyond credibility "that Massachusetts, on the good faith and aid of little Rhode-island will undertake a war against the rest of the Union."[100]

That the author of the Kentucky Resolution denounced the Hartford secessionists was not surprising. More remarkable was the fact that Jefferson was now calling for the sort of security measures he had denounced in 1798–99, the activation of domestic police powers, more vigorous government regulation of foreign trade, and a stronger military. "The late war has indeed terminated most honorably," he wrote to George W. Campbell in October of 1815, "yet it has sufficiently proved that our military system is not in a form adequate to our safety in a state of war." He called for a reform of the financial system in order to pay off the war debts, and he radically proposed that the monetary system be removed from the private sector and placed under national control:

> the basis of this can only be by taking the circulating medium into the hands of the nation to whom it belongs, out of that of private adventurers, who have so

[100] Jefferson to Elizabeth Trist, December 26, 1814.

managed it for their own profit as to leave us without any common measure of the value of property, and to subject all private fortunes to the fluctuations of their swindling projects. the coining of paper money by private authority is a higher degree of treason than the coining of precious metals.[101]

In his economic policies, he sounded like the prophet of Henry Clay's "American System," and this was only partially a response to the embarrassments of the late war. Jefferson's attitudes on industry and commerce cannot be deduced from a few lines in *Notes on Virginia*, and his "federalism," as some scholars have defined it, was sporadically present throughout his career.[102] Jefferson's federalism, like Madison's, flourished when he and his friends were in office, and waned when the government was in the hands of others.[103]

Jefferson is responsible for the cliché that it was only the Napoleonic wars and the War of 1812 that had led him to pursue American industrial self-sufficiency. He had, of course, been an industrial entrepreneur since his return to Monticello in 1795, and his First Annual Message, on December 8, 1801, had announced that "Agriculture, manufactures, commerce, and navigation, the four pillars of our prosperity, are the most thriving when left most free to individual enterprise." It was true that historical circumstances had led Jefferson to modify his rhetoric, but opinions published in 1785 had nothing to do with unfolding events. The wars between France and Great Britain had made it impossible for him to sustain his agrarian hyperbole. There had been a time, he wrote to Benjamin Austin in 1816, when his words about leaving workshops in Europe might have been quoted "with more candor":

But who in 1785 could foresee the rapid depravity which was to render the close of that century the disgrace of the history of man? Who could have imagined that the two most distinguished in the rank of nations, for science and civilization, would have suddenly descended from that honorable eminence, and setting at defiance all those moral laws established by the Author of nature between nation and nation, as between man and man, would cover earth and sea with robberies and piracies, merely because strong enough to do it with temporal impunity.[104]

[101] Jefferson to George W. Campbell, October 15, 1815.

[102] Again, I cite Onuf's "Thomas Jefferson Federalist" in *The Mind of Thomas Jefferson* (see note 15 above).

[103] Wood, "Is There a Madison Problem?" in *Revolutionary Characters*, p. 151, defends Madison from the charge of ideological inconsistency and seeks to reconcile the "fervent nationalist" with the "strict constructionist, states' rights defender of the Democratic Republican Party."

[104] Jefferson to Benjamin Austin, Esq., January 9, 1816.

The war between England and France was unnatural; war was a departure from the moral laws of nature and nature's God. America had been forced by fiendish and unnatural conditions to bring its workshops home, and on November 28, 1814, he wrote to William Short, saying, "Our enemy has indeed the consolation of Satan on removing our first parents from Paradise: from a peaceable and agricultural nation, he makes us a military and manufacturing one." But it was not only the "unnatural" state of war existing between England and France that had forced the United States to develop its own manufactures. Industrial development was already under way at Monticello, augmented by a plantation entrepreneur who had been struggling for years to operate a nailery.

MONROE AND EXPANSIONISM

With James Monroe succeeding Madison, the presidency remained safely in the hands of a Virginian, and Jefferson trusted the hands of Virginians. True enough, Robert Livingston, a New Yorker, had laid the groundwork for the Louisiana Purchase, and John Quincy Adams of Massachusetts was about to advance the policy that came to be known as the Monroe doctrine.[105] The downfall of Napoleon had brought an end to the impressment of American seamen, and now the British were proposing an Anglo-American pact in response to the "Holy Alliance," a move initiated by Tsarist Russia to discourage revolutions in the New World and prop up the crumbling Spanish Empire. Secretary of State John Quincy Adams advised that it would be "more dignified, to avow our principles explicitly to Russia and France, than to come in as a cock-boat in the wake of the British man-of-war."[106] Thus the Monroe doctrine was an exercise in bravado, for Americans were temporarily dependent on the might of the British Navy to enforce it. Nonetheless, it allowed Americans to assume a dignified posture.

Jefferson wrote cautiously to Monroe that "acceding to her proposition" would bring Great Britain's "mighty weight into the scale of free government . . . Great Britain is the nation which can do us the most harm of any one, or all on earth; and with her on our side we need not fear the

105 For Monroe's correspondence with Jefferson and Madison, see James P. Lucier, ed., *The Political Writings of James Monroe* (Washington, DC: Regnery Publishing, 2001), pp. 632–637.

106 Robert V. Remini, *John Quincy Adams* (New York: Henry Holt, 2002), p. 60.

whole world." He envisioned an opportunity to expand "our American system," possibly even acquiring "any one or more of the Spanish providences." He candidly confessed to Monroe that he had:

> ever looked on Cuba as the most interesting addition which could ever be made to our system of states. the controul which, with Florida point this island would give us over the Gulph of Mexico, and the countries and the Isthmus bordering on it, as well as all those whose waters flow into it, would fill up the measure of our political well-being.

With Great Britain, "then, we should most sedulously cherish a cordial friendship; and nothing would tend more to knit our affections than to be fighting once more, side by side, in the same cause."[107] Thus, with unintended irony, he attached an appendix to his letter to Robert Livingston of April 18, 1802, expressing the possibility that we might someday "marry ourselves to the British Fleet."[108]

UNDERMINING JOHN QUINCY ADAMS

President John Quincy Adams was a man of arts and letters who could boast a record of public service that began during the Revolution when, at the age of 14, he served as a French translator to the American mission in St. Petersburg. But despite shared intellectual interests there was little meeting of minds between him and Jefferson. The second President Adams proposed that Congress fund a national observatory, noting that Europe had over 130 "lighthouses of the skies; while throughout the whole American hemisphere, there is not one." Jefferson's party, opposed, as ever, to public spending, greeted the phrase "lighthouses of the skies" with ridicule, and there is no record of the scientific Jefferson leaping to the defense of his fellow dilettante.

John Quincy Adams had been sympathetic to the Jefferson administration while serving as a senator from Massachusetts, supporting the president on such important issues as the Louisiana Purchase and the Embargo Act. In this so-called Era of Good Feelings, the United States briefly became virtually a one-party nation. It seemed momentarily as if the

[107] Jefferson to James Monroe, October 24, 1823.

[108] The Monroe doctrine was anticipated by Jefferson's letter to Livingston, April 18, 1802, and supplemented by the "Roosevelt Corollary" of 1904, in which Theodore Roosevelt effectively proclaimed that no country in Latin America had any sovereignty that the United States was obliged to respect. In defense of this principle, John F. Kennedy was prepared to launch a nuclear war against the Soviet Union that would almost certainly have destroyed modern civilization.

conflicts between Virginia and Massachusetts had been resolved, as the younger Adams was nominally a Democratic Republican and was serving as Monroe's Secretary of State. Despite the resumption of amiable personal relations between Jefferson and the senior Adams, Jefferson remained suspicious of both father and son, as he revealed in a letter to William Short in the same year that John Quincy Adams was running as one of the Republican candidates for the presidency.

He recalled olden times, the dinner in his Philadelphia apartment when, at his own table, "as well as elsewhere," many had heard Hamilton and Adams "both avow their preference of monarchy, and especially that of England." He recalled how both had discussed the British constitution as a model government, with Adams adding only "if its corruptions were done away" and Hamilton saying that "with these corruptions it was perfect, and without them it would be an impractical government." Once again the spectre of royalism was haunting America:

> Can any one read mr Adams's Defence of the American constitutions without seeing that he was a monarchist? and John Quincy Adams, his son, was more complicit than the father, in his answer to Paine's Rights of man. so much for leaders. their followers were divided. some went the same lengths, others, and I believe the greater part, only wished a stronger Executive.[109]

Thus Jefferson, while outwardly silent, revealed himself in his intimate letters to be nurturing his ancient paranoia concerning monarchism and, even worse, harboring fears that John Quincy Adams, who now occupied the White House, might be a threat to republicanism. Adams' administration presented dangers with its centralizing proclivities.

The correspondence between Jefferson and Madison at the end of 1825 casts a shadow on the cordial and sentimental communications between Jefferson and John Adams. The patriotic narrative of their cosy relationship at the end is almost mystical, culminating with their deaths on the fiftieth anniversary of the Declaration. In reality, Jefferson remained suspicious. His letters reveal the emotions accompanying the junior Adams' migration from the Federalist to the Democratic Republican to the Whig Party, and the coming replacement of the "Virginia dynasty" by the Democratic Party of Andrew Jackson.

The nation's primal conflicts were recycled, sometimes in almost farcical form, during the Whig interregnum of John Quincy Adams and the democratic reign of "King Andy." The erratic and irascible Jackson was destined

[109] Jefferson to William Short, January 8, 1825.

to appear as a Jeffersonian when he vetoed the Bank Bill and as a Whig when he responded to South Carolina's Nullification Proclamation. Years later, the aging James Madison, approached by states-rightists in his capacity as the venerable author of the Virginia Resolution, would be placed in a difficult position when asked, once again, to take the side of states' rights in the Nullification Crisis of 1832. But many years had passed, and Madison, the last of the Founders, disappointed them by refusing to oppose Jackson's nationalistic position in the heat of that confrontation.

We do not know how Jefferson would have responded to that crisis. Jefferson had stated in 1802 that the Constitution was an "act of the whole American people." Intentionally or not, he laid the grounds for Jackson's position in 1832 that the Constitution works not through the medium of the states, but directly on the people of the United States.[110] Jackson declared that the Constitution "forms a government and not a league," and that it "operates directly on the people individually." Lincoln's First Inaugural Address was to reiterate Jackson's position on nullification, but the roots of Jackson's and Lincoln's position could be found in Jefferson's 1802 letter to the Danbury Clergy.

Jefferson did not retire from politics when he left Washington, DC, at the age of 66, in accord with the legend cultivated by himself. Despite his continuing claims that he was too old and tired for political activism, he did whatever he could to undermine the presidency of John Quincy Adams. He sharpened his stiletto, engaging in attempts to engage the press, the Virginia legislature, and his old allies in sabotaging the son of his old friend. The Sage of Monticello worked through James Madison, while Madison conspired with Thomas Ritchie, editor of the *Richmond Enquirer*, and wrote to an old cantankerous ally, William Branch Giles, to oppose the policies of the junior Adams. Madison persuaded Jefferson to suppress his final brilliant, lucid, and immoderate treatise, "The Solemn Declaration and Protest" of Virginia against the consolidation of power by the federal government in Washington.

110 I deal with this matter of the Constitution as an act of the people, not the states, in the discussion (in Chapter 9 above) of Jefferson's letter to Nehemiah Dodge (January 1, 1802), which asserts that the Constitution is an act of "the whole American people" and defers to individual conscience in matters of religion; but his letter to Samuel Miller (January 23, 1808) asserts that the Constitution does not limit the power of the states respecting an establishment of religion. Thus, in his letter to Dodge, Jefferson concedes the point that Jackson later makes in his Nullification Proclamation that the Constitution "forms a government not a league" and "operates directly on the people individually." In his letter to Miller he reverses himself.

Jefferson's intellectual brilliance had not diminished one iota, and he continued to flourish his Machiavellian pen in a letter to Giles on matters "not intended for the public eye." The day after Christmas, 1825, he expressed his fears that the "federal court" and "the doctrines of the President" were "in combination" to strip away the constitutional powers of the states. The "Solemn Declaration" that he had sent to Madison for his perusal two days earlier, like the letter to Giles was a spontaneous and almost immediate overreaction to the relatively innocuous words of John Quincy Adams' First Annual Message to Congress. Adams had maneuvered himself into the presidency and faithfully served the Monroe administration while wearing the mantle of a Democratic Republican, but now, in Jefferson's perception, he was revealing himself to be a Whig.

John Quincy Adams had spoken of involving the federal government in the promotion of "agriculture, commerce, and manufactures, the cultivation and encouragement of the mechanic and the elegant arts, the advancement of literature, and the progress of the sciences, ornamental and profound." Those proposals were modest and vague in comparison to the elaborate plans once issued by Jefferson's own Secretary of the Treasury, Albert Gallatin. And these, as outlined in Madison's 1815 Address to Congress, were what James Morton Smith calls "positive, even vigorous, federal activity accepted by both Madison and Jefferson."[111] Madison even resurrected Washington's call for the establishment of a national university, in face of the fact that a main purpose of the University of Virginia was to shelter young men from cosmopolitan influences. In terms of federal activism, John Quincy Adams was no less a Jeffersonian than Madison or Monroe, never purchasing an empire by executive order or imposing an embargo. In terms of his scientific curiosity and intellectual vigor, the "little applejohn" from Massachusetts rivaled Jefferson himself. In this respect, he stood markedly in contrast to his successor, Andrew Jackson.

JEFFERSON, JACKSON, AND THE POWER OF WASHINGTON, DC

Jefferson's opinion of Andrew Jackson is a matter of controversy. Merrill Peterson notes "the acute sensibility of political leaders to the value of

[111] Adams, in State of the Union Address, December 6, 1825: James Morton Smith, *The Republic of Letters: The Correspondence between Thomas Jefferson and James Madison, 1776–1826* (New York: Norton, 1995), vol. III, p. 1771.

Jefferson's benediction."[112] Jackson passed through Charlottesville on his way to Congress in November, 1823, without making a side-trip to Monticello, but afterwards wrote to Jefferson apologizing for not stopping. A letter from Jefferson to Jackson was included in the Ford edition of his correspondence, but has not yet received the *nihil obstat* of the Princeton editors as "an authoritative final version." The letter indicates that Jefferson travelled to Charlottesville, hoping to meet with the general, but he had already passed through. It concludes:

> I recall with pleasure the remembrance of our joint labors while in the Senate together in times of great trial and of hard battling, battles indeed of words, not of blood, as those you have since fought so much for your own glory & that of your country; with the assurance that my attempts continue undiminished, accept that of my great respect & consideration.

Jefferson favored William Crawford in the election of 1824, and in that year he is supposed to have told Daniel Webster, during a visit to Monticello:

> I feel much alarmed at the prospect of seeing General Jackson President. He is one of the most unfit men I know of for such a place. He has had very little respect for laws or constitutions, and is, in fact, an able military chief. His passions are terrible. When I was President of the Senate he was a Senator; and he could never speak on account of the rashness of his feelings. I have seen him attempt it repeatedly, and as often choke with rage. His passions are no doubt cooler now; he has been much tried since I knew him, but he is a dangerous man.[113]

Jefferson and Jackson both vacillated between a vigorous advocacy of states' rights and pontifications that the national Constitution worked directly on the individual citizen.[114] Both men could be unpredictable and opportunistic.

[112] Merrill Peterson, *The Jefferson Image in the American Mind* (Charlottesville, VA: University of Virginia Press, 1998), pp. 25–27.

[113] George Ticknor Curtis, *Life of Daniel Webster*, 2 vols. (New York: D. Appleton & Co., 1870), vol. I, p. 222. Thomas Jefferson supposedly said this to Webster during the latter's visit to Monticello in 1824. Jefferson's support of Crawford in Peterson, *Thomas Jefferson and the New Nation*, p. 1002.

[114] I discuss elsewhere in this volume Jefferson's January 2, 1802, letter to Nehemiah Dodge which refers to the Constitution as "an act of the whole American people," and Jackson's of December 10, 1832, that the Constitution "operates directly on the people individually, not upon the states."

ENLIGHTENED DESPOT OR CITIZEN KING?

Jefferson recalled his election in 1800 "as real a revolution in the principles of our government as that of 1776 was in its form."[115] At his inauguration, he notably spoke the conciliatory words, "We are all Republicans; we are all Federalists." Henry Adams and Theodore Roosevelt saw his administration as consolidating the strong national state. Hamilton had noted that he was "generally for a large construction of the Executive authority" and was unlikely to do anything that would diminish its value. He was the first imperial president, which was evident as early as *Notes on Virginia*, when he cast his eyes west of the Mississippi, decades before the term Manifest Destiny became fashionable.

The strength of Jeffersonian democracy was its paradoxical departure from the mythological underpinnings of Jeffersonian democracy – its inadvertent nationalism and empire-building. Professor Pocock disclosed an unintended irony when he situated Jefferson in his "Machiavellian Moment." The genealogy traced by Arthur Schlesinger from Jefferson to Jackson to the New Deal was an ironic fulfillment of Hamilton's sarcastic prophecy.

The Count of Monticello was an aristocrat in robe and slippers when answering the White House door in ostentatious humility, and disdainful of rank when seating the British ambassador's wife at the foot of his table. He was a tyrant when threatening his slaves with a whip in the presence of Constantine Volney.[116] He displayed the hereditary might of his equestrian class when inspecting his plantations on horseback. In office, he wielded his powers more independently than George III, who had failed miserably in striving towards the ideal of Henry Bolingbroke's "patriot king." Jefferson is more deserving than France's Louis Philippe I of the soubriquet "Citizen King," but his *bonhomie* nonetheless masked the presence of a vigorous executive, the subtle provocateur of the Chase impeachment, the independent purchaser of Louisiana, the vindictive prosecutor of Aaron Burr, and the executive who signed the Embargo Act. His proletarian preachments were less significant than his imperial grasp. His handsome face, his legendary elegance on the dance floor, his debonair bearing, his "Palladian" mansion, made Jefferson the

[115] Jefferson to Spencer Roane, September 6, 1819.

[116] For the incident regarding Ambassador and Mrs. Merry, see Henry Adams, *History of the United States during the Administrations of Thomas Jefferson*, pp. 553ff. Volney's diary is excerpted in the original French by Fawn Brodie in her *Thomas Jefferson*, pp. 288 and 353 note 3.

Renaissance prince, the "blessed patriarch," the enlightened despot. But he was neither the sole incarnation of "ambition and opulence" nor the ultimate embodiment of "conspicuous consumption" on whom the masses of the American people were destined to lavish their adulation.[117]

BEARER OF LIGHT AND TRICKSTER GOD

Jefferson's preamble to the Declaration of Independence, despite what Jeremy Bentham recognized as its independence from Aristotelian logic and its unfastening from the moorings of empiricism, has nonetheless been an inspiration to many subsequent anti-colonial movements. Its celebration of "life, liberty and the pursuit of happiness" and its "self-evident" truth that "all men are created equal" by mandate of "the Laws of Nature and of Nature's God" is without competition as the prime philosophical statement, as well as the basis, of much political ideology in modern world history. The words have become so sacred that any recollection of Samuel Johnson's contemporary remarks on them, namely "the loudest yelps for freedom come from the drivers of Negroes," is denounced by American patriotic historians as "presentist" and irrelevant. A repetition of Dr. Johnson's words at a Donald Trump campaign rally, or any mention of Sally Hemings, would invite, quite literally, a fist in the mouth.

Be that as it may, the Patriotic Evangelical Right has an uncomfortably sneaking suspicion that Jefferson is guilty of major crimes. Despite the sacred fire he kindled with the Declaration of Independence, he was guilty of the offense of supporting tax-funded public education. Thanks to Donald Trump's administration, public schools and universities are being weakened to the point of becoming an endangered species. Although great mischief was set afoot by Jefferson's heretical doctrine of "a wall of separation between church and state," Tea Party Patriots can derive comfort from the fact that the doctrine has no basis in the Constitution of the United States. Despite any quibbles, the people of America have "builded him an altar in the evening dews and damps." His graven image has been set up in a Roman temple in the Potomac riverbed, where it is threatened by global warming. Jefferson, despite his

[117] Parton on Jefferson's elegance, cf. Senator William McClay on Jefferson's awkwardness, diary entry, May 24, 1790, cited in Gore Vidal, *Inventing a Nation: Washington, Adams, Jefferson* (New Haven, CT: Yale University Press, 2003), p. 78. On beating a horse, Meacham, *Thomas Jefferson,* pp. 289–290, quotes Henry Stevens Randall, *The Life of Thomas Jefferson* (New York: Derby and Jackson, 1858), p. 675.

heresies, is a demigod to mainstream Christian America, and they are willing to forgive his blasphemous proclamation on the "separation of Church and state" in light of his invocation of God in the nation's founding document.

It is a little-known fact, and one that is hidden only from the culturally illiterate, that in his *Notes on Virginia* he counseled against "putting the Bible and Testament into the hands of the children, at an age when their judgments are not sufficiently matured for religious enquiries."

What mainstream Evangelical America perceives as Jefferson's most offensive liberal heterodoxies can be overlooked, for Jefferson undeniably had his virtues. These were revisited with the secession of the Confederate States and reinvigorated with the election of Donald Trump. Like Jefferson, he opportunistically advocated an interpretation of federalism that called for the atomization of the nation state and that opposed vigorous central government, except when he and his friends were in power. Jefferson reinforced a populist provincialism based on xenophobic localism, with minimal, if any, taxation. He supported the rise of Daniel Shays' citizen militia against the Massachusetts government. These positions alone would have compensated for his sins, but Evangelical America heaps additional praise upon him for his hostility to a national system of regulated banking, and they give secretive but strong support to his firm belief that black and white people cannot coexist, unless it is under an oppressive white supremacy. Many Americans also admire Jefferson's prophetic act of sending the United States Marines to the "shores of Tripoli," a Muslim country. This Crusade is one of his most enduring legacies, along with Jefferson's aborted plan in 1812 to bring Canada under complete domination by the United States.

Jefferson was an imperfect champion of the rights to life, liberty, and pursuit of happiness. He endowed us with a heritage of ideals that inspired Lincoln at Gettysburg. He also sent others onto battlefields where he dared not tread. He kept slaves, coveted his neighbour's wife, and apparently impregnated a teenager. If it is wrong to condemn him for being a creature of his times, it is equally wrong to regard him as an oracle whose words and deeds have timeless validity. As tortured as Mary Shelley's "Modern Prometheus" he could not speak to everyone in his times or our own. If Jefferson Davis and Theodore Roosevelt were agreed on anything, it was that he ignited the fires of Secession. I have said in the preface to this work that Jefferson exemplified Joseph Campbell's "Hero with a Thousand Faces." He was both a Bearer of Light and a Trickster God, a modern Prometheus.

Index